THE SNAKEPIT BOOK

BY BEN SNAKEPIT

Originally published by Gorsky Press, 2004

Second Edition released May 1, 2014

Microcosm Publishing
2752 N Williams Ave
Portland, OR 97227
www.microcosmpublishing.com

THE SNAKE PIT BOOK

BY BEN SNAKEPIT

INTRODUCTION

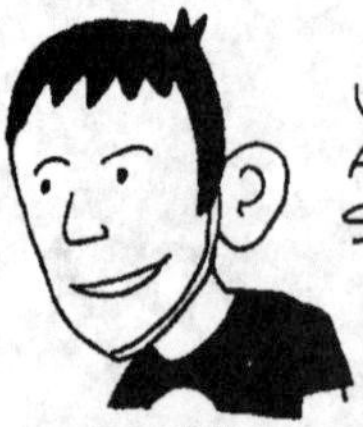

WELL, HELLO EVERYONE. I'M BEN AND THIS IS MY BOOK OF LITTLE COMIC STRIPS ABOUT WHAT I'VE DONE EVERY DAY FOR THE LAST THREE YEARS. I DREW THE FIRST SNAKEPIT STRIP ON JULY 17, 2000. I TRIED TO STICK TO IT EVERY DAY BUT I DIDN'T HAVE THE KIND OF WILLPOWER I NEEDED. IT WAS MY NEW YEAR'S RESOLUTION FOR 2001 TO NEVER MISS ANOTHER DAY OF DRAWING, AND THREE YEARS LATER I'M STILL ROCKING OUT ON IT. SO IT SEEMED MORE LOGICAL TO ME TO HAVE THIS BOOK START THEN, AND JUST CONSIDER THE SECOND HALF OF 2000 TO BE PRACTICE. (BY THE WAY, I HAVE <u>NO</u> INTENTION OF EVER PUBLISHING THOSE EARLY COMICS AGAIN. I THINK THEY'RE HORRIBLE, SO DONT ASK.) GOING BACK AND LOOKING AT THESE COMICS, ONE DAY AT A TIME, IT DOESN'T SEEM LIKE ANYTHING ABOUT MY LIFE HAS CHANGED. BUT WHEN I HAVE IT ALL IN ONE CHUNK, THERE ARE DRAMATIC DIFFERENCES. I'M A VERY DIFFERENT PERSON THAN I WAS THE FIRST TIME I RODE MY BIKE OUT TO THE WEST END KINKO'S IN RICHMOND TO PUT TOGETHER A ZINE. BUT AT THE SAME TIME I'M EXACTLY THE SAME. IT'S A WEIRD FEELING TO HOLD THREE YEARS OF YOUR LIFE IN YOUR HAND; TO WATCH YOURSELF GROW FROM YOUR MID-TWENTIES TO YOUR LATE TWENTIES IN JUST AN HOUR OR SO. I ALWAYS THOUGHT MY GREATEST ACCOMPLISHMENT WOULD BE BEING THE "ITS FREE AND I LIVE RIGHT OVER THERE" KID IN THE FUGAZI MOVIE. I THINK THIS BOOK IS A LOT COOLER, ESPECIALLY SINCE NOWHERE IN THIS BOOK AM I WEARING A BACKWARDS BASEBALL CAP. IT'S NEAT, THOUGH, TO SIT DOWN AND REVIEW EVERYTHING IVE DONE, THE PLACES I'VE BEEN, THE PEOPLE THAT HAVE DRIFTED IN AND OUT OF MY LIFE; ALWAYS CHANGING AND ALWAYS STAYING THE SAME.

I GUESS THE MOST OBVIOUS THING ABOUT THESE COMICS IS THAT YOU GET TO WATCH MY DRAWING SKILLS IMPROVE OVER THREE YEARS, NOT THAT THEY REALLY IMPROVE THAT MUCH, BUT I AT LEAST FEEL LIKE I'M DOING A LITTLE BETTER NOW. THAT KINDA GOES FOR MORE THAN JUST MY DRAWING SKILLS. I FEEL LIKE I'M DOING BETTER IN JUST ABOUT EVERY ASPECT IN MY LIFE, DUE IN NO SMALL PART TO THE COMICS IN THIS BOOK. SO PUT THIS BOOK IN YOUR BATHROOM, NEXT TO THE TOILET, AND READ IT WHEN YOU'RE TAKING A CRAP. THAT'S WHAT IT'S INTENDED FOR. I HOPE READING ABOUT HOW STUPID MY LIFE IS WILL MAKE YOU FEEL BETTER ABOUT YOURS, CUZ IN A WAY, ALL OUR LIVES ARE THE SAME, MONOTONOUS DAY AFTER DAY, PUNCTUATED WITH THE OCCASIONAL MISHAP OR FUN THING, AND IT'S IMPORTANT FOR US ALL TO REMEMBER OUR LIVES IN THEIR ENTIRETY, THE GOOD WITH THE BAD, THE SWEET WITH THE SOUR; AND HOPE WHEN IT'S ALL OVER WE WILL HAVE NO (OR AT LEAST VERY FEW) REGRETS AND A GOOD STORY TO TELL. I GUESS.

ENJOY THE COMICS,

A LETTER FROM AARON

DEAR BEN,   3/13/2003

I SEE THE SUBTITLE OF YOUR NEW QUARTERLY IS "CHEWING GUM, HOLDING HANDS". PERHAPS A REFERENCE TO A SONG BY MY OLD BAND? I STILL LIKE THE SONG, BUT KICK MYSELF NOW FOR BEING DISHONEST, OR NOT WHOLLY HONEST, IN PAINTING THAT PICTURE. THE TRUTH WAS, WE WERE CHEWING GUM, HOLDING HANDS, AND HIGH AS A KITE ON COCAINE! THE DIFFERENCE BETWEEN MY SONG AND YOUR COMICS IS THAT YOU'RE NOT AFRAID TO SHOW, AND APPRECIATE, THE WHOLE PICTURE. YOU KNOW THAT LIFE IS MORE BEAUTIFUL WITH ALL THE SEEDINESS AND AWKWARDNESS, THE HOPELESS-NESS AND REGRET. ONLY AFTER FINISHING THAT 4-COURSE MEAL CAN YOU REALLY, TRULY APPRECIATE THE SWEET TASTES OF INNOCENCE AND IDEALISM AND ROMANCE. YOUR COMICS TELL THAT STORY AGAIN AND AGAIN, WITH TENDERNESS AND DECEPTIVE DIRECTNESS, WITH THE GIRL AND WITH THE COCAINE, GODDAMMIT, UNTIL THEY BOTH RUN OUT. IF YOU HADN'T GUESSED BY NOW, THIS LETTER IS ALSO THE INTRODUCTION FOR YOUR BOOK, IF YOU CARE TO USE IT AS SUCH. I KNOW, I TOLD YOU EARLIER TONIGHT AT YOUR SHOW THAT I ALWAYS SKIP INTRODUCTIONS, THAT I REALLY LIKE YOUR WORK AND WOULDN'T WANT IT CHEAPENED BY

SOMEONE EXPLAINING OR QUALIFYING IT, EVEN IF THAT SOMEONE WAS ME. BUT YOU CAPTURE SOME MOMENTS AND MOODS OF OUR LIVES SO WELL, LIKE A GREAT SONG, AND WHEN IT CAME DOWN TO IT, I COULDN'T RESIST SINGING ALONG. CONGRATULATIONS ON THE COLLECTION!

X—AARON (COMETBUS)

2001

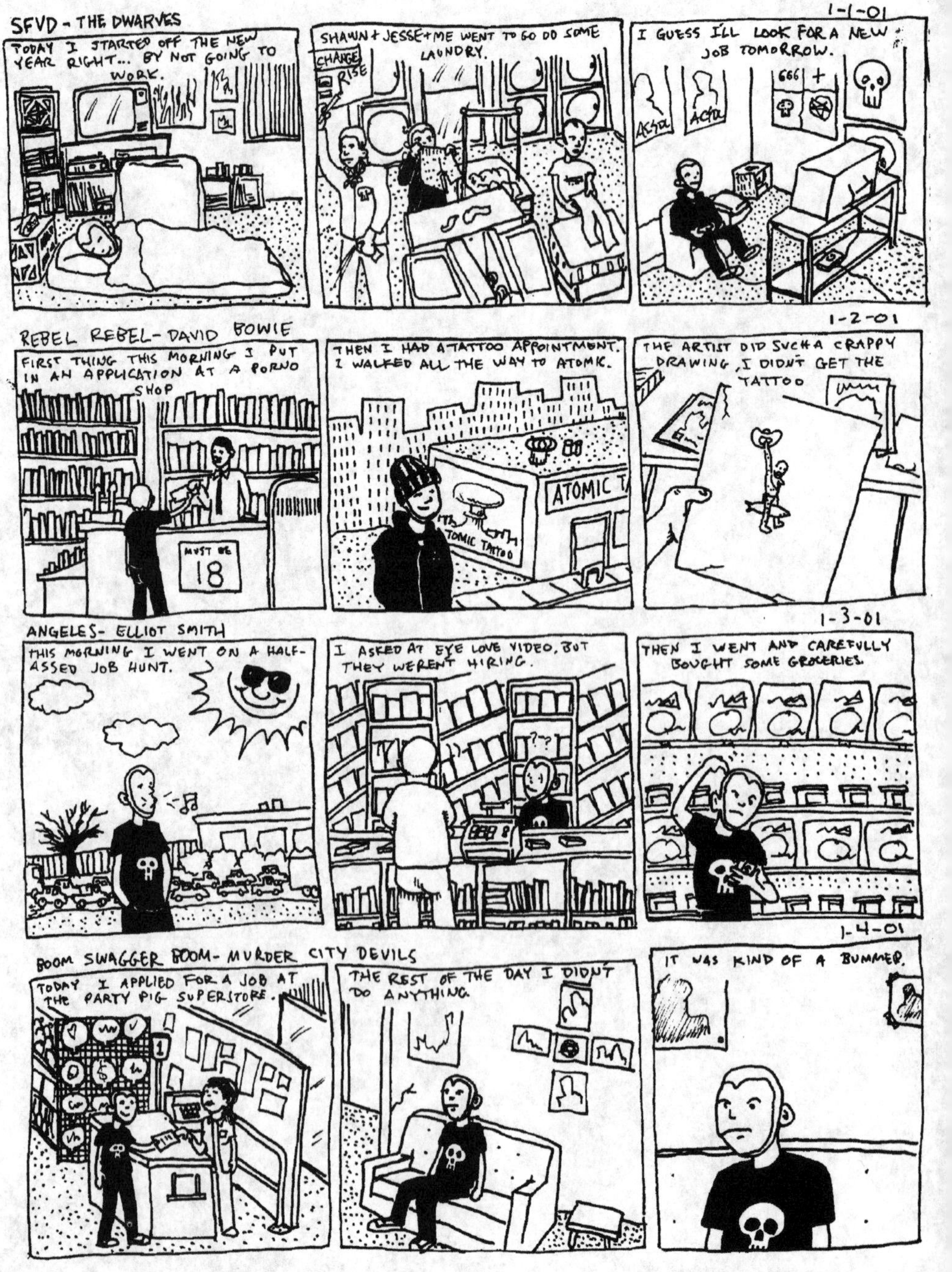
SFVD - THE DWARVES
1-1-01
TODAY I STARTED OFF THE NEW YEAR RIGHT... BY NOT GOING TO WORK.
SHAWN + JESSE + ME WENT TO GO DO SOME LAUNDRY.
CHANGE
RISE
I GUESS I'LL LOOK FOR A NEW JOB TOMORROW.
666
REBEL REBEL - DAVID BOWIE
1-2-01
FIRST THING THIS MORNING I PUT IN AN APPLICATION AT A PORNO SHOP
MUST BE 18
THEN I HAD A TATTOO APPOINTMENT. I WALKED ALL THE WAY TO ATOMIC.
ATOMIC T
TOMIC TATTOO
THE ARTIST DID SUCH A CRAPPY DRAWING, I DIDN'T GET THE TATTOO
1-3-01
ANGELES - ELLIOT SMITH
THIS MORNING I WENT ON A HALF-ASSED JOB HUNT.
I ASKED AT EYE LOVE VIDEO, BUT THEY WEREN'T HIRING.
?-?
THEN I WENT AND CAREFULLY BOUGHT SOME GROCERIES.
1-4-01
BOOM SWAGGER BOOM - MURDER CITY DEVILS
TODAY I APPLIED FOR A JOB AT THE PARTY PIG SUPERSTORE.
THE REST OF THE DAY I DIDN'T DO ANYTHING.
IT WAS KIND OF A BUMMER.

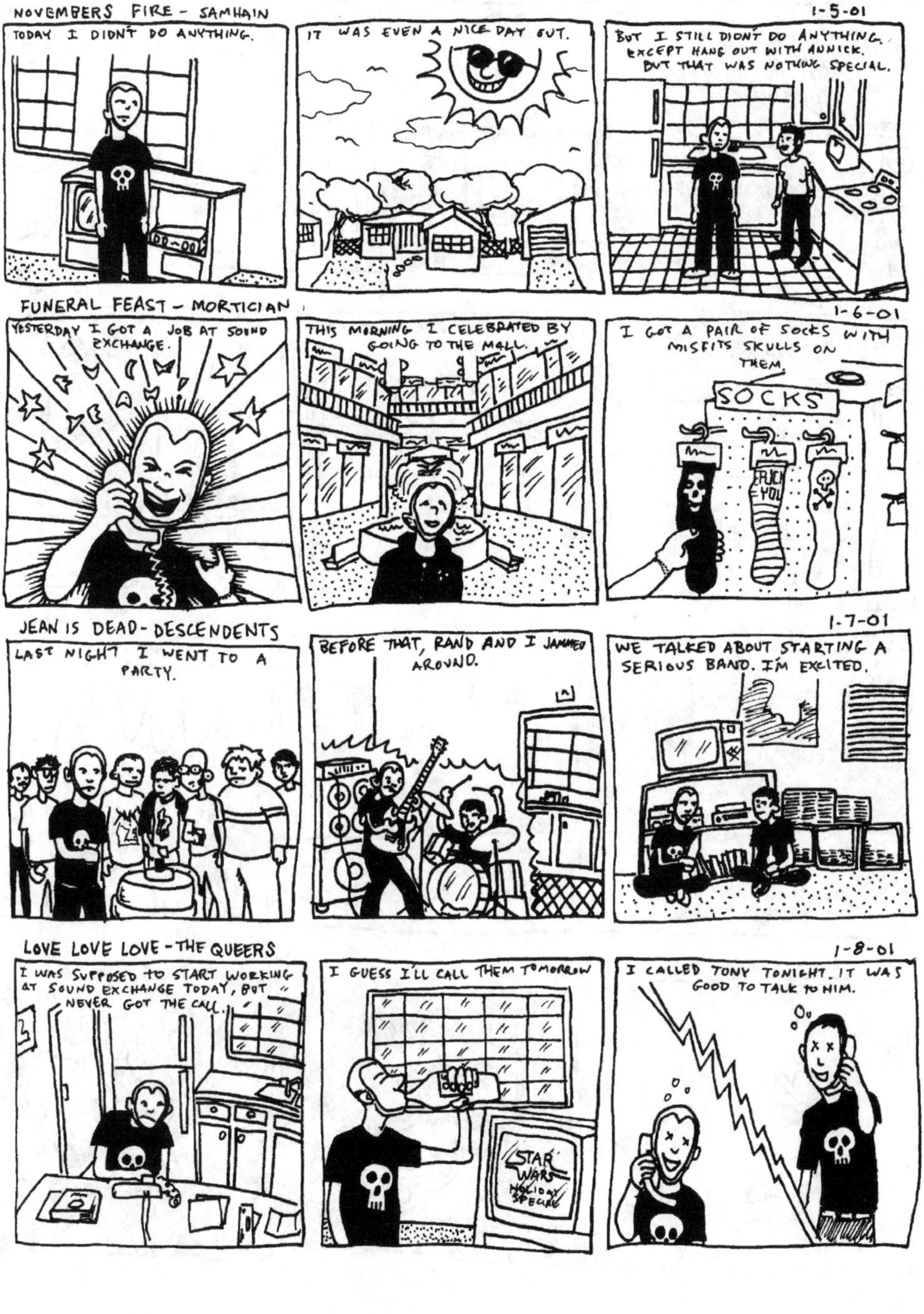
NOVEMBERS FIRE - SAMHAIN
1-5-01
TODAY I DIDN'T DO ANYTHING.
IT WAS EVEN A NICE DAY OUT.
BUT I STILL DIDN'T DO ANYTHING. EXCEPT HANG OUT WITH ANNICK. BUT THAT WAS NOTHING SPECIAL.
FUNERAL FEAST - MORTICIAN
1-6-01
YESTERDAY I GOT A JOB AT SOUND EXCHANGE.
THIS MORNING I CELEBRATED BY GOING TO THE MALL.
I GOT A PAIR OF SOCKS WITH MISFITS SKULLS ON THEM.
SOCKS
FUCK YOU
JEAN IS DEAD - DESCENDENTS
1-7-01
LAST NIGHT I WENT TO A PARTY.
BEFORE THAT, RAND AND I JAMMED AROUND.
WE TALKED ABOUT STARTING A SERIOUS BAND. I'M EXCITED.
LOVE LOVE LOVE - THE QUEERS
1-8-01
I WAS SUPPOSED TO START WORKING AT SOUND EXCHANGE TODAY, BUT NEVER GOT THE CALL.
I GUESS I'LL CALL THEM TOMORROW
STAR WARS HOLIDAY SPECIAL
I CALLED TONY TONIGHT. IT WAS GOOD TO TALK TO HIM.

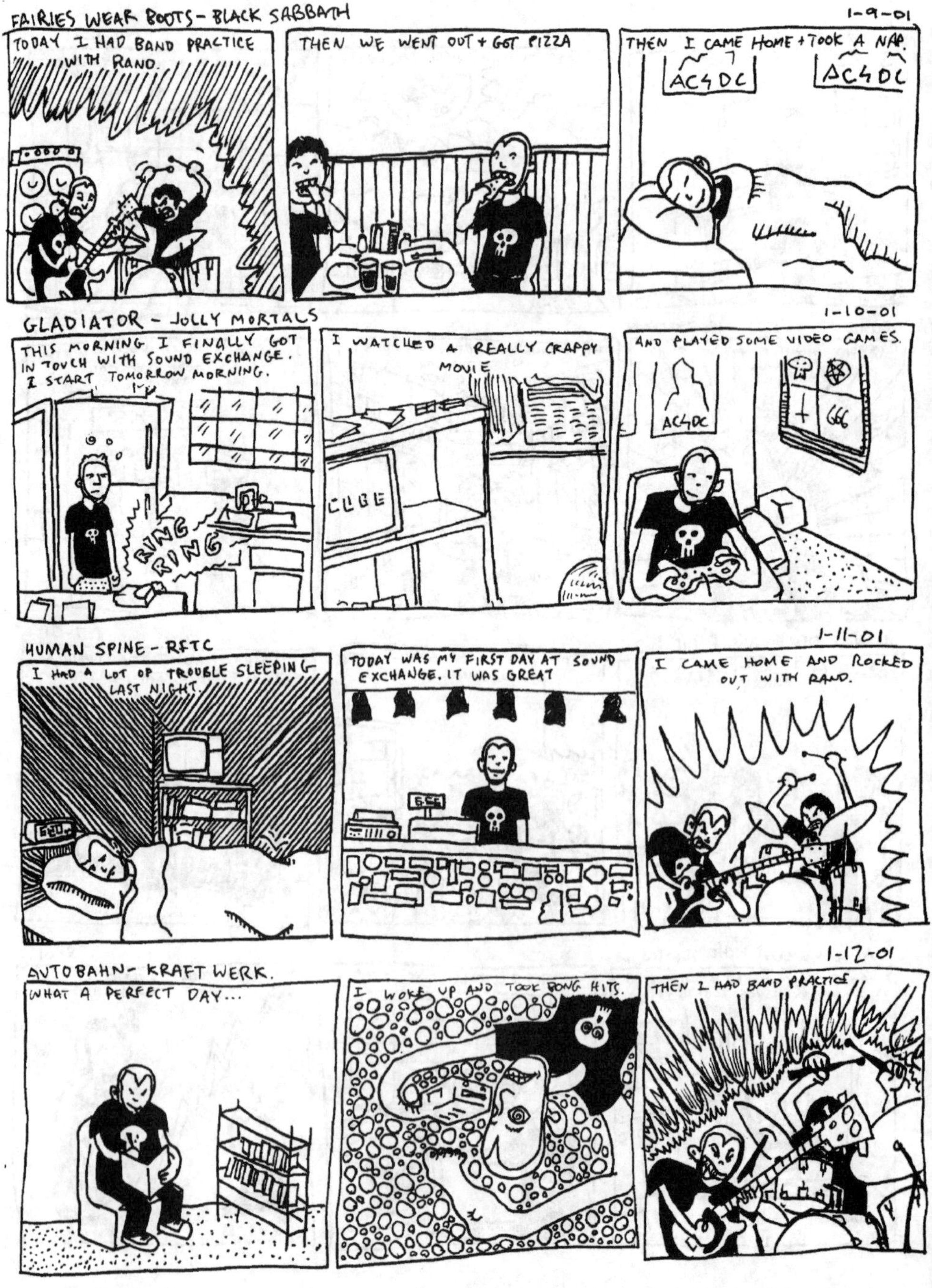

FAIRIES WEAR BOOTS - BLACK SABBATH
1-9-01
TODAY I HAD BAND PRACTICE WITH RAND.
THEN WE WENT OUT + GOT PIZZA
THEN I CAME HOME + TOOK A NAP.
AC/DC
AC/DC
GLADIATOR - JOLLY MORTALS
1-10-01
THIS MORNING I FINALLY GOT IN TOUCH WITH SOUND EXCHANGE. I START TOMORROW MORNING.
RING RING
I WATCHED A REALLY CRAPPY MOVIE
CUBE
AND PLAYED SOME VIDEO GAMES.
AC/DC
666
HUMAN SPINE - RFTC
1-11-01
I HAD A LOT OF TROUBLE SLEEPING LAST NIGHT.
TODAY WAS MY FIRST DAY AT SOUND EXCHANGE. IT WAS GREAT
I CAME HOME AND ROCKED OUT WITH RAND.
AUTOBAHN - KRAFTWERK.
1-12-01
WHAT A PERFECT DAY...
I WOKE UP AND TOOK BONG HITS.
THEN I HAD BAND PRACTICE

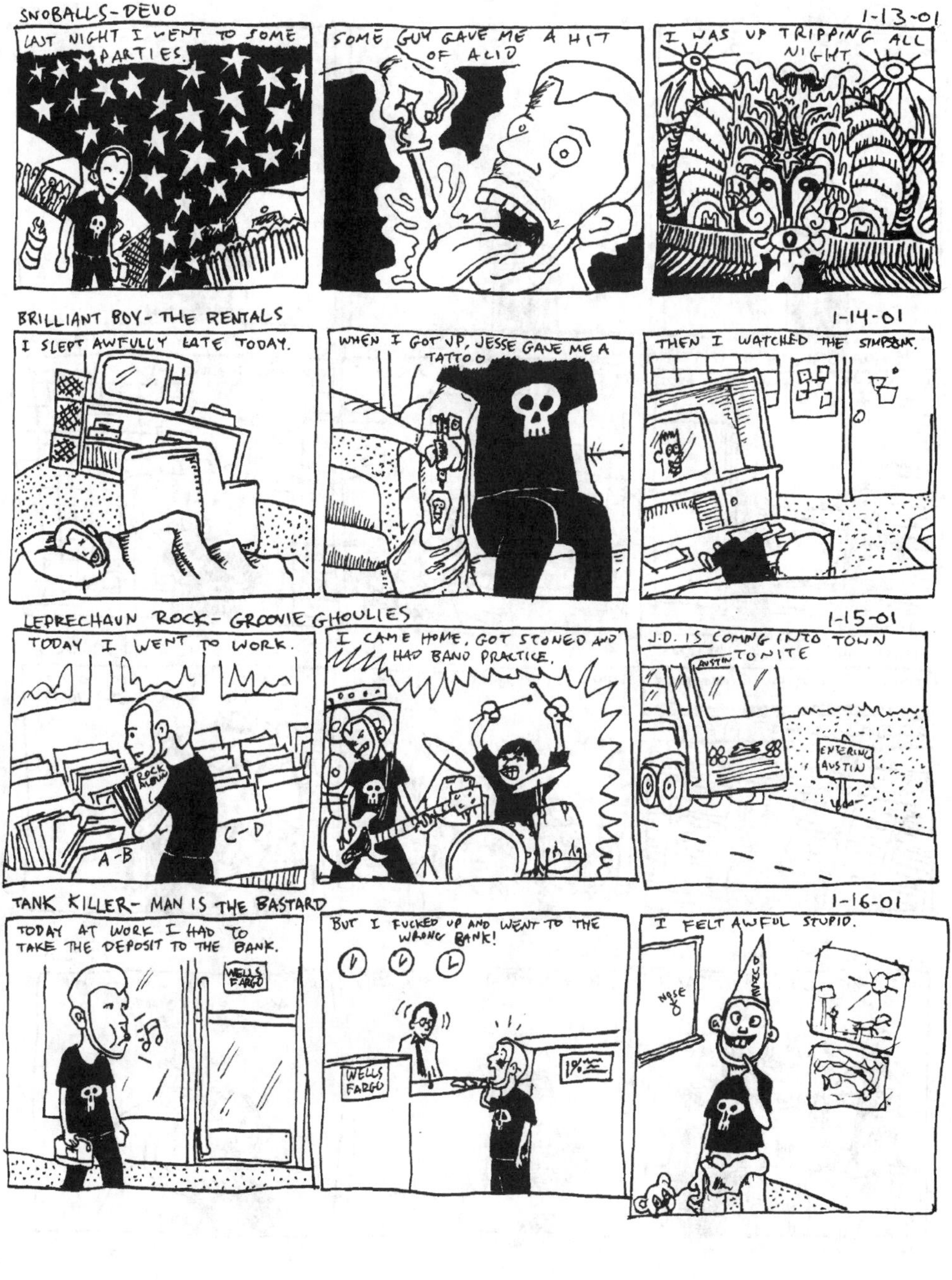

SNOBALLS-DEVO
1-13-01
LAST NIGHT I WENT TO SOME PARTIES.
SOME GUY GAVE ME A HIT OF ACID
I WAS UP TRIPPING ALL NIGHT.
BRILLIANT BOY- THE RENTALS
1-14-01
I SLEPT AWFULLY LATE TODAY.
WHEN I GOT UP, JESSE GAVE ME A TATTOO
THEN I WATCHED THE SIMPSONS.
LEPRECHAUN ROCK- GROOVIE GHOULIES
1-15-01
TODAY I WENT TO WORK.
ROCK ALBUMS
A-B
C-D
I CAME HOME, GOT STONED AND HAD BAND PRACTICE.
J.D. IS COMING INTO TOWN TONITE
AUSTIN
ENTERING AUSTIN
TANK KILLER- MAN IS THE BASTARD
1-16-01
TODAY AT WORK I HAD TO TAKE THE DEPOSIT TO THE BANK.
WELLS FARGO
BUT I FUCKED UP AND WENT TO THE WRONG BANK!
WELLS FARGO
I FELT AWFUL STUPID.
DUNCE
NOSE

I WANNA - PINHEAD GUNPOWDER 1-17-001

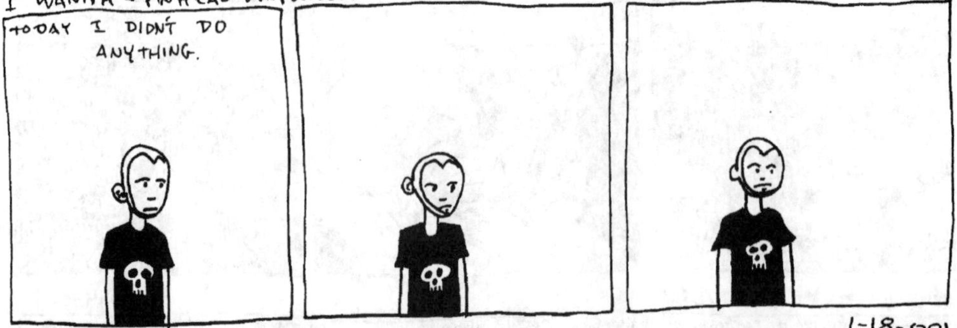
TODAY I DIDN'T DO ANYTHING.

MINNESOTA STRIP - DICTATORS 1-18-001

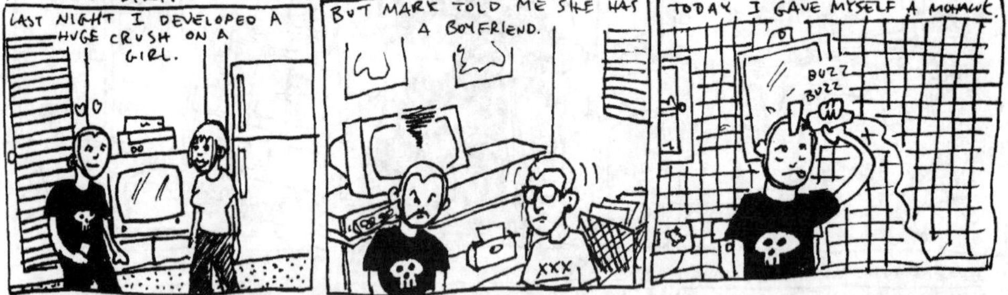
LAST NIGHT I DEVELOPED A HUGE CRUSH ON A GIRL.
BUT MARK TOLD ME SHE HAS A BOYFRIEND.
XXX
TODAY I GAVE MYSELF A MOHAWK.
BUZZ BUZZ

LIGHTS OUT - ANGRY SAMOANS 1-19-001

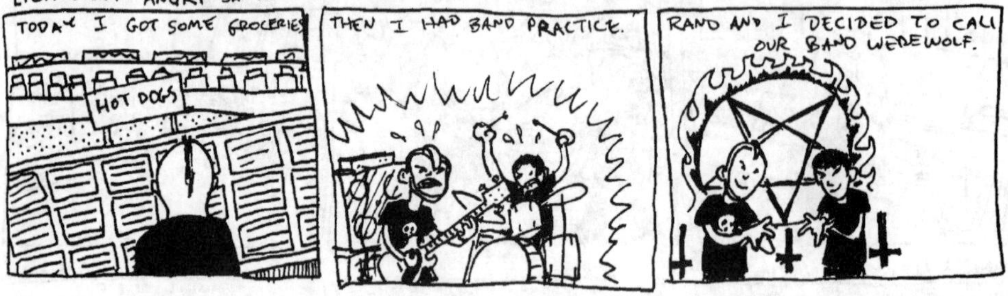
TODAY I GOT SOME GROCERIES
HOT DOGS
THEN I HAD BAND PRACTICE.
RAND AND I DECIDED TO CALL OUR BAND WEREWOLF.

MURDER IN THE BRADY HOUSE - THE QUEERS 1-20-001

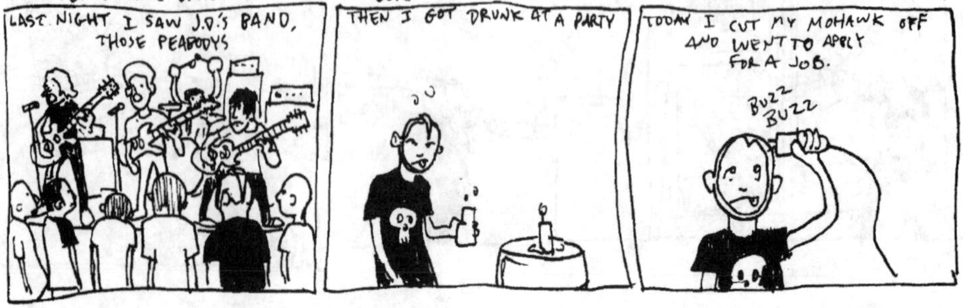
LAST NIGHT I SAW J.D.'S BAND, THOSE PEABODYS
THEN I GOT DRUNK AT A PARTY
TODAY I CUT MY MOHAWK OFF AND WENT TO APPLY FOR A JOB.
BUZZ BUZZ

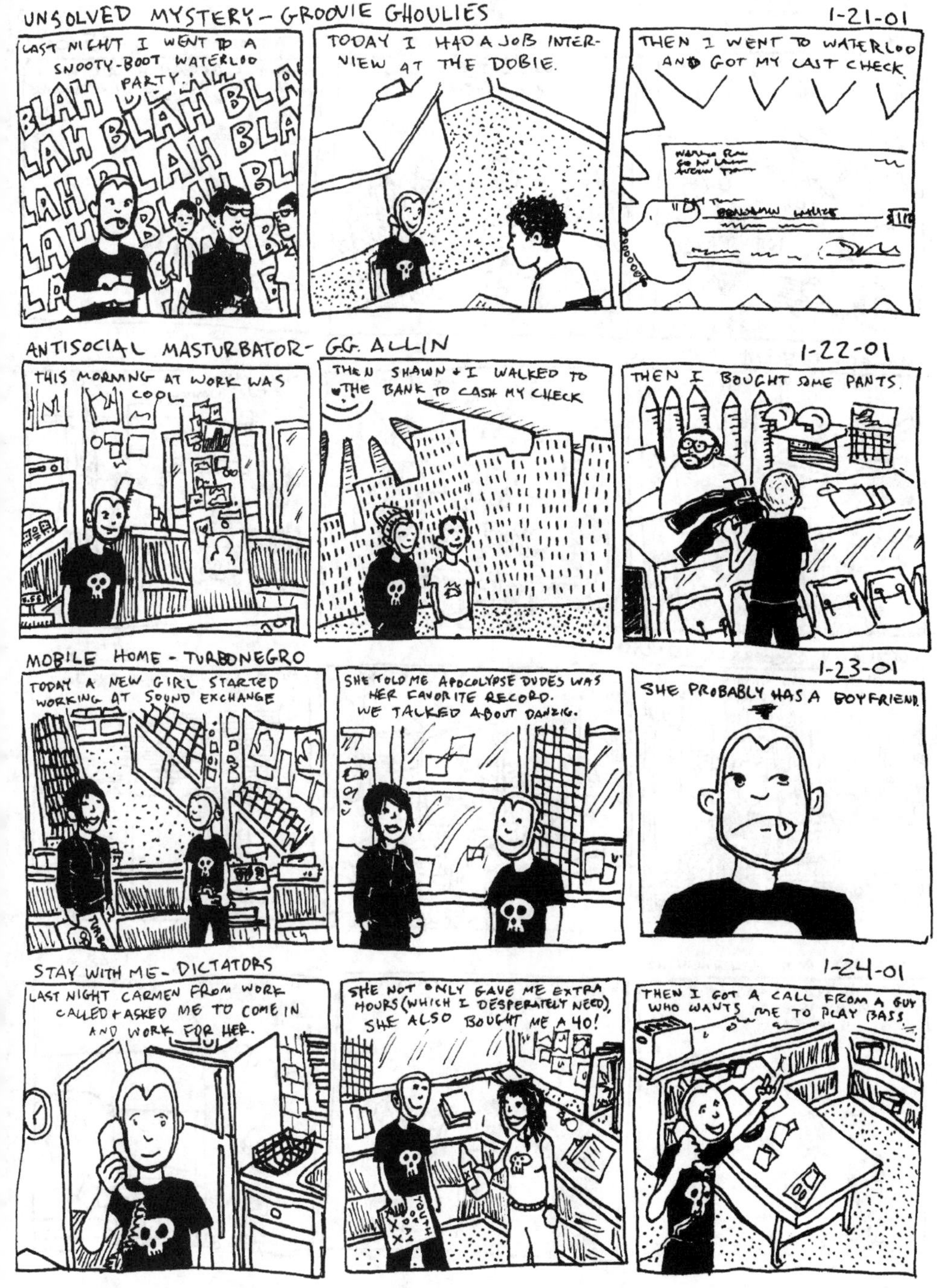
UNSOLVED MYSTERY - GROOVIE GHOULIES
1-21-01
LAST NIGHT I WENT TO A SNOOTY-BOOT WATERLOO PARTY.
BLAH BLAH BLAH BLAH BLAH BLAH BLAH BLAH BLAH BLAH
TODAY I HAD A JOB INTERVIEW AT THE DOBIE.
THEN I WENT TO WATERLOO AND GOT MY LAST CHECK.
ANTISOCIAL MASTURBATOR - G.G. ALLIN
1-22-01
THIS MORNING AT WORK WAS COOL.
THEN SHAWN + I WALKED TO THE BANK TO CASH MY CHECK
THEN I BOUGHT SOME PANTS.
MOBILE HOME - TURBONEGRO
1-23-01
TODAY A NEW GIRL STARTED WORKING AT SOUND EXCHANGE
SHE TOLD ME APOCOLYPSE DUDES WAS HER FAVORITE RECORD.
WE TALKED ABOUT DANZIG.
SHE PROBABLY HAS A BOYFRIEND.
STAY WITH ME - DICTATORS
1-24-01
LAST NIGHT CARMEN FROM WORK CALLED + ASKED ME TO COME IN AND WORK FOR HER.
SHE NOT ONLY GAVE ME EXTRA HOURS (WHICH I DESPERATELY NEED), SHE ALSO BOUGHT ME A 40!
YOUTH OF TODAY
THEN I GOT A CALL FROM A GUY WHO WANTS ME TO PLAY BASS

LETS FUCK - THE DWARVES.

LAST NIGHT STEVE PICKED ME UP TO GO TRY OUT FOR HIS BAND, THE PINK SWORDS

TODAYS EPISODE WAS DRAWN ON A TOILET.   1-25-01

WE ROCKED OUT & IT WAS AWESOME!

TODAY I GOT AN EMAIL FROM NORA THAT PUT ME IN A TERRIBLE MOOD.

MYAGE - DESCENDENTS   1-26-01

LAST NIGHT I HAD TO WORK A BIG IN-STORE.

THEN JESSE + I WENT TO SEE SHAWN AT WORK.

TODAY MARK JESSE AND I CLEANED THE HOUSE

CLASH CITY ROCKERS - THE CLASH   1-27-01

LAST NIGHT WORK WAS SLOW. I WORKED WITH STEPHANIE.

I CAME HOME AND GOT DRUNK AND WATCHED "BEYOND THE MAT".

TODAY IT WAS COLD OUT SO I STAYED INSIDE.

PANDORA'S BOX - LEATHERFACE   1-28-01

LAST NIGHT JUSTY+SHADES AND I DESPERATELY TRIED TO FIND A GOOD PARTY.

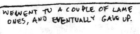

WE WENT TO A COUPLE OF LAME ONES, AND EVENTUALLY GAVE UP.

THIS MORNING I WENT TO TACO BELL

DRIVE THRU

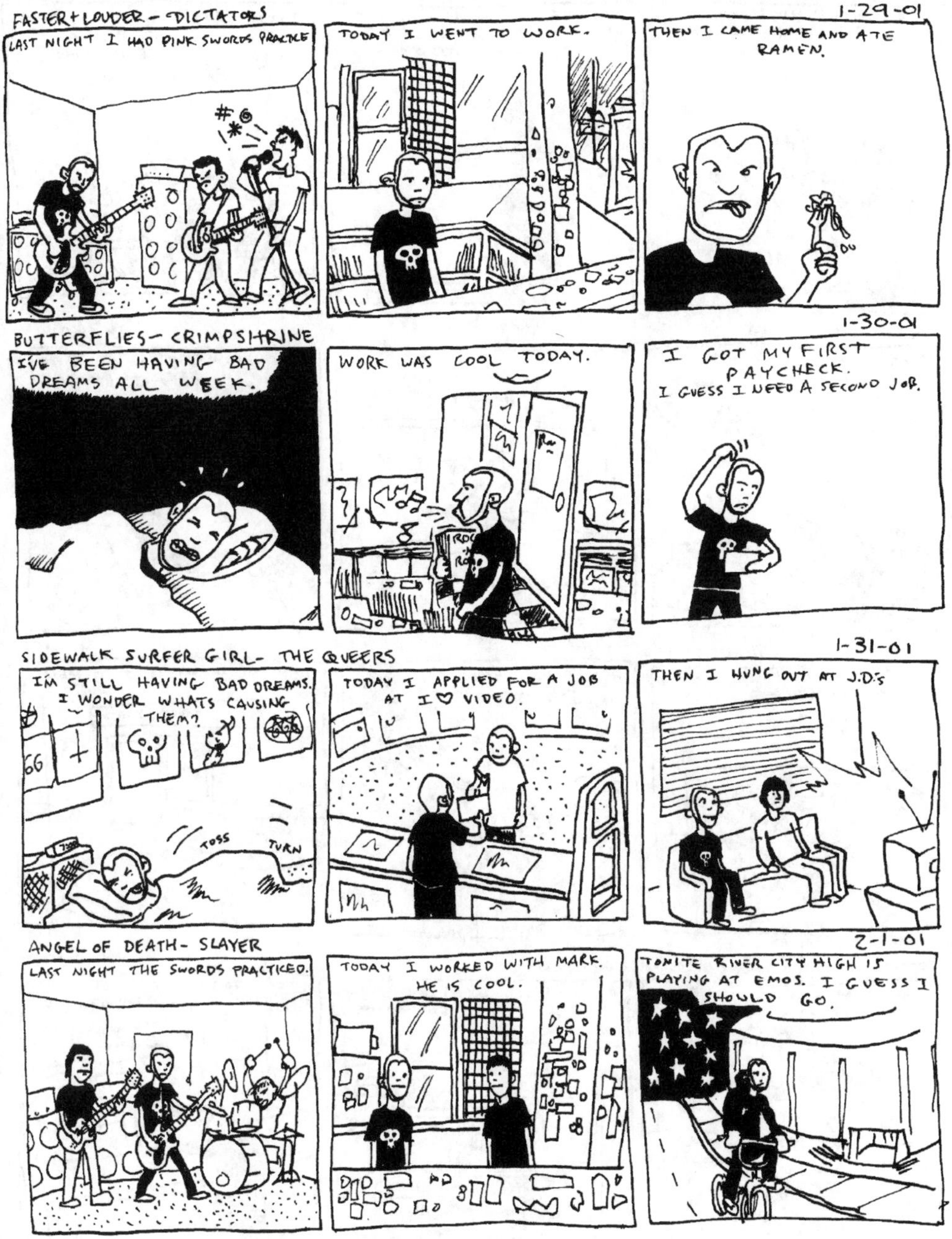
FASTER + LOUDER - DICTATORS
1-29-01
LAST NIGHT I HAD PINK SWORDS PRACTICE
TODAY I WENT TO WORK.
THEN I CAME HOME AND ATE RAMEN.
1-30-01
BUTTERFLIES - CRIMPSHRINE
I'VE BEEN HAVING BAD DREAMS ALL WEEK.
WORK WAS COOL TODAY.
I GOT MY FIRST PAYCHECK.
I GUESS I NEED A SECOND JOB.
SIDEWALK SURFER GIRL - THE QUEERS
1-31-01
I'M STILL HAVING BAD DREAMS. I WONDER WHATS CAUSING THEM?
TOSS
TURN
TODAY I APPLIED FOR A JOB AT I ♡ VIDEO.
THEN I HUNG OUT AT J.D.'s
ANGEL OF DEATH - SLAYER
2-1-01
LAST NIGHT THE SWORDS PRACTICED.
TODAY I WORKED WITH MARK. HE IS COOL.
TONITE RIVER CITY HIGH IS PLAYING AT EMOS. I GUESS I SHOULD GO.

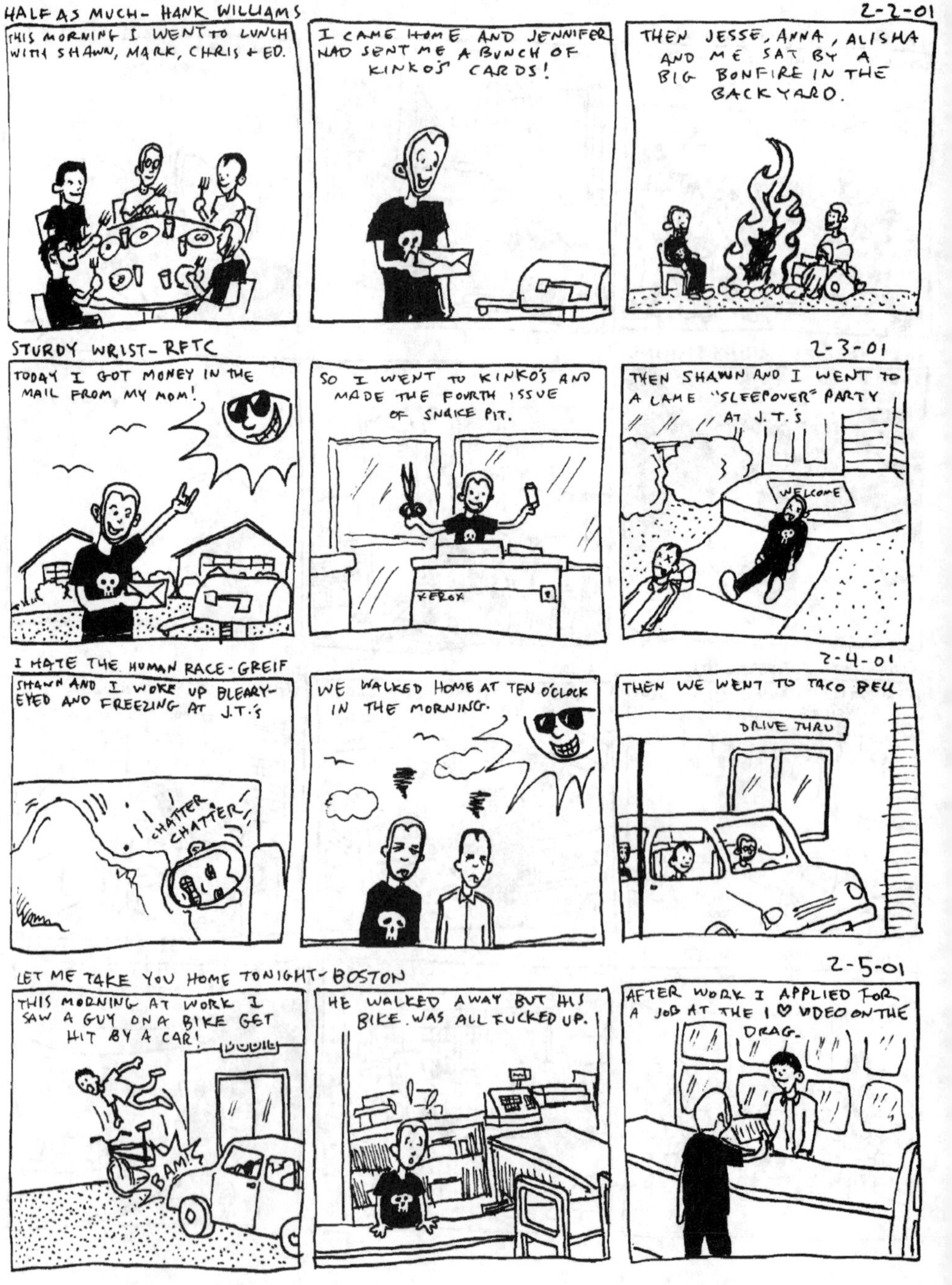
HALF AS MUCH- HANK WILLIAMS
2-2-01
THIS MORNING I WENT TO LUNCH WITH SHAWN, MARK, CHRIS + ED.
I CAME HOME AND JENNIFER HAD SENT ME A BUNCH OF KINKO'S CARDS!
THEN JESSE, ANNA, ALISHA AND ME SAT BY A BIG BONFIRE IN THE BACKYARD.
STURDY WRIST- RFTC
2-3-01
TODAY I GOT MONEY IN THE MAIL FROM MY MOM!
SO I WENT TO KINKO'S AND MADE THE FOURTH ISSUE OF SNAKE PIT.
XEROX
THEN SHAWN AND I WENT TO A LAME "SLEEPOVER" PARTY AT J.T.'S
WELCOME
I HATE THE HUMAN RACE-GREIF
2-4-01
SHAWN AND I WOKE UP BLEARY-EYED AND FREEZING AT J.T.'S
CHATTER CHATTER
WE WALKED HOME AT TEN O'CLOCK IN THE MORNING.
THEN WE WENT TO TACO BELL
DRIVE THRU
LET ME TAKE YOU HOME TONIGHT- BOSTON
2-5-01
THIS MORNING AT WORK I SAW A GUY ON A BIKE GET HIT BY A CAR!
BAM!
HE WALKED AWAY BUT HIS BIKE WAS ALL FUCKED UP.
AFTER WORK I APPLIED FOR A JOB AT THE I ♥ VIDEO ON THE DRAG.

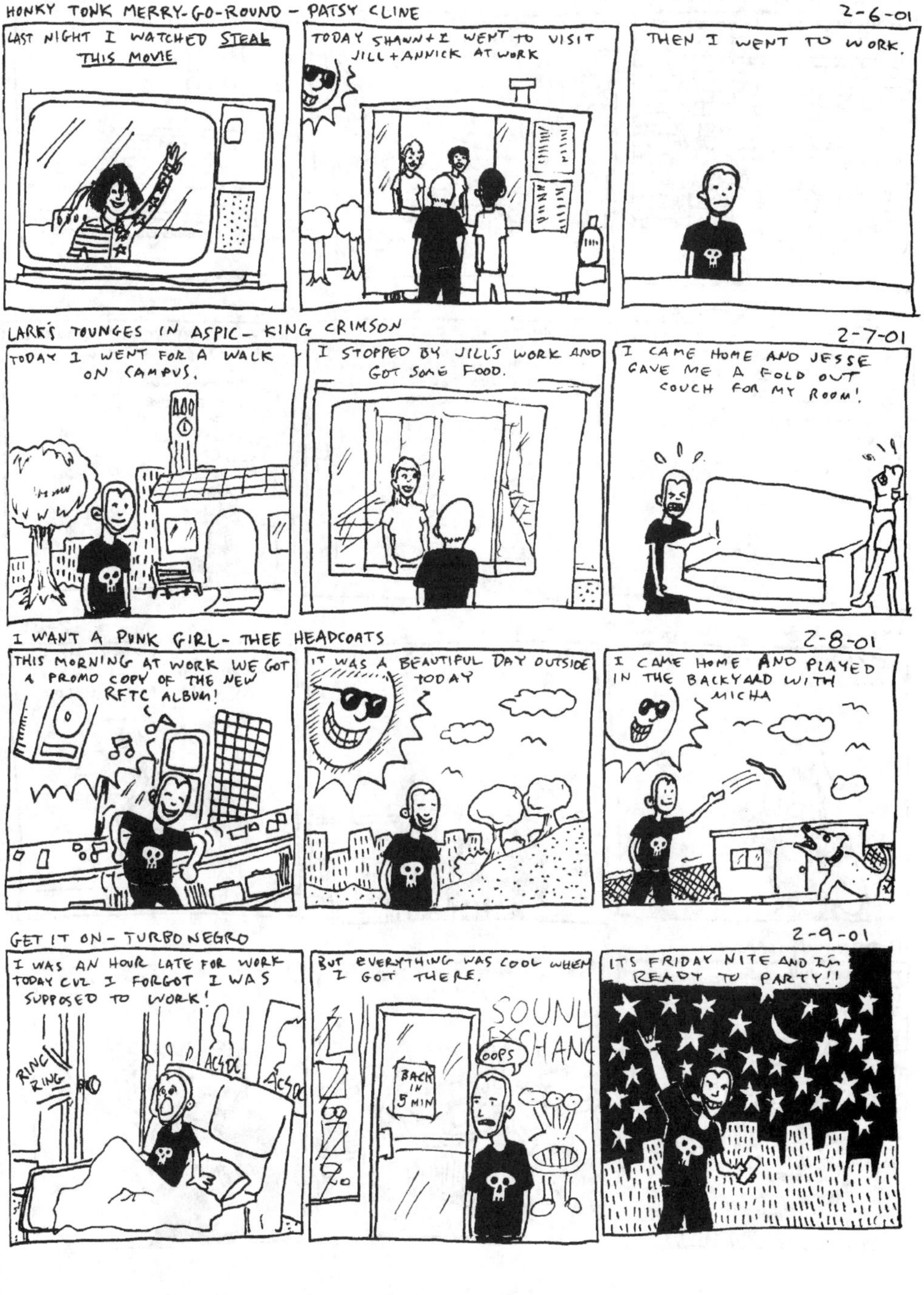
HONKY TONK MERRY-GO-ROUND - PATSY CLINE
2-6-01
LAST NIGHT I WATCHED STEAL THIS MOVIE
TODAY SHAWN+I WENT TO VISIT JILL+ANNICK AT WORK
THEN I WENT TO WORK.
LARK'S TOUNGES IN ASPIC - KING CRIMSON
2-7-01
TODAY I WENT FOR A WALK ON CAMPUS.
I STOPPED BY JILL'S WORK AND GOT SOME FOOD.
I CAME HOME AND JESSE GAVE ME A FOLD OUT COUCH FOR MY ROOM!
I WANT A PUNK GIRL - THEE HEADCOATS
2-8-01
THIS MORNING AT WORK WE GOT A PROMO COPY OF THE NEW RFTC ALBUM!
IT WAS A BEAUTIFUL DAY OUTSIDE TODAY
I CAME HOME AND PLAYED IN THE BACKYARD WITH MICHA
GET IT ON - TURBONEGRO
2-9-01
I WAS AN HOUR LATE FOR WORK TODAY CUZ I FORGOT I WAS SUPPOSED TO WORK!
RING RING
AC/DC
AC/DC
BUT EVERYTHING WAS COOL WHEN I GOT THERE.
BACK IN 5 MIN
OOPS
ITS FRIDAY NITE AND I'M READY TO PARTY!!

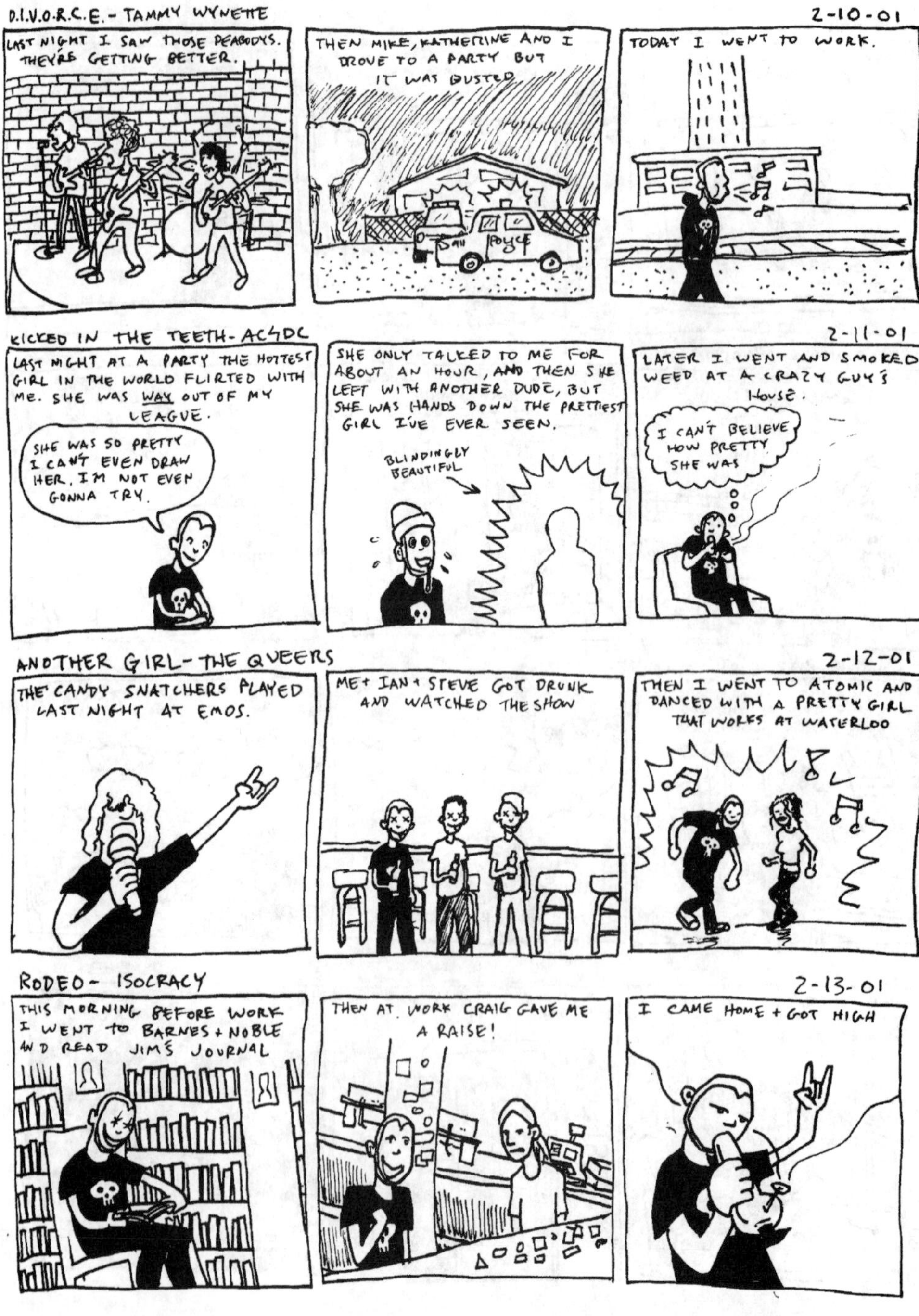
D.I.V.O.R.C.E. - TAMMY WYNETTE
2-10-01
LAST NIGHT I SAW THOSE PEABODYS. THEY'RE GETTING BETTER.
THEN MIKE, KATHERINE AND I DROVE TO A PARTY BUT IT WAS BUSTED
POLICE
TODAY I WENT TO WORK.
KICKED IN THE TEETH - AC/DC
2-11-01
LAST NIGHT AT A PARTY THE HOTTEST GIRL IN THE WORLD FLIRTED WITH ME. SHE WAS WAY OUT OF MY LEAGUE.
SHE WAS SO PRETTY I CAN'T EVEN DRAW HER. I'M NOT EVEN GONNA TRY.
SHE ONLY TALKED TO ME FOR ABOUT AN HOUR, AND THEN SHE LEFT WITH ANOTHER DUDE, BUT SHE WAS HANDS DOWN THE PRETTIEST GIRL I'VE EVER SEEN.
BLINDINGLY BEAUTIFUL
LATER I WENT AND SMOKED WEED AT A CRAZY GUY'S HOUSE.
I CAN'T BELIEVE HOW PRETTY SHE WAS
ANOTHER GIRL - THE QUEERS
2-12-01
THE CANDY SNATCHERS PLAYED LAST NIGHT AT EMOS.
ME + IAN + STEVE GOT DRUNK AND WATCHED THE SHOW
THEN I WENT TO ATOMIC AND DANCED WITH A PRETTY GIRL THAT WORKS AT WATERLOO
RODEO - ISOCRACY
2-13-01
THIS MORNING BEFORE WORK I WENT TO BARNES + NOBLE AND READ JIM'S JOURNAL
THEN AT WORK CRAIG GAVE ME A RAISE!
I CAME HOME + GOT HIGH

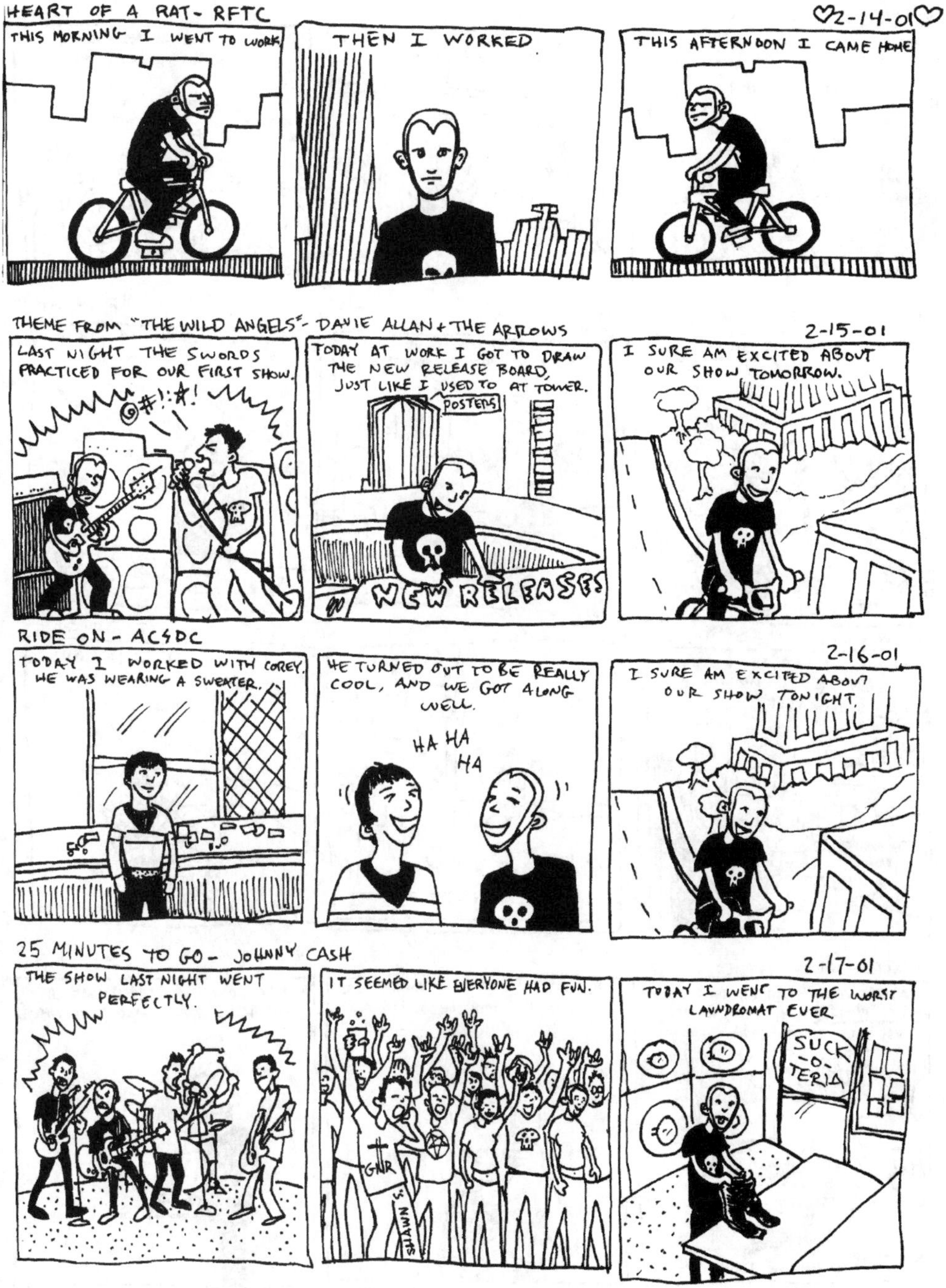
HEART OF A RAT - RFTC
♡2-14-01♡
THIS MORNING I WENT TO WORK
THEN I WORKED
THIS AFTERNOON I CAME HOME
THEME FROM "THE WILD ANGELS" - DAVIE ALLAN + THE ARROWS
2-15-01
LAST NIGHT THE SWORDS PRACTICED FOR OUR FIRST SHOW.
@#!:*!
TODAY AT WORK I GOT TO DRAW THE NEW RELEASE BOARD, JUST LIKE I USED TO AT TOWER.
POSTERS
NEW RELEASES
I SURE AM EXCITED ABOUT OUR SHOW TOMORROW.
RIDE ON - AC/DC
2-16-01
TODAY I WORKED WITH COREY. HE WAS WEARING A SWEATER.
HE TURNED OUT TO BE REALLY COOL, AND WE GOT ALONG WELL.
HA HA HA
I SURE AM EXCITED ABOUT OUR SHOW TONIGHT.
25 MINUTES TO GO - JOHNNY CASH
2-17-01
THE SHOW LAST NIGHT WENT PERFECTLY.
IT SEEMED LIKE EVERYONE HAD FUN.
GNR
TODAY I WENT TO THE WORST LAUNDROMAT EVER
SUCK -O- TERIA

CRIMINALLY INSANE - SLAYER

LAST NIGHT I STAYED AT HOME AND HAD SOME "PERSONAL TIME"

THIS MORNING I GOT MY VAN RUNNING AND GOT SOME GROCERIES.

THEN I CAME HOME AND HAD SOME MORE "PERSONAL TIME"

ENTER TO THE REALM OF SATAN

40 BOYS IN 40 NIGHTS - THE DONNAS

2-19-01

LAST NIGHT WE HAD SWORDS PRACTICE

THEN WE WENT TO STEVE'S HOUSE AND LISTENED TO SLAYER.

TODAY I WENT TO WORK.

THAW (COLD WORLD) - SEPTIC DEATH

2-20-01

AT WORK TODAY SOME GUY BOUGHT $350 WORTH OF POSTERS

THEN THE ENIGMA CAME IN! HE WANTED TO PUT A FLYER UP.

HE LET ME TOUCH ONE OF HIS HORNS!

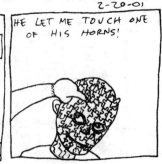

NO ACTION - ELVIS COSTELLO

2-21-01

YESTERDAY I STARTED READING HIGH FIDELITY BY NICK HORNSBY. I USUALLY DON'T READ BOOKS.

BUT I REALLY LIKE THIS ONE

THEN I TALKED TO BETH FOR THE FIRST TIME IN 3 MONTHS.

THEN TODAY AFTER WORK I CAME HOME & ATE MACARONI + CHEESE

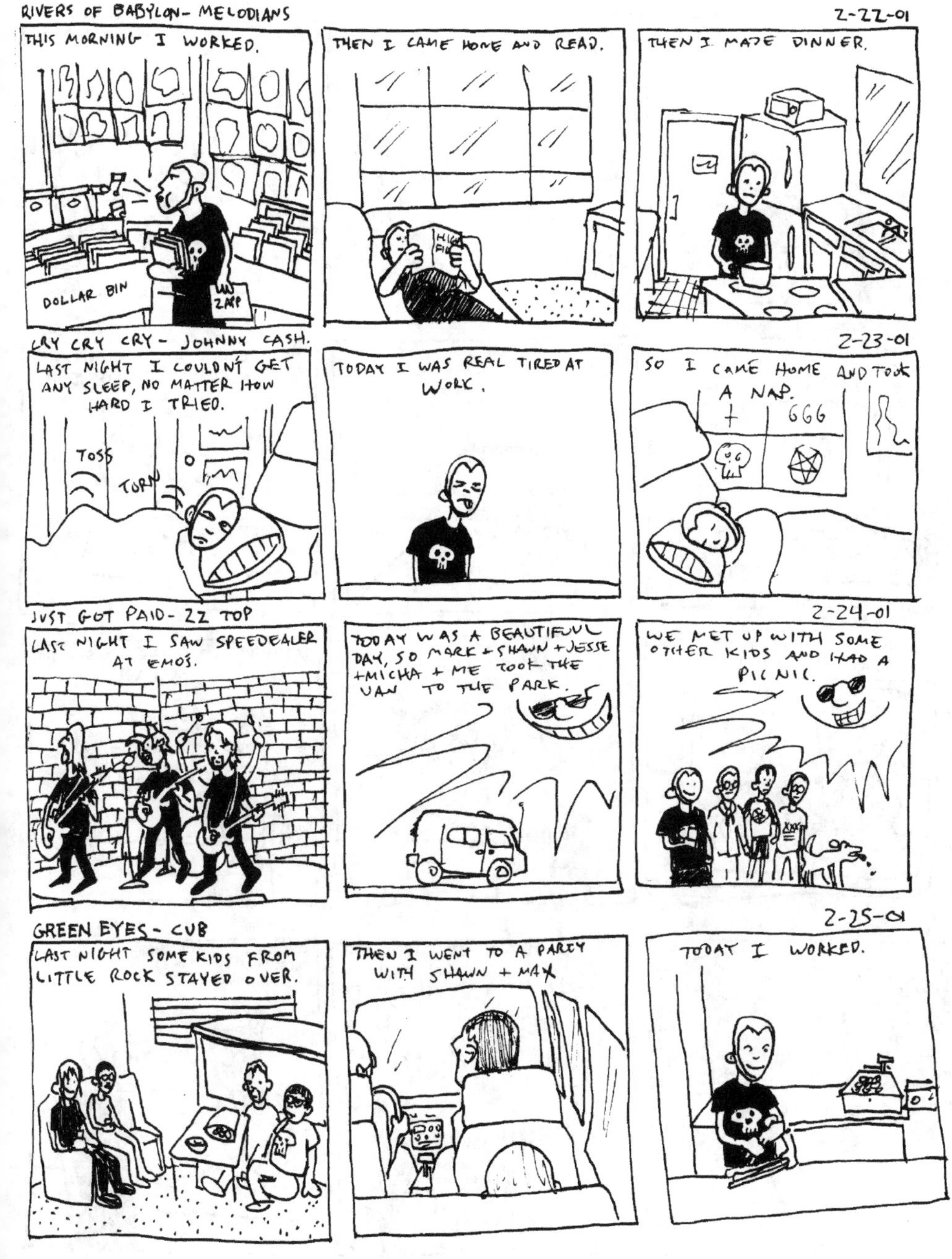
RIVERS OF BABYLON- MELODIANS
2-22-01
THIS MORNING I WORKED.
DOLLAR BIN
ZAPP
THEN I CAME HOME AND READ.
THEN I MADE DINNER.
CRY CRY CRY - JOHNNY CASH.
2-23-01
LAST NIGHT I COULDN'T GET ANY SLEEP, NO MATTER HOW HARD I TRIED.
TOSS
TURN
TODAY I WAS REAL TIRED AT WORK.
SO I CAME HOME AND TOOK A NAP.
666
JUST GOT PAID - ZZ TOP
2-24-01
LAST NIGHT I SAW SPEEDEALER AT EMO'S.
TODAY WAS A BEAUTIFUL DAY, SO MARK + SHAWN + JESSE +MICHA + ME TOOK THE VAN TO THE PARK.
WE MET UP WITH SOME OTHER KIDS AND HAD A PICNIC.
XXX
GREEN EYES - CUB
2-25-01
LAST NIGHT SOME KIDS FROM LITTLE ROCK STAYED OVER.
THEN I WENT TO A PARTY WITH SHAWN + MAX
TODAY I WORKED.

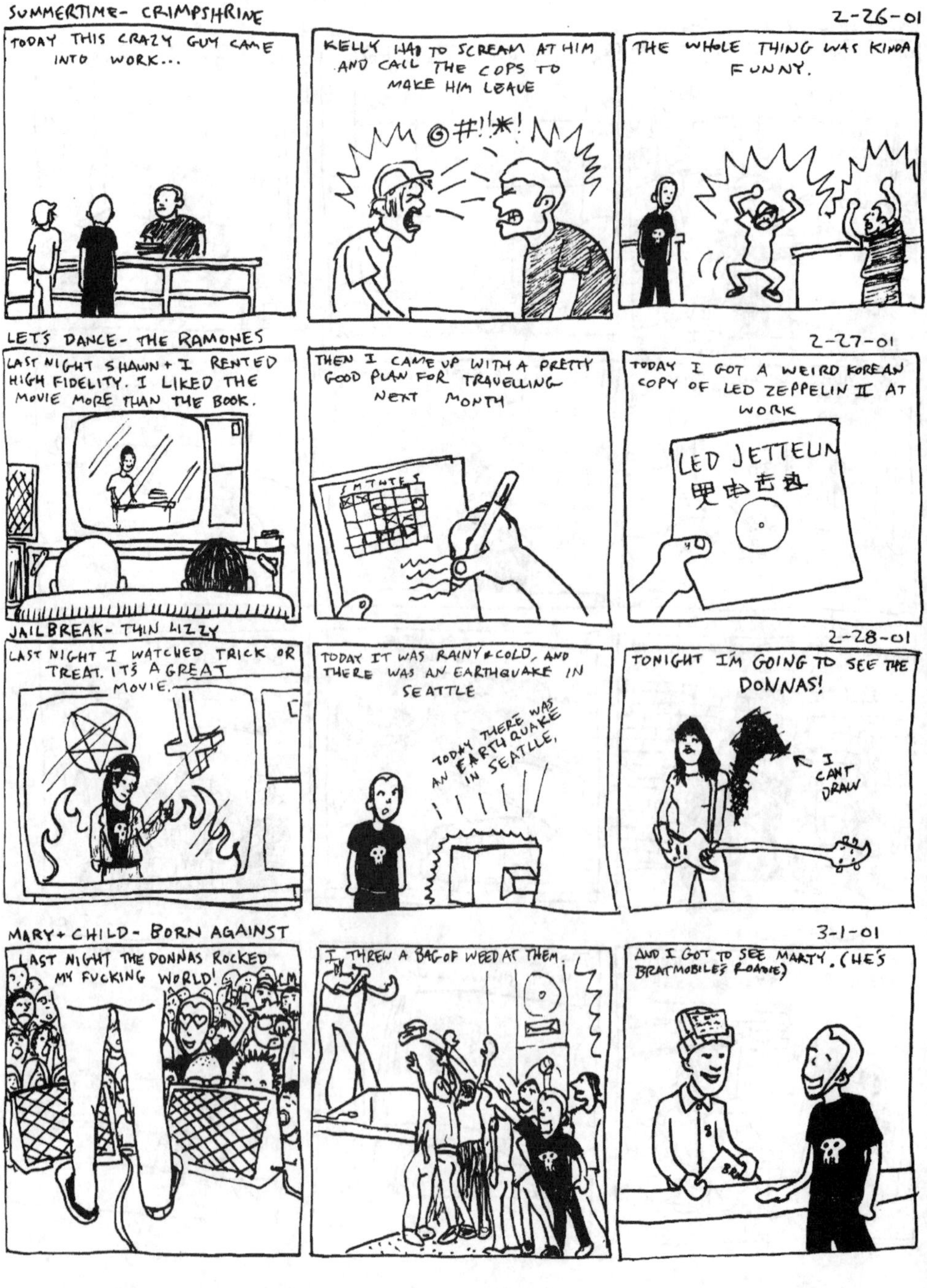
SUMMERTIME- CRIMPSHRINE
2-26-01
TODAY THIS CRAZY GUY CAME INTO WORK...
KELLY HAD TO SCREAM AT HIM AND CALL THE COPS TO MAKE HIM LEAVE
@#!!*!
THE WHOLE THING WAS KINDA FUNNY.
LET'S DANCE- THE RAMONES
2-27-01
LAST NIGHT SHAWN + I RENTED HIGH FIDELITY. I LIKED THE MOVIE MORE THAN THE BOOK.
THEN I CAME UP WITH A PRETTY GOOD PLAN FOR TRAVELLING NEXT MONTH
S M T W T F S
TODAY I GOT A WEIRD KOREAN COPY OF LED ZEPPELIN II AT WORK
LED JETTELIN
JAILBREAK- THIN LIZZY
2-28-01
LAST NIGHT I WATCHED TRICK OR TREAT. IT'S A GREAT MOVIE.
TODAY IT WAS RAINY + COLD, AND THERE WAS AN EARTHQUAKE IN SEATTLE
TODAY THERE WAS AN EARTHQUAKE IN SEATTLE,
TONIGHT I'M GOING TO SEE THE DONNAS!
I CANT DRAW
MARY + CHILD- BORN AGAINST
3-1-01
LAST NIGHT THE DONNAS ROCKED MY FUCKING WORLD!
I THREW A BAG OF WEED AT THEM.
AND I GOT TO SEE MARTY. (HE'S BRATMOBILE'S ROADIE)

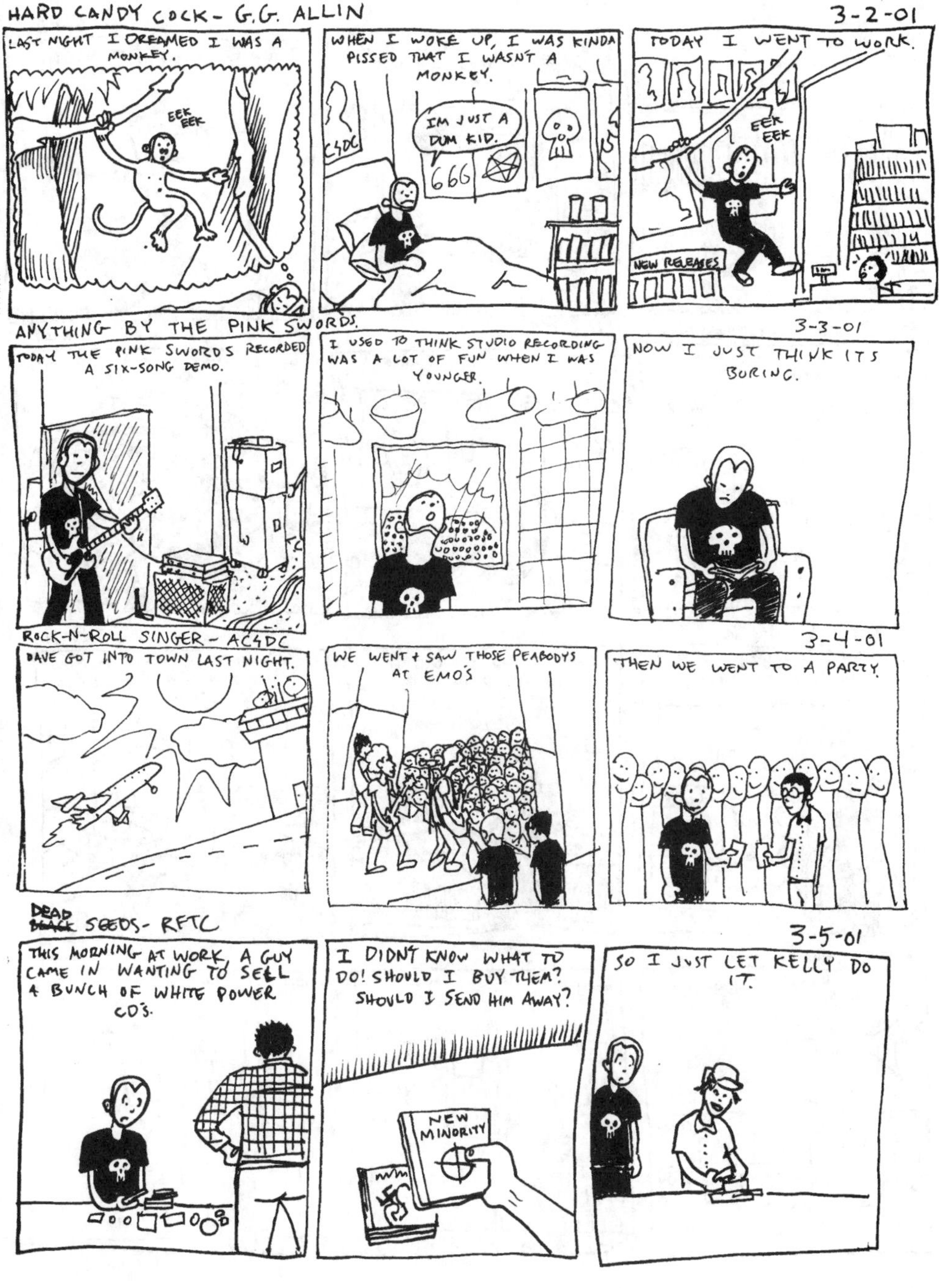
HARD CANDY COCK- G.G. ALLIN
3-2-01
LAST NIGHT I DREAMED I WAS A MONKEY.
EEK EEK
WHEN I WOKE UP, I WAS KINDA PISSED THAT I WASN'T A MONKEY.
I'M JUST A DUM KID.
666
AC/DC
TODAY I WENT TO WORK.
EEK EEK
NEW RELEASES
ANYTHING BY THE PINK SWORDS.
3-3-01
TODAY THE PINK SWORDS RECORDED A SIX-SONG DEMO.
I USED TO THINK STUDIO RECORDING WAS A LOT OF FUN WHEN I WAS YOUNGER.
NOW I JUST THINK ITS BORING.
ROCK-N-ROLL SINGER - AC/DC
3-4-01
DAVE GOT INTO TOWN LAST NIGHT.
WE WENT + SAW THOSE PEABODYS AT EMO'S
THEN WE WENT TO A PARTY.
DEAD ~~BLACK~~ SEEDS- RFTC
3-5-01
THIS MORNING AT WORK, A GUY CAME IN WANTING TO SELL A BUNCH OF WHITE POWER CD'S.
I DIDN'T KNOW WHAT TO DO! SHOULD I BUY THEM? SHOULD I SEND HIM AWAY?
NEW MINORITY
SO I JUST LET KELLY DO IT.

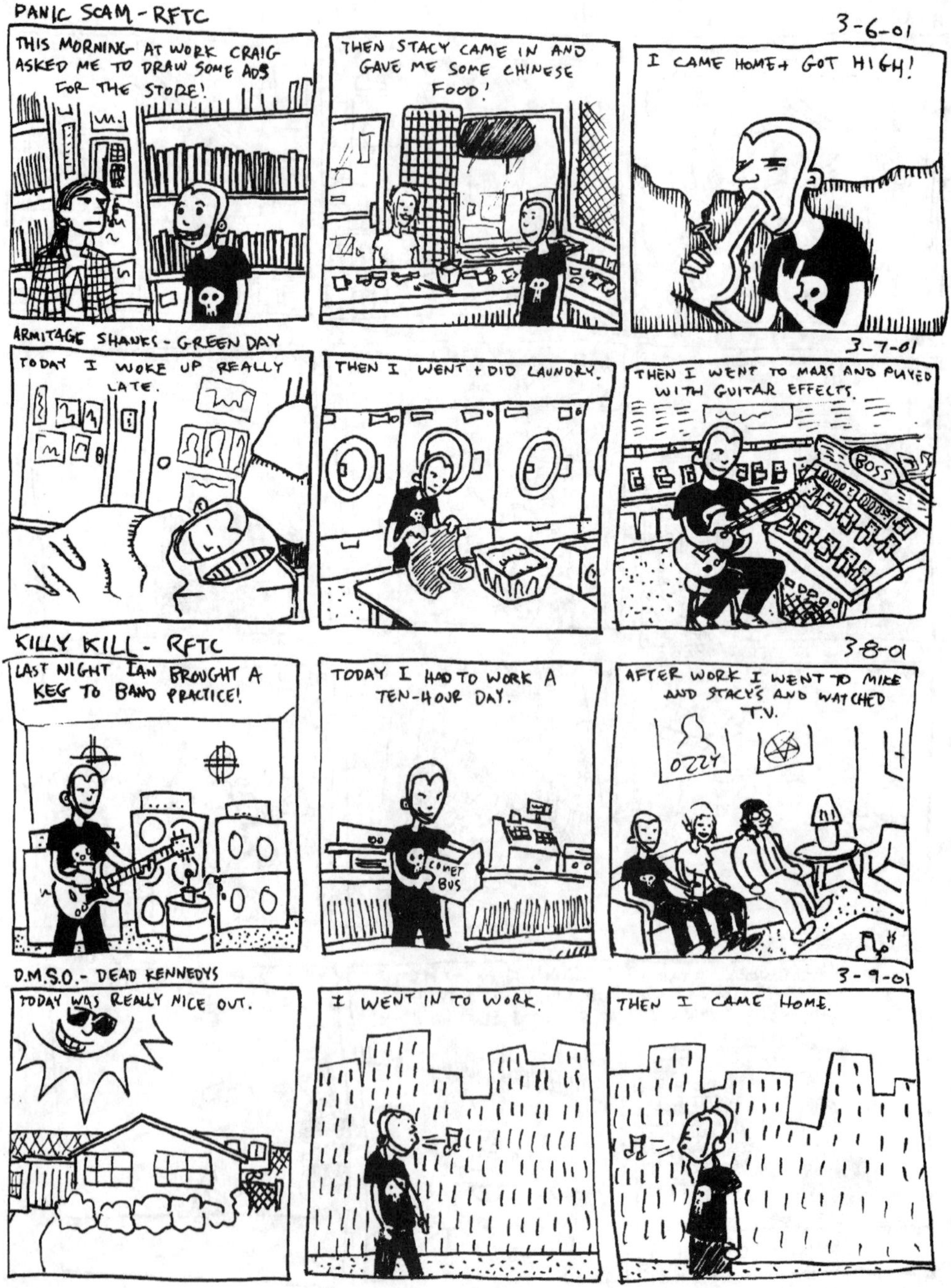
PANIC SCAM - RFTC
3-6-01
THIS MORNING AT WORK CRAIG ASKED ME TO DRAW SOME ADS FOR THE STORE!
THEN STACY CAME IN AND GAVE ME SOME CHINESE FOOD!
I CAME HOME + GOT HIGH!
ARMITAGE SHANKS - GREEN DAY
3-7-01
TODAY I WOKE UP REALLY LATE.
THEN I WENT + DID LAUNDRY.
THEN I WENT TO MARS AND PLAYED WITH GUITAR EFFECTS.
BOSS
KILLY KILL - RFTC
3-8-01
LAST NIGHT IAN BROUGHT A KEG TO BAND PRACTICE!
TODAY I HAD TO WORK A TEN-HOUR DAY.
COMET BUS
AFTER WORK I WENT TO MIKE AND STACY'S AND WATCHED T.V.
OZZY
D.M.S.O. - DEAD KENNEDYS
3-9-01
TODAY WAS REALLY NICE OUT.
I WENT IN TO WORK.
THEN I CAME HOME.

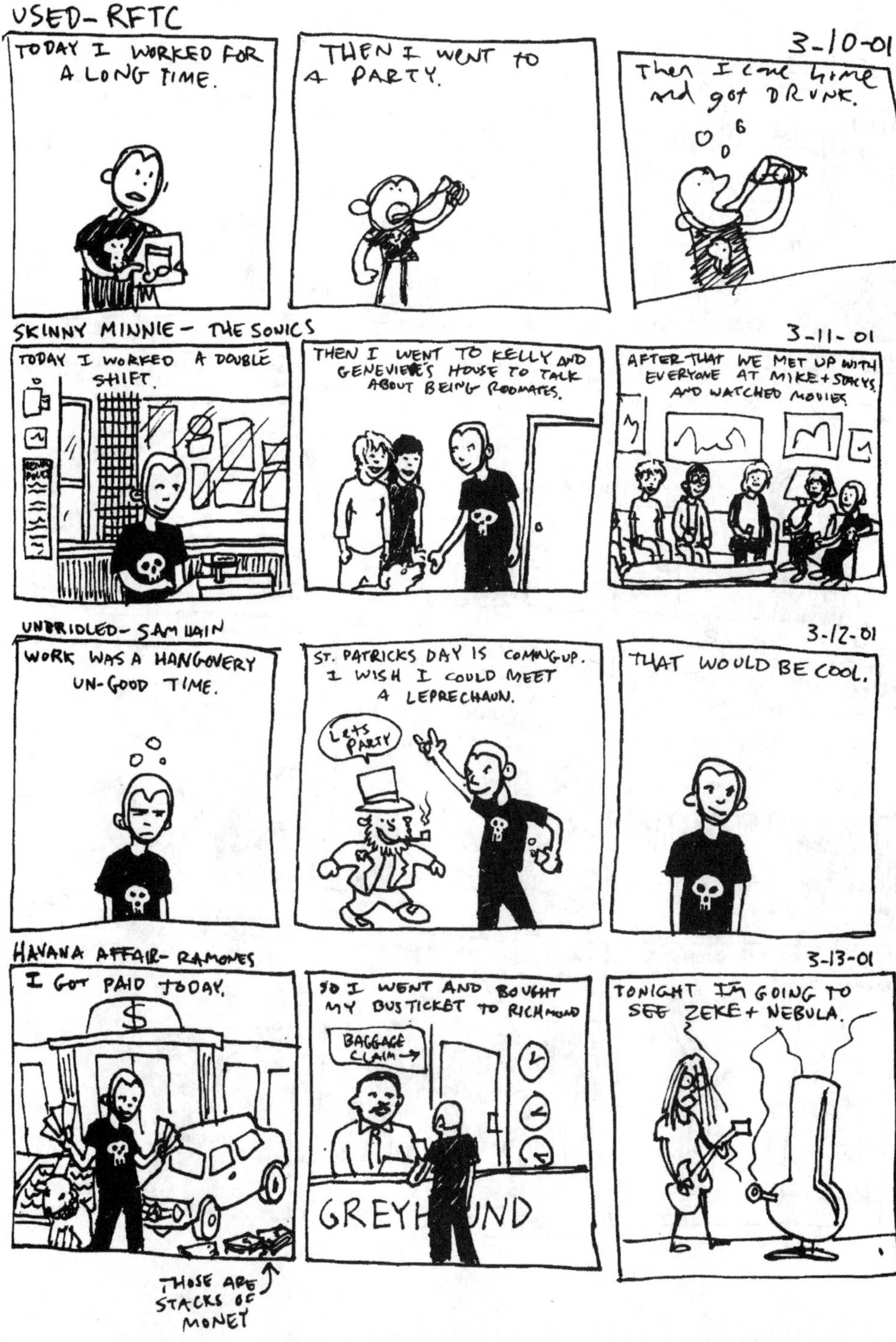

USED- RFTC
3-10-01
TODAY I WORKED FOR A LONG TIME.
THEN I WENT TO A PARTY.
Then I came home and got DRUNK.
SKINNY MINNIE- THE SONICS
3-11-01
TODAY I WORKED A DOUBLE SHIFT.
THEN I WENT TO KELLY AND GENEVIEVE'S HOUSE TO TALK ABOUT BEING ROOMATES.
AFTER THAT WE MET UP WITH EVERYONE AT MIKE + STACY'S AND WATCHED MOVIES.
UNBRIDLED- SAMHAIN
3-12-01
WORK WAS A HANGOVERY UN-GOOD TIME.
ST. PATRICKS DAY IS COMING UP. I WISH I COULD MEET A LEPRECHAUN.
Lets PARTY
THAT WOULD BE COOL.
HAVANA AFFAIR- RAMONES
3-13-01
I GOT PAID TODAY.
$
THOSE ARE STACKS OF MONEY
SO I WENT AND BOUGHT MY BUSTICKET TO RICHMOND
BAGGAGE CLAIM
GREYHOUND
TONIGHT I'M GOING TO SEE ZEKE + NEBULA.

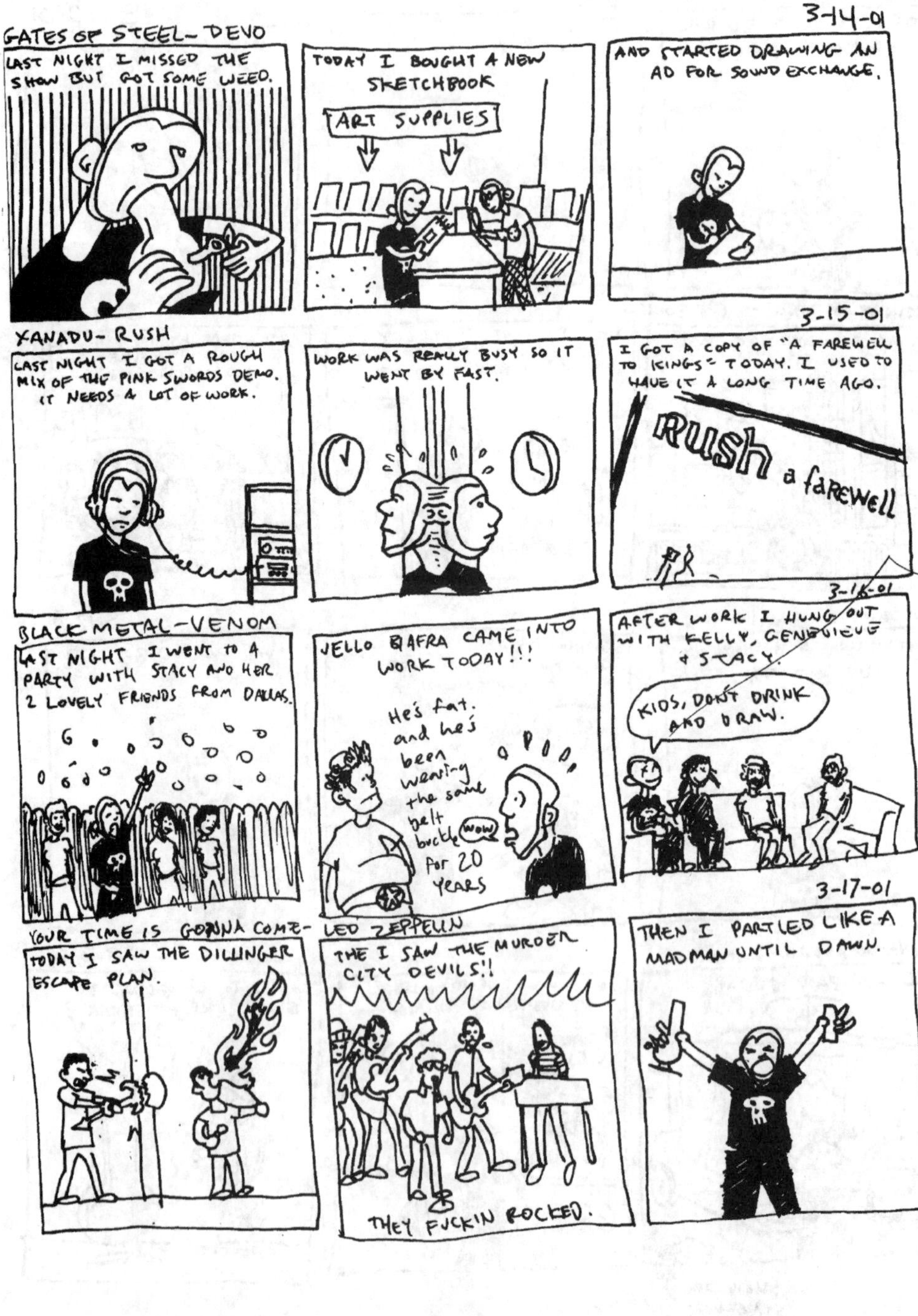

3-14-01
GATES OF STEEL - DEVO
LAST NIGHT I MISSED THE SHOW BUT GOT SOME WEED.
TODAY I BOUGHT A NEW SKETCHBOOK
ART SUPPLIES
AND STARTED DRAWING AN AD FOR SOUND EXCHANGE.
3-15-01
XANADU - RUSH
LAST NIGHT I GOT A ROUGH MIX OF THE PINK SWORDS DEMO. IT NEEDS A LOT OF WORK.
WORK WAS REALLY BUSY SO IT WENT BY FAST.
I GOT A COPY OF "A FAREWELL TO KINGS" TODAY. I USED TO HAVE IT A LONG TIME AGO.
Rush a farewell
3-16-01
BLACK METAL - VENOM
LAST NIGHT I WENT TO A PARTY WITH STACY AND HER 2 LOVELY FRIENDS FROM DALLAS.
JELLO BIAFRA CAME INTO WORK TODAY!!!
He's fat. and he's been wearing the same belt buckle for 20 years
WOW
AFTER WORK I HUNG OUT WITH KELLY, GENEVIEVE & STACY.
KIDS, DON'T DRINK AND DRAW.
3-17-01
YOUR TIME IS GONNA COME - LED ZEPPELIN
TODAY I SAW THE DILLINGER ESCAPE PLAN.
THE I SAW THE MURDER CITY DEVILS!!
THEY FUCKIN ROCKED.
THEN I PARTIED LIKE A MADMAN UNTIL DAWN.

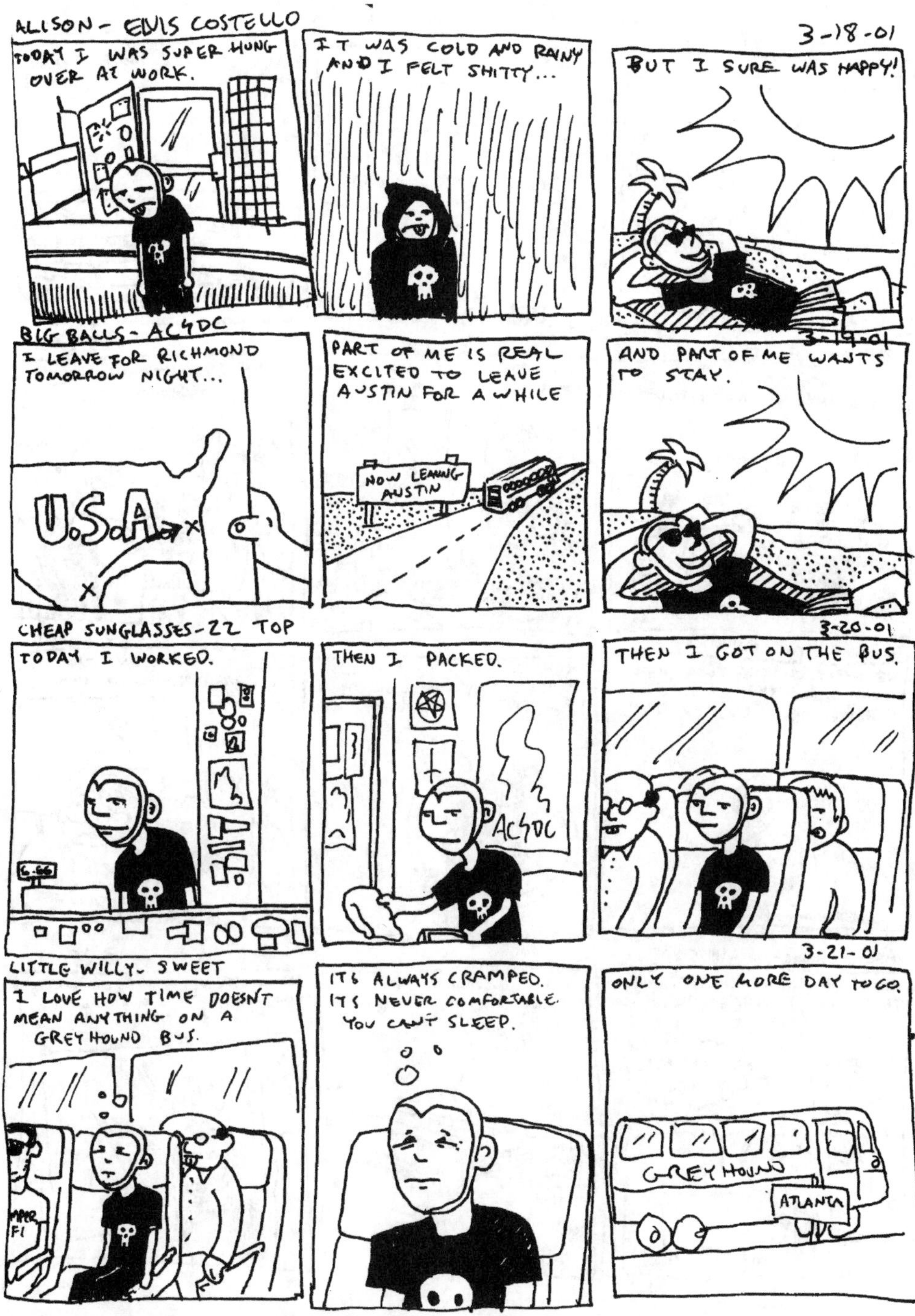
ALLISON - ELVIS COSTELLO
3-18-01
TODAY I WAS SUPER HUNG OVER AT WORK.
IT WAS COLD AND RAINY AND I FELT SHITTY...
BUT I SURE WAS HAPPY!
BIG BALLS - AC/DC
3-19-01
I LEAVE FOR RICHMOND TOMORROW NIGHT...
U.S.A
PART OF ME IS REAL EXCITED TO LEAVE AUSTIN FOR A WHILE
NOW LEAVING AUSTIN
AND PART OF ME WANTS TO STAY.
CHEAP SUNGLASSES - ZZ TOP
3-20-01
TODAY I WORKED.
THEN I PACKED.
AC/DC
THEN I GOT ON THE BUS.
LITTLE WILLY - SWEET
3-21-01
I LOVE HOW TIME DOESNT MEAN ANYTHING ON A GREYHOUND BUS.
ITS ALWAYS CRAMPED. ITS NEVER COMFORTABLE. YOU CANT SLEEP.
ONLY ONE MORE DAY TO GO.
GREYHOUND
ATLANTA

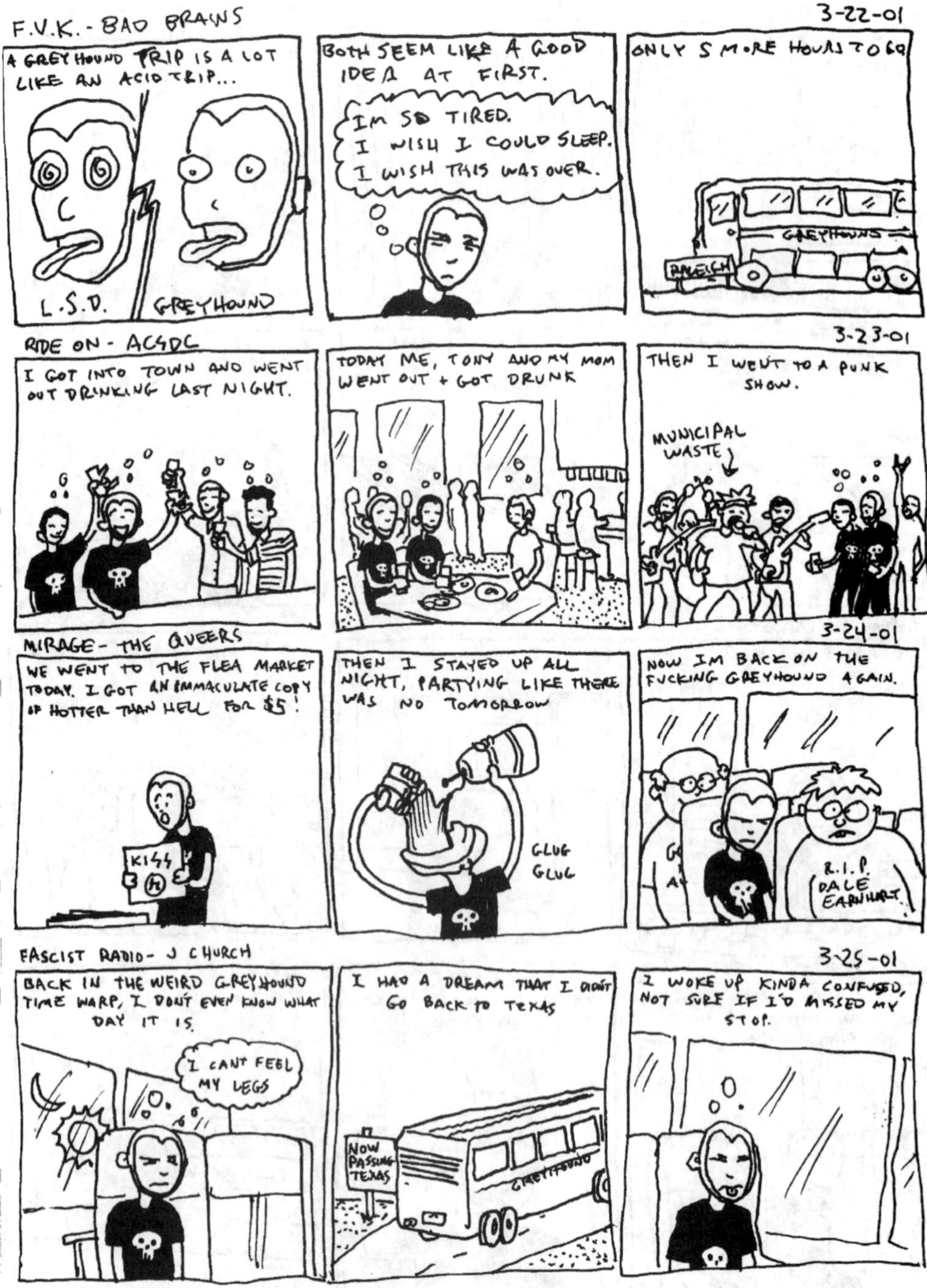
F.V.K. - BAD BRAINS
3-22-01
A GREYHOUND TRIP IS A LOT LIKE AN ACID TRIP...
L.S.D.
GREYHOUND
BOTH SEEM LIKE A GOOD IDEA AT FIRST.
I'M SO TIRED. I WISH I COULD SLEEP. I WISH THIS WAS OVER.
ONLY 5 MORE HOURS TO GO
GREYHOUND
RALEIGH
RIDE ON - AC/DC
3-23-01
I GOT INTO TOWN AND WENT OUT DRINKING LAST NIGHT.
TODAY ME, TONY AND MY MOM WENT OUT + GOT DRUNK
THEN I WENT TO A PUNK SHOW.
MUNICIPAL WASTE
MIRAGE - THE QUEERS
3-24-01
WE WENT TO THE FLEA MARKET TODAY. I GOT AN IMMACULATE COPY OF HOTTER THAN HELL FOR $5!
KISS
THEN I STAYED UP ALL NIGHT, PARTYING LIKE THERE WAS NO TOMORROW
GLUG GLUG
NOW I'M BACK ON THE FUCKING GREYHOUND AGAIN.
R.I.P. DALE EARNHART
FASCIST RADIO - J CHURCH
3-25-01
BACK IN THE WEIRD GREYHOUND TIME WARP, I DON'T EVEN KNOW WHAT DAY IT IS.
I CAN'T FEEL MY LEGS
I HAD A DREAM THAT I DIDN'T GO BACK TO TEXAS
NOW PASSING TEXAS
GREYHOUND
I WOKE UP KINDA CONFUSED, NOT SURE IF I'D MISSED MY STOP.

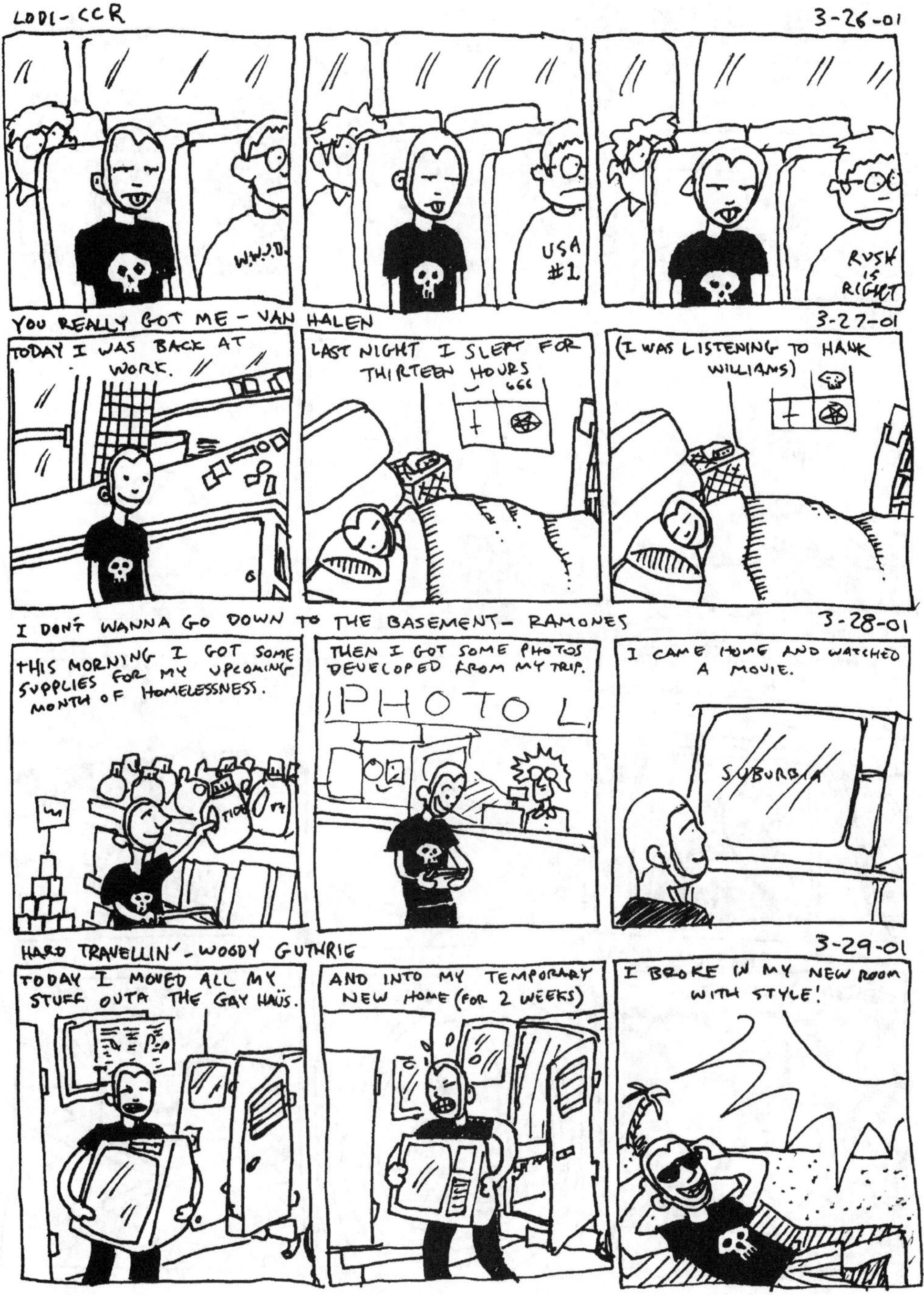

LODI - CCR
3-26-01
W.W.J.D.
USA #1
RUSH IS RIGHT
YOU REALLY GOT ME - VAN HALEN
3-27-01
TODAY I WAS BACK AT WORK.
LAST NIGHT I SLEPT FOR THIRTEEN HOURS
666
(I WAS LISTENING TO HANK WILLIAMS)
I DON'T WANNA GO DOWN TO THE BASEMENT - RAMONES
3-28-01
THIS MORNING I GOT SOME SUPPLIES FOR MY UPCOMING MONTH OF HOMELESSNESS.
TIDE
THEN I GOT SOME PHOTOS DEVELOPED FROM MY TRIP.
PHOTO
I CAME HOME AND WATCHED A MOVIE.
SUBURBIA
HARD TRAVELLIN' - WOODY GUTHRIE
3-29-01
TODAY I MOVED ALL MY STUFF OUTA THE GAY HAÜS.
AND INTO MY TEMPORARY NEW HOME (FOR 2 WEEKS)
I BROKE IN MY NEW ROOM WITH STYLE!

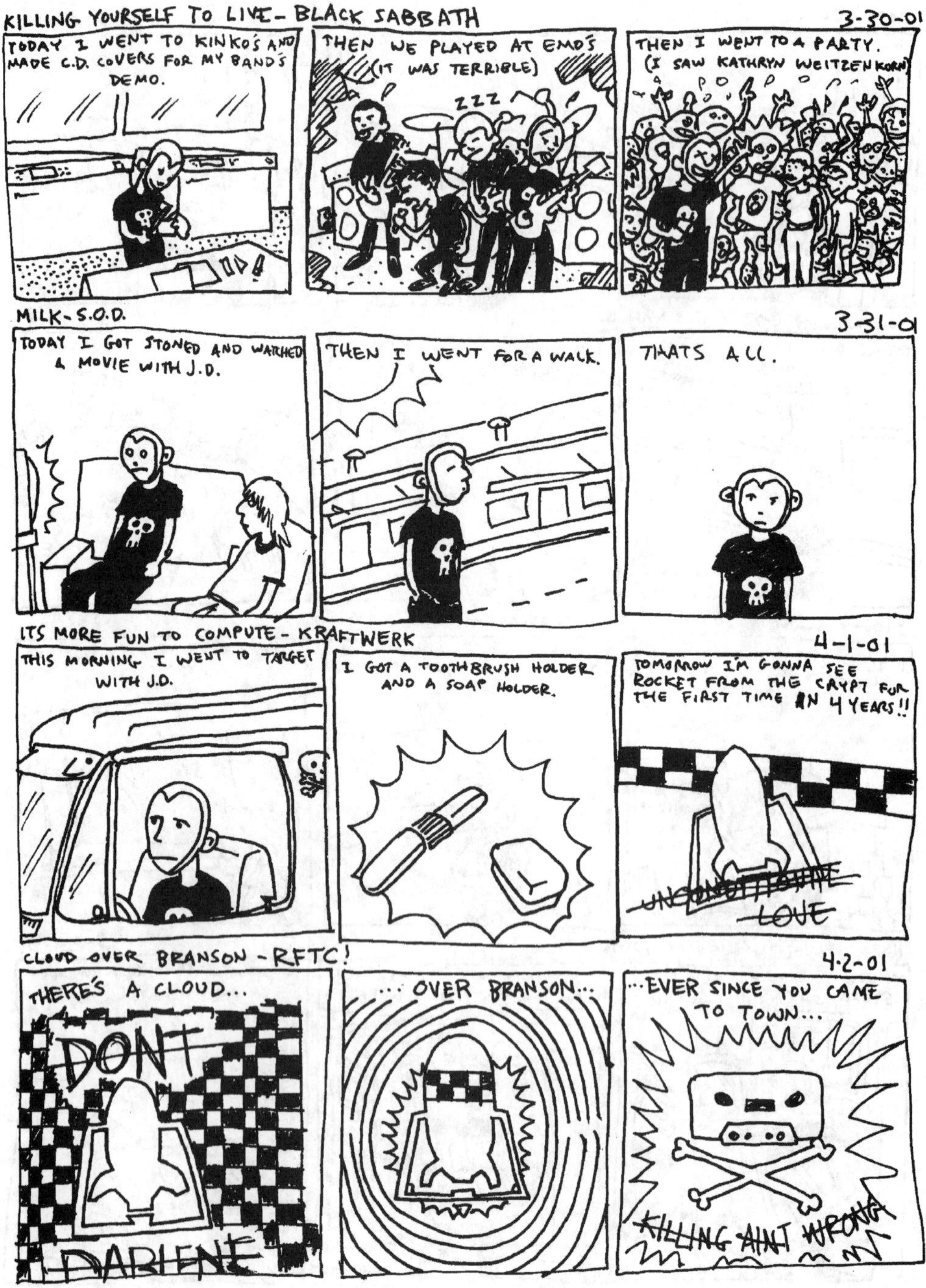

KILLING YOURSELF TO LIVE - BLACK SABBATH
3-30-01
TODAY I WENT TO KINKO'S AND MADE C.D. COVERS FOR MY BAND'S DEMO.
THEN WE PLAYED AT EMO'S (IT WAS TERRIBLE)
ZZZ
THEN I WENT TO A PARTY. (I SAW KATHRYN WEITZENKORN)
MILK - S.O.D.
3-31-01
TODAY I GOT STONED AND WATCHED A MOVIE WITH J.D.
THEN I WENT FOR A WALK.
THATS ALL.
ITS MORE FUN TO COMPUTE - KRAFTWERK
4-1-01
THIS MORNING I WENT TO TARGET WITH J.D.
I GOT A TOOTHBRUSH HOLDER AND A SOAP HOLDER.
TOMORROW I'M GONNA SEE ROCKET FROM THE CRYPT FOR THE FIRST TIME IN 4 YEARS!!
LOVE
CLOUD OVER BRANSON - RFTC!
4-2-01
THERE'S A CLOUD...
DONT
DARLENE
... OVER BRANSON...
... EVER SINCE YOU CAME TO TOWN...
KILLING AINT WRONG

ROCKNROLL OUTLAW - ROSE TATTOO

4-3-01

THE SHOW LAST NIGHT WAS AWESOME.

TODAY I WORKED.

THEN I CAME HOME AND TOOK A SHOWER.

NEVER SAY DIE - OZZY

4-4-01

TODAY I DID LAUNDRY

THEN I TOOK A SHOWER (MY HOUSE HAS THE BEST SHOWER I'VE EVER USED)

THEN I WENT TO BAND PRACTICE. I THINK I MIGHT QUIT MY BAND. ???

HELLO THERE - CHEAP TRICK

4-5-01

TODAY AFTER WORK I TOOK SOME BONG HITS.

THEN ROSA MARIA'S + JD'S TEAPOTS CAME TO LIFE AND GOT IN A FIGHT!!

WOW, THAT WAS GOOD WEED.

SOUND SYSTEM - OP IVY

4-6-01

LAST NIGHT I GOT DRUNK AND GAVE MYSELF A DUMB TATTOO

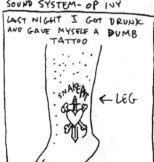

SNAKE ← LEG

TODAY I WENT FOR A WALK

I FOUND A NEAT LITTLE TRAIL IN THE WOODS.

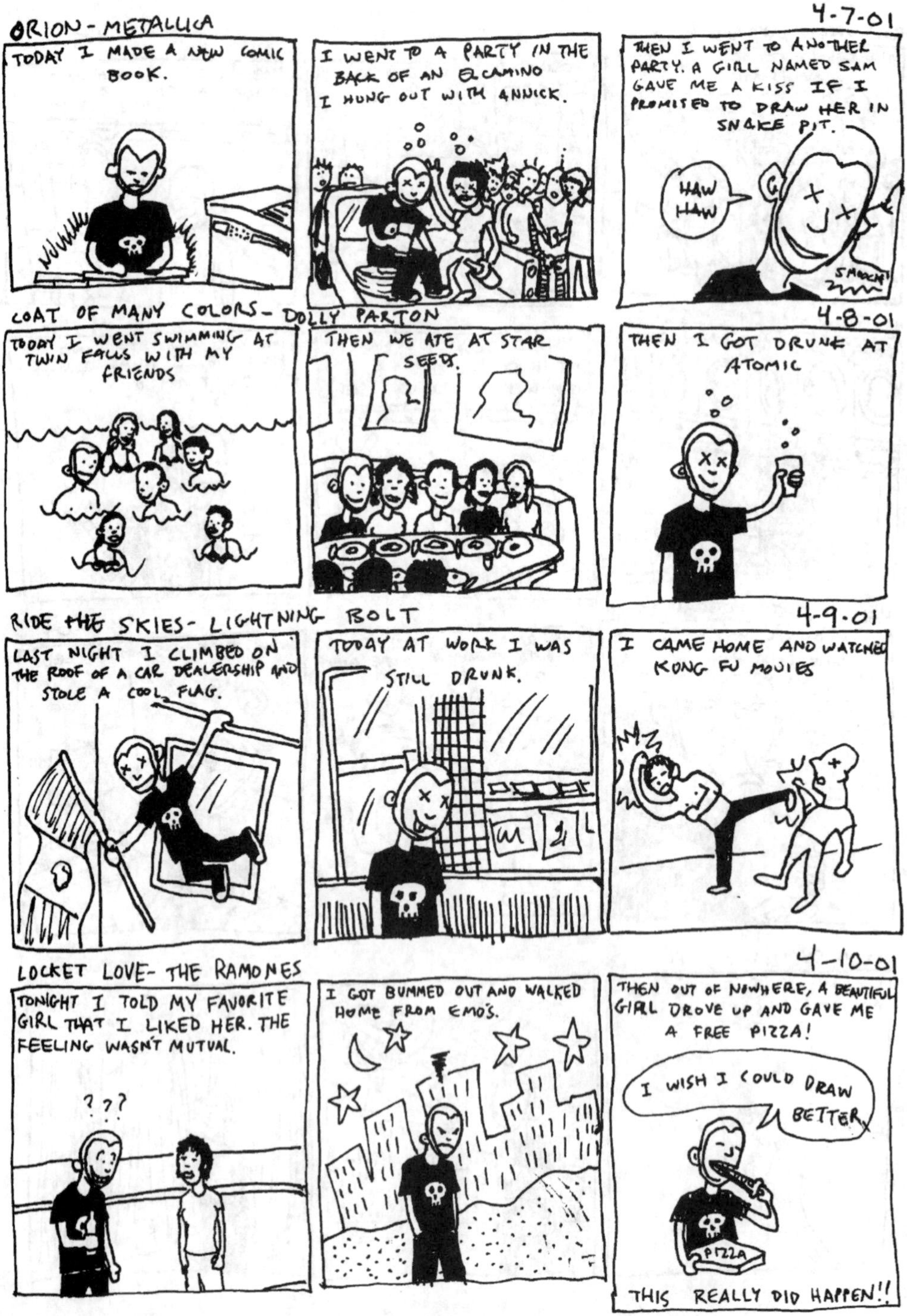
ORION - METALLICA
4-7-01
TODAY I MADE A NEW COMIC BOOK.
I WENT TO A PARTY IN THE BACK OF AN EL CAMINO
I HUNG OUT WITH ANNICK.
THEN I WENT TO ANOTHER PARTY. A GIRL NAMED SAM GAVE ME A KISS IF I PROMISED TO DRAW HER IN SNAKE PIT.
HAW HAW
SMOOCH
COAT OF MANY COLORS - DOLLY PARTON
4-8-01
TODAY I WENT SWIMMING AT TWIN FALLS WITH MY FRIENDS
THEN WE ATE AT STAR SEEDS.
THEN I GOT DRUNK AT ATOMIC
RIDE THE SKIES - LIGHTNING BOLT
4-9-01
LAST NIGHT I CLIMBED ON THE ROOF OF A CAR DEALERSHIP AND STOLE A COOL FLAG.
TODAY AT WORK I WAS STILL DRUNK.
I CAME HOME AND WATCHED KUNG FU MOVIES
LOCKET LOVE - THE RAMONES
4-10-01
TONIGHT I TOLD MY FAVORITE GIRL THAT I LIKED HER. THE FEELING WASN'T MUTUAL.
???
I GOT BUMMED OUT AND WALKED HOME FROM EMO'S.
THEN OUT OF NOWHERE, A BEAUTIFUL GIRL DROVE UP AND GAVE ME A FREE PIZZA!
I WISH I COULD DRAW BETTER.
PIZZA
THIS REALLY DID HAPPEN!!

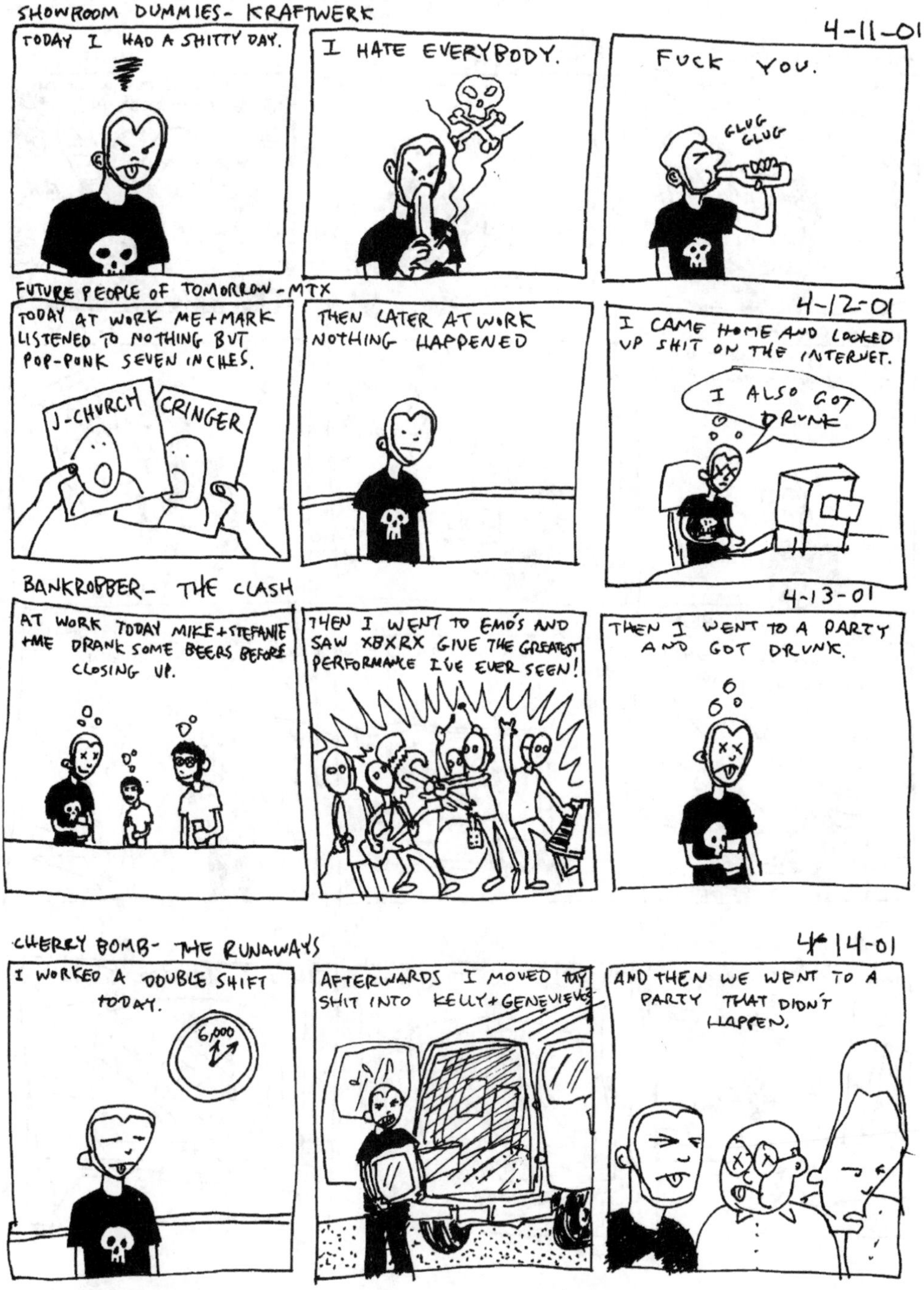
SHOWROOM DUMMIES- KRAFTWERK
4-11-01
TODAY I HAD A SHITTY DAY.
I HATE EVERYBODY.
FUCK YOU.
GLUG GLUG
FUTURE PEOPLE OF TOMORROW - MTX
4-12-01
TODAY AT WORK ME+MARK LISTENED TO NOTHING BUT POP-PUNK SEVEN INCHES.
J-CHURCH
CRINGER
THEN LATER AT WORK NOTHING HAPPENED
I CAME HOME AND LOOKED UP SHIT ON THE INTERNET.
I ALSO GOT DRUNK
BANKROBBER- THE CLASH
4-13-01
AT WORK TODAY MIKE+STEFANIE +ME DRANK SOME BEERS BEFORE CLOSING UP.
THEN I WENT TO EMO'S AND SAW XBXRX GIVE THE GREATEST PERFORMANCE I'VE EVER SEEN!
THEN I WENT TO A PARTY AND GOT DRUNK.
CHERRY BOMB- THE RUNAWAYS
4-14-01
I WORKED A DOUBLE SHIFT TODAY.
6,000
AFTERWARDS I MOVED MY SHIT INTO KELLY+GENEVIEVE'S
AND THEN WE WENT TO A PARTY THAT DIDN'T HAPPEN.

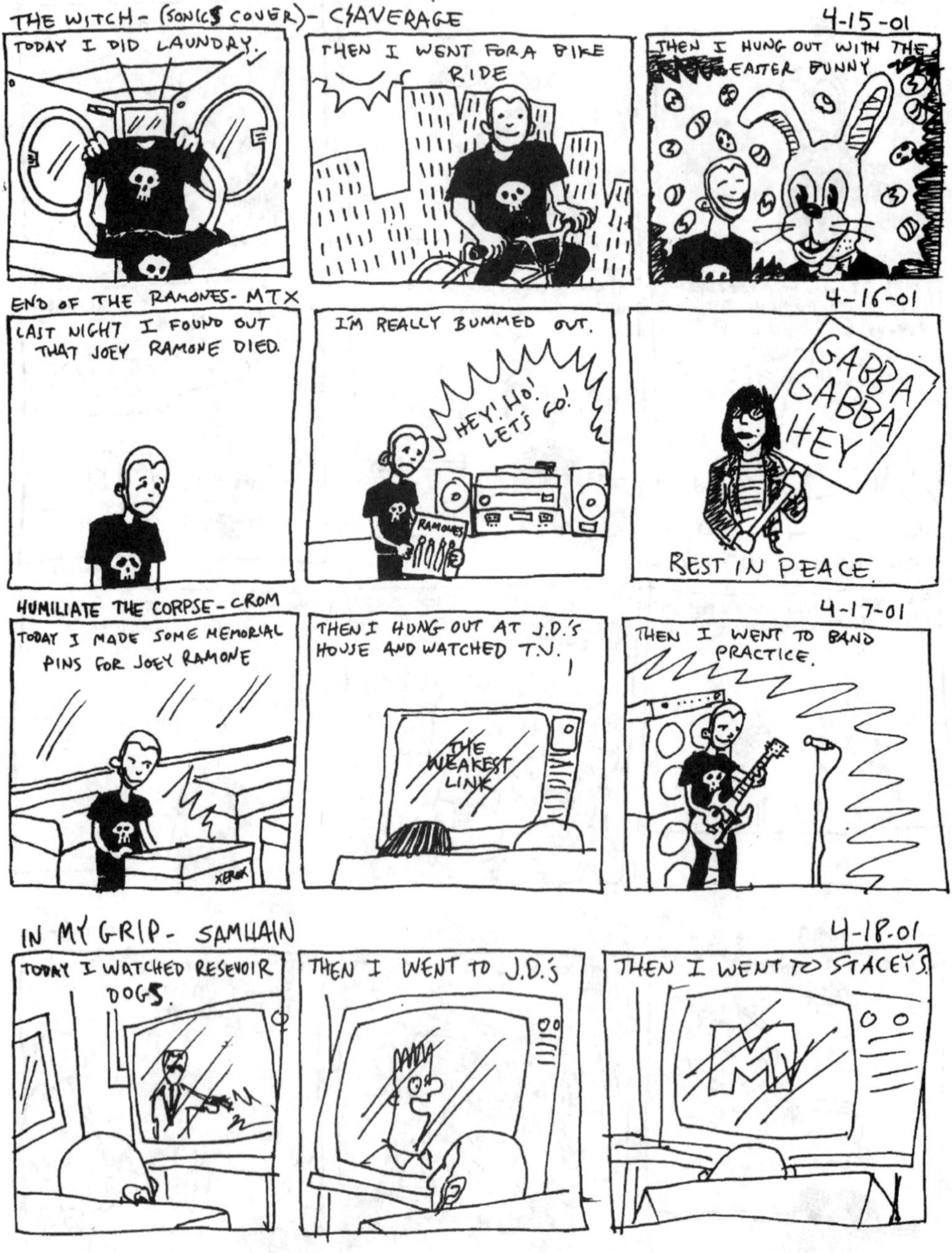

THE WITCH - (SONICS COVER) - C/AVERAGE
4-15-01
TODAY I DID LAUNDRY.
THEN I WENT FOR A BIKE RIDE
THEN I HUNG OUT WITH THE EASTER BUNNY
END OF THE RAMONES - MTX
4-16-01
LAST NIGHT I FOUND OUT THAT JOEY RAMONE DIED.
I'M REALLY BUMMED OUT.
HEY! HO! LET'S GO!
RAMONES
GABBA GABBA HEY
REST IN PEACE.
HUMILIATE THE CORPSE - CROM
4-17-01
TODAY I MADE SOME MEMORIAL PINS FOR JOEY RAMONE
XEROX
THEN I HUNG OUT AT J.D.'S HOUSE AND WATCHED T.V.
THE WEAKEST LINK
THEN I WENT TO BAND PRACTICE.
IN MY GRIP - SAMHAIN
4-18-01
TODAY I WATCHED RESEVOIR DOGS.
THEN I WENT TO J.D.'S
THEN I WENT TO STACEY'S.
MTV

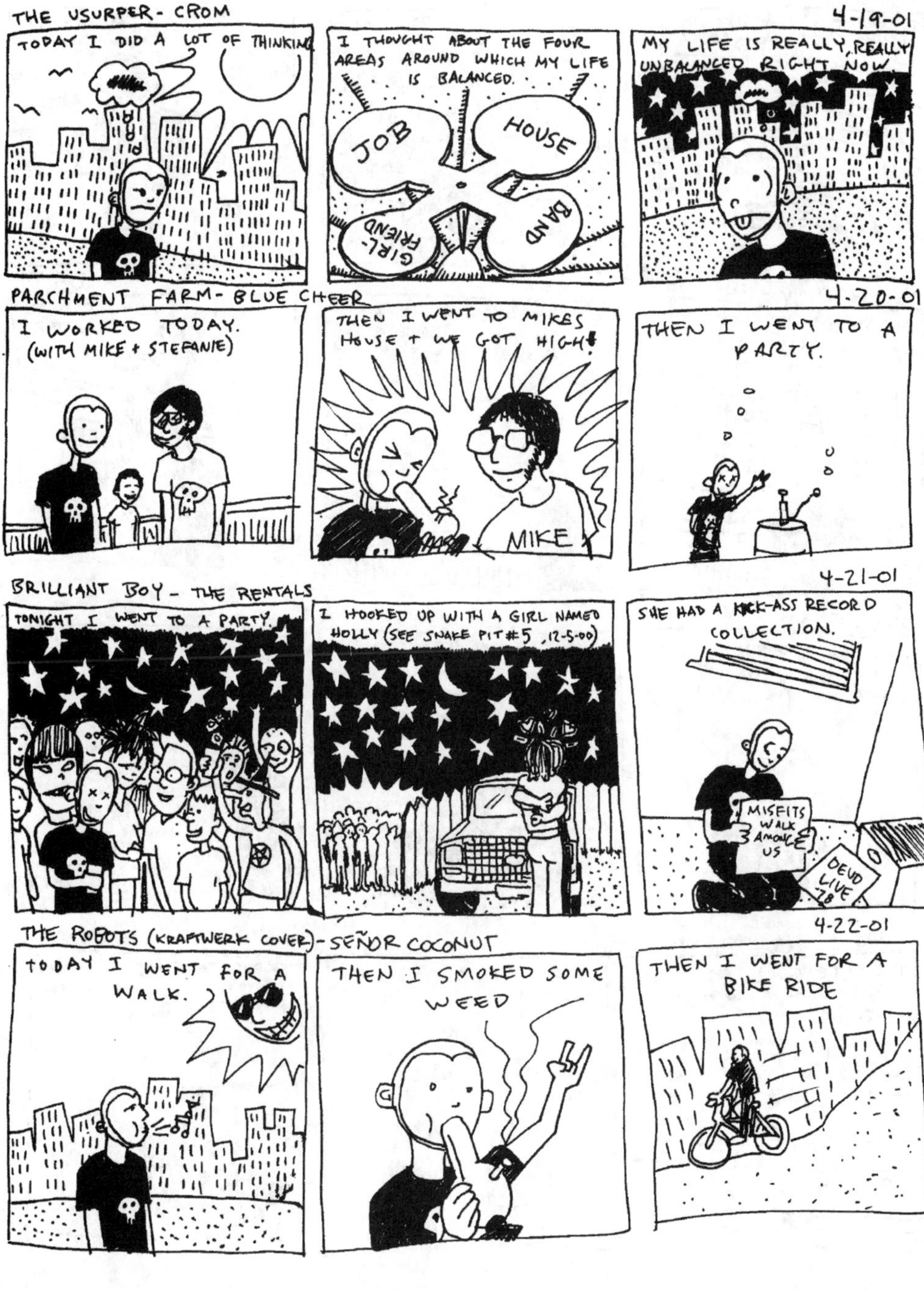
THE USURPER - CROM
4-19-01
TODAY I DID A LOT OF THINKING
I THOUGHT ABOUT THE FOUR AREAS AROUND WHICH MY LIFE IS BALANCED.
JOB
HOUSE
GIRL-FRIEND
BAND
MY LIFE IS REALLY, REALLY UNBALANCED RIGHT NOW.
PARCHMENT FARM - BLUE CHEER
4-20-01
I WORKED TODAY. (WITH MIKE + STEFANIE)
THEN I WENT TO MIKES HOUSE + WE GOT HIGH!
MIKE
THEN I WENT TO A PARTY.
BRILLIANT BOY - THE RENTALS
4-21-01
TONIGHT I WENT TO A PARTY
I HOOKED UP WITH A GIRL NAMED HOLLY (SEE SNAKE PIT #5, 12-5-00)
SHE HAD A KICK-ASS RECORD COLLECTION.
MISFITS WALK AMONG US
DEVO LIVE '78
THE ROBOTS (KRAFTWERK COVER) - SEÑOR COCONUT
4-22-01
TODAY I WENT FOR A WALK.
THEN I SMOKED SOME WEED
THEN I WENT FOR A BIKE RIDE

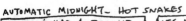

I HAVENT HAD A DECENT NIGHTS SLEEP IN OVER A WEEK.

ARF ARF

ITS NOT THAT I DONT LIKE KELLY'S DOGS, THEY JUST BARK TOO MUCH AT NIGHT

ARF ARF ARF ARF ARF ARF ARF ARF ARF ARF ARF ARF ARF ARF ARF ARF ARF ARF ARF ARF ARF ARF ARF ARF ARF ARF ARF ARF ARF ARF ARF

I WONDER HOW MUCH MORE I CAN DEAL WITH.

ARF ARF ARF ARF

HE'S WAITING- THE SONICS

TODAY I WORKED.

I ASKED MIKE IF I CAN CRASH AT HIS PLACE FOR A FEW DAYS.

? ? ?

I MOVED MY STUFF OUT OF KELLY + GENEVIEVES THIS AFTERNOON

CYGNUS X-1 - RUSH

TODAY I HAD THE DAY OFF, SO I WALKED AROUND, KINDA LOOKING FOR A HOME.

BUT I GOT REAL BAD SUN BURN

THROB OW

THEN I SAW A REALLY CUTE GIRL AT THE FUCKING CHAMPS SHOW.

WHAT I SEE- BLACK FLAG

THE CUTE GIRL FROM LAST NIGHT CAME INTO THE STORE TODAY...

A-B   C-D

... WITH HER BOYFRIEND.

I SWEAR TO GOD, IF I MEET ONE MORE COOL GIRL WITH A BOYFRIEND I'M GONNA KILL SOMEBODY.

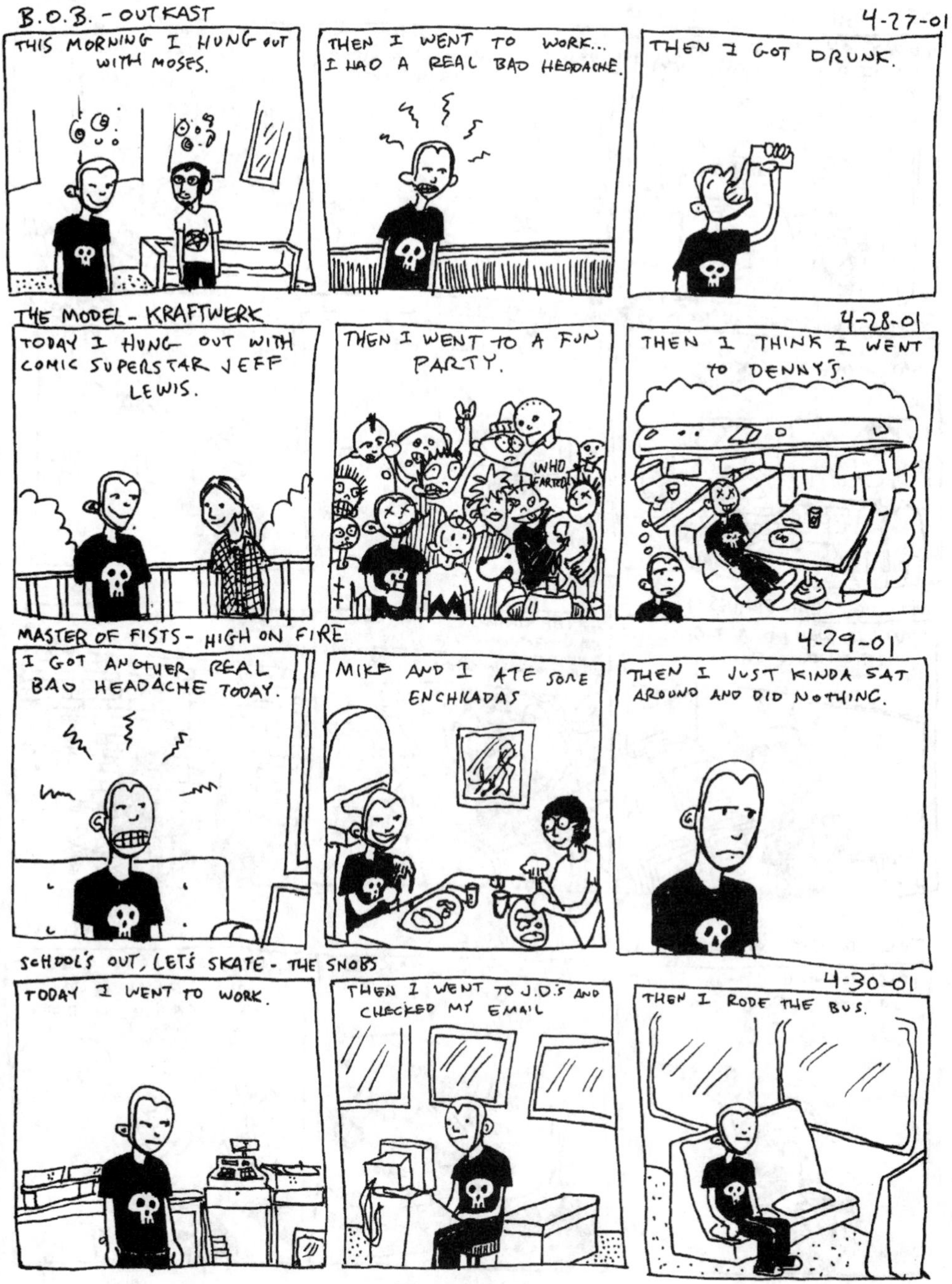

B.O.B. - OUTKAST
4-27-01
THIS MORNING I HUNG OUT WITH MOSES.
THEN I WENT TO WORK... I HAD A REAL BAD HEADACHE.
THEN I GOT DRUNK.
THE MODEL - KRAFTWERK
4-28-01
TODAY I HUNG OUT WITH COMIC SUPERSTAR JEFF LEWIS.
THEN I WENT TO A FUN PARTY.
WHO FARTED?
THEN I THINK I WENT TO DENNY'S.
MASTER OF FISTS - HIGH ON FIRE
4-29-01
I GOT ANOTHER REAL BAD HEADACHE TODAY.
MIKE AND I ATE SOME ENCHILADAS
THEN I JUST KINDA SAT AROUND AND DID NOTHING.
SCHOOL'S OUT, LET'S SKATE - THE SNOBS
4-30-01
TODAY I WENT TO WORK.
THEN I WENT TO J.D.'S AND CHECKED MY EMAIL
THEN I RODE THE BUS.

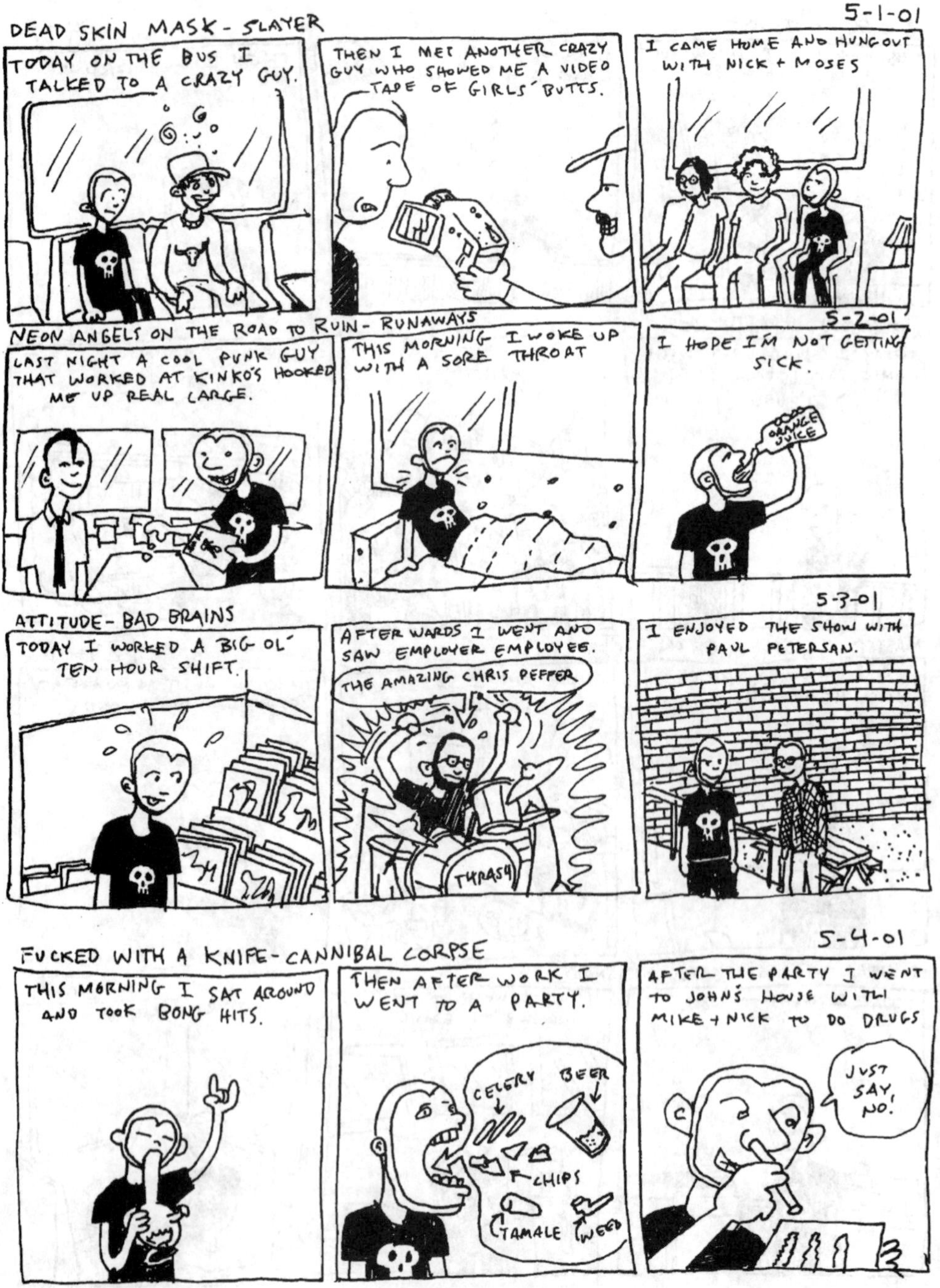
DEAD SKIN MASK - SLAYER
5-1-01
TODAY ON THE BUS I TALKED TO A CRAZY GUY.
THEN I MET ANOTHER CRAZY GUY WHO SHOWED ME A VIDEO TAPE OF GIRLS' BUTTS.
I CAME HOME AND HUNG OUT WITH NICK + MOSES
NEON ANGELS ON THE ROAD TO RUIN - RUNAWAYS
5-2-01
LAST NIGHT A COOL PUNK GUY THAT WORKED AT KINKO'S HOOKED ME UP REAL LARGE.
THIS MORNING I WOKE UP WITH A SORE THROAT
I HOPE I'M NOT GETTING SICK.
ORANGE JUICE
ATTITUDE - BAD BRAINS
5-3-01
TODAY I WORKED A BIG OL' TEN HOUR SHIFT.
AFTERWARDS I WENT AND SAW EMPLOYER EMPLOYEE.
THE AMAZING CHRIS PEFFER
THRASH
I ENJOYED THE SHOW WITH PAUL PETERSAN.
FUCKED WITH A KNIFE - CANNIBAL CORPSE
5-4-01
THIS MORNING I SAT AROUND AND TOOK BONG HITS.
THEN AFTER WORK I WENT TO A PARTY.
CELERY
BEER
CHIPS
TAMALE
WEED
AFTER THE PARTY I WENT TO JOHN'S HOUSE WITH MIKE + NICK TO DO DRUGS
JUST SAY NO!

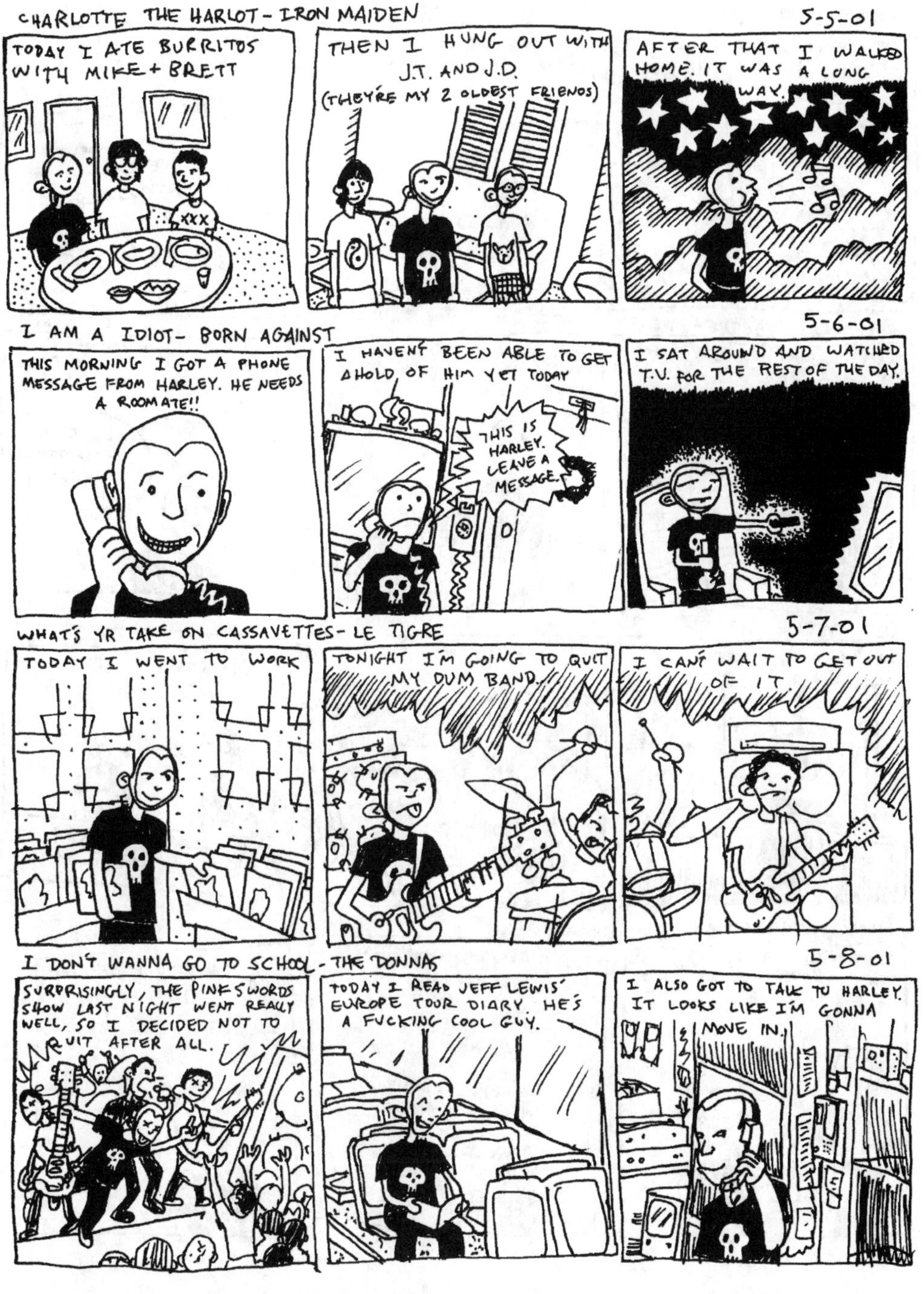
CHARLOTTE THE HARLOT - IRON MAIDEN
5-5-01
TODAY I ATE BURRITOS WITH MIKE + BRETT
XXX
THEN I HUNG OUT WITH J.T. AND J.D. (THEY'RE MY 2 OLDEST FRIENDS)
AFTER THAT I WALKED HOME. IT WAS A LONG WAY.
I AM A IDIOT - BORN AGAINST
5-6-01
THIS MORNING I GOT A PHONE MESSAGE FROM HARLEY. HE NEEDS A ROOMATE!!
I HAVEN'T BEEN ABLE TO GET AHOLD OF HIM YET TODAY
THIS IS HARLEY. LEAVE A MESSAGE.
I SAT AROUND AND WATCHED T.V. FOR THE REST OF THE DAY.
WHAT'S YR TAKE ON CASSAVETTES - LE TIGRE
5-7-01
TODAY I WENT TO WORK
TONIGHT I'M GOING TO QUIT MY DUM BAND.
I CAN'T WAIT TO GET OUT OF IT.
I DON'T WANNA GO TO SCHOOL - THE DONNAS
5-8-01
SURPRISINGLY, THE PINK SWORDS SHOW LAST NIGHT WENT REALLY WELL, SO I DECIDED NOT TO QUIT AFTER ALL.
TODAY I READ JEFF LEWIS' EUROPE TOUR DIARY. HE'S A FUCKING COOL GUY.
I ALSO GOT TO TALK TO HARLEY. IT LOOKS LIKE I'M GONNA MOVE IN.

WHISTLE BAIT- MTX

LAST NIGHT I STAYED AT J.D's HOUSE + PLAYED MARIO 64

TODAY I READ SOME JOHN PORCELLINO COMIX.

THEN I SMOKED WEED AND WATCHED TV

A SHOW ABOUT SERIAL KILLERS

GOING DOWN TO DIE- DANZIG

TODAY ONE OF THE GIRLS IN MY GRAB BAG CAME INTO THE STORE.

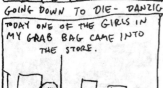

GRAB BAG: THE LIST OF ABOUT FIVE GIRLS IN TOWN I WANNA HOOK UP WITH.

I KNOW ITS KIND OF A GROSS THING, BUT I REALLY WANT A GIRLFRIEND.

ALL I CAN DO IS THINK WISHFULLY

RED TAPE- CIRCLE JERKS

TODAY I WORKED

THEN I WENT TO A PARTY.

AFTERWARDS I ATE AT STAR SEEDS WITH J.T.

FUCK ARMAGEDDON- BAD RELIGION

LAST NIGHT I TALKED TO JOHN ABOUT MOVING INTO HIS HOUSE.

(ITS CHEAPER THAN HARLEYS PLACE)

COUNTING MONEY

I'M SUPPOSED TO GO LOOK AT IT TONIGHT.

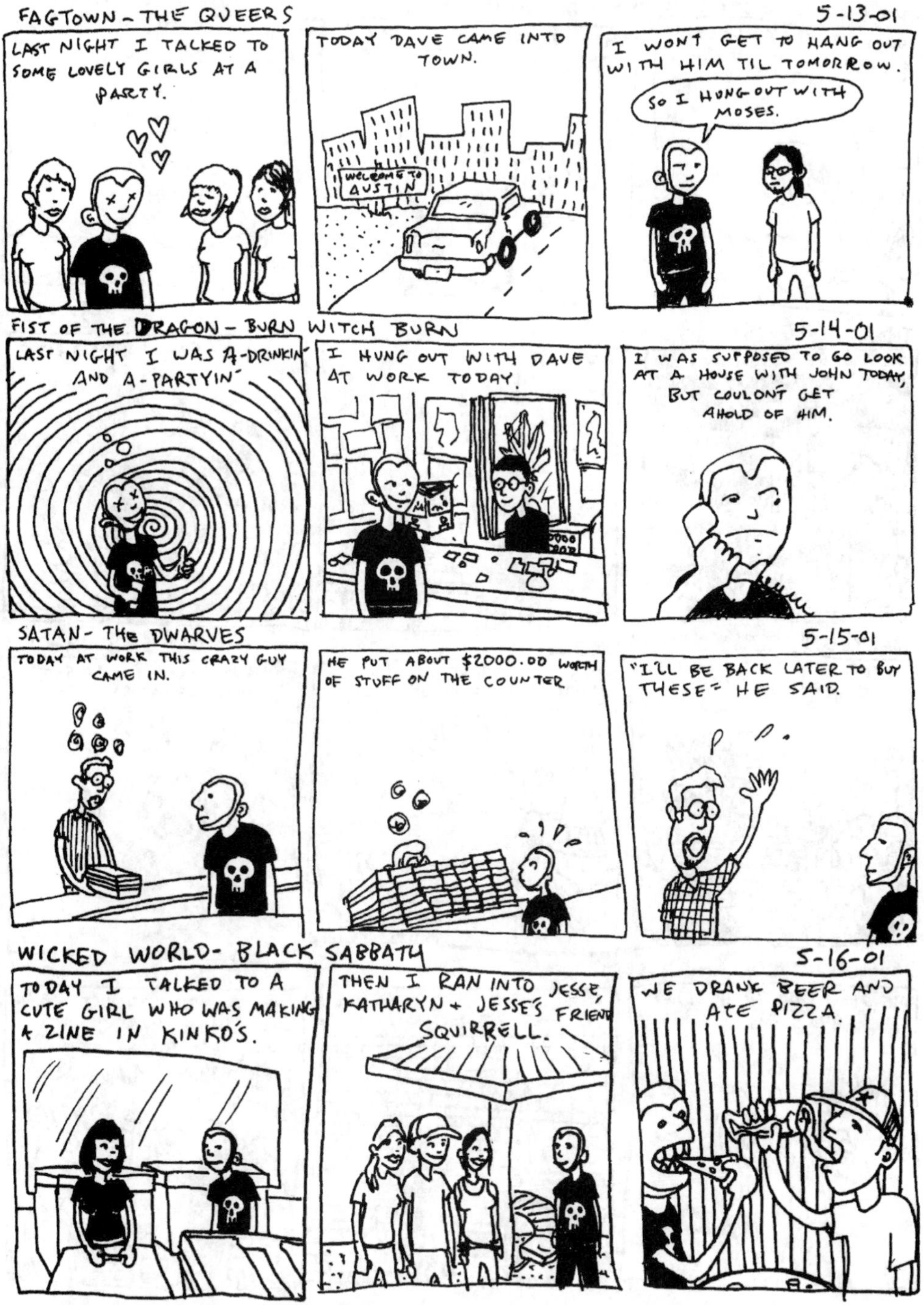

FAGTOWN - THE QUEERS
5-13-01
LAST NIGHT I TALKED TO SOME LOVELY GIRLS AT A PARTY.
TODAY DAVE CAME INTO TOWN.
WELCOME TO AUSTIN
I WONT GET TO HANG OUT WITH HIM TIL TOMORROW.
SO I HUNG OUT WITH MOSES.
FIST OF THE DRAGON - BURN WITCH BURN
5-14-01
LAST NIGHT I WAS A-DRINKIN' AND A-PARTYIN'
I HUNG OUT WITH DAVE AT WORK TODAY.
I WAS SUPPOSED TO GO LOOK AT A HOUSE WITH JOHN TODAY, BUT COULDN'T GET AHOLD OF HIM.
SATAN - THE DWARVES
5-15-01
TODAY AT WORK THIS CRAZY GUY CAME IN.
HE PUT ABOUT $2000.00 WORTH OF STUFF ON THE COUNTER
"I'LL BE BACK LATER TO BUY THESE" HE SAID.
WICKED WORLD - BLACK SABBATH
5-16-01
TODAY I TALKED TO A CUTE GIRL WHO WAS MAKING A ZINE IN KINKO'S.
THEN I RAN INTO JESSE, KATHARYN + JESSE'S FRIEND SQUIRRELL.
WE DRANK BEER AND ATE PIZZA.

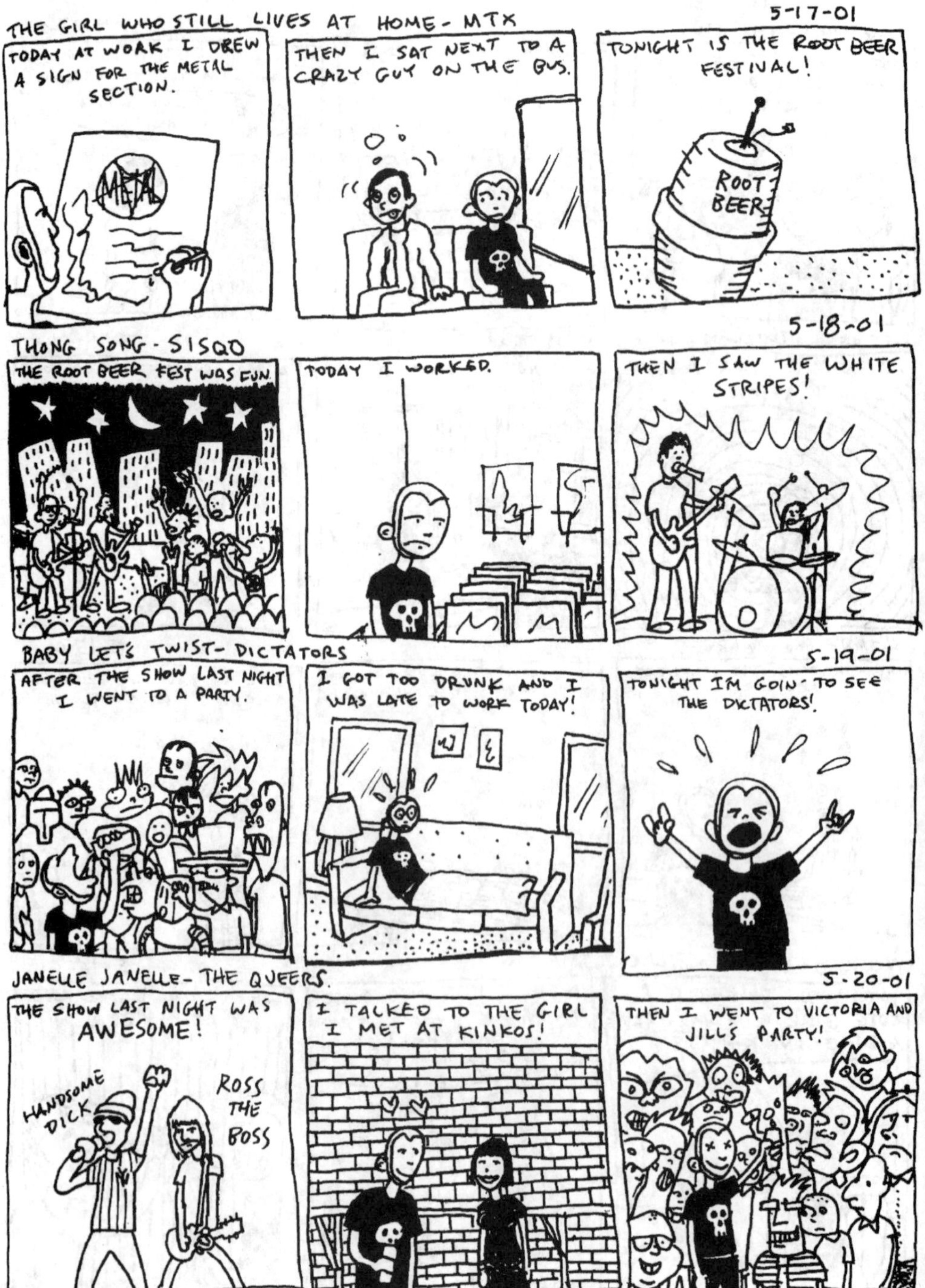
THE GIRL WHO STILL LIVES AT HOME - MTX
5-17-01
TODAY AT WORK I DREW A SIGN FOR THE METAL SECTION.
METAL
THEN I SAT NEXT TO A CRAZY GUY ON THE BUS.
TONIGHT IS THE ROOT BEER FESTIVAL!
ROOT BEER
THONG SONG - SISQO
5-18-01
THE ROOT BEER FEST WAS FUN.
TODAY I WORKED.
THEN I SAW THE WHITE STRIPES!
BABY LET'S TWIST - DICTATORS
5-19-01
AFTER THE SHOW LAST NIGHT I WENT TO A PARTY.
I GOT TOO DRUNK AND I WAS LATE TO WORK TODAY!
TONIGHT I'M GOIN' TO SEE THE DICTATORS!
JANELLE JANELLE - THE QUEERS.
5-20-01
THE SHOW LAST NIGHT WAS AWESOME!
HANDSOME DICK
ROSS THE BOSS
I TALKED TO THE GIRL I MET AT KINKOS!
THEN I WENT TO VICTORIA AND JILL'S PARTY!

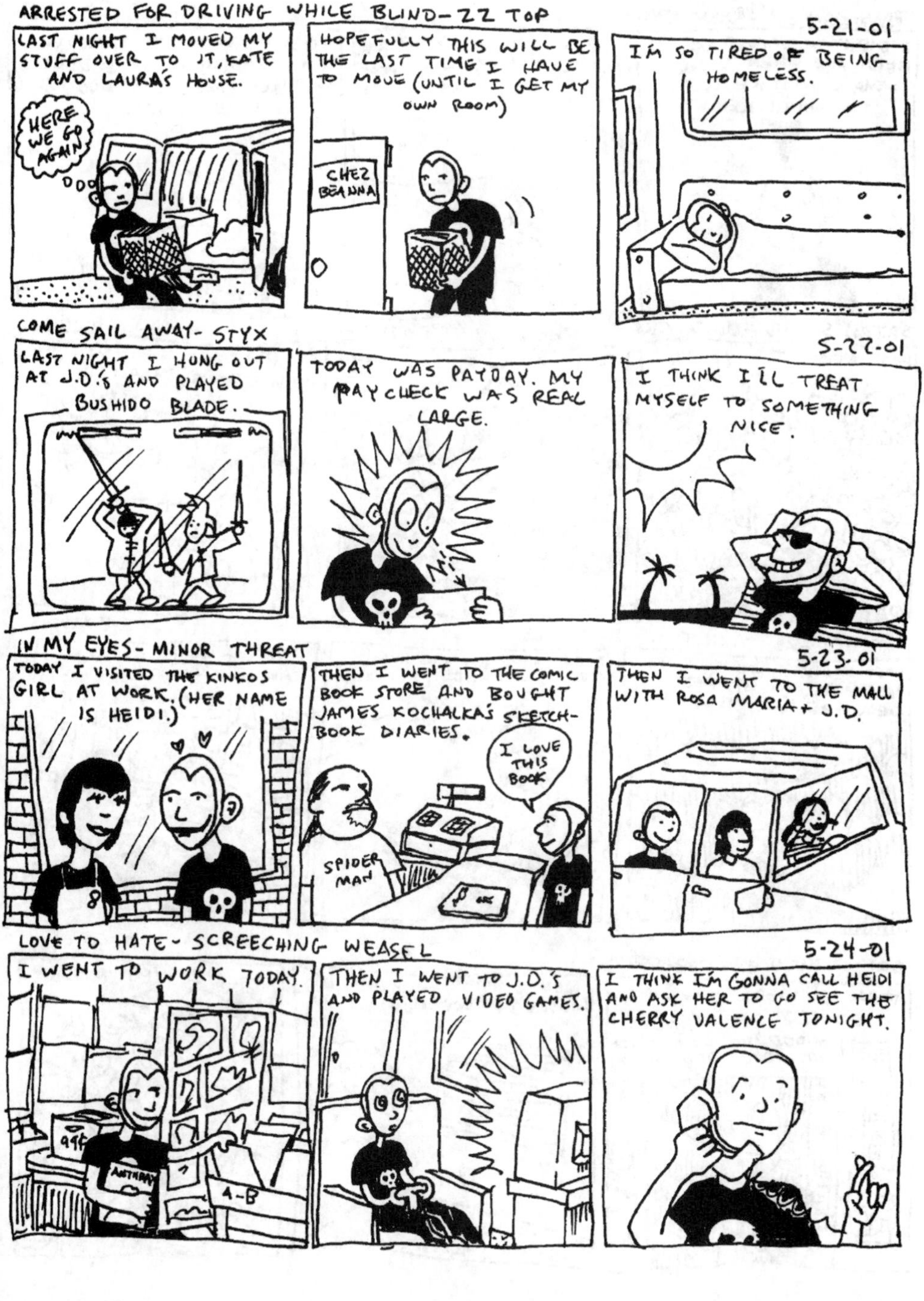
ARRESTED FOR DRIVING WHILE BLIND – ZZ TOP
5-21-01
LAST NIGHT I MOVED MY STUFF OVER TO JT, KATE AND LAURA'S HOUSE.
HERE WE GO AGAIN
HOPEFULLY THIS WILL BE THE LAST TIME I HAVE TO MOVE (UNTIL I GET MY OWN ROOM)
CHEZ BEANNA
I'M SO TIRED OF BEING HOMELESS.
COME SAIL AWAY – STYX
5-22-01
LAST NIGHT I HUNG OUT AT J.D.'S AND PLAYED BUSHIDO BLADE.
TODAY WAS PAYDAY. MY PAYCHECK WAS REAL LARGE.
I THINK I'LL TREAT MYSELF TO SOMETHING NICE.
IN MY EYES – MINOR THREAT
5-23-01
TODAY I VISITED THE KINKOS GIRL AT WORK. (HER NAME IS HEIDI.)
THEN I WENT TO THE COMIC BOOK STORE AND BOUGHT JAMES KOCHALKA'S SKETCH-BOOK DIARIES.
I LOVE THIS BOOK
SPIDER MAN
THEN I WENT TO THE MALL WITH ROSA MARIA + J.D.
LOVE TO HATE – SCREECHING WEASEL
5-24-01
I WENT TO WORK TODAY.
99¢
ANTHRAX
A-B
THEN I WENT TO J.D.'S AND PLAYED VIDEO GAMES.
I THINK I'M GONNA CALL HEIDI AND ASK HER TO GO SEE THE CHERRY VALENCE TONIGHT.

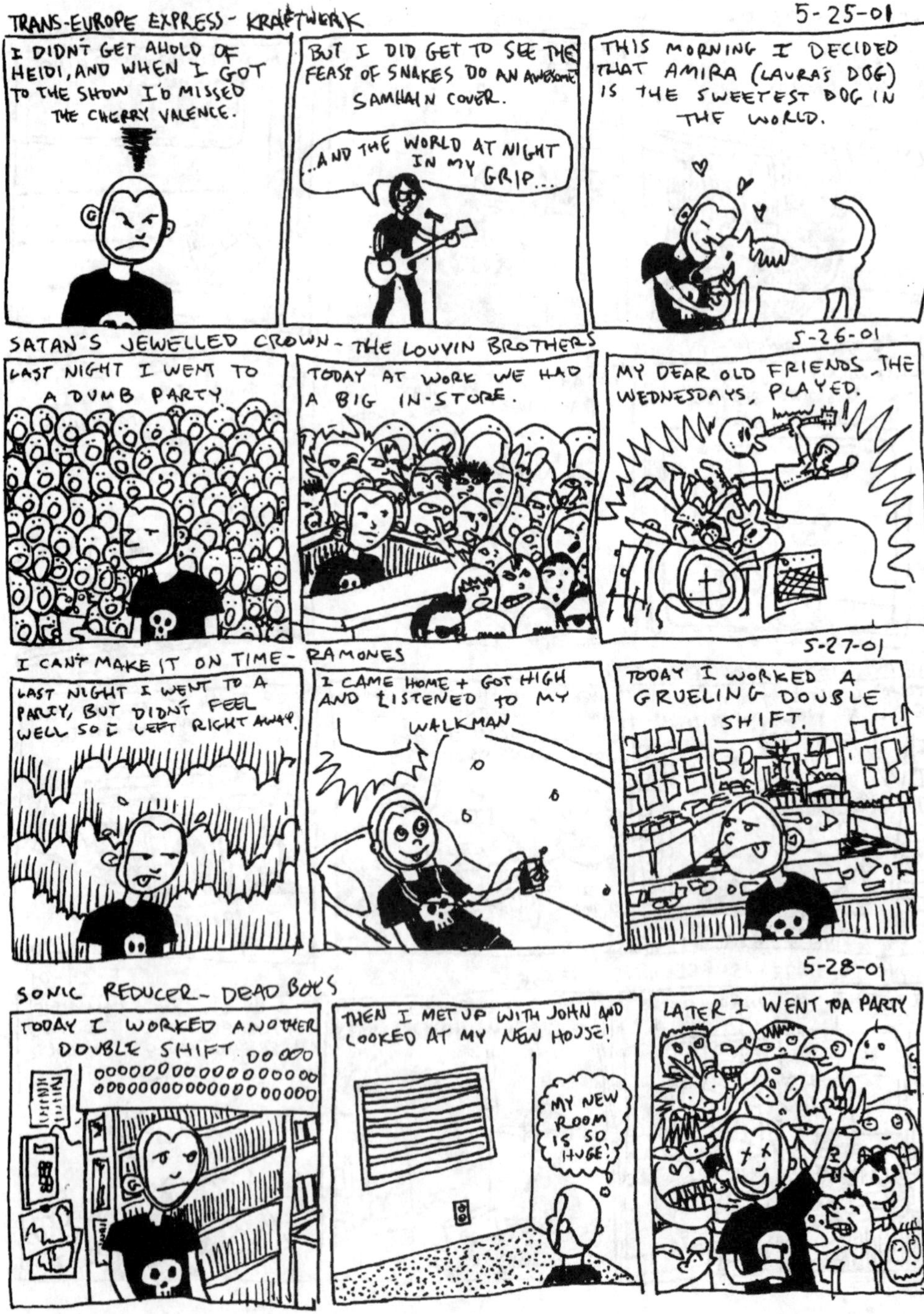
TRANS-EUROPE EXPRESS - KRAFTWERK
5-25-01
I DIDN'T GET AHOLD OF HEIDI, AND WHEN I GOT TO THE SHOW I'D MISSED THE CHERRY VALENCE.
BUT I DID GET TO SEE THE FEAST OF SNAKES DO AN AWESOME SAMHAIN COVER.
...AND THE WORLD AT NIGHT IN MY GRIP...
THIS MORNING I DECIDED THAT AMIRA (LAURA'S DOG) IS THE SWEETEST DOG IN THE WORLD.
SATAN'S JEWELLED CROWN - THE LOUVIN BROTHERS
5-26-01
LAST NIGHT I WENT TO A DUMB PARTY.
TODAY AT WORK WE HAD A BIG IN-STORE.
MY DEAR OLD FRIENDS, THE WEDNESDAYS, PLAYED.
I CAN'T MAKE IT ON TIME - RAMONES
5-27-01
LAST NIGHT I WENT TO A PARTY, BUT DIDN'T FEEL WELL SO I LEFT RIGHT AWAY.
I CAME HOME + GOT HIGH AND LISTENED TO MY WALKMAN
TODAY I WORKED A GRUELING DOUBLE SHIFT.
5-28-01
SONIC REDUCER - DEAD BOYS
TODAY I WORKED ANOTHER DOUBLE SHIFT
THEN I MET UP WITH JOHN AND LOOKED AT MY NEW HOUSE!
MY NEW ROOM IS SO HUGE!
LATER I WENT TO A PARTY

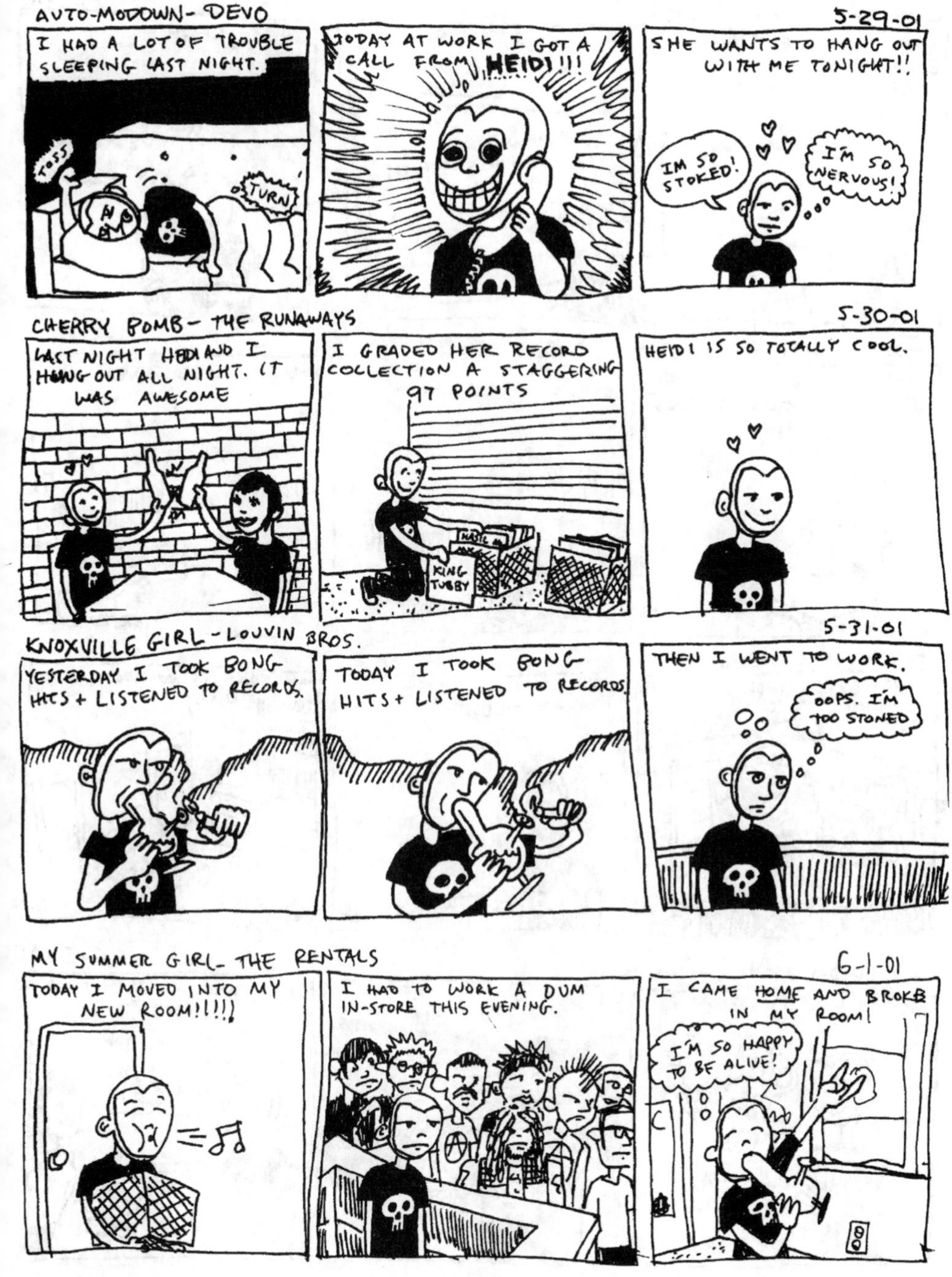
AUTO-MODOWN- DEVO
5-29-01
I HAD A LOT OF TROUBLE SLEEPING LAST NIGHT.
TOSS
TURN
TODAY AT WORK I GOT A CALL FROM HEIDI!!!
SHE WANTS TO HANG OUT WITH ME TONIGHT!!
IM SO STOKED!
I'M SO NERVOUS!
CHERRY BOMB- THE RUNAWAYS
5-30-01
LAST NIGHT HEIDI AND I HUNG OUT ALL NIGHT. IT WAS AWESOME
I GRADED HER RECORD COLLECTION A STAGGERING 97 POINTS
KING TUBBY
HEIDI IS SO TOTALLY COOL.
KNOXVILLE GIRL - LOUVIN BROS.
5-31-01
YESTERDAY I TOOK BONG HITS + LISTENED TO RECORDS.
TODAY I TOOK BONG HITS + LISTENED TO RECORDS.
THEN I WENT TO WORK.
OOPS. I'M TOO STONED
MY SUMMER GIRL- THE RENTALS
6-1-01
TODAY I MOVED INTO MY NEW ROOM!!!!!
I HAD TO WORK A DUM IN-STORE THIS EVENING.
I CAME HOME AND BROKE IN MY ROOM!
I'M SO HAPPY TO BE ALIVE!

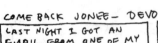

COME BACK JONEE— DEVO

5-2-01

LAST NIGHT I GOT AN EMAIL FROM ONE OF MY HEROES, JAMES KOCHACKA!

HE SAID I DRAW TOO SLOPPY

DEAR BEN,
YOU DRAW TOO SLOPPY.
LOVE,
JAMES.

HE'S RIGHT.

OOPS. I GOTTA DRAW A COMIC

FOLSOM PRISON BLUES — JOHNNY CASH

6-3-01

THIS MORNING JOHN GAVE ME HIS OLD DRAWING TABLE!

IT'S TIME FOR ME TO GET SERIOUS ABOUT ART!

UH... WHATEVER.

FLESHRIPPER — MORTICIAN

6-4-01

TODAY AFTER WORK I HELPED OLLIE MOVE IN.

AT THE STORAGE SPACE, I FOUND A DRESSER!!

MY ROOM IS COMING ALONG NICELY

JUST BECAUSE— THE COLLINS KIDS

6-5-01

TODAY I GOT PAID!!

THEN I WENT TO SEE A MOVIE WITH HEIDI

THEN WE WENT OUT TO DINNER

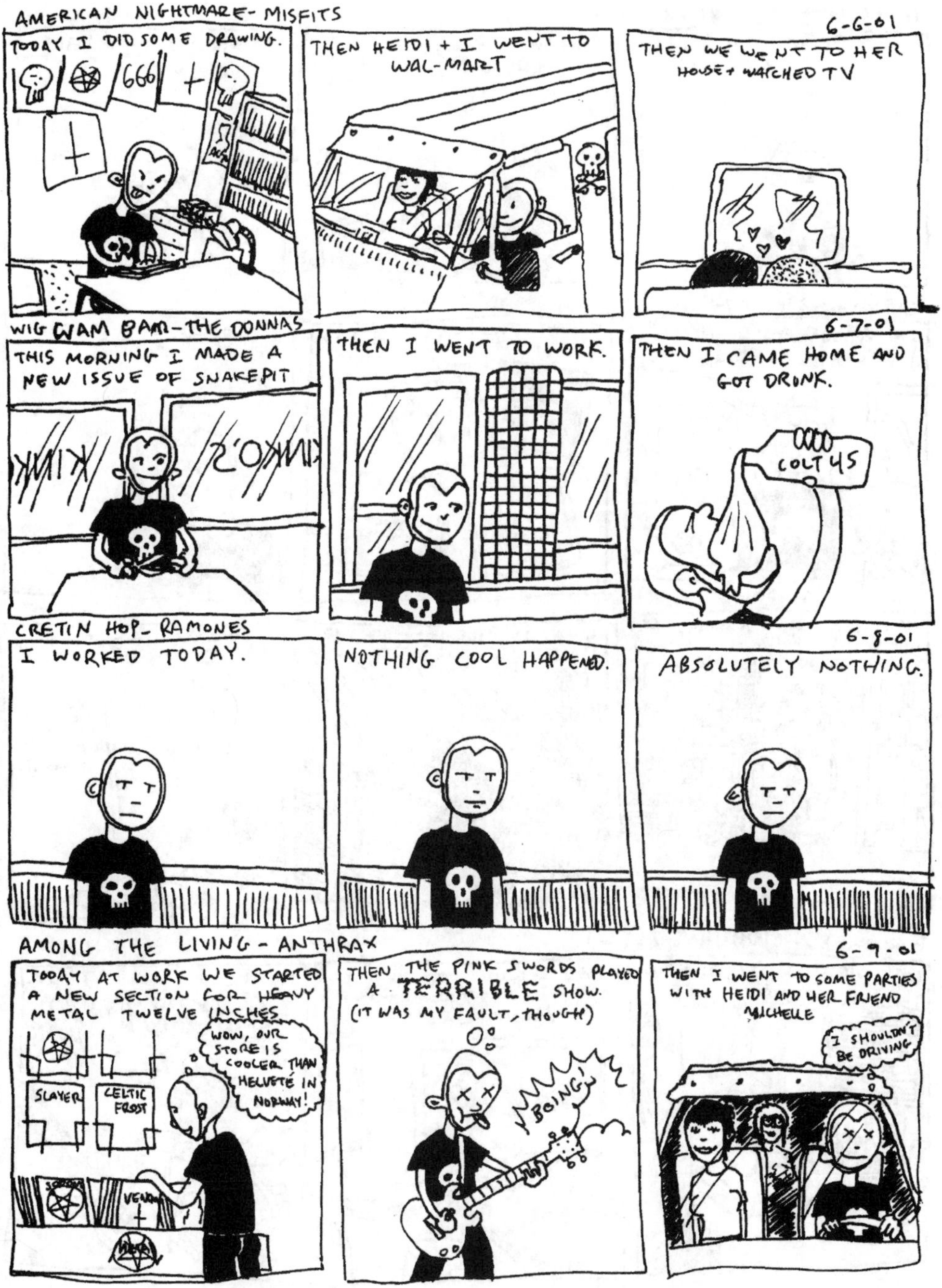

AMERICAN NIGHTMARE - MISFITS
6-6-01
TODAY I DID SOME DRAWING.
666
THEN HEIDI + I WENT TO WAL-MART
THEN WE WENT TO HER HOUSE + WATCHED TV
WIG WAM BAM - THE DONNAS
6-7-01
THIS MORNING I MADE A NEW ISSUE OF SNAKEPIT
KINKO'S
THEN I WENT TO WORK.
THEN I CAME HOME AND GOT DRUNK.
COLT 45
CRETIN HOP - RAMONES
6-8-01
I WORKED TODAY.
NOTHING COOL HAPPENED.
ABSOLUTELY NOTHING.
AMONG THE LIVING - ANTHRAX
6-9-01
TODAY AT WORK WE STARTED A NEW SECTION FOR HEAVY METAL TWELVE INCHES
WOW, OUR STORE IS COOLER THAN HELVETE IN NORWAY!
SLAYER
CELTIC FROST
VENOM
THEN THE PINK SWORDS PLAYED A TERRIBLE SHOW. (IT WAS MY FAULT, THOUGH)
BOING!
THEN I WENT TO SOME PARTIES WITH HEIDI AND HER FRIEND MICHELLE
I SHOULDN'T BE DRIVING

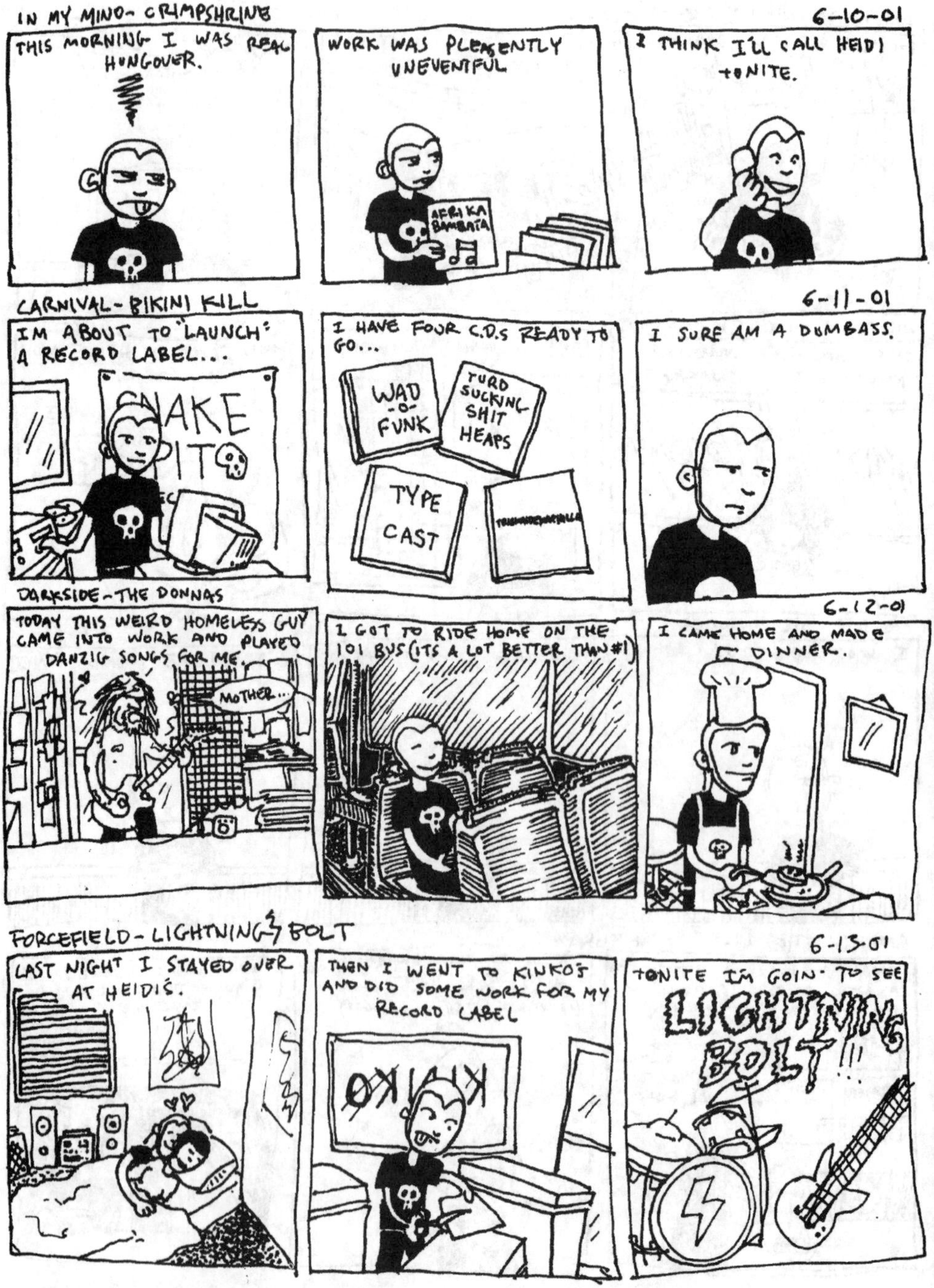
IN MY MIND - CRIMPSHRINE
6-10-01
THIS MORNING I WAS REAL HUNGOVER.
WORK WAS PLEASENTLY UNEVENTFUL
AFRIKA BAMBATA
I THINK I'LL CALL HEIDI TONITE.
CARNIVAL - BIKINI KILL
6-11-01
IM ABOUT TO "LAUNCH" A RECORD LABEL...
I HAVE FOUR C.D.S READY TO GO...
WAD -O- FUNK
TURD SUCKING SHIT HEAPS
TYPE CAST
I SURE AM A DUMBASS.
DARKSIDE - THE DONNAS
6-12-01
TODAY THIS WEIRD HOMELESS GUY CAME INTO WORK AND PLAYED DANZIG SONGS FOR ME.
MOTHER...
I GOT TO RIDE HOME ON THE 101 BUS (ITS A LOT BETTER THAN #1)
I CAME HOME AND MADE DINNER.
FORCEFIELD - LIGHTNING BOLT
6-13-01
LAST NIGHT I STAYED OVER AT HEIDI'S.
THEN I WENT TO KINKO'S AND DID SOME WORK FOR MY RECORD LABEL
KINKO
TONITE I'M GOIN' TO SEE LIGHTNING BOLT!!!

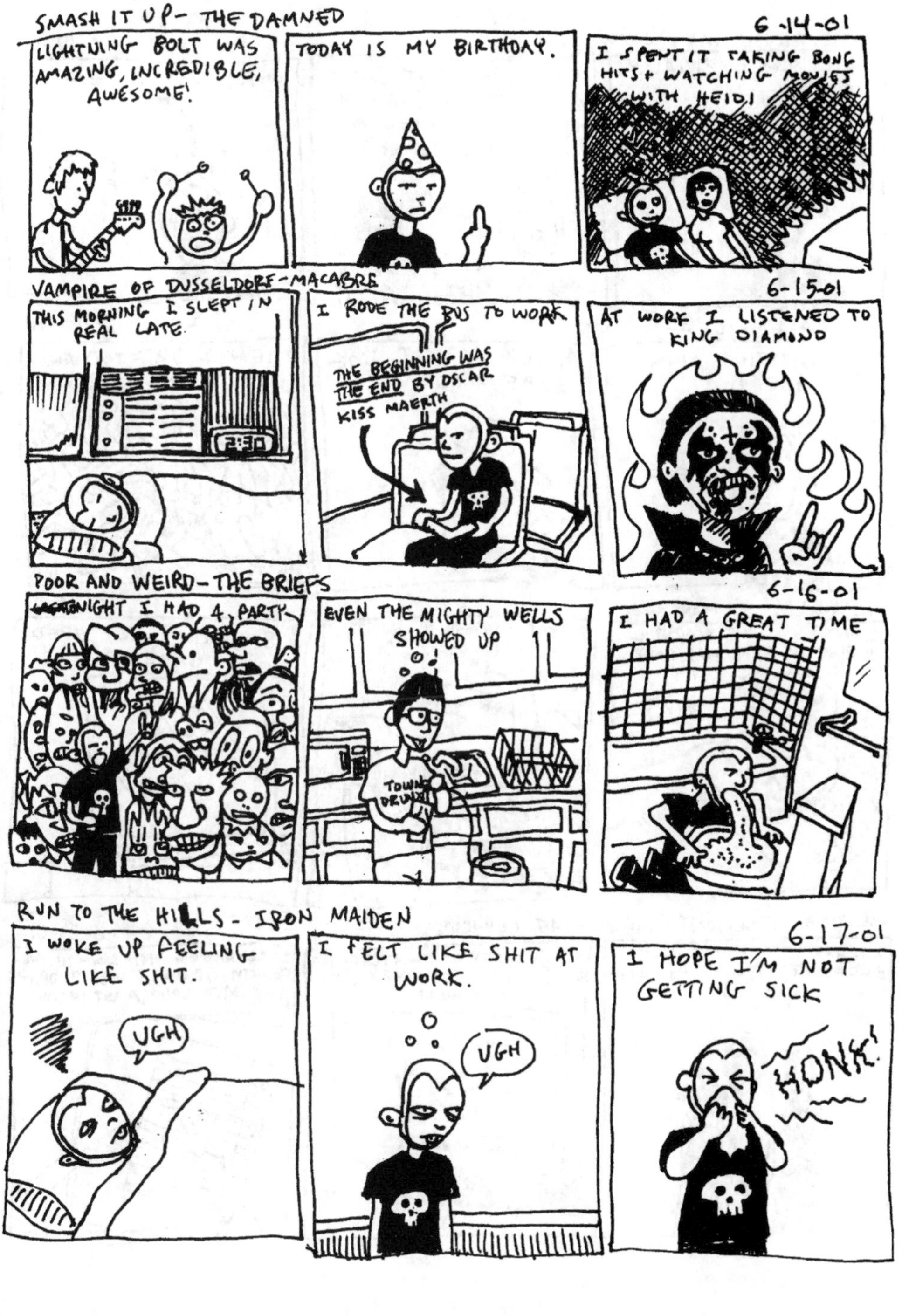

SMASH IT UP- THE DAMNED
6-14-01
LIGHTNING BOLT WAS AMAZING, INCREDIBLE, AWESOME!
TODAY IS MY BIRTHDAY.
I SPENT IT TAKING BONG HITS + WATCHING MOVIES WITH HEIDI
VAMPIRE OF DUSSELDORF-MACABRE
6-15-01
THIS MORNING I SLEPT IN REAL LATE.
2:30
I RODE THE BUS TO WORK
THE BEGINNING WAS THE END BY OSCAR KISS MAERTH
AT WORK I LISTENED TO KING DIAMOND
POOR AND WEIRD- THE BRIEFS
6-16-01
TONIGHT I HAD A PARTY
EVEN THE MIGHTY WELLS SHOWED UP
TOWN DRUNK
I HAD A GREAT TIME
RUN TO THE HILLS - IRON MAIDEN
6-17-01
I WOKE UP FEELING LIKE SHIT.
UGH
I FELT LIKE SHIT AT WORK.
UGH
I HOPE I'M NOT GETTING SICK
HONK!

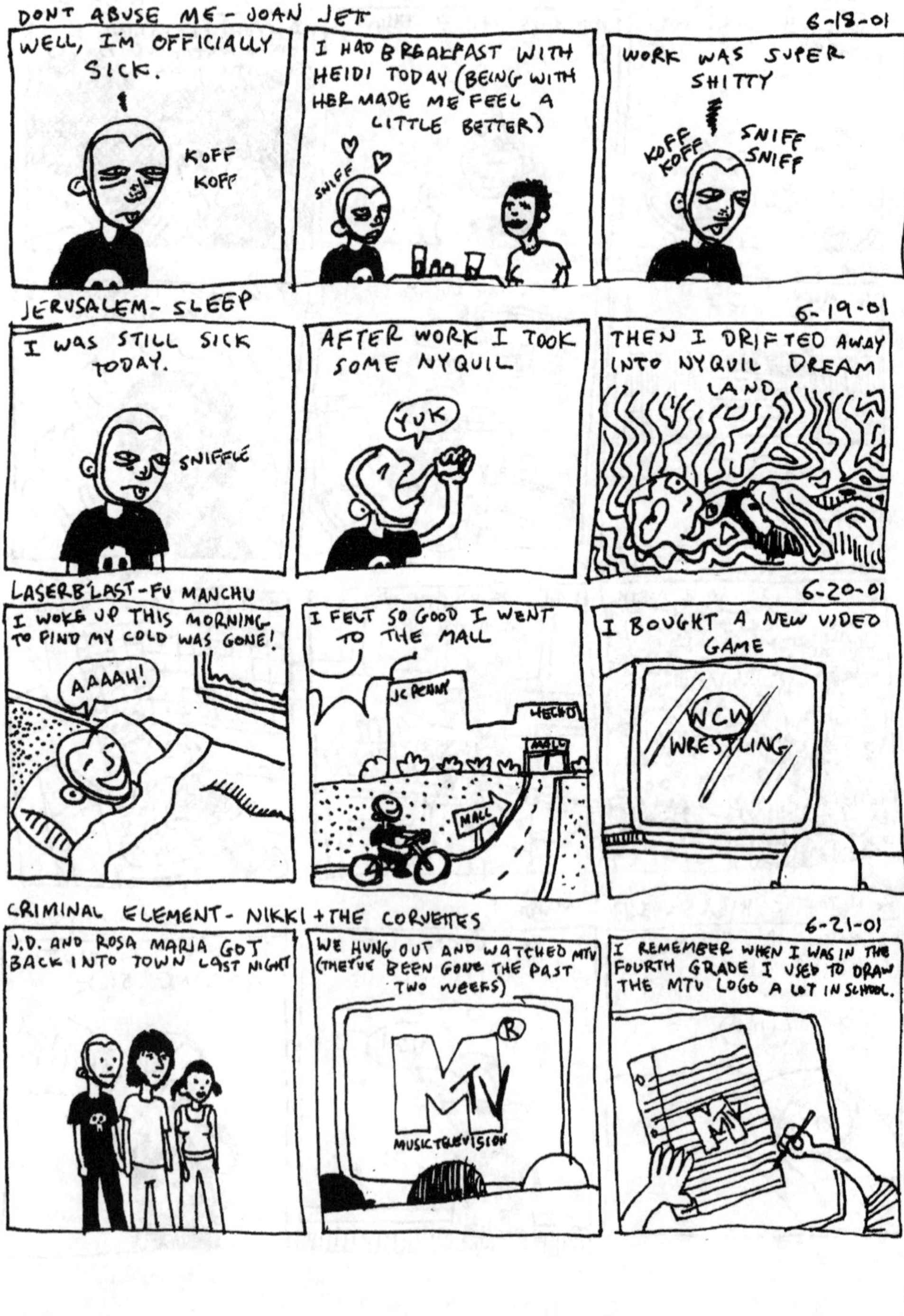
DONT ABUSE ME - JOAN JETT
6-18-01
WELL, I'M OFFICIALLY SICK.
KOFF KOFF
I HAD BREAKFAST WITH HEIDI TODAY (BEING WITH HER MADE ME FEEL A LITTLE BETTER)
SNIFF
WORK WAS SUPER SHITTY
KOFF KOFF
SNIFF SNIFF
JERUSALEM - SLEEP
6-19-01
I WAS STILL SICK TODAY.
SNIFFLE
AFTER WORK I TOOK SOME NYQUIL
YUK
THEN I DRIFTED AWAY INTO NYQUIL DREAM LAND
LASERBLAST - FU MANCHU
6-20-01
I WOKE UP THIS MORNING TO FIND MY COLD WAS GONE!
AAAAH!
I FELT SO GOOD I WENT TO THE MALL
JC PENNY
HECHTS
MALL
MALL
I BOUGHT A NEW VIDEO GAME
WCW WRESTLING
CRIMINAL ELEMENT - NIKKI + THE CORVETTES
6-21-01
J.D. AND ROSA MARIA GOT BACK INTO TOWN LAST NIGHT
WE HUNG OUT AND WATCHED MTV (THEY'VE BEEN GONE THE PAST TWO WEEKS)
MTV
MUSIC TELEVISION
I REMEMBER WHEN I WAS IN THE FOURTH GRADE I USED TO DRAW THE MTV LOGO A LOT IN SCHOOL.
MTV

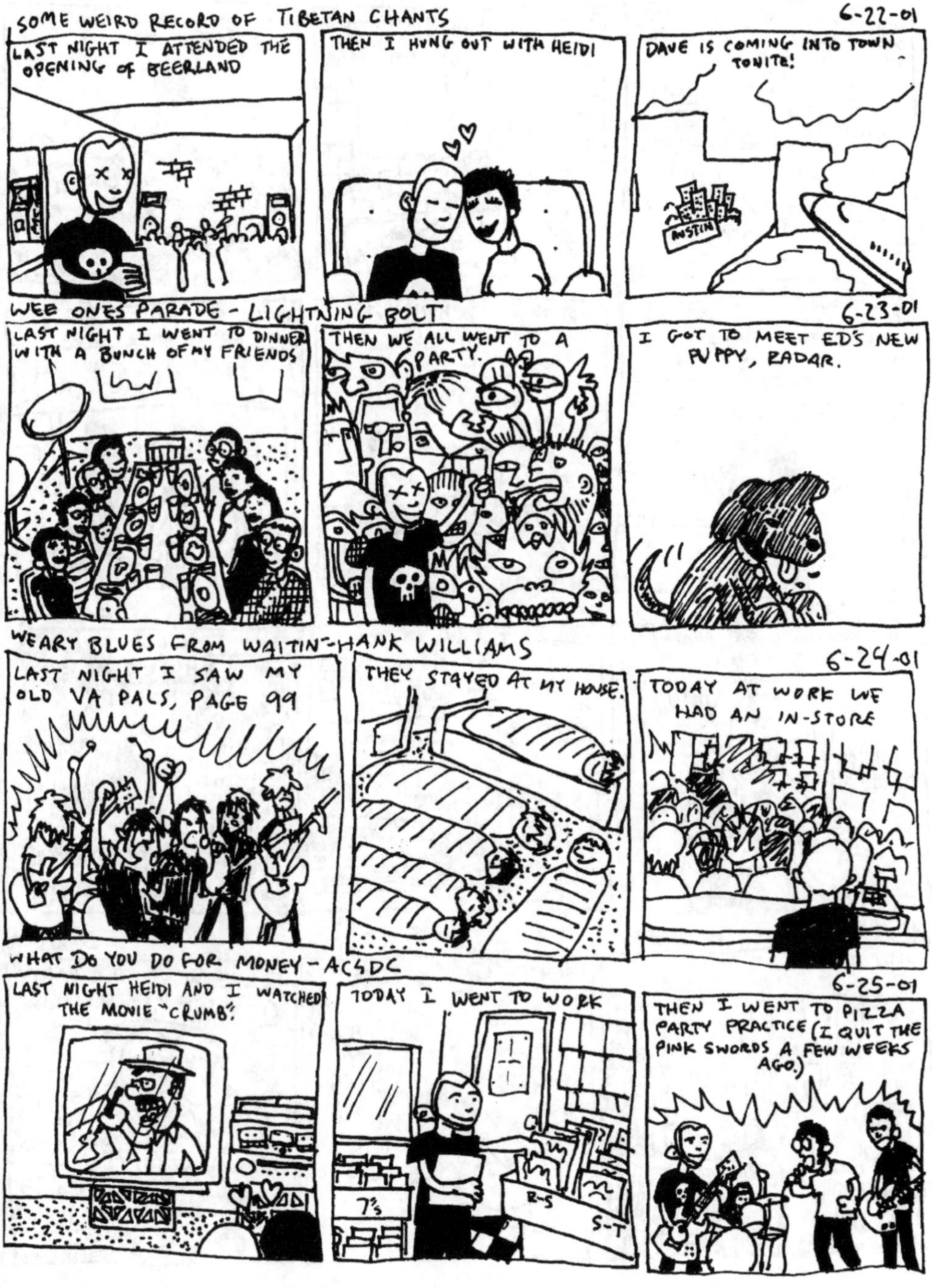

SOME WEIRD RECORD OF TIBETAN CHANTS
6-22-01
LAST NIGHT I ATTENDED THE OPENING OF BEERLAND
THEN I HUNG OUT WITH HEIDI
DAVE IS COMING INTO TOWN TONITE!
AUSTIN
WEE ONES PARADE - LIGHTNING BOLT
6-23-01
LAST NIGHT I WENT TO DINNER WITH A BUNCH OF MY FRIENDS
THEN WE ALL WENT TO A PARTY.
I GOT TO MEET ED'S NEW PUPPY, RADAR.
WEARY BLUES FROM WAITIN'-HANK WILLIAMS
6-24-01
LAST NIGHT I SAW MY OLD VA PALS, PAGE 99
THEY STAYED AT MY HOUSE.
TODAY AT WORK WE HAD AN IN-STORE
WHAT DO YOU DO FOR MONEY - AC/DC
6-25-01
LAST NIGHT HEIDI AND I WATCHED THE MOVIE "CRUMB".
TODAY I WENT TO WORK
7"s
R-S
S-T
THEN I WENT TO PIZZA PARTY PRACTICE (I QUIT THE PINK SWORDS A FEW WEEKS AGO.)

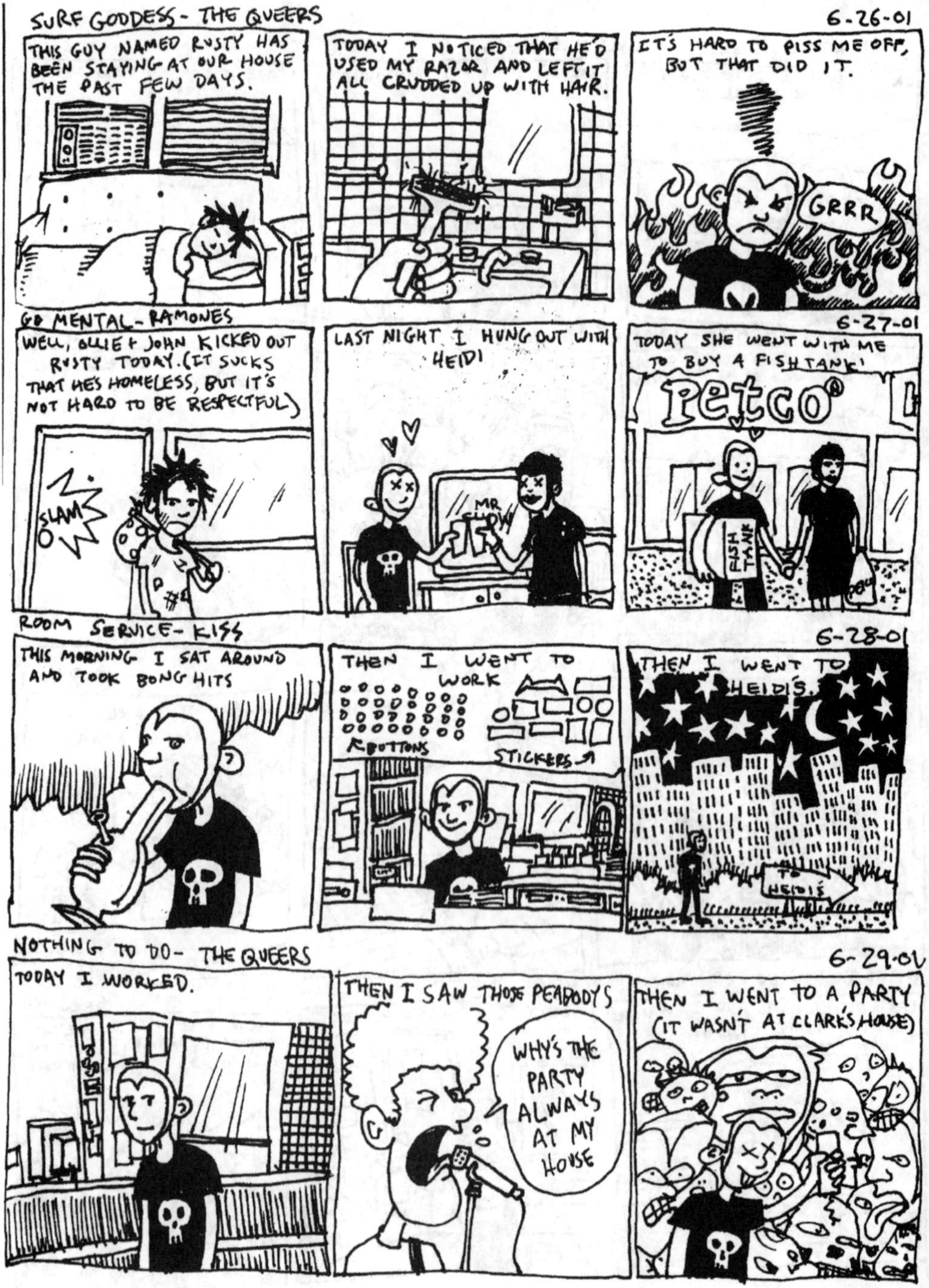
SURF GODDESS - THE QUEERS
6-26-01
THIS GUY NAMED RUSTY HAS BEEN STAYING AT OUR HOUSE THE PAST FEW DAYS.
TODAY I NOTICED THAT HE'D USED MY RAZOR AND LEFT IT ALL CRUDDED UP WITH HAIR.
IT'S HARD TO PISS ME OFF, BUT THAT DID IT.
GRRR
GO MENTAL - RAMONES
6-27-01
WELL, OLLIE + JOHN KICKED OUT RUSTY TODAY. (IT SUCKS THAT HE'S HOMELESS, BUT IT'S NOT HARD TO BE RESPECTFUL)
SLAM
LAST NIGHT I HUNG OUT WITH HEIDI
TODAY SHE WENT WITH ME TO BUY A FISH TANK!
petco®
FISH TANK
ROOM SERVICE - KISS
6-28-01
THIS MORNING I SAT AROUND AND TOOK BONG HITS
THEN I WENT TO WORK
BUTTONS
STICKERS
THEN I WENT TO HEIDI'S.
TO HEIDI'S
NOTHING TO DO - THE QUEERS
6-29-01
TODAY I WORKED.
THEN I SAW THOSE PEABODYS
WHY'S THE PARTY ALWAYS AT MY HOUSE
THEN I WENT TO A PARTY (IT WASN'T AT CLARK'S HOUSE)

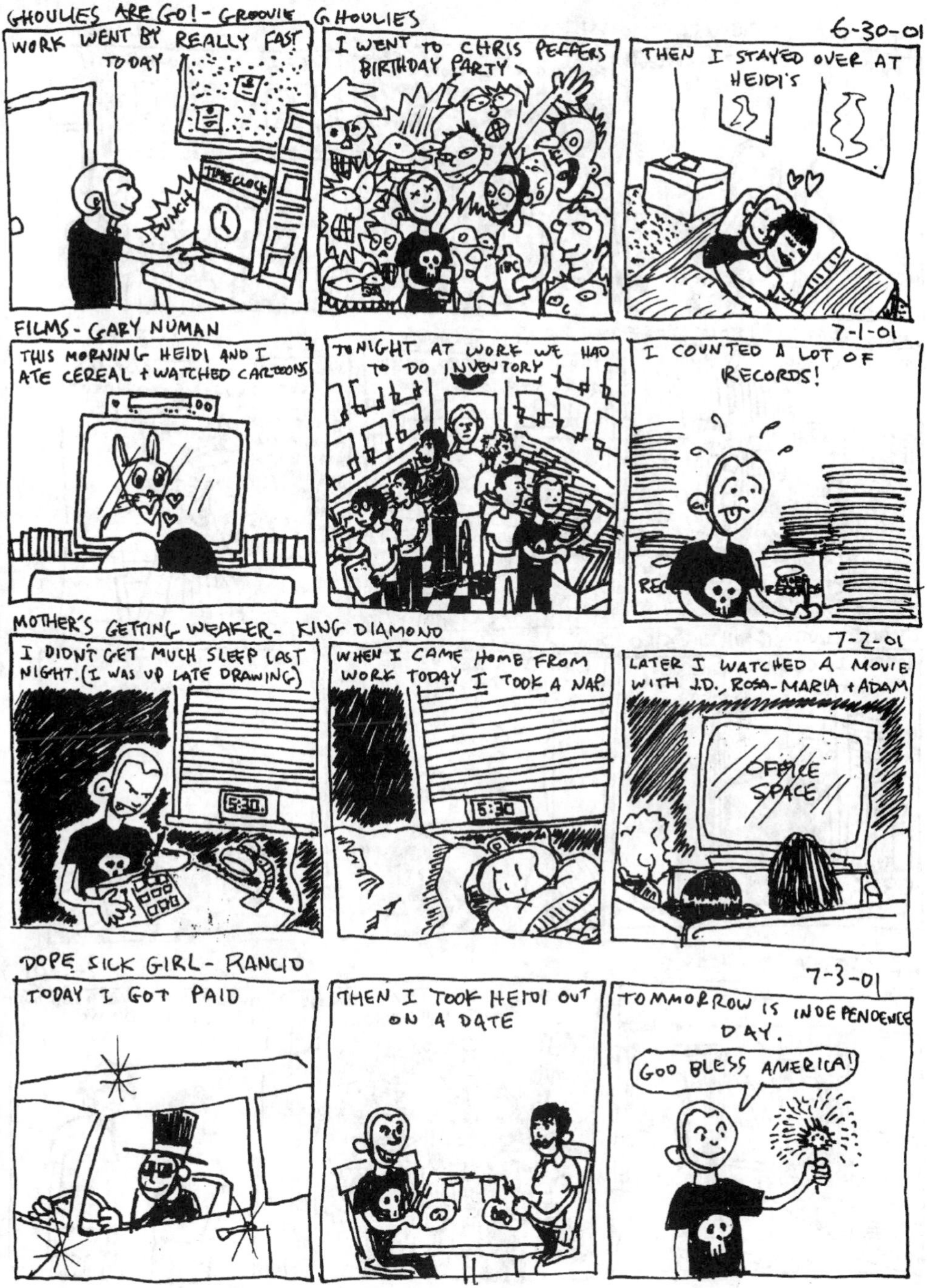
GHOULIES ARE GO! - GROOVIE GHOULIES
6-30-01
WORK WENT BY REALLY FAST TODAY
TIME CLOCK
PUNCH
I WENT TO CHRIS PEFFERS BIRTHDAY PARTY
THEN I STAYED OVER AT HEIDI'S
FILMS - GARY NUMAN
7-1-01
THIS MORNING HEIDI AND I ATE CEREAL + WATCHED CARTOONS
TONIGHT AT WORK WE HAD TO DO INVENTORY
I COUNTED A LOT OF RECORDS!
MOTHER'S GETTING WEAKER - KING DIAMOND
7-2-01
I DIDN'T GET MUCH SLEEP LAST NIGHT. (I WAS UP LATE DRAWING)
5:30
WHEN I CAME HOME FROM WORK TODAY I TOOK A NAP.
5:30
LATER I WATCHED A MOVIE WITH J.D., ROSA-MARIA + ADAM
OFFICE SPACE
DOPE SICK GIRL - RANCID
7-3-01
TODAY I GOT PAID
THEN I TOOK HEIDI OUT ON A DATE
TOMMORROW IS INDEPENDENCE DAY.
GOD BLESS AMERICA!

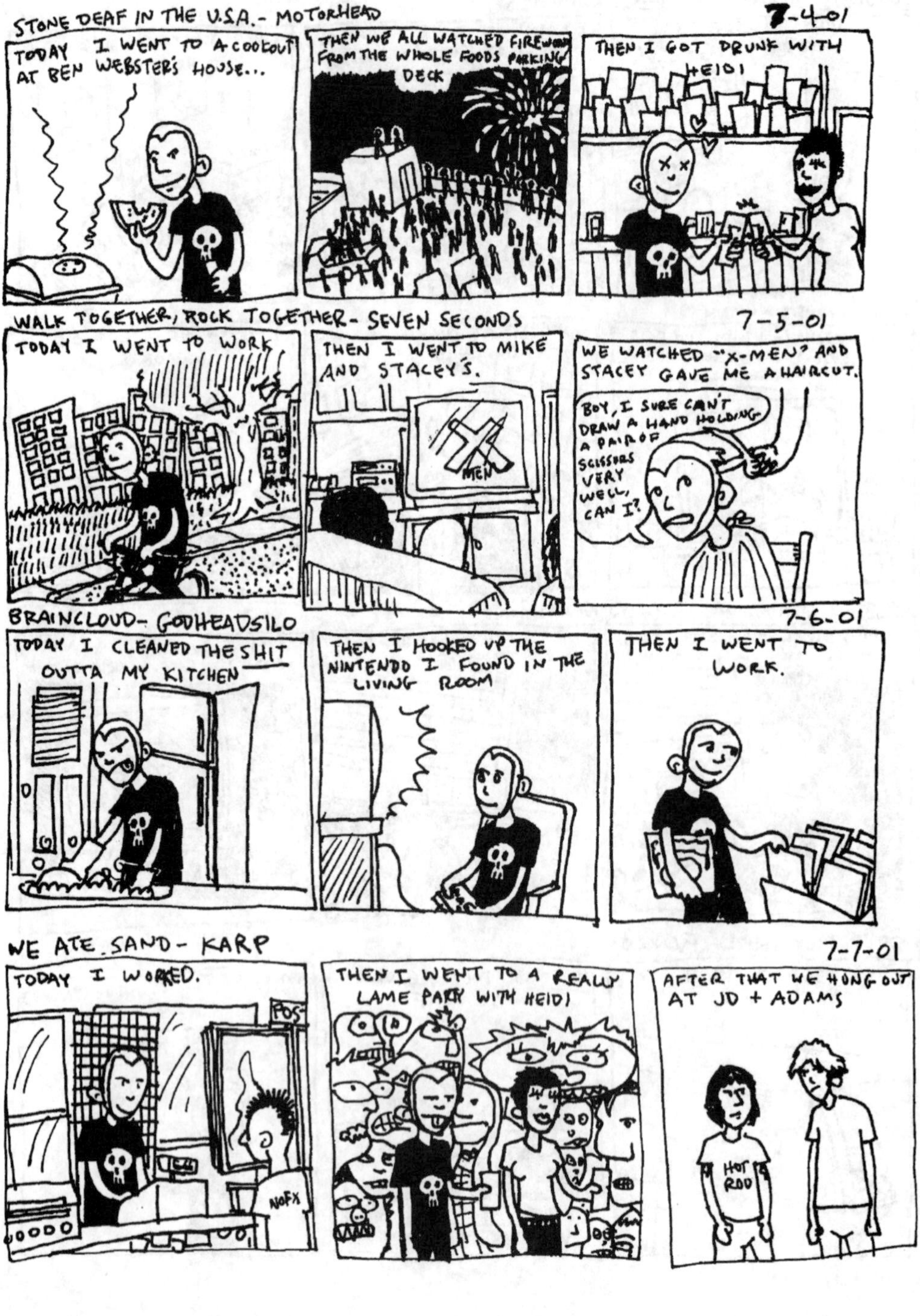
STONE DEAF IN THE U.S.A. - MOTORHEAD
7-4-01
TODAY I WENT TO A COOKOUT AT BEN WEBSTER'S HOUSE...
THEN WE ALL WATCHED FIREW FROM THE WHOLE FOODS PARKING DECK
THEN I GOT DRUNK WITH HEIDI
WALK TOGETHER, ROCK TOGETHER - SEVEN SECONDS
7-5-01
TODAY I WENT TO WORK
THEN I WENT TO MIKE AND STACEY'S.
MEN
WE WATCHED "X-MEN" AND STACEY GAVE ME A HAIRCUT.
BOY, I SURE CAN'T DRAW A HAND HOLDING A PAIR OF SCISSORS VERY WELL, CAN I?
BRAINCLOUD - GODHEADSILO
7-6-01
TODAY I CLEANED THE SHIT OUTTA MY KITCHEN
THEN I HOOKED UP THE NINTENDO I FOUND IN THE LIVING ROOM
THEN I WENT TO WORK.
WE ATE SAND - KARP
7-7-01
TODAY I WORKED.
POS-
NOFX
THEN I WENT TO A REALLY LAME PARTY WITH HEIDI
AFTER THAT WE HUNG OUT AT JD + ADAMS
HOT ROD

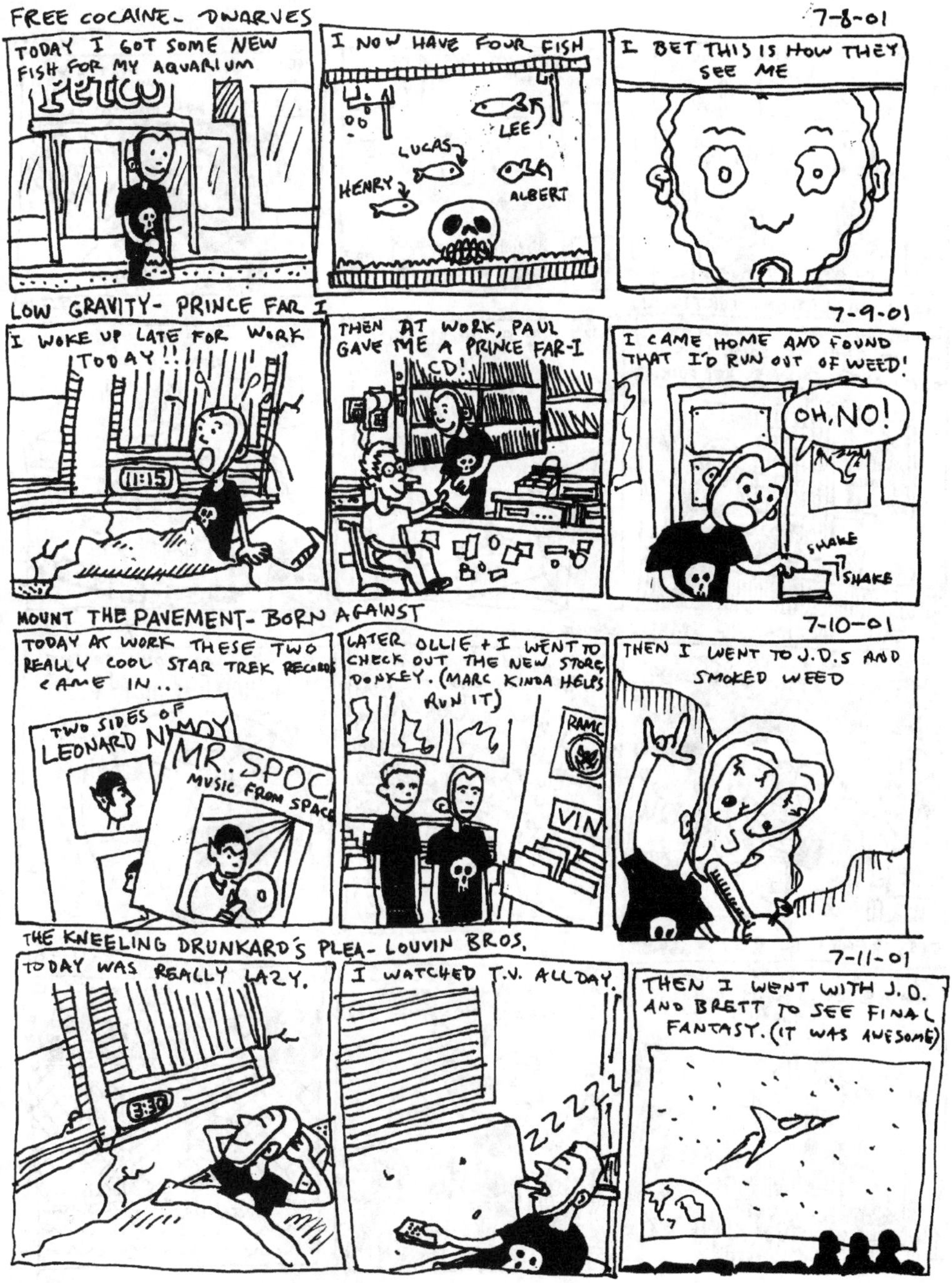
FREE COCAINE - DWARVES
7-8-01
TODAY I GOT SOME NEW FISH FOR MY AQUARIUM
PETCO
I NOW HAVE FOUR FISH
LEE
LUCAS
HENRY
ALBERT
I BET THIS IS HOW THEY SEE ME
LOW GRAVITY - PRINCE FAR I
7-9-01
I WOKE UP LATE FOR WORK TODAY!!
11:15
THEN AT WORK, PAUL GAVE ME A PRINCE FAR-I CD!
I CAME HOME AND FOUND THAT I'D RUN OUT OF WEED!
OH, NO!
SHAKE
SHAKE
MOUNT THE PAVEMENT - BORN AGAINST
7-10-01
TODAY AT WORK THESE TWO REALLY COOL STAR TREK RECORDS CAME IN...
TWO SIDES OF LEONARD NIMOY
MR. SPOCK MUSIC FROM SPACE
LATER OLLIE + I WENT TO CHECK OUT THE NEW STORE, DONKEY. (MARC KINDA HELPS RUN IT)
VIN
THEN I WENT TO J.D.S AND SMOKED WEED
THE KNEELING DRUNKARD'S PLEA - LOUVIN BROS.
7-11-01
TODAY WAS REALLY LAZY.
3:30
I WATCHED T.V. ALL DAY.
ZZZZZ
THEN I WENT WITH J.D. AND BRETT TO SEE FINAL FANTASY. (IT WAS AWESOME)

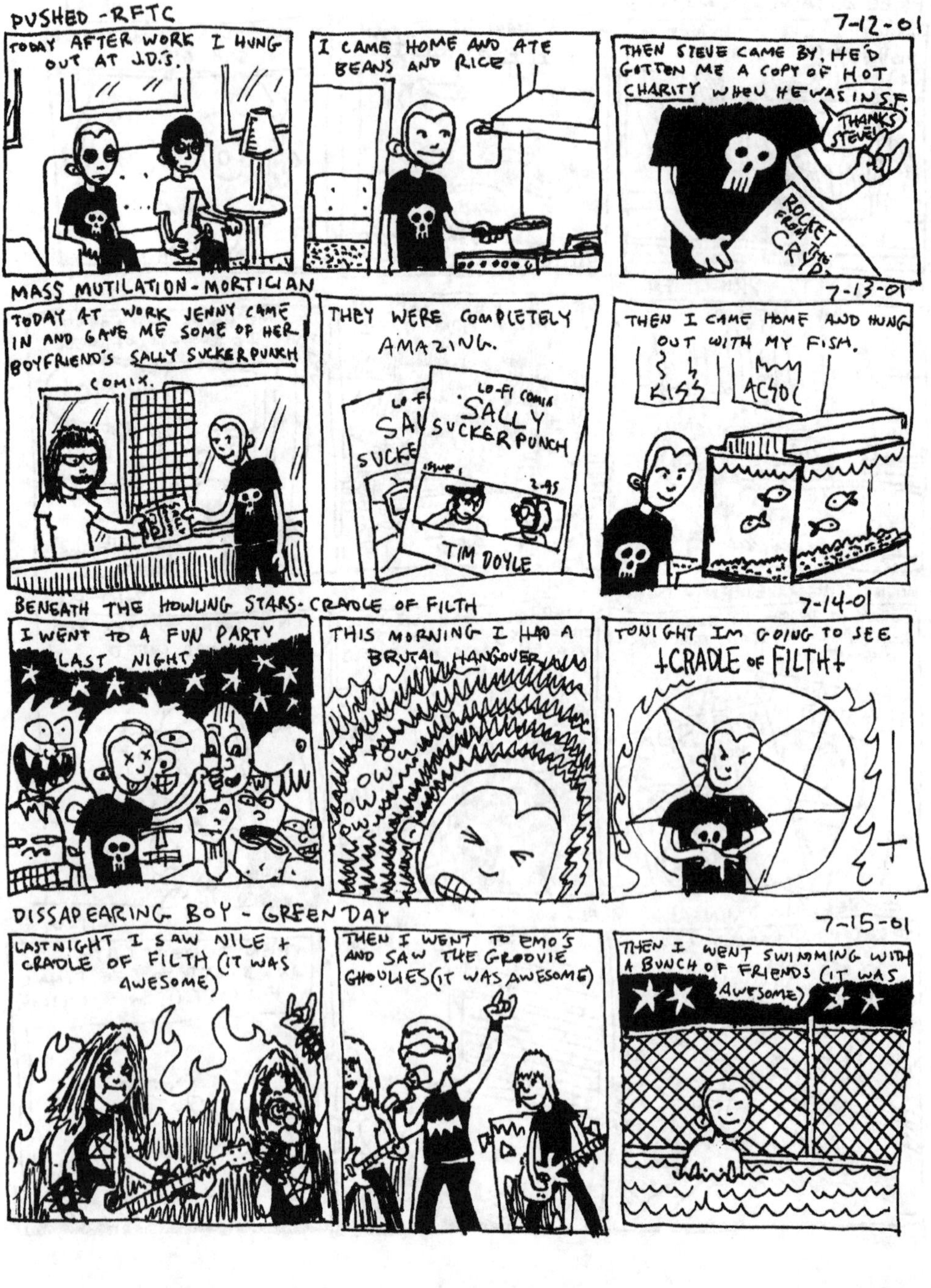
PUSHED - RFTC
7-12-01
TODAY AFTER WORK I HUNG OUT AT J.D.'S.
I CAME HOME AND ATE BEANS AND RICE
THEN STEVE CAME BY. HE'D GOTTEN ME A COPY OF HOT CHARITY WHEN HE WAS IN S.F.
THANKS STEVE!
ROCKET FROM THE CRYPT
MASS MUTILATION - MORTICIAN
7-13-01
TODAY AT WORK JENNY CAME IN AND GAVE ME SOME OF HER BOYFRIEND'S SALLY SUCKERPUNCH COMIX.
THEY WERE COMPLETELY AMAZING.
LO-FI COMIX
SALLY SUCKERPUNCH
ISSUE 1
2.95
TIM DOYLE
THEN I CAME HOME AND HUNG OUT WITH MY FISH.
KISS
AC/DC
BENEATH THE HOWLING STARS - CRADLE OF FILTH
7-14-01
I WENT TO A FUN PARTY LAST NIGHT
THIS MORNING I HAD A BRUTAL HANGOVER
OW OW OW OW
TONIGHT IM GOING TO SEE
†CRADLE OF FILTH†
DISSAPEARING BOY - GREEN DAY
7-15-01
LAST NIGHT I SAW NILE + CRADLE OF FILTH (IT WAS AWESOME)
THEN I WENT TO EMO'S AND SAW THE GROOVIE GHOULIES (IT WAS AWESOME)
THEN I WENT SWIMMING WITH A BUNCH OF FRIENDS (IT WAS AWESOME)

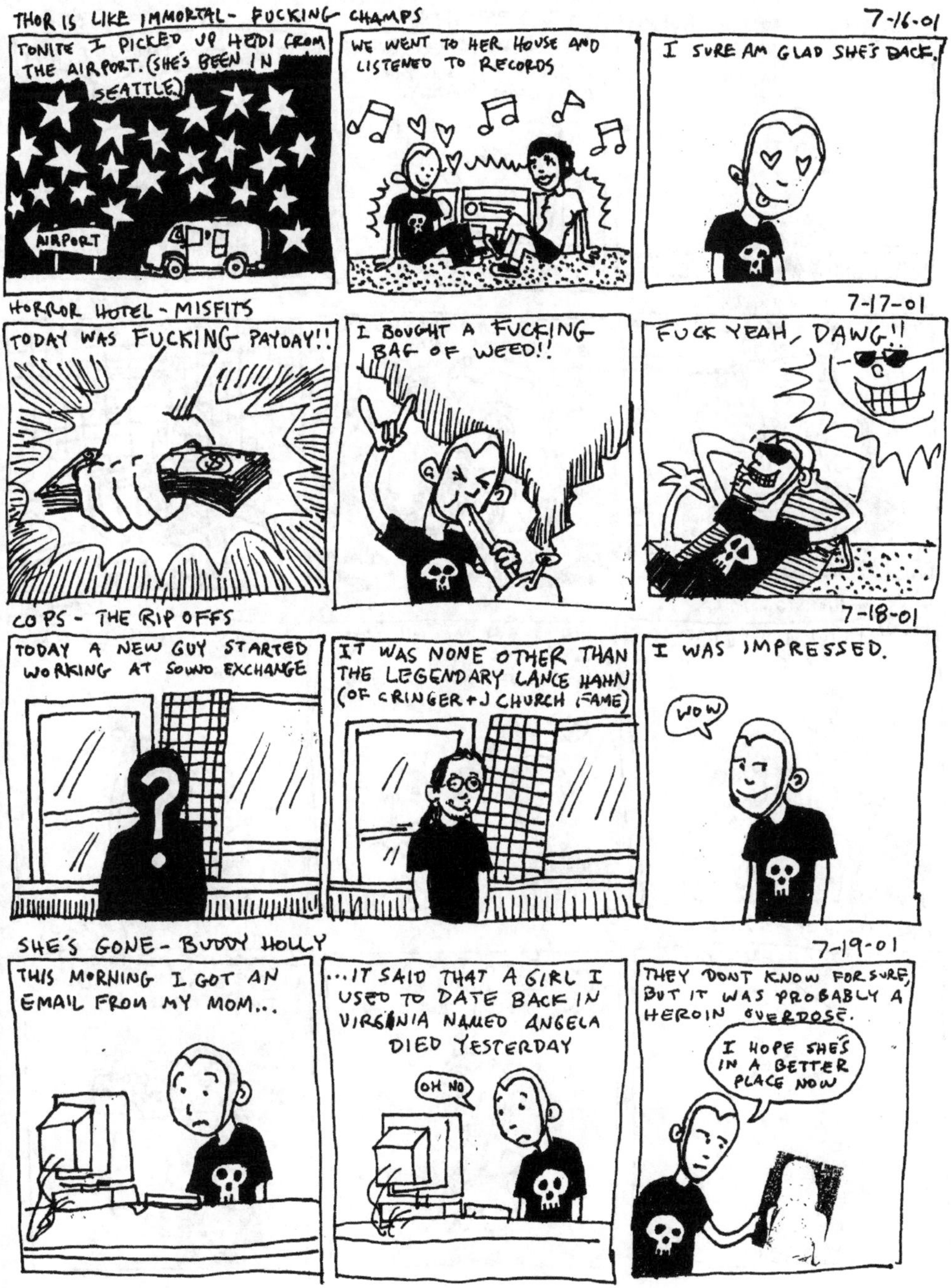
THOR IS LIKE IMMORTAL - FUCKING CHAMPS
7-16-01
TONITE I PICKED UP HEIDI FROM THE AIRPORT. (SHE'S BEEN IN SEATTLE)
AIRPORT
WE WENT TO HER HOUSE AND LISTENED TO RECORDS
I SURE AM GLAD SHE'S BACK.
HORROR HOTEL - MISFITS
7-17-01
TODAY WAS FUCKING PAYDAY!!
I BOUGHT A FUCKING BAG OF WEED!!
FUCK YEAH, DAWG!!
COPS - THE RIP OFFS
7-18-01
TODAY A NEW GUY STARTED WORKING AT SOUND EXCHANGE
IT WAS NONE OTHER THAN THE LEGENDARY LANCE HAHN (OF CRINGER + J CHURCH FAME)
I WAS IMPRESSED.
WOW
SHE'S GONE - BUDDY HOLLY
7-19-01
THIS MORNING I GOT AN EMAIL FROM MY MOM...
...IT SAID THAT A GIRL I USED TO DATE BACK IN VIRGINIA NAMED ANGELA DIED YESTERDAY
OH NO
THEY DONT KNOW FOR SURE, BUT IT WAS PROBABLY A HEROIN OVERDOSE.
I HOPE SHE'S IN A BETTER PLACE NOW

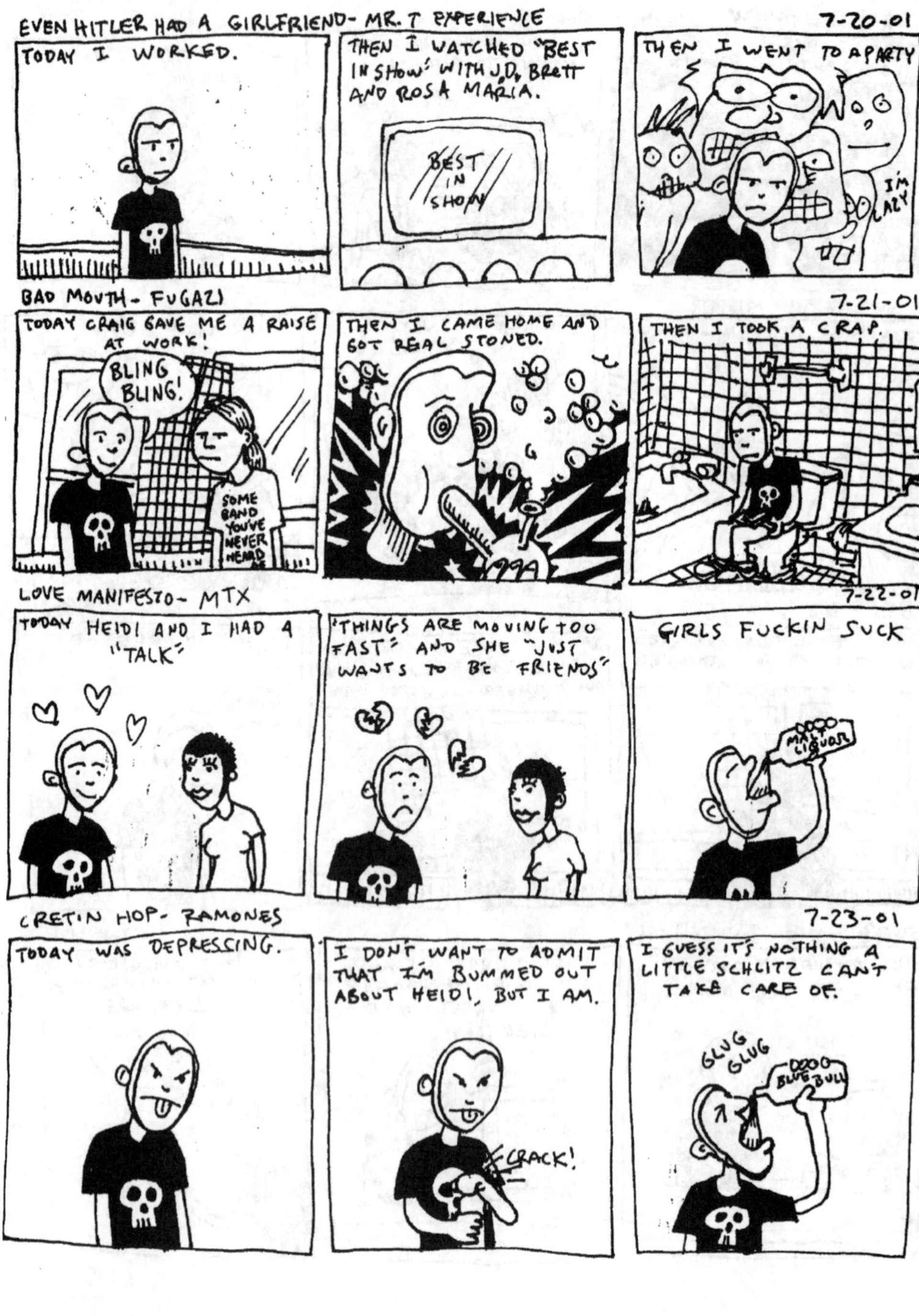

EVEN HITLER HAD A GIRLFRIEND- MR. T EXPERIENCE
7-20-01
TODAY I WORKED.
THEN I WATCHED "BEST IN SHOW" WITH J.D., BRETT AND ROSA MARIA.
BEST IN SHOW
THEN I WENT TO A PARTY
IM LAZY
BAD MOUTH- FUGAZI
7-21-01
TODAY CRAIG GAVE ME A RAISE AT WORK!
BLING BLING!
SOME BAND YOU'VE NEVER HEARD OF
THEN I CAME HOME AND GOT REAL STONED.
THEN I TOOK A CRAP.
LOVE MANIFESTO- MTX
7-22-01
TODAY HEIDI AND I HAD A "TALK"
"THINGS ARE MOVING TOO FAST" AND SHE "JUST WANTS TO BE FRIENDS"
GIRLS FUCKIN SUCK
MALT LIQUOR
CRETIN HOP- RAMONES
7-23-01
TODAY WAS DEPRESSING.
I DON'T WANT TO ADMIT THAT I'M BUMMED OUT ABOUT HEIDI, BUT I AM.
CRACK!
I GUESS IT'S NOTHING A LITTLE SCHLITZ CAN'T TAKE CARE OF.
GLUG GLUG
BLUE BULL

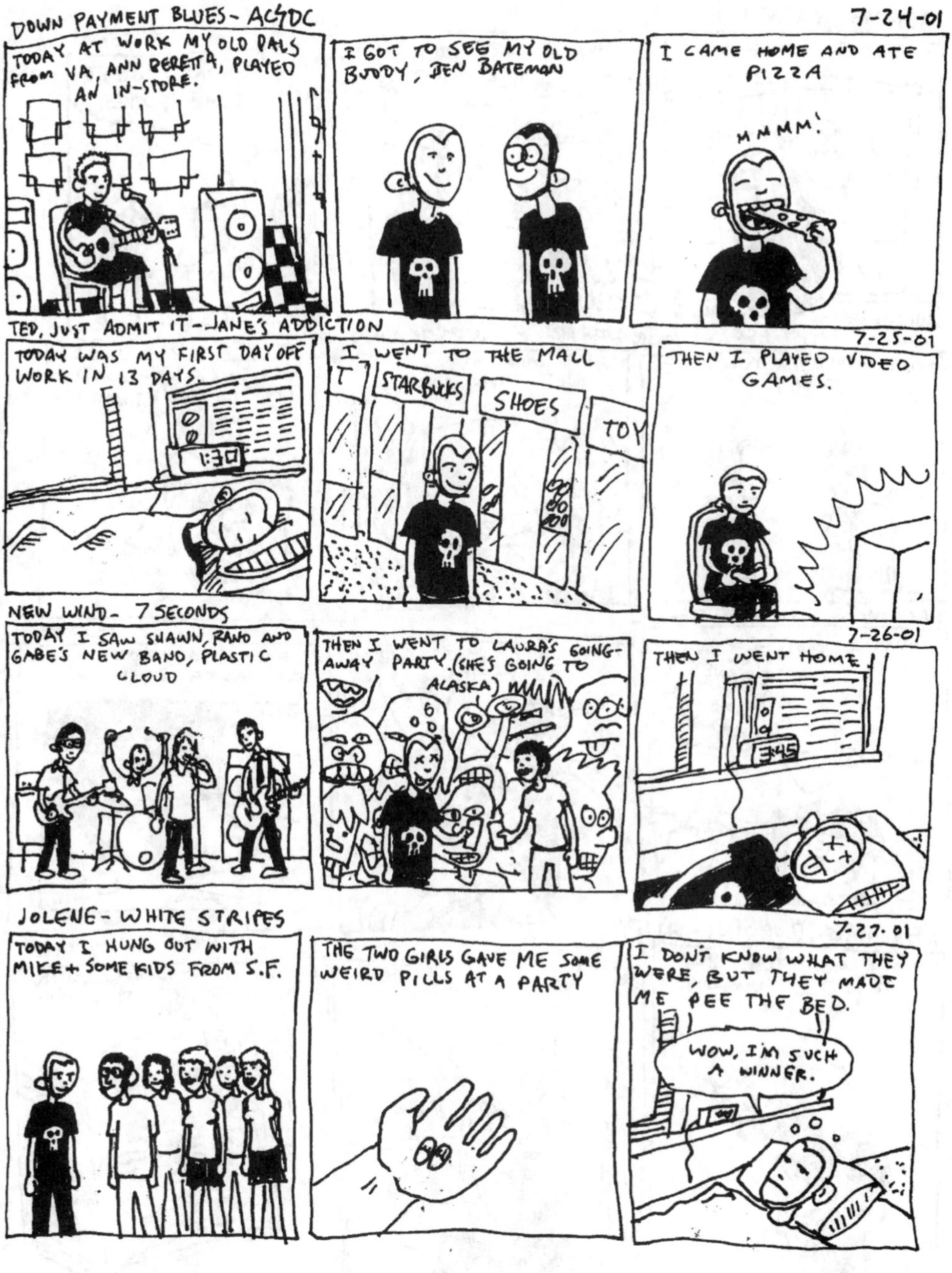
DOWN PAYMENT BLUES - AC/DC
7-24-01
TODAY AT WORK MY OLD PALS FROM VA, ANN BERETTA, PLAYED AN IN-STORE.
I GOT TO SEE MY OLD BUDDY, BEN BATEMAN
I CAME HOME AND ATE PIZZA
MMMM!
TED, JUST ADMIT IT - JANE'S ADDICTION
7-25-01
TODAY WAS MY FIRST DAY OFF WORK IN 13 DAYS.
1:30
I WENT TO THE MALL
STARBUCKS
SHOES
TOY
THEN I PLAYED VIDEO GAMES.
NEW WIND - 7 SECONDS
7-26-01
TODAY I SAW SHAWN, RAND AND GABE'S NEW BAND, PLASTIC CLOUD
THEN I WENT TO LAURA'S GOING-AWAY PARTY. (SHE'S GOING TO ALASKA)
THEN I WENT HOME
3:45
JOLENE - WHITE STRIPES
7-27-01
TODAY I HUNG OUT WITH MIKE + SOME KIDS FROM S.F.
THE TWO GIRLS GAVE ME SOME WEIRD PILLS AT A PARTY
I DON'T KNOW WHAT THEY WERE, BUT THEY MADE ME PEE THE BED.
WOW, I'M SUCH A WINNER.

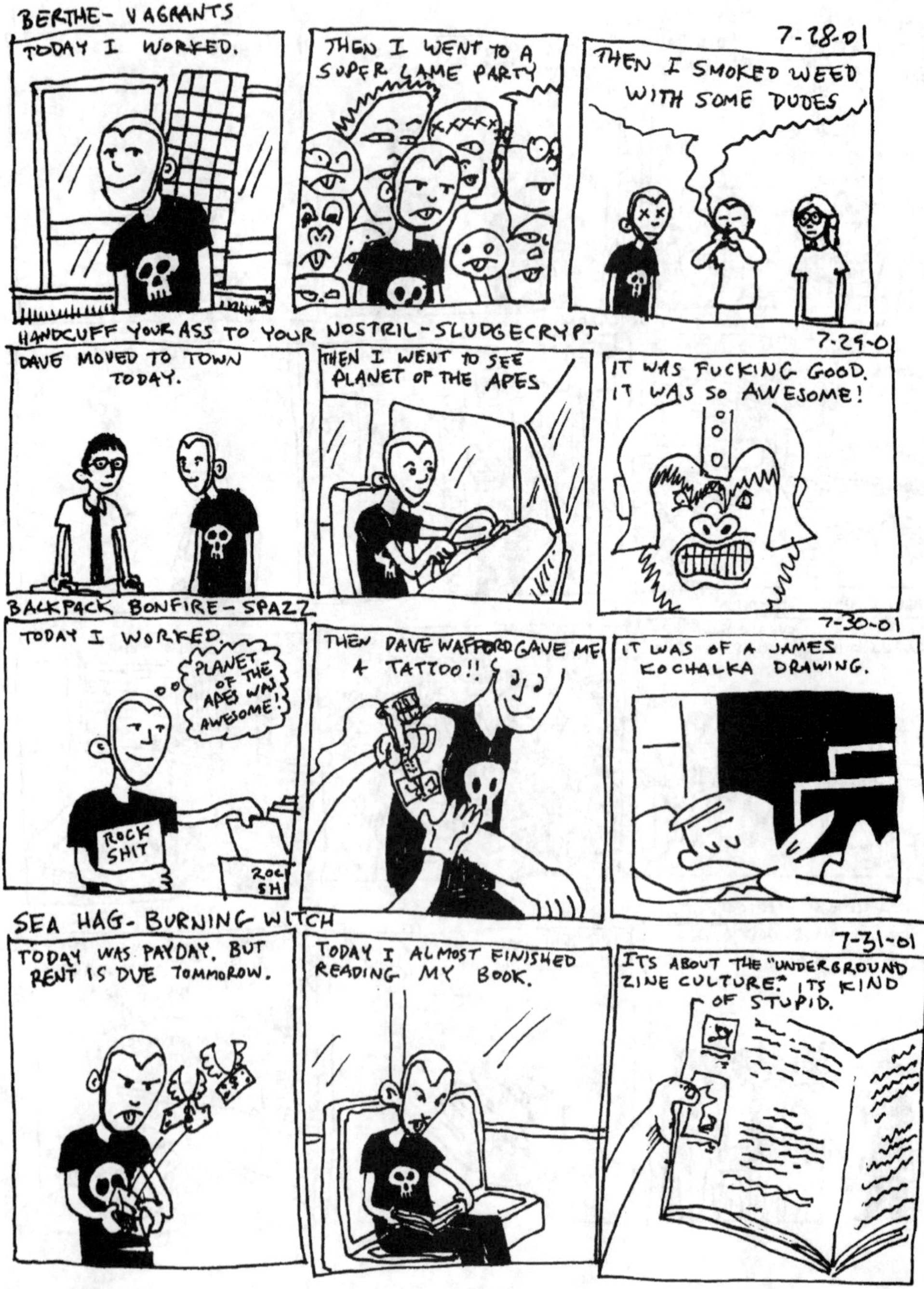
BERTHE- VAGRANTS
7-28-01
TODAY I WORKED.
THEN I WENT TO A SUPER LAME PARTY
THEN I SMOKED WEED WITH SOME DUDES
HANDCUFF YOUR ASS TO YOUR NOSTRIL- SLUDGECRYPT
7-29-01
DAVE MOVED TO TOWN TODAY.
THEN I WENT TO SEE PLANET OF THE APES
IT WAS FUCKING GOOD. IT WAS SO AWESOME!
BACKPACK BONFIRE- SPAZZ
7-30-01
TODAY I WORKED.
PLANET OF THE APES WAS AWESOME!
ROCK SHIT
THEN DAVE WAFFORD GAVE ME A TATTOO!!
IT WAS OF A JAMES KOCHALKA DRAWING.
SEA HAG- BURNING WITCH
7-31-01
TODAY WAS PAYDAY. BUT RENT IS DUE TOMMOROW.
TODAY I ALMOST FINISHED READING MY BOOK.
ITS ABOUT THE "UNDERGROUND ZINE CULTURE." ITS KIND OF STUPID.

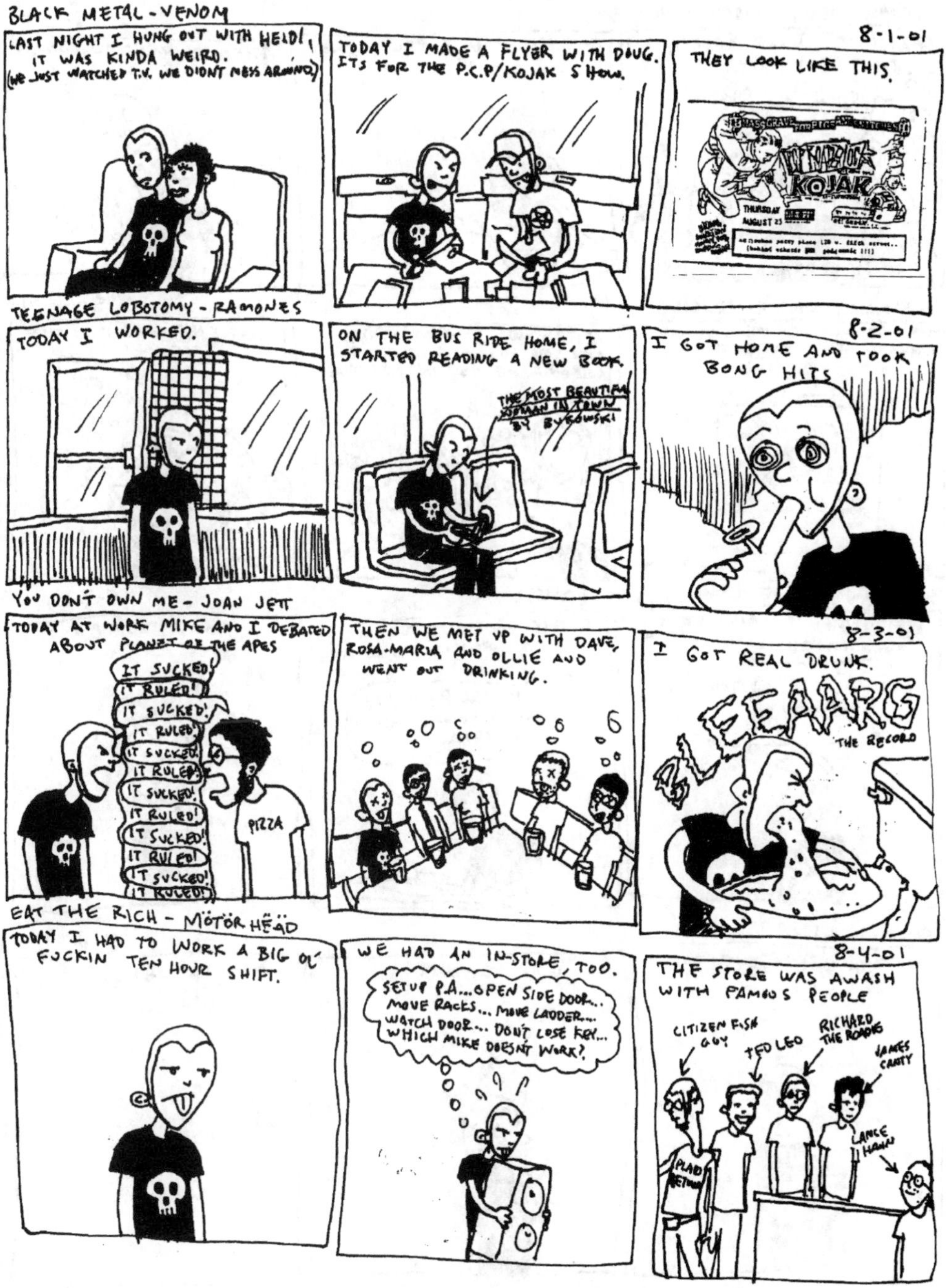

BLACK METAL - VENOM
8-1-01
LAST NIGHT I HUNG OUT WITH HEIDI, IT WAS KINDA WEIRD.
(WE JUST WATCHED T.V. WE DIDN'T MESS AROUND)
TODAY I MADE A FLYER WITH DOUG. ITS FOR THE P.C.P/KOJAK SHOW.
THEY LOOK LIKE THIS.
KOJAK
THURSDAY
AUGUST 23
TEENAGE LOBOTOMY - RAMONES
8-2-01
TODAY I WORKED.
ON THE BUS RIDE HOME, I STARTED READING A NEW BOOK.
THE MOST BEAUTIFUL WOMAN IN TOWN BY BUKOWSKI
I GOT HOME AND TOOK BONG HITS
YOU DON'T OWN ME - JOAN JETT
8-3-01
TODAY AT WORK MIKE AND I DEBATED ABOUT PLANET OF THE APES
IT SUCKED!
IT RULED!
IT SUCKED!
IT RULED!
IT SUCKED!
IT RULED!
IT SUCKED!
IT RULED!
IT SUCKED!
IT RULED!
IT SUCKED!
IT RULED!
PIZZA
THEN WE MET UP WITH DAVE, ROSA-MARIA AND OLLIE AND WENT OUT DRINKING.
I GOT REAL DRUNK.
BLEEAARG
THE RECORD
EAT THE RICH - MÖTÖRHËAD
8-4-01
TODAY I HAD TO WORK A BIG OL' FUCKIN TEN HOUR SHIFT.
WE HAD AN IN-STORE, TOO.
SETUP P.A... OPEN SIDE DOOR... MOVE RACKS... MOVE LADDER... WATCH DOOR... DON'T LOSE KEY... WHICH MIKE DOESN'T WORK?
THE STORE WAS AWASH WITH FAMOUS PEOPLE
CITIZEN FISH GUY
TED LEO
RICHARD THE ROADIE
JAMES CANTY
PLAID RETINA
LANCE HAHN

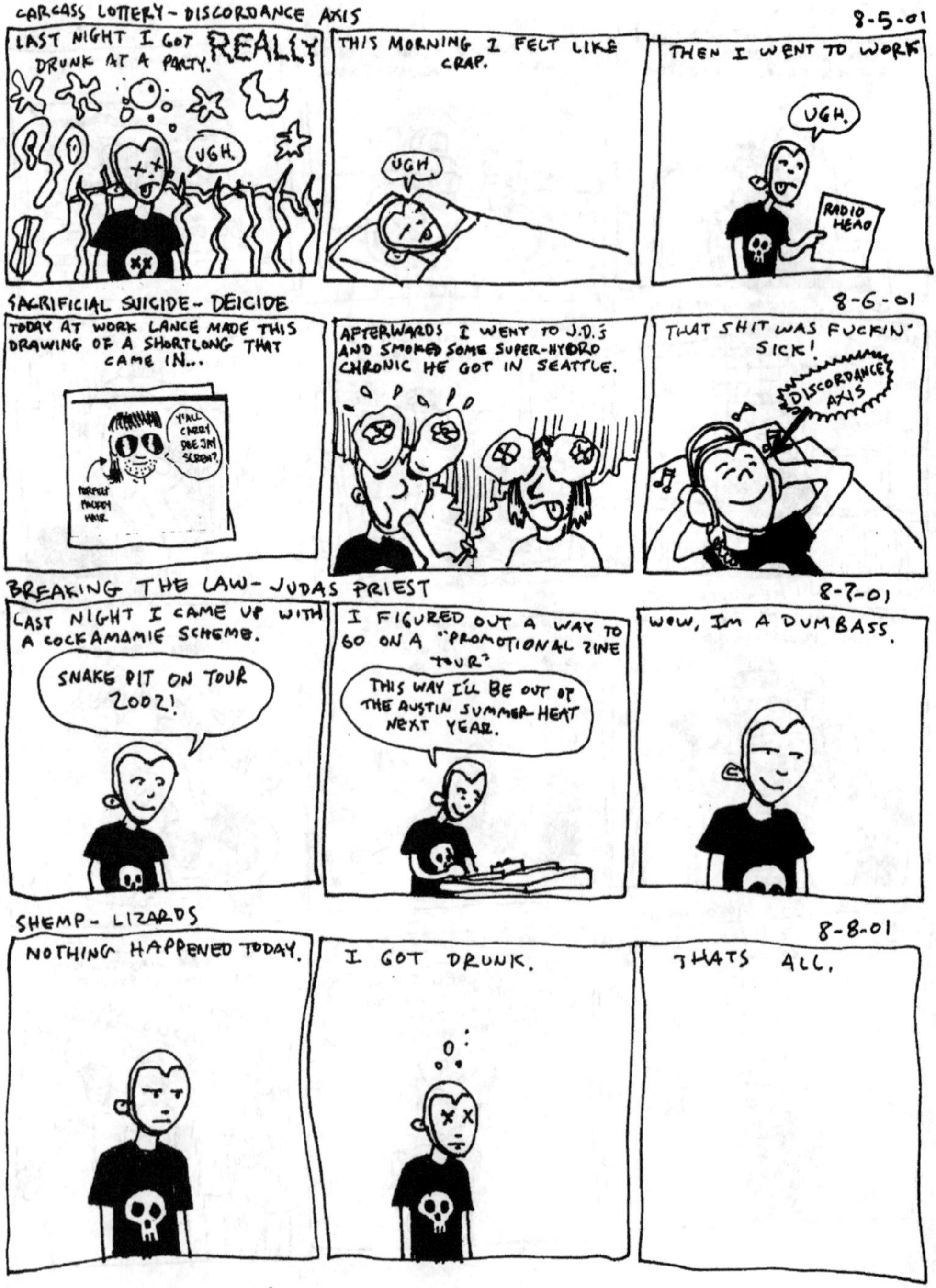
CARCASS LOTTERY - DISCORDANCE AXIS
8-5-01
LAST NIGHT I GOT REALLY DRUNK AT A PARTY.
UGH.
THIS MORNING I FELT LIKE CRAP.
UGH.
THEN I WENT TO WORK
UGH.
RADIO HEAD
SACRIFICIAL SUICIDE - DEICIDE
8-6-01
TODAY AT WORK LANCE MADE THIS DRAWING OF A SHORTLONG THAT CAME IN...
AFTERWARDS I WENT TO J.D.'S AND SMOKED SOME SUPER-HYDRO CHRONIC HE GOT IN SEATTLE.
THAT SHIT WAS FUCKIN' SICK!
DISCORDANCE AXIS
BREAKING THE LAW - JUDAS PRIEST
8-7-01
LAST NIGHT I CAME UP WITH A COCKAMAMIE SCHEME.
SNAKE PIT ON TOUR 2002!
I FIGURED OUT A WAY TO GO ON A "PROMOTIONAL ZINE TOUR"
THIS WAY I'LL BE OUT OF THE AUSTIN SUMMER HEAT NEXT YEAR.
WOW, IM A DUMBASS.
SHEMP - LIZARDS
8-8-01
NOTHING HAPPENED TODAY.
I GOT DRUNK.
THATS ALL.

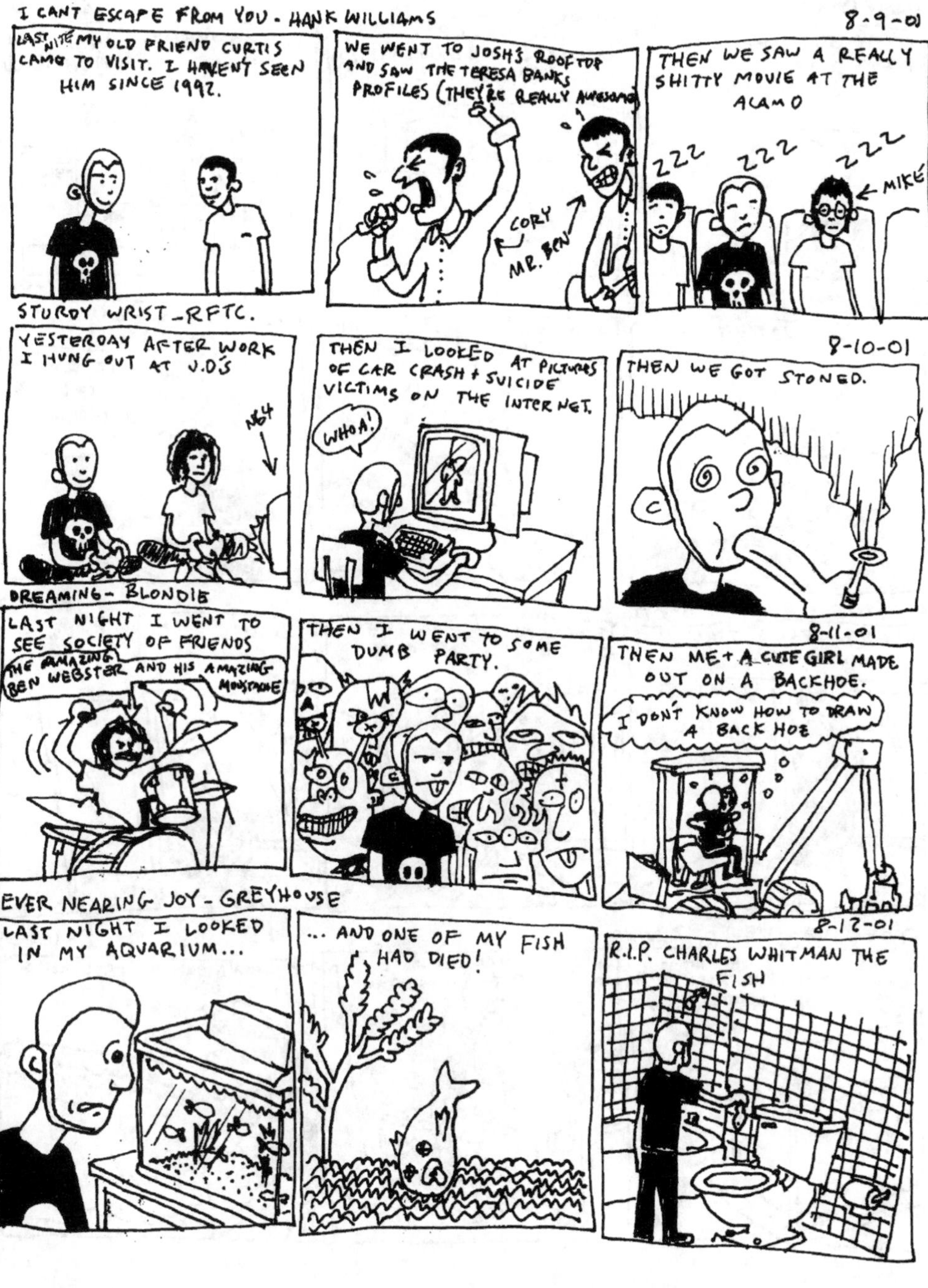
I CANT ESCAPE FROM YOU - HANK WILLIAMS
8-9-01
LAST NITE MY OLD FRIEND CURTIS CAME TO VISIT. I HAVEN'T SEEN HIM SINCE 1992.
WE WENT TO JOSH'S ROOFTOP AND SAW THE TERESA BANKS PROFILES (THEY'RE REALLY AWESOME)
CORY
MR. BEN
THEN WE SAW A REALLY SHITTY MOVIE AT THE ALAMO
ZZZ
ZZZ
ZZZ
MIKE
STURDY WRIST - RFTC.
8-10-01
YESTERDAY AFTER WORK I HUNG OUT AT J.D'S
N64
THEN I LOOKED AT PICTURES OF CAR CRASH + SUICIDE VICTIMS ON THE INTERNET.
WHOA!
THEN WE GOT STONED.
DREAMING - BLONDIE
8-11-01
LAST NIGHT I WENT TO SEE SOCIETY OF FRIENDS
THE AMAZING BEN WEBSTER AND HIS AMAZING MOUSTACHE
THEN I WENT TO SOME DUMB PARTY.
THEN ME + A CUTE GIRL MADE OUT ON A BACKHOE.
I DON'T KNOW HOW TO DRAW A BACK HOE
EVER NEARING JOY - GREYHOUSE
8-12-01
LAST NIGHT I LOOKED IN MY AQUARIUM...
... AND ONE OF MY FISH HAD DIED!
R.I.P. CHARLES WHITMAN THE FISH

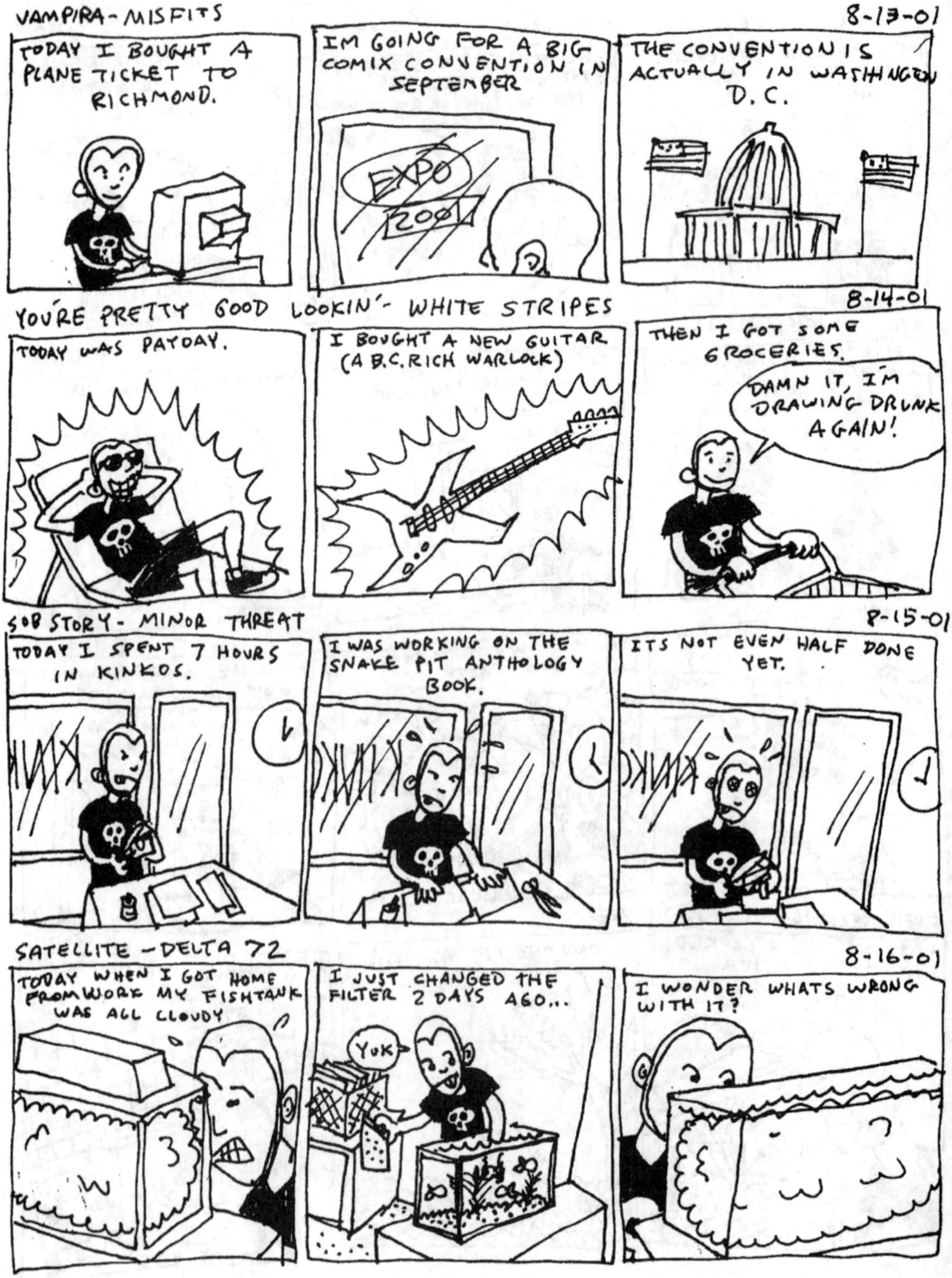
VAMPIRA - MISFITS
8-13-01
TODAY I BOUGHT A PLANE TICKET TO RICHMOND.
IM GOING FOR A BIG COMIX CONVENTION IN SEPTEMBER
EXPO 2001
THE CONVENTION IS ACTUALLY IN WASHINGTON D.C.
YOU'RE PRETTY GOOD LOOKIN' - WHITE STRIPES
8-14-01
TODAY WAS PAYDAY.
I BOUGHT A NEW GUITAR (A B.C. RICH WARLOCK)
THEN I GOT SOME GROCERIES.
DAMN IT, I'M DRAWING DRUNK AGAIN!
SOB STORY - MINOR THREAT
8-15-01
TODAY I SPENT 7 HOURS IN KINKOS.
I WAS WORKING ON THE SNAKE PIT ANTHOLOGY BOOK.
ITS NOT EVEN HALF DONE YET.
SATELLITE - DELTA 72
8-16-01
TODAY WHEN I GOT HOME FROM WORK MY FISHTANK WAS ALL CLOUDY
I JUST CHANGED THE FILTER 2 DAYS AGO...
YUK
I WONDER WHATS WRONG WITH IT?

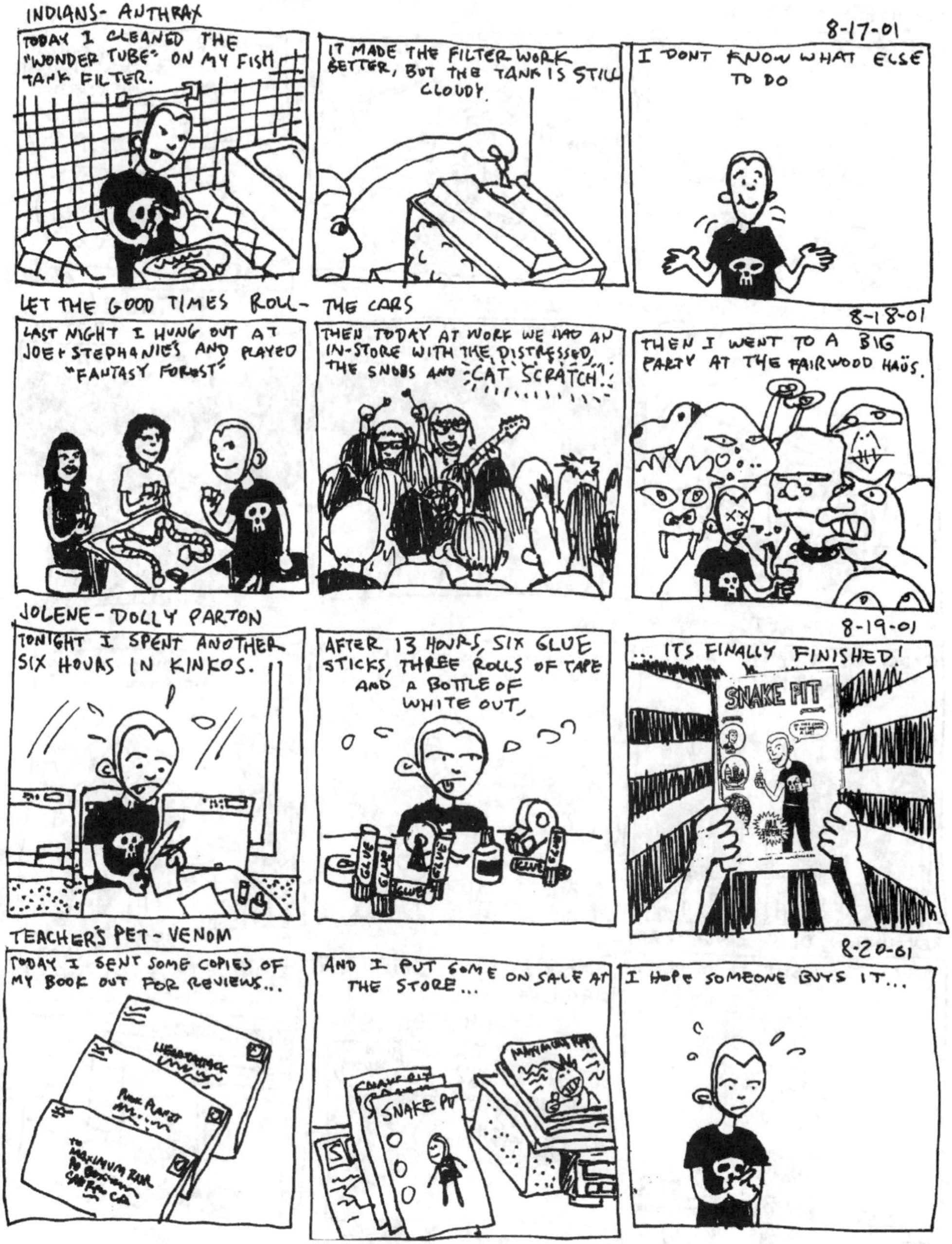
INDIANS- ANTHRAX
8-17-01
TODAY I CLEANED THE "WONDER TUBE" ON MY FISH TANK FILTER.
IT MADE THE FILTER WORK BETTER, BUT THE TANK IS STILL CLOUDY.
I DONT KNOW WHAT ELSE TO DO
LET THE GOOD TIMES ROLL- THE CARS
8-18-01
LAST NIGHT I HUNG OUT AT JOE+STEPHANIE'S AND PLAYED "FANTASY FOREST"
THEN TODAY AT WORK WE HAD AN IN-STORE WITH THE DISTRESSED, THE SNOBS AND CAT SCRATCH!
THEN I WENT TO A BIG PARTY AT THE FAIRWOOD HAÜS.
JOLENE- DOLLY PARTON
8-19-01
TONIGHT I SPENT ANOTHER SIX HOURS IN KINKOS.
AFTER 13 HOURS, SIX GLUE STICKS, THREE ROLLS OF TAPE AND A BOTTLE OF WHITE OUT,
GLUE
GLUE
GLUE
GLUE
GLUE
GLUE
... ITS FINALLY FINISHED!
SNAKE PIT
TEACHER'S PET- VENOM
8-20-01
TODAY I SENT SOME COPIES OF MY BOOK OUT FOR REVIEWS...
TO MAXIMUM RNR
AND I PUT SOME ON SALE AT THE STORE...
SNAKE PIT
I HOPE SOMEONE BUYS IT...

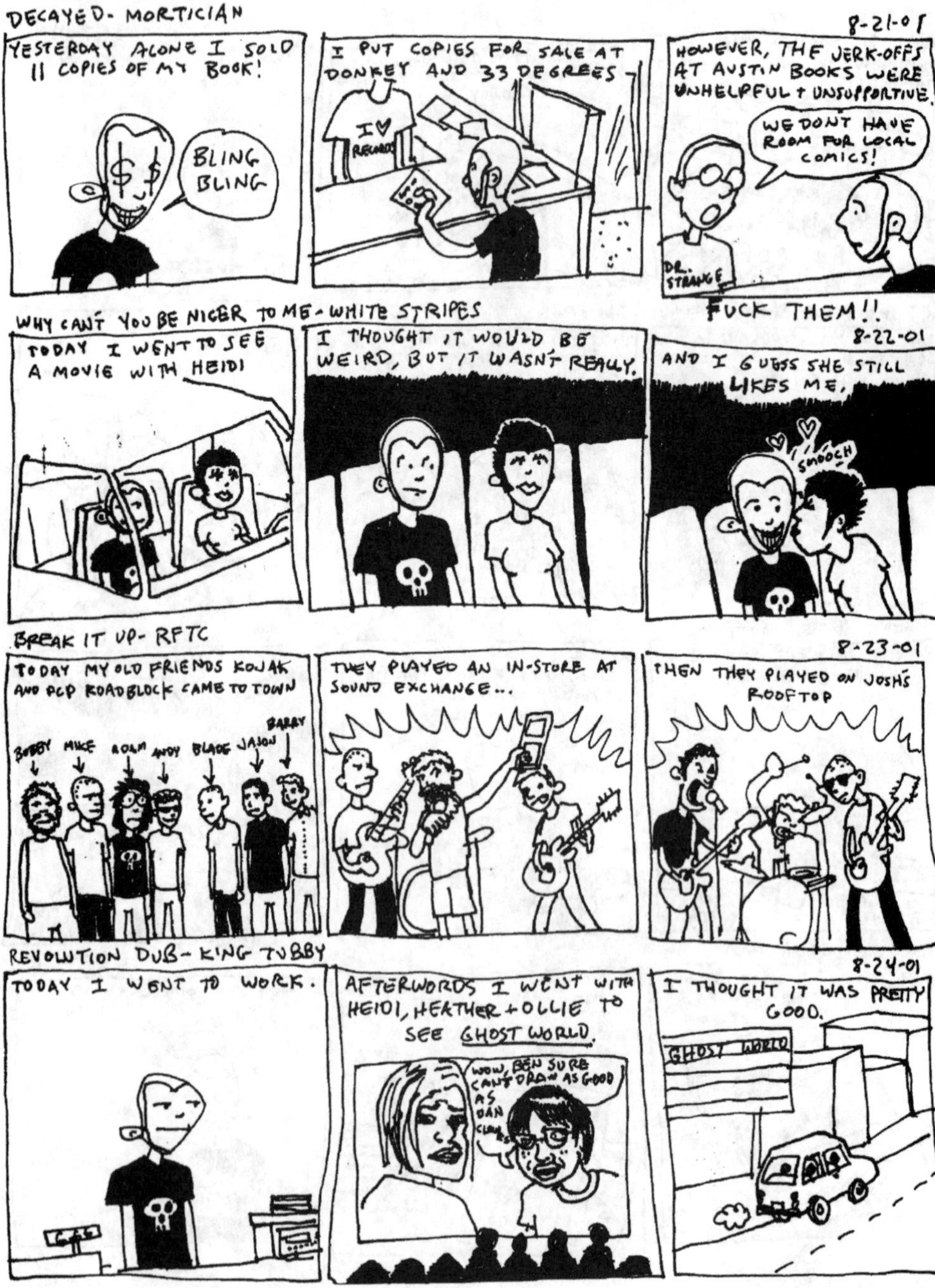

DECAYED- MORTICIAN
8-21-01
YESTERDAY ALONE I SOLD 11 COPIES OF MY BOOK!
BLING BLING
I PUT COPIES FOR SALE AT DONKEY AND 33 DEGREES -
I ♥ RECORDS
HOWEVER, THE JERK-OFFS AT AUSTIN BOOKS WERE UNHELPFUL + UNSUPPORTIVE.
WE DONT HAVE ROOM FOR LOCAL COMICS!
DR. STRANGE
FUCK THEM!!
WHY CAN'T YOU BE NICER TO ME- WHITE STRIPES
8-22-01
TODAY I WENT TO SEE A MOVIE WITH HEIDI
I THOUGHT IT WOULD BE WEIRD, BUT IT WASN'T REALLY.
AND I GUESS SHE STILL LIKES ME.
SMOOCH
BREAK IT UP- RFTC
8-23-01
TODAY MY OLD FRIENDS KOJAK AND PCP ROADBLOCK CAME TO TOWN
BOBBY
MIKE
ADAM
ANDY
BLADE
JASON
BARRY
THEY PLAYED AN IN-STORE AT SOUND EXCHANGE...
THEN THEY PLAYED ON JOSH'S ROOFTOP
REVOLUTION DUB- KING TUBBY
8-24-01
TODAY I WENT TO WORK.
AFTERWORDS I WENT WITH HEIDI, HEATHER + OLLIE TO SEE GHOST WORLD.
WOW, BEN SURE CAN'T DRAW AS GOOD AS DAN CLOWES
I THOUGHT IT WAS PRETTY GOOD.
GHOST WORLD

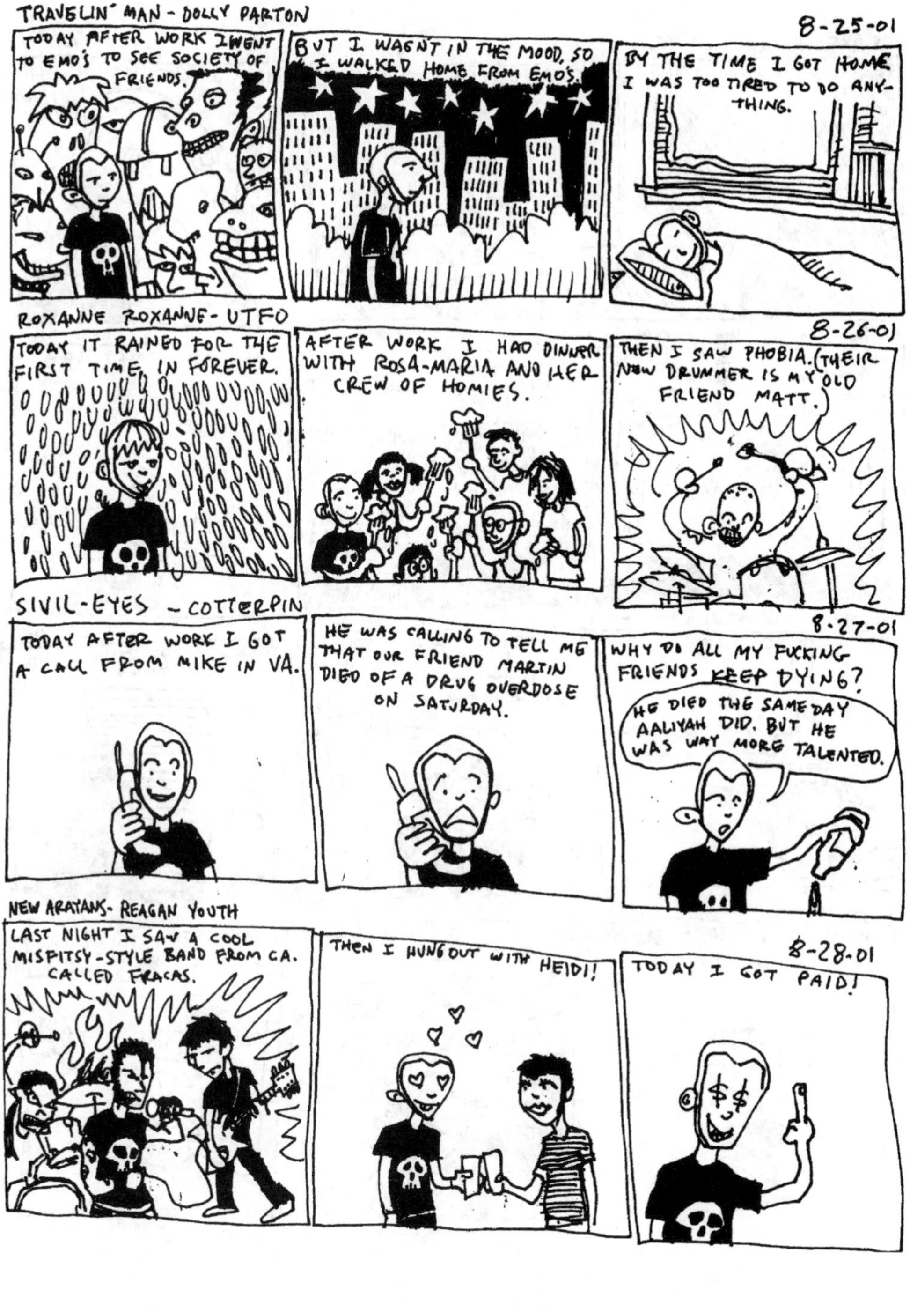

TRAVELIN' MAN - DOLLY PARTON
8-25-01
TODAY AFTER WORK I WENT TO EMO'S TO SEE SOCIETY OF FRIENDS.
BUT I WASN'T IN THE MOOD, SO I WALKED HOME FROM EMO'S.
BY THE TIME I GOT HOME I WAS TOO TIRED TO DO ANYTHING.
ROXANNE ROXANNE - UTFO
8-26-01
TODAY IT RAINED FOR THE FIRST TIME IN FOREVER.
AFTER WORK I HAD DINNER WITH ROSA-MARIA AND HER CREW OF HOMIES.
THEN I SAW PHOBIA. (THEIR NEW DRUMMER IS MY OLD FRIEND MATT.)
SIVIL-EYES - COTTERPIN
8-27-01
TODAY AFTER WORK I GOT A CALL FROM MIKE IN VA.
HE WAS CALLING TO TELL ME THAT OUR FRIEND MARTIN DIED OF A DRUG OVERDOSE ON SATURDAY.
WHY DO ALL MY FUCKING FRIENDS KEEP DYING?
HE DIED THE SAME DAY AALIYAH DID. BUT HE WAS WAY MORE TALENTED.
NEW ARAYANS - REAGAN YOUTH
LAST NIGHT I SAW A COOL MISFITSY-STYLE BAND FROM CA. CALLED FRACAS.
THEN I HUNG OUT WITH HEIDI!
8-28-01
TODAY I GOT PAID!

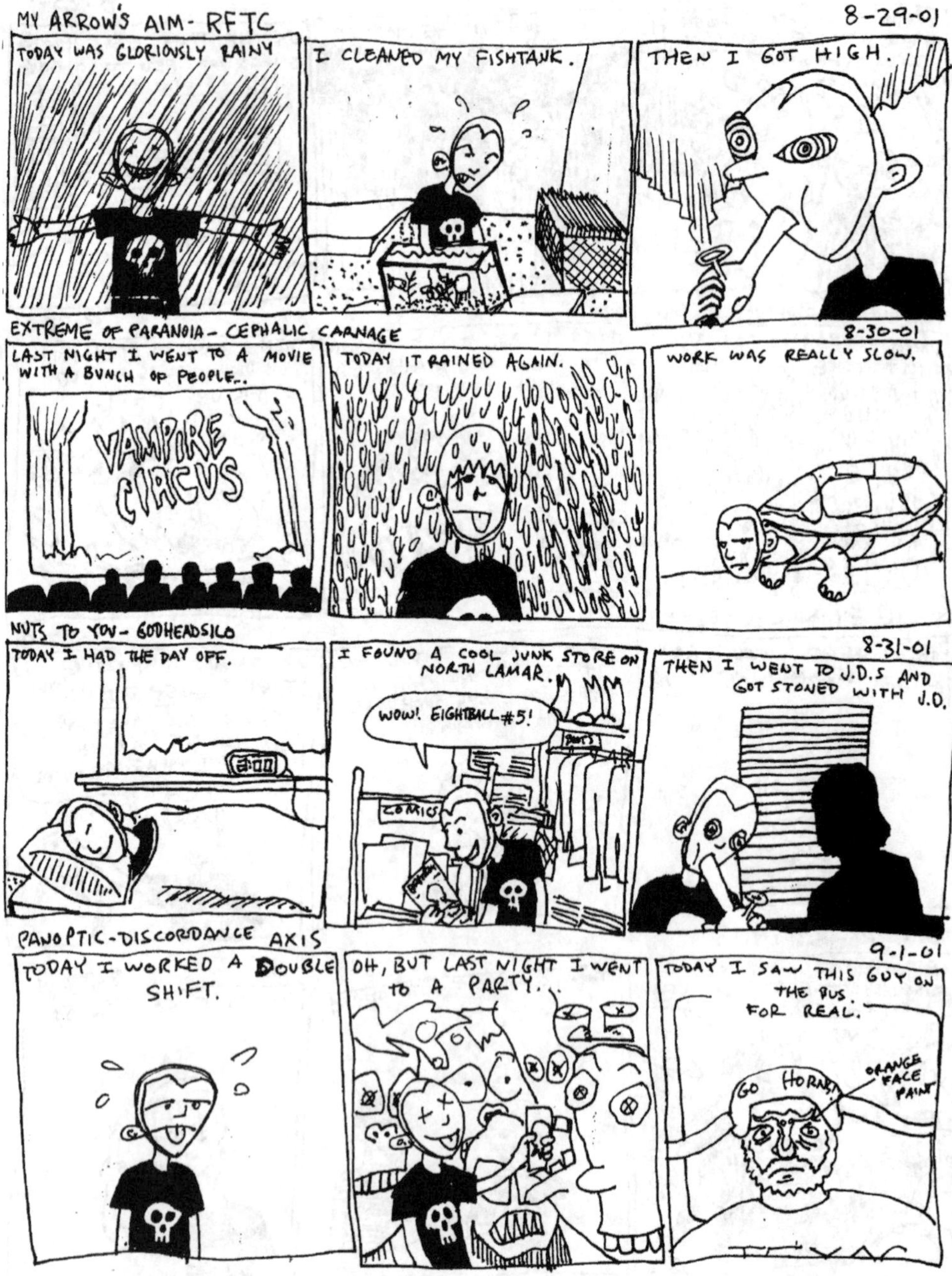
MY ARROW'S AIM - RFTC
8-29-01
TODAY WAS GLORIOUSLY RAINY
I CLEANED MY FISHTANK.
THEN I GOT HIGH.
EXTREME OF PARANOIA - CEPHALIC CARNAGE
8-30-01
LAST NIGHT I WENT TO A MOVIE WITH A BUNCH OF PEOPLE..
VAMPIRE CIRCUS
TODAY IT RAINED AGAIN.
WORK WAS REALLY SLOW.
NUTS TO YOU - GODHEADSILO
8-31-01
TODAY I HAD THE DAY OFF.
I FOUND A COOL JUNK STORE ON NORTH LAMAR.
WOW! EIGHTBALL #5!
COMICS
THEN I WENT TO J.D.S AND GOT STONED WITH J.D.
PANOPTIC - DISCORDANCE AXIS
9-1-01
TODAY I WORKED A DOUBLE SHIFT.
OH, BUT LAST NIGHT I WENT TO A PARTY...
TODAY I SAW THIS GUY ON THE BUS FOR REAL.
GO HORNS!
ORANGE FACE PAINT

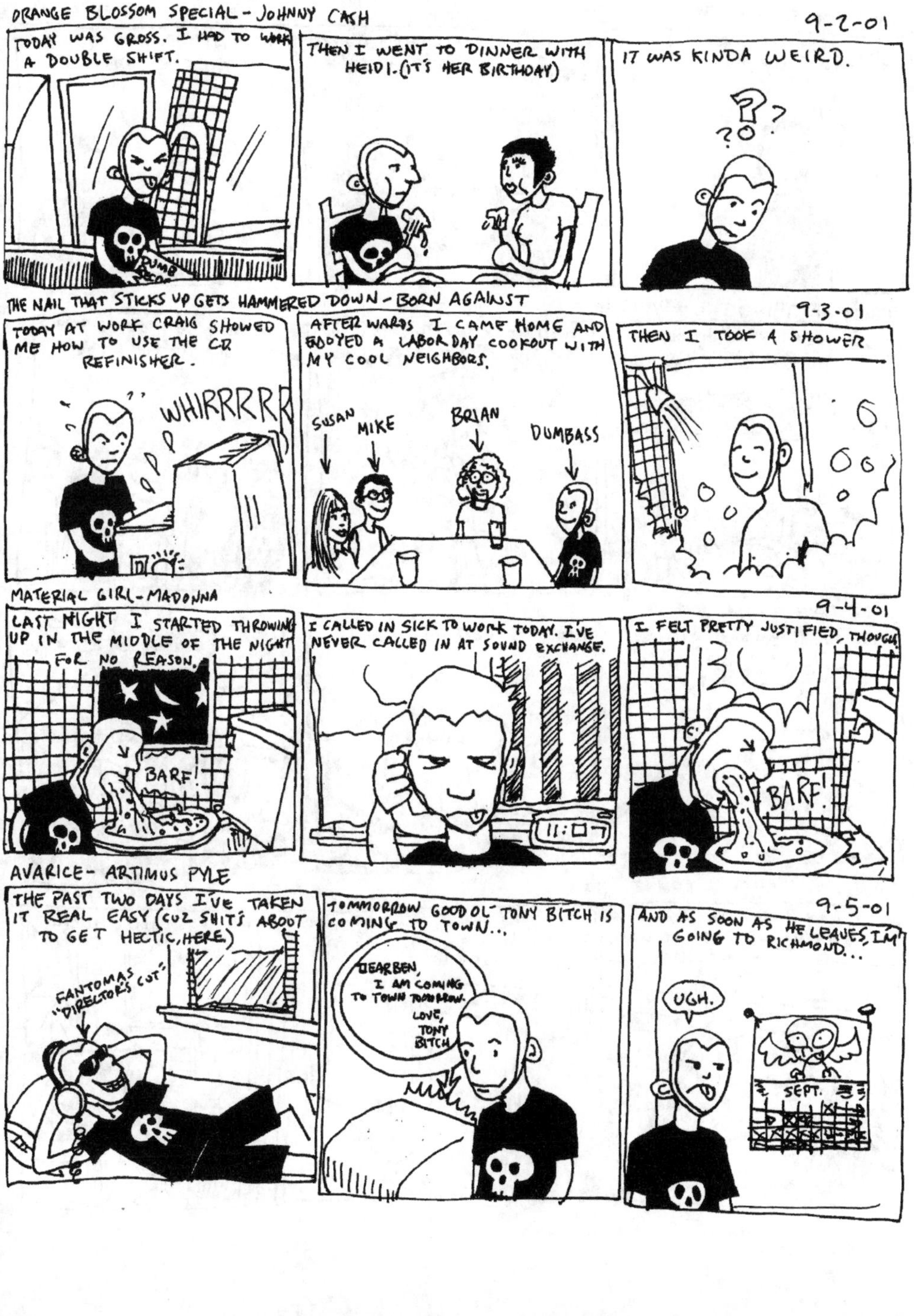
ORANGE BLOSSOM SPECIAL - JOHNNY CASH
9-2-01
TODAY WAS GROSS. I HAD TO WORK A DOUBLE SHIFT.
DUMB
THEN I WENT TO DINNER WITH HEIDI. (IT'S HER BIRTHDAY)
IT WAS KINDA WEIRD.
THE NAIL THAT STICKS UP GETS HAMMERED DOWN - BORN AGAINST
9-3-01
TODAY AT WORK CRAIG SHOWED ME HOW TO USE THE CD REFINISHER.
WHIRRRRR
AFTERWARDS I CAME HOME AND ENJOYED A LABOR DAY COOKOUT WITH MY COOL NEIGHBORS.
SUSAN
MIKE
BRIAN
DUMBASS
THEN I TOOK A SHOWER
MATERIAL GIRL - MADONNA
9-4-01
LAST NIGHT I STARTED THROWING UP IN THE MIDDLE OF THE NIGHT FOR NO REASON.
BARF!
I CALLED IN SICK TO WORK TODAY. I'VE NEVER CALLED IN AT SOUND EXCHANGE.
11:07
I FELT PRETTY JUSTIFIED, THOUGH.
BARF!
AVARICE - ARTIMUS PYLE
9-5-01
THE PAST TWO DAYS I'VE TAKEN IT REAL EASY (CUZ SHIT'S ABOUT TO GET HECTIC, HERE.)
FANTOMAS "DIRECTOR'S CUT"
TOMMORROW GOOD OL' TONY BITCH IS COMING TO TOWN...
DEAR BEN, I AM COMING TO TOWN TOMORROW. LOVE, TONY BITCH
AND AS SOON AS HE LEAVES, I'M GOING TO RICHMOND...
UGH.
SEPT.

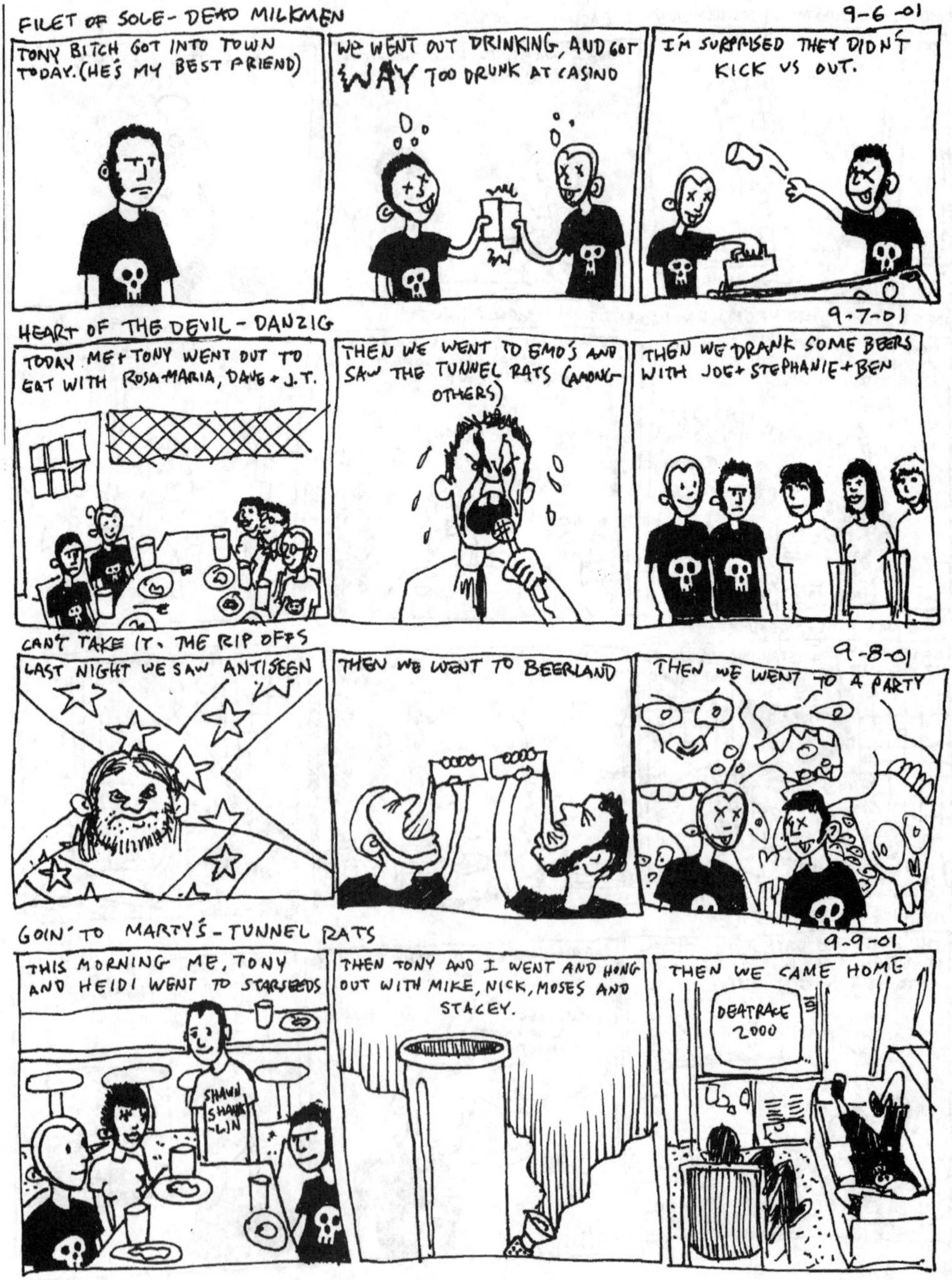
FILET OF SOLE - DEAD MILKMEN
9-6-01
TONY BITCH GOT INTO TOWN TODAY. (HE'S MY BEST FRIEND)
WE WENT OUT DRINKING, AND GOT WAY TOO DRUNK AT CASINO
I'M SURPRISED THEY DIDN'T KICK US OUT.
HEART OF THE DEVIL - DANZIG
9-7-01
TODAY ME + TONY WENT OUT TO EAT WITH ROSA-MARIA, DAVE + J.T.
THEN WE WENT TO EMO'S AND SAW THE TUNNEL RATS (AMONG-OTHERS)
THEN WE DRANK SOME BEERS WITH JOE + STEPHANIE + BEN
CAN'T TAKE IT - THE RIP OFFS
9-8-01
LAST NIGHT WE SAW ANTISEEN
THEN WE WENT TO BEERLAND
THEN WE WENT TO A PARTY
GOIN' TO MARTY'S - TUNNEL RATS
9-9-01
THIS MORNING ME, TONY AND HEIDI WENT TO STARSEEDS
SHAW SHAW -LIN
THEN TONY AND I WENT AND HUNG OUT WITH MIKE, NICK, MOSES AND STACEY.
THEN WE CAME HOME
DEATRACE 2000

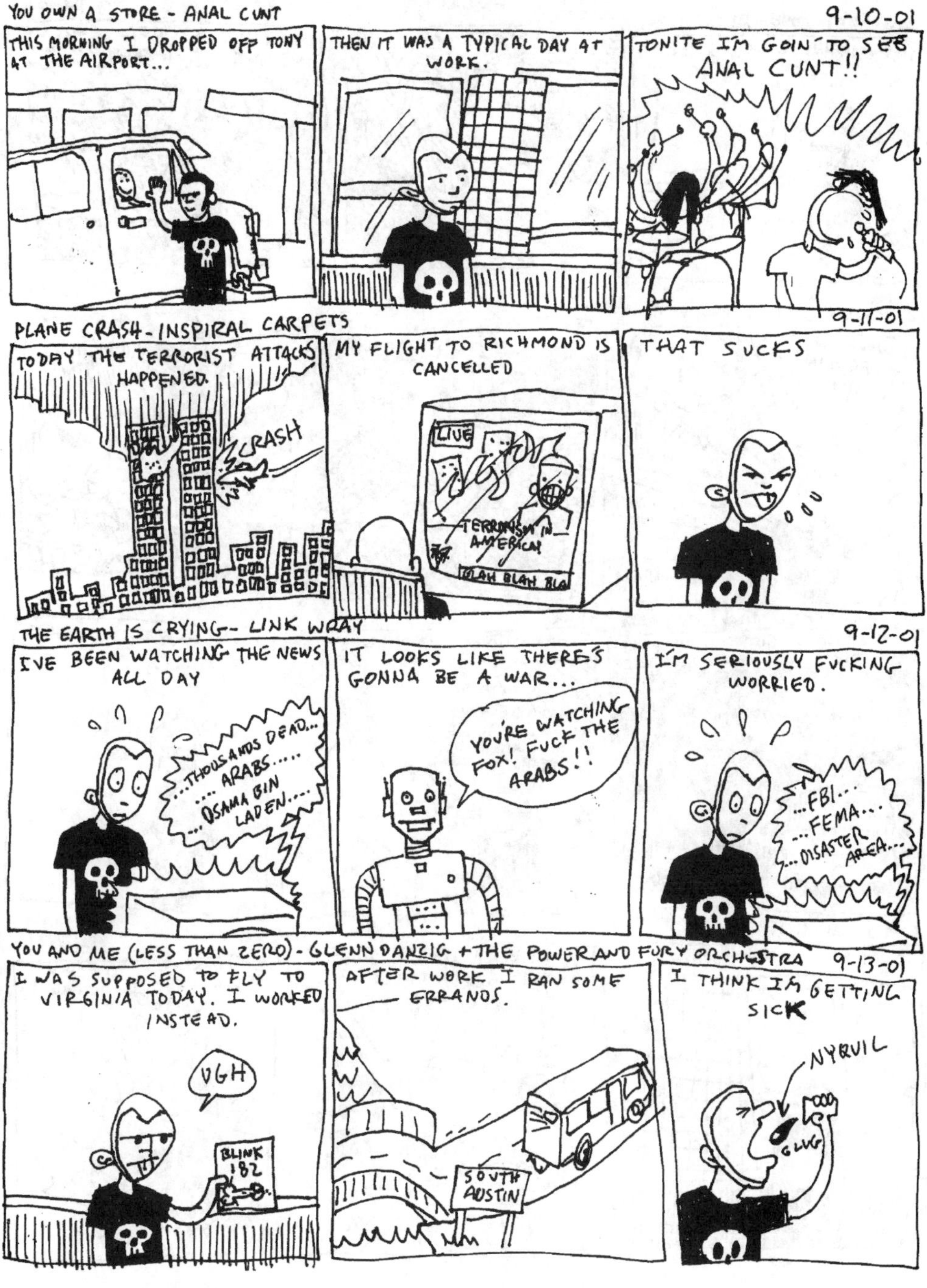
YOU OWN A STORE - ANAL CUNT
9-10-01
THIS MORNING I DROPPED OFF TONY AT THE AIRPORT...
THEN IT WAS A TYPICAL DAY AT WORK.
TONITE I'M GOIN' TO SEE ANAL CUNT!!
PLANE CRASH - INSPIRAL CARPETS
9-11-01
TODAY THE TERRORIST ATTACKS HAPPENED.
CRASH
MY FLIGHT TO RICHMOND IS CANCELLED
LIVE
TERRORISM IN AMERICA!
BLAH BLAH BLA
THAT SUCKS
THE EARTH IS CRYING - LINK WRAY
9-12-01
I'VE BEEN WATCHING THE NEWS ALL DAY
...THOUSANDS DEAD... .... ARABS..... ... OSAMA BIN LADEN....
IT LOOKS LIKE THERE'S GONNA BE A WAR...
YOU'RE WATCHING FOX! FUCK THE ARABS!!
I'M SERIOUSLY FUCKING WORRIED.
...FBI... ...FEMA... ...DISASTER AREA...
YOU AND ME (LESS THAN ZERO) - GLENN DANZIG + THE POWER AND FURY ORCHESTRA
9-13-01
I WAS SUPPOSED TO FLY TO VIRGINIA TODAY. I WORKED INSTEAD.
UGH
BLINK 182
AFTER WORK I RAN SOME ERRANDS.
SOUTH AUSTIN
I THINK I'M GETTING SICK
NYQUIL
GLUG

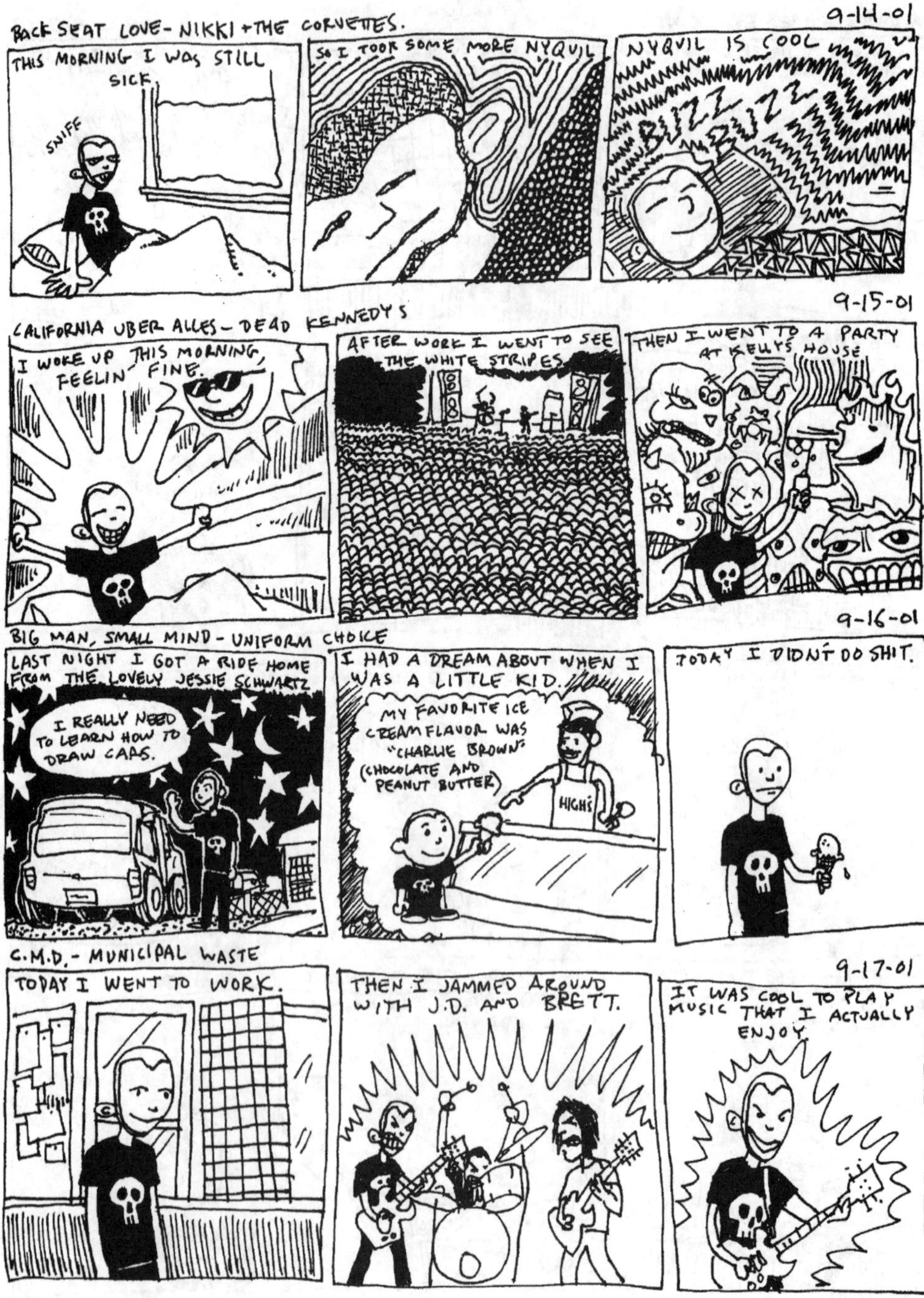

BACK SEAT LOVE - NIKKI + THE CORVETTES.
9-14-01
THIS MORNING I WAS STILL SICK.
SNIFF
SO I TOOK SOME MORE NYQUIL.
NYQUIL IS COOL
BUZZ
BUZZ
CALIFORNIA UBER ALLES - DEAD KENNEDYS
9-15-01
I WOKE UP THIS MORNING, FEELIN' FINE.
AFTER WORK I WENT TO SEE THE WHITE STRIPES.
THEN I WENT TO A PARTY AT KELLY'S HOUSE
BIG MAN, SMALL MIND - UNIFORM CHOICE
9-16-01
LAST NIGHT I GOT A RIDE HOME FROM THE LOVELY JESSIE SCHWARTZ
I REALLY NEED TO LEARN HOW TO DRAW CARS.
I HAD A DREAM ABOUT WHEN I WAS A LITTLE KID.
MY FAVORITE ICE CREAM FLAVOR WAS "CHARLIE BROWN" (CHOCOLATE AND PEANUT BUTTER)
HIGH'S
TODAY I DIDN'T DO SHIT.
C.M.D. - MUNICIPAL WASTE
9-17-01
TODAY I WENT TO WORK.
THEN I JAMMED AROUND WITH J.D. AND BRETT.
IT WAS COOL TO PLAY MUSIC THAT I ACTUALLY ENJOY.

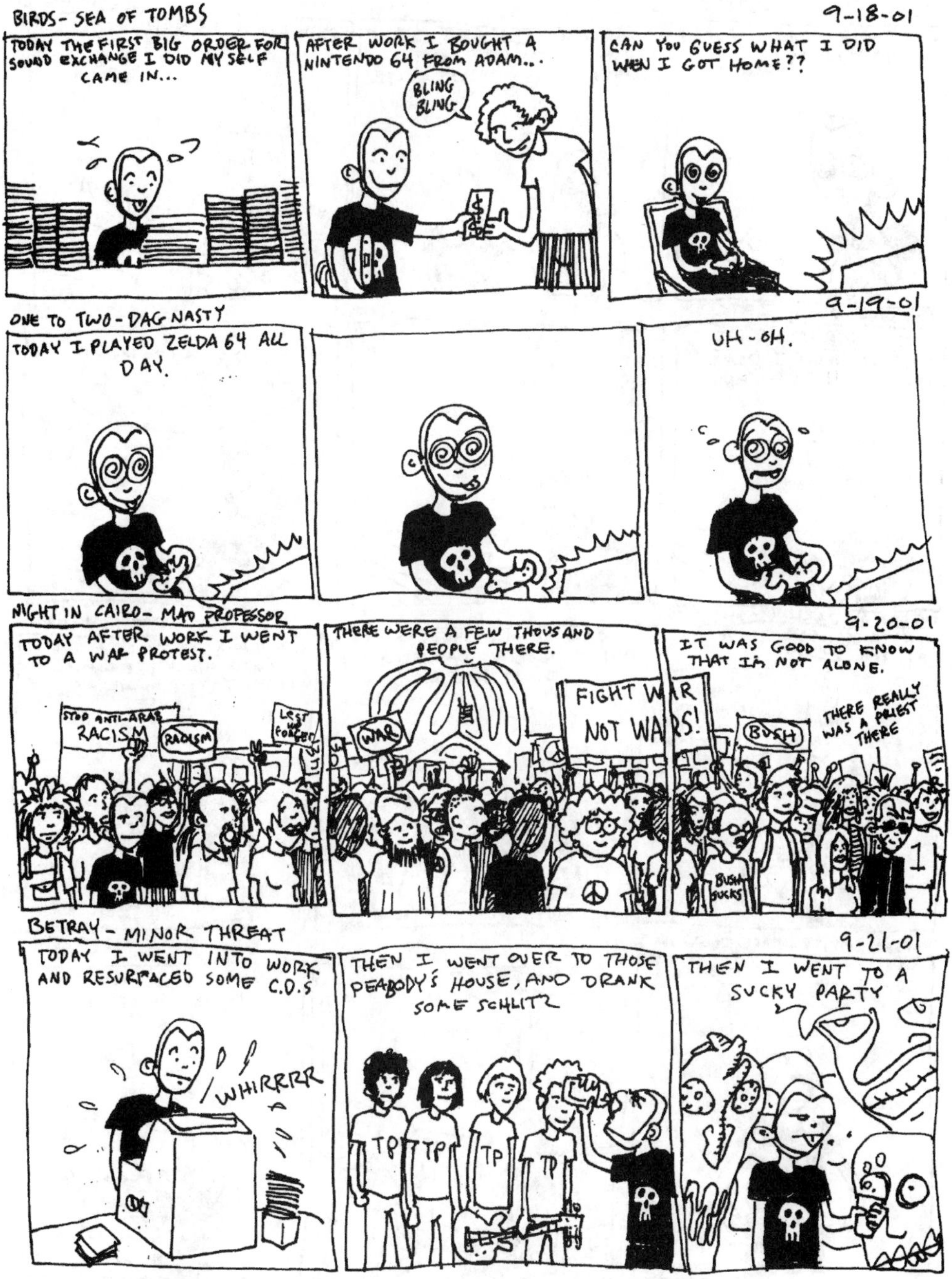
BIRDS - SEA OF TOMBS
9-18-01
TODAY THE FIRST BIG ORDER FOR SOUND EXCHANGE I DID MYSELF CAME IN...
AFTER WORK I BOUGHT A NINTENDO 64 FROM ADAM...
BLING BLING
CAN YOU GUESS WHAT I DID WHEN I GOT HOME??
ONE TO TWO - DAG NASTY
9-19-01
TODAY I PLAYED ZELDA 64 ALL DAY.
UH-OH.
NIGHT IN CAIRO - MAD PROFESSOR
9-20-01
TODAY AFTER WORK I WENT TO A WAR PROTEST.
STOP ANTI-ARAB RACISM
RACISM
LEST WE FORGET
THERE WERE A FEW THOUSAND PEOPLE THERE.
WAR
FIGHT WAR NOT WARS!
IT WAS GOOD TO KNOW THAT I'M NOT ALONE.
BUSH
THERE REALLY WAS A PRIEST THERE
BUSH SUCKS
BETRAY - MINOR THREAT
9-21-01
TODAY I WENT INTO WORK AND RESURFACED SOME C.D.S
WHIRRRR
THEN I WENT OVER TO THOSE PEABODY'S HOUSE, AND DRANK SOME SCHLITZ
TP
TP
TP
TP
THEN I WENT TO A SUCKY PARTY

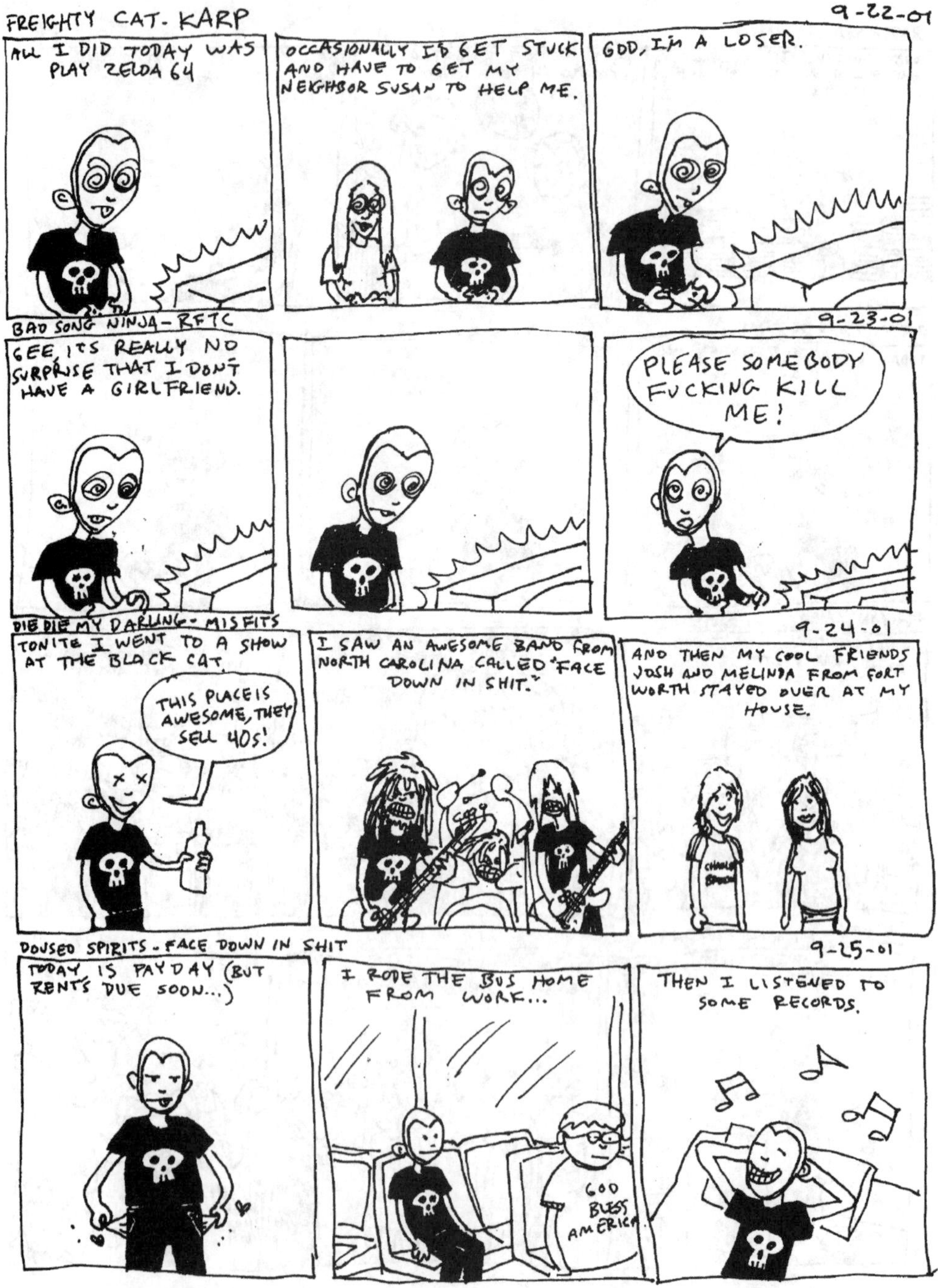

FREIGHTY CAT - KARP
9-22-01
ALL I DID TODAY WAS PLAY ZELDA 64
OCCASIONALLY I'D GET STUCK AND HAVE TO GET MY NEIGHBOR SUSAN TO HELP ME.
GOD, I'M A LOSER.
BAD SONG NINJA - RFTC
9-23-01
GEE, ITS REALLY NO SURPRISE THAT I DON'T HAVE A GIRLFRIEND.
PLEASE SOMEBODY FUCKING KILL ME!
DIE DIE MY DARLING - MISFITS
9-24-01
TONITE I WENT TO A SHOW AT THE BLACK CAT.
THIS PLACE IS AWESOME, THEY SELL 40s!
I SAW AN AWESOME BAND FROM NORTH CAROLINA CALLED "FACE DOWN IN SHIT."
AND THEN MY COOL FRIENDS JOSH AND MELINDA FROM FORT WORTH STAYED OVER AT MY HOUSE.
DOUSED SPIRITS - FACE DOWN IN SHIT
9-25-01
TODAY IS PAYDAY (BUT RENT'S DUE SOON...)
I RODE THE BUS HOME FROM WORK...
GOD BLESS AMERICA
THEN I LISTENED TO SOME RECORDS.

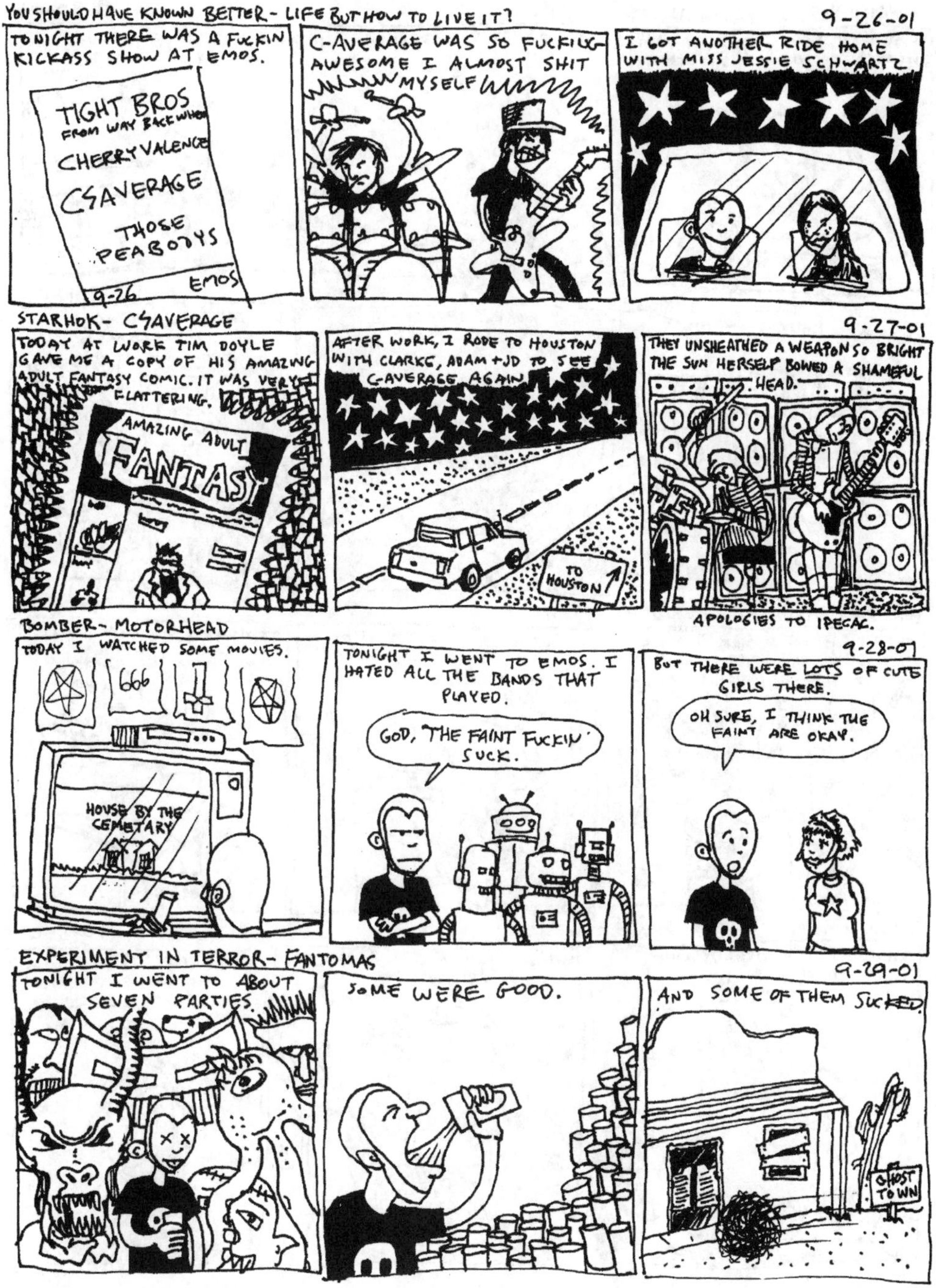

YOU SHOULD HAVE KNOWN BETTER - LIFE BUT HOW TO LIVE IT?
9-26-01
TONIGHT THERE WAS A FUCKIN KICKASS SHOW AT EMOS.
TIGHT BROS FROM WAY BACK WHEN
CHERRY VALENCE
C-AVERAGE
THOSE PEABODYS
9-26
EMOS
C-AVERAGE WAS SO FUCKING AWESOME I ALMOST SHIT MYSELF
I GOT ANOTHER RIDE HOME WITH MISS JESSIE SCHWARTZ
STARHOK - C-AVERAGE
9-27-01
TODAY AT WORK TIM DOYLE GAVE ME A COPY OF HIS AMAZING ADULT FANTASY COMIC. IT WAS VERY FLATTERING.
AMAZING ADULT FANTASY
AFTER WORK, I RODE TO HOUSTON WITH CLARKE, ADAM + JD TO SEE C-AVERAGE AGAIN.
TO HOUSTON
THEY UNSHEATHED A WEAPON SO BRIGHT THE SUN HERSELF BOWED A SHAMEFUL HEAD.
APOLOGIES TO IPECAC.
BOMBER - MOTORHEAD
9-28-01
TODAY I WATCHED SOME MOVIES.
666
HOUSE BY THE CEMETARY
TONIGHT I WENT TO EMOS. I HATED ALL THE BANDS THAT PLAYED.
GOD, THE FAINT FUCKIN' SUCK.
BUT THERE WERE LOTS OF CUTE GIRLS THERE.
OH SURE, I THINK THE FAINT ARE OKAY.
EXPERIMENT IN TERROR - FANTOMAS
9-29-01
TONIGHT I WENT TO ABOUT SEVEN PARTIES.
SOME WERE GOOD.
AND SOME OF THEM SUCKED.
GHOST TOWN

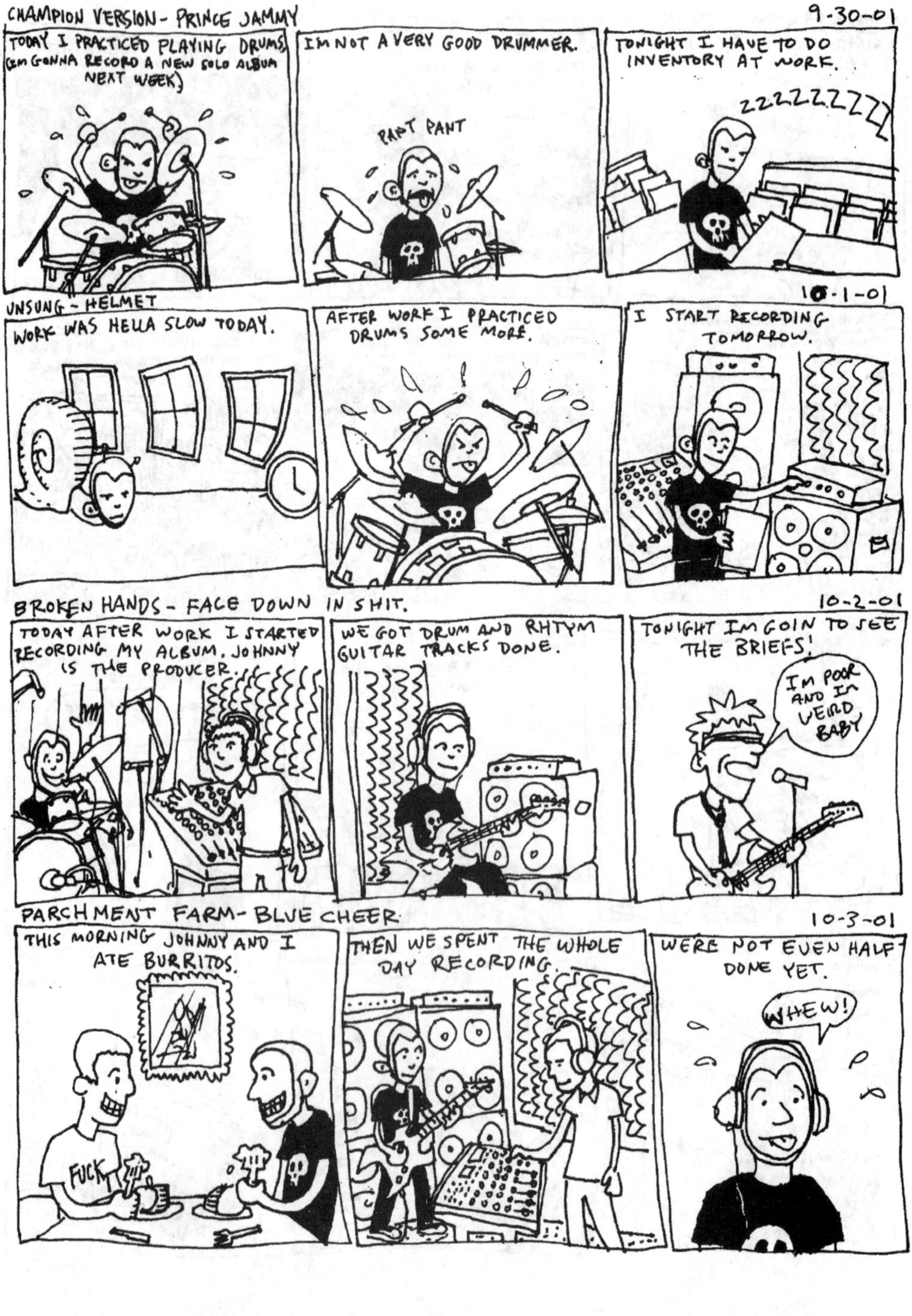
CHAMPION VERSION - PRINCE JAMMY
9-30-01
TODAY I PRACTICED PLAYING DRUMS. (I'M GONNA RECORD A NEW SOLO ALBUM NEXT WEEK)
I'M NOT A VERY GOOD DRUMMER.
PANT PANT
TONIGHT I HAVE TO DO INVENTORY AT WORK.
ZZZZZZZZZ
UNSUNG - HELMET
10-1-01
WORK WAS HELLA SLOW TODAY.
AFTER WORK I PRACTICED DRUMS SOME MORE.
I START RECORDING TOMORROW.
BROKEN HANDS - FACE DOWN IN SHIT.
10-2-01
TODAY AFTER WORK I STARTED RECORDING MY ALBUM. JOHNNY IS THE PRODUCER.
WE GOT DRUM AND RHTYM GUITAR TRACKS DONE.
TONIGHT I'M GOIN TO SEE THE BRIEFS!
I'M POOR AND I'M WEIRD BABY
PARCHMENT FARM - BLUE CHEER
10-3-01
THIS MORNING JOHNNY AND I ATE BURRITOS.
FUCK
THEN WE SPENT THE WHOLE DAY RECORDING.
WERE NOT EVEN HALF DONE YET.
WHEW!

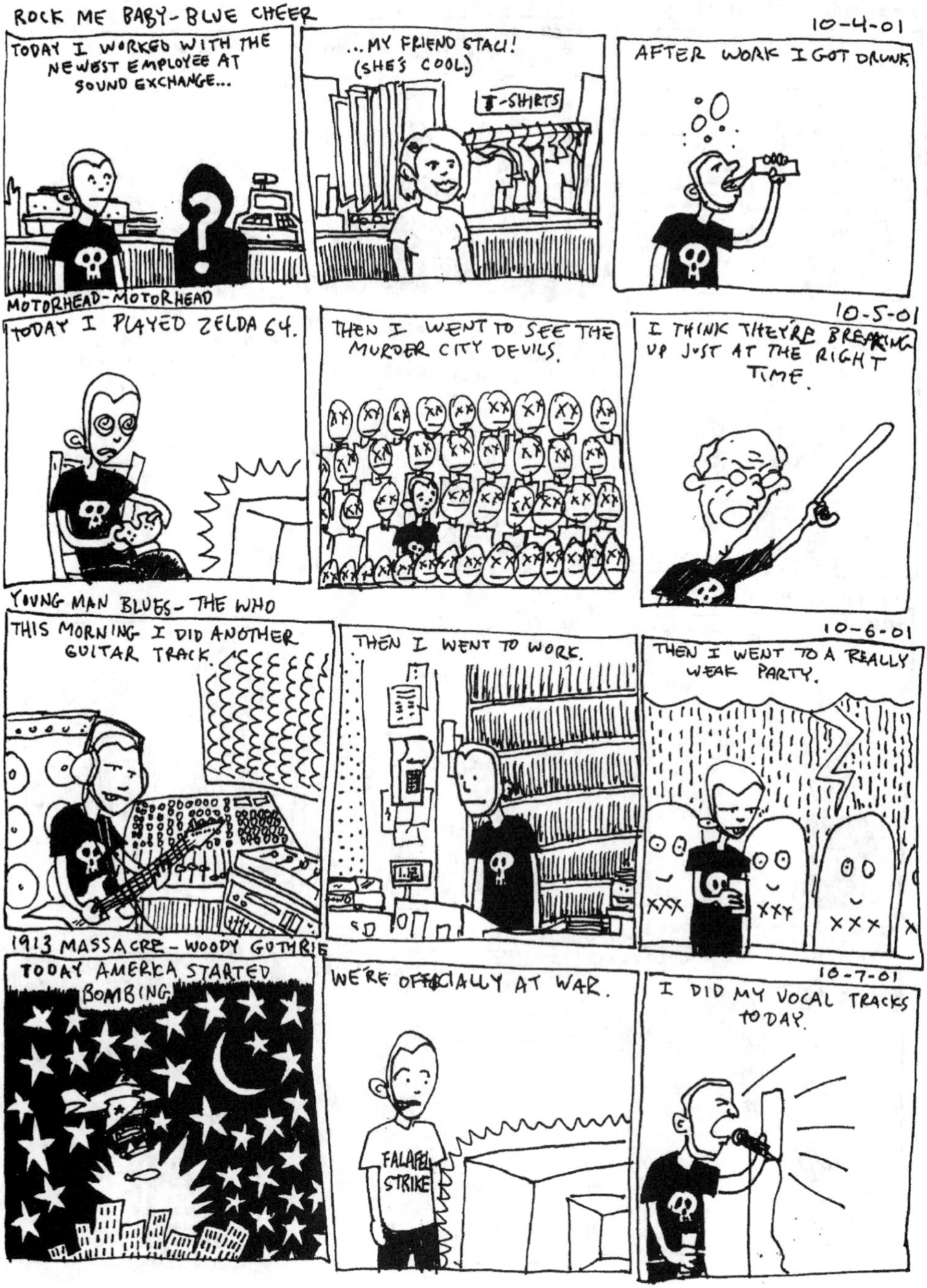
ROCK ME BABY - BLUE CHEER
10-4-01
TODAY I WORKED WITH THE NEWEST EMPLOYEE AT SOUND EXCHANGE...
...MY FRIEND STACI! (SHE'S COOL.)
T-SHIRTS
AFTER WORK I GOT DRUNK.
MOTORHEAD - MOTORHEAD
10-5-01
TODAY I PLAYED ZELDA 64.
THEN I WENT TO SEE THE MURDER CITY DEVILS.
I THINK THEY'RE BREAKING UP JUST AT THE RIGHT TIME.
YOUNG MAN BLUES - THE WHO
10-6-01
THIS MORNING I DID ANOTHER GUITAR TRACK.
THEN I WENT TO WORK.
THEN I WENT TO A REALLY WEAK PARTY.
1913 MASSACRE - WOODY GUTHRIE
10-7-01
TODAY AMERICA STARTED BOMBING.
WE'RE OFFICIALLY AT WAR.
FALAFEL STRIKE
I DID MY VOCAL TRACKS TODAY.

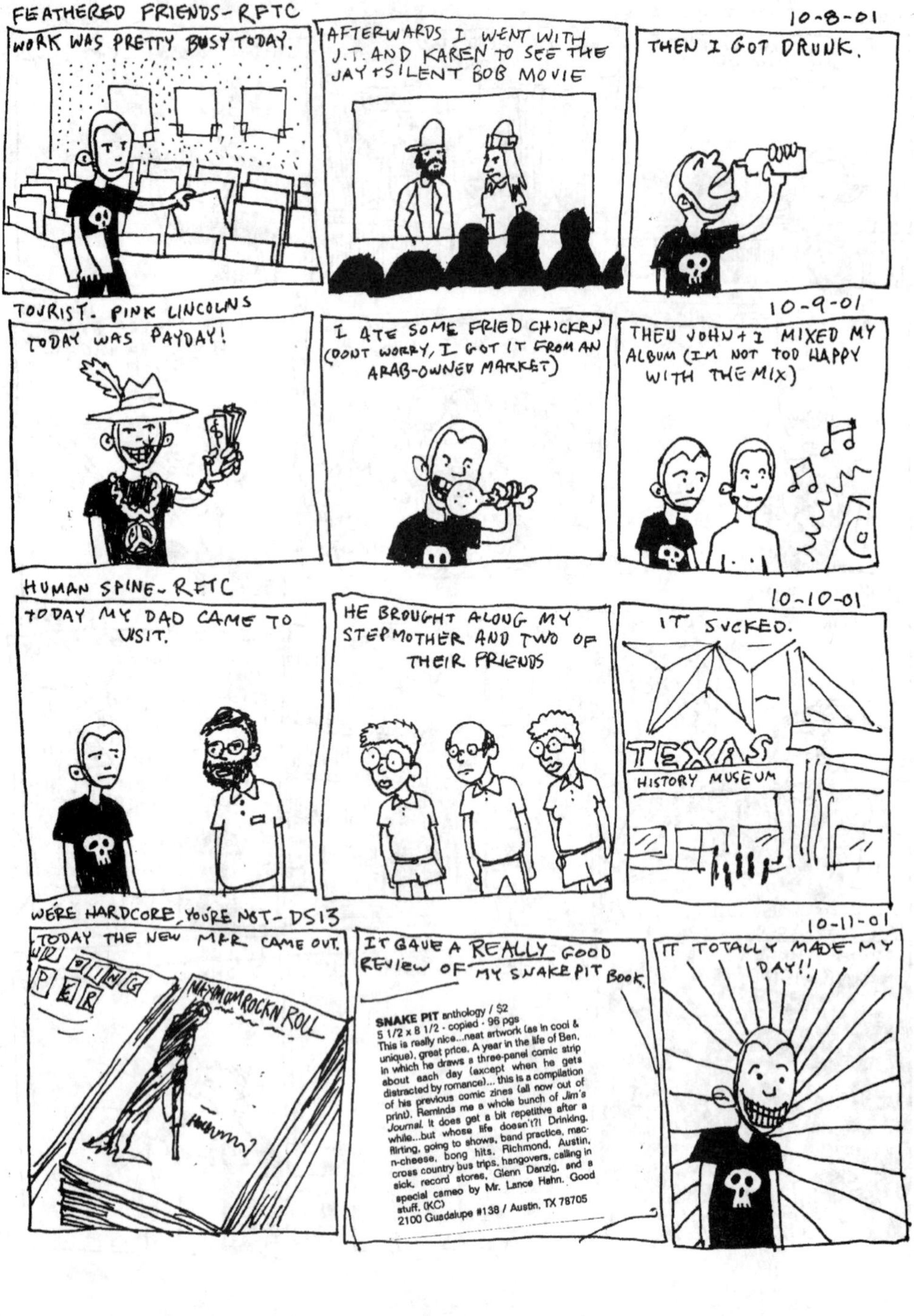
FEATHERED FRIENDS - RFTC
10-8-01
WORK WAS PRETTY BUSY TODAY.
AFTERWARDS I WENT WITH J.T. AND KAREN TO SEE THE JAY + SILENT BOB MOVIE
THEN I GOT DRUNK.
TOURIST - PINK LINCOLNS
10-9-01
TODAY WAS PAYDAY!
I ATE SOME FRIED CHICKEN (DONT WORRY, I GOT IT FROM AN ARAB-OWNED MARKET)
THEN JOHN + I MIXED MY ALBUM (IM NOT TOO HAPPY WITH THE MIX)
HUMAN SPINE - RFTC
10-10-01
TODAY MY DAD CAME TO VISIT.
HE BROUGHT ALONG MY STEPMOTHER AND TWO OF THEIR FRIENDS
IT SUCKED.
TEXAS
HISTORY MUSEUM
WE'RE HARDCORE, YOU'RE NOT - DS13
10-11-01
TODAY THE NEW MRR CAME OUT.
MAXIMUMROCKNROLL
IT GAVE A REALLY GOOD REVIEW OF MY SNAKE PIT BOOK.
SNAKE PIT anthology / $2
5 1/2 x 8 1/2 - copied - 96 pgs
This is really nice...neat artwork (as in cool & unique), great price. A year in the life of Ben, in which he draws a three-panel comic strip about each day (except when he gets distracted by romance)... this is a compilation of his previous comic zines (all now out of print). Reminds me a whole bunch of Jim's Journal. It does get a bit repetitive after a while...but whose life doesn't?! Drinking, flirting, going to shows, band practice, mac-n-cheese, bong hits, Richmond, Austin, cross country bus trips, hangovers, calling in sick, record stores, Glenn Danzig, and a special cameo by Mr. Lance Hahn. Good stuff. (KC)
2100 Guadalupe #138 / Austin, TX 78705
IT TOTALLY MADE MY DAY!!

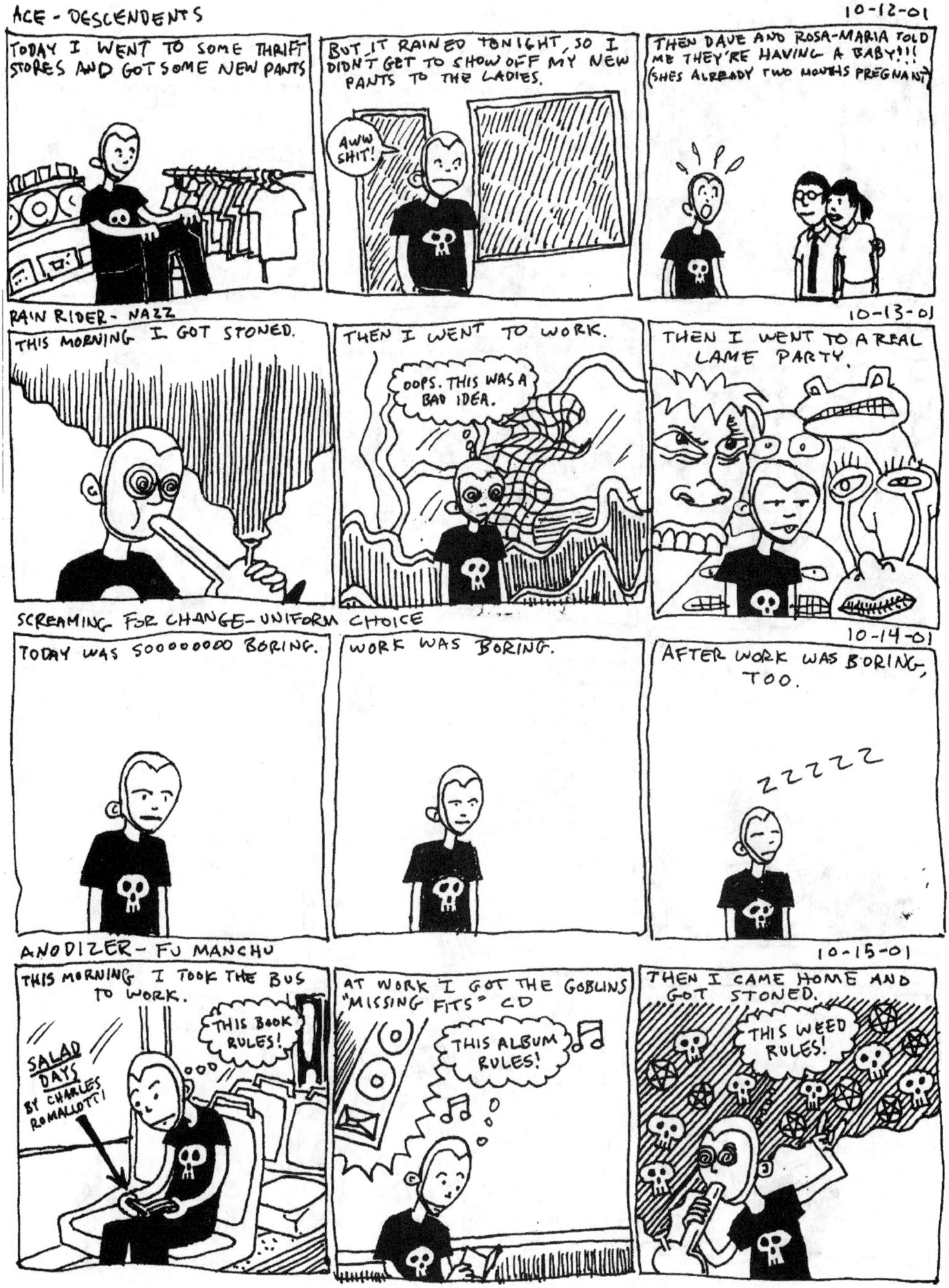
ACE - DESCENDENTS
10-12-01
TODAY I WENT TO SOME THRIFT STORES AND GOT SOME NEW PANTS
BUT IT RAINED TONIGHT, SO I DIDN'T GET TO SHOW OFF MY NEW PANTS TO THE LADIES.
AWW SHIT!
THEN DAVE AND ROSA-MARIA TOLD ME THEY'RE HAVING A BABY!!! (SHES ALREADY TWO MONTHS PREGNANT)
RAIN RIDER - NAZZ
10-13-01
THIS MORNING I GOT STONED.
THEN I WENT TO WORK.
OOPS. THIS WAS A BAD IDEA.
THEN I WENT TO A REAL LAME PARTY.
SCREAMING FOR CHANGE - UNIFORM CHOICE
10-14-01
TODAY WAS SOOOOOOOO BORING.
WORK WAS BORING.
AFTER WORK WAS BORING, TOO.
ZZZZZ
ANODIZER - FU MANCHU
10-15-01
THIS MORNING I TOOK THE BUS TO WORK.
THIS BOOK RULES!
SALAD DAYS BY CHARLES ROMALLOTTI
AT WORK I GOT THE GOBLINS "MISSING FITS" CD
THIS ALBUM RULES!
THEN I CAME HOME AND GOT STONED.
THIS WEED RULES!

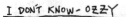

I DON'T KNOW - OZZY
10-16-01
I SAW ON THE NEWS TODAY ~~THAT~~ EVERYONE'S GETTING ANTHRAX
MOSH MOSH MOSH MOSH MOSH MOSH MOSH MOSH
TIPEKANSNIK UFESIN
NOT
AFTER WORK I WAS KINDLY FRONTED SOME WEED BY A PERSON YOU DON'T NEED TO KNOW.
STONER TIP: HIDE WEED IN YOUR POCKETS SO COPS WONT SEE IT.
I CAME HOME AND LISTENED TO THE GOBLINS "MISSING FITS" ALBUM LIKE TWENTY TIMES.
THIS THING IS SO FUCKIN' AWESOME!
HEART OF GLASS - BLONDIE
10-17-01
I DIDNT DO JACK FUCKIN SHIT TODAY.
I STARTED THINKING THAT MAYBE I SMOKE POT TOO MUCH...
ALWAYS LATE...
...ALWAYS STUPID...
...ALWAYS BROKE...
...ALWAYS FORGETTING STUFF...
THINKING SUCKS.
THESE IMPORTANT YEARS - HUSKER DU
10-18-01
I STARED AT THIS BLANK PANEL TODAY FOR ABOUT AN HOUR.
MY LIFE IS USUALLY SO STUPID AND TRIVIAL, THAT WHEN SOMETHING IMPORTANT ACTUALLY HAPPENS I DONT KNOW HOW TO DRAW IT.
TODAY ROSA MARIA TOLD ME THAT SHE + DAVE ARE MARRIED (AND HAVE BEEN FOR A WHILE)
THE INVISIBLE GUEST - KING DIAMOND
10-19-01
TODAY I HAVE LIVED IN AUSTIN FOR ONE YEAR.
THERE WAS A PARTY AT LARA, KATE + JTS HOUSE
AND I TALKED TO A REALLY CUTE GIRL

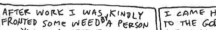

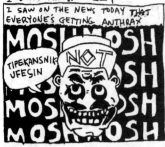

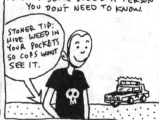

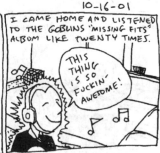

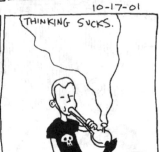

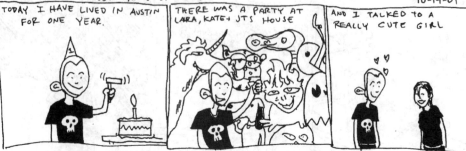

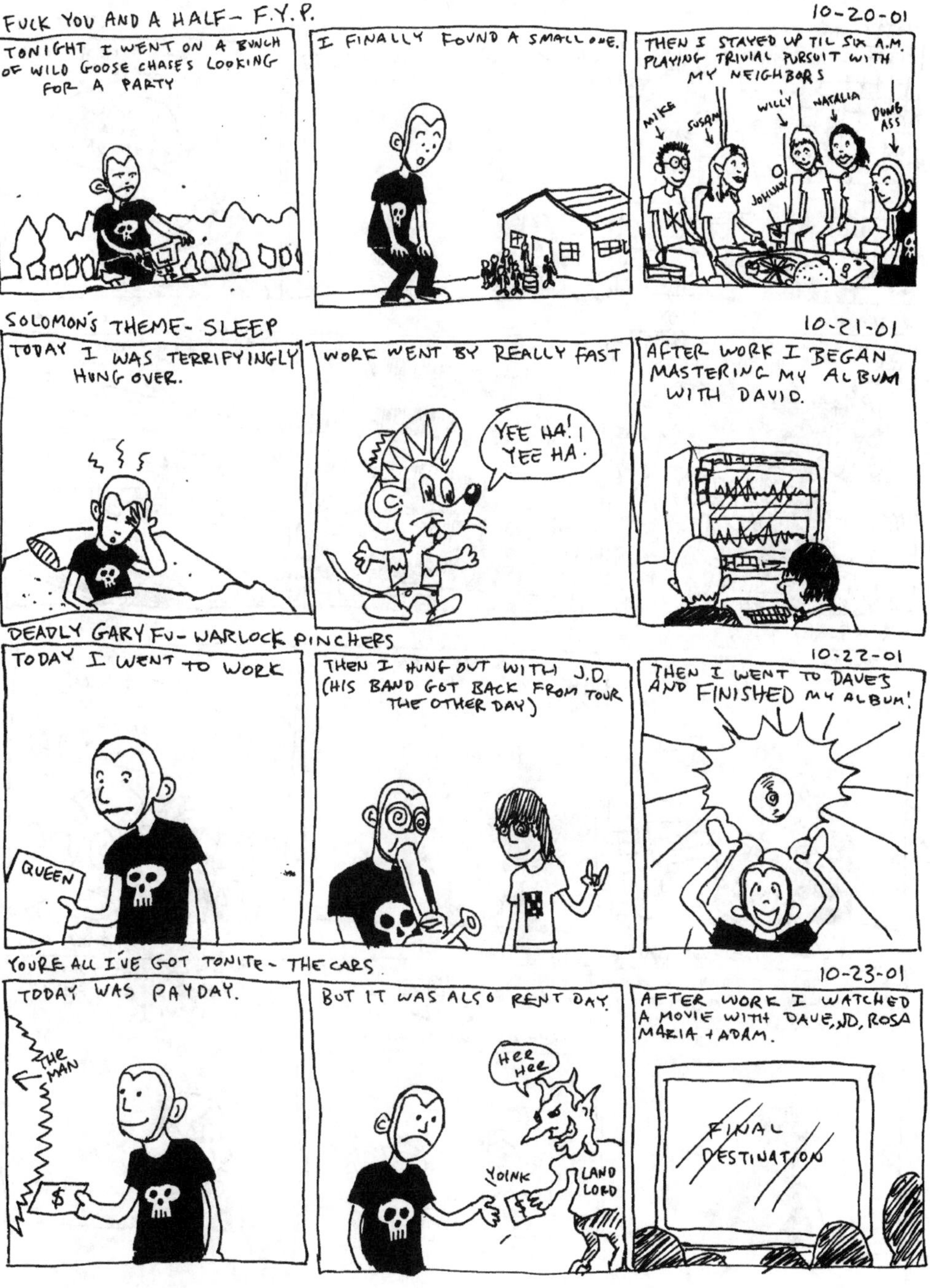

FUCK YOU AND A HALF - F.Y.P.
10-20-01
TONIGHT I WENT ON A BUNCH OF WILD GOOSE CHASES LOOKING FOR A PARTY
I FINALLY FOUND A SMALL ONE.
THEN I STAYED UP TIL SIX A.M. PLAYING TRIVIAL PURSUIT WITH MY NEIGHBORS
MIKE
SUSAN
WILLY
NATALIA
DUNG ASS
JOHNNY
SOLOMON'S THEME - SLEEP
10-21-01
TODAY I WAS TERRIFYINGLY HUNG OVER.
WORK WENT BY REALLY FAST
YEE HA! YEE HA.
AFTER WORK I BEGAN MASTERING MY ALBUM WITH DAVID.
DEADLY GARY FU - WARLOCK PINCHERS
10-22-01
TODAY I WENT TO WORK
QUEEN
THEN I HUNG OUT WITH J.D. (HIS BAND GOT BACK FROM TOUR THE OTHER DAY)
THEN I WENT TO DAVE'S AND FINISHED MY ALBUM!
YOU'RE ALL I'VE GOT TONITE - THE CARS
10-23-01
TODAY WAS PAYDAY.
THE MAN
$
BUT IT WAS ALSO RENT DAY.
HEE HEE
YOINK
LAND LORD
AFTER WORK I WATCHED A MOVIE WITH DAVE, JD, ROSA MARIA + ADAM.
FINAL DESTINATION

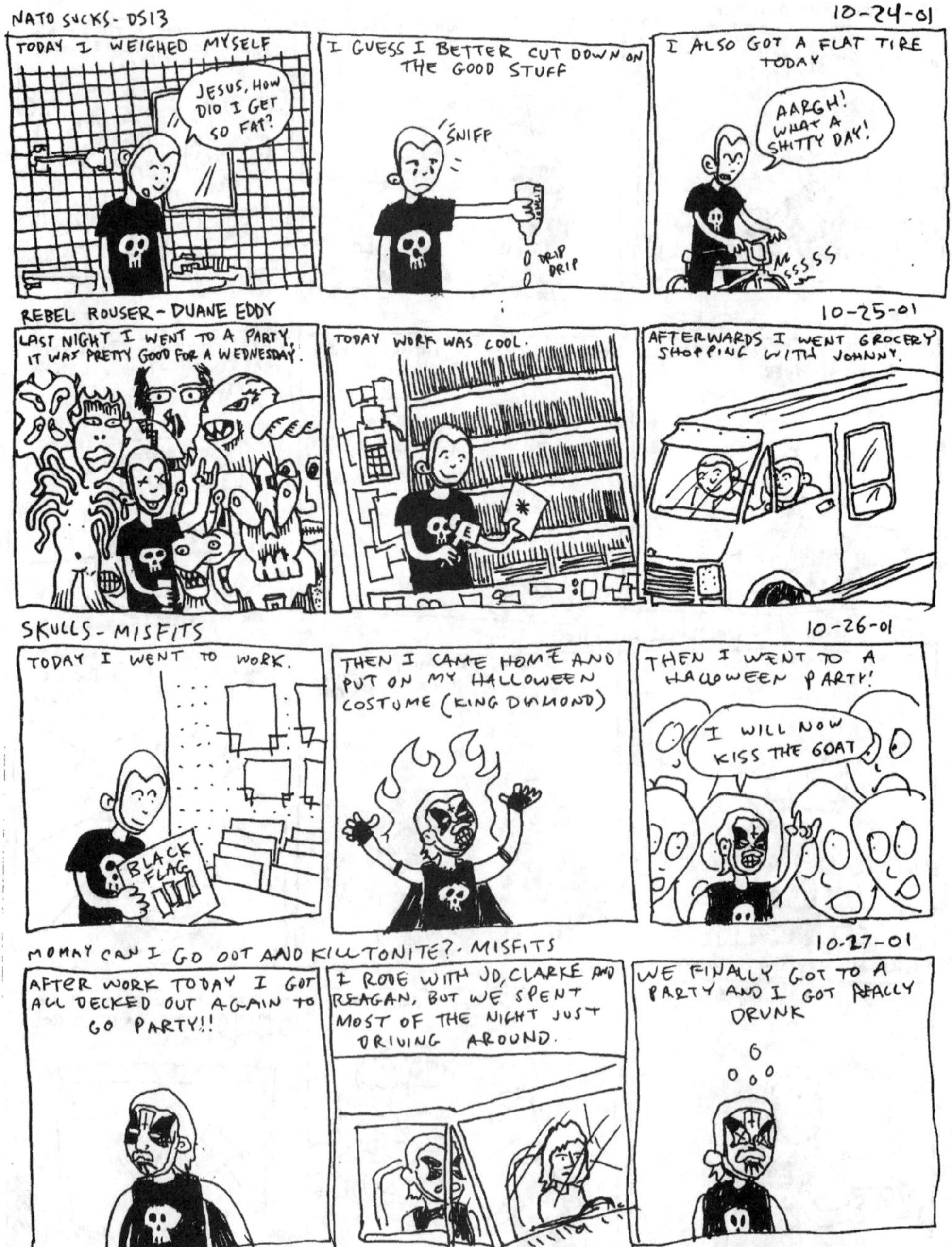
NATO SUCKS - DS13
10-24-01
TODAY I WEIGHED MYSELF
JESUS, HOW DID I GET SO FAT?
I GUESS I BETTER CUT DOWN ON THE GOOD STUFF
SNIFF
DRIP DRIP
I ALSO GOT A FLAT TIRE TODAY
AARGH! WHAT A SHITTY DAY!
SSSSS
REBEL ROUSER - DUANE EDDY
10-25-01
LAST NIGHT I WENT TO A PARTY, IT WAS PRETTY GOOD FOR A WEDNESDAY.
TODAY WORK WAS COOL.
AFTERWARDS I WENT GROCERY SHOPPING WITH JOHNNY.
SKULLS - MISFITS
10-26-01
TODAY I WENT TO WORK.
BLACK FLAG
THEN I CAME HOME AND PUT ON MY HALLOWEEN COSTUME (KING DIAMOND)
THEN I WENT TO A HALLOWEEN PARTY!
I WILL NOW KISS THE GOAT
MOMMY CAN I GO OUT AND KILL TONITE? - MISFITS
10-27-01
AFTER WORK TODAY I GOT ALL DECKED OUT AGAIN TO GO PARTY!!
I RODE WITH JD, CLARKE AND REAGAN, BUT WE SPENT MOST OF THE NIGHT JUST DRIVING AROUND.
WE FINALLY GOT TO A PARTY AND I GOT REALLY DRUNK

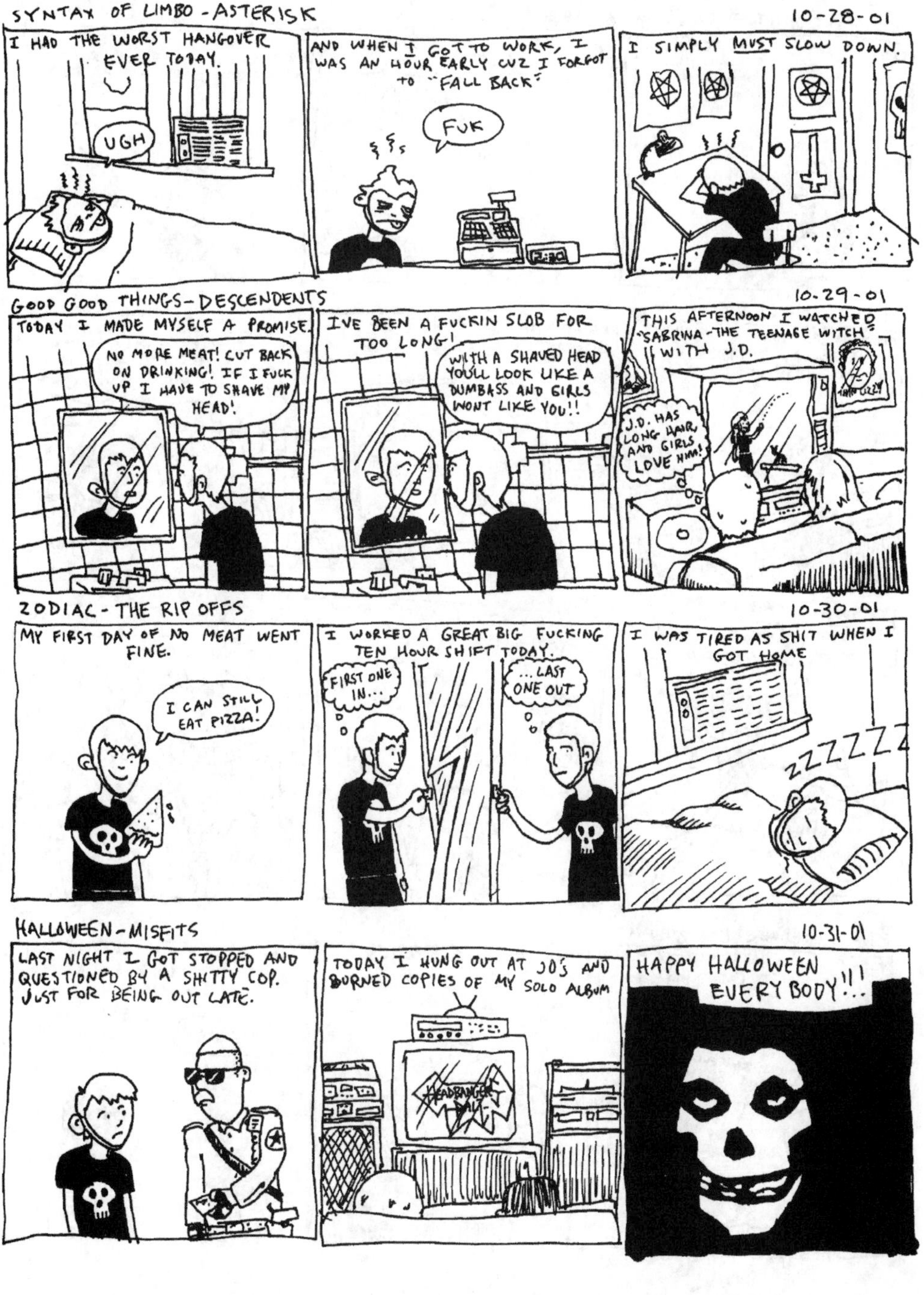

SYNTAX OF LIMBO - ASTERISK
10-28-01
I HAD THE WORST HANGOVER EVER TODAY.
UGH
AND WHEN I GOT TO WORK, I WAS AN HOUR EARLY CUZ I FORGOT TO "FALL BACK"
FUK
I SIMPLY MUST SLOW DOWN.
GOOD GOOD THINGS - DESCENDENTS
10-29-01
TODAY I MADE MYSELF A PROMISE.
NO MORE MEAT! CUT BACK ON DRINKING! IF I FUCK UP I HAVE TO SHAVE MY HEAD!
IVE BEEN A FUCKIN SLOB FOR TOO LONG!
WITH A SHAVED HEAD YOU'LL LOOK LIKE A DUMBASS AND GIRLS WONT LIKE YOU!!
THIS AFTERNOON I WATCHED "SABRINA - THE TEENAGE WITCH" WITH J.D.
J.D. HAS LONG HAIR AND GIRLS LOVE HIM!
ZODIAC - THE RIP OFFS
10-30-01
MY FIRST DAY OF NO MEAT WENT FINE.
I CAN STILL EAT PIZZA!
I WORKED A GREAT BIG FUCKING TEN HOUR SHIFT TODAY.
FIRST ONE IN...
... LAST ONE OUT
I WAS TIRED AS SHIT WHEN I GOT HOME
ZZZZZZ
HALLOWEEN - MISFITS
10-31-01
LAST NIGHT I GOT STOPPED AND QUESTIONED BY A SHITTY COP. JUST FOR BEING OUT LATE.
TODAY I HUNG OUT AT JD'S AND BURNED COPIES OF MY SOLO ALBUM
HAPPY HALLOWEEN EVERYBODY!!!

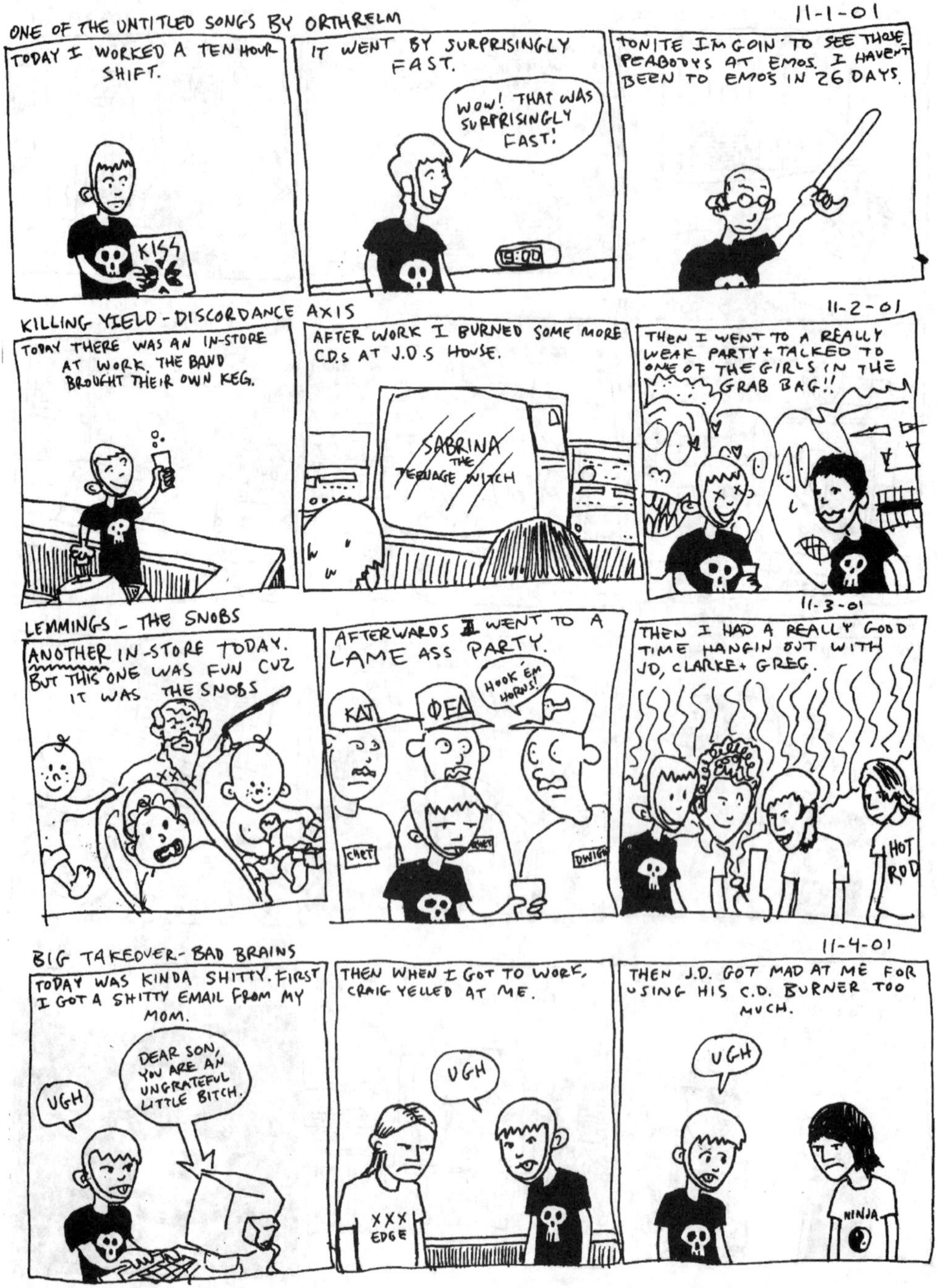
ONE OF THE UNTITLED SONGS BY ORTHRELM
11-1-01
TODAY I WORKED A TEN HOUR SHIFT.
KISS
IT WENT BY SURPRISINGLY FAST.
WOW! THAT WAS SURPRISINGLY FAST!
19:00
TONITE I'M GOIN' TO SEE THOSE PEABODYS AT EMOS. I HAVEN'T BEEN TO EMOS IN 26 DAYS.
KILLING YIELD - DISCORDANCE AXIS
11-2-01
TODAY THERE WAS AN IN-STORE AT WORK. THE BAND BROUGHT THEIR OWN KEG.
AFTER WORK I BURNED SOME MORE C.D.S AT J.D.S HOUSE.
SABRINA THE TEENAGE WITCH
THEN I WENT TO A REALLY WEAK PARTY + TALKED TO ONE OF THE GIRLS IN THE GRAB BAG!!
LEMMINGS - THE SNOBS
11-3-01
ANOTHER IN-STORE TODAY. BUT THIS ONE WAS FUN CUZ IT WAS THE SNOBS
AFTERWARDS I WENT TO A LAME ASS PARTY.
HOOK 'EM HORNS!
KΔT
ΦEΔ
CHET
DWIGHT
THEN I HAD A REALLY GOOD TIME HANGIN OUT WITH JD, CLARKE + GREG.
HOT ROD
BIG TAKEOVER - BAD BRAINS
11-4-01
TODAY WAS KINDA SHITTY. FIRST I GOT A SHITTY EMAIL FROM MY MOM.
UGH
DEAR SON, YOU ARE AN UNGRATEFUL LITTLE BITCH.
THEN WHEN I GOT TO WORK, CRAIG YELLED AT ME.
UGH
XXX EDGE
THEN J.D. GOT MAD AT ME FOR USING HIS C.D. BURNER TOO MUCH.
UGH
NINJA

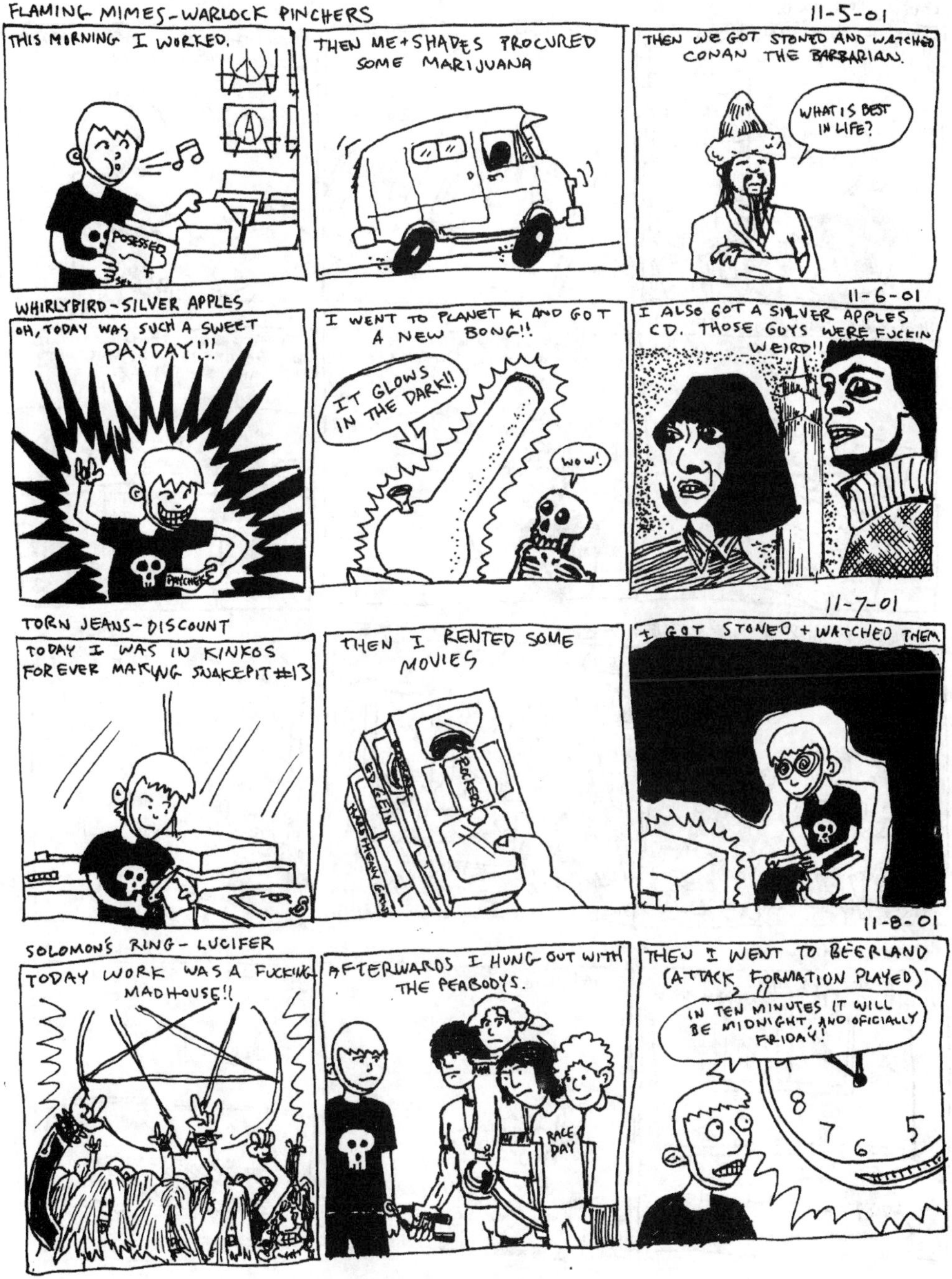

FLAMING MIMES-WARLOCK PINCHERS
11-5-01
THIS MORNING I WORKED.
POSSESSED
THEN ME+SHADES PROCURED SOME MARIJUANA
THEN WE GOT STONED AND WATCHED CONAN THE BARBARIAN.
WHAT IS BEST IN LIFE?
WHIRLYBIRD-SILVER APPLES
11-6-01
OH, TODAY WAS SUCH A SWEET PAYDAY!!!
PAYCHECK
I WENT TO PLANET K AND GOT A NEW BONG!!
IT GLOWS IN THE DARK!!
WOW!
I ALSO GOT A SILVER APPLES CD. THOSE GUYS WERE FUCKIN WEIRD!!
TORN JEANS-DISCOUNT
11-7-01
TODAY I WAS IN KINKOS FOREVER MAKING SNAKEPIT #13
THEN I RENTED SOME MOVIES
ED GEIN
I GOT STONED + WATCHED THEM
SOLOMON'S RING-LUCIFER
11-8-01
TODAY WORK WAS A FUCKING MADHOUSE!!
AFTERWARDS I HUNG OUT WITH THE PEABODYS.
RACE DAY
THEN I WENT TO BEERLAND (ATTACK FORMATION PLAYED)
IN TEN MINUTES IT WILL BE MIDNIGHT, AND OFICIALLY FRIDAY!

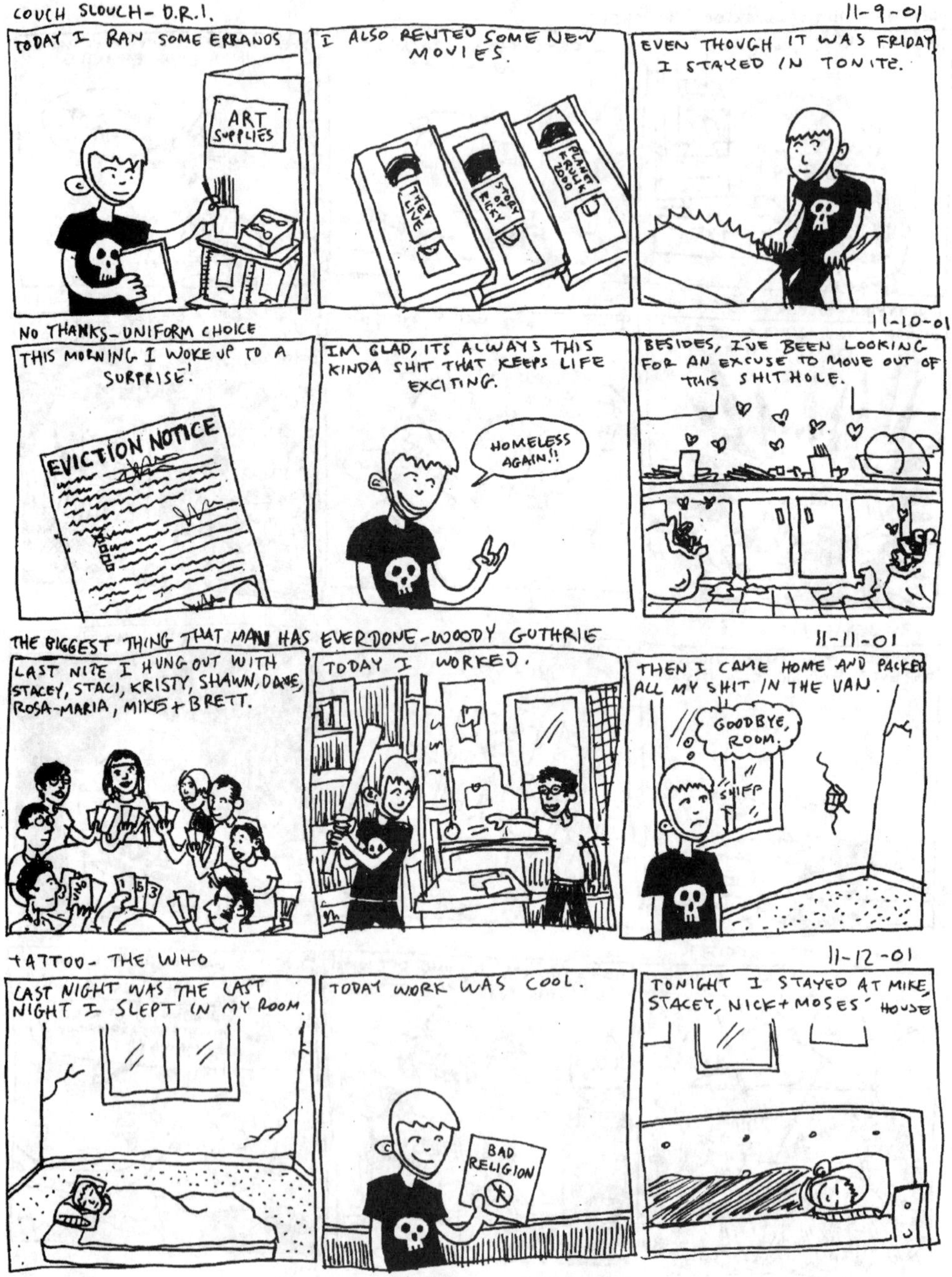
COUCH SLOUCH- D.R.I.
11-9-01
TODAY I RAN SOME ERRANDS
ART SUPPLIES
I ALSO RENTED SOME NEW MOVIES.
THEY LIVE
STORY OF RICKY
EVEN THOUGH IT WAS FRIDAY, I STAYED IN TONITE.
NO THANKS_UNIFORM CHOICE
11-10-01
THIS MORNING I WOKE UP TO A SURPRISE!
EVICTION NOTICE
IM GLAD, ITS ALWAYS THIS KINDA SHIT THAT KEEPS LIFE EXCITING.
HOMELESS AGAIN!!
BESIDES, I'VE BEEN LOOKING FOR AN EXCUSE TO MOVE OUT OF THIS SHITHOLE.
THE BIGGEST THING THAT MAN HAS EVERDONE-WOODY GUTHRIE
11-11-01
LAST NITE I HUNG OUT WITH STACEY, STACI, KRISTY, SHAWN, DAVE, ROSA-MARIA, MIKE + BRETT.
TODAY I WORKED.
THEN I CAME HOME AND PACKED ALL MY SHIT IN THE VAN.
GOODBYE, ROOM.
SNIFF
TATTOO- THE WHO
11-12-01
LAST NIGHT WAS THE LAST NIGHT I SLEPT IN MY ROOM.
TODAY WORK WAS COOL.
BAD RELIGION
TONIGHT I STAYED AT MIKE, STACEY, NICK + MOSES' HOUSE

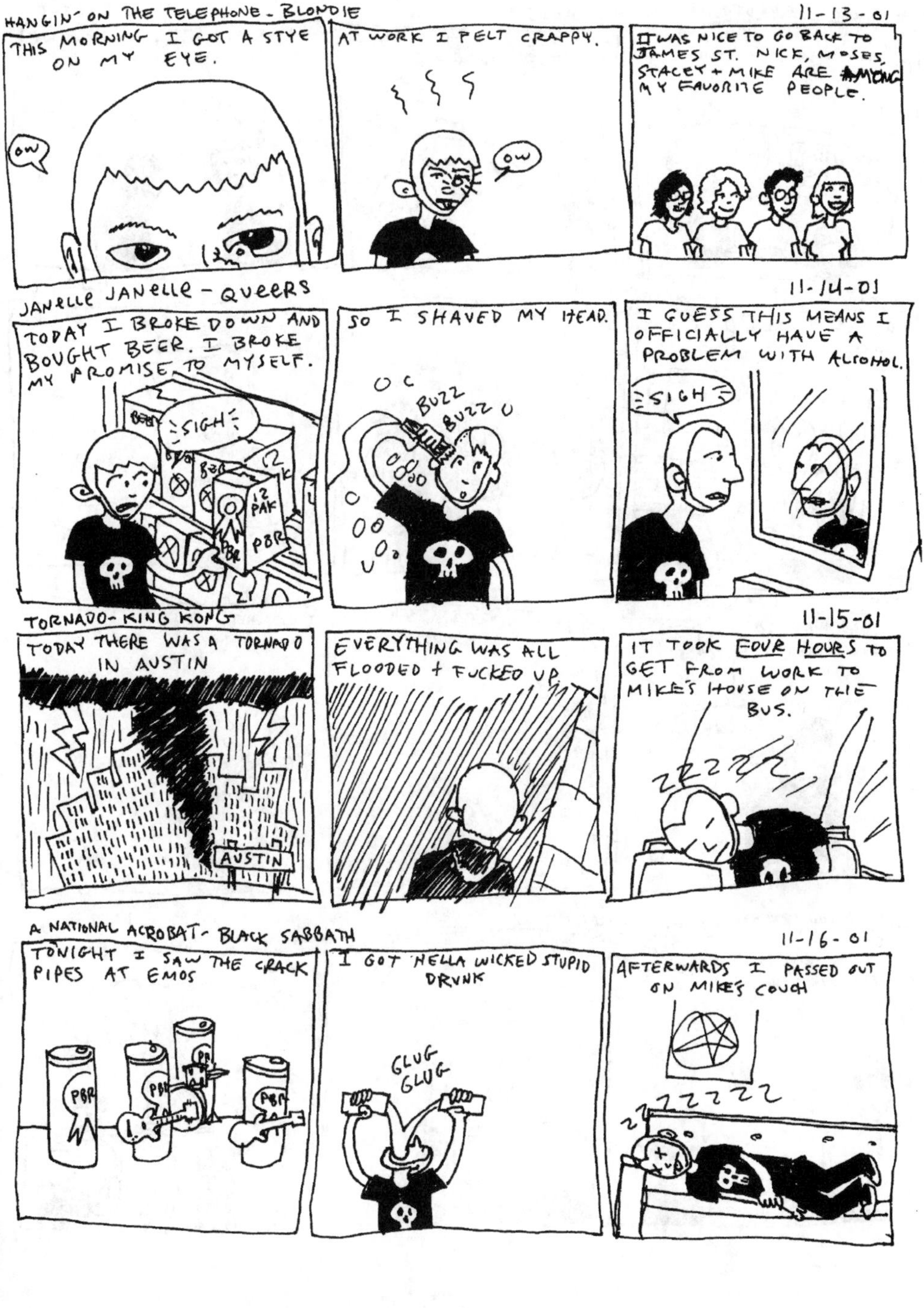
HANGIN' ON THE TELEPHONE - BLONDIE
11-13-01
THIS MORNING I GOT A STYE ON MY EYE.
OW
AT WORK I FELT CRAPPY.
OW
IT WAS NICE TO GO BACK TO JAMES ST. NICK, MOSES, STACEY + MIKE ARE AMONG MY FAVORITE PEOPLE.
JANELLE JANELLE - QUEERS
11-14-01
TODAY I BROKE DOWN AND BOUGHT BEER. I BROKE MY PROMISE TO MYSELF.
SIGH
12 PAK
PBR
SO I SHAVED MY HEAD.
BUZZ
BUZZ
I GUESS THIS MEANS I OFFICIALLY HAVE A PROBLEM WITH ALCOHOL.
SIGH
TORNADO - KING KONG
11-15-01
TODAY THERE WAS A TORNADO IN AUSTIN
AUSTIN
EVERYTHING WAS ALL FLOODED + FUCKED UP.
IT TOOK FOUR HOURS TO GET FROM WORK TO MIKE'S HOUSE ON THE BUS.
ZZZZZ
A NATIONAL ACROBAT - BLACK SABBATH
11-16-01
TONIGHT I SAW THE CRACK PIPES AT EMOS
PBR
I GOT HELLA WICKED STUPID DRUNK
GLUG
GLUG
AFTERWARDS I PASSED OUT ON MIKE'S COUCH
ZZZZZZZ

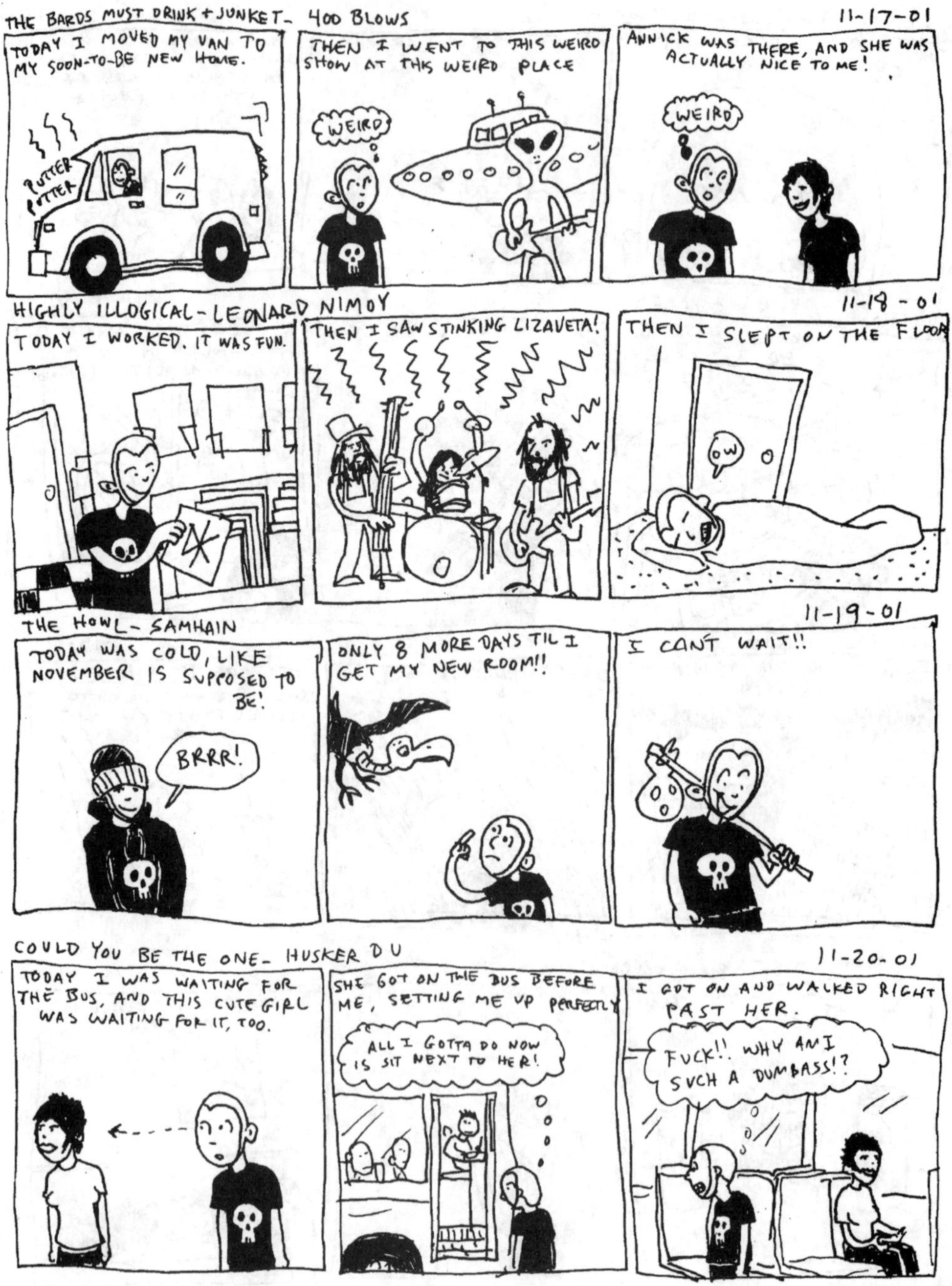
THE BARDS MUST DRINK + JUNKET - 400 BLOWS
11-17-01
TODAY I MOVED MY VAN TO MY SOON-TO-BE NEW HOME.
PUTTER PUTTER
THEN I WENT TO THIS WEIRD SHOW AT THIS WEIRD PLACE
WEIRD
ANNICK WAS THERE, AND SHE WAS ACTUALLY NICE TO ME!
WEIRD
HIGHLY ILLOGICAL - LEONARD NIMOY
11-18-01
TODAY I WORKED. IT WAS FUN.
THEN I SAW STINKING LIZAVETA!
THEN I SLEPT ON THE FLOOR
OW
THE HOWL - SAMHAIN
11-19-01
TODAY WAS COLD, LIKE NOVEMBER IS SUPPOSED TO BE!
BRRR!
ONLY 8 MORE DAYS TIL I GET MY NEW ROOM!!
I CAN'T WAIT!!
COULD YOU BE THE ONE - HUSKER DU
11-20-01
TODAY I WAS WAITING FOR THE BUS, AND THIS CUTE GIRL WAS WAITING FOR IT, TOO.
SHE GOT ON THE BUS BEFORE ME, SETTING ME UP PERFECTLY
ALL I GOTTA DO NOW IS SIT NEXT TO HER!
I GOT ON AND WALKED RIGHT PAST HER.
FUCK!! WHY AM I SUCH A DUMBASS!?

OH CAROLINA - PRINCE BUSTER

TODAY WORK WAS FUN.

AFTER WORK I WENT TO CICI'S WITH MIKE & J.D.

THEN WE WENT TO CASINO AND I HIT ON A GIRL.

I GOT HER NUMBER. HOW DO YOU LIKE THEM APPLES?

ALL THIS AND MORE - DEAD BOYS

THIS MORNING I MADE SOME THANKSGIVING COOKIES.

THEN I HAD THANKSGIVING DINNER AT NICOLE'S (THE GIRL I MET AT CASINO)

SHE'S VERY NICE, BUT SHE'S NOT EXACTLY MY TYPE.

ZZZZ

KILLER WOLF - DANZIG

TODAY I GOT THE NEW ISSUE OF AUSTIN CELEBRITY PROFILES. RAY GAVE SNAKEPIT A GOOD REVIEW.

WOW! THANKS RAY!

THEN MIKE+JD+ME CALLED EVERYONE WE KNOW, DESPERATELY TRYING TO FIND A PARTY.

IT WAS ALL FOR NAUGHT.

ZZZ

HELLO THERE - CHEAP TRICK

TODAY I PUT A NEW TIRE ON MY BIKE!!!

READY TO ROCK!

I WENT TO WORK.

I NEED TO PRACTICE DRAWING BIKES!

THEN I CAME HOME AND WATCHED STARSHIP TROOPERS

THE ENEMY CANNOT PUSH A BUTTON IF YOU DISABLE HIS HAND!

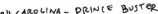

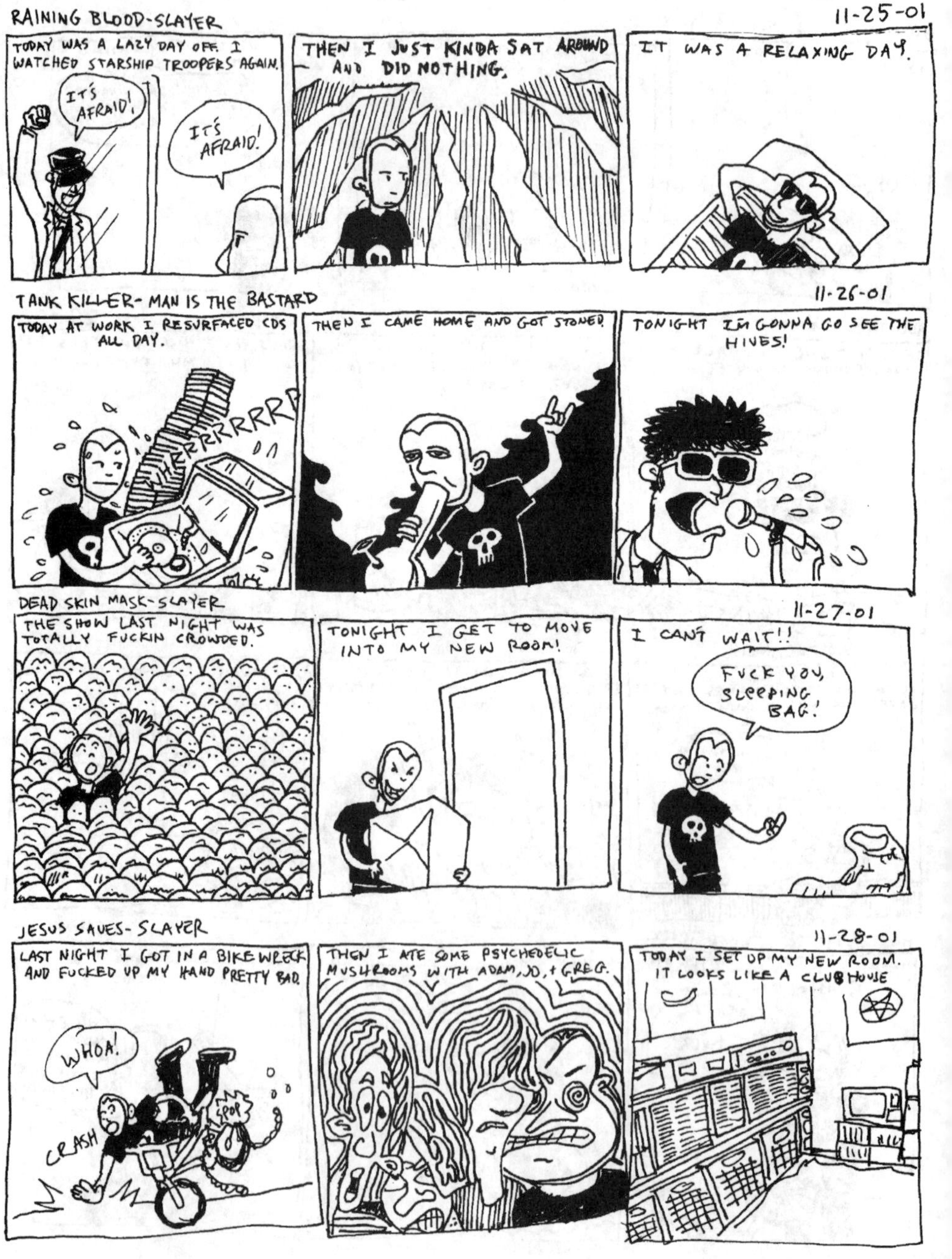
RAINING BLOOD-SLAYER
11-25-01
TODAY WAS A LAZY DAY OFF. I WATCHED STARSHIP TROOPERS AGAIN.
IT'S AFRAID!
IT'S AFRAID!
THEN I JUST KINDA SAT AROUND AND DID NOTHING.
IT WAS A RELAXING DAY.
TANK KILLER-MAN IS THE BASTARD
11-26-01
TODAY AT WORK I RESURFACED CDS ALL DAY.
RRRRRRRRP
THEN I CAME HOME AND GOT STONED.
TONIGHT I'M GONNA GO SEE THE HIVES!
DEAD SKIN MASK-SLAYER
11-27-01
THE SHOW LAST NIGHT WAS TOTALLY FUCKIN CROWDED.
TONIGHT I GET TO MOVE INTO MY NEW ROOM!
I CAN'T WAIT!!
FUCK YOU, SLEEPING BAG!
JESUS SAVES-SLAYER
11-28-01
LAST NIGHT I GOT IN A BIKE WRECK AND FUCKED UP MY HAND PRETTY BAD.
WHOA!
CRASH
SPOP
THEN I ATE SOME PSYCHEDELIC MUSHROOMS WITH ADAM, JD, + GREG.
TODAY I SET UP MY NEW ROOM. IT LOOKS LIKE A CLUBHOUSE

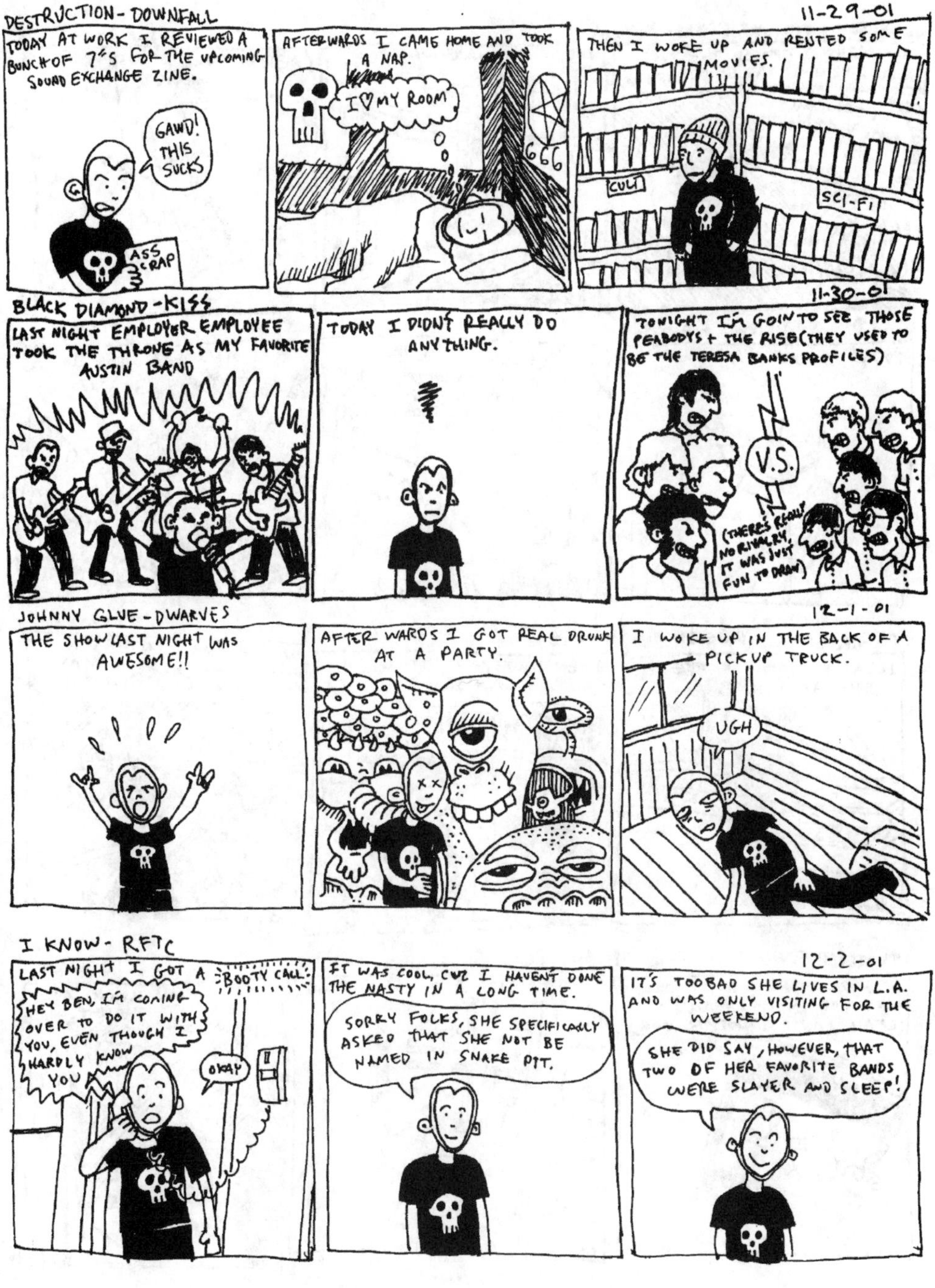
DESTRUCTION - DOWNFALL
11-29-01
TODAY AT WORK I REVIEWED A BUNCH OF 7"S FOR THE UPCOMING SOUND EXCHANGE ZINE.
GAWD! THIS SUCKS
ASS CRAP
AFTERWARDS I CAME HOME AND TOOK A NAP.
I ♡ MY ROOM
666
THEN I WOKE UP AND RENTED SOME MOVIES.
CULT
SCI-FI
BLACK DIAMOND - KISS
11-30-01
LAST NIGHT EMPLOYER EMPLOYEE TOOK THE THRONE AS MY FAVORITE AUSTIN BAND
TODAY I DIDN'T REALLY DO ANYTHING.
TONIGHT I'M GOIN TO SEE THOSE PEABODYS + THE RISE (THEY USED TO BE THE TERESA BANKS PROFILES)
V.S.
(THERE'S REALLY NO RIVALRY, IT WAS JUST FUN TO DRAW)
JOHNNY GLUE - DWARVES
12-1-01
THE SHOW LAST NIGHT WAS AWESOME!!
AFTERWARDS I GOT REAL DRUNK AT A PARTY.
I WOKE UP IN THE BACK OF A PICKUP TRUCK.
UGH
I KNOW - RFTC
12-2-01
LAST NIGHT I GOT A BOOTY CALL
HEY BEN, I'M COMING OVER TO DO IT WITH YOU, EVEN THOUGH I HARDLY KNOW YOU
OKAY
IT WAS COOL, CUZ I HAVEN'T DONE THE NASTY IN A LONG TIME.
SORRY FOLKS, SHE SPECIFICALLY ASKED THAT SHE NOT BE NAMED IN SNAKE PIT.
IT'S TOO BAD SHE LIVES IN L.A. AND WAS ONLY VISITING FOR THE WEEKEND.
SHE DID SAY, HOWEVER, THAT TWO OF HER FAVORITE BANDS WERE SLAYER AND SLEEP!

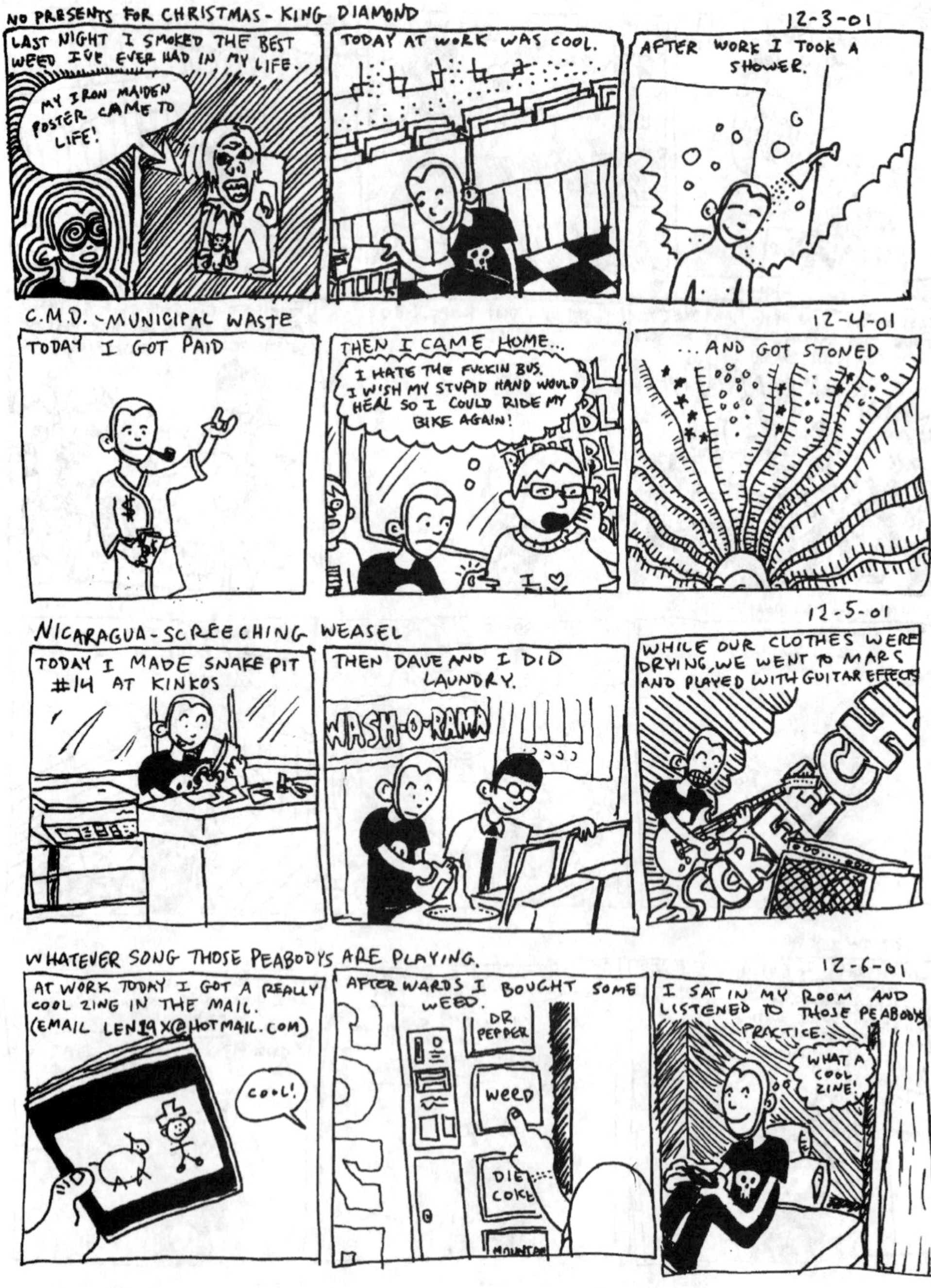
NO PRESENTS FOR CHRISTMAS - KING DIAMOND
12-3-01
LAST NIGHT I SMOKED THE BEST WEED I'VE EVER HAD IN MY LIFE...
MY IRON MAIDEN POSTER CAME TO LIFE!
TODAY AT WORK WAS COOL.
AFTER WORK I TOOK A SHOWER.
C.M.D. - MUNICIPAL WASTE
12-4-01
TODAY I GOT PAID
THEN I CAME HOME...
I HATE THE FUCKIN BUS. I WISH MY STUPID HAND WOULD HEAL SO I COULD RIDE MY BIKE AGAIN!
...AND GOT STONED
NICARAGUA - SCREECHING WEASEL
12-5-01
TODAY I MADE SNAKE PIT #14 AT KINKOS
THEN DAVE AND I DID LAUNDRY.
WASH-O-RAMA
WHILE OUR CLOTHES WERE DRYING, WE WENT TO MARS AND PLAYED WITH GUITAR EFFECTS
SCREECH
WHATEVER SONG THOSE PEABODYS ARE PLAYING.
12-6-01
AT WORK TODAY I GOT A REALLY COOL ZINE IN THE MAIL. (EMAIL LEN19X@HOTMAIL.COM)
COOL!
AFTERWARDS I BOUGHT SOME WEED.
DR PEPPER
WEED
COKE
I SAT IN MY ROOM AND LISTENED TO THOSE PEABODYS PRACTICE.
WHAT A COOL ZINE!

BORN IN FUCKING CHAINS - FACE DOWN IN SHIT
12-7-01
TODAY I WENT TO KINKO'S AND PRINTED UP SOME MORE ANTOLOGY ZINES.
XEROX
THEN I COLLATED THEM.
TIP TO ZINE EDITORS: USE HAND LOTION TO KEEP FROM GETTING PAPER CUTS!
THEN I WENT TO A TOTALLY SHITTY PARTY.
UGH.
SPECIES OF CRUELTY - ERIC WOOD
12-8-01
THIS EVENING I WORKED.
CRIMP SHRINE
THEN I SAW LONG WALKS ON THE BEACH PLAY THEIR LAST SHOW. (IT IS MOVING TO NEW YORK.)
LWOTB
R.I.P.
THEN I WENT TO A PARTY IN THE BACK OF A RENTED TRUCK.
FUCK EVERYTHING - RICH OLIVER
12-9-01
I WAS HUNG OVER TODAY.
UGH.
I RENTED SOME MOVIES.
HELLS BELLS PT1
HELLS BELLS PT2
STAR TREK BLOOPERS
PARADISE LOST II
AND STAYED IN ALL DAY.
Z Z Z Z Z Z
DROP THE ATTITUDE FUCKER - THE QUEERS
12-10-01
WORK WAS COOL TODAY.
BLACK FLAG
AFTER WORDS I STAPLED MY ANTHOLOGY ZINES.
THEN I FELL ASLEEP
666

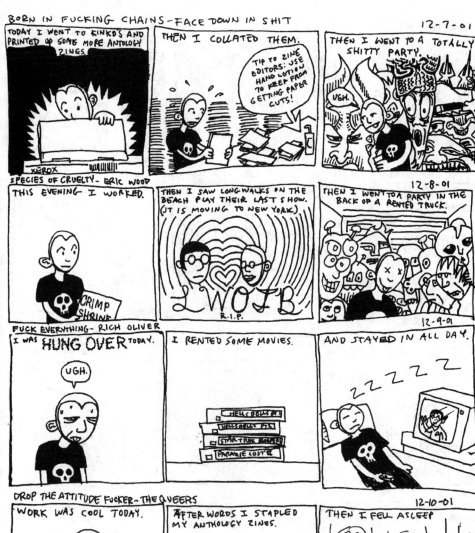

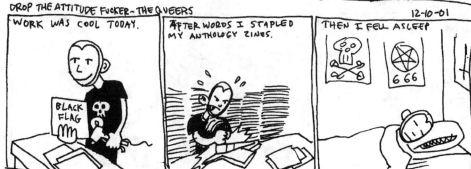

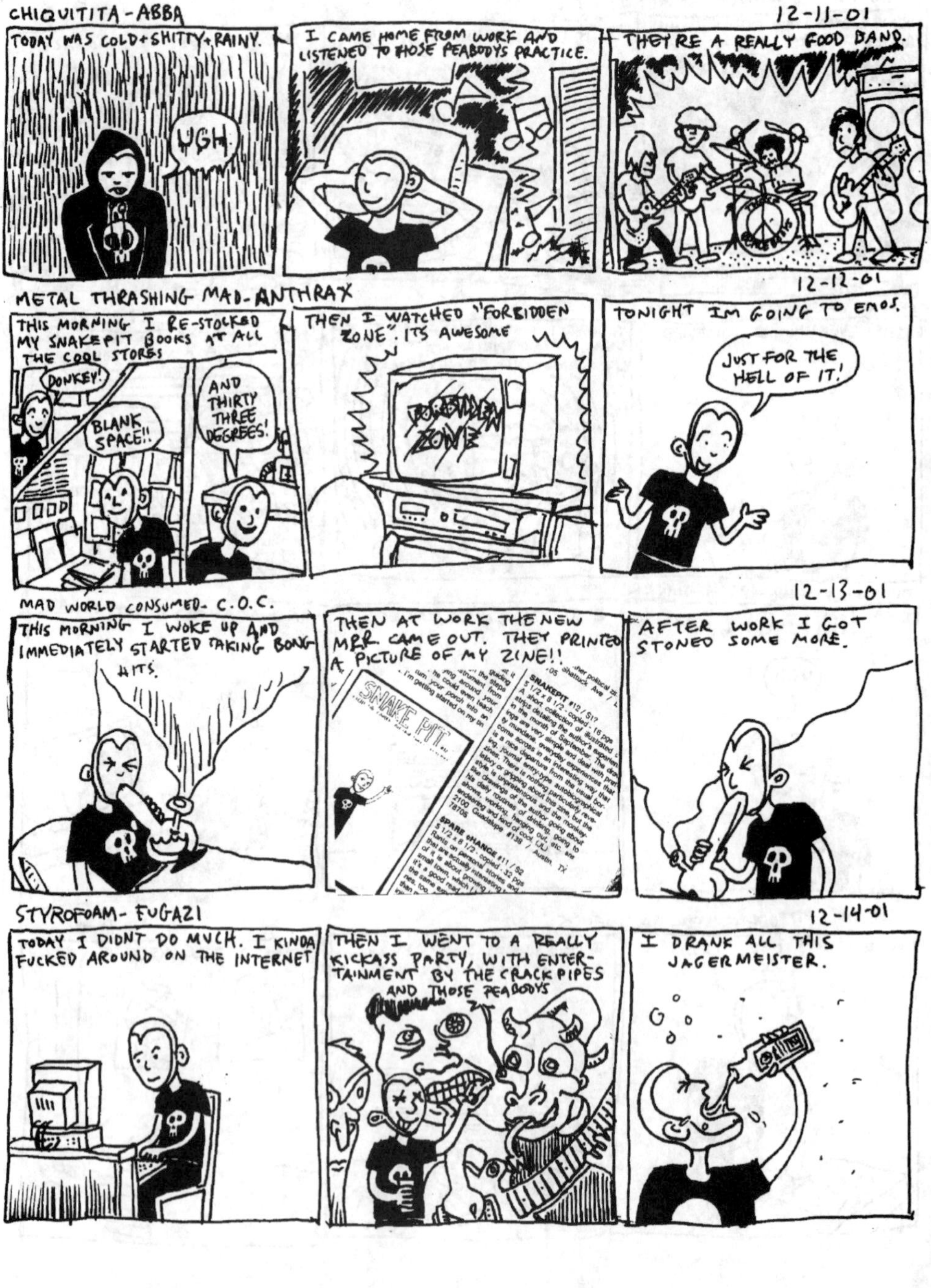
CHIQUITITA - ABBA
12-11-01
TODAY WAS COLD+SHITTY+RAINY.
UGH.
I CAME HOME FROM WORK AND LISTENED TO THOSE PEABODYS PRACTICE.
THEYRE A REALLY GOOD BAND.
METAL THRASHING MAD - ANTHRAX
12-12-01
THIS MORNING I RE-STOCKED MY SNAKEPIT BOOKS AT ALL THE COOL STORES
DONKEY!
BLANK SPACE!!
AND THIRTY THREE DEGREES!
THEN I WATCHED "FORBIDDEN ZONE". ITS AWESOME
FORBIDDEN ZONE
TONIGHT IM GOING TO EMOS.
JUST FOR THE HELL OF IT!
MAD WORLD CONSUMED - C.O.C.
12-13-01
THIS MORNING I WOKE UP AND IMMEDIATELY STARTED TAKING BONG HITS.
THEN AT WORK THE NEW MRR CAME OUT. THEY PRINTED A PICTURE OF MY ZINE!!
SNAKE PIT
AFTER WORK I GOT STONED SOME MORE.
STYROFOAM - FUGAZI
12-14-01
TODAY I DIDNT DO MUCH. I KINDA FUCKED AROUND ON THE INTERNET
THEN I WENT TO A REALLY KICKASS PARTY, WITH ENTERTAINMENT BY THE CRACKPIPES AND THOSE PEABODYS
I DRANK ALL THIS JAGERMEISTER.

A+ IN ARSON CLASS - RFTC 12-15-01

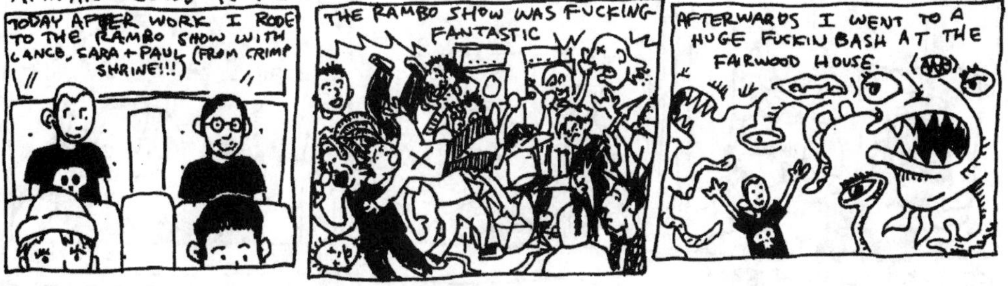
TODAY AFTER WORK I RODE TO THE RAMBO SHOW WITH LANCE, SARA + PAUL (FROM CRIMP SHRINE!!!)
THE RAMBO SHOW WAS FUCKING FANTASTIC
AFTERWARDS I WENT TO A HUGE FUCKIN BASH AT THE FAIRWOOD HOUSE.

SCATTERD REMAINS, SPLATTERED BRAINS - CANNIBAL CORPSE 12-16-01

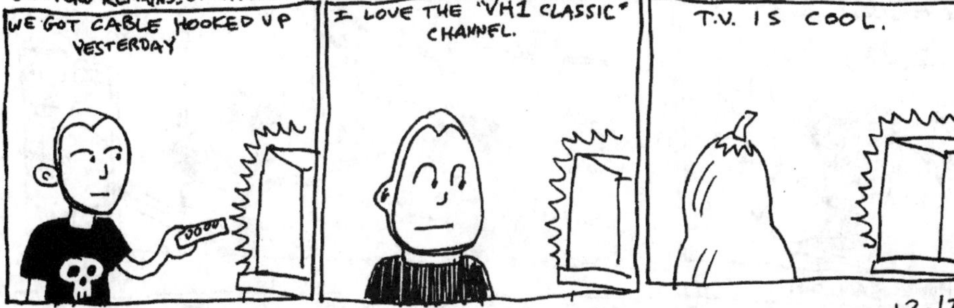
WE GOT CABLE HOOKED UP YESTERDAY
I LOVE THE "VH1 CLASSIC" CHANNEL.
T.V. IS COOL.

I LOVE IT LOUD - KISS 12-17-01

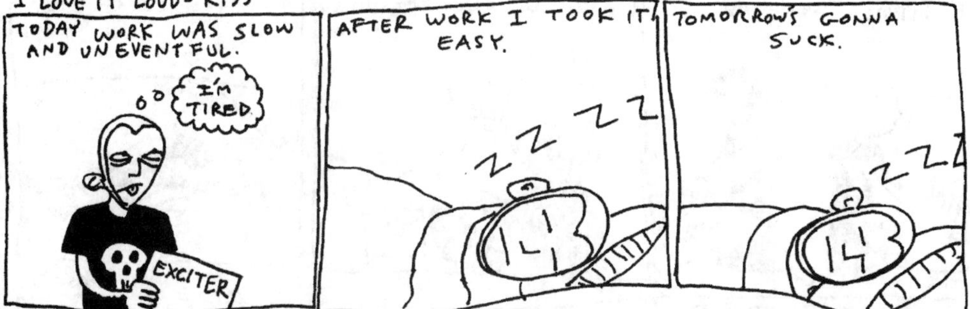
TODAY WORK WAS SLOW AND UNEVENTFUL.
I'M TIRED
EXCITER
AFTER WORK I TOOK IT EASY.
Z Z Z Z
TOMORROW'S GONNA SUCK.
Z Z Z

PLANET ROCK - AFRIKA BAMBAATAA 12-18-01

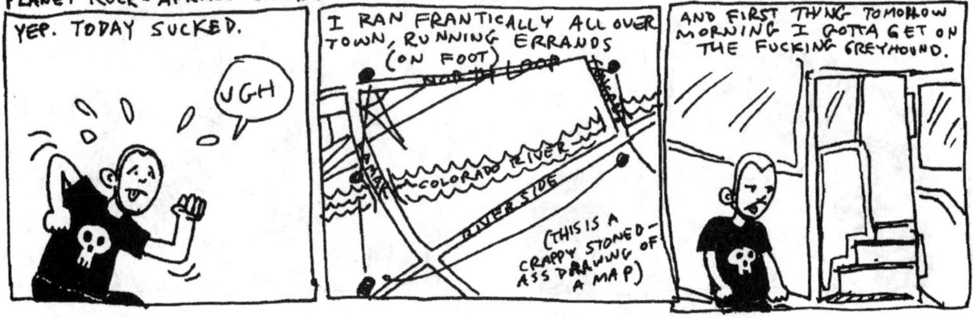
YEP. TODAY SUCKED.
UGH
I RAN FRANTICALLY ALL OVER TOWN, RUNNING ERRANDS (ON FOOT)
COLORADO RIVER
RIVERSIDE
(THIS IS A CRAPPY STONED-ASS DRAWING OF A MAP)
AND FIRST THING TOMORROW MORNING I GOTTA GET ON THE FUCKING GREYHOUND.

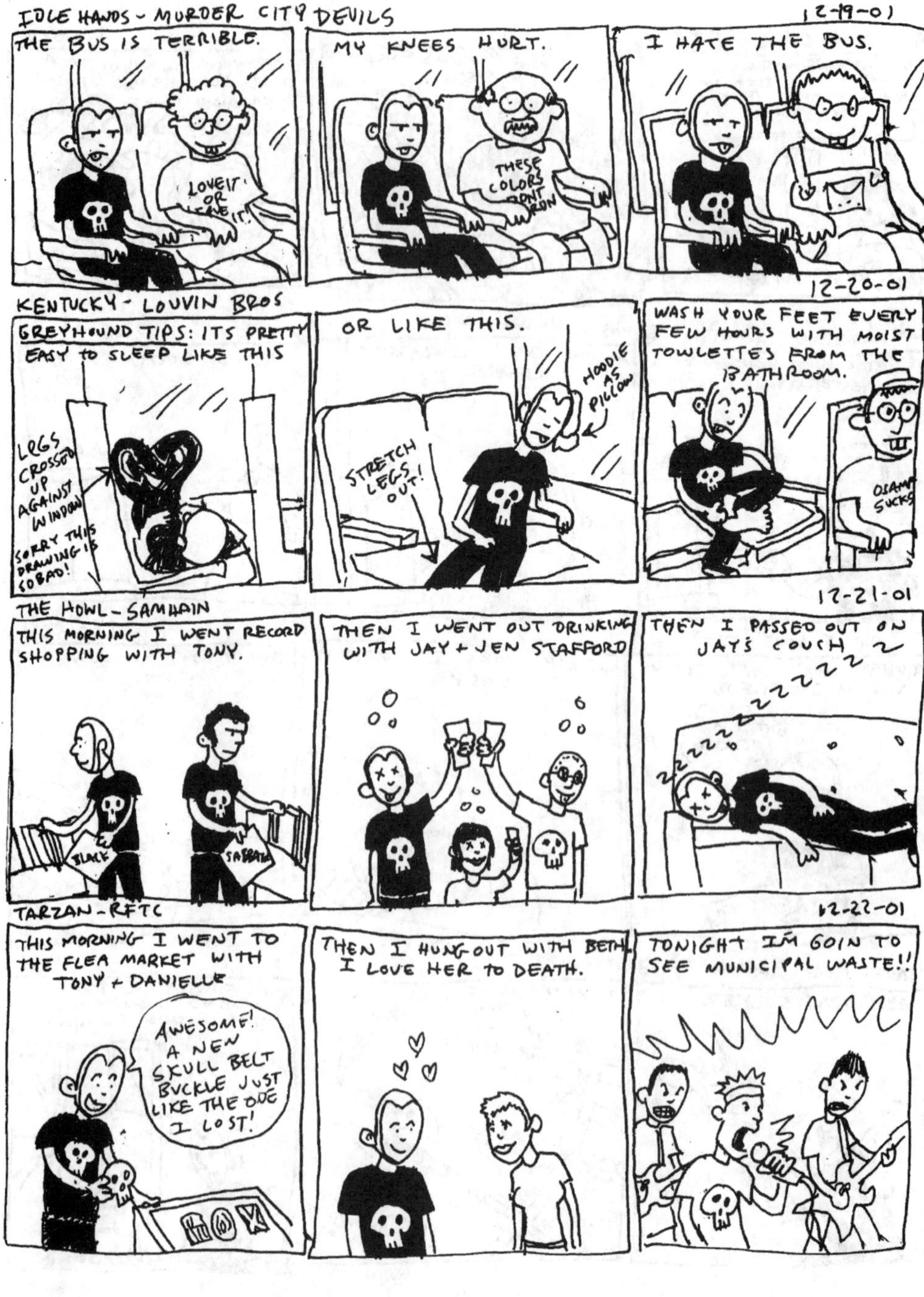
IDLE HANDS - MURDER CITY DEVILS
12-19-01
THE BUS IS TERRIBLE.
LOVE IT OR LEAVE IT!
MY KNEES HURT.
THESE COLORS DONT RUN
I HATE THE BUS.
KENTUCKY - LOUVIN BROS
12-20-01
GREYHOUND TIPS: ITS PRETTY EASY TO SLEEP LIKE THIS
LEGS CROSSED UP AGAINST WINDOW
SORRY THIS DRAWING IS SO BAD!
OR LIKE THIS.
HOODIE AS PILLOW
STRETCH LEGS OUT!
WASH YOUR FEET EVERY FEW HOURS WITH MOIST TOWLETTES FROM THE BATHROOM.
OSAMA SUCKS
THE HOWL - SAMHAIN
12-21-01
THIS MORNING I WENT RECORD SHOPPING WITH TONY.
BLACK
SABBATH
THEN I WENT OUT DRINKING WITH JAY + JEN STAFFORD
THEN I PASSED OUT ON JAY'S COUCH
ZZZZZZZZZZZZZZZ
TARZAN - RFTC
12-22-01
THIS MORNING I WENT TO THE FLEA MARKET WITH TONY + DANIELLE
AWESOME! A NEW SKULL BELT BUCKLE JUST LIKE THE ONE I LOST!
THEN I HUNG OUT WITH BETH. I LOVE HER TO DEATH.
TONIGHT I'M GOIN TO SEE MUNICIPAL WASTE!!

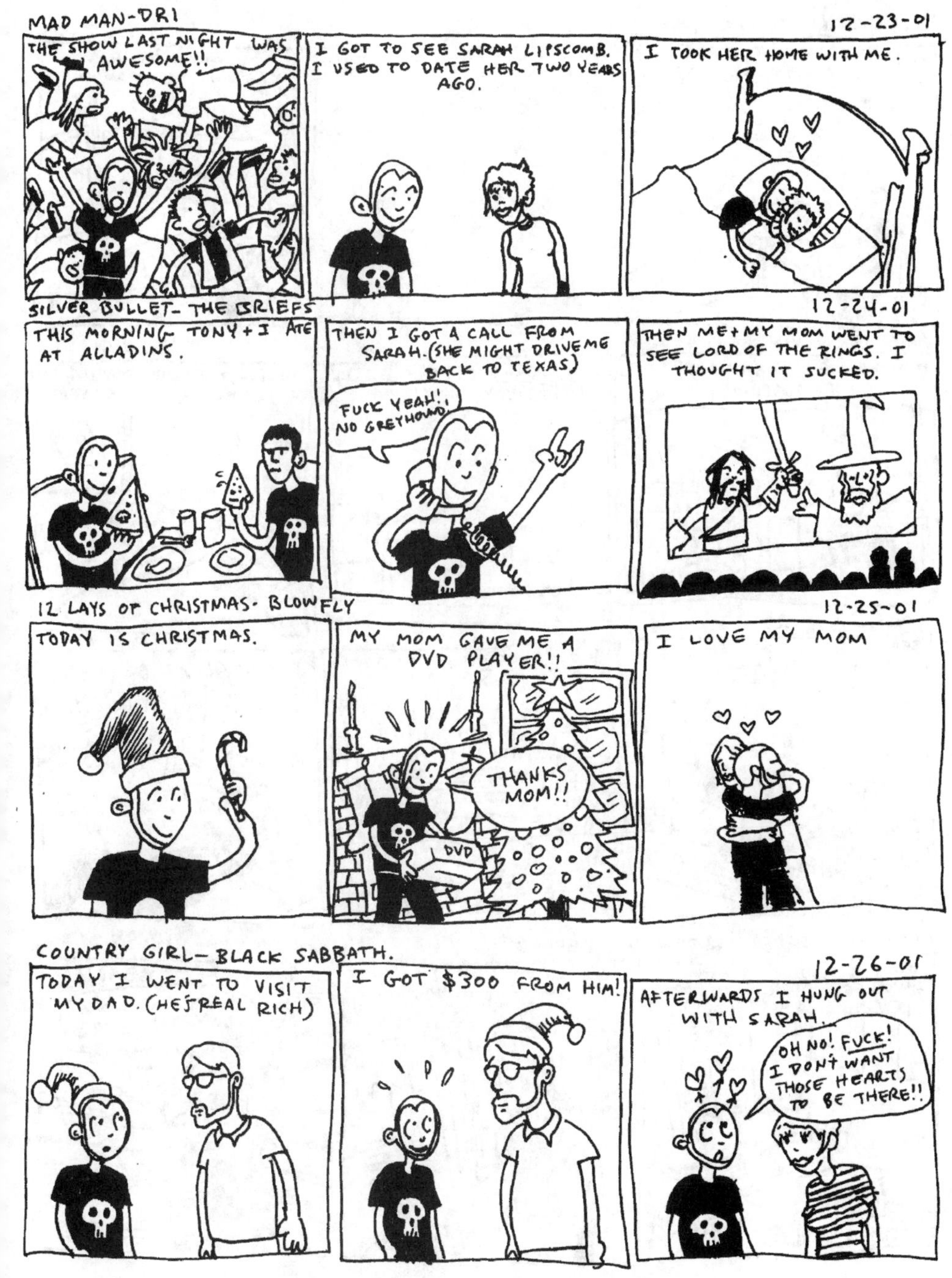
MAD MAN-DRI
12-23-01
THE SHOW LAST NIGHT WAS AWESOME!!
I GOT TO SEE SARAH LIPSCOMB. I USED TO DATE HER TWO YEARS AGO.
I TOOK HER HOME WITH ME.
SILVER BULLET- THE BRIEFS
12-24-01
THIS MORNING TONY + I ATE AT ALLADINS.
THEN I GOT A CALL FROM SARAH. (SHE MIGHT DRIVE ME BACK TO TEXAS)
FUCK YEAH! NO GREYHOUND.
THEN ME + MY MOM WENT TO SEE LORD OF THE RINGS. I THOUGHT IT SUCKED.
12 LAYS OF CHRISTMAS- BLOWFLY
12-25-01
TODAY IS CHRISTMAS.
MY MOM GAVE ME A DVD PLAYER!!
THANKS MOM!!
DVD
I LOVE MY MOM
COUNTRY GIRL- BLACK SABBATH.
12-26-01
TODAY I WENT TO VISIT MY DAD. (HE'S REAL RICH)
I GOT $300 FROM HIM!
AFTERWARDS I HUNG OUT WITH SARAH.
OH NO! FUCK! I DON'T WANT THOSE HEARTS TO BE THERE!!

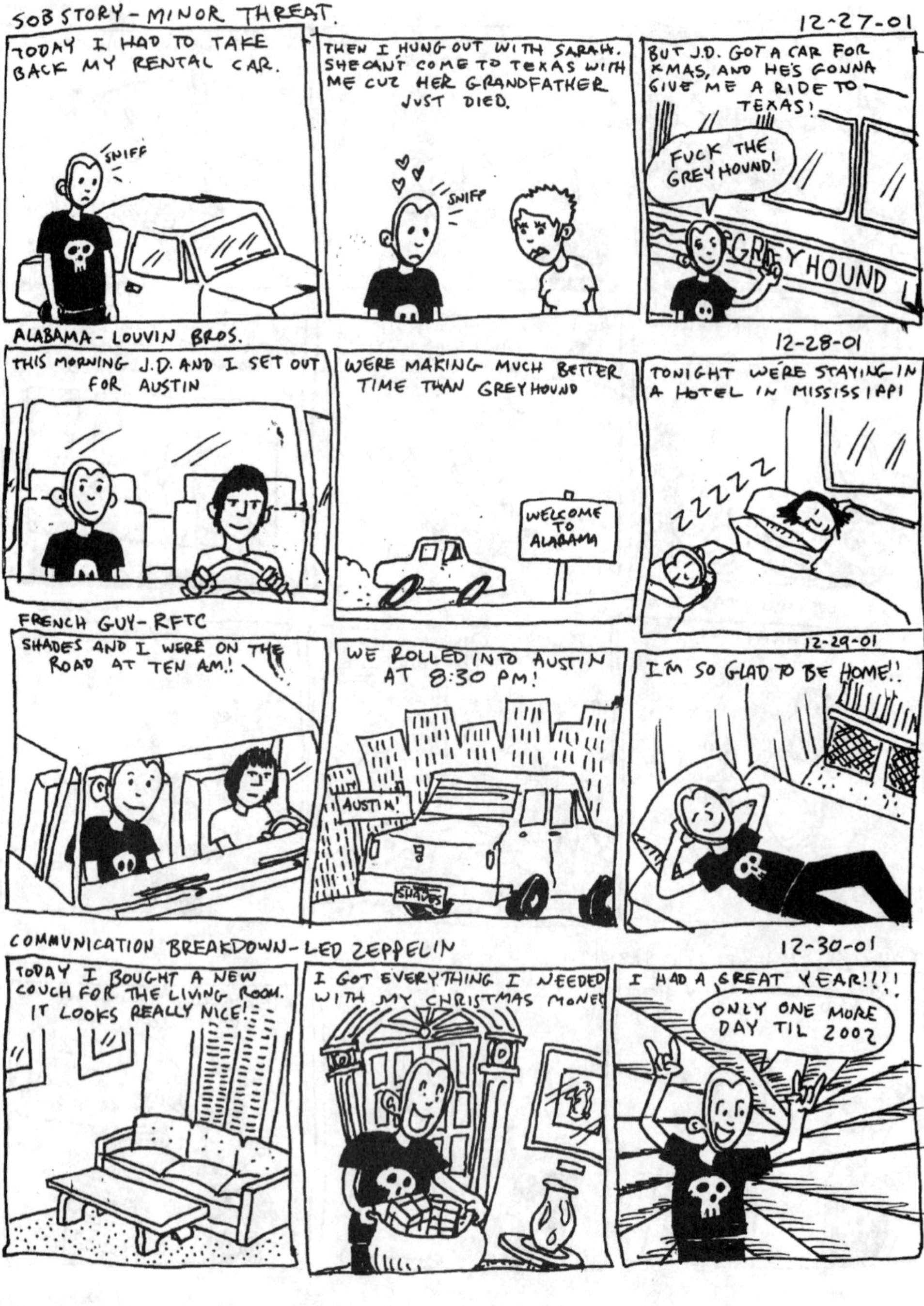
SOB STORY - MINOR THREAT.
12-27-01
TODAY I HAD TO TAKE BACK MY RENTAL CAR.
SNIFF
THEN I HUNG OUT WITH SARAH. SHE CAN'T COME TO TEXAS WITH ME CUZ HER GRANDFATHER JUST DIED.
SNIFF
BUT J.D. GOT A CAR FOR XMAS, AND HE'S GONNA GIVE ME A RIDE TO TEXAS!
FUCK THE GREYHOUND!
GREYHOUND
ALABAMA - LOUVIN BROS.
12-28-01
THIS MORNING J.D. AND I SET OUT FOR AUSTIN
WERE MAKING MUCH BETTER TIME THAN GREYHOUND
WELCOME TO ALABAMA
TONIGHT WE'RE STAYING IN A HOTEL IN MISSISSIPPI
ZZZZZZ
FRENCH GUY - RFTC
12-29-01
SHADES AND I WERE ON THE ROAD AT TEN AM!
WE ROLLED INTO AUSTIN AT 8:30 PM!
AUSTIN!
SHADES
I'M SO GLAD TO BE HOME!
COMMUNICATION BREAKDOWN - LED ZEPPELIN
12-30-01
TODAY I BOUGHT A NEW COUCH FOR THE LIVING ROOM. IT LOOKS REALLY NICE!
I GOT EVERYTHING I NEEDED WITH MY CHRISTMAS MONEY
I HAD A GREAT YEAR!!!!
ONLY ONE MORE DAY TIL 2002

ATTITUDE - BAD BRAINS

12-31-01

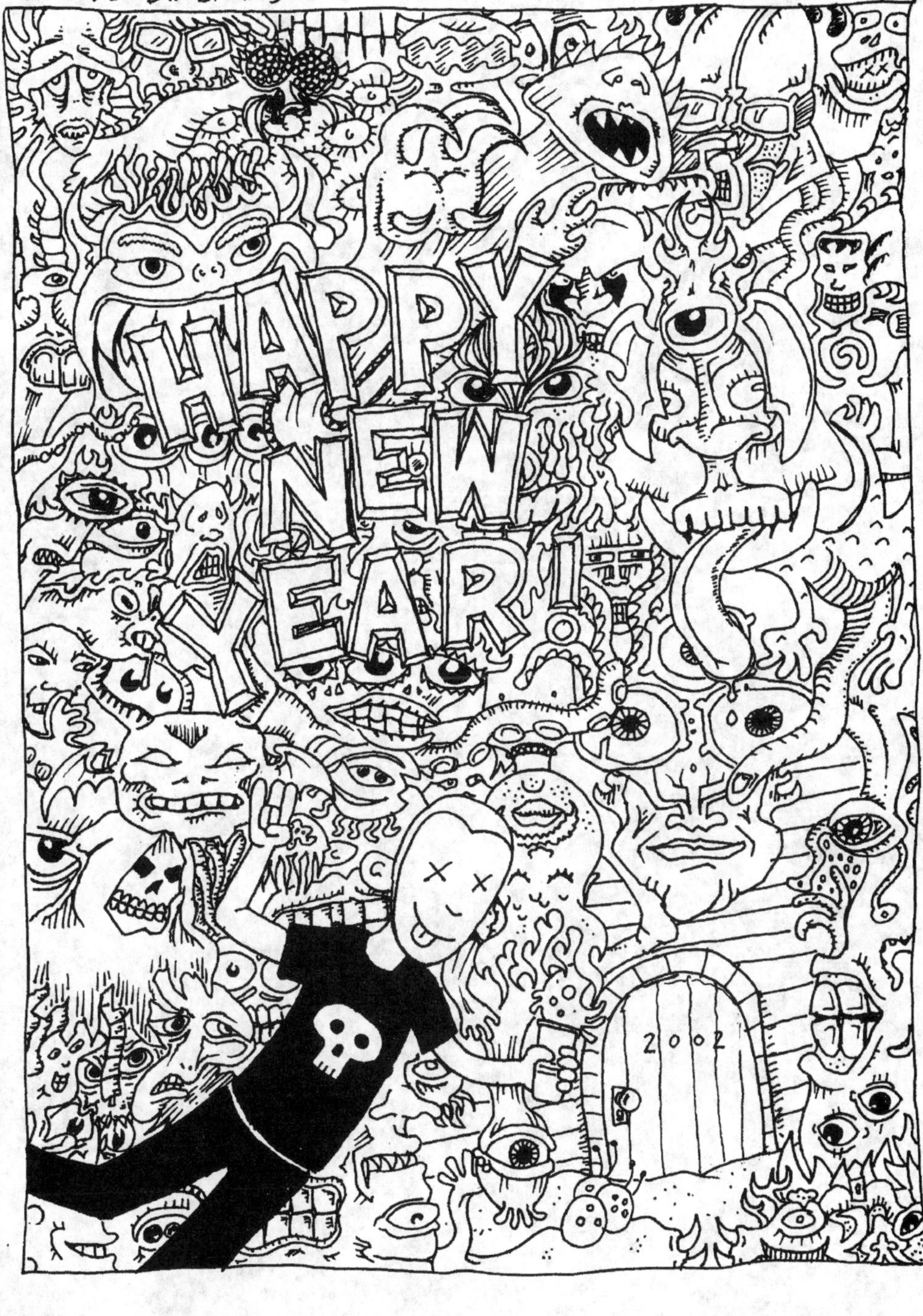

HAPPY NEW YEAR!
2002

2002

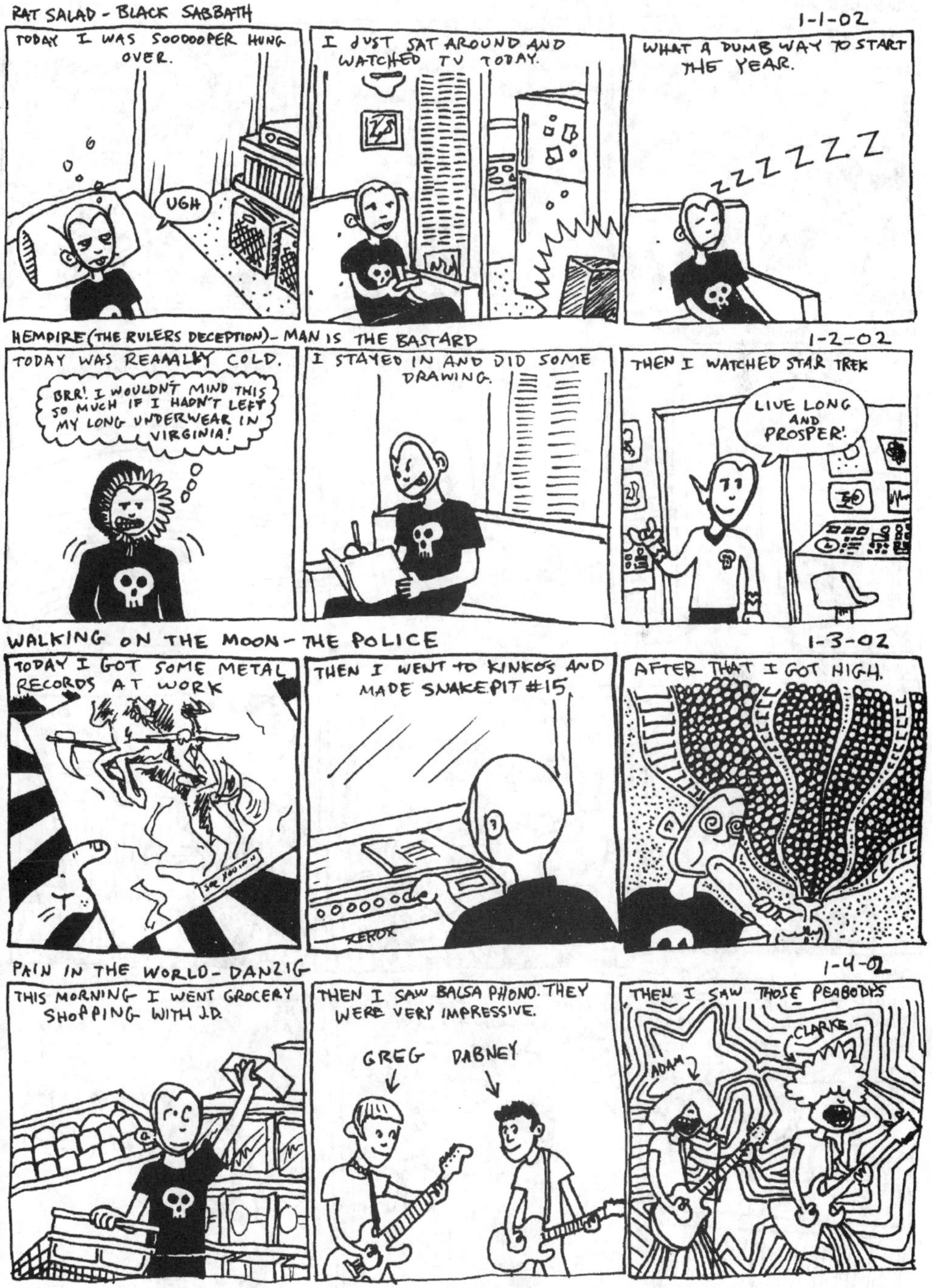
RAT SALAD - BLACK SABBATH
1-1-02
TODAY I WAS SOOOOOPER HUNG OVER.
UGH
I JUST SAT AROUND AND WATCHED TV TODAY.
WHAT A DUMB WAY TO START THE YEAR.
ZZZZZZZ
HEMPIRE (THE RULERS DECEPTION) - MAN IS THE BASTARD
1-2-02
TODAY WAS REAAALLY COLD.
BRR! I WOULDN'T MIND THIS SO MUCH IF I HADN'T LEFT MY LONG UNDERWEAR IN VIRGINIA!
I STAYED IN AND DID SOME DRAWING.
THEN I WATCHED STAR TREK
LIVE LONG AND PROSPER!
WALKING ON THE MOON - THE POLICE
1-3-02
TODAY I GOT SOME METAL RECORDS AT WORK
THEN I WENT TO KINKO'S AND MADE SNAKEPIT #15
XEROX
AFTER THAT I GOT HIGH.
PAIN IN THE WORLD - DANZIG
1-4-02
THIS MORNING I WENT GROCERY SHOPPING WITH J.D.
THEN I SAW BALSA PHONO. THEY WERE VERY IMPRESSIVE.
GREG
DABNEY
THEN I SAW THOSE PEABODYS
ADAM
CLARKE

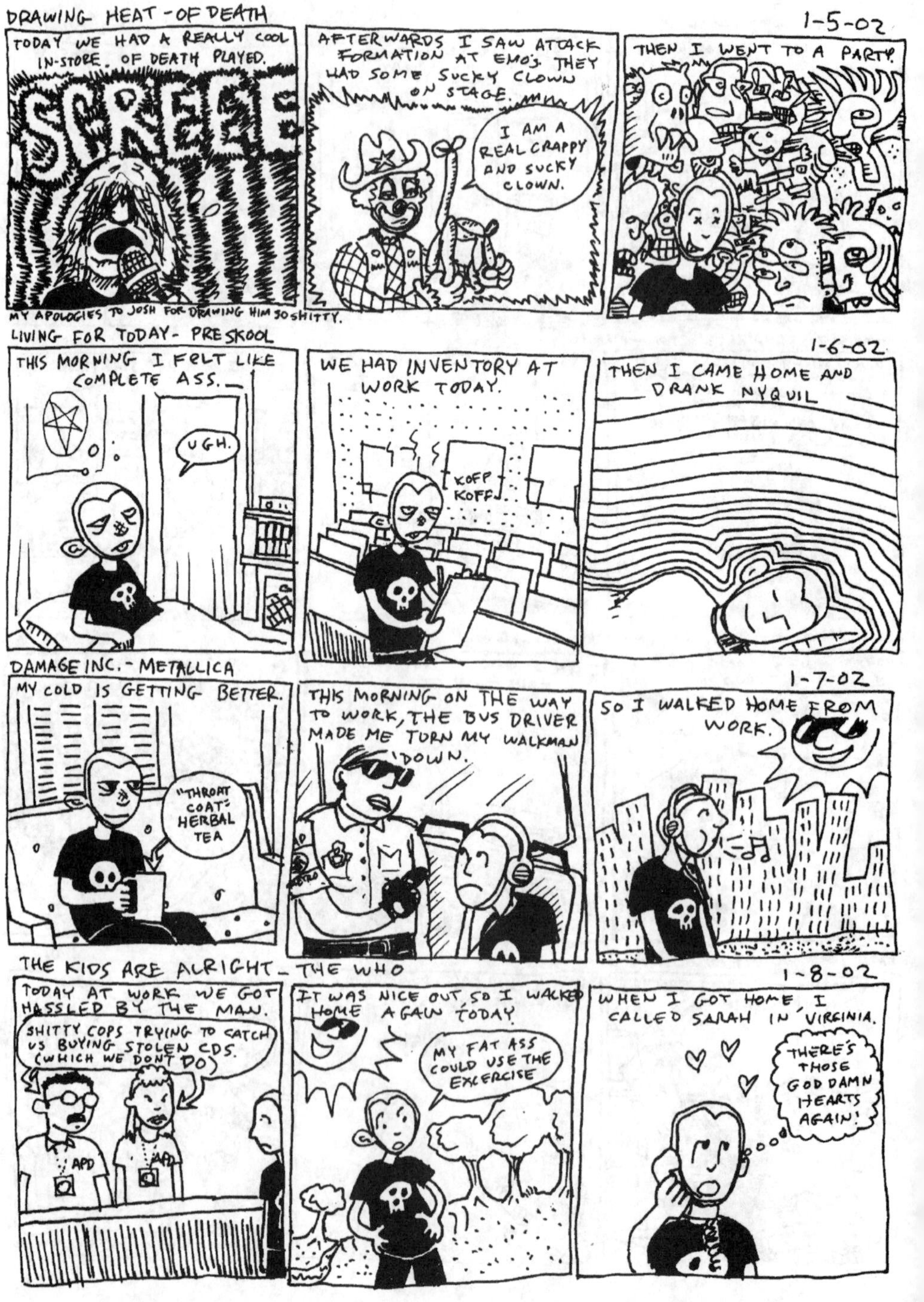

DRAWING HEAT - OF DEATH
1-5-02
TODAY WE HAD A REALLY COOL IN-STORE. OF DEATH PLAYED.
SCREEE
AFTERWARDS I SAW ATTACK FORMATION AT EMO'S. THEY HAD SOME SUCKY CLOWN ON STAGE.
I AM A REAL CRAPPY AND SUCKY CLOWN.
THEN I WENT TO A PARTY.
MY APOLOGIES TO JOSH FOR DRAWING HIM SO SHITTY.
LIVING FOR TODAY - PRESKOOL
1-6-02
THIS MORNING I FELT LIKE COMPLETE ASS.
UGH.
WE HAD INVENTORY AT WORK TODAY.
KOFF KOFF
THEN I CAME HOME AND DRANK NYQUIL
DAMAGE INC. - METALLICA
1-7-02
MY COLD IS GETTING BETTER.
"THROAT COAT" HERBAL TEA
THIS MORNING ON THE WAY TO WORK, THE BUS DRIVER MADE ME TURN MY WALKMAN DOWN.
SO I WALKED HOME FROM WORK.
THE KIDS ARE ALRIGHT - THE WHO
1-8-02
TODAY AT WORK WE GOT HASSLED BY THE MAN.
SHITTY COPS TRYING TO CATCH US BUYING STOLEN CDS. (WHICH WE DONT DO)
APD
APD
IT WAS NICE OUT SO I WALKED HOME AGAIN TODAY.
MY FAT ASS COULD USE THE EXCERCISE
WHEN I GOT HOME, I CALLED SARAH IN VIRGINIA.
THERE'S THOSE GOD DAMN HEARTS AGAIN!

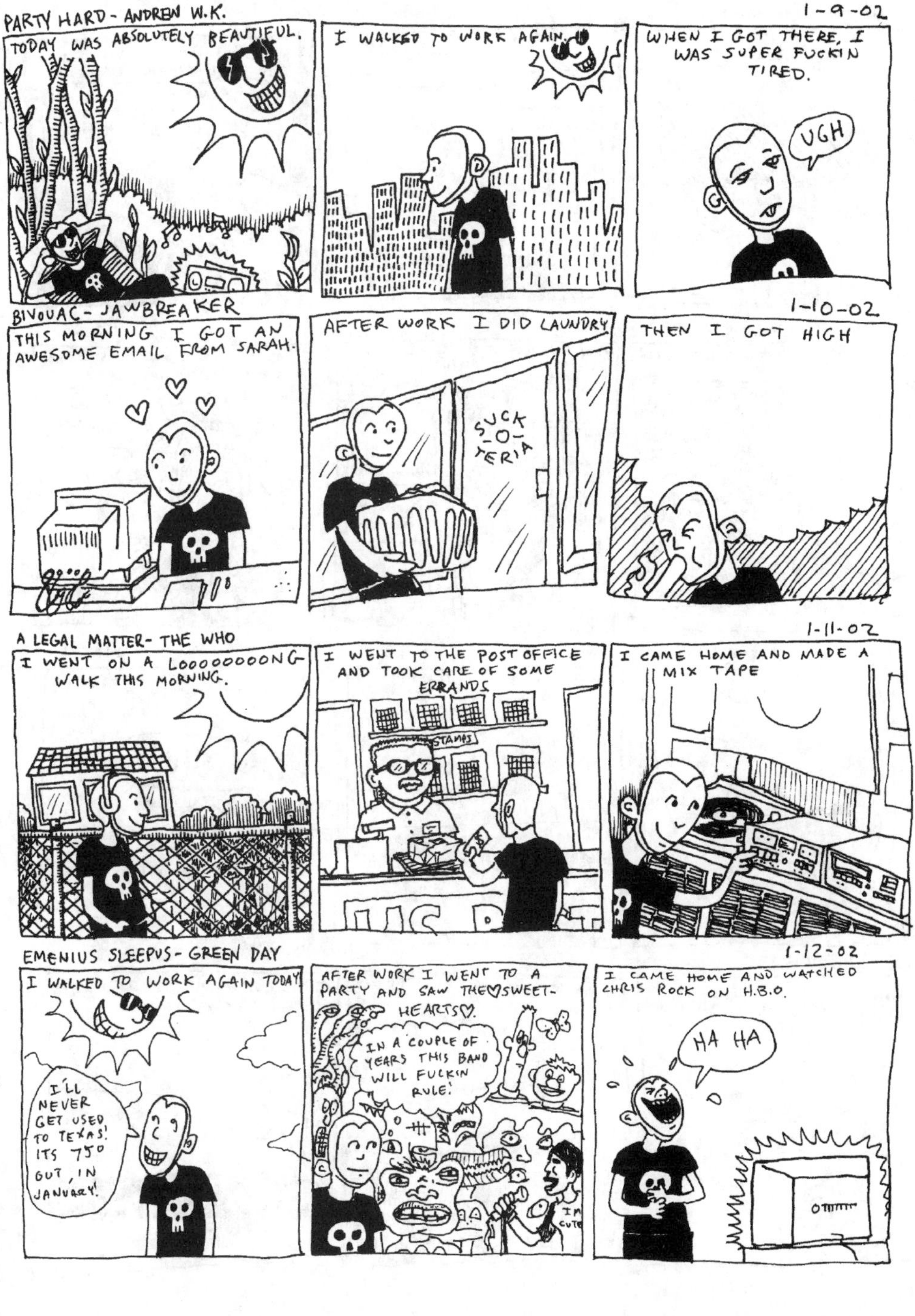
PARTY HARD - ANDREW W.K.
1-9-02
TODAY WAS ABSOLUTELY BEAUTIFUL.
I WALKED TO WORK AGAIN.
WHEN I GOT THERE, I WAS SUPER FUCKIN TIRED.
UGH
BIVOUAC - JAWBREAKER
1-10-02
THIS MORNING I GOT AN AWESOME EMAIL FROM SARAH.
AFTER WORK I DID LAUNDRY
SUCK -O- TERIA
THEN I GOT HIGH
A LEGAL MATTER - THE WHO
1-11-02
I WENT ON A LOOOOOOOONG WALK THIS MORNING.
I WENT TO THE POST OFFICE AND TOOK CARE OF SOME ERRANDS
STAMPS
I CAME HOME AND MADE A MIX TAPE
EMENIUS SLEEPUS - GREEN DAY
1-12-02
I WALKED TO WORK AGAIN TODAY!
I'LL NEVER GET USED TO TEXAS! ITS 75° OUT, IN JANUARY!
AFTER WORK I WENT TO A PARTY AND SAW THE♡SWEET-HEARTS♡.
IN A COUPLE OF YEARS THIS BAND WILL FUCKIN RULE!
I'M CUTE
I CAME HOME AND WATCHED CHRIS ROCK ON H.B.O.
HA HA

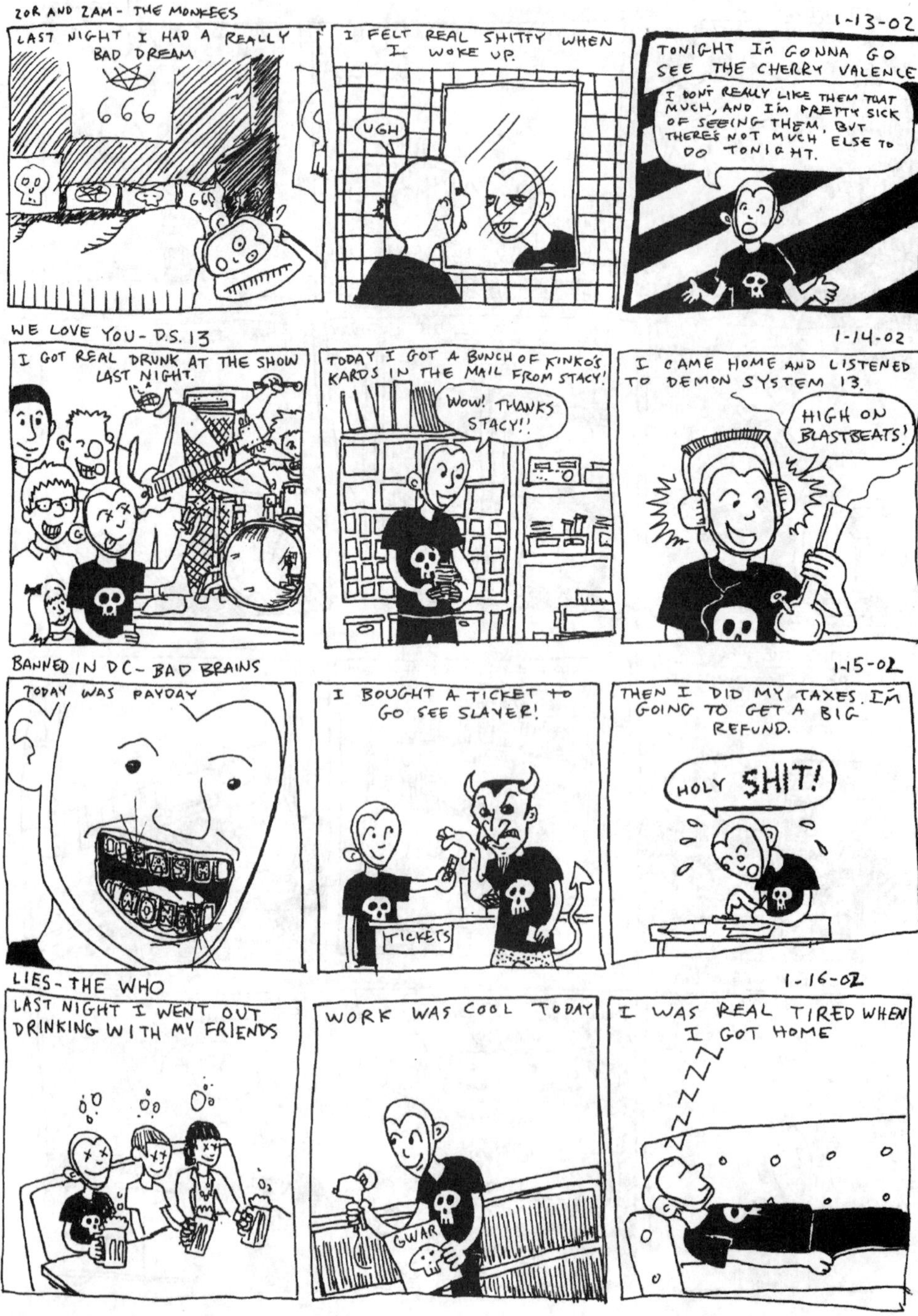

ZOR AND ZAM - THE MONKEES
1-13-02
LAST NIGHT I HAD A REALLY BAD DREAM
666
666
I FELT REAL SHITTY WHEN I WOKE UP.
UGH
TONIGHT I'M GONNA GO SEE THE CHERRY VALENCE.
I DON'T REALLY LIKE THEM THAT MUCH, AND I'M PRETTY SICK OF SEEING THEM, BUT THERE'S NOT MUCH ELSE TO DO TONIGHT.
WE LOVE YOU - D.S. 13
1-14-02
I GOT REAL DRUNK AT THE SHOW LAST NIGHT.
TODAY I GOT A BUNCH OF KINKO'S KARDS IN THE MAIL FROM STACY!
WOW! THANKS STACY!!
I CAME HOME AND LISTENED TO DEMON SYSTEM 13.
HIGH ON BLASTBEATS!
BANNED IN DC - BAD BRAINS
1-15-02
TODAY WAS PAYDAY
I BOUGHT A TICKET TO GO SEE SLAYER!
TICKETS
THEN I DID MY TAXES. I'M GOING TO GET A BIG REFUND.
HOLY SHIT!
LIES - THE WHO
1-16-02
LAST NIGHT I WENT OUT DRINKING WITH MY FRIENDS
WORK WAS COOL TODAY
GWAR
I WAS REAL TIRED WHEN I GOT HOME
ZZZZZ

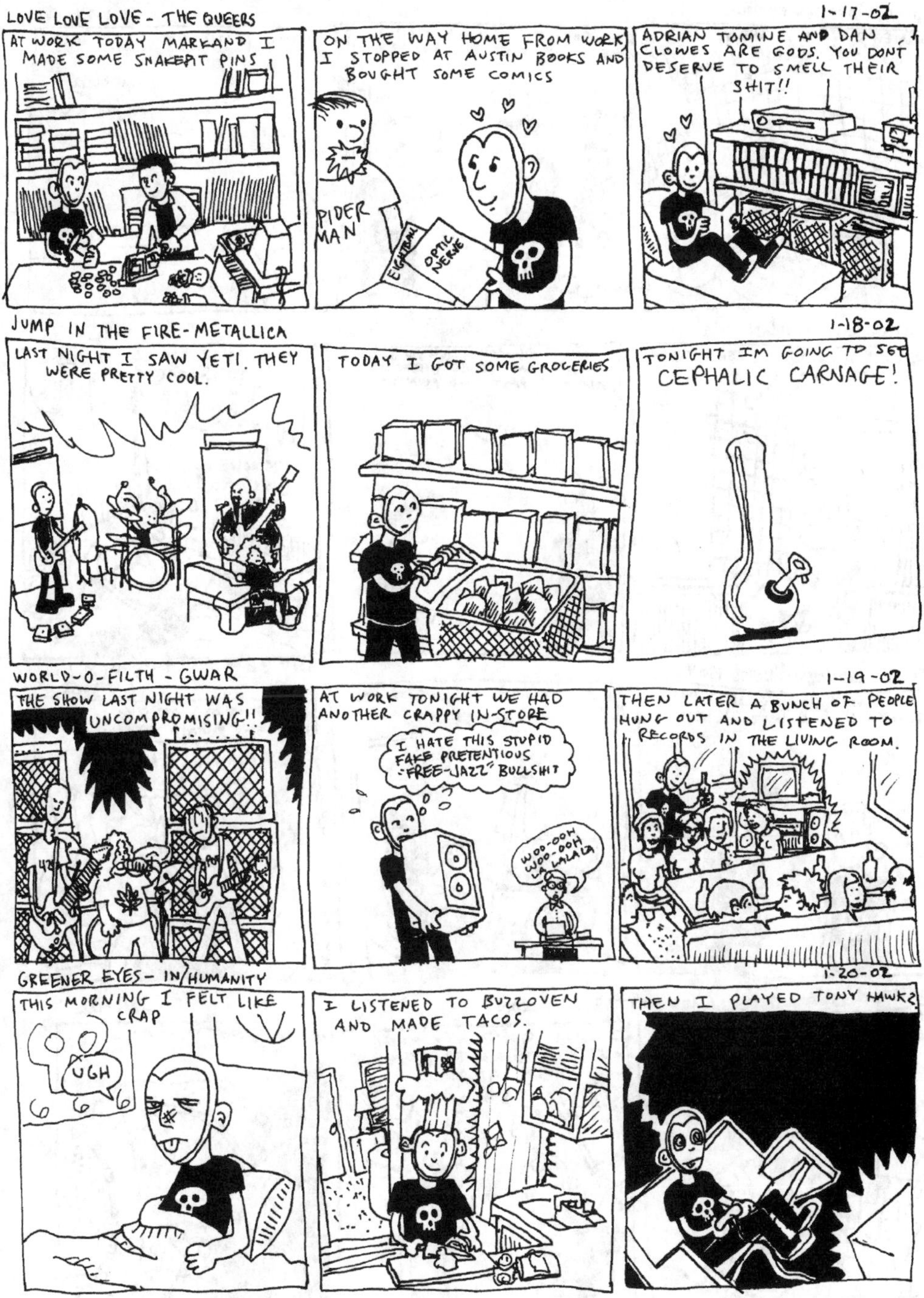
LOVE LOVE LOVE - THE QUEERS
1-17-02
AT WORK TODAY MARK AND I MADE SOME SNAKEPIT PINS
ON THE WAY HOME FROM WORK I STOPPED AT AUSTIN BOOKS AND BOUGHT SOME COMICS
PIDER MAN
EIGHTBALL
OPTIC NERVE
ADRIAN TOMINE AND DAN CLOWES ARE GODS. YOU DON'T DESERVE TO SMELL THEIR SHIT!!
JUMP IN THE FIRE - METALLICA
1-18-02
LAST NIGHT I SAW YETI. THEY WERE PRETTY COOL.
TODAY I GOT SOME GROCERIES
TONIGHT IM GOING TO SEE CEPHALIC CARNAGE!
WORLD-O-FILTH - GWAR
1-19-02
THE SHOW LAST NIGHT WAS UNCOMPROMISING!!
AT WORK TONIGHT WE HAD ANOTHER CRAPPY IN-STORE
I HATE THIS STUPID FAKE PRETENTIOUS "FREE-JAZZ" BULLSHIT
WOO-OOH WOO-OOH LA LALALA
THEN LATER A BUNCH OF PEOPLE HUNG OUT AND LISTENED TO RECORDS IN THE LIVING ROOM.
GREENER EYES - IN/HUMANITY
1-20-02
THIS MORNING I FELT LIKE CRAP
UGH
6 6 6
I LISTENED TO BUZZOVEN AND MADE TACOS.
THEN I PLAYED TONY HAWK2

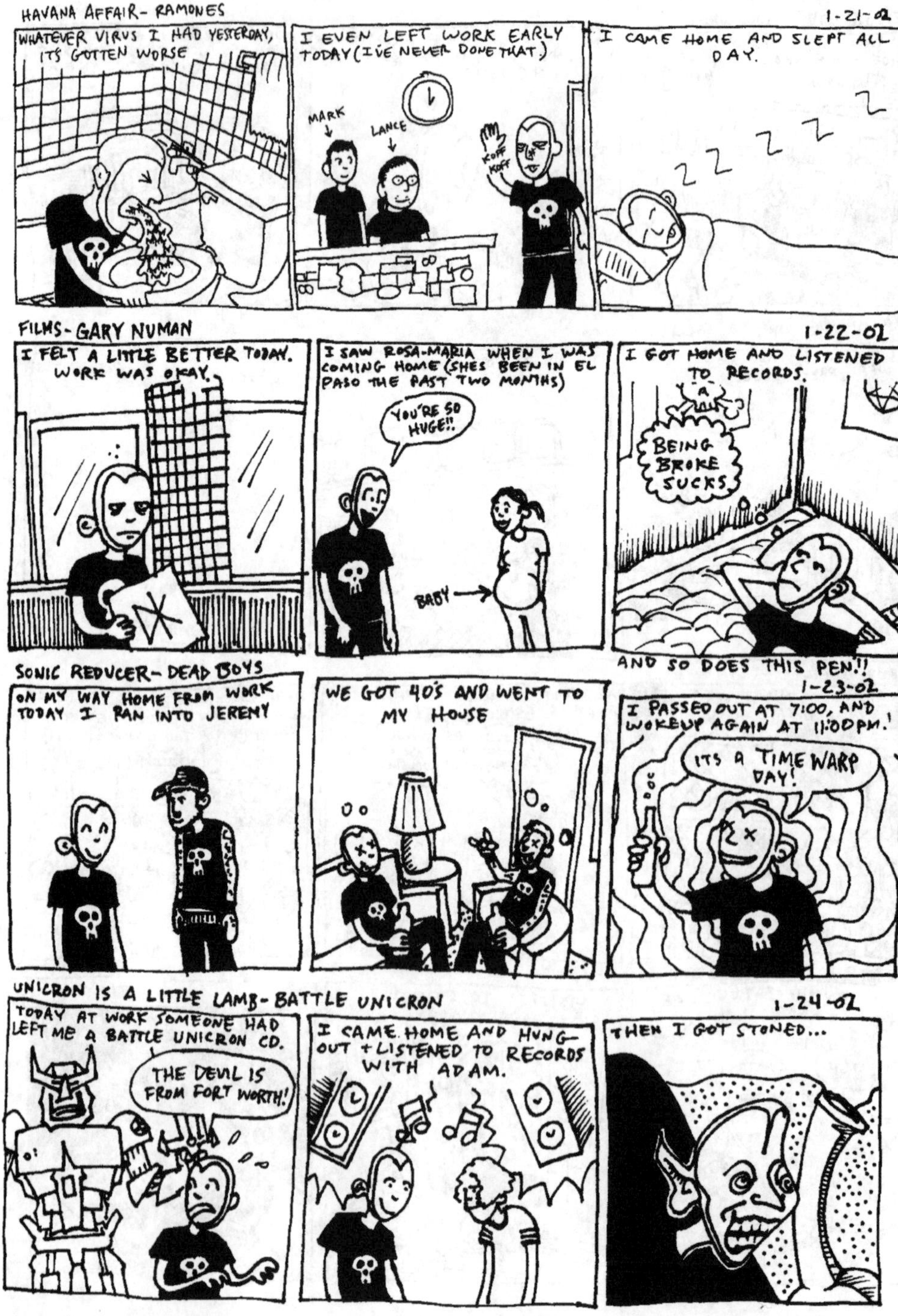
HAVANA AFFAIR- RAMONES
1-21-02
WHATEVER VIRUS I HAD YESTERDAY, ITS GOTTEN WORSE
I EVEN LEFT WORK EARLY TODAY (I'VE NEVER DONE THAT.)
MARK
LANCE
KOFF KOFF
I CAME HOME AND SLEPT ALL DAY.
Z Z Z Z Z
FILMS- GARY NUMAN
1-22-02
I FELT A LITTLE BETTER TODAY. WORK WAS OKAY.
I SAW ROSA-MARIA WHEN I WAS COMING HOME (SHES BEEN IN EL PASO THE PAST TWO MONTHS)
YOU'RE SO HUGE!!
BABY
I GOT HOME AND LISTENED TO RECORDS.
BEING BROKE SUCKS
AND SO DOES THIS PEN!!
SONIC REDUCER- DEAD BOYS
1-23-02
ON MY WAY HOME FROM WORK TODAY I RAN INTO JEREMY
WE GOT 40'S AND WENT TO MY HOUSE
I PASSED OUT AT 7:00, AND WOKEUP AGAIN AT 11:00PM.
ITS A TIME WARP DAY!
UNICRON IS A LITTLE LAMB- BATTLE UNICRON
1-24-02
TODAY AT WORK SOMEONE HAD LEFT ME A BATTLE UNICRON CD.
THE DEVIL IS FROM FORT WORTH!
I CAME HOME AND HUNG-OUT + LISTENED TO RECORDS WITH ADAM.
THEN I GOT STONED...

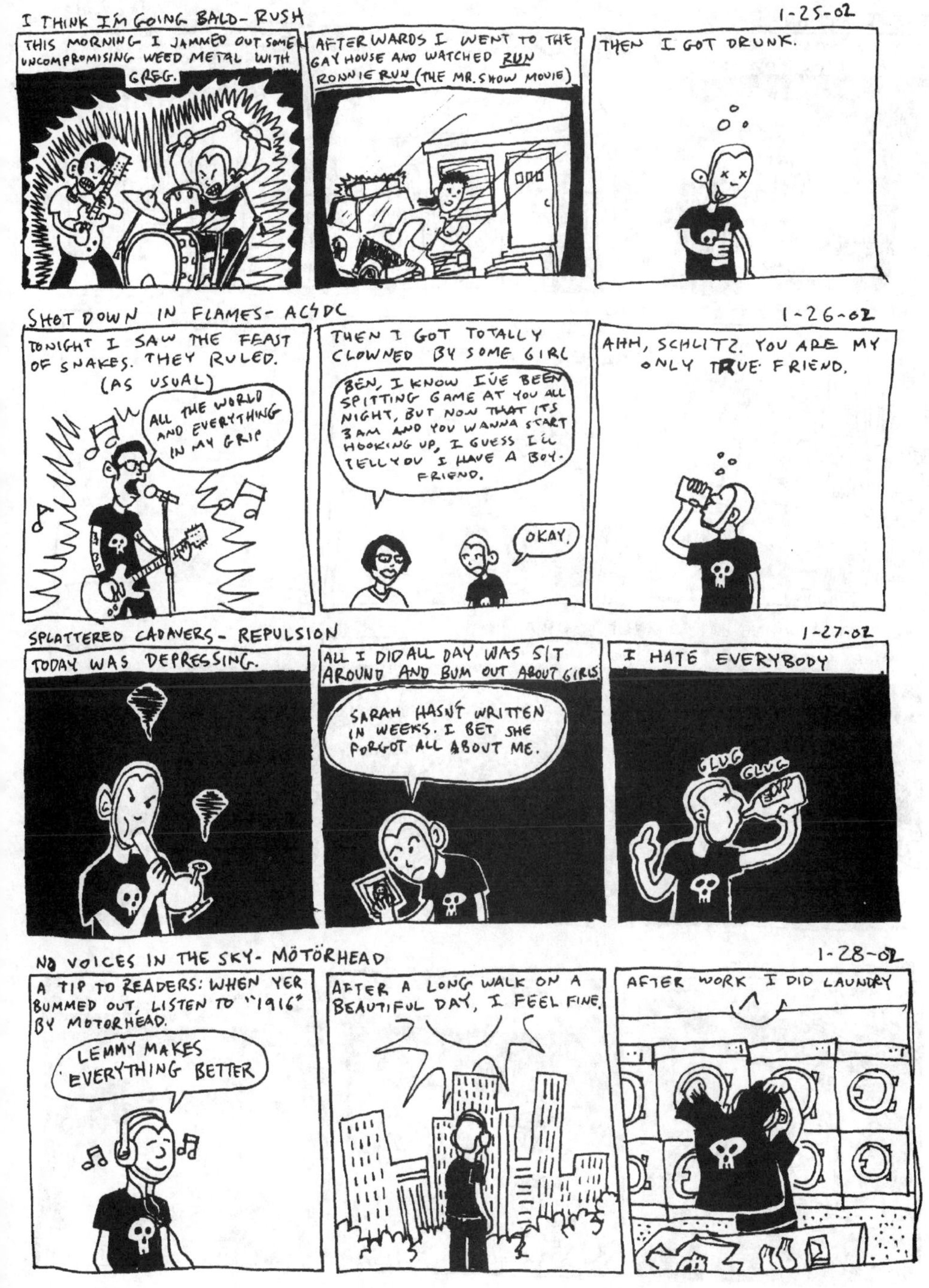
I THINK I'M GOING BALD- RUSH
1-25-02
THIS MORNING I JAMMED OUT SOME UNCOMPROMISING WEED METAL WITH GREG.
AFTERWARDS I WENT TO THE GAY HOUSE AND WATCHED RUN RONNIE RUN (THE MR. SHOW MOVIE)
THEN I GOT DRUNK.
SHOT DOWN IN FLAMES- AC/DC
1-26-02
TONIGHT I SAW THE FEAST OF SNAKES. THEY RULED. (AS USUAL)
ALL THE WORLD AND EVERYTHING IN MY GRIP
THEN I GOT TOTALLY CLOWNED BY SOME GIRL
BEN, I KNOW I'VE BEEN SPITTING GAME AT YOU ALL NIGHT, BUT NOW THAT ITS 3AM AND YOU WANNA START HOOKING UP, I GUESS I'LL TELL YOU I HAVE A BOYFRIEND.
OKAY.
AHH, SCHLITZ. YOU ARE MY ONLY TRUE FRIEND.
SPLATTERED CADAVERS- REPULSION
1-27-02
TODAY WAS DEPRESSING.
ALL I DID ALL DAY WAS SIT AROUND AND BUM OUT ABOUT GIRLS
SARAH HASN'T WRITTEN IN WEEKS. I BET SHE FORGOT ALL ABOUT ME.
I HATE EVERYBODY
GLUG GLUG
NO VOICES IN THE SKY- MÖTÖRHEAD
1-28-02
A TIP TO READERS: WHEN YER BUMMED OUT, LISTEN TO "1916" BY MOTORHEAD.
LEMMY MAKES EVERYTHING BETTER
AFTER A LONG WALK ON A BEAUTIFUL DAY, I FEEL FINE.
AFTER WORK I DID LAUNDRY

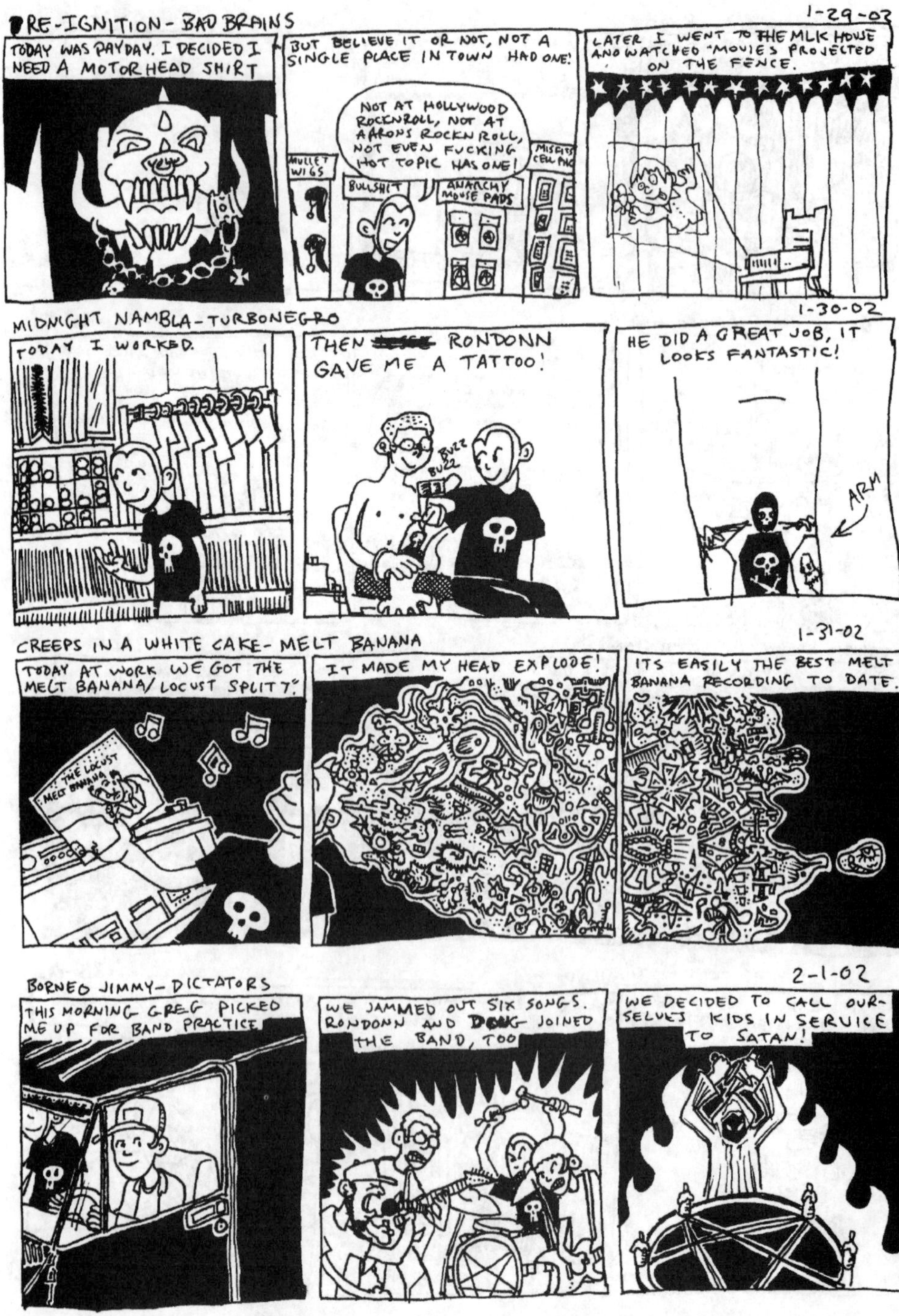

RE-IGNITION - BAD BRAINS
1-29-02
TODAY WAS PAYDAY. I DECIDED I NEED A MOTORHEAD SHIRT
BUT BELIEVE IT OR NOT, NOT A SINGLE PLACE IN TOWN HAD ONE!
NOT AT HOLLYWOOD ROCKNROLL, NOT AT AARONS ROCKNROLL, NOT EVEN FUCKING HOT TOPIC HAS ONE!
MULLET WIGS
BULLSHIT
ANARCHY MOUSE PADS
MISFITS CELL PHO
LATER I WENT TO THE MLK HOUSE AND WATCHED "MOVIES PROJECTED ON THE FENCE.
MIDNIGHT NAMBLA - TURBONEGRO
1-30-02
TODAY I WORKED.
THEN [redacted] RONDONN GAVE ME A TATTOO!
BUZZ
BUZZ
HE DID A GREAT JOB, IT LOOKS FANTASTIC!
ARM
CREEPS IN A WHITE CAKE - MELT BANANA
1-31-02
TODAY AT WORK WE GOT THE MELT BANANA / LOCUST SPLIT 7".
THE LOCUST
MELT BANANA
IT MADE MY HEAD EXPLODE!
ITS EASILY THE BEST MELT BANANA RECORDING TO DATE.
BORNEO JIMMY - DICTATORS
2-1-02
THIS MORNING GREG PICKED ME UP FOR BAND PRACTICE
WE JAMMED OUT SIX SONGS. RONDONN AND [redacted] JOINED THE BAND, TOO
WE DECIDED TO CALL OURSELVES KIDS IN SERVICE TO SATAN!

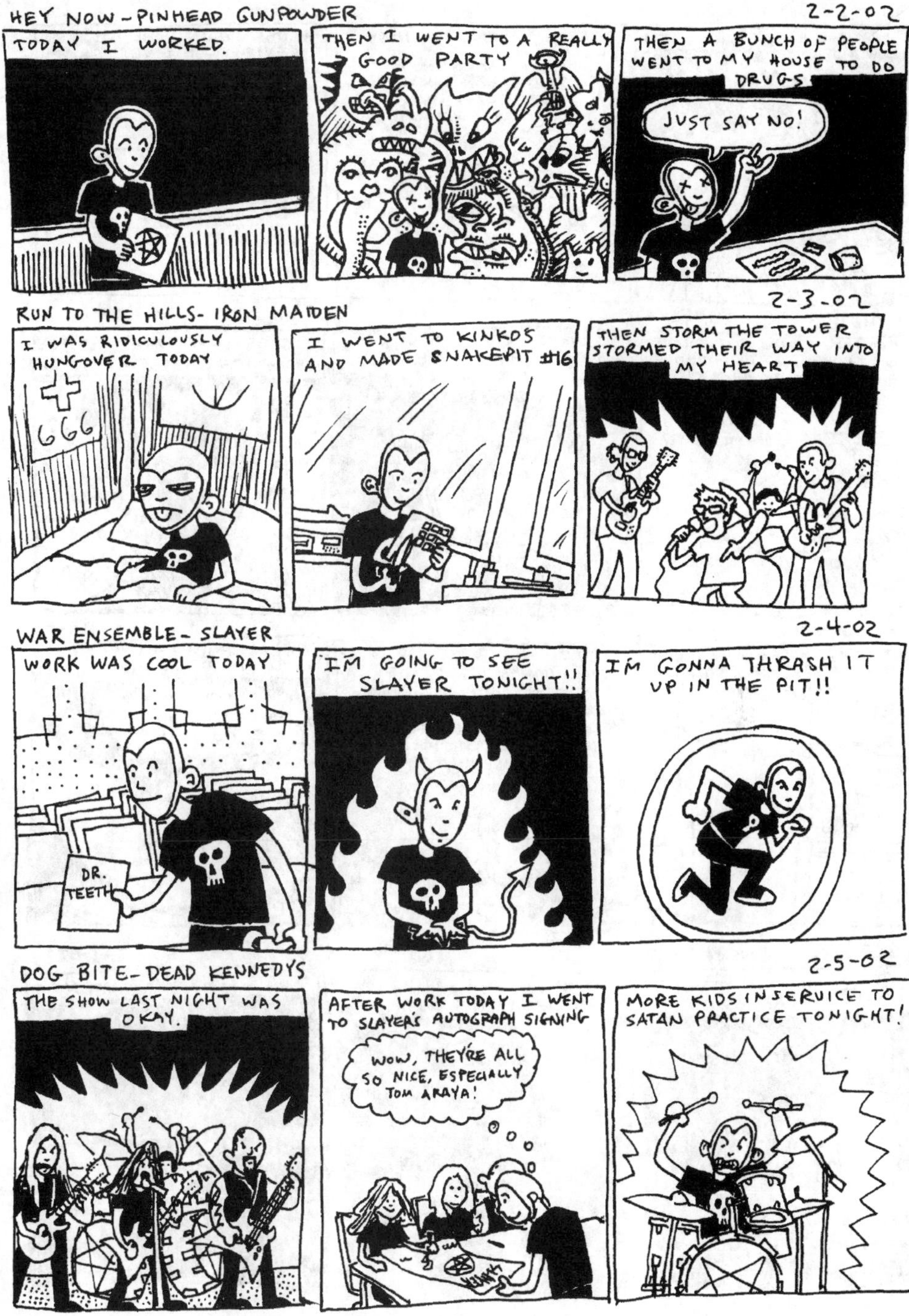
HEY NOW - PINHEAD GUNPOWDER
2-2-02
TODAY I WORKED.
THEN I WENT TO A REALLY GOOD PARTY
THEN A BUNCH OF PEOPLE WENT TO MY HOUSE TO DO DRUGS
JUST SAY NO!
RUN TO THE HILLS - IRON MAIDEN
2-3-02
I WAS RIDICULOUSLY HUNGOVER TODAY
666
I WENT TO KINKOS AND MADE SNAKEPIT #16
THEN STORM THE TOWER STORMED THEIR WAY INTO MY HEART
WAR ENSEMBLE - SLAYER
2-4-02
WORK WAS COOL TODAY
DR. TEETH
I'M GOING TO SEE SLAYER TONIGHT!!
I'M GONNA THRASH IT UP IN THE PIT!!
DOG BITE - DEAD KENNEDYS
2-5-02
THE SHOW LAST NIGHT WAS OKAY.
AFTER WORK TODAY I WENT TO SLAYER'S AUTOGRAPH SIGNING
WOW, THEY'RE ALL SO NICE, ESPECIALLY TOM ARAYA!
MORE KIDS IN SERVICE TO SATAN PRACTICE TONIGHT!

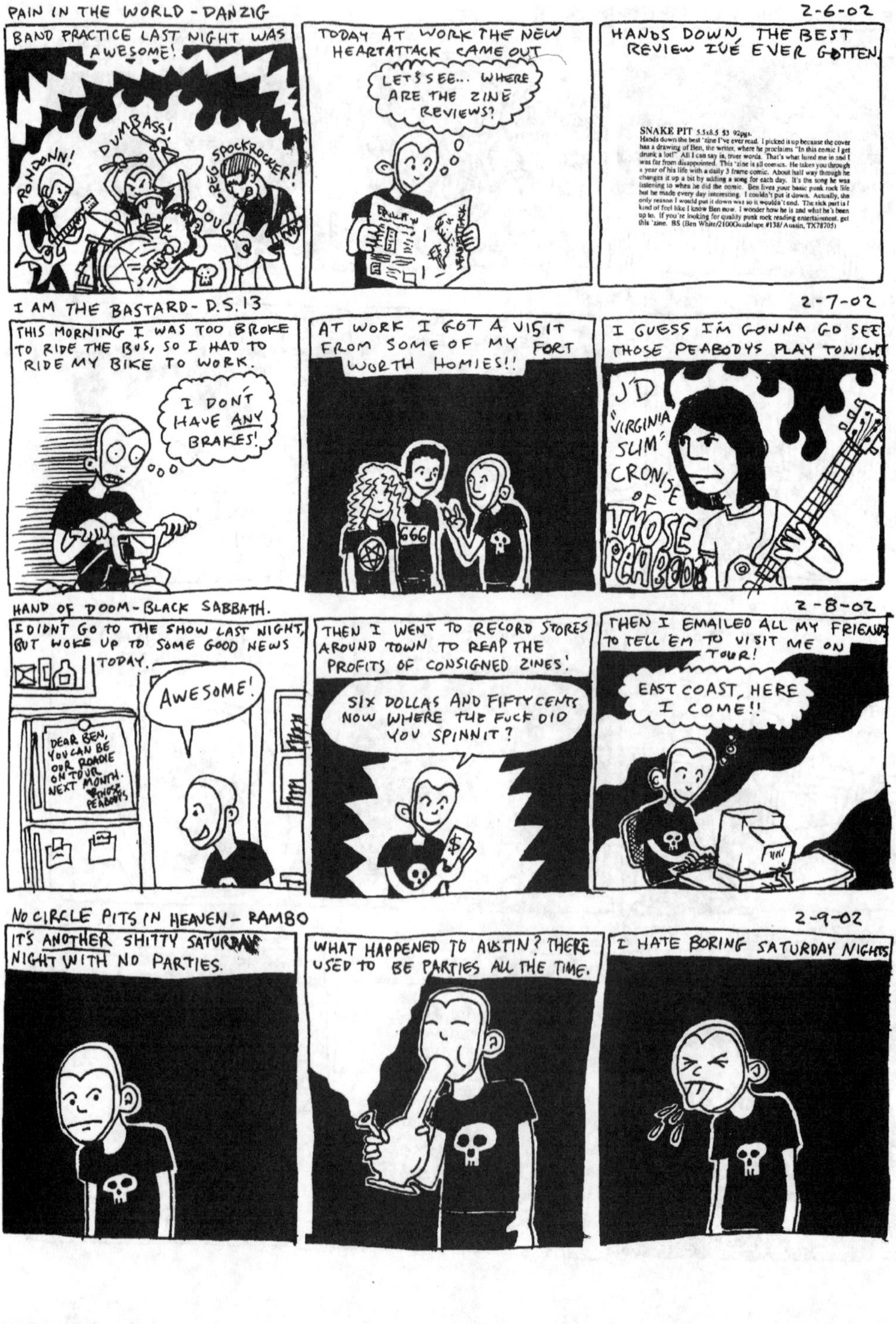
PAIN IN THE WORLD - DANZIG
2-6-02
BAND PRACTICE LAST NIGHT WAS AWESOME!
DUMBASS!
RONDONN!
GREG SPOCKROCKER!
DOUG
TODAY AT WORK THE NEW HEARTATTACK CAME OUT
LET'S SEE... WHERE ARE THE ZINE REVIEWS?
HANDS DOWN, THE BEST REVIEW I'VE EVER GOTTEN.
SNAKE PIT 5.5x8.5 $3 92pgs.
Hands down the best 'zine I've ever read. I picked it up because the cover has a drawing of Ben, the writer, where he proclaims "In this comic I get drunk a lot!" All I can say is, truer words. That's what lured me in and I was far from disappointed. This 'zine is all comics. He takes you through a year of his life with a daily 3 frame comic. About half way through he changes it up a bit by adding a song for each day. It's the song he was listening to when he did the comic. Ben lives your basic punk rock life but he made every day interesting. I couldn't put it down. Actually, the only reason I would put it down was so it wouldn't end. The sick part is I kind of feel like I know Ben now. I wonder how he is and what he's been up to. If you're looking for quality punk rock reading entertainment, get this 'zine. BS (Ben White/2100Guadalupe #138/ Austin, TX78705)
I AM THE BASTARD - D.S.13
2-7-02
THIS MORNING I WAS TOO BROKE TO RIDE THE BUS, SO I HAD TO RIDE MY BIKE TO WORK.
I DON'T HAVE ANY BRAKES!
AT WORK I GOT A VISIT FROM SOME OF MY FORT WORTH HOMIES!!
666
I GUESS I'M GONNA GO SEE THOSE PEABODYS PLAY TONIGHT
J'D "VIRGINIA SLIM" CRONISE OF THOSE PEABODYS
HAND OF DOOM - BLACK SABBATH.
2-8-02
I DIDN'T GO TO THE SHOW LAST NIGHT, BUT WOKE UP TO SOME GOOD NEWS TODAY.
DEAR BEN, YOU CAN BE OUR ROADIE ON TOUR NEXT MONTH. ♥THOSE PEABODYS
AWESOME!
THEN I WENT TO RECORD STORES AROUND TOWN TO REAP THE PROFITS OF CONSIGNED ZINES!
SIX DOLLAS AND FIFTY CENTS NOW WHERE THE FUCK DID YOU SPINNIT?
$
THEN I EMAILED ALL MY FRIENDS TO TELL 'EM TO VISIT ME ON TOUR!
EAST COAST, HERE I COME!!
NO CIRCLE PITS IN HEAVEN - RAMBO
2-9-02
IT'S ANOTHER SHITTY SATURDAY NIGHT WITH NO PARTIES.
WHAT HAPPENED TO AUSTIN? THERE USED TO BE PARTIES ALL THE TIME.
I HATE BORING SATURDAY NIGHTS.

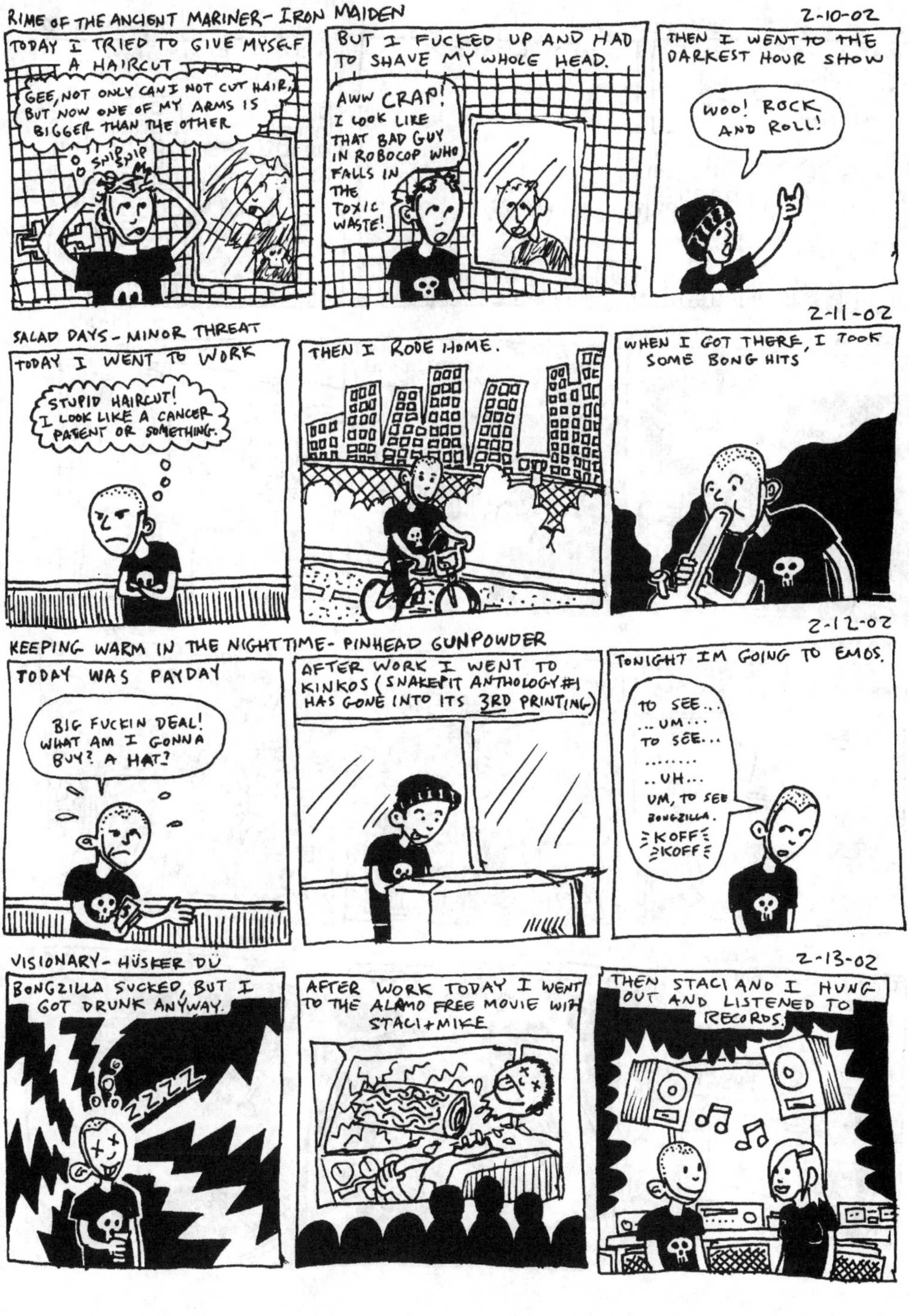
RIME OF THE ANCIENT MARINER - IRON MAIDEN
2-10-02
TODAY I TRIED TO GIVE MYSELF A HAIRCUT
GEE, NOT ONLY CAN I NOT CUT HAIR, BUT NOW ONE OF MY ARMS IS BIGGER THAN THE OTHER
SNIP SNIP
BUT I FUCKED UP AND HAD TO SHAVE MY WHOLE HEAD.
AWW CRAP! I LOOK LIKE THAT BAD GUY IN ROBOCOP WHO FALLS IN THE TOXIC WASTE!
THEN I WENT TO THE DARKEST HOUR SHOW
WOO! ROCK AND ROLL!
SALAD DAYS - MINOR THREAT
2-11-02
TODAY I WENT TO WORK
STUPID HAIRCUT! I LOOK LIKE A CANCER PATIENT OR SOMETHING.
THEN I RODE HOME.
WHEN I GOT THERE, I TOOK SOME BONG HITS
KEEPING WARM IN THE NIGHTTIME - PINHEAD GUNPOWDER
2-12-02
TODAY WAS PAYDAY
BIG FUCKIN DEAL! WHAT AM I GONNA BUY? A HAT?
AFTER WORK I WENT TO KINKOS (SNAKEPIT ANTHOLOGY #1 HAS GONE INTO ITS 3RD PRINTING)
TONIGHT IM GOING TO EMOS.
TO SEE... ...UM... TO SEE... ....UH... UM, TO SEE BONGZILLA.
KOFF KOFF
VISIONARY - HÜSKER DÜ
2-13-02
BONGZILLA SUCKED, BUT I GOT DRUNK ANYWAY.
ZZZZ
AFTER WORK TODAY I WENT TO THE ALAMO FREE MOVIE WITH STACI + MIKE
THEN STACI AND I HUNG OUT AND LISTENED TO RECORDS.

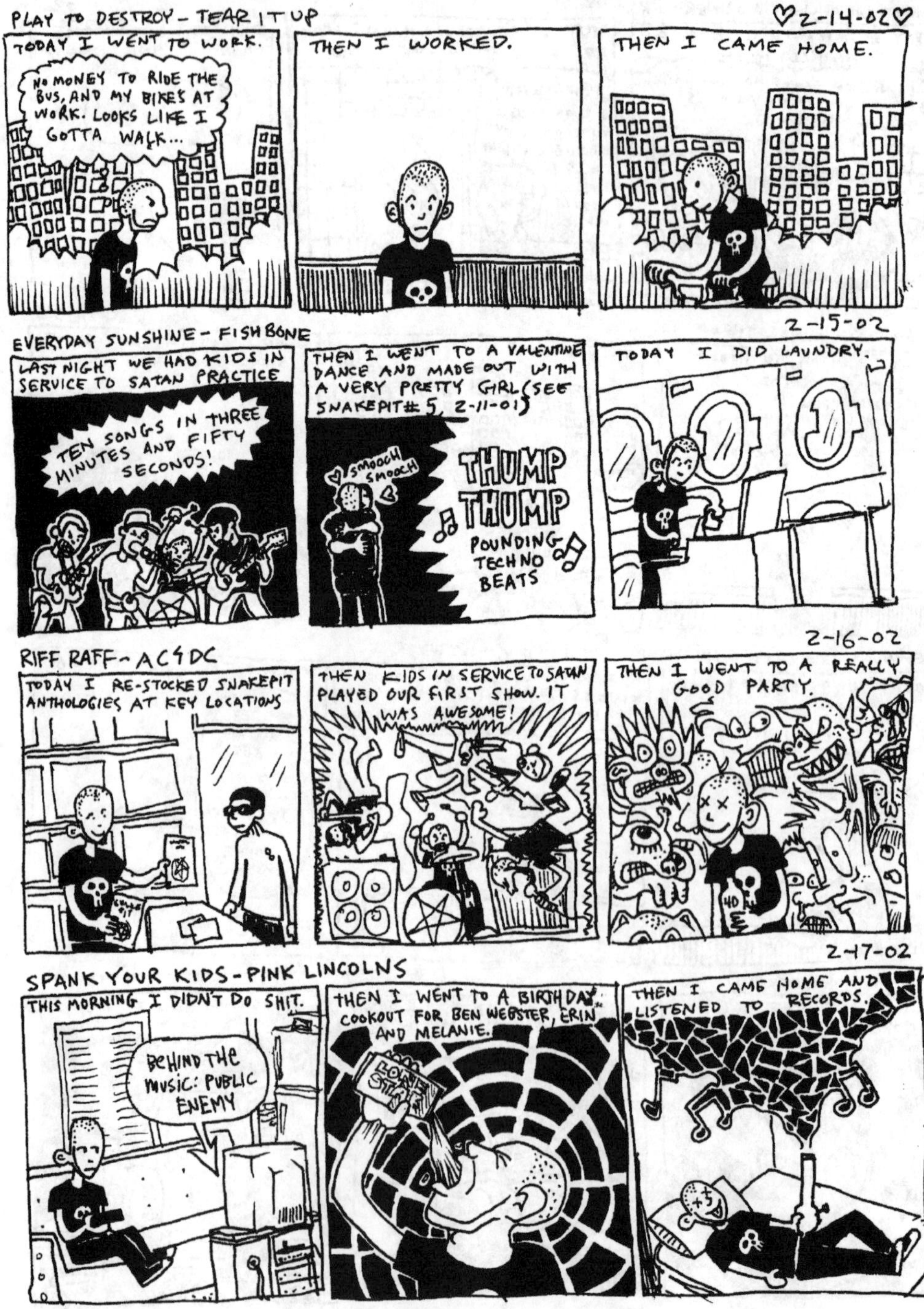
PLAY TO DESTROY - TEAR IT UP
♡2-14-02♡
TODAY I WENT TO WORK.
NO MONEY TO RIDE THE BUS, AND MY BIKE'S AT WORK. LOOKS LIKE I GOTTA WALK...
THEN I WORKED.
THEN I CAME HOME.
2-15-02
EVERYDAY SUNSHINE - FISHBONE
LAST NIGHT WE HAD KIDS IN SERVICE TO SATAN PRACTICE
TEN SONGS IN THREE MINUTES AND FIFTY SECONDS!
THEN I WENT TO A VALENTINE DANCE AND MADE OUT WITH A VERY PRETTY GIRL (SEE SNAKEPIT #5, 2-11-01)
SMOOCH SMOOCH
THUMP THUMP
POUNDING TECHNO BEATS
TODAY I DID LAUNDRY.
2-16-02
RIFF RAFF - AC/DC
TODAY I RE-STOCKED SNAKEPIT ANTHOLOGIES AT KEY LOCATIONS
THEN KIDS IN SERVICE TO SATAN PLAYED OUR FIRST SHOW. IT WAS AWESOME!
THEN I WENT TO A REALLY GOOD PARTY.
40
2-17-02
SPANK YOUR KIDS - PINK LINCOLNS
THIS MORNING I DIDN'T DO SHIT.
BEHIND THE MUSIC: PUBLIC ENEMY
THEN I WENT TO A BIRTHDAY COOKOUT FOR BEN WEBSTER, ERIN AND MELANIE.
THEN I CAME HOME AND LISTENED TO RECORDS.

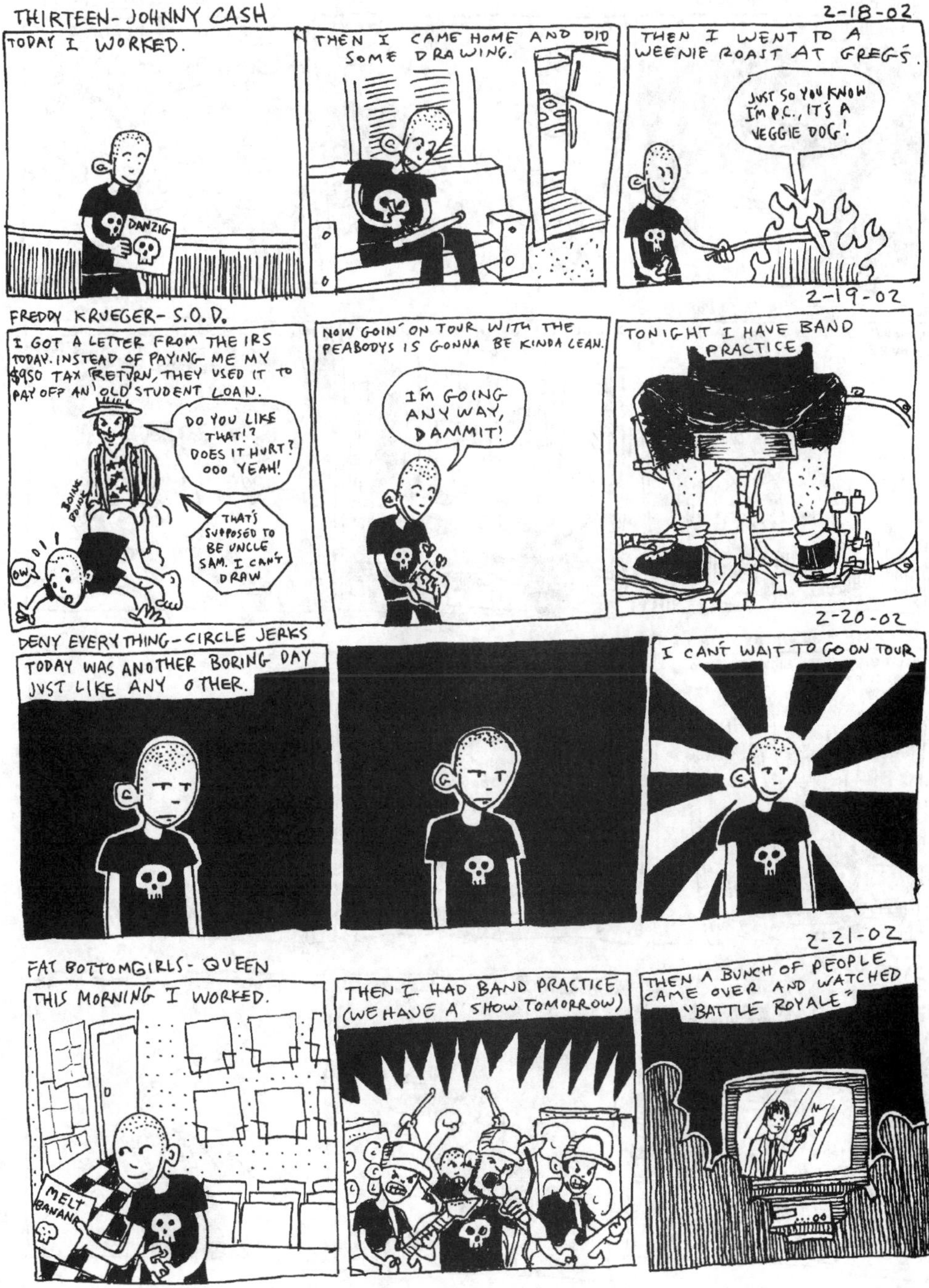
THIRTEEN- JOHNNY CASH
2-18-02
TODAY I WORKED.
DANZIG
THEN I CAME HOME AND DID SOME DRAWING.
THEN I WENT TO A WEENIE ROAST AT GREG'S.
JUST SO YOU KNOW I'M P.C., IT'S A VEGGIE DOG!
2-19-02
FREDDY KRUEGER- S.O.D.
I GOT A LETTER FROM THE IRS TODAY. INSTEAD OF PAYING ME MY $950 TAX RETURN, THEY USED IT TO PAY OFF AN OLD STUDENT LOAN.
DO YOU LIKE THAT!? DOES IT HURT? OOO YEAH!
BOING BOING
OW
THAT'S SUPPOSED TO BE UNCLE SAM. I CAN'T DRAW
NOW GOIN' ON TOUR WITH THE PEABODYS IS GONNA BE KINDA LEAN.
I'M GOING ANYWAY, DAMMIT!
TONIGHT I HAVE BAND PRACTICE
2-20-02
DENY EVERYTHING- CIRCLE JERKS
TODAY WAS ANOTHER BORING DAY JUST LIKE ANY OTHER.
I CAN'T WAIT TO GO ON TOUR
2-21-02
FAT BOTTOM GIRLS- QUEEN
THIS MORNING I WORKED.
MELT BANANA
THEN I HAD BAND PRACTICE (WE HAVE A SHOW TOMORROW)
THEN A BUNCH OF PEOPLE CAME OVER AND WATCHED "BATTLE ROYALE"

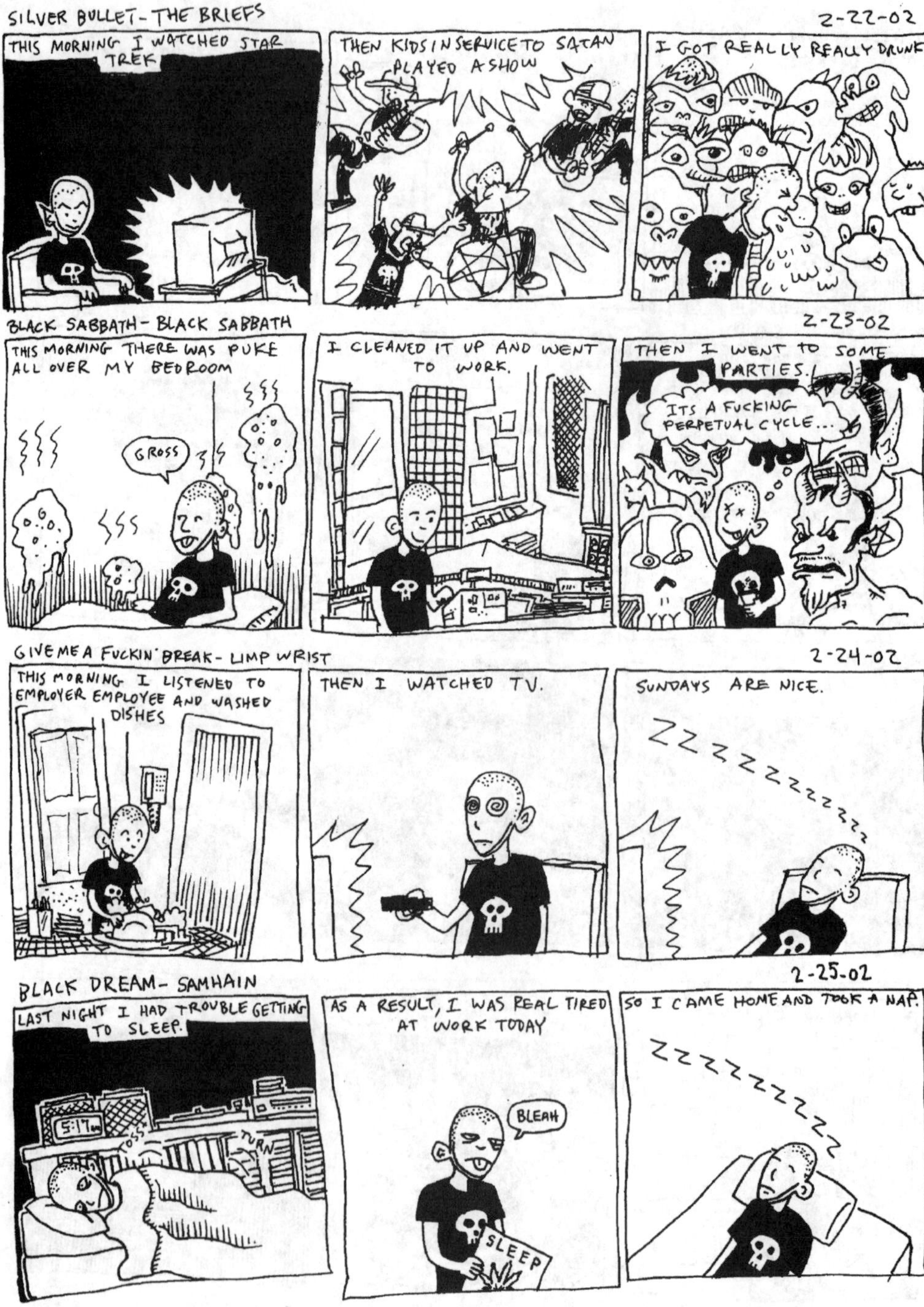
SILVER BULLET - THE BRIEFS
2-22-02
THIS MORNING I WATCHED STAR TREK
THEN KIDS IN SERVICE TO SATAN PLAYED A SHOW
I GOT REALLY REALLY DRUNK.
BLACK SABBATH - BLACK SABBATH
2-23-02
THIS MORNING THERE WAS PUKE ALL OVER MY BEDROOM
GROSS
I CLEANED IT UP AND WENT TO WORK.
THEN I WENT TO SOME PARTIES.
ITS A FUCKING PERPETUAL CYCLE...
GIVE ME A FUCKIN' BREAK - LIMP WRIST
2-24-02
THIS MORNING I LISTENED TO EMPLOYER EMPLOYEE AND WASHED DISHES
THEN I WATCHED T.V.
SUNDAYS ARE NICE.
ZZZZZZZZZZZ
BLACK DREAM - SAMHAIN
2-25-02
LAST NIGHT I HAD TROUBLE GETTING TO SLEEP.
5:17
TOSS
TURN
AS A RESULT, I WAS REAL TIRED AT WORK TODAY
BLEAH
SLEEP
SO I CAME HOME AND TOOK A NAP.
ZZZZZZZZZZ

THE ROLLER-MAN IS THE BASTARD. 2-26-02

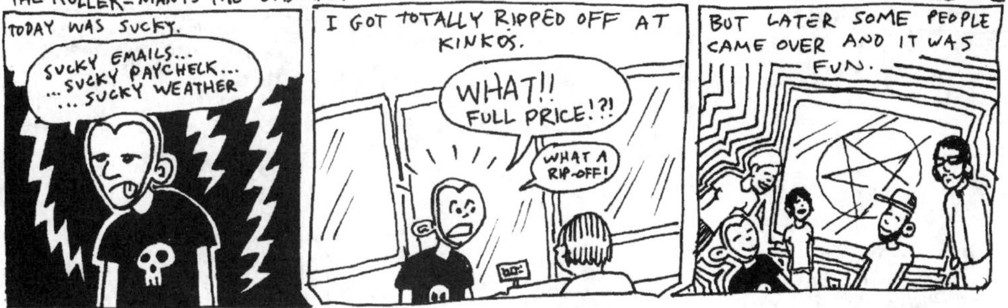
TODAY WAS SUCKY.
SUCKY EMAILS... SUCKY PAYCHECK... ...SUCKY WEATHER
I GOT TOTALLY RIPPED OFF AT KINKOS.
WHAT!! FULL PRICE!?!
WHAT A RIP-OFF!
BUT LATER SOME PEOPLE CAME OVER AND IT WAS FUN.

NEW GIRLFRIEND - MTX 2-27-02

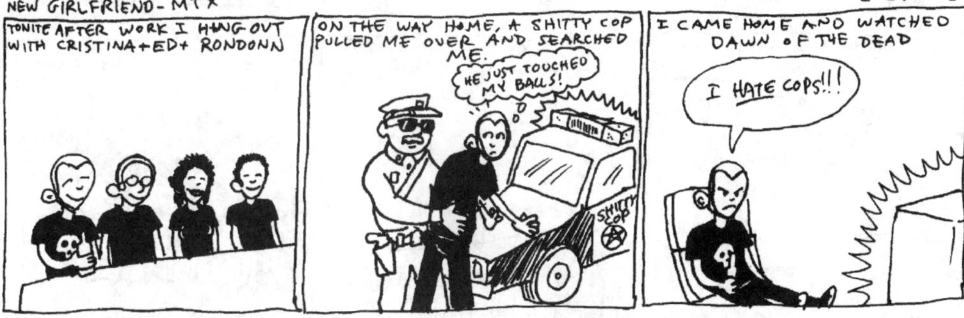
TONITE AFTER WORK I HUNG OUT WITH CRISTINA + ED + RONDONN
ON THE WAY HOME, A SHITTY COP PULLED ME OVER AND SEARCHED ME.
HE JUST TOUCHED MY BALLS!
SHITTY COP
I CAME HOME AND WATCHED DAWN OF THE DEAD
I HATE COPS!!!

SCANTRON SLAMATHON - MUNICIPAL WASTE 2-28-02

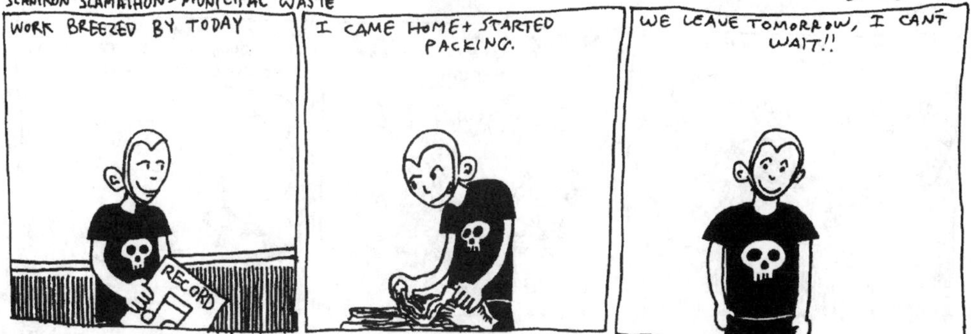
WORK BREEZED BY TODAY
RECORD
I CAME HOME + STARTED PACKING.
WE LEAVE TOMORROW, I CANT WAIT!!

GET RID OF THAT GIRL - THE DONNAS (THOSE PEABODYS/TRAIL OF DEAD TOUR) 3-1-02

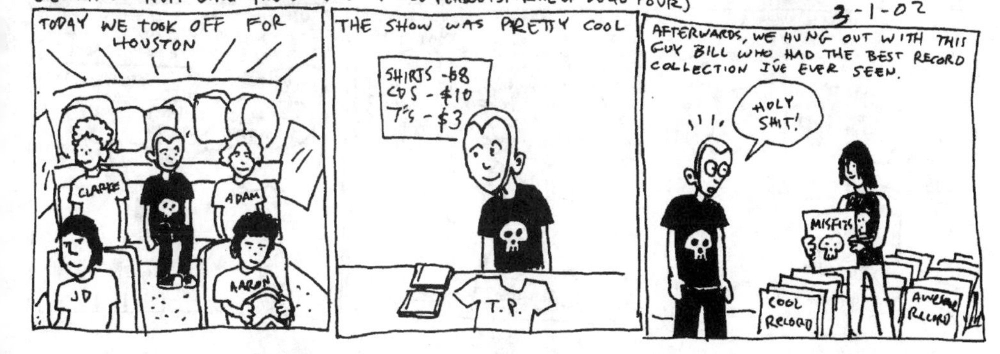
TODAY WE TOOK OFF FOR HOUSTON
CLARKE
ADAM
JD
AARON
THE SHOW WAS PRETTY COOL
SHIRTS - $8
CDS - $10
7"S - $3
T.P.
AFTERWARDS, WE HUNG OUT WITH THIS GUY BILL WHO HAD THE BEST RECORD COLLECTION I'VE EVER SEEN.
HOLY SHIT!
MISFITS
COOL RECORD
AWESOME RECORD

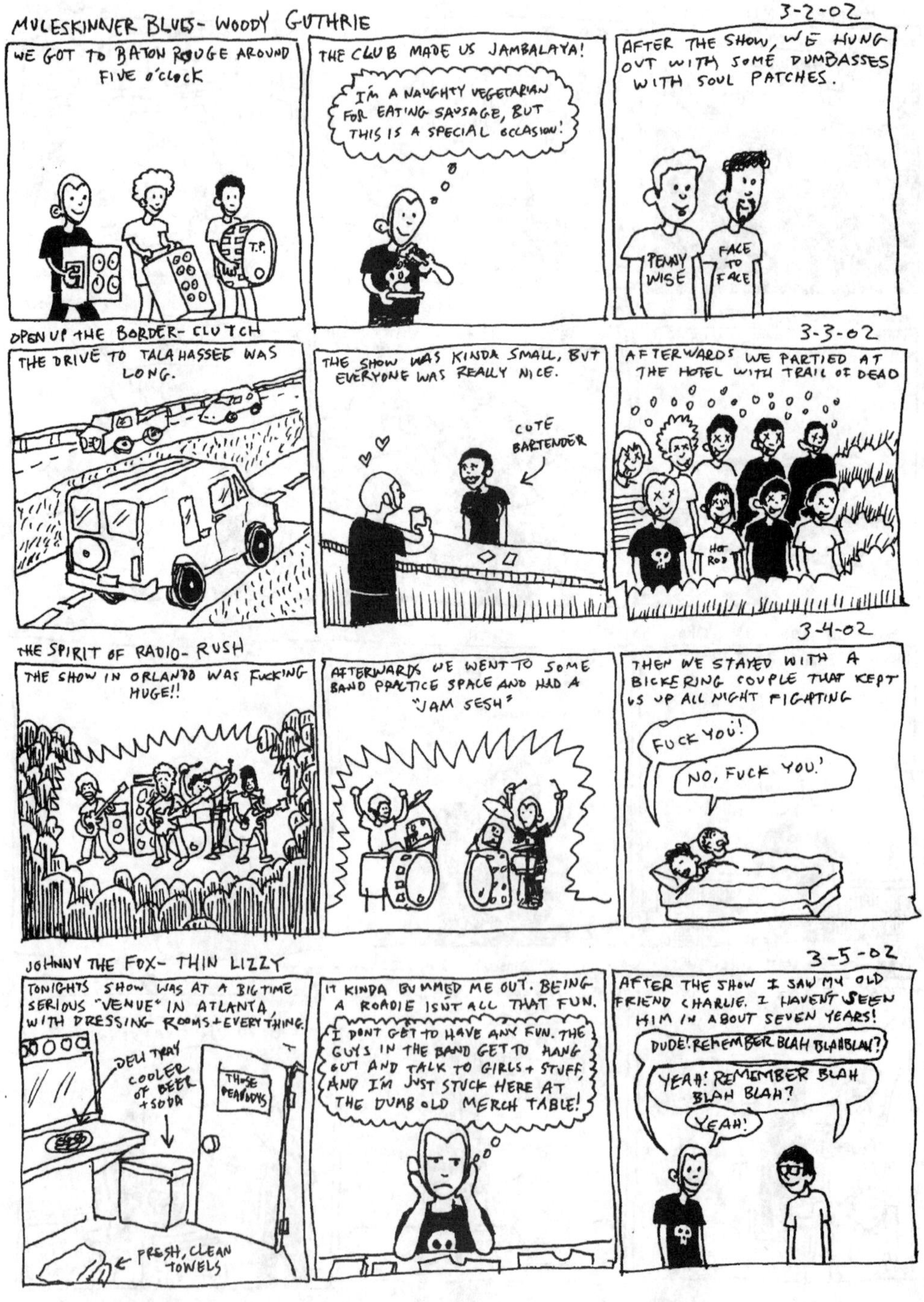
MULESKINNER BLUES- WOODY GUTHRIE
3-2-02
WE GOT TO BATON ROUGE AROUND FIVE O'CLOCK
T.P.
THE CLUB MADE US JAMBALAYA!
I'M A NAUGHTY VEGETARIAN FOR EATING SAUSAGE, BUT THIS IS A SPECIAL OCCASION!
AFTER THE SHOW, WE HUNG OUT WITH SOME DUMBASSES WITH SOUL PATCHES.
PENNY WISE
FACE TO FACE
OPEN UP THE BORDER- CLUTCH
3-3-02
THE DRIVE TO TALAHASSEE WAS LONG.
THE SHOW WAS KINDA SMALL, BUT EVERYONE WAS REALLY NICE.
CUTE BARTENDER
AFTERWARDS WE PARTIED AT THE HOTEL WITH TRAIL OF DEAD
HOT ROD
THE SPIRIT OF RADIO- RUSH
3-4-02
THE SHOW IN ORLANDO WAS FUCKING HUGE!!
AFTERWARDS WE WENT TO SOME BAND PRACTICE SPACE AND HAD A "JAM SESH"
THEN WE STAYED WITH A BICKERING COUPLE THAT KEPT US UP ALL NIGHT FIGHTING
FUCK YOU!
NO, FUCK YOU!
JOHNNY THE FOX- THIN LIZZY
3-5-02
TONIGHTS SHOW WAS AT A BIG TIME SERIOUS "VENUE" IN ATLANTA, WITH DRESSING ROOMS + EVERYTHING.
DELI TRAY
COOLER OF BEER + SODA
THOSE PEABODYS
FRESH, CLEAN TOWELS
IT KINDA BUMMED ME OUT. BEING A ROADIE ISN'T ALL THAT FUN.
I DONT GET TO HAVE ANY FUN. THE GUYS IN THE BAND GET TO HANG OUT AND TALK TO GIRLS + STUFF, AND I'M JUST STUCK HERE AT THE DUMB OLD MERCH TABLE!
AFTER THE SHOW I SAW MY OLD FRIEND CHARLIE. I HAVENT SEEN HIM IN ABOUT SEVEN YEARS!
DUDE! REMEMBER BLAH BLAH BLAH?
YEAH! REMEMBER BLAH BLAH BLAH?
YEAH!

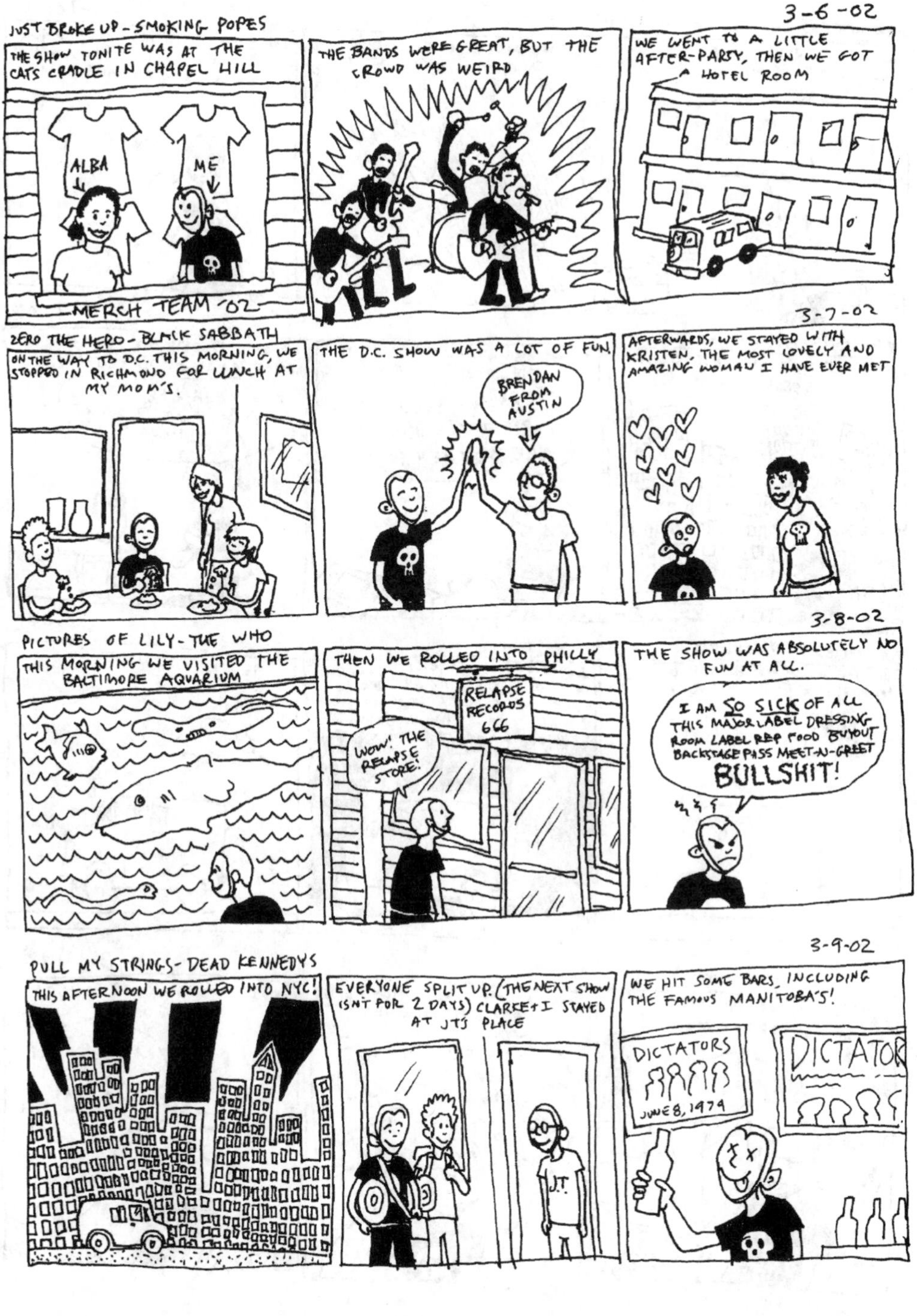
3-6-02
JUST BROKE UP - SMOKING POPES
THE SHOW TONITE WAS AT THE CATS CRADLE IN CHAPEL HILL
ALBA
ME
MERCH TEAM '02
THE BANDS WERE GREAT, BUT THE CROWD WAS WEIRD
WE WENT TO A LITTLE AFTER-PARTY, THEN WE GOT A HOTEL ROOM
3-7-02
ZERO THE HERO - BLACK SABBATH
ON THE WAY TO D.C. THIS MORNING, WE STOPPED IN RICHMOND FOR LUNCH AT MY MOM'S.
THE D.C. SHOW WAS A LOT OF FUN.
BRENDAN FROM AUSTIN
AFTERWARDS, WE STAYED WITH KRISTEN, THE MOST LOVELY AND AMAZING WOMAN I HAVE EVER MET
3-8-02
PICTURES OF LILY - THE WHO
THIS MORNING WE VISITED THE BALTIMORE AQUARIUM
THEN WE ROLLED INTO PHILLY
RELAPSE RECORDS 666
WOW! THE RELAPSE STORE!
THE SHOW WAS ABSOLUTELY NO FUN AT ALL.
I AM SO SICK OF ALL THIS MAJOR LABEL DRESSING ROOM LABEL REP FOOD BUYOUT BACKSTAGE PASS MEET-N-GREET BULLSHIT!
3-9-02
PULL MY STRINGS - DEAD KENNEDYS
THIS AFTERNOON WE ROLLED INTO NYC!
EVERYONE SPLIT UP. (THE NEXT SHOW ISN'T FOR 2 DAYS) CLARKE + I STAYED AT JT'S PLACE
J.T.
WE HIT SOME BARS, INCLUDING THE FAMOUS MANITOBA'S!
DICTATORS
JUNE 8, 1974
DICTATOR

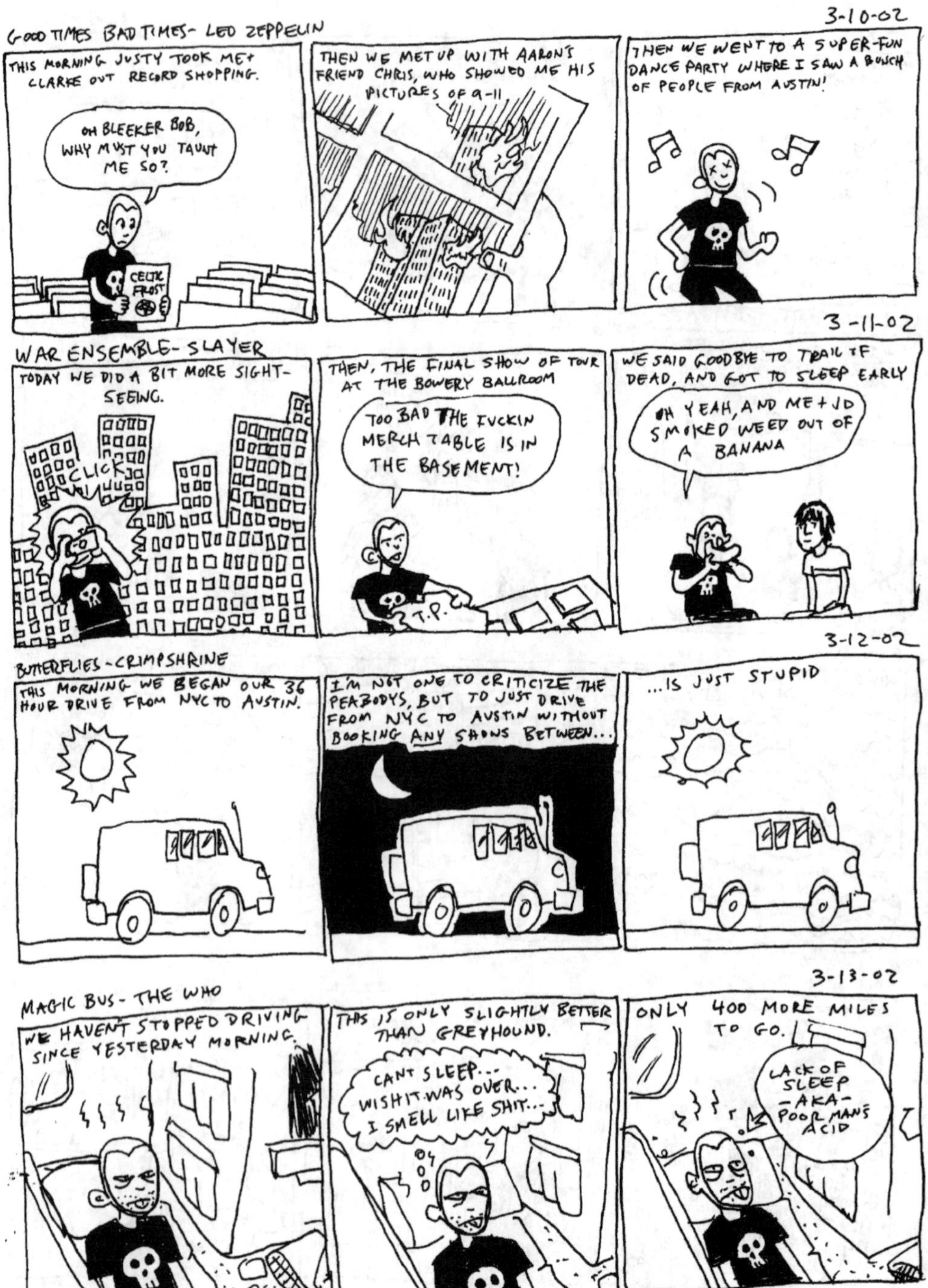
3-10-02
GOOD TIMES BAD TIMES- LED ZEPPELIN
THIS MORNING JUSTY TOOK ME + CLARKE OUT RECORD SHOPPING.
OH BLEEKER BOB, WHY MUST YOU TAUNT ME SO?
CELTIC FROST
THEN WE MET UP WITH AARON'S FRIEND CHRIS, WHO SHOWED ME HIS
PICTURES OF 9-11
THEN WE WENT TO A SUPER-FUN DANCE PARTY WHERE I SAW A BUNCH OF PEOPLE FROM AUSTIN!
3-11-02
WAR ENSEMBLE- SLAYER
TODAY WE DID A BIT MORE SIGHT-SEEING.
CLICK
THEN, THE FINAL SHOW OF TOUR AT THE BOWERY BALLROOM
TOO BAD THE FUCKIN MERCH TABLE IS IN THE BASEMENT!
T.P.
WE SAID GOODBYE TO TRAIL OF DEAD, AND GOT TO SLEEP EARLY
OH YEAH, AND ME + JD SMOKED WEED OUT OF A BANANA
3-12-02
BUTTERFLIES - CRIMPSHRINE
THIS MORNING WE BEGAN OUR 36 HOUR DRIVE FROM NYC TO AUSTIN.
I'M NOT ONE TO CRITICIZE THE PEABODYS, BUT TO JUST DRIVE FROM NYC TO AUSTIN WITHOUT BOOKING ANY SHOWS BETWEEN...
...IS JUST STUPID
3-13-02
MAGIC BUS - THE WHO
WE HAVEN'T STOPPED DRIVING SINCE YESTERDAY MORNING.
THIS IS ONLY SLIGHTLY BETTER THAN GREYHOUND.
CAN'T SLEEP... WISH IT WAS OVER... I SMELL LIKE SHIT...
ONLY 400 MORE MILES TO GO.
LACK OF SLEEP -AKA- POOR MANS ACID

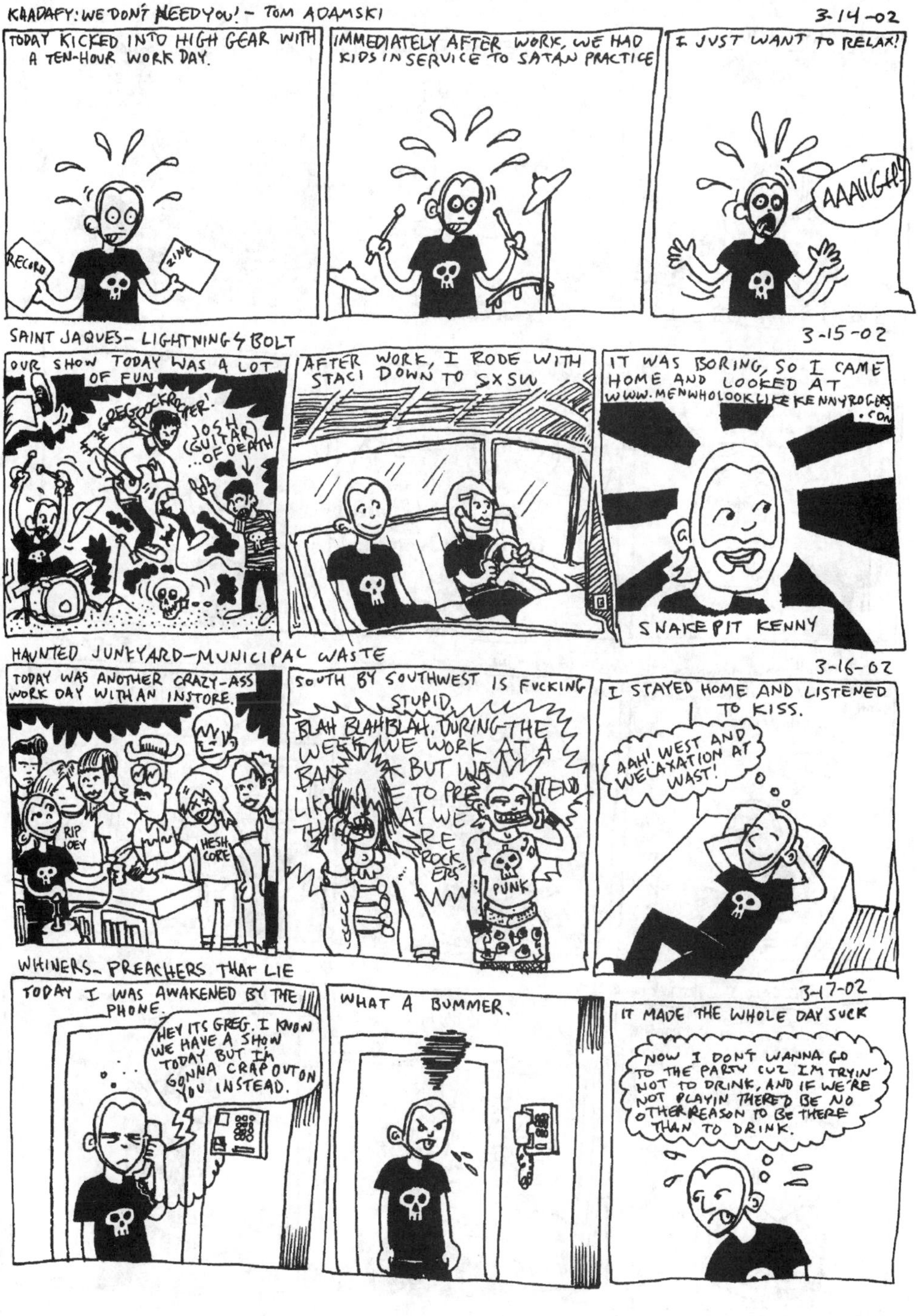
KAADAFY: WE DON'T NEED YOU! - TOM ADAMSKI
3-14-02
TODAY KICKED INTO HIGH GEAR WITH A TEN-HOUR WORK DAY.
RECORD
ZINE
IMMEDIATELY AFTER WORK, WE HAD KIDS IN SERVICE TO SATAN PRACTICE
I JUST WANT TO RELAX!
AAAIIGH!
SAINT JAQUES - LIGHTNING BOLT
3-15-02
OUR SHOW TODAY WAS A LOT OF FUN
GREG ROCKROCKER!
JOSH (GUITAR) ...OF DEATH
AFTER WORK, I RODE WITH STACI DOWN TO SXSW
IT WAS BORING, SO I CAME HOME AND LOOKED AT WWW.MENWHOLOOKLIKEKENNYROGERS.COM
SNAKEPIT KENNY
HAUNTED JUNKYARD - MUNICIPAL WASTE
3-16-02
TODAY WAS ANOTHER CRAZY-ASS WORK DAY WITH AN INSTORE.
RIP JOEY
HESH CORE
SOUTH BY SOUTHWEST IS FUCKING STUPID.
BLAH BLAH BLAH. DURING THE WEEK WE WORK AT A
ROCKERS
PUNK
I STAYED HOME AND LISTENED TO KISS.
AAH! WEST AND WELAXATION AT WAST!
WHINERS - PREACHERS THAT LIE
3-17-02
TODAY I WAS AWAKENED BY THE PHONE.
HEY ITS GREG. I KNOW WE HAVE A SHOW TODAY BUT I'M GONNA CRAP OUT ON YOU INSTEAD.
WHAT A BUMMER.
IT MADE THE WHOLE DAY SUCK
NOW I DON'T WANNA GO TO THE PARTY CUZ I'M TRYIN' NOT TO DRINK, AND IF WE'RE NOT PLAYIN THERE'D BE NO OTHER REASON TO BE THERE THAN TO DRINK.

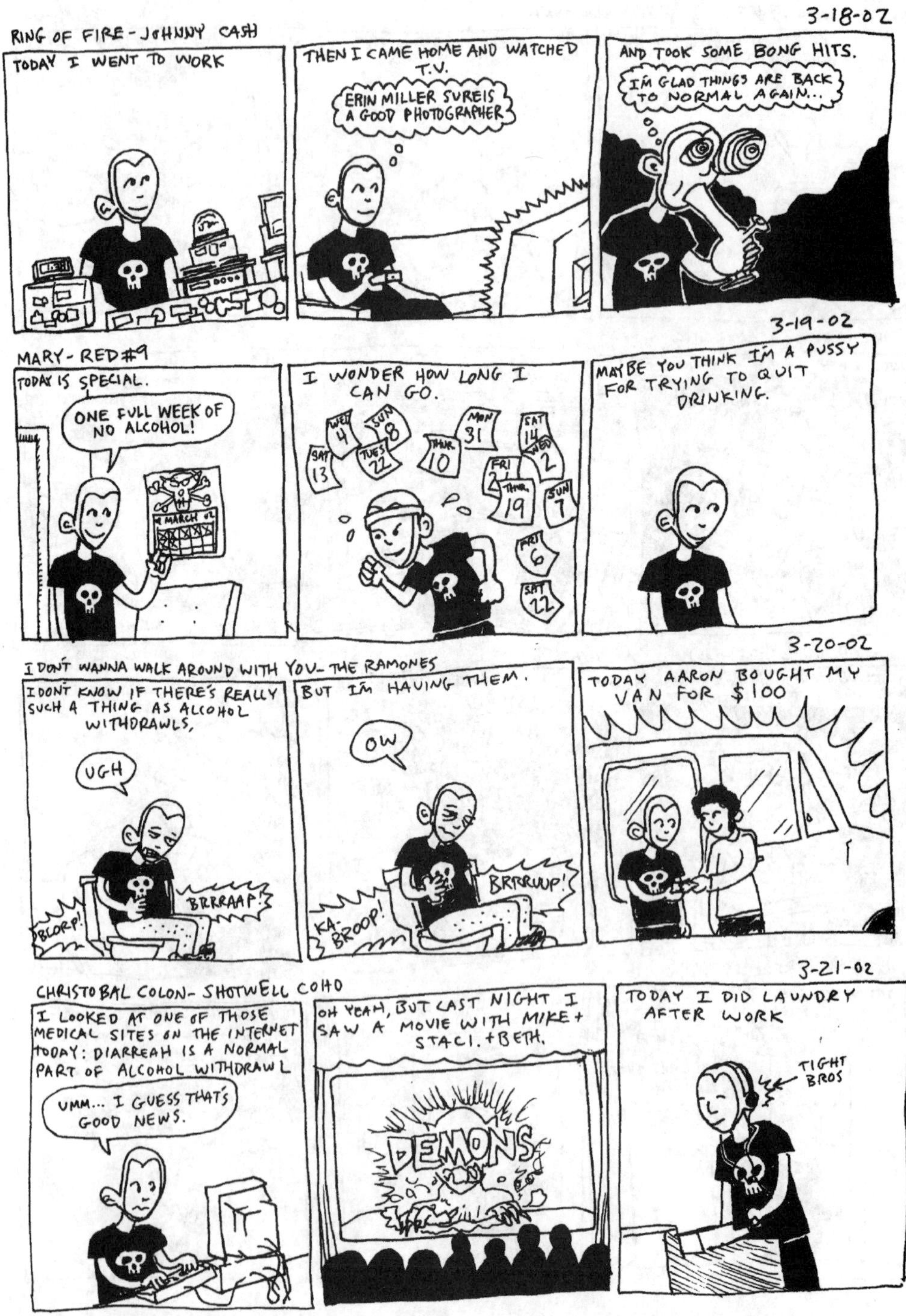
3-18-02
RING OF FIRE - JOHNNY CASH
TODAY I WENT TO WORK
THEN I CAME HOME AND WATCHED T.V.
ERIN MILLER SURE IS A GOOD PHOTOGRAPHER
AND TOOK SOME BONG HITS.
I'M GLAD THINGS ARE BACK TO NORMAL AGAIN...
3-19-02
MARY - RED #9
TODAY IS SPECIAL.
ONE FULL WEEK OF NO ALCOHOL!
MARCH 02
I WONDER HOW LONG I CAN GO.
WED 4
SUN 8
MON 31
SAT 14
SAT 13
TUES 22
THUR 10
FRI 2
WED 2
THUR 19
SUN 7
FRI 6
SAT 22
MAYBE YOU THINK I'M A PUSSY FOR TRYING TO QUIT DRINKING.
3-20-02
I DON'T WANNA WALK AROUND WITH YOU - THE RAMONES
I DON'T KNOW IF THERE'S REALLY SUCH A THING AS ALCOHOL WITHDRAWLS,
UGH
BLORP!
BRRRAAP!
BUT I'M HAVING THEM.
OW
KA-BROOP!
BRRRUUP!
TODAY AARON BOUGHT MY VAN FOR $100
3-21-02
CHRISTOBAL COLON - SHOTWELL COHO
I LOOKED AT ONE OF THOSE MEDICAL SITES ON THE INTERNET TODAY: DIARREAH IS A NORMAL PART OF ALCOHOL WITHDRAWL
UMM... I GUESS THAT'S GOOD NEWS.
OH YEAH, BUT LAST NIGHT I SAW A MOVIE WITH MIKE + STACI + BETH.
DEMONS
TODAY I DID LAUNDRY AFTER WORK
TIGHT BROS

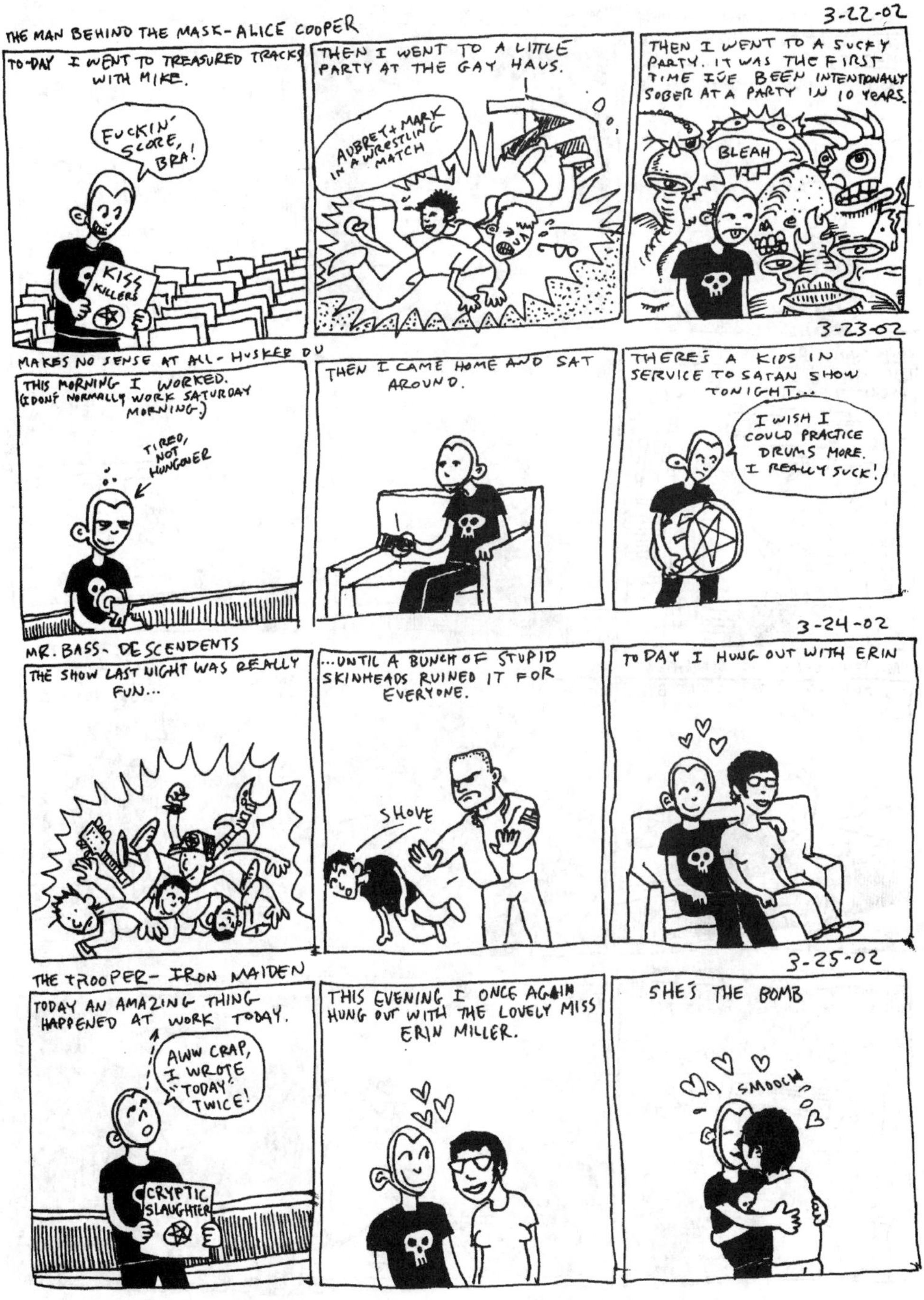
3-22-02
THE MAN BEHIND THE MASK - ALICE COOPER
TO-DAY I WENT TO TREASURED TRACKS WITH MIKE.
FUCKIN' SCORE, BRA!
KISS KILLERS
THEN I WENT TO A LITTLE PARTY AT THE GAY HAUS.
AUBREY + MARK IN A WRESTLING MATCH
THEN I WENT TO A SUCKY PARTY. IT WAS THE FIRST TIME I'VE BEEN INTENTIONALLY SOBER AT A PARTY IN 10 YEARS.
BLEAH
3-23-02
MAKES NO SENSE AT ALL - HUSKER DU
THIS MORNING I WORKED. (I DON'T NORMALLY WORK SATURDAY MORNING.)
TIRED, NOT HUNGOVER
THEN I CAME HOME AND SAT AROUND.
THERE'S A KIDS IN SERVICE TO SATAN SHOW TONIGHT...
I WISH I COULD PRACTICE DRUMS MORE. I REALLY SUCK!
3-24-02
MR. BASS - DESCENDENTS
THE SHOW LAST NIGHT WAS REALLY FUN...
...UNTIL A BUNCH OF STUPID SKINHEADS RUINED IT FOR EVERYONE.
SHOVE
TODAY I HUNG OUT WITH ERIN
3-25-02
THE TROOPER - IRON MAIDEN
TODAY AN AMAZING THING HAPPENED AT WORK TODAY.
AWW CRAP, I WROTE "TODAY" TWICE!
CRYPTIC SLAUGHTER
THIS EVENING I ONCE AGAIN HUNG OUT WITH THE LOVELY MISS ERIN MILLER.
SHE'S THE BOMB
SMOOCH

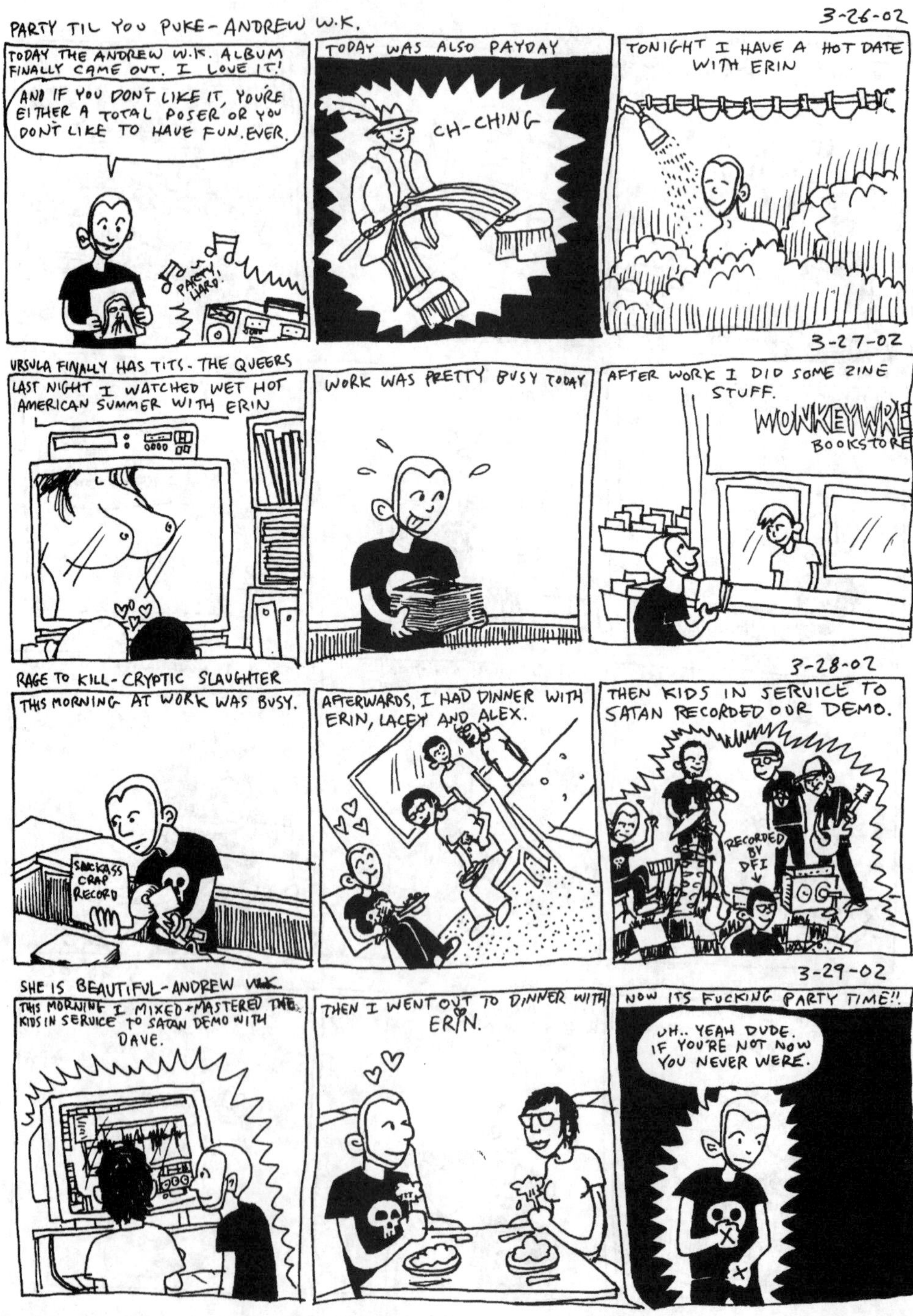
PARTY TIL YOU PUKE - ANDREW W.K.
3-26-02
TODAY THE ANDREW W.K. ALBUM FINALLY CAME OUT. I LOVE IT!
AND IF YOU DON'T LIKE IT, YOU'RE EITHER A TOTAL POSER OR YOU DON'T LIKE TO HAVE FUN. EVER.
PARTY HARD!
TODAY WAS ALSO PAYDAY
CH-CHING
TONIGHT I HAVE A HOT DATE WITH ERIN
3-27-02
URSULA FINALLY HAS TITS - THE QUEERS
LAST NIGHT I WATCHED WET HOT AMERICAN SUMMER WITH ERIN
WORK WAS PRETTY BUSY TODAY
AFTER WORK I DID SOME ZINE STUFF.
MONKEYWRE
BOOKSTORE
3-28-02
RAGE TO KILL - CRYPTIC SLAUGHTER
THIS MORNING AT WORK WAS BUSY.
SUCKASS CRAP RECORD
AFTERWARDS, I HAD DINNER WITH ERIN, LACEY AND ALEX.
THEN KIDS IN SERVICE TO SATAN RECORDED OUR DEMO.
RECORDED BY DFI
3-29-02
SHE IS BEAUTIFUL - ANDREW W.K.
THIS MORNING I MIXED + MASTERED THE KIDS IN SERVICE TO SATAN DEMO WITH DAVE.
THEN I WENT OUT TO DINNER WITH ERIN.
NOW ITS FUCKING PARTY TIME!!
UH.. YEAH DUDE. IF YOU'RE NOT NOW YOU NEVER WERE.

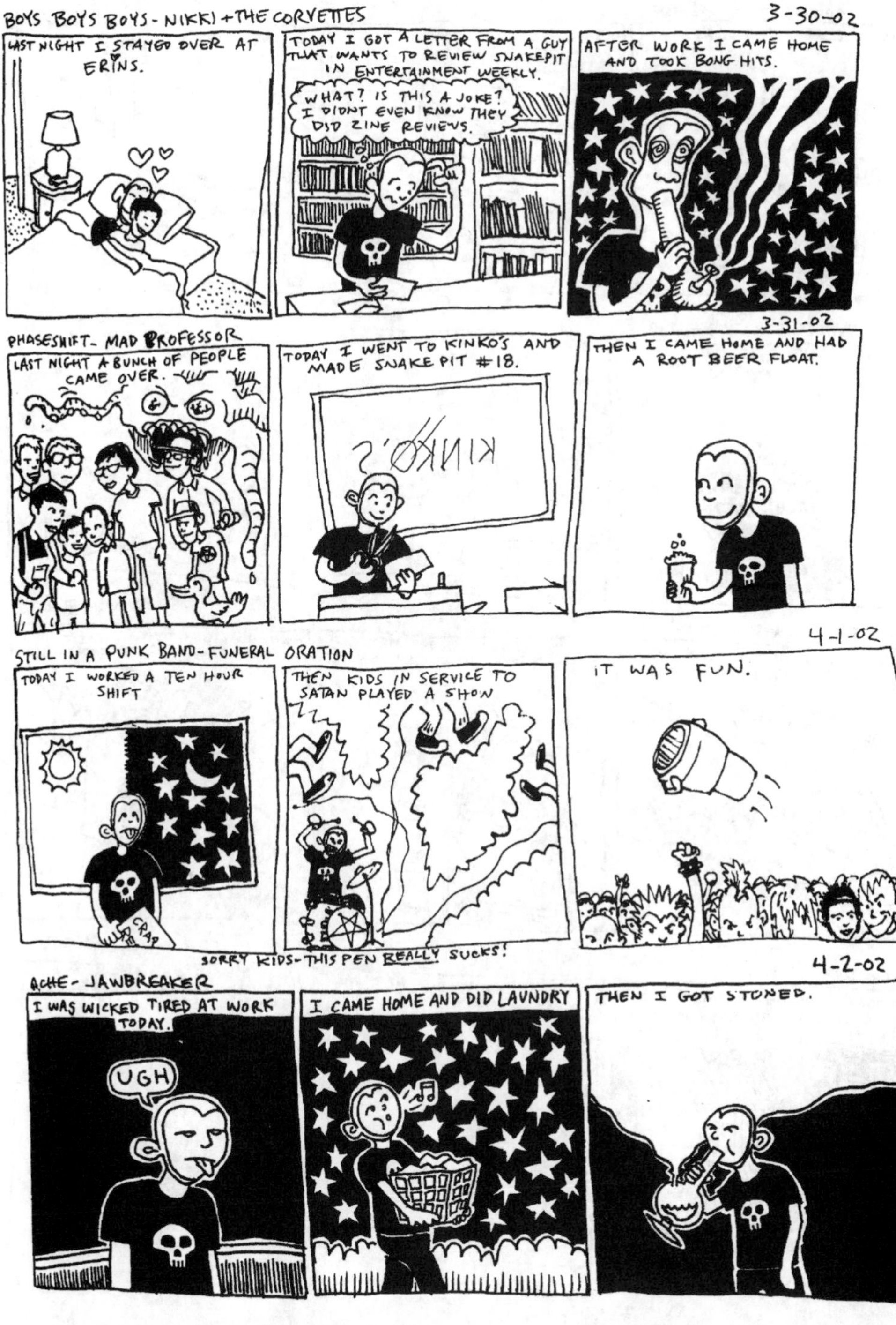
BOYS BOYS BOYS - NIKKI + THE CORVETTES
3-30-02
LAST NIGHT I STAYED OVER AT ERINS.
TODAY I GOT A LETTER FROM A GUY THAT WANTS TO REVIEW SNAKEPIT IN ENTERTAINMENT WEEKLY.
WHAT? IS THIS A JOKE? I DIDNT EVEN KNOW THEY DID ZINE REVIEWS.
AFTER WORK I CAME HOME AND TOOK BONG HITS.
3-31-02
PHASESHIFT - MAD PROFESSOR
LAST NIGHT A BUNCH OF PEOPLE CAME OVER.
TODAY I WENT TO KINKO'S AND MADE SNAKE PIT #18.
KINKO'S
THEN I CAME HOME AND HAD A ROOT BEER FLOAT.
4-1-02
STILL IN A PUNK BAND - FUNERAL ORATION
TODAY I WORKED A TEN HOUR SHIFT
CRAP
THEN KIDS IN SERVICE TO SATAN PLAYED A SHOW
IT WAS FUN.
SORRY KIDS - THIS PEN REALLY SUCKS!
4-2-02
ACHE - JAWBREAKER
I WAS WICKED TIRED AT WORK TODAY.
UGH
I CAME HOME AND DID LAUNDRY
THEN I GOT STONED.

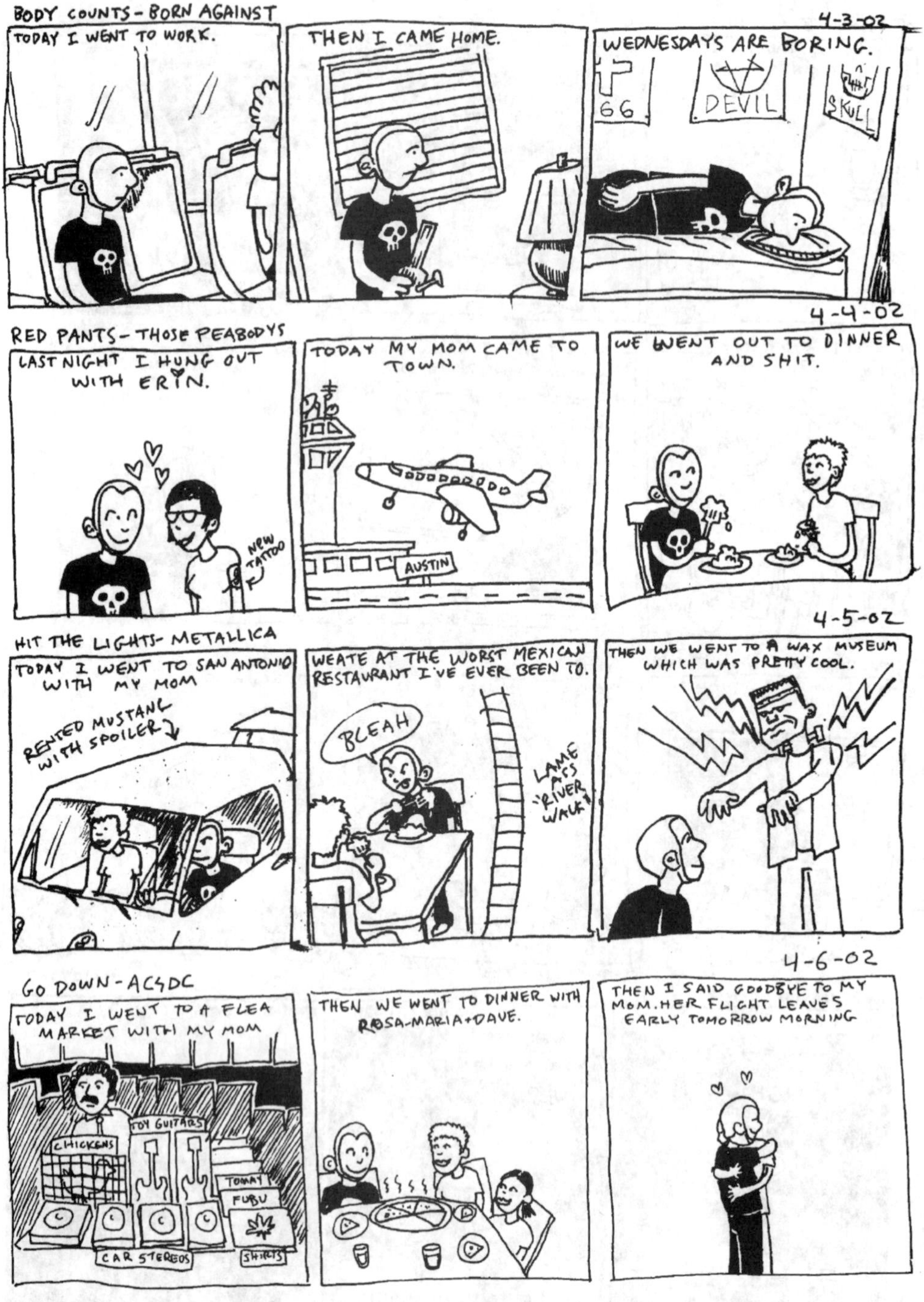
BODY COUNTS - BORN AGAINST
4-3-02
TODAY I WENT TO WORK.
THEN I CAME HOME.
WEDNESDAYS ARE BORING.
66
DEVIL
SKULL
RED PANTS - THOSE PEABODYS
4-4-02
LAST NIGHT I HUNG OUT WITH ERIN.
NEW TATTOO
TODAY MY MOM CAME TO TOWN.
AUSTIN
WE WENT OUT TO DINNER AND SHIT.
HIT THE LIGHTS - METALLICA
4-5-02
TODAY I WENT TO SAN ANTONIO WITH MY MOM
RENTED MUSTANG WITH SPOILER
WE ATE AT THE WORST MEXICAN RESTAURANT I'VE EVER BEEN TO.
BLEAH
LAME ASS "RIVER WALK"
THEN WE WENT TO A WAX MUSEUM WHICH WAS PRETTY COOL.
GO DOWN - AC&DC
4-6-02
TODAY I WENT TO A FLEA MARKET WITH MY MOM
CHICKENS
TOY GUITARS
TOMMY
FUBU
CAR STEREOS
SHIRTS
THEN WE WENT TO DINNER WITH ROSA-MARIA + DAVE.
THEN I SAID GOODBYE TO MY MOM. HER FLIGHT LEAVES EARLY TOMORROW MORNING

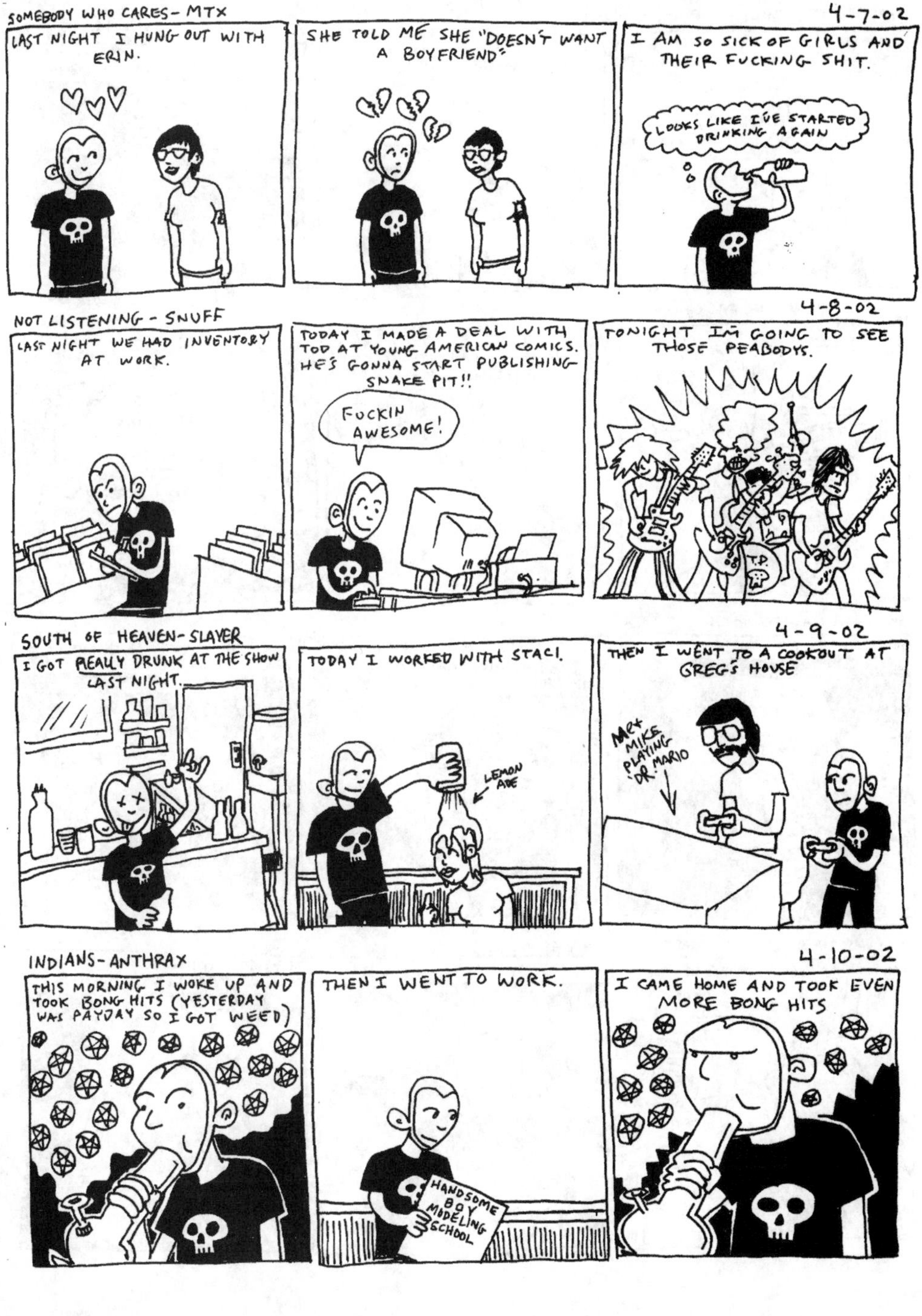
SOMEBODY WHO CARES - MTX
4-7-02
LAST NIGHT I HUNG OUT WITH ERIN.
SHE TOLD ME SHE "DOESN'T WANT A BOYFRIEND"
I AM SO SICK OF GIRLS AND THEIR FUCKING SHIT.
LOOKS LIKE I'VE STARTED DRINKING AGAIN
NOT LISTENING - SNUFF
4-8-02
LAST NIGHT WE HAD INVENTORY AT WORK.
TODAY I MADE A DEAL WITH TOD AT YOUNG AMERICAN COMICS. HE'S GONNA START PUBLISHING SNAKE PIT!!
FUCKIN AWESOME!
TONIGHT I'M GOING TO SEE THOSE PEABODYS.
T.P.
SOUTH OF HEAVEN - SLAYER
4-9-02
I GOT REALLY DRUNK AT THE SHOW LAST NIGHT.
TODAY I WORKED WITH STACI.
LEMON ADE
THEN I WENT TO A COOKOUT AT GREG'S HOUSE
ME + MIKE PLAYING 'DR. MARIO
INDIANS - ANTHRAX
4-10-02
THIS MORNING I WOKE UP AND TOOK BONG HITS (YESTERDAY WAS PAYDAY SO I GOT WEED)
THEN I WENT TO WORK.
HANDSOME BOY MODELING SCHOOL
I CAME HOME AND TOOK EVEN MORE BONG HITS

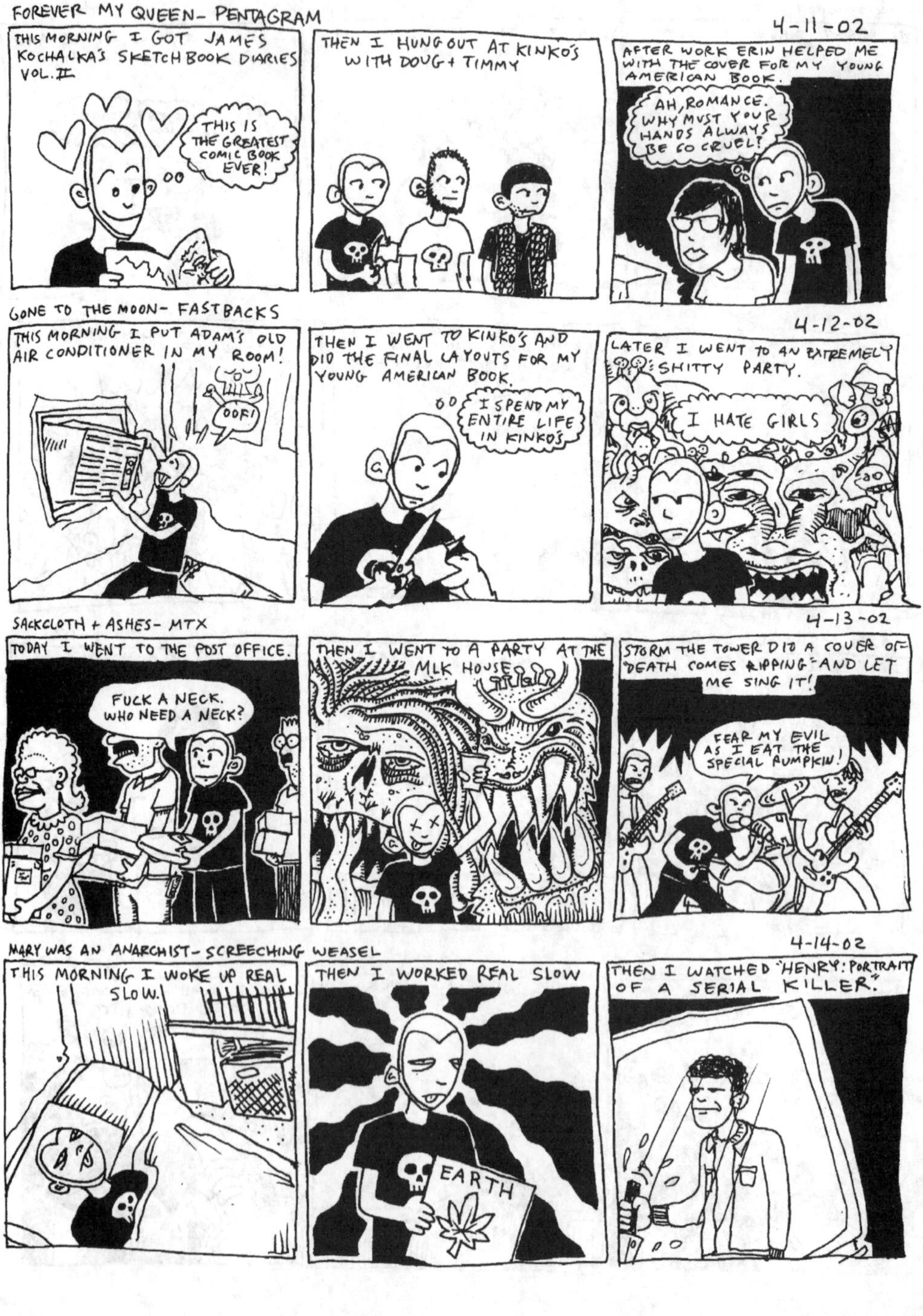
FOREVER MY QUEEN- PENTAGRAM
4-11-02
THIS MORNING I GOT JAMES KOCHALKA'S SKETCHBOOK DIARIES VOL. II
THIS IS THE GREATEST COMIC BOOK EVER!
THEN I HUNG OUT AT KINKO'S WITH DOUG + TIMMY
AFTER WORK ERIN HELPED ME WITH THE COVER FOR MY YOUNG AMERICAN BOOK.
AH, ROMANCE. WHY MUST YOUR HANDS ALWAYS BE SO CRUEL?
GONE TO THE MOON- FASTBACKS
4-12-02
THIS MORNING I PUT ADAM'S OLD AIR CONDITIONER IN MY ROOM!
OOF!
THEN I WENT TO KINKO'S AND DID THE FINAL LAYOUTS FOR MY YOUNG AMERICAN BOOK.
I SPEND MY ENTIRE LIFE IN KINKO'S
LATER I WENT TO AN EXTREMELY SHITTY PARTY.
I HATE GIRLS
SACKCLOTH + ASHES- MTX
4-13-02
TODAY I WENT TO THE POST OFFICE.
FUCK A NECK. WHO NEED A NECK?
THEN I WENT TO A PARTY AT THE MLK HOUSE
STORM THE TOWER DID A COVER OF "DEATH COMES RIPPING" AND LET ME SING IT!
FEAR MY EVIL AS I EAT THE SPECIAL PUMPKIN!
MARY WAS AN ANARCHIST- SCREECHING WEASEL
4-14-02
THIS MORNING I WOKE UP REAL SLOW.
THEN I WORKED REAL SLOW
EARTH
THEN I WATCHED "HENRY: PORTRAIT OF A SERIAL KILLER".

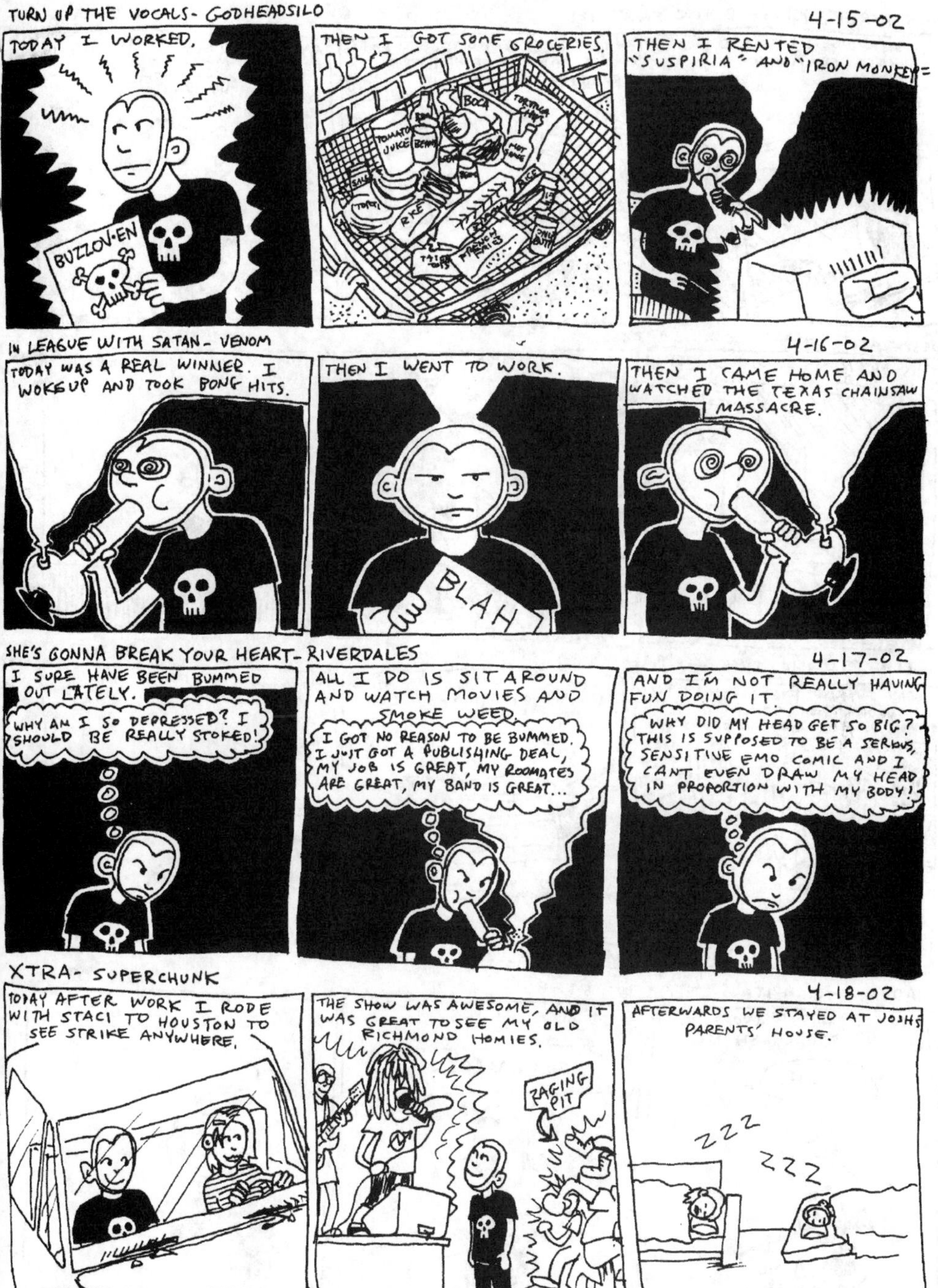

TURN UP THE VOCALS- GODHEADSILO
4-15-02
TODAY I WORKED.
BUZZOV•EN
THEN I GOT SOME GROCERIES.
TOMATO JUICE
BOCA
THEN I RENTED "SUSPIRIA" AND "IRON MONKEY"
IN LEAGUE WITH SATAN- VENOM
4-16-02
TODAY WAS A REAL WINNER. I WOKEUP AND TOOK BONG HITS.
THEN I WENT TO WORK.
BLAH
THEN I CAME HOME AND WATCHED THE TEXAS CHAINSAW MASSACRE.
SHE'S GONNA BREAK YOUR HEART- RIVERDALES
4-17-02
I SURE HAVE BEEN BUMMED OUT LATELY.
WHY AM I SO DEPRESSED? I SHOULD BE REALLY STOKED!
ALL I DO IS SIT AROUND AND WATCH MOVIES AND SMOKE WEED.
I GOT NO REASON TO BE BUMMED. I JUST GOT A PUBLISHING DEAL, MY JOB IS GREAT, MY ROOMATES ARE GREAT, MY BAND IS GREAT...
AND I'M NOT REALLY HAVING FUN DOING IT.
WHY DID MY HEAD GET SO BIG? THIS IS SUPPOSED TO BE A SERIOUS, SENSITIVE EMO COMIC AND I CANT EVEN DRAW MY HEAD IN PROPORTION WITH MY BODY!
XTRA- SUPERCHUNK
4-18-02
TODAY AFTER WORK I RODE WITH STACI TO HOUSTON TO SEE STRIKE ANYWHERE.
THE SHOW WAS AWESOME, AND IT WAS GREAT TO SEE MY OLD RICHMOND HOMIES.
RAGING PIT
AFTERWARDS WE STAYED AT JOSH'S PARENTS' HOUSE.
ZZZ
ZZZ

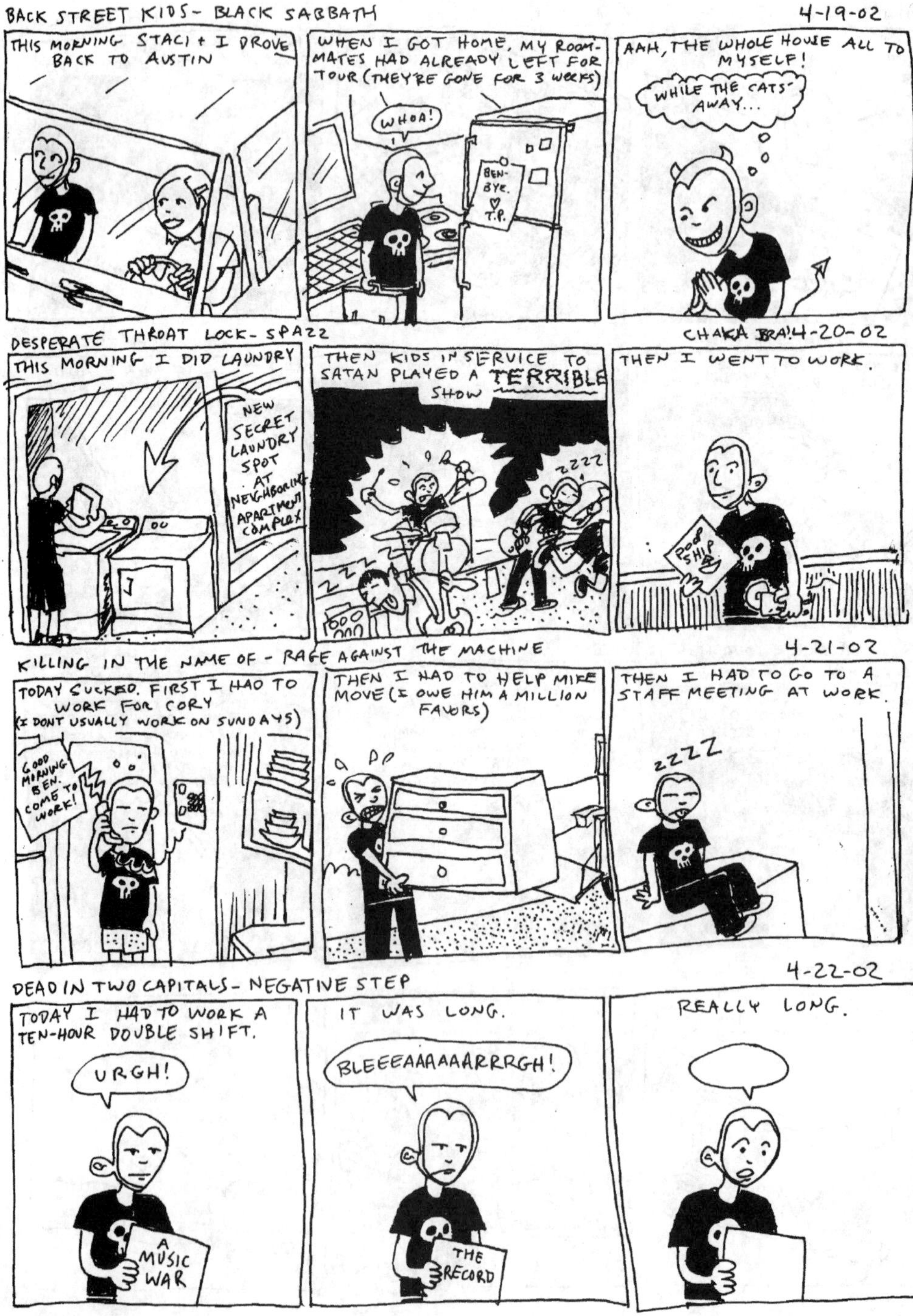
BACK STREET KIDS - BLACK SABBATH
4-19-02
THIS MORNING STACI + I DROVE BACK TO AUSTIN
WHEN I GOT HOME, MY ROOM-MATES HAD ALREADY LEFT FOR TOUR (THEY'RE GONE FOR 3 WEEKS)
WHOA!
BEN- BYE. ♥ T.P.
AAH, THE WHOLE HOUSE ALL TO MYSELF!
WHILE THE CATS' AWAY...
DESPERATE THROAT LOCK - SPAZZ
CHAKA BRA! 4-20-02
THIS MORNING I DID LAUNDRY
NEW SECRET LAUNDRY SPOT AT NEIGHBORING APARTMENT COMPLEX
THEN KIDS IN SERVICE TO SATAN PLAYED A TERRIBLE SHOW
ZZZZ
ZZZ
THEN I WENT TO WORK.
POD SHIP
KILLING IN THE NAME OF - RAGE AGAINST THE MACHINE
4-21-02
TODAY SUCKED. FIRST I HAD TO WORK FOR CORY (I DONT USUALLY WORK ON SUNDAYS)
GOOD MORNING BEN. COME TO WORK!
THEN I HAD TO HELP MIKE MOVE (I OWE HIM A MILLION FAVORS)
THEN I HAD TO GO TO A STAFF MEETING AT WORK.
ZZZZ
DEAD IN TWO CAPITALS - NEGATIVE STEP
4-22-02
TODAY I HAD TO WORK A TEN-HOUR DOUBLE SHIFT.
URGH!
A MUSIC WAR
IT WAS LONG.
BLEEEAAAAAARRRGH!
THE RECORD
REALLY LONG.

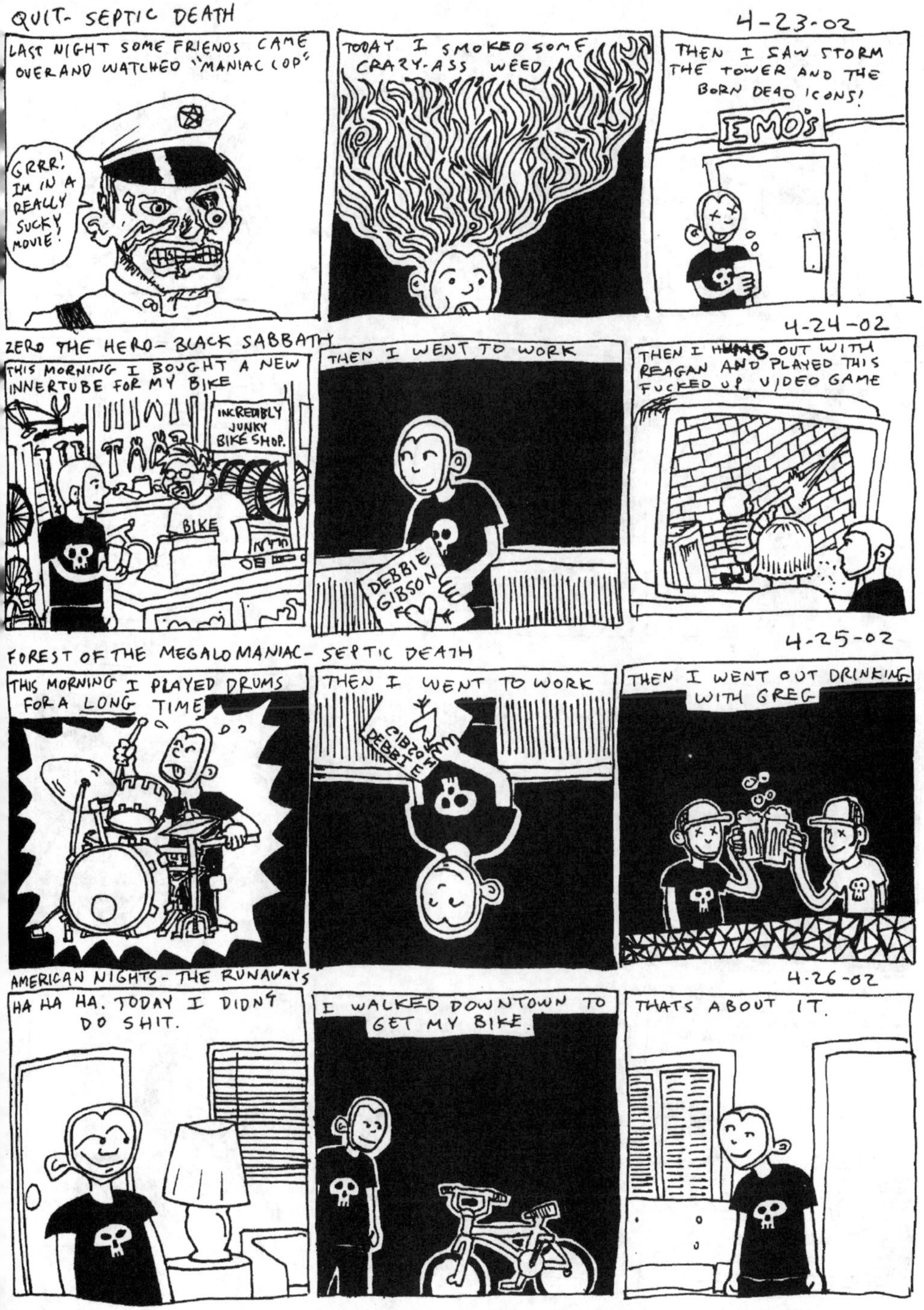
QUIT- SEPTIC DEATH
4-23-02
LAST NIGHT SOME FRIENDS CAME OVER AND WATCHED "MANIAC COP"
GRRR! IM IN A REALLY SUCKY MOVIE!
TODAY I SMOKED SOME CRAZY-ASS WEED
THEN I SAW STORM THE TOWER AND THE BORN DEAD ICONS!
EMO'S
ZERO THE HERO- BLACK SABBATH
4-24-02
THIS MORNING I BOUGHT A NEW INNERTUBE FOR MY BIKE
INCREDIBLY JUNKY BIKE SHOP.
BIKE
THEN I WENT TO WORK
DEBBIE GIBSON
THEN I HUNG OUT WITH REAGAN AND PLAYED THIS FUCKED UP VIDEO GAME
FOREST OF THE MEGALOMANIAC- SEPTIC DEATH
4-25-02
THIS MORNING I PLAYED DRUMS FOR A LONG TIME
THEN I WENT TO WORK
DEBBIE GIBSON
THEN I WENT OUT DRINKING WITH GREG
AMERICAN NIGHTS- THE RUNAWAYS
4-26-02
HA HA HA. TODAY I DIDN'T DO SHIT.
I WALKED DOWNTOWN TO GET MY BIKE.
THATS ABOUT IT.

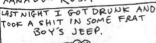

XANADU- RUSH

4-27-02

LAST NIGHT I GOT DRUNK AND TOOK A SHIT IN SOME FRAT BOY'S JEEP.

TODAY AFTER WORK I SAW ✝DARK FUNERAL✝

AND CANNIBAL CORPSE!

PETROLEUM DISTILLATION - FIFTEEN

4-28-02

TODAY I WENT TO ROSA-MARIA'S BABY SHOWER.

SHE'S SUPER PREGNANT

THEN I WATCHED HOUSE BY THE CEMETARY. IT KINDA SUCKED.

=YAWN=

THAT'S ALL.

ZZZZZZ

BLACK FOREST - GOBLIN

4-29-02

TODAY WORK WAS KINDA WEIRD.

CHEEP CHEEP! THE FUTURE IS UNCERTAIN! CHEEP CHEEP!

I CAME HOME AND PLAYED THE DRUMS

THEN I TOOK BONG HITS.

=GURGLE GURGLE= THE FUTURE IS UNCERTAIN! =GURGLE=

BROWN EYES- WOODY GUTHRIE

4-30-02

TODAY MIKE AND I WENT TO ARANDA'S + ATE ENCHLADAS

THEN I GOT A COPY OF DELAINE'S MY SMALL DIARY COMIC (DELANCEL3@HOTMAIL.com)

WHAT A GREAT COMIC!

THEN I RODE MY BIKE HOME

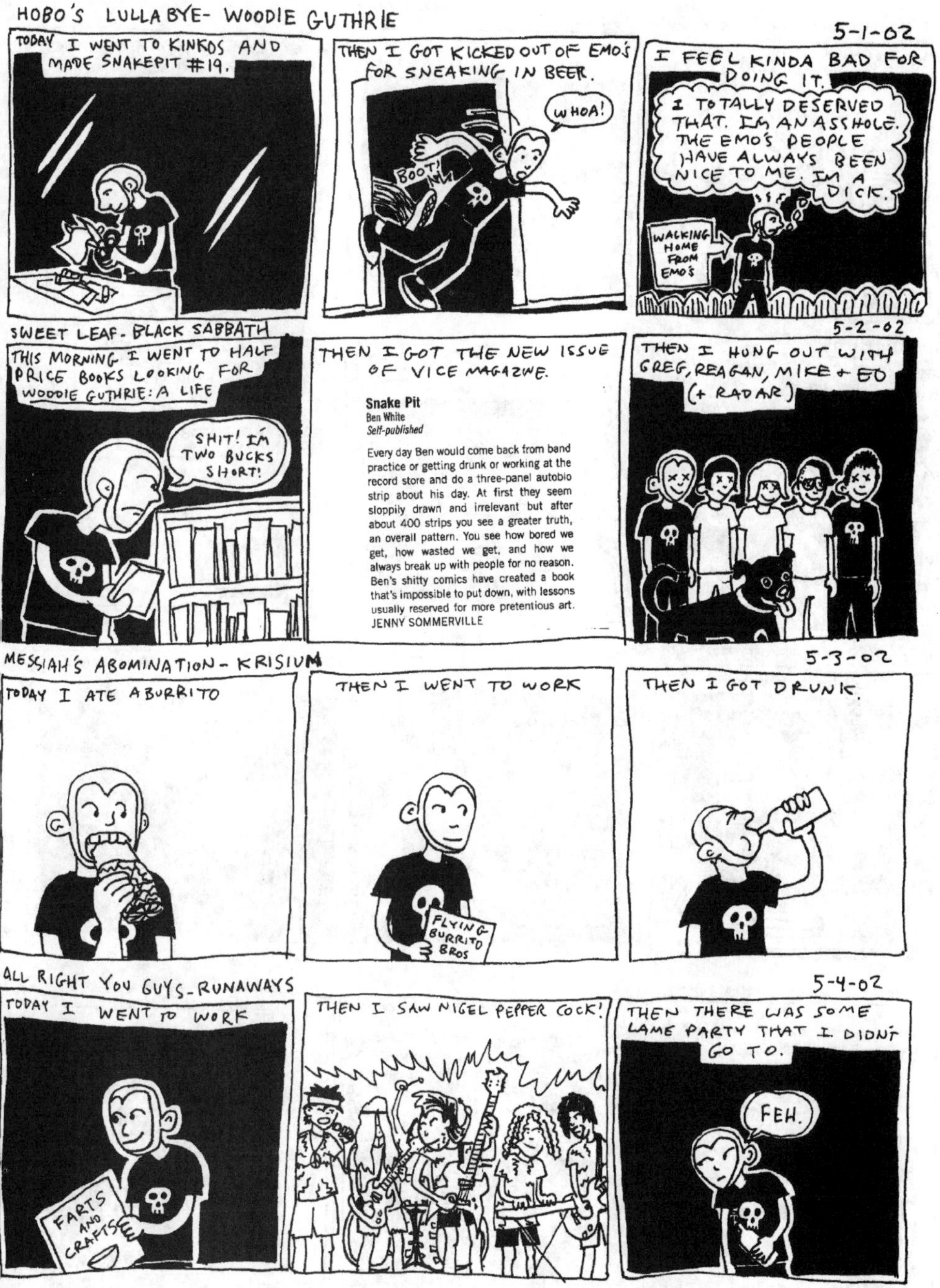
HOBO'S LULLABYE- WOODIE GUTHRIE
5-1-02
TODAY I WENT TO KINKOS AND MADE SNAKEPIT #19.
THEN I GOT KICKED OUT OF EMO'S FOR SNEAKING IN BEER.
WHOA!
BOOT!
I FEEL KINDA BAD FOR DOING IT.
I TOTALLY DESERVED THAT. I'M AN ASSHOLE. THE EMO'S PEOPLE HAVE ALWAYS BEEN NICE TO ME. I'M A DICK.
WALKING HOME FROM EMO'S
SWEET LEAF - BLACK SABBATH
5-2-02
THIS MORNING I WENT TO HALF PRICE BOOKS LOOKING FOR WOODIE GUTHRIE: A LIFE
SHIT! I'M TWO BUCKS SHORT!
THEN I GOT THE NEW ISSUE OF VICE MAGAZINE.
Snake Pit
Ben White
Self-published
Every day Ben would come back from band practice or getting drunk or working at the record store and do a three-panel autobio strip about his day. At first they seem sloppily drawn and irrelevant but after about 400 strips you see a greater truth, an overall pattern. You see how bored we get, how wasted we get, and how we always break up with people for no reason. Ben's shitty comics have created a book that's impossible to put down, with lessons usually reserved for more pretentious art.
JENNY SOMMERVILLE
THEN I HUNG OUT WITH GREG, REAGAN, MIKE + ED (+ RADAR)
MESSIAH'S ABOMINATION - KRISIUM
5-3-02
TODAY I ATE A BURRITO
THEN I WENT TO WORK
FLYING BURRITO BROS
THEN I GOT DRUNK.
ALL RIGHT YOU GUYS - RUNAWAYS
5-4-02
TODAY I WENT TO WORK
FARTS AND CRAFTS
THEN I SAW NIGEL PEPPER COCK!
THEN THERE WAS SOME LAME PARTY THAT I DIDN'T GO TO.
FEH.

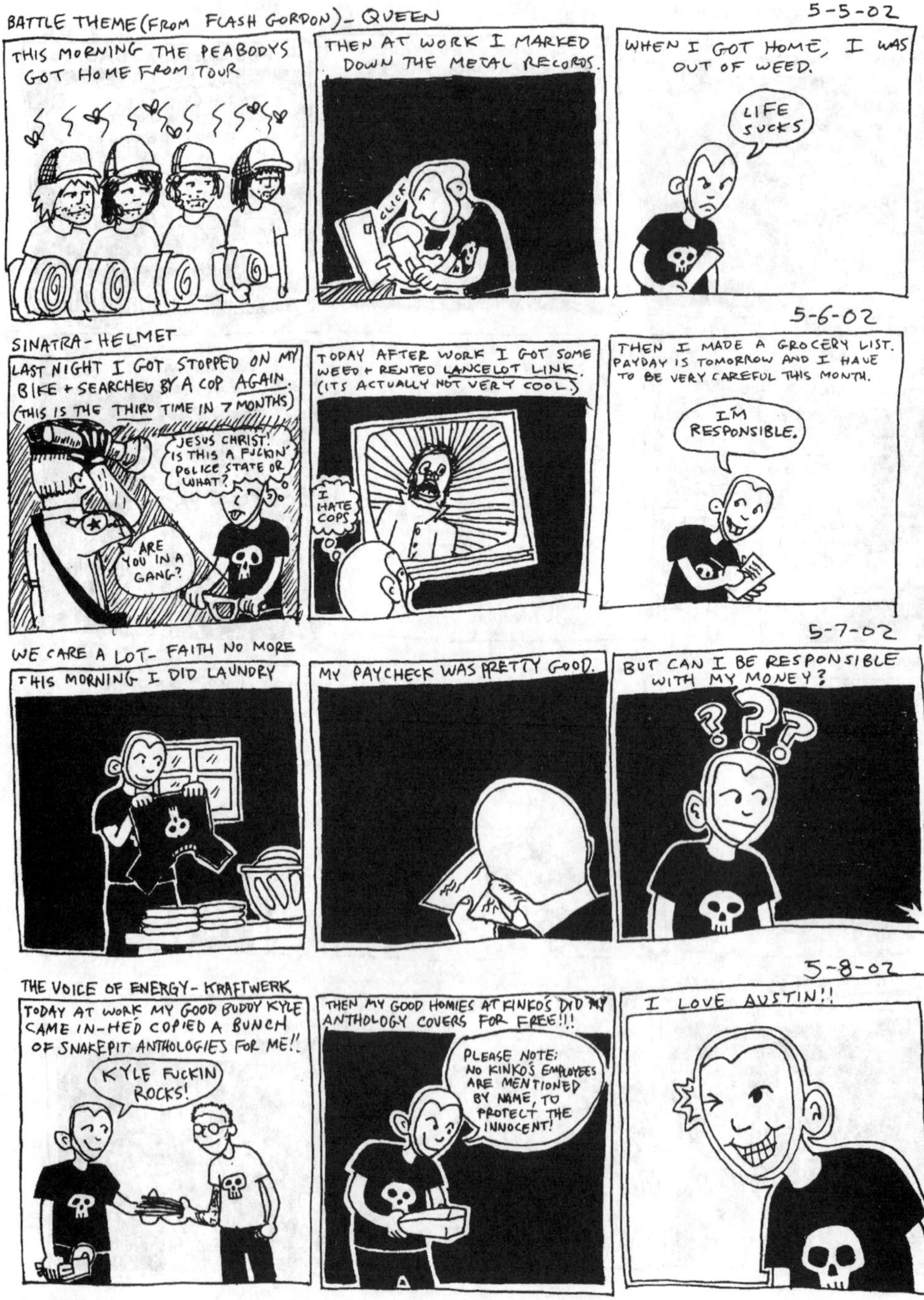
BATTLE THEME (FROM FLASH GORDON) - QUEEN
5-5-02
THIS MORNING THE PEABODYS GOT HOME FROM TOUR
THEN AT WORK I MARKED DOWN THE METAL RECORDS.
CLICK
WHEN I GOT HOME, I WAS OUT OF WEED.
LIFE SUCKS
5-6-02
SINATRA - HELMET
LAST NIGHT I GOT STOPPED ON MY BIKE + SEARCHED BY A COP AGAIN. (THIS IS THE THIRD TIME IN 7 MONTHS)
JESUS CHRIST! IS THIS A FUCKIN' POLICE STATE OR WHAT?
ARE YOU IN A GANG?
TODAY AFTER WORK I GOT SOME WEED + RENTED LANCELOT LINK. (ITS ACTUALLY NOT VERY COOL.)
I HATE COPS
THEN I MADE A GROCERY LIST. PAYDAY IS TOMORROW AND I HAVE TO BE VERY CAREFUL THIS MONTH.
I'M RESPONSIBLE.
5-7-02
WE CARE A LOT - FAITH NO MORE
THIS MORNING I DID LAUNDRY
MY PAYCHECK WAS PRETTY GOOD.
BUT CAN I BE RESPONSIBLE WITH MY MONEY?
???
5-8-02
THE VOICE OF ENERGY - KRAFTWERK
TODAY AT WORK MY GOOD BUDDY KYLE CAME IN - HE'D COPIED A BUNCH OF SNAKEPIT ANTHOLOGIES FOR ME!!
KYLE FUCKIN ROCKS!
THEN MY GOOD HOMIES AT KINKO'S DID MY ANTHOLOGY COVERS FOR FREE!!!
PLEASE NOTE: NO KINKO'S EMPLOYEES ARE MENTIONED BY NAME, TO PROTECT THE INNOCENT!
I LOVE AUSTIN!!

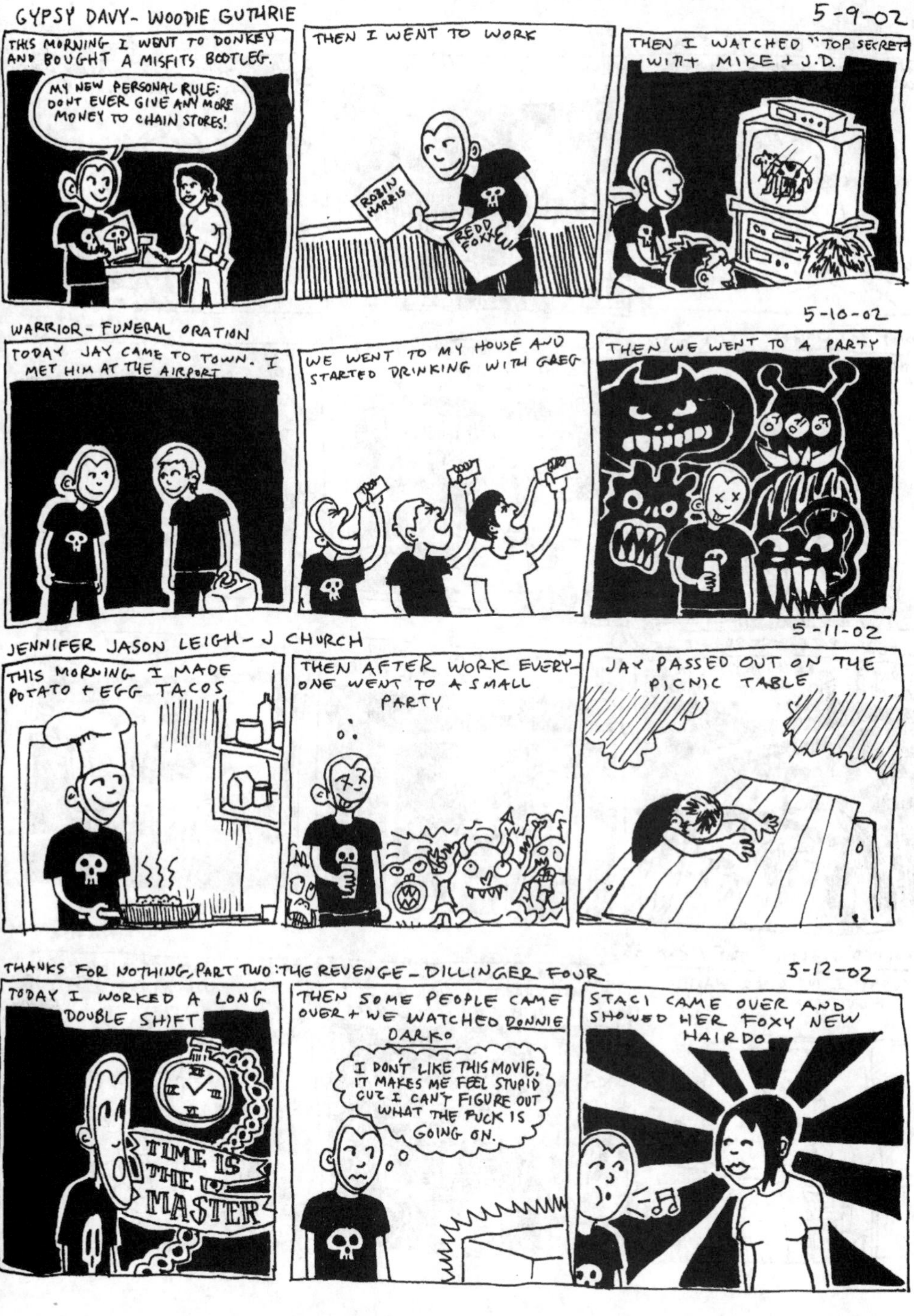
GYPSY DAVY - WOODIE GUTHRIE
5-9-02
THIS MORNING I WENT TO DONKEY AND BOUGHT A MISFITS BOOTLEG.
MY NEW PERSONAL RULE: DONT EVER GIVE ANY MORE MONEY TO CHAIN STORES!
THEN I WENT TO WORK
ROBIN HARRIS
REDD FOXX
THEN I WATCHED "TOP SECRET" WITH MIKE + J.D.
WARRIOR - FUNERAL ORATION
5-10-02
TODAY JAY CAME TO TOWN. I MET HIM AT THE AIRPORT
WE WENT TO MY HOUSE AND STARTED DRINKING WITH GREG
THEN WE WENT TO A PARTY
JENNIFER JASON LEIGH - J CHURCH
5-11-02
THIS MORNING I MADE POTATO + EGG TACOS
THEN AFTER WORK EVERYONE WENT TO A SMALL PARTY
JAY PASSED OUT ON THE PICNIC TABLE
THANKS FOR NOTHING, PART TWO: THE REVENGE - DILLINGER FOUR
5-12-02
TODAY I WORKED A LONG DOUBLE SHIFT
TIME IS THE MASTER
THEN SOME PEOPLE CAME OVER + WE WATCHED DONNIE DARKO
I DON'T LIKE THIS MOVIE, IT MAKES ME FEEL STUPID CUZ I CAN'T FIGURE OUT WHAT THE FUCK IS GOING ON.
STACI CAME OVER AND SHOWED HER FOXY NEW HAIRDO

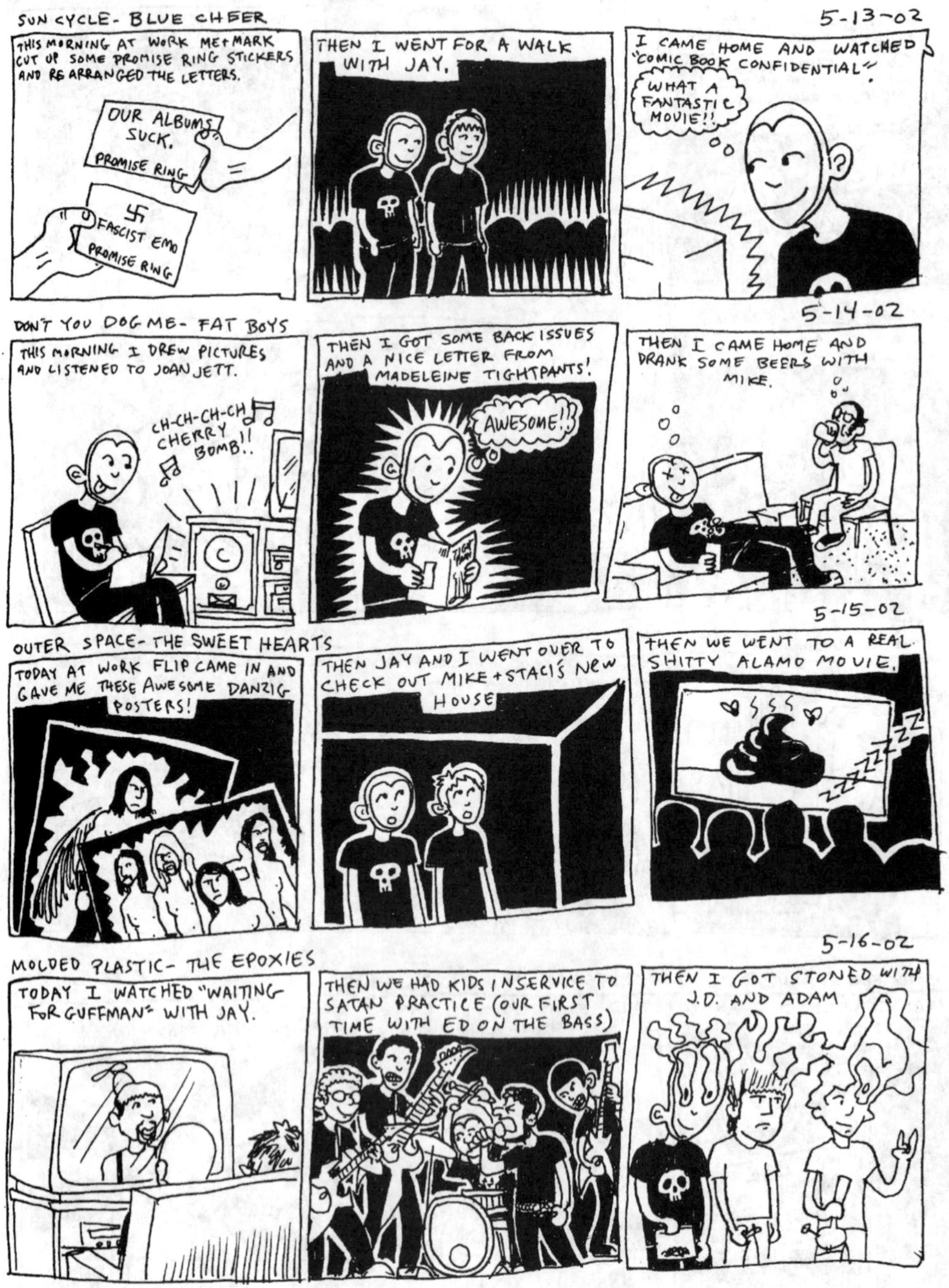
SUN CYCLE- BLUE CHEER
5-13-02
THIS MORNING AT WORK ME+MARK CUT UP SOME PROMISE RING STICKERS AND RE ARRANGED THE LETTERS.
OUR ALBUMS SUCK.
PROMISE RING
FASCIST EMO
PROMISE RING
THEN I WENT FOR A WALK WITH JAY.
I CAME HOME AND WATCHED "COMIC BOOK CONFIDENTIAL".
WHAT A FANTASTIC MOVIE!!
DON'T YOU DOG ME- FAT BOYS
5-14-02
THIS MORNING I DREW PICTURES AND LISTENED TO JOAN JETT.
CH-CH-CH-CH CHERRY BOMB!!
THEN I GOT SOME BACK ISSUES AND A NICE LETTER FROM MADELEINE TIGHTPANTS!
AWESOME!
THEN I CAME HOME AND DRANK SOME BEERS WITH MIKE.
5-15-02
OUTER SPACE- THE SWEET HEARTS
TODAY AT WORK FLIP CAME IN AND GAVE ME THESE AWESOME DANZIG POSTERS!
THEN JAY AND I WENT OVER TO CHECK OUT MIKE+STACI'S NEW HOUSE
THEN WE WENT TO A REAL SHITTY ALAMO MOVIE.
ZZZZZZZ
5-16-02
MOLDED PLASTIC- THE EPOXIES
TODAY I WATCHED "WAITING FOR GUFFMAN" WITH JAY.
THEN WE HAD KIDS IN SERVICE TO SATAN PRACTICE (OUR FIRST TIME WITH ED ON THE BASS)
THEN I GOT STONED WITH J.D. AND ADAM

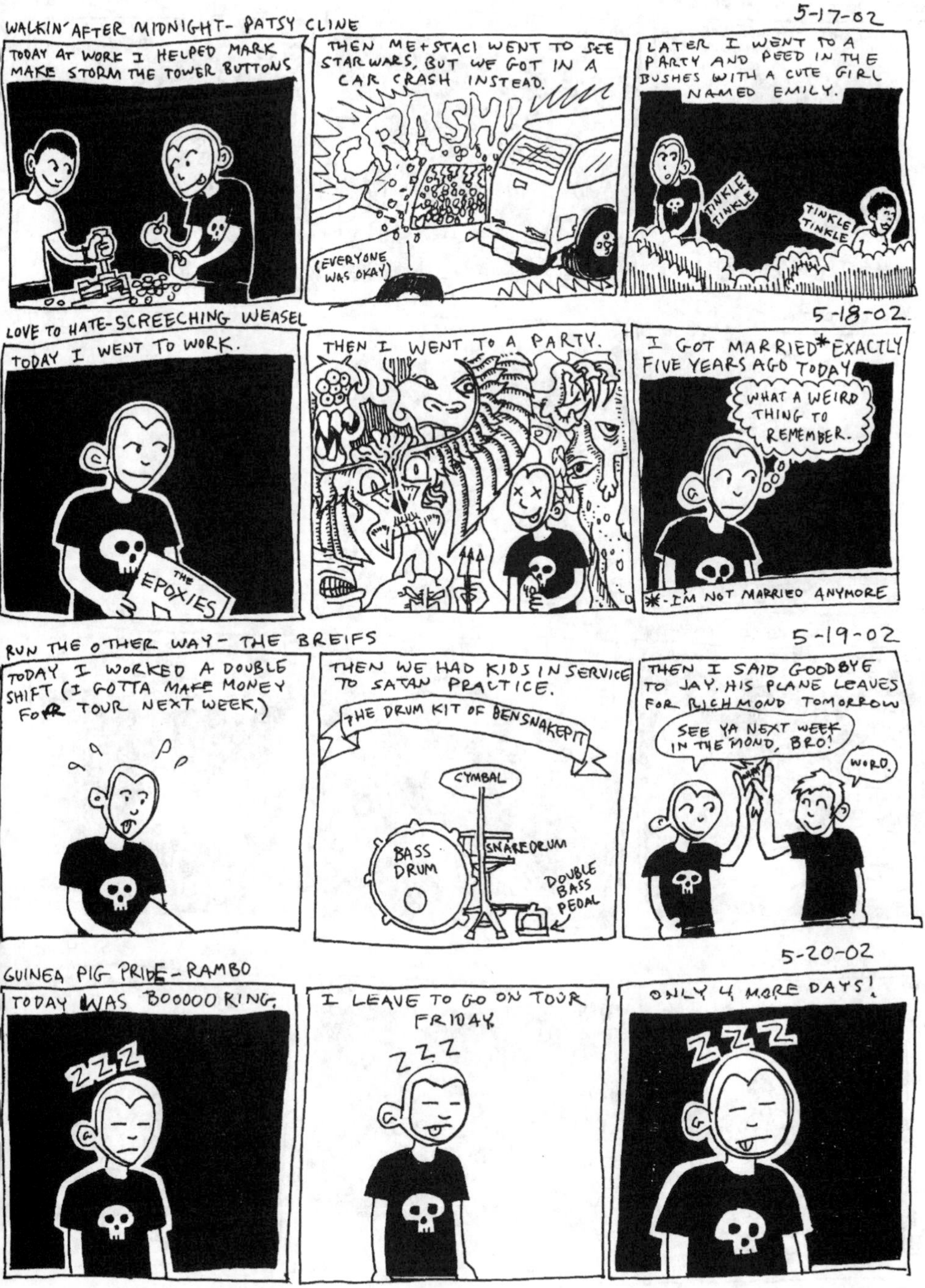

WALKIN' AFTER MIDNIGHT- PATSY CLINE
5-17-02
TODAY AT WORK I HELPED MARK MAKE STORM THE TOWER BUTTONS
THEN ME+STACI WENT TO SEE STAR WARS, BUT WE GOT IN A CAR CRASH INSTEAD.
CRASH!
(EVERYONE WAS OKAY)
LATER I WENT TO A PARTY AND PEED IN THE BUSHES WITH A CUTE GIRL NAMED EMILY.
TINKLE TINKLE
TINKLE TINKLE
LOVE TO HATE-SCREECHING WEASEL
5-18-02
TODAY I WENT TO WORK.
THE EPOXIES
THEN I WENT TO A PARTY.
I GOT MARRIED* EXACTLY FIVE YEARS AGO TODAY
WHAT A WEIRD THING TO REMEMBER.
*-I'M NOT MARRIED ANYMORE
RUN THE OTHER WAY- THE BREIFS
5-19-02
TODAY I WORKED A DOUBLE SHIFT (I GOTTA MAKE MONEY FOR TOUR NEXT WEEK.)
THEN WE HAD KIDS IN SERVICE TO SATAN PRACTICE.
THE DRUM KIT OF BEN SNAKEPIT
CYMBAL
BASS DRUM
SNAREDRUM
DOUBLE BASS PEDAL
THEN I SAID GOODBYE TO JAY. HIS PLANE LEAVES FOR RICHMOND TOMORROW
SEE YA NEXT WEEK IN THE MOND, BRO!
WORD.
GUINEA PIG PRIDE - RAMBO
5-20-02
TODAY WAS BOOOOORING.
ZZZ
I LEAVE TO GO ON TOUR FRIDAY.
ZZZ
ONLY 4 MORE DAYS!
ZZZ

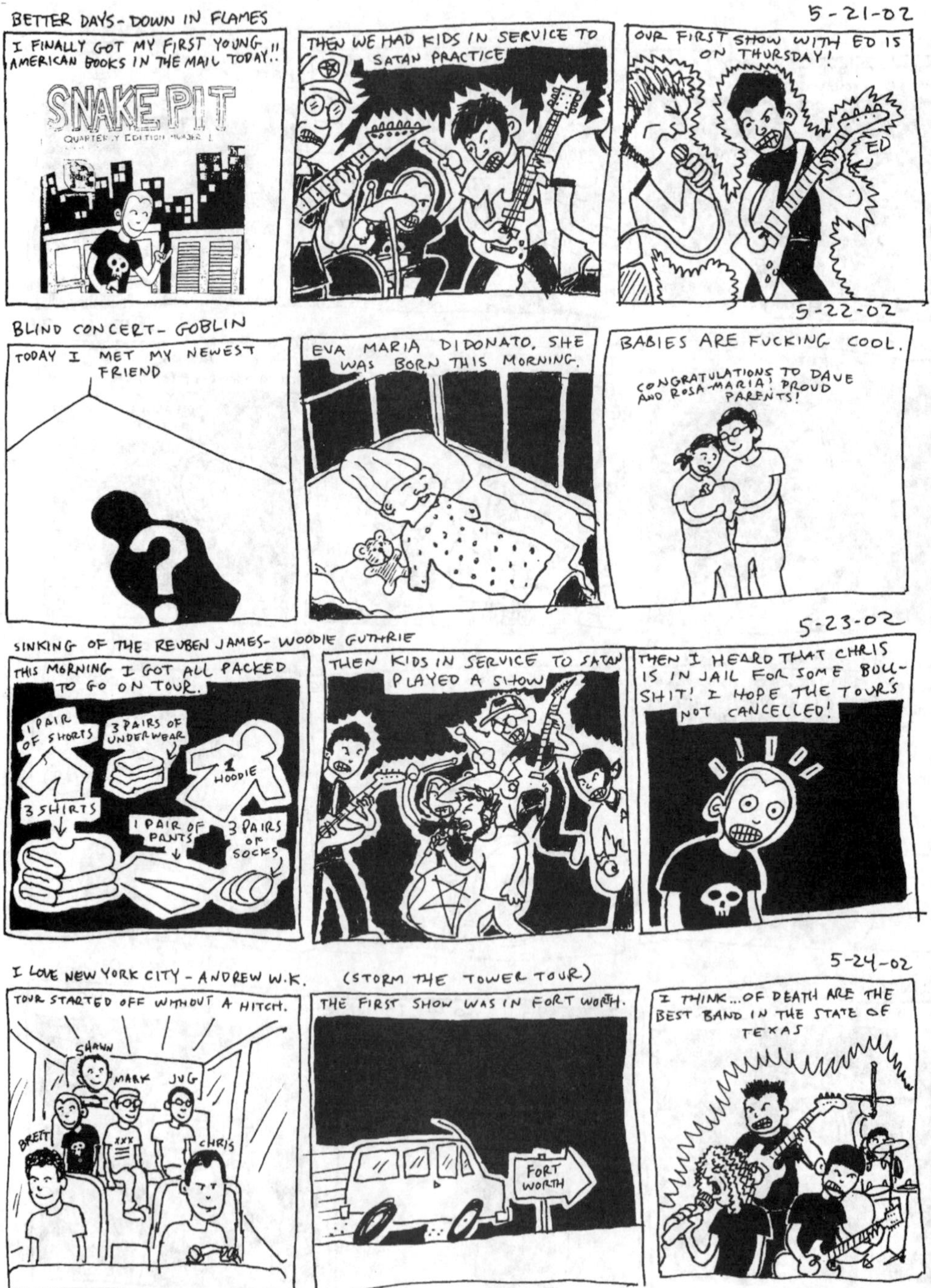
BETTER DAYS - DOWN IN FLAMES
5-21-02
I FINALLY GOT MY FIRST YOUNG AMERICAN BOOKS IN THE MAIL TODAY!!
SNAKE PIT
THEN WE HAD KIDS IN SERVICE TO SATAN PRACTICE
OUR FIRST SHOW WITH ED IS ON THURSDAY!
ED
5-22-02
BLIND CONCERT - GOBLIN
TODAY I MET MY NEWEST FRIEND
EVA MARIA DIDONATO, SHE WAS BORN THIS MORNING.
BABIES ARE FUCKING COOL.
CONGRATULATIONS TO DAVE AND ROSA-MARIA! PROUD PARENTS!
5-23-02
SINKING OF THE REUBEN JAMES - WOODIE GUTHRIE
THIS MORNING I GOT ALL PACKED TO GO ON TOUR.
1 PAIR OF SHORTS
3 PAIRS OF UNDERWEAR
1 HOODIE
3 SHIRTS
1 PAIR OF PANTS
3 PAIRS OF SOCKS
THEN KIDS IN SERVICE TO SATAN PLAYED A SHOW
THEN I HEARD THAT CHRIS IS IN JAIL FOR SOME BULL-SHIT! I HOPE THE TOUR'S NOT CANCELLED!
5-24-02
I LOVE NEW YORK CITY - ANDREW W.K. (STORM THE TOWER TOUR)
TOUR STARTED OFF WITHOUT A HITCH.
SHAWN
MARK
JUG
BRETT
CHRIS
XXX
THE FIRST SHOW WAS IN FORT WORTH.
FORT WORTH
I THINK ...OF DEATH ARE THE BEST BAND IN THE STATE OF TEXAS

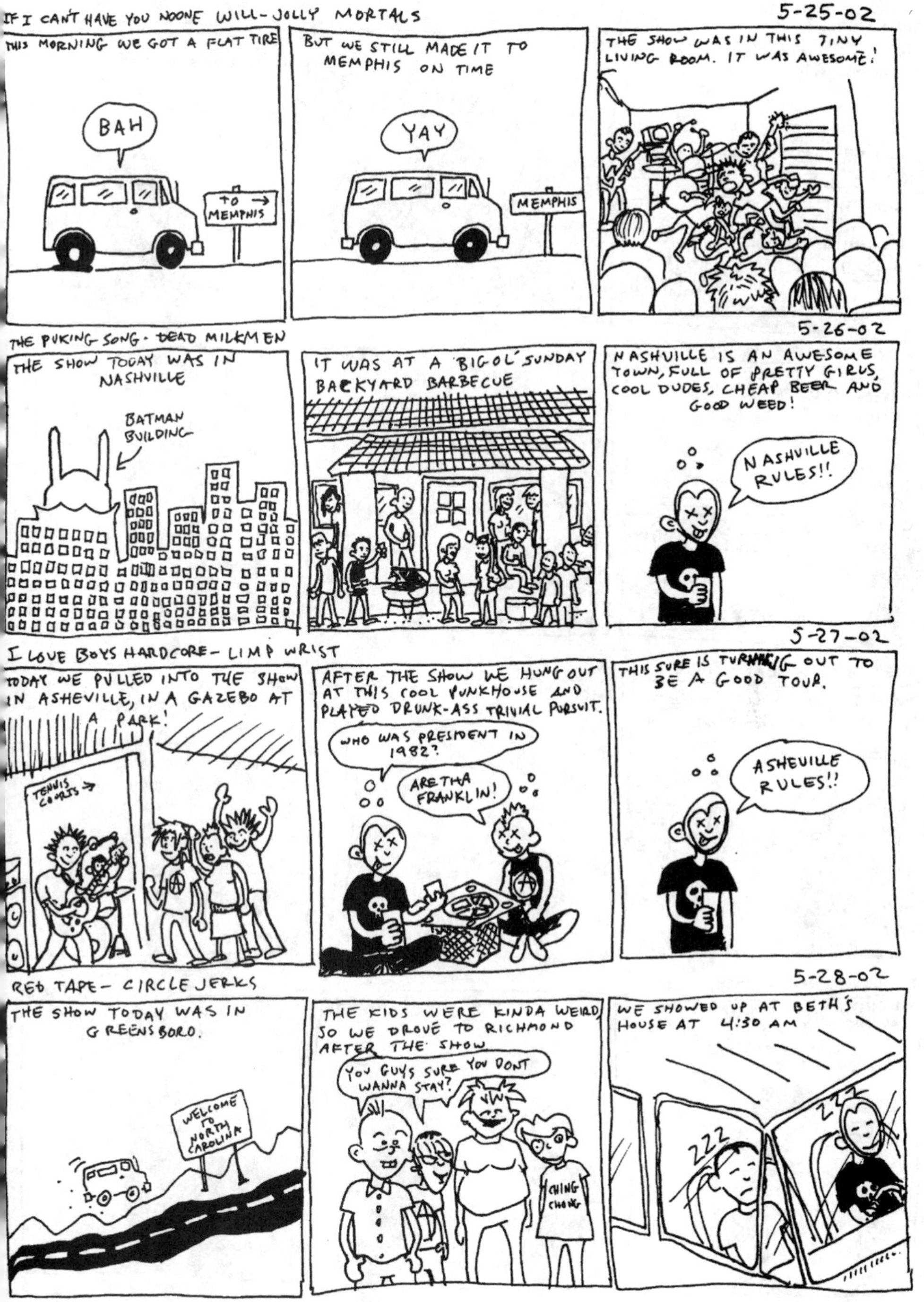
IF I CAN'T HAVE YOU NOONE WILL - JOLLY MORTALS
5-25-02
THIS MORNING WE GOT A FLAT TIRE
BAH
TO → MEMPHIS
BUT WE STILL MADE IT TO MEMPHIS ON TIME
YAY
MEMPHIS
THE SHOW WAS IN THIS TINY LIVING ROOM. IT WAS AWESOME!
THE PUKING SONG - DEAD MILKMEN
5-26-02
THE SHOW TODAY WAS IN NASHVILLE
BATMAN BUILDING
IT WAS AT A BIG OL' SUNDAY BACKYARD BARBECUE
NASHVILLE IS AN AWESOME TOWN, FULL OF PRETTY GIRLS, COOL DUDES, CHEAP BEER AND GOOD WEED!
NASHVILLE RULES!!
5-27-02
I LOVE BOYS HARDCORE - LIMP WRIST
TODAY WE PULLED INTO THE SHOW IN ASHEVILLE, IN A GAZEBO AT A PARK!
TENNIS COURTS →
AFTER THE SHOW WE HUNG OUT AT THIS COOL PUNKHOUSE AND PLAYED DRUNK-ASS TRIVIAL PURSUIT.
WHO WAS PRESIDENT IN 1982?
ARETHA FRANKLIN!
THIS SURE IS TURNING OUT TO BE A GOOD TOUR.
ASHEVILLE RULES!!
RED TAPE - CIRCLE JERKS
5-28-02
THE SHOW TODAY WAS IN GREENSBORO.
WELCOME TO NORTH CAROLINA
THE KIDS WERE KINDA WEIRD SO WE DROVE TO RICHMOND AFTER THE SHOW
YOU GUYS SURE YOU DONT WANNA STAY?
CHING CHONG
WE SHOWED UP AT BETH'S HOUSE AT 4:30 AM
ZZZ

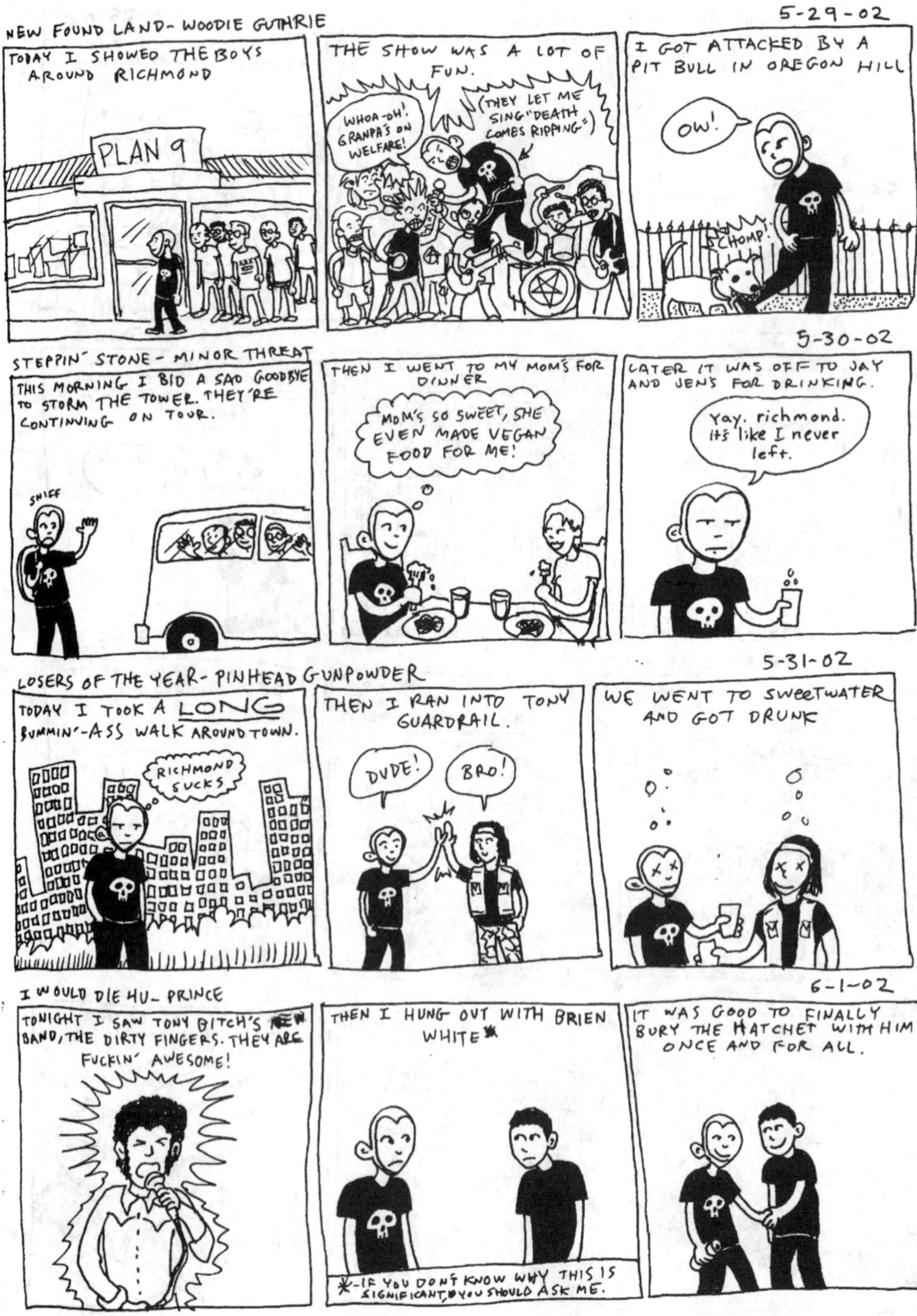

NEW FOUND LAND - WOODIE GUTHRIE
5-29-02
TODAY I SHOWED THE BOYS AROUND RICHMOND
PLAN 9
THE SHOW WAS A LOT OF FUN.
WHOA-OH! GRANPA'S ON WELFARE!
(THEY LET ME SING "DEATH COMES RIPPING")
I GOT ATTACKED BY A PIT BULL IN OREGON HILL
OW!
CHOMP!
STEPPIN' STONE - MINOR THREAT
5-30-02
THIS MORNING I BID A SAD GOODBYE TO STORM THE TOWER. THEY'RE CONTINUING ON TOUR.
SNIFF
THEN I WENT TO MY MOM'S FOR DINNER
MOM'S SO SWEET, SHE EVEN MADE VEGAN FOOD FOR ME!
LATER IT WAS OFF TO JAY AND JEN'S FOR DRINKING.
Yay. richmond. it's like I never left.
LOSERS OF THE YEAR - PINHEAD GUNPOWDER
5-31-02
TODAY I TOOK A LONG BUMMIN'-ASS WALK AROUND TOWN.
RICHMOND SUCKS
THEN I RAN INTO TONY GUARDRAIL.
DUDE!
BRO!
WE WENT TO SWEETWATER AND GOT DRUNK
I WOULD DIE 4U - PRINCE
6-1-02
TONIGHT I SAW TONY BITCH'S NEW BAND, THE DIRTY FINGERS. THEY ARE FUCKIN' AWESOME!
THEN I HUNG OUT WITH BRIEN WHITE*
*-IF YOU DON'T KNOW WHY THIS IS SIGNIFICANT, YOU SHOULD ASK ME.
IT WAS GOOD TO FINALLY BURY THE HATCHET WITH HIM ONCE AND FOR ALL.

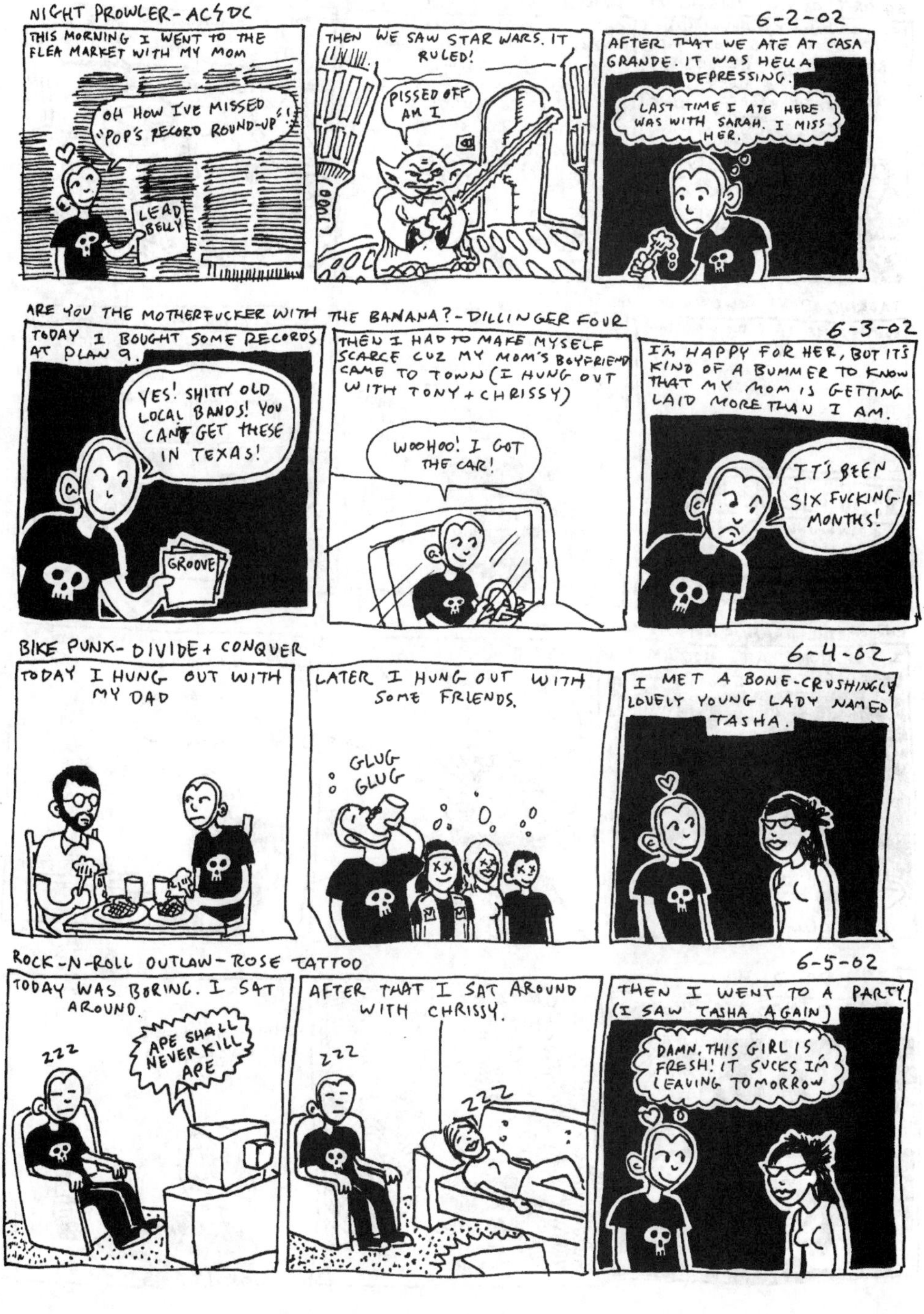
NIGHT PROWLER - AC/DC
6-2-02
THIS MORNING I WENT TO THE FLEA MARKET WITH MY MOM
OH HOW I'VE MISSED "POP'S RECORD ROUND-UP"!
LEAD BELLY
THEN WE SAW STAR WARS. IT RULED!
PISSED OFF AM I
AFTER THAT WE ATE AT CASA GRANDE. IT WAS HELLA DEPRESSING.
LAST TIME I ATE HERE WAS WITH SARAH. I MISS HER.
ARE YOU THE MOTHERFUCKER WITH THE BANANA? - DILLINGER FOUR
6-3-02
TODAY I BOUGHT SOME RECORDS AT PLAN 9.
YES! SHITTY OLD LOCAL BANDS! YOU CAN'T GET THESE IN TEXAS!
GROOVE
THEN I HAD TO MAKE MYSELF SCARCE CUZ MY MOM'S BOYFRIEND CAME TO TOWN (I HUNG OUT WITH TONY + CHRISSY)
WOOHOO! I GOT THE CAR!
I'M HAPPY FOR HER, BUT IT'S KIND OF A BUMMER TO KNOW THAT MY MOM IS GETTING LAID MORE THAN I AM.
IT'S BEEN SIX FUCKING MONTHS!
BIKE PUNX - DIVIDE + CONQUER
6-4-02
TODAY I HUNG OUT WITH MY DAD
LATER I HUNG OUT WITH SOME FRIENDS.
GLUG GLUG
I MET A BONE-CRUSHINGLY LOVELY YOUNG LADY NAMED TASHA.
ROCK-N-ROLL OUTLAW - ROSE TATTOO
6-5-02
TODAY WAS BORING. I SAT AROUND.
ZZZ
APE SHALL NEVER KILL APE
AFTER THAT I SAT AROUND WITH CHRISSY.
ZZZ
ZZZ
THEN I WENT TO A PARTY. (I SAW TASHA AGAIN)
DAMN, THIS GIRL IS FRESH! IT SUCKS I'M LEAVING TOMORROW

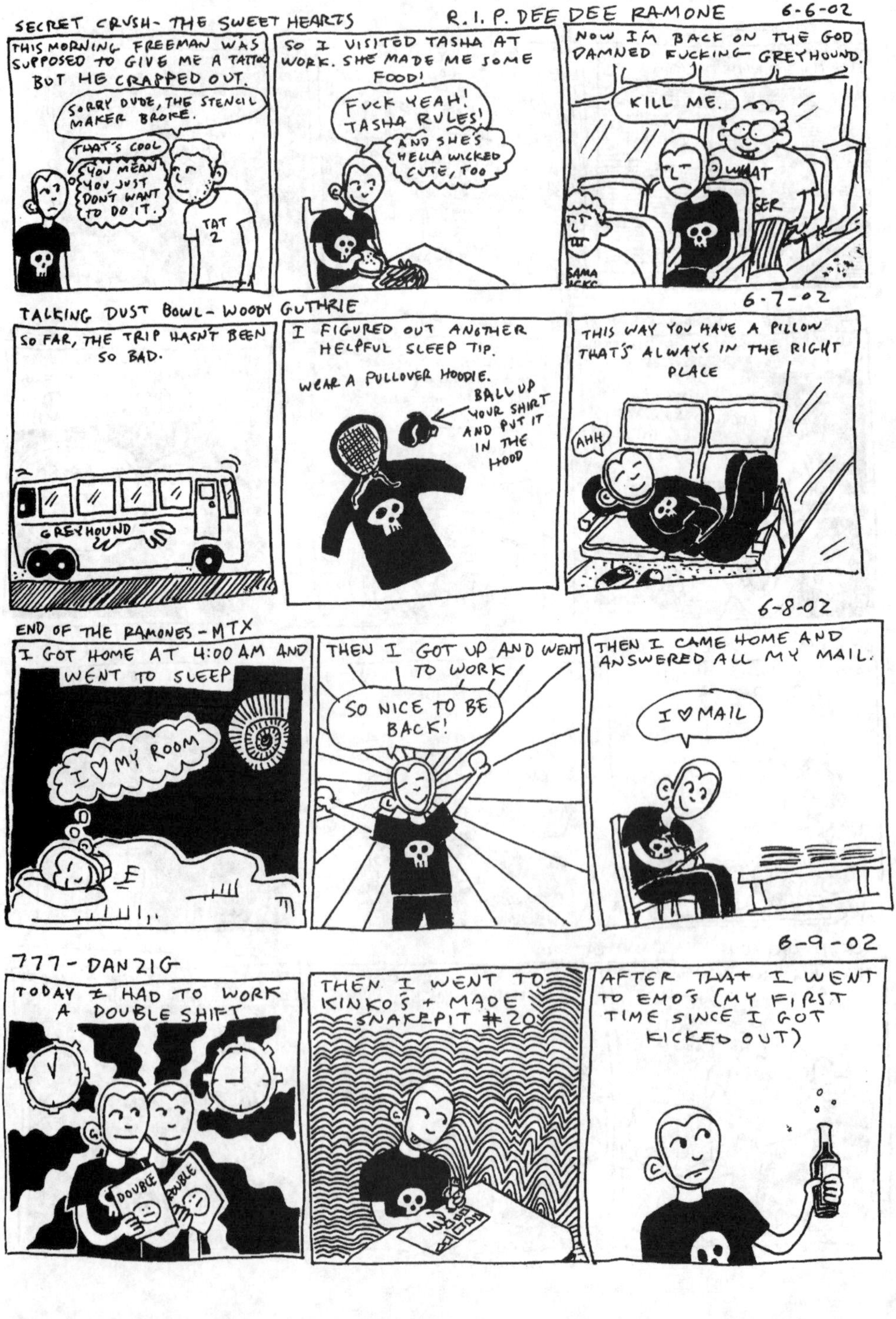
SECRET CRUSH - THE SWEETHEARTS
R.I.P. DEE DEE RAMONE
6-6-02
THIS MORNING FREEMAN WAS SUPPOSED TO GIVE ME A TATTOO BUT HE CRAPPED OUT.
SORRY DUDE, THE STENCIL MAKER BROKE.
THAT'S COOL
YOU MEAN YOU JUST DON'T WANT TO DO IT.
TAT 2
SO I VISITED TASHA AT WORK. SHE MADE ME SOME FOOD!
FUCK YEAH! TASHA RULES!
AND SHE'S HELLA WICKED CUTE, TOO
NOW I'M BACK ON THE GOD DAMNED FUCKING GREYHOUND.
KILL ME.
TALKING DUST BOWL - WOODY GUTHRIE
6-7-02
SO FAR, THE TRIP HASN'T BEEN SO BAD.
GREYHOUND
I FIGURED OUT ANOTHER HELPFUL SLEEP TIP.
WEAR A PULLOVER HOODIE.
BALL UP YOUR SHIRT AND PUT IT IN THE HOOD
THIS WAY YOU HAVE A PILLOW THAT'S ALWAYS IN THE RIGHT PLACE
AHH
END OF THE RAMONES - MTX
6-8-02
I GOT HOME AT 4:00 AM AND WENT TO SLEEP
I ♡ MY ROOM
THEN I GOT UP AND WENT TO WORK
SO NICE TO BE BACK!
THEN I CAME HOME AND ANSWERED ALL MY MAIL.
I ♡ MAIL
777 - DANZIG
6-9-02
TODAY I HAD TO WORK A DOUBLE SHIFT
DOUBLE
DOUBLE
THEN I WENT TO KINKO'S + MADE SNAKEPIT #20
AFTER THAT I WENT TO EMO'S (MY FIRST TIME SINCE I GOT KICKED OUT)

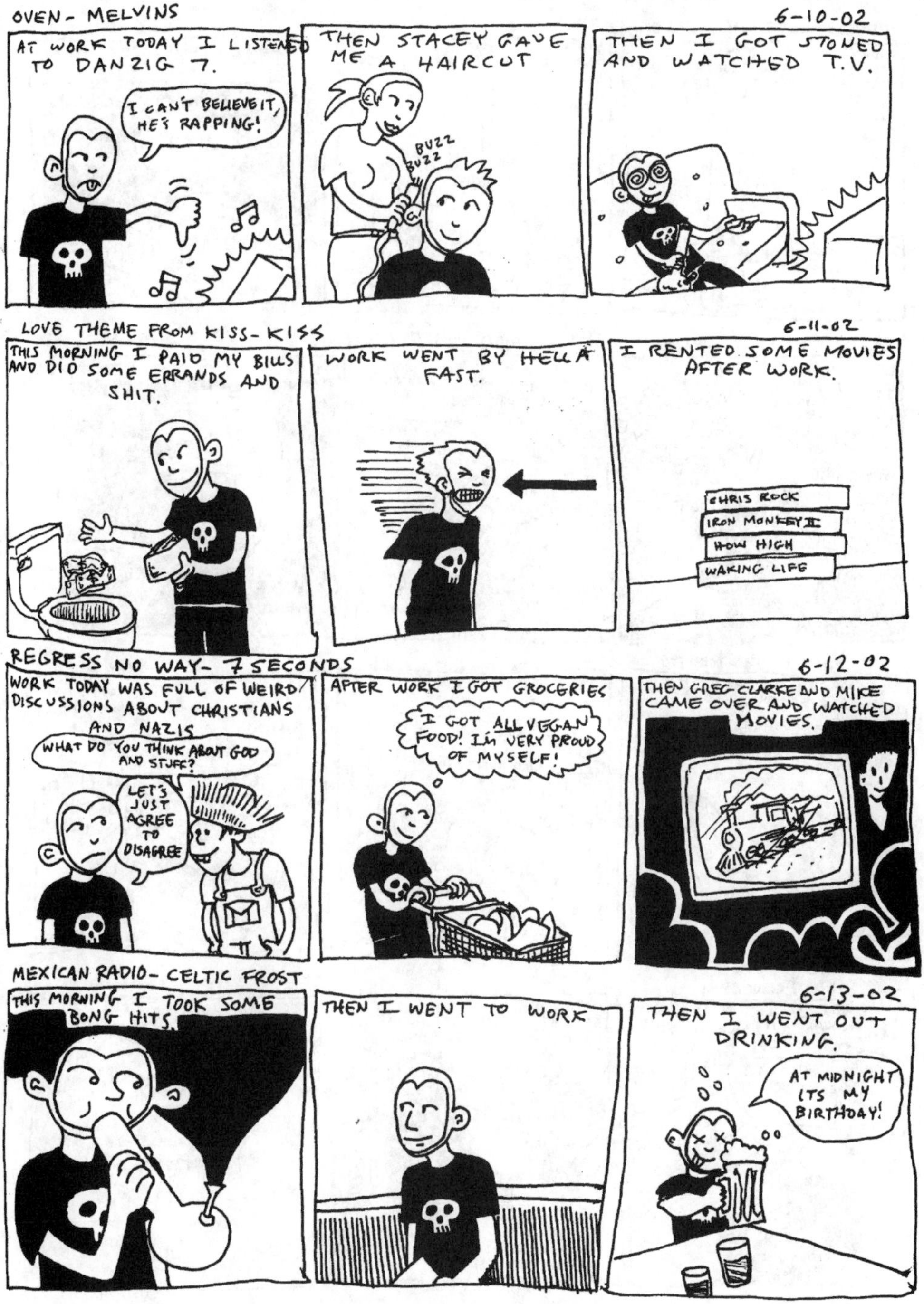
OVEN - MELVINS
6-10-02
AT WORK TODAY I LISTENED TO DANZIG 7.
I CAN'T BELIEVE IT, HE'S RAPPING!
THEN STACEY GAVE ME A HAIRCUT
BUZZ BUZZ
THEN I GOT STONED AND WATCHED T.V.
LOVE THEME FROM KISS - KISS
6-11-02
THIS MORNING I PAID MY BILLS AND DID SOME ERRANDS AND SHIT.
WORK WENT BY HELLA FAST.
I RENTED SOME MOVIES AFTER WORK.
CHRIS ROCK
IRON MONKEY II
HOW HIGH
WAKING LIFE
REGRESS NO WAY - 7 SECONDS
6-12-02
WORK TODAY WAS FULL OF WEIRD DISCUSSIONS ABOUT CHRISTIANS AND NAZIS
WHAT DO YOU THINK ABOUT GOD AND STUFF?
LET'S JUST AGREE TO DISAGREE
AFTER WORK I GOT GROCERIES
I GOT ALL VEGAN FOOD! I'M VERY PROUD OF MYSELF!
THEN GREG CLARKE AND MIKE CAME OVER AND WATCHED MOVIES.
MEXICAN RADIO - CELTIC FROST
6-13-02
THIS MORNING I TOOK SOME BONG HITS.
THEN I WENT TO WORK
THEN I WENT OUT DRINKING.
AT MIDNIGHT ITS MY BIRTHDAY!

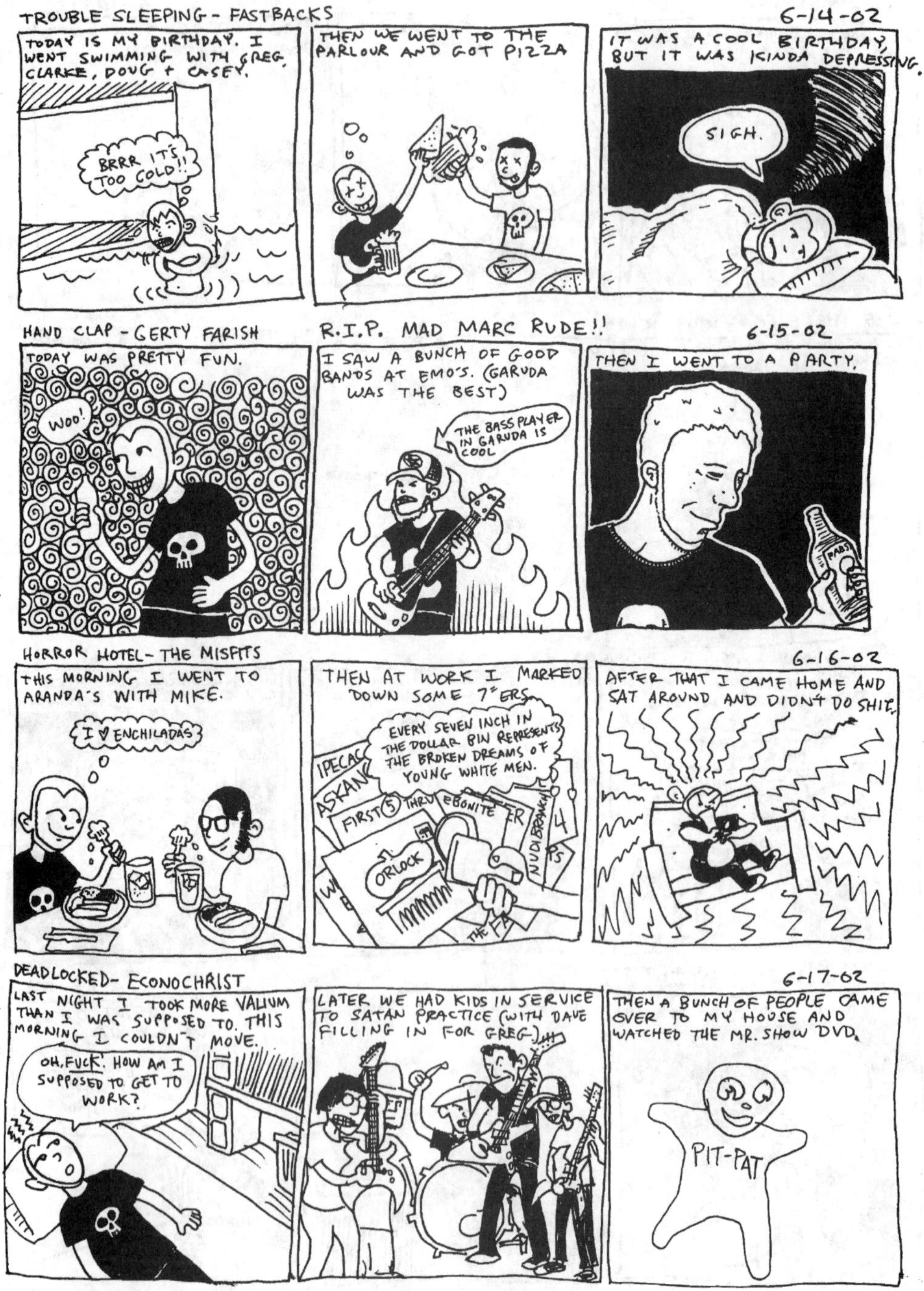
TROUBLE SLEEPING - FASTBACKS
6-14-02
TODAY IS MY BIRTHDAY. I WENT SWIMMING WITH GREG, CLARKE, DOUG + CASEY.
BRRR IT'S TOO COLD!!
THEN WE WENT TO THE PARLOUR AND GOT PIZZA
IT WAS A COOL BIRTHDAY, BUT IT WAS KINDA DEPRESSING.
SIGH.
HAND CLAP - GERTY FARISH
R.I.P. MAD MARC RUDE!!
6-15-02
TODAY WAS PRETTY FUN.
WOO!
I SAW A BUNCH OF GOOD BANDS AT EMO'S. (GARUDA WAS THE BEST)
THE BASS PLAYER IN GARUDA IS COOL
THEN I WENT TO A PARTY.
PABST
HORROR HOTEL - THE MISFITS
6-16-02
THIS MORNING I WENT TO ARANDA'S WITH MIKE.
I ♥ ENCHILADAS
THEN AT WORK I MARKED DOWN SOME 7"ERS
EVERY SEVEN INCH IN THE DOLLAR BIN REPRESENTS THE BROKEN DREAMS OF YOUNG WHITE MEN.
IPECAC
ASKAN
FIRST 5 THRU
EBONITE
NUDIBRANCH
ORLOCK
AFTER THAT I CAME HOME AND SAT AROUND AND DIDN'T DO SHIT.
DEADLOCKED - ECONOCHRIST
6-17-02
LAST NIGHT I TOOK MORE VALIUM THAN I WAS SUPPOSED TO. THIS MORNING I COULDN'T MOVE.
OH, FUCK. HOW AM I SUPPOSED TO GET TO WORK?
LATER WE HAD KIDS IN SERVICE TO SATAN PRACTICE (WITH DAVE FILLING IN FOR GREG.)
THEN A BUNCH OF PEOPLE CAME OVER TO MY HOUSE AND WATCHED THE MR. SHOW DVD.
PIT-PAT

WE ARE THE CHAMPIONS - THE OATH   6-18-02

TODAY WAS PAYDAY.

THAT'S FUCKIN STUPID HELLA WICKED TIGHT, DOG.
PLAYA PLAYA

AFTER WORK I WORKED ON ZINE STUFF

XEROX

AND MORE ZINE STUFF

A.L.F. ~ VAMPIRE LEZBOS   6-19-02

I WAS KINDA DEPRESSED TODAY.

BLEAH

AFTER WORK I DID SOME KINKO'S SHIT.

LANIER
THE KING OF COPY MACHINES

THEN WE HAD KIDS IN SERVICE TO SATAN PRACTICE

I'M THE WORST DRUMMER EVER!

ON THE BALCONY - PRE-SKOOL   6-20-02

THIS MORNING I WENT ALL OVER TOWN LOOKING FOR THE MR. SHOW DVD. NOBODY HAD IT.

HIGHLAND MALL
BEST BUY
TOWER RECORDS
VIDEO
AUSTIN
TARGET
WATER LOO VIDEO

THEN I WENT TO WORK...

I WANNA GO TO THE PORTLAND ZINE SYMPOSIUM SO BAD, BUT I CAN'T AFFORD IT!

AFTER THAT I HUNG OUT AT KYLE'S HOUSE AND GOT STOOOOOONED.

PRESIDENT OF THE ANARCHIST CLUB - SEWERTROUT   6-21-02

THIS MORNING AS I WAS RIDING THE BUS TO WORK, I SAW THE MOST BEAUTIFUL GIRL I'D EVER SEEN.

SHE MUST WORK AT TOWER. IT LOOKS LIKE SHE'S ON A SMOKE BREAK.
TOWER

I DECIDED TO GO TO TOWER AND GIVE HER A FLYER FOR THE SHOW TOMORROW, BUT I CHICKENED OUT.
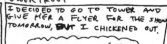

UH, THE TIMING'S NOT RIGHT. I'LL NEVER GET TO MEET HER.

TONIGHT AT A PARTY, MEASON INTRODUCED HER TO ME.

BEN, THIS IS ROSALIE. SHE JUST MOVED TO TOWN.
HI

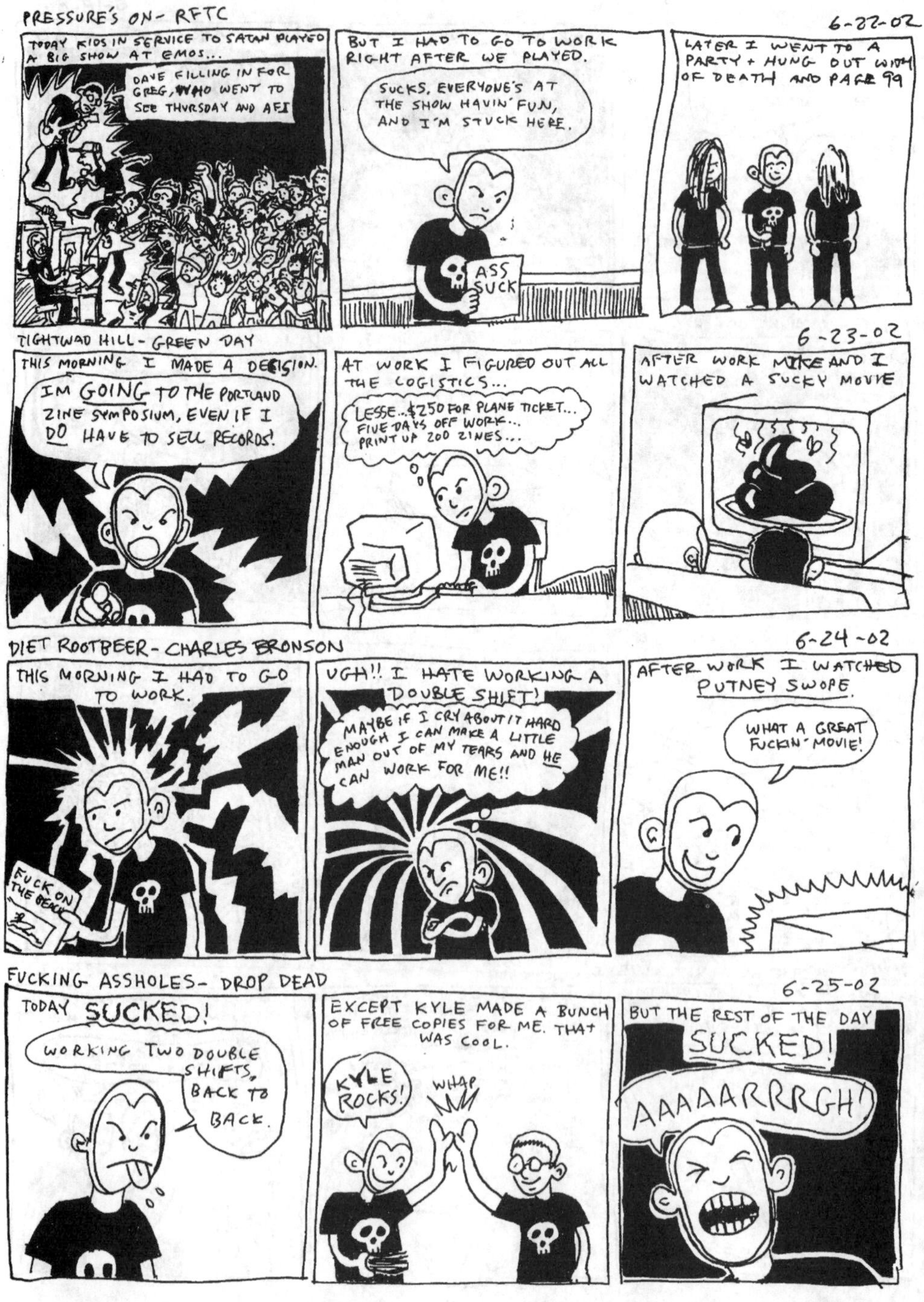
PRESSURE'S ON- RFTC
6-22-02
TODAY KIDS IN SERVICE TO SATAN PLAYED A BIG SHOW AT EMOS...
DAVE FILLING IN FOR GREG, WHO WENT TO SEE THURSDAY AND AFI
BUT I HAD TO GO TO WORK RIGHT AFTER WE PLAYED.
SUCKS. EVERYONE'S AT THE SHOW HAVIN' FUN, AND I'M STUCK HERE.
ASS SUCK
LATER I WENT TO A PARTY + HUNG OUT WITH OF DEATH AND PAGE 99
TIGHTWAD HILL- GREEN DAY
6-23-02
THIS MORNING I MADE A DECISION.
IM GOING TO THE PORTLAND ZINE SYMPOSIUM, EVEN IF I DO HAVE TO SELL RECORDS!
AT WORK I FIGURED OUT ALL THE LOGISTICS...
LESSE...$250 FOR PLANE TICKET... FIVE DAYS OFF WORK... PRINT UP 200 ZINES...
AFTER WORK MIKE AND I WATCHED A SUCKY MOVIE
DIET ROOTBEER- CHARLES BRONSON
6-24-02
THIS MORNING I HAD TO GO TO WORK.
FUCK ON THE BEACH
UGH!! I HATE WORKING A DOUBLE SHIFT!
MAYBE IF I CRY ABOUT IT HARD ENOUGH I CAN MAKE A LITTLE MAN OUT OF MY TEARS AND HE CAN WORK FOR ME!!
AFTER WORK I WATCHED PUTNEY SWOPE.
WHAT A GREAT FUCKIN' MOVIE!
FUCKING ASSHOLES- DROP DEAD
6-25-02
TODAY SUCKED!
WORKING TWO DOUBLE SHIFTS, BACK TO BACK.
EXCEPT KYLE MADE A BUNCH OF FREE COPIES FOR ME. THAT WAS COOL.
KYLE ROCKS!
WHAP
BUT THE REST OF THE DAY SUCKED!
AAAAARRRGH!

THE ROLLER - MAN IS THE BASTARD

6-26-02

WORK WAS OKAY THIS MORNING

AFTERWARD I BOUGHT MY PLANE TICKET TO PORTLAND

THEN I SAW E.T.A. PLAY AN AWESOME SHOW!

A CHEYENNE WAR DANCE FROM A NATIVE AMERICAN RECORD

6-27-02

TODAY THE KIDS IN SERVICE TO SATAN PLAYED A TERRIBLE SHOW.

AFTERWARD, THAT GIRL ROSALEE FROM A COUPLE OF PAGES AGO GAVE ME HER NUMBER.

GIMMIE A CALL IF YOU WANNA HANG OUT SOMETIME.

WORD!

THEN WE HAD A PARTY AT MY HOUSE AND WATCHED THE NEW LIGHTNING BOLT DVD

GREG'S BACK!

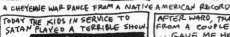

I WON'T EAT IT - E.T.A.

6-28-02

TODAY I WORKED.

THEN I SAT AROUND

THEN I WENT TO SOME LAME-ASS PARTY.

TAKE -A- SHIT

ZZZZ

IT WAS SO LAME ITS NOT EVEN WORTH DRAWING.

LONG TIME - BOSTON

TONIGHT AT WORK WE HAD AN IN-STORE.

AFTER IT WAS OVER, FORSTELLA FORD'S FUCKING ASSHOLE ROADIE YELLED AT ME FOR LIKE 20 MINUTES.

THIS SHOW SUCKS! NOBODY IS HERE! THERE WERE NO FLIERS! YOU'RE WASTING EVERYONE'S TIME! NOBODY COOKS FOR THE BANDS!

I'M NOT A PROMOTER. I JUST WORK HERE.

6-29-02

LATER I HUNG OUT WITH GREG, CLARKE, KYLE AND J.D.

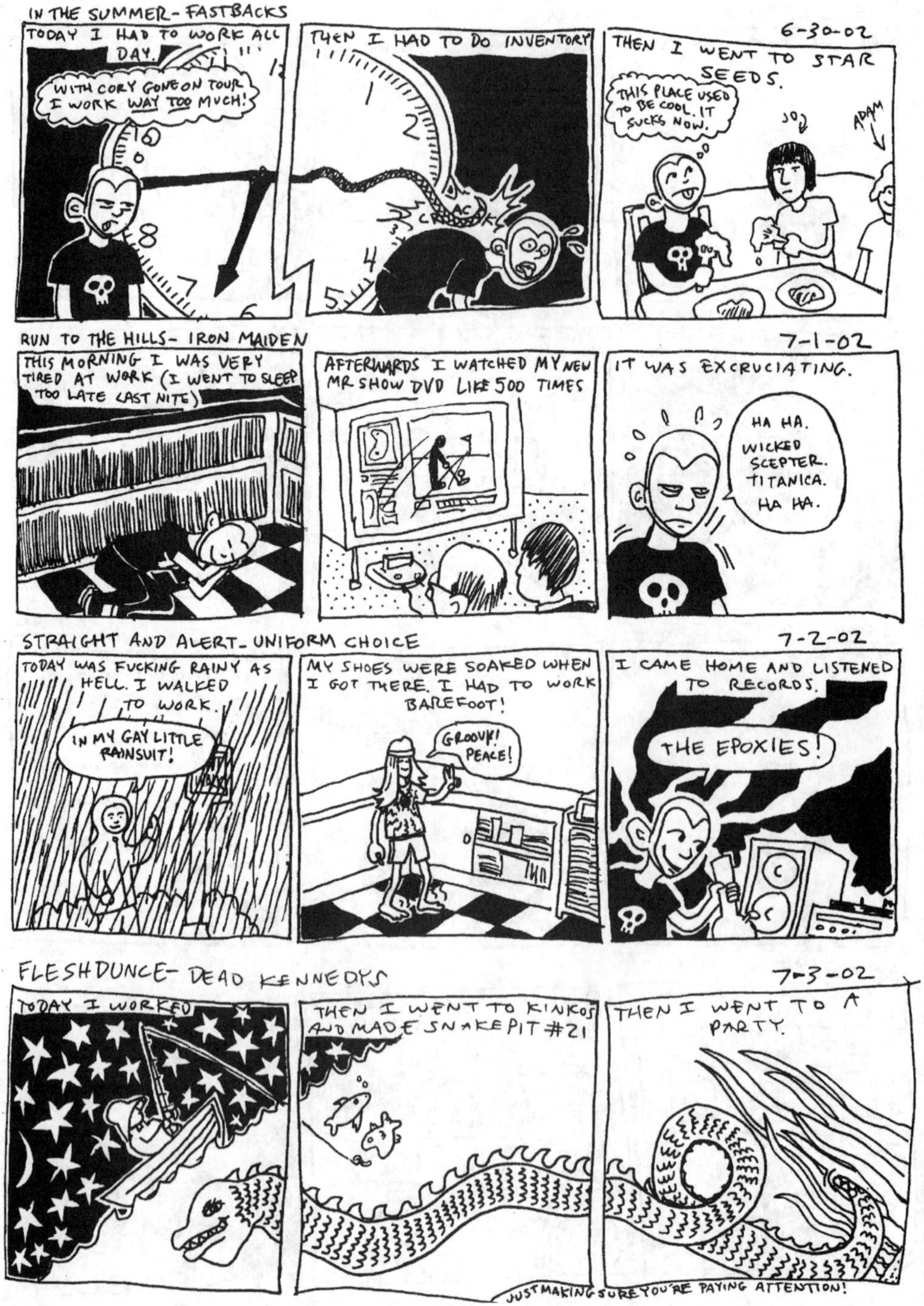

IN THE SUMMER- FASTBACKS
6-30-02
TODAY I HAD TO WORK ALL DAY.
WITH CORY GONE ON TOUR I WORK WAY TOO MUCH!
THEN I HAD TO DO INVENTORY
CRAACK
THEN I WENT TO STAR SEEDS.
THIS PLACE USED TO BE COOL. IT SUCKS NOW.
JO
ADAM
RUN TO THE HILLS- IRON MAIDEN
7-1-02
THIS MORNING I WAS VERY TIRED AT WORK (I WENT TO SLEEP TOO LATE LAST NITE)
AFTERWARDS I WATCHED MY NEW MR SHOW DVD LIKE 500 TIMES
IT WAS EXCRUCIATING.
HA HA. WICKED SCEPTER. TITANICA. HA HA.
STRAIGHT AND ALERT- UNIFORM CHOICE
7-2-02
TODAY WAS FUCKING RAINY AS HELL. I WALKED TO WORK.
IN MY GAY LITTLE RAINSUIT!
MY SHOES WERE SOAKED WHEN I GOT THERE. I HAD TO WORK BAREFOOT!
GROOVY! PEACE!
I CAME HOME AND LISTENED TO RECORDS.
THE EPOXIES!
FLESHDUNCE- DEAD KENNEDYS
7-3-02
TODAY I WORKED
THEN I WENT TO KINKOS AND MADE SNAKEPIT #21
THEN I WENT TO A PARTY.
JUST MAKING SURE YOU'RE PAYING ATTENTION!

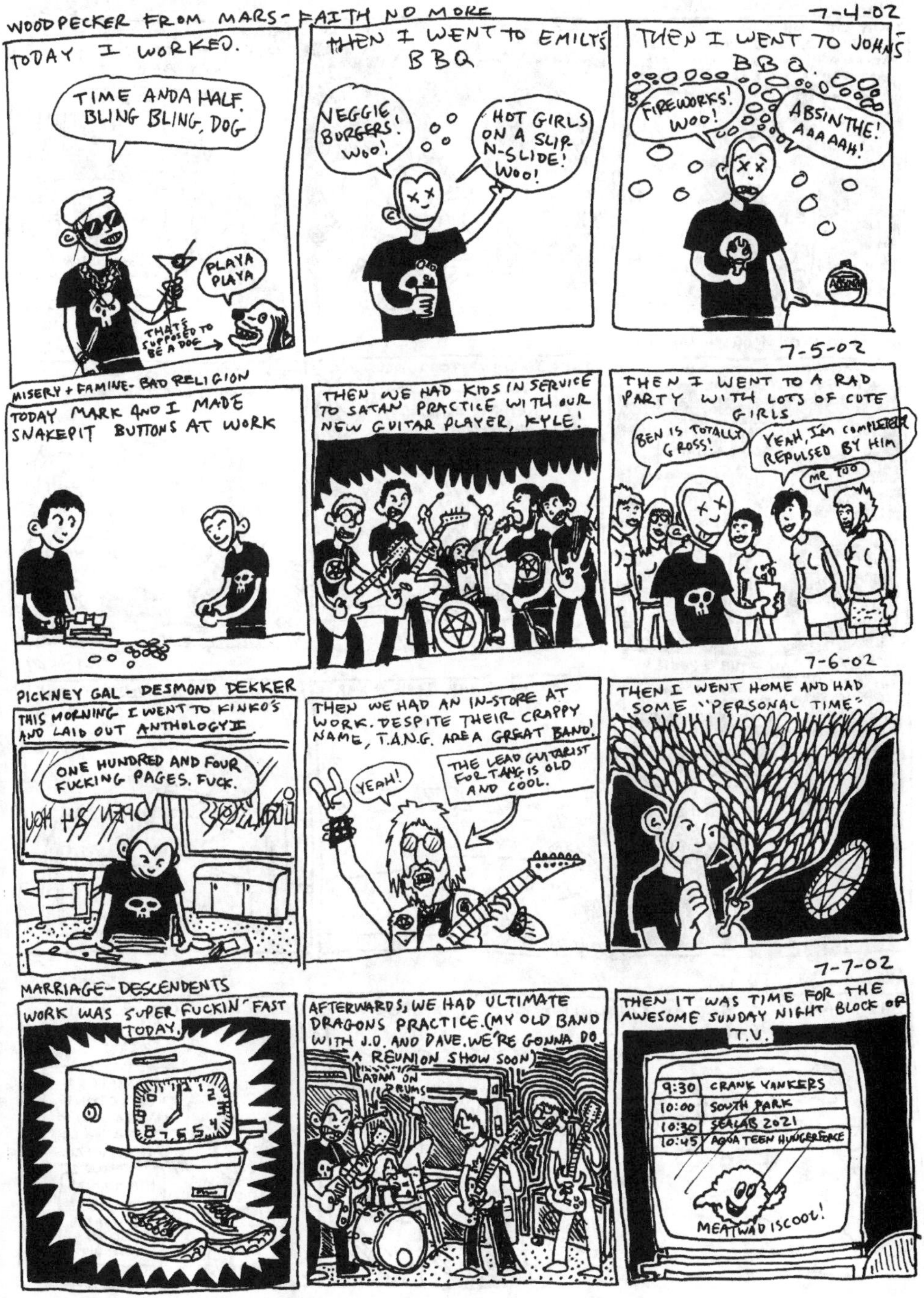
WOODPECKER FROM MARS - FAITH NO MORE
7-4-02
TODAY I WORKED.
TIME AND A HALF. BLING BLING, DOG
PLAYA PLAYA
THAT'S SUPPOSED TO BE A DOG
THEN I WENT TO EMILY'S BBQ
VEGGIE BURGERS! WOO!
HOT GIRLS ON A SLIP-N-SLIDE! WOO!
THEN I WENT TO JOHN'S BBQ.
FIREWORKS! WOO!
ABSINTHE! AAAAAH!
7-5-02
MISERY + FAMINE - BAD RELIGION
TODAY MARK AND I MADE SNAKEPIT BUTTONS AT WORK
THEN WE HAD KIDS IN SERVICE TO SATAN PRACTICE WITH OUR NEW GUITAR PLAYER, KYLE!
THEN I WENT TO A RAD PARTY WITH LOTS OF CUTE GIRLS
BEN IS TOTALLY GROSS!
YEAH, I'M COMPLETELY REPULSED BY HIM
ME TOO
7-6-02
PICKNEY GAL - DESMOND DEKKER
THIS MORNING I WENT TO KINKO'S AND LAID OUT ANTHOLOGY II
ONE HUNDRED AND FOUR FUCKING PAGES. FUCK.
THEN WE HAD AN IN-STORE AT WORK. DESPITE THEIR CRAPPY NAME, T.A.N.G. ARE A GREAT BAND!
YEAH!
THE LEAD GUITARIST FOR TANG IS OLD AND COOL.
THEN I WENT HOME AND HAD SOME "PERSONAL TIME"
7-7-02
MARRIAGE - DESCENDENTS
WORK WAS SUPER FUCKIN' FAST TODAY.
AFTERWARDS, WE HAD ULTIMATE DRAGONS PRACTICE. (MY OLD BAND WITH J.D. AND DAVE. WE'RE GONNA DO A REUNION SHOW SOON)
ADAM ON DRUMS
THEN IT WAS TIME FOR THE AWESOME SUNDAY NIGHT BLOCK OF T.V.
9:30 CRANK YANKERS
10:00 SOUTH PARK
10:30 SEALAB 2021
10:45 AQUA TEEN HUNGER FORCE
MEATWAD IS COOL!

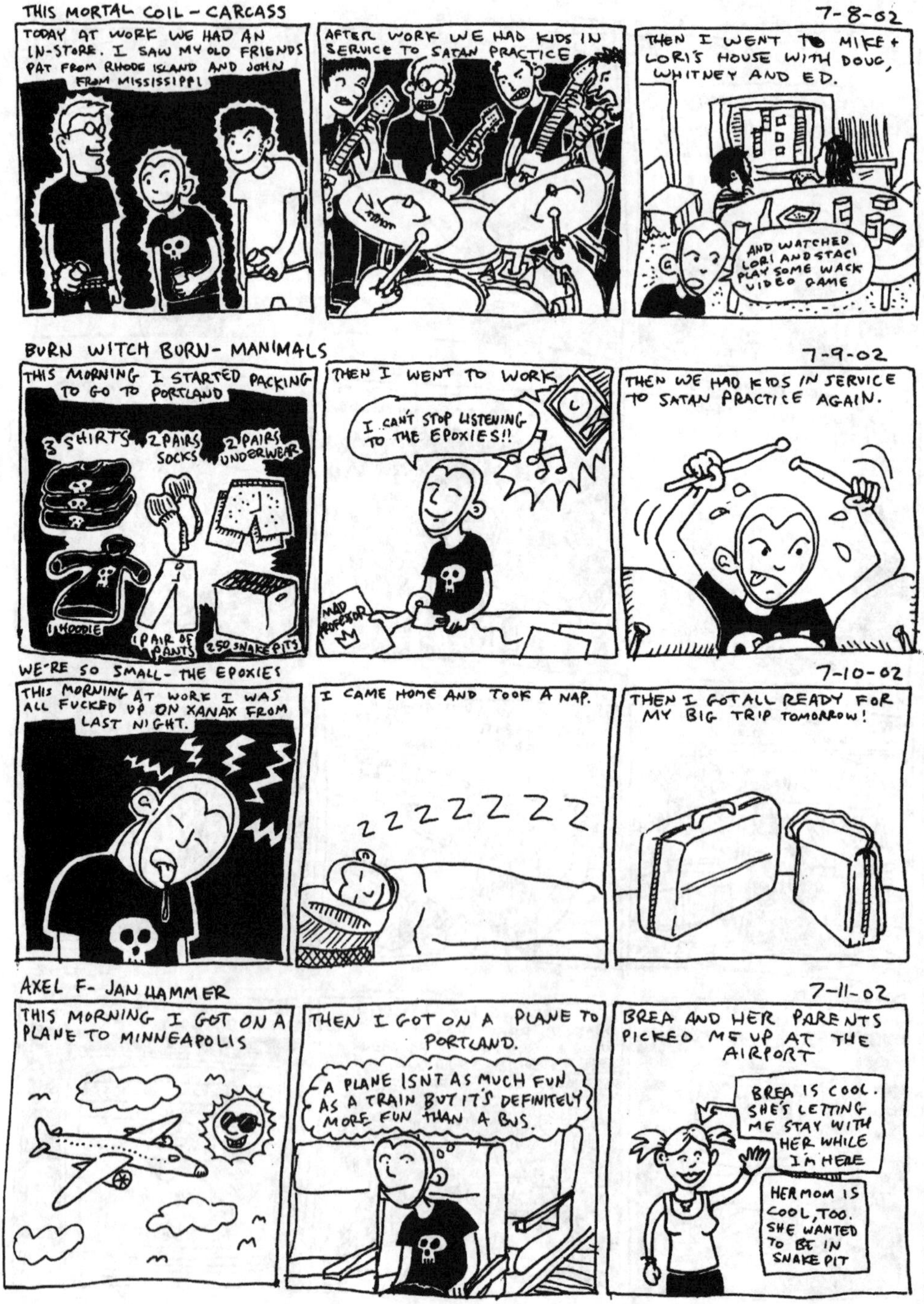
THIS MORTAL COIL - CARCASS
7-8-02
TODAY AT WORK WE HAD AN IN-STORE. I SAW MY OLD FRIENDS PAT FROM RHODE ISLAND AND JOHN FROM MISSISSIPPI
AFTER WORK WE HAD KIDS IN SERVICE TO SATAN PRACTICE
THEN I WENT TO MIKE + LORI'S HOUSE WITH DOUG, WHITNEY AND ED.
AND WATCHED LORI AND STACI PLAY SOME WACK VIDEO GAME
BURN WITCH BURN - MANIMALS
7-9-02
THIS MORNING I STARTED PACKING TO GO TO PORTLAND
3 SHIRTS
2 PAIRS SOCKS
2 PAIRS UNDERWEAR
1 HOODIE
1 PAIR OF PANTS
250 SNAKE PITS
THEN I WENT TO WORK
I CAN'T STOP LISTENING TO THE EPOXIES!!
MAD PROFESSOR
THEN WE HAD KIDS IN SERVICE TO SATAN PRACTICE AGAIN.
WE'RE SO SMALL - THE EPOXIES
7-10-02
THIS MORNING AT WORK I WAS ALL FUCKED UP ON XANAX FROM LAST NIGHT.
I CAME HOME AND TOOK A NAP.
ZZZZZZZ
THEN I GOT ALL READY FOR MY BIG TRIP TOMORROW!
AXEL F - JAN HAMMER
7-11-02
THIS MORNING I GOT ON A PLANE TO MINNEAPOLIS
THEN I GOT ON A PLANE TO PORTLAND.
A PLANE ISN'T AS MUCH FUN AS A TRAIN BUT IT'S DEFINITELY MORE FUN THAN A BUS.
BREA AND HER PARENTS PICKED ME UP AT THE AIRPORT
BREA IS COOL. SHE'S LETTING ME STAY WITH HER WHILE I'M HERE
HER MOM IS COOL, TOO. SHE WANTED TO BE IN SNAKE PIT

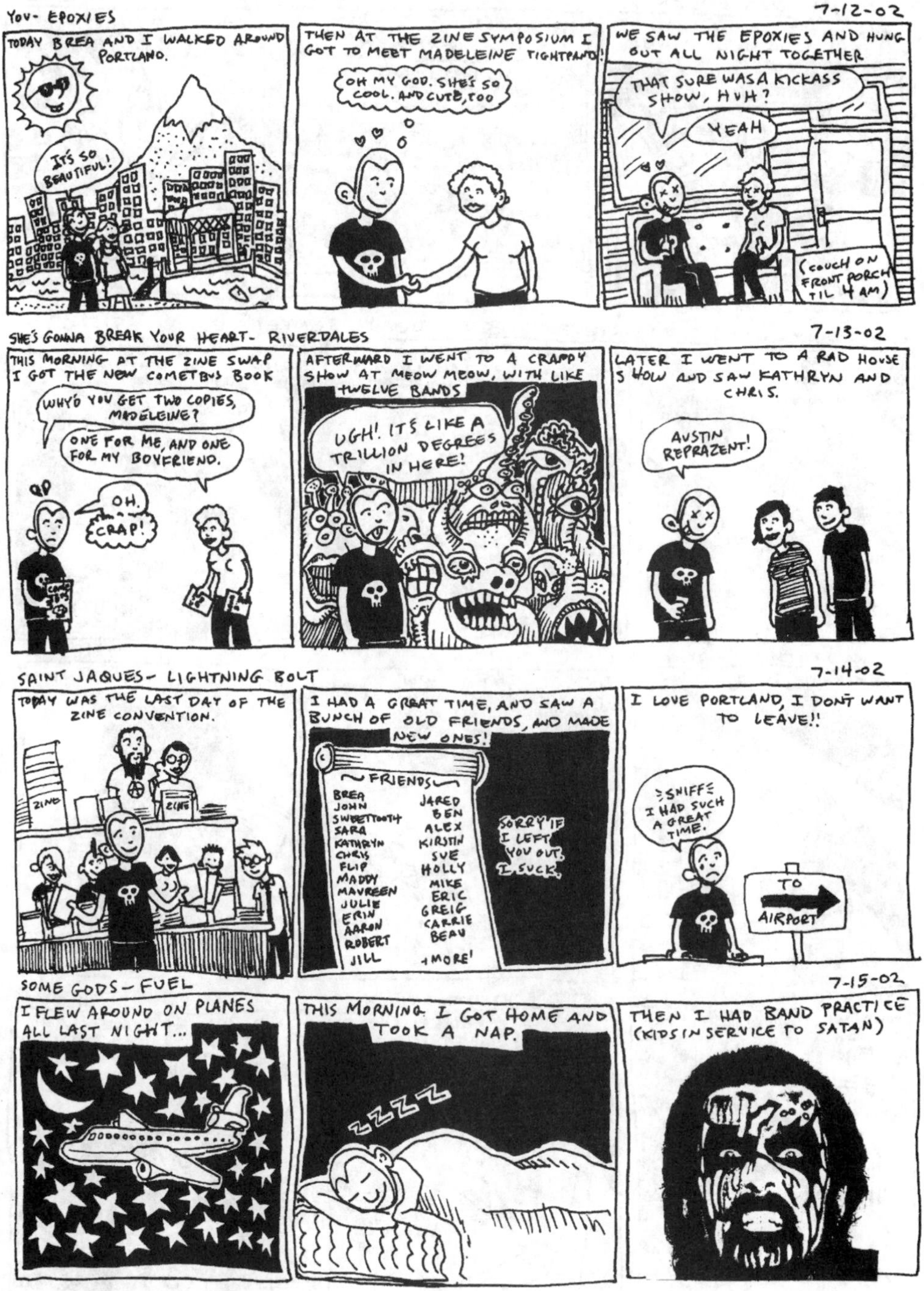
YOU- EPOXIES
7-12-02
TODAY BREA AND I WALKED AROUND PORTLAND.
IT'S SO BEAUTIFUL!
THEN AT THE ZINE SYMPOSIUM I GOT TO MEET MADELEINE TIGHTPANTS!
OH MY GOD. SHE'S SO COOL. AND CUTE, TOO
WE SAW THE EPOXIES AND HUNG OUT ALL NIGHT TOGETHER
THAT SURE WAS A KICKASS SHOW, HUH?
YEAH
(COUCH ON FRONT PORCH TIL 4 AM)
SHE'S GONNA BREAK YOUR HEART- RIVERDALES
7-13-02
THIS MORNING AT THE ZINE SWAP I GOT THE NEW COMETBUS BOOK
WHY'D YOU GET TWO COPIES, MADELEINE?
ONE FOR ME, AND ONE FOR MY BOYFRIEND.
OH.
CRAP!
AFTERWARD I WENT TO A CRAPPY SHOW AT MEOW MEOW, WITH LIKE TWELVE BANDS
UGH! IT'S LIKE A TRILLION DEGREES IN HERE!
LATER I WENT TO A RAD HOUSE SHOW AND SAW KATHRYN AND CHRIS.
AUSTIN REPRAZENT!
SAINT JAQUES- LIGHTNING BOLT
7-14-02
TODAY WAS THE LAST DAY OF THE ZINE CONVENTION.
ZINE
ZINE
I HAD A GREAT TIME, AND SAW A BUNCH OF OLD FRIENDS, AND MADE NEW ONES!
~FRIENDS~
BREA
JOHN
SWEETTOOTH
SARA
KATHRYN
CHRIS
FLIP
MADDY
MAUREEN
JULIE
ERIN
AARON
ROBERT
JILL
JARED
BEN
ALEX
KIRSTIN
SUE
HOLLY
MIKE
ERIC
GREIG
CARRIE
BEAU
+MORE!
SORRY IF I LEFT YOU OUT. I SUCK.
I LOVE PORTLAND, I DON'T WANT TO LEAVE!!
SNIFF
I HAD SUCH A GREAT TIME.
TO AIRPORT
SOME GODS-FUEL
7-15-02
I FLEW AROUND ON PLANES ALL LAST NIGHT...
THIS MORNING I GOT HOME AND TOOK A NAP.
ZZZZ
THEN I HAD BAND PRACTICE (KIDS IN SERVICE TO SATAN)

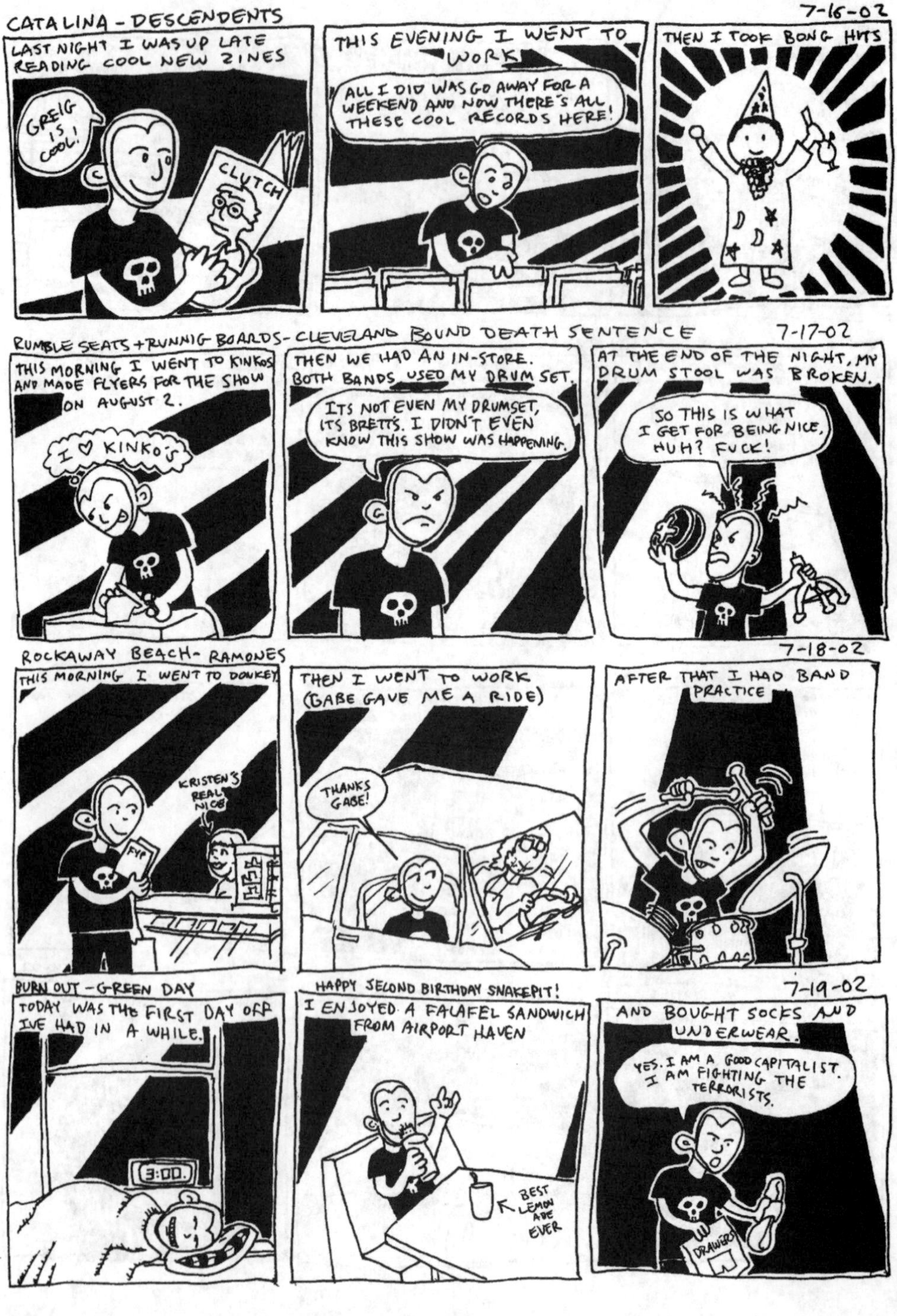
CATALINA - DESCENDENTS
7-16-02
LAST NIGHT I WAS UP LATE READING COOL NEW ZINES
GREIG IS COOL!
CLUTCH
THIS EVENING I WENT TO WORK
ALL I DID WAS GO AWAY FOR A WEEKEND AND NOW THERE'S ALL THESE COOL RECORDS HERE!
THEN I TOOK BONG HITS
RUMBLE SEATS + RUNNING BOARDS - CLEVELAND BOUND DEATH SENTENCE
7-17-02
THIS MORNING I WENT TO KINKOS AND MADE FLYERS FOR THE SHOW ON AUGUST 2.
I ♡ KINKO'S
THEN WE HAD AN IN-STORE. BOTH BANDS USED MY DRUM SET.
ITS NOT EVEN MY DRUMSET, ITS BRETT'S. I DIDN'T EVEN KNOW THIS SHOW WAS HAPPENING.
AT THE END OF THE NIGHT, MY DRUM STOOL WAS BROKEN.
SO THIS IS WHAT I GET FOR BEING NICE, HUH? FUCK!
ROCKAWAY BEACH - RAMONES
7-18-02
THIS MORNING I WENT TO DONKEY
KRISTEN'S REAL NICE
FYP
THEN I WENT TO WORK (GABE GAVE ME A RIDE)
THANKS GABE!
AFTER THAT I HAD BAND PRACTICE
BURN OUT - GREEN DAY
HAPPY SECOND BIRTHDAY SNAKEPIT!
7-19-02
TODAY WAS THE FIRST DAY OFF IVE HAD IN A WHILE.
3:00.
I ENJOYED A FALAFEL SANDWICH FROM AIRPORT HAVEN
BEST LEMONADE EVER
AND BOUGHT SOCKS AND UNDERWEAR.
YES. I AM A GOOD CAPITALIST. I AM FIGHTING THE TERRORISTS.
DRAWERS

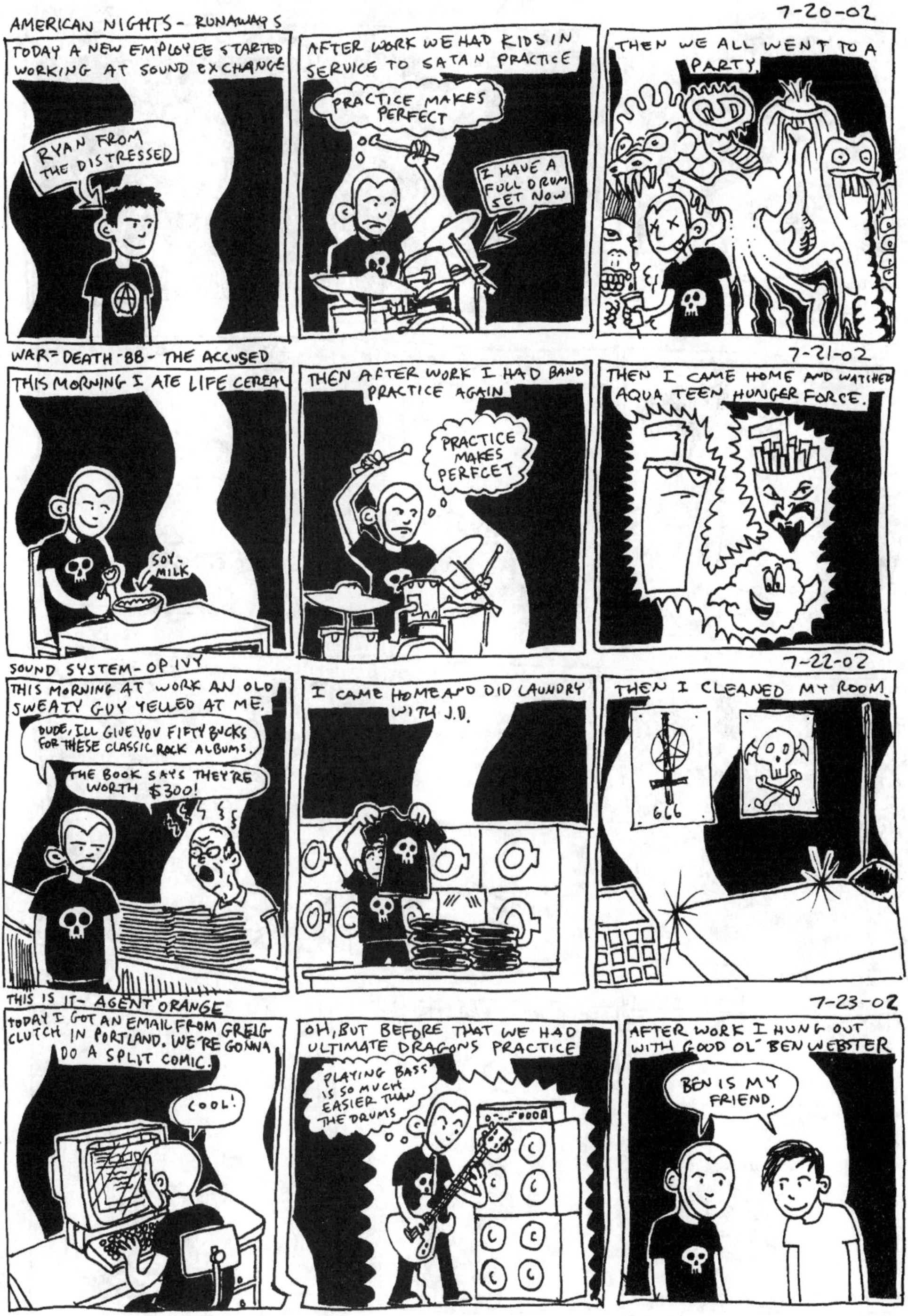
AMERICAN NIGHTS - RUNAWAYS
7-20-02
TODAY A NEW EMPLOYEE STARTED WORKING AT SOUND EXCHANGE
RYAN FROM THE DISTRESSED
AFTER WORK WE HAD KIDS IN SERVICE TO SATAN PRACTICE
PRACTICE MAKES PERFECT
I HAVE A FULL DRUM SET NOW
THEN WE ALL WENT TO A PARTY.
WAR = DEATH - 88 - THE ACCUSED
7-21-02
THIS MORNING I ATE LIFE CEREAL
SOY-MILK
THEN AFTER WORK I HAD BAND PRACTICE AGAIN
PRACTICE MAKES PERFCET
THEN I CAME HOME AND WATCHED AQUA TEEN HUNGER FORCE.
SOUND SYSTEM - OP IVY
7-22-02
THIS MORNING AT WORK AN OLD SWEATY GUY YELLED AT ME.
DUDE, ILL GIVE YOU FIFTY BUCKS FOR THESE CLASSIC ROCK ALBUMS.
THE BOOK SAYS THEY'RE WORTH $300!
I CAME HOME AND DID LAUNDRY WITH J.D.
THEN I CLEANED MY ROOM.
666
THIS IS IT - AGENT ORANGE
7-23-02
TODAY I GOT AN EMAIL FROM GREIG CLUTCH IN PORTLAND. WE'RE GONNA DO A SPLIT COMIC.
COOL!
OH, BUT BEFORE THAT WE HAD ULTIMATE DRAGONS PRACTICE
PLAYING BASS IS SO MUCH EASIER THAN THE DRUMS
AFTER WORK I HUNG OUT WITH GOOD OL' BEN WEBSTER
BEN IS MY FRIEND.

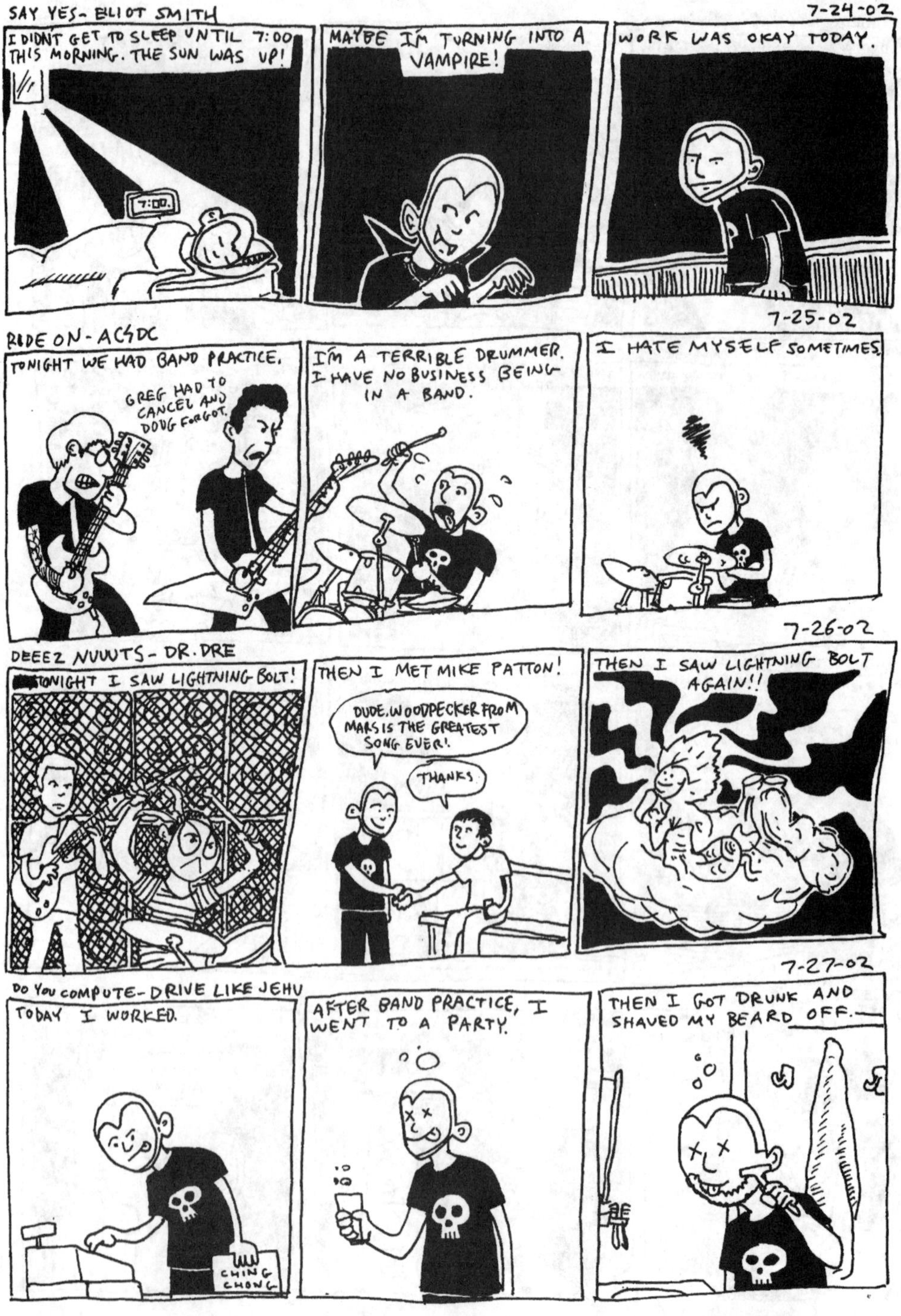
SAY YES - ELLIOT SMITH
7-24-02
I DIDN'T GET TO SLEEP UNTIL 7:00 THIS MORNING. THE SUN WAS UP!
7:00.
MAYBE I'M TURNING INTO A VAMPIRE!
WORK WAS OKAY TODAY.
7-25-02
RIDE ON - AC/DC
TONIGHT WE HAD BAND PRACTICE.
GREG HAD TO CANCEL AND DOUG FORGOT.
I'M A TERRIBLE DRUMMER. I HAVE NO BUSINESS BEING IN A BAND.
I HATE MYSELF SOMETIMES.
7-26-02
DEEEZ NUUUTS - DR. DRE
[redacted]TONIGHT I SAW LIGHTNING BOLT!
THEN I MET MIKE PATTON!
DUDE, WOODPECKER FROM MARS IS THE GREATEST SONG EVER!
THANKS.
THEN I SAW LIGHTNING BOLT AGAIN!!
7-27-02
DO YOU COMPUTE - DRIVE LIKE JEHU
TODAY I WORKED.
CHING CHONG
AFTER BAND PRACTICE, I WENT TO A PARTY.
THEN I GOT DRUNK AND SHAVED MY BEARD OFF.

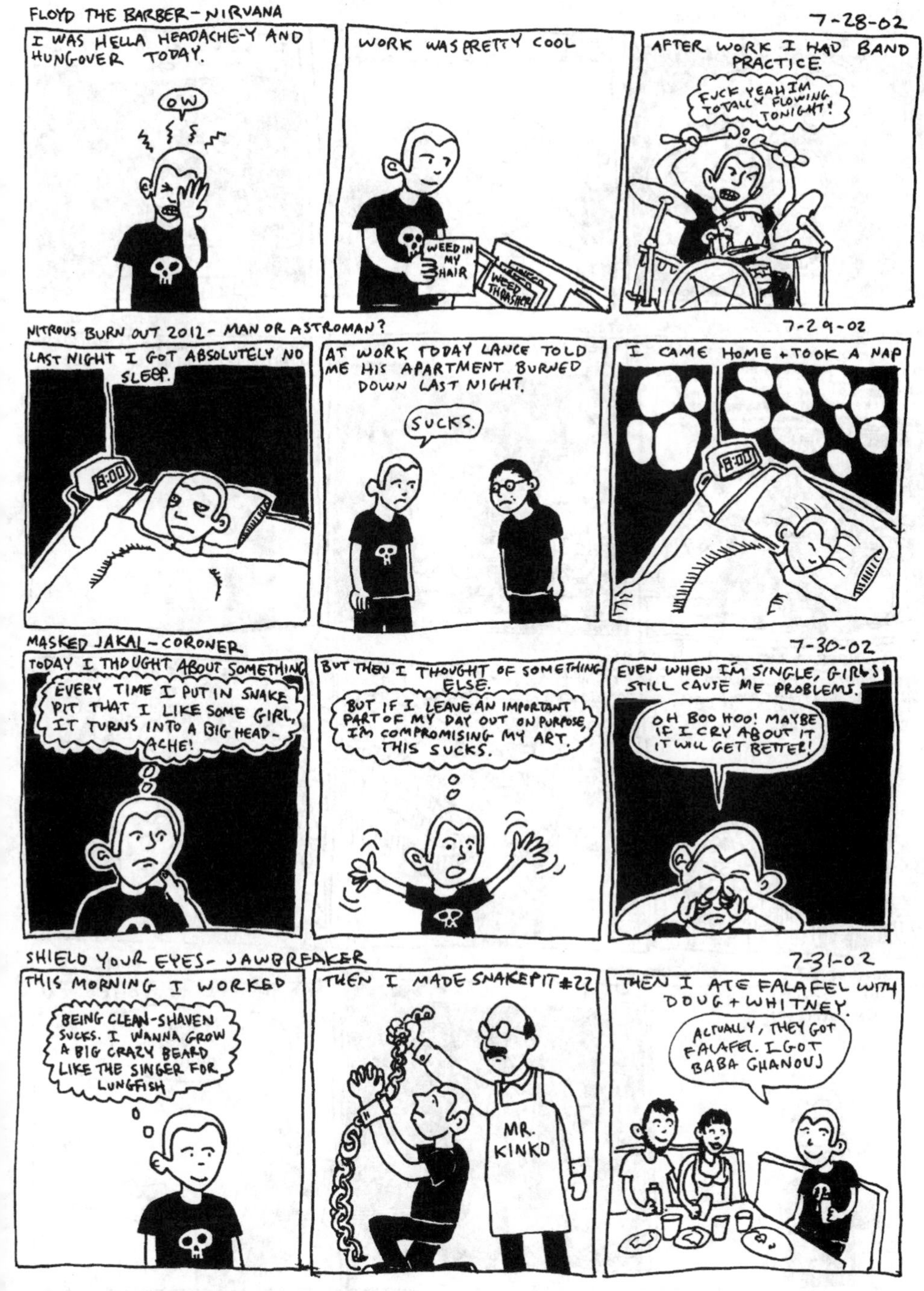

FLOYD THE BARBER - NIRVANA
7-28-02
I WAS HELLA HEADACHE-Y AND HUNGOVER TODAY.
OW
WORK WAS PRETTY COOL
WEED IN MY HAIR
WEED THRASHER
AFTER WORK I HAD BAND PRACTICE.
FUCK YEAH I'M TOTALLY FLOWING TONIGHT!
NITROUS BURN OUT 2012 - MAN OR ASTROMAN?
7-29-02
LAST NIGHT I GOT ABSOLUTELY NO SLEEP.
8:00
AT WORK TODAY LANCE TOLD ME HIS APARTMENT BURNED DOWN LAST NIGHT.
SUCKS.
I CAME HOME + TOOK A NAP
8:00
MASKED JAKAL - CORONER
7-30-02
TODAY I THOUGHT ABOUT SOMETHING
EVERY TIME I PUT IN SNAKE PIT THAT I LIKE SOME GIRL, IT TURNS INTO A BIG HEAD-ACHE!
BUT THEN I THOUGHT OF SOMETHING ELSE.
BUT IF I LEAVE AN IMPORTANT PART OF MY DAY OUT ON PURPOSE, I'M COMPROMISING MY ART. THIS SUCKS.
EVEN WHEN I'M SINGLE, GIRLS STILL CAUSE ME PROBLEMS.
OH BOO HOO! MAYBE IF I CRY ABOUT IT IT WILL GET BETTER!
SHIELD YOUR EYES - JAWBREAKER
7-31-02
THIS MORNING I WORKED
BEING CLEAN-SHAVEN SUCKS. I WANNA GROW A BIG CRAZY BEARD LIKE THE SINGER FOR LUNGFISH
THEN I MADE SNAKEPIT #22
MR. KINKO
THEN I ATE FALAFEL WITH DOUG + WHITNEY.
ACTUALLY, THEY GOT FALAFEL. I GOT BABA GHANOUJ

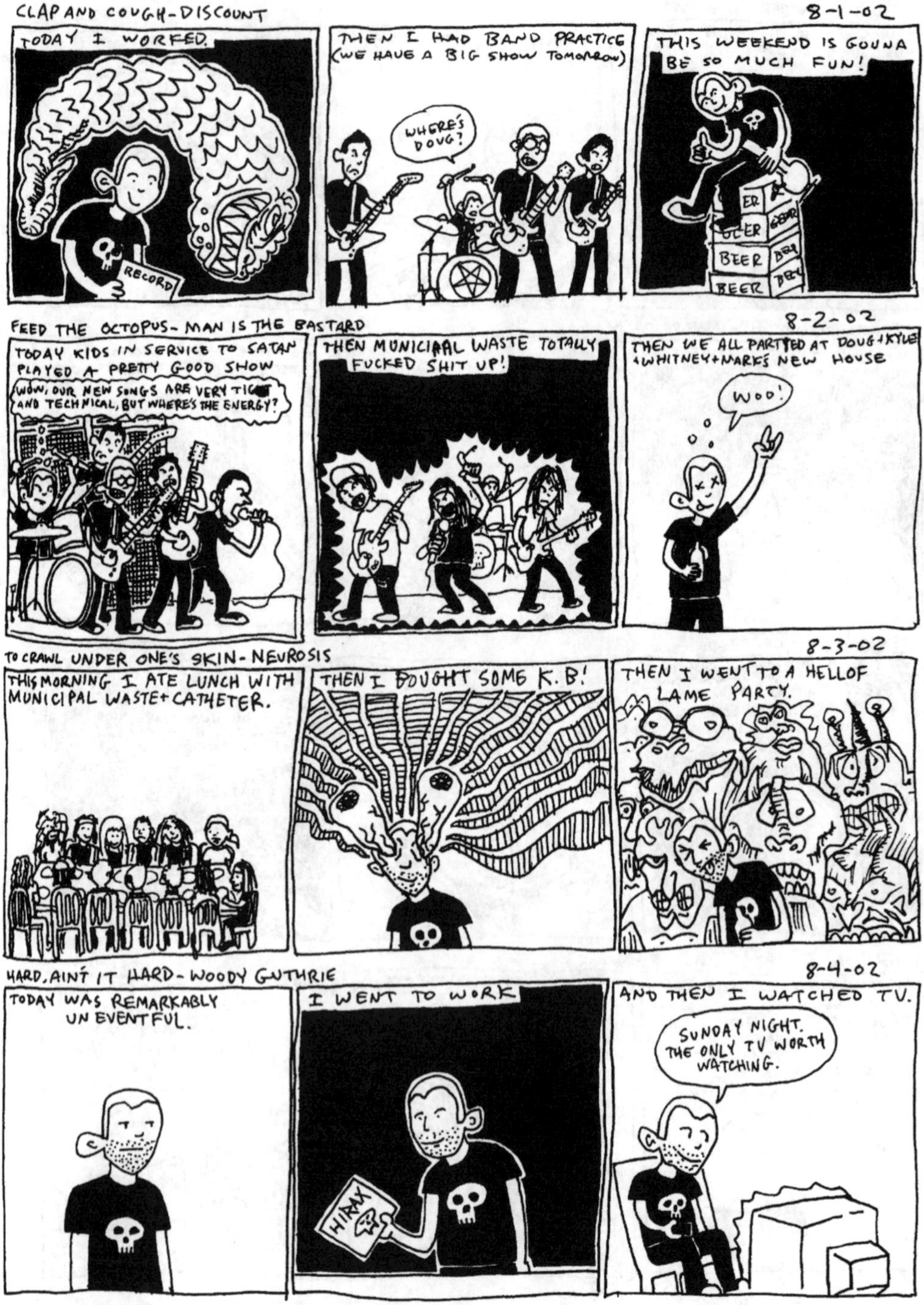
CLAP AND COUGH - DISCOUNT
8-1-02
TODAY I WORKED.
RECORD
THEN I HAD BAND PRACTICE (WE HAVE A BIG SHOW TOMORROW)
WHERE'S DOUG?
THIS WEEKEND IS GONNA BE SO MUCH FUN!
BEER
BEER
FEED THE OCTOPUS - MAN IS THE BASTARD
8-2-02
TODAY KIDS IN SERVICE TO SATAN PLAYED A PRETTY GOOD SHOW
WOW, OUR NEW SONGS ARE VERY TIGHT AND TECHNICAL, BUT WHERE'S THE ENERGY?
THEN MUNICIPAL WASTE TOTALLY FUCKED SHIT UP!
THEN WE ALL PARTYED AT DOUG+KYLE +WHITNEY+MARK'S NEW HOUSE
WOO!
TO CRAWL UNDER ONE'S SKIN - NEUROSIS
8-3-02
THIS MORNING I ATE LUNCH WITH MUNICIPAL WASTE+CATHETER.
THEN I BOUGHT SOME K.B!
THEN I WENT TO A HELLOF LAME PARTY.
HARD, AIN'T IT HARD - WOODY GUTHRIE
8-4-02
TODAY WAS REMARKABLY UNEVENTFUL.
I WENT TO WORK
HIRAX
AND THEN I WATCHED TV.
SUNDAY NIGHT. THE ONLY TV WORTH WATCHING.

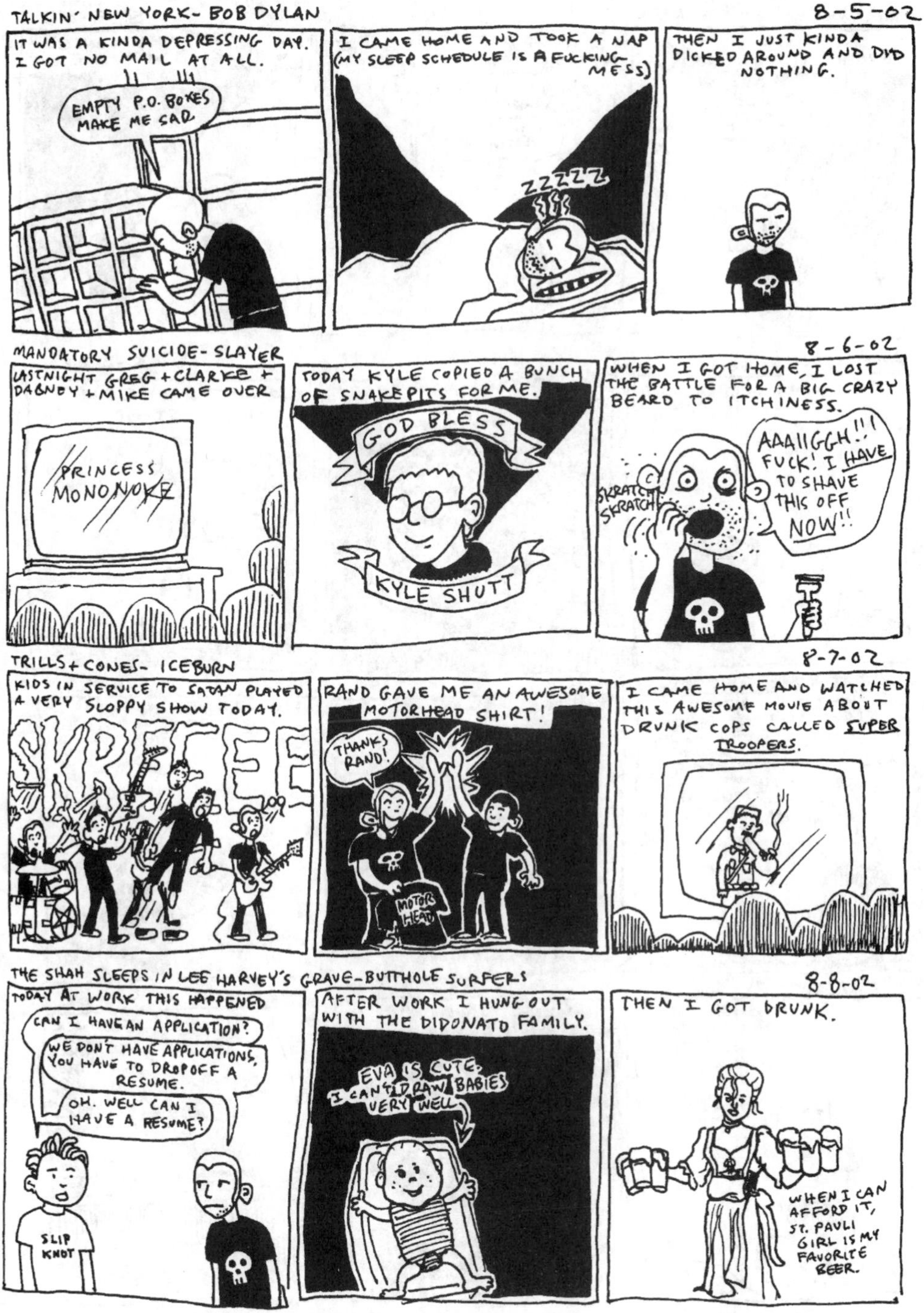
TALKIN' NEW YORK- BOB DYLAN
8-5-02
IT WAS A KINDA DEPRESSING DAY. I GOT NO MAIL AT ALL.
EMPTY P.O. BOXES MAKE ME SAD
I CAME HOME AND TOOK A NAP (MY SLEEP SCHEDULE IS A FUCKING MESS)
ZZZZZ
THEN I JUST KINDA DICKED AROUND AND DID NOTHING.
MANDATORY SUICIDE- SLAYER
8-6-02
LAST NIGHT GREG + CLARKE + DAGNEY + MIKE CAME OVER
PRINCESS MONONOKE
TODAY KYLE COPIED A BUNCH OF SNAKEPITS FOR ME.
GOD BLESS
KYLE SHUTT
WHEN I GOT HOME, I LOST THE BATTLE FOR A BIG CRAZY BEARD TO ITCHINESS.
SKRATCH SKRATCH
AAAIIGGH!!! FUCK! I HAVE TO SHAVE THIS OFF NOW!!
TRILLS + CONES- ICEBURN
8-7-02
KIDS IN SERVICE TO SATAN PLAYED A VERY SLOPPY SHOW TODAY.
SKREEEE
RAND GAVE ME AN AWESOME MOTORHEAD SHIRT!
THANKS RAND!
MOTOR HEAD
I CAME HOME AND WATCHED THIS AWESOME MOVIE ABOUT DRUNK COPS CALLED SUPER TROOPERS.
THE SHAH SLEEPS IN LEE HARVEY'S GRAVE- BUTTHOLE SURFERS
8-8-02
TODAY AT WORK THIS HAPPENED
CAN I HAVE AN APPLICATION?
WE DON'T HAVE APPLICATIONS, YOU HAVE TO DROP OFF A RESUME.
OH. WELL CAN I HAVE A RESUME?
SLIP KNOT
AFTER WORK I HUNG OUT WITH THE DIDONATO FAMILY.
EVA IS CUTE. I CAN'T DRAW BABIES VERY WELL
THEN I GOT DRUNK.
WHEN I CAN AFFORD IT, ST. PAULI GIRL IS MY FAVORITE BEER.

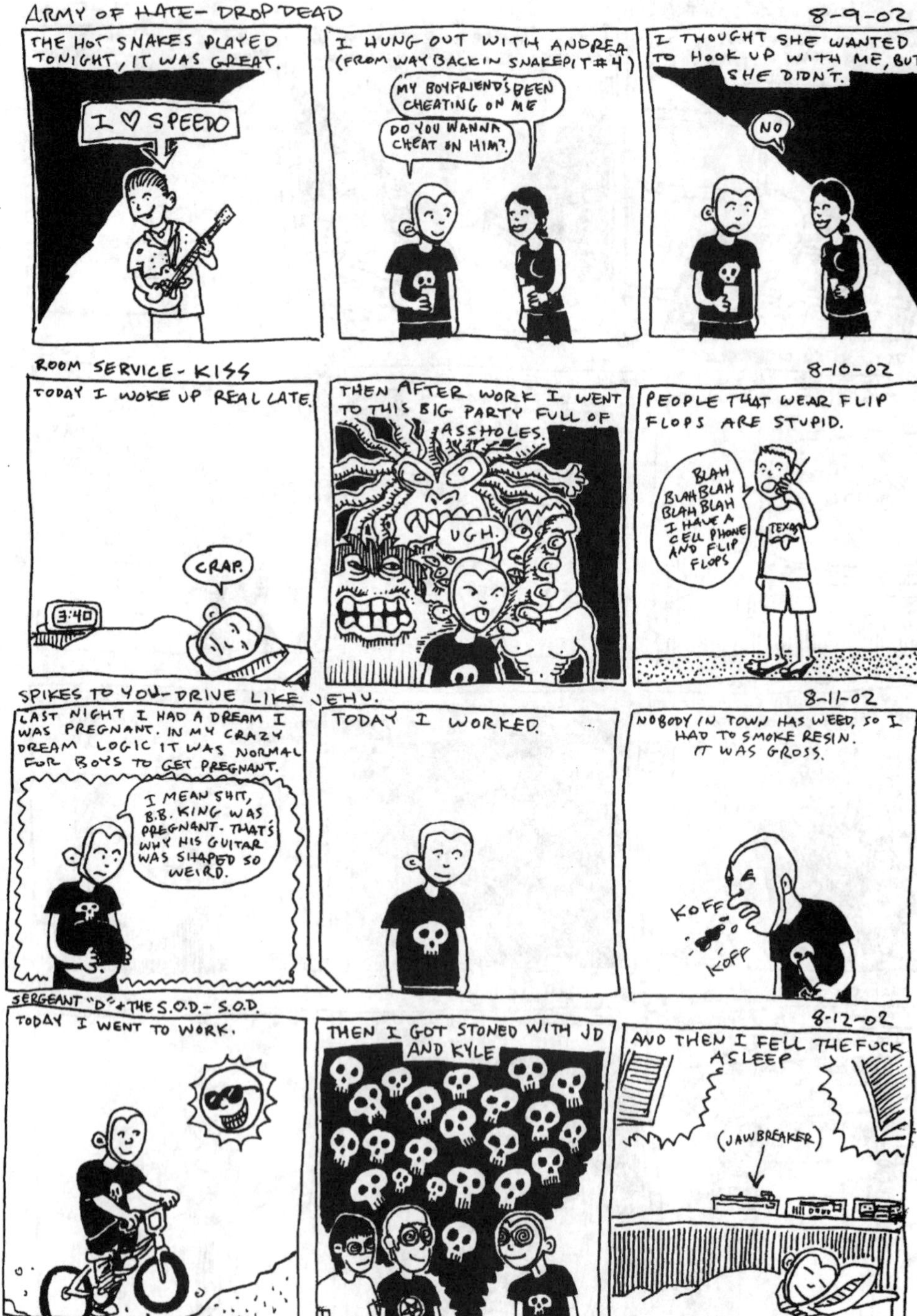
ARMY OF HATE- DROP DEAD
8-9-02
THE HOT SNAKES PLAYED TONIGHT, IT WAS GREAT.
I ♥ SPEEDO
I HUNG OUT WITH ANDREA (FROM WAY BACK IN SNAKEPIT #4)
MY BOYFRIEND'S BEEN CHEATING ON ME
DO YOU WANNA CHEAT ON HIM?
I THOUGHT SHE WANTED TO HOOK UP WITH ME, BUT SHE DIDN'T.
NO
ROOM SERVICE- KISS
8-10-02
TODAY I WOKE UP REAL LATE.
CRAP.
3:40
THEN AFTER WORK I WENT TO THIS BIG PARTY FULL OF ASSHOLES.
UGH.
PEOPLE THAT WEAR FLIP FLOPS ARE STUPID.
BLAH BLAH BLAH BLAH BLAH I HAVE A CELL PHONE AND FLIP FLOPS
TEXAS
SPIKES TO YOU- DRIVE LIKE JEHU.
8-11-02
LAST NIGHT I HAD A DREAM I WAS PREGNANT. IN MY CRAZY DREAM LOGIC IT WAS NORMAL FOR BOYS TO GET PREGNANT.
I MEAN SHIT, B.B. KING WAS PREGNANT. THAT'S WHY HIS GUITAR WAS SHAPED SO WEIRD.
TODAY I WORKED.
NOBODY IN TOWN HAS WEED, SO I HAD TO SMOKE RESIN. IT WAS GROSS.
KOFF
KOFF
SERGEANT "D" + THE S.O.D.- S.O.D.
8-12-02
TODAY I WENT TO WORK.
THEN I GOT STONED WITH JD AND KYLE
AND THEN I FELL THE FUCK ASLEEP
(JAWBREAKER)

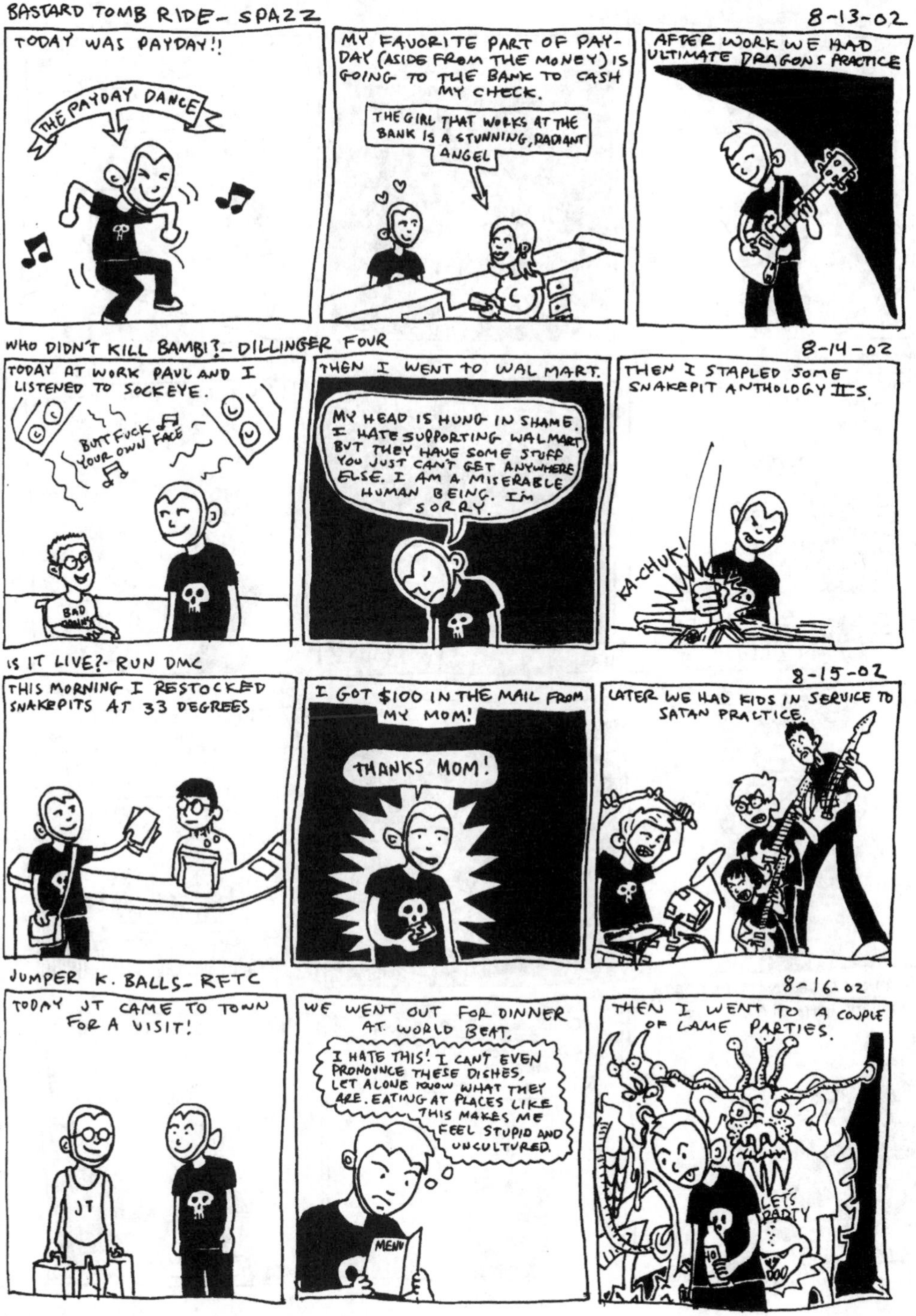

BASTARD TOMB RIDE- SPAZZ
8-13-02
TODAY WAS PAYDAY!!
THE PAYDAY DANCE
MY FAVORITE PART OF PAY-DAY (ASIDE FROM THE MONEY) IS GOING TO THE BANK TO CASH MY CHECK.
THE GIRL THAT WORKS AT THE BANK IS A STUNNING, RADIANT ANGEL
AFTER WORK WE HAD ULTIMATE DRAGONS PRACTICE
WHO DIDN'T KILL BAMBI?- DILLINGER FOUR
8-14-02
TODAY AT WORK PAUL AND I LISTENED TO SOCKEYE.
BUTT FUCK YOUR OWN FACE
BAD
THEN I WENT TO WAL MART.
MY HEAD IS HUNG IN SHAME. I HATE SUPPORTING WALMART BUT THEY HAVE SOME STUFF YOU JUST CAN'T GET ANYWHERE ELSE. I AM A MISERABLE HUMAN BEING. I'M SORRY.
THEN I STAPLED SOME SNAKEPIT ANTHOLOGY IIS.
KA-CHUK!
IS IT LIVE?- RUN DMC
8-15-02
THIS MORNING I RESTOCKED SNAKEPITS AT 33 DEGREES
I GOT $100 IN THE MAIL FROM MY MOM!
THANKS MOM!
LATER WE HAD KIDS IN SERVICE TO SATAN PRACTICE.
JUMPER K. BALLS- RFTC
8-16-02
TODAY JT CAME TO TOWN FOR A VISIT!
JT
WE WENT OUT FOR DINNER AT WORLD BEAT.
I HATE THIS! I CAN'T EVEN PRONOUNCE THESE DISHES, LET ALONE KNOW WHAT THEY ARE. EATING AT PLACES LIKE THIS MAKES ME FEEL STUPID AND UNCULTURED.
MENU
THEN I WENT TO A COUPLE OF LAME PARTIES.
LETS PARTY

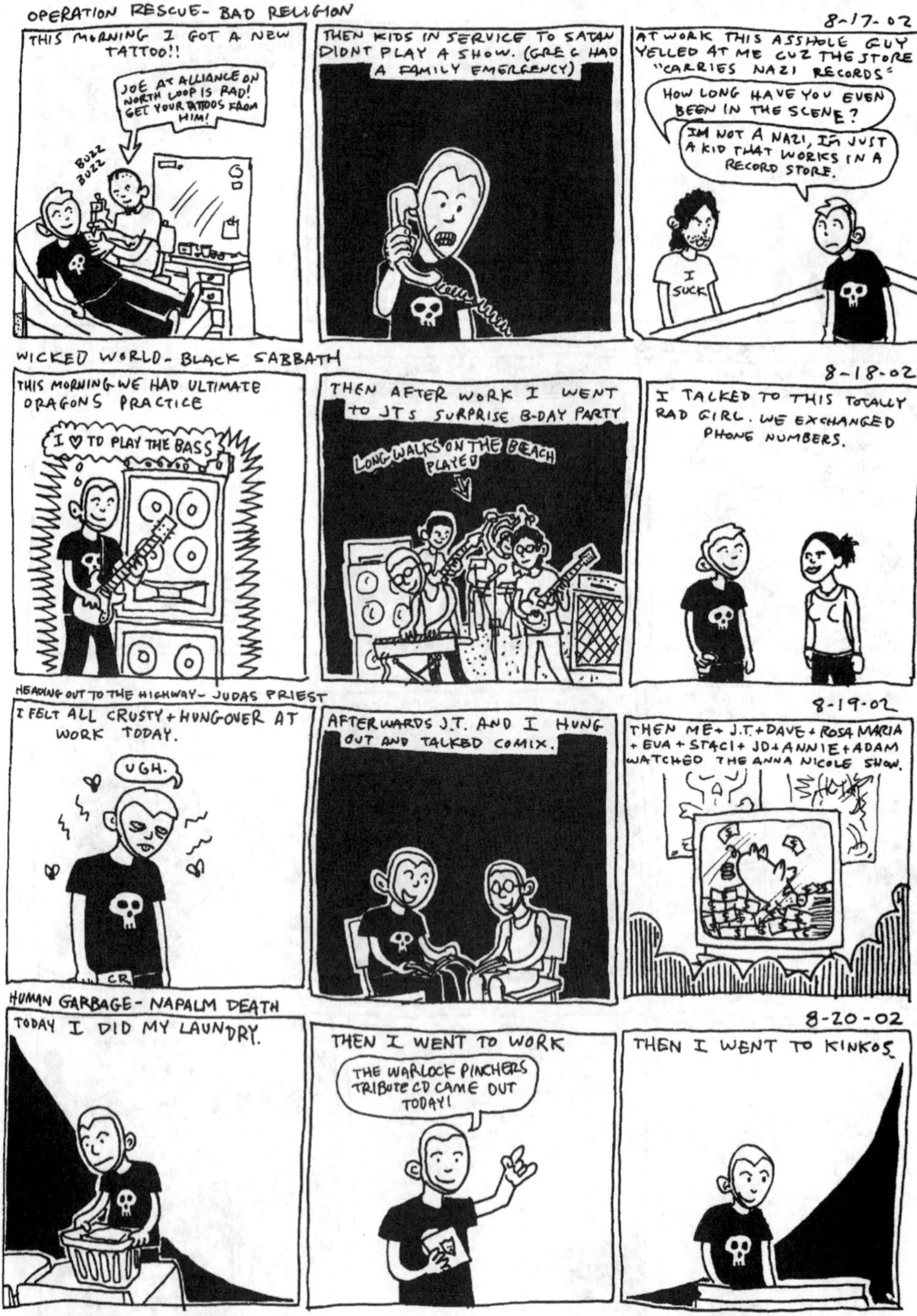

OPERATION RESCUE- BAD RELIGION
8-17-02
THIS MORNING I GOT A NEW TATTOO!!
JOE AT ALLIANCE ON NORTH LOOP IS RAD! GET YOUR TATTOOS FROM HIM!
BUZZ BUZZ
THEN KIDS IN SERVICE TO SATAN DIDNT PLAY A SHOW. (GREG HAD A FAMILY EMERGENCY)
AT WORK THIS ASSHOLE GUY YELLED AT ME CUZ THE STORE "CARRIES NAZI RECORDS"
HOW LONG HAVE YOU EVEN BEEN IN THE SCENE?
IM NOT A NAZI, IM JUST A KID THAT WORKS IN A RECORD STORE.
I SUCK
WICKED WORLD- BLACK SABBATH
8-18-02
THIS MORNING WE HAD ULTIMATE DRAGONS PRACTICE
I ♥ TO PLAY THE BASS
THEN AFTER WORK I WENT TO JTS SURPRISE B-DAY PARTY
LONG WALKS ON THE BEACH PLAYED
I TALKED TO THIS TOTALLY RAD GIRL. WE EXCHANGED PHONE NUMBERS.
HEADING OUT TO THE HIGHWAY- JUDAS PRIEST
8-19-02
I FELT ALL CRUSTY + HUNGOVER AT WORK TODAY.
UGH.
CR
AFTERWARDS J.T. AND I HUNG OUT AND TALKED COMIX.
THEN ME + J.T. + DAVE + ROSA MARIA + EVA + STACI + JD + ANNIE + ADAM WATCHED THE ANNA NICOLE SHOW.
HUMAN GARBAGE- NAPALM DEATH
8-20-02
TODAY I DID MY LAUNDRY.
THEN I WENT TO WORK
THE WARLOCK PINCHERS TRIBUTE CD CAME OUT TODAY!
THEN I WENT TO KINKOS

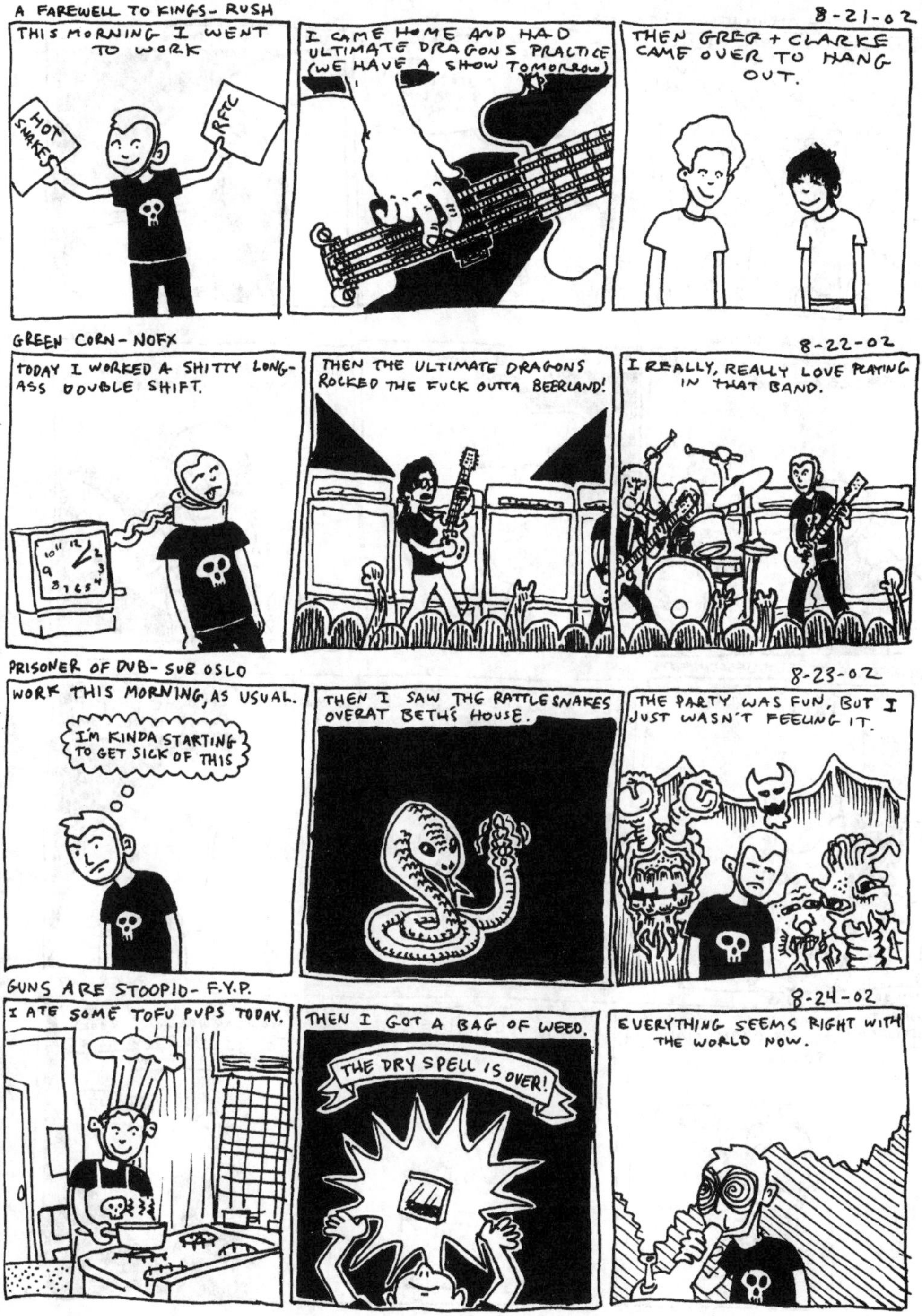
A FAREWELL TO KINGS - RUSH
8-21-02
THIS MORNING I WENT TO WORK
HOT SNAKES
RFTC
I CAME HOME AND HAD ULTIMATE DRAGONS PRACTICE (WE HAVE A SHOW TOMORROW)
THEN GREG + CLARKE CAME OVER TO HANG OUT.
GREEN CORN - NOFX
8-22-02
TODAY I WORKED A SHITTY LONG-ASS DOUBLE SHIFT.
THEN THE ULTIMATE DRAGONS ROCKED THE FUCK OUTTA BEERLAND!
I REALLY, REALLY LOVE PLAYING IN THAT BAND.
PRISONER OF DUB - SUB OSLO
8-23-02
WORK THIS MORNING, AS USUAL.
I'M KINDA STARTING TO GET SICK OF THIS
THEN I SAW THE RATTLESNAKES OVERAT BETH'S HOUSE.
THE PARTY WAS FUN, BUT I JUST WASN'T FEELING IT.
GUNS ARE STOOPID - F.Y.P.
8-24-02
I ATE SOME TOFU PUPS TODAY.
THEN I GOT A BAG OF WEED.
THE DRY SPELL IS OVER!
EVERYTHING SEEMS RIGHT WITH THE WORLD NOW.

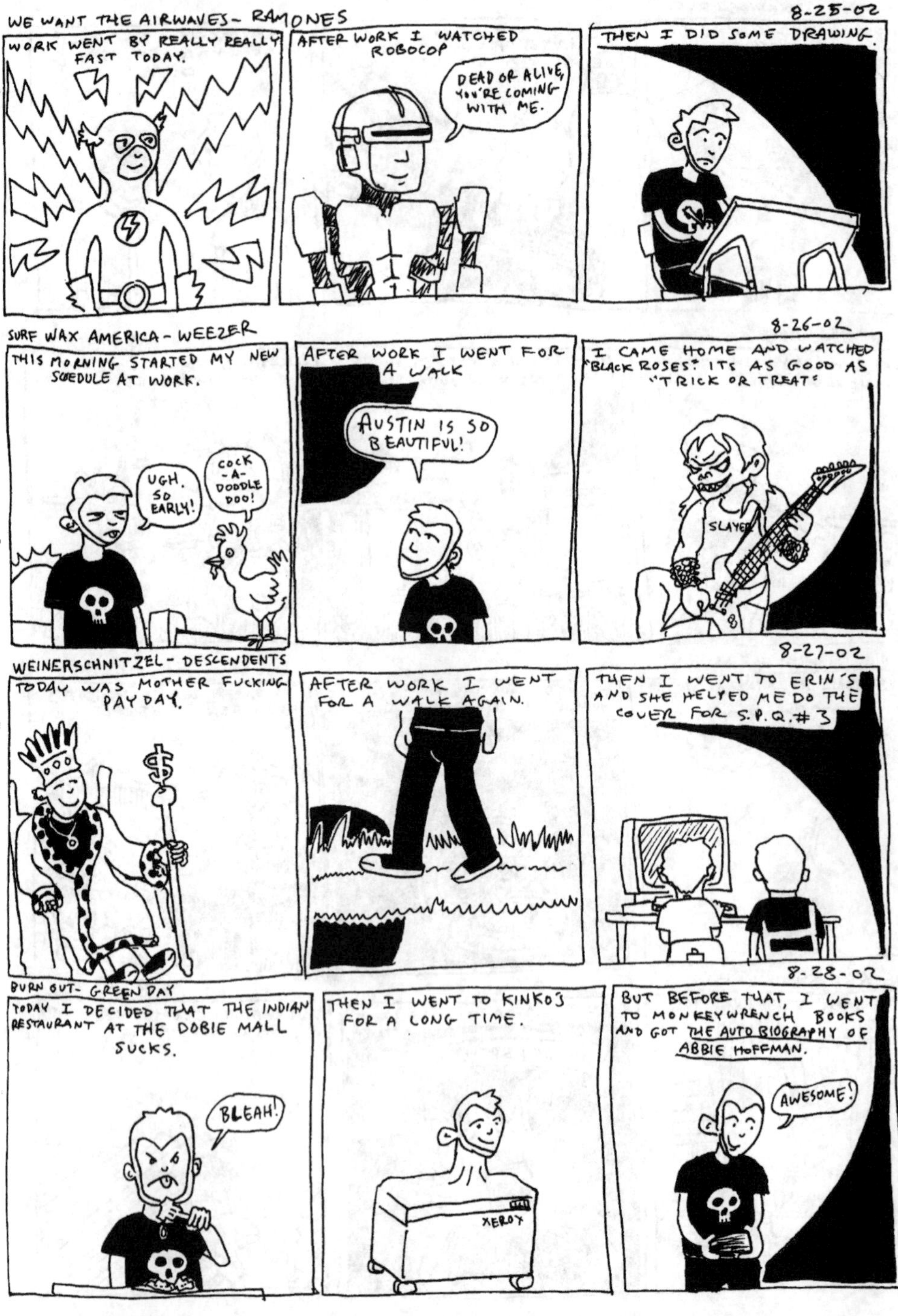

WE WANT THE AIRWAVES - RAMONES
8-25-02
WORK WENT BY REALLY REALLY FAST TODAY.
AFTER WORK I WATCHED ROBOCOP
DEAD OR ALIVE, YOU'RE COMING WITH ME.
THEN I DID SOME DRAWING.
SURF WAX AMERICA - WEEZER
8-26-02
THIS MORNING STARTED MY NEW SCEDULE AT WORK.
UGH. SO EARLY!
COCK -A- DOODLE DOO!
AFTER WORK I WENT FOR A WALK
AUSTIN IS SO BEAUTIFUL!
I CAME HOME AND WATCHED "BLACK ROSES." ITS AS GOOD AS "TRICK OR TREAT"
SLAYER
WEINERSCHNITZEL - DESCENDENTS
8-27-02
TODAY WAS MOTHER FUCKING PAYDAY.
AFTER WORK I WENT FOR A WALK AGAIN.
THEN I WENT TO ERIN'S AND SHE HELPED ME DO THE COVER FOR S.P.Q. #3
BURN OUT - GREEN DAY
8-28-02
TODAY I DECIDED THAT THE INDIAN RESTAURANT AT THE DOBIE MALL SUCKS.
BLEAH!
THEN I WENT TO KINKO'S FOR A LONG TIME.
XEROX
BUT BEFORE THAT, I WENT TO MONKEYWRENCH BOOKS AND GOT THE AUTOBIOGRAPHY OF ABBIE HOFFMAN.
AWESOME!

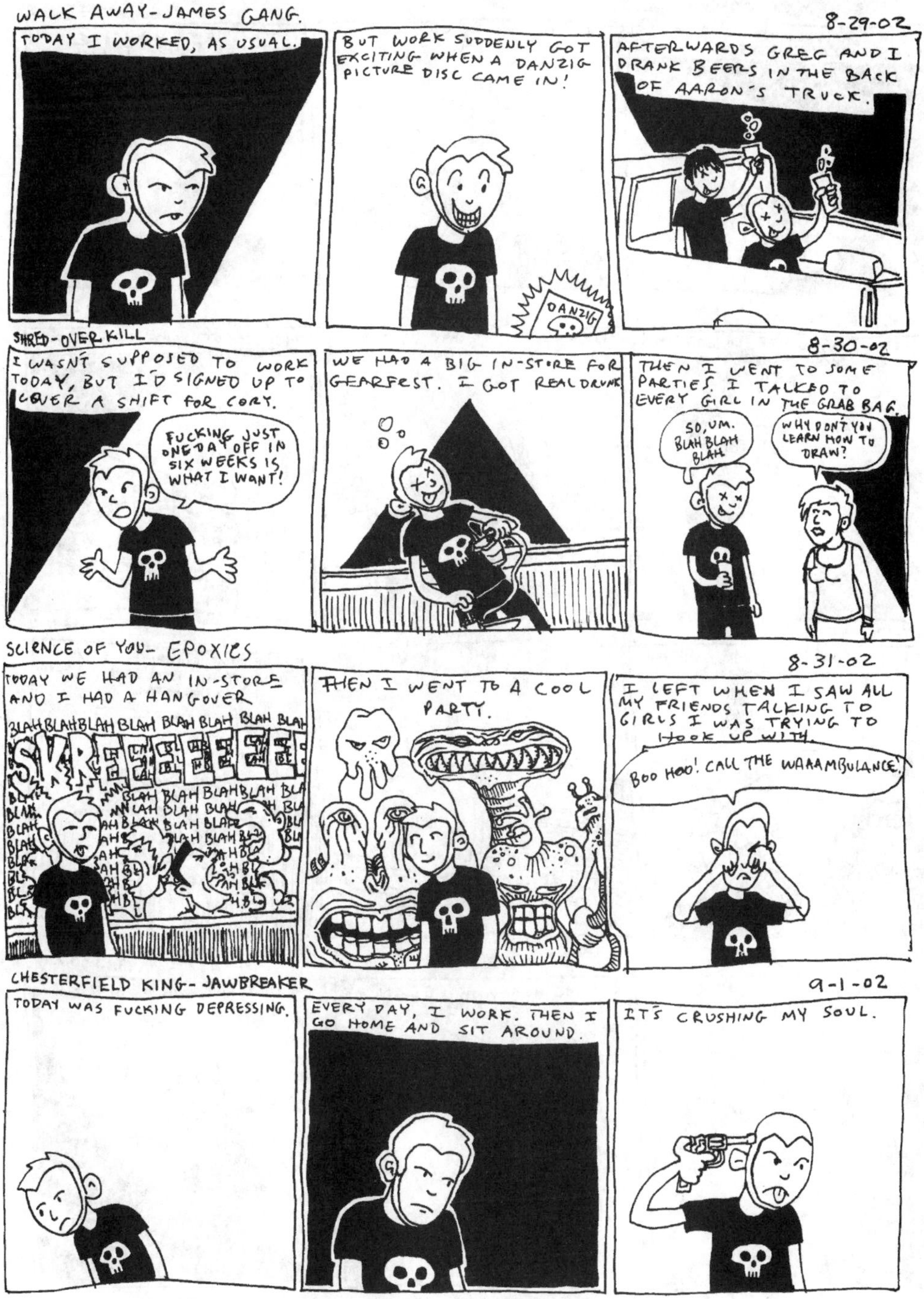
WALK AWAY-JAMES GANG.
8-29-02
TODAY I WORKED, AS USUAL.
BUT WORK SUDDENLY GOT EXCITING WHEN A DANZIG PICTURE DISC CAME IN!
DANZIG
AFTERWARDS GREG AND I DRANK BEERS IN THE BACK OF AARON'S TRUCK.
SHRED-OVERKILL
8-30-02
I WASN'T SUPPOSED TO WORK TODAY, BUT I'D SIGNED UP TO COVER A SHIFT FOR CORY.
FUCKING JUST ONE DAY OFF IN SIX WEEKS IS WHAT I WANT!
WE HAD A BIG IN-STORE FOR GEARFEST. I GOT REAL DRUNK
THEN I WENT TO SOME PARTIES. I TALKED TO EVERY GIRL IN THE GRAB BAG.
SO, UM. BLAH BLAH BLAH
WHY DON'T YOU LEARN HOW TO DRAW?
SCIENCE OF YOU- EPOXIES
8-31-02
TODAY WE HAD AN IN-STORE AND I HAD A HANGOVER
BLAH BLAH BLAH BLAH BLAH BLAH BLAH BLAH
SKREEEEEEE
BLAH BLAH BLAH BLAH BLAH
THEN I WENT TO A COOL PARTY.
I LEFT WHEN I SAW ALL MY FRIENDS TALKING TO GIRLS I WAS TRYING TO HOOK UP WITH.
BOO HOO! CALL THE WAAAMBULANCE!
CHESTERFIELD KING- JAWBREAKER
9-1-02
TODAY WAS FUCKING DEPRESSING.
EVERY DAY, I WORK. THEN I GO HOME AND SIT AROUND.
IT'S CRUSHING MY SOUL.

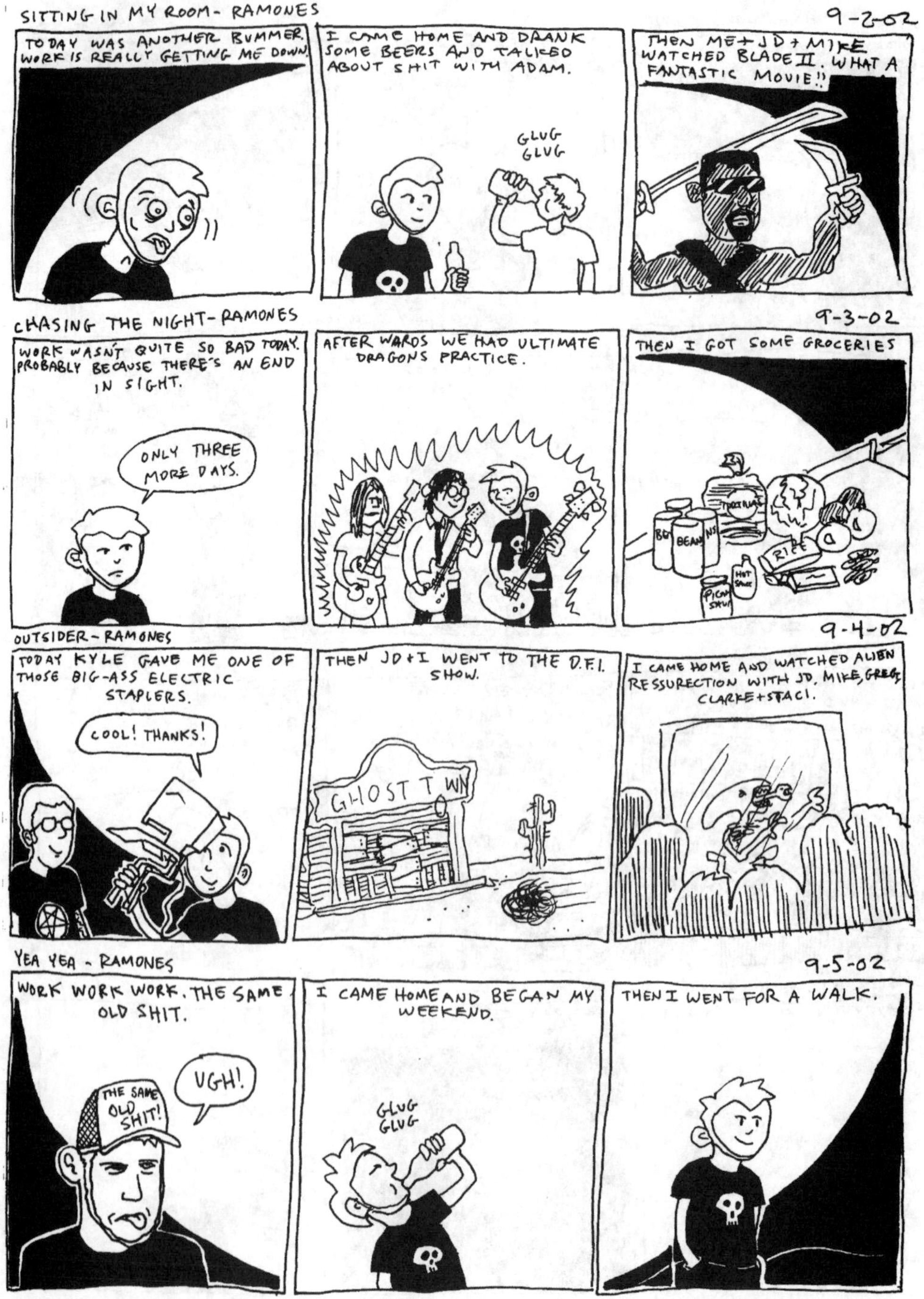
SITTING IN MY ROOM - RAMONES
9-2-02
TODAY WAS ANOTHER BUMMER. WORK IS REALLY GETTING ME DOWN.
I CAME HOME AND DRANK SOME BEERS AND TALKED ABOUT SHIT WITH ADAM.
GLUG GLUG
THEN ME + JD + MIKE WATCHED BLADE II. WHAT A FANTASTIC MOVIE!!
CHASING THE NIGHT - RAMONES
9-3-02
WORK WASN'T QUITE SO BAD TODAY. PROBABLY BECAUSE THERE'S AN END IN SIGHT.
ONLY THREE MORE DAYS.
AFTER WARDS WE HAD ULTIMATE DRAGONS PRACTICE.
THEN I GOT SOME GROCERIES
BEANS
RICE
HOT SAUCE
OUTSIDER - RAMONES
9-4-02
TODAY KYLE GAVE ME ONE OF THOSE BIG-ASS ELECTRIC STAPLERS.
COOL! THANKS!
THEN JD + I WENT TO THE D.F.I. SHOW.
GHOST T WN
I CAME HOME AND WATCHED ALIEN RESSURECTION WITH JD, MIKE, GREG, CLARKE + STACI.
YEA YEA - RAMONES
9-5-02
WORK WORK WORK. THE SAME OLD SHIT.
THE SAME OLD SHIT!
UGH!
I CAME HOME AND BEGAN MY WEEKEND.
GLUG GLUG
THEN I WENT FOR A WALK.

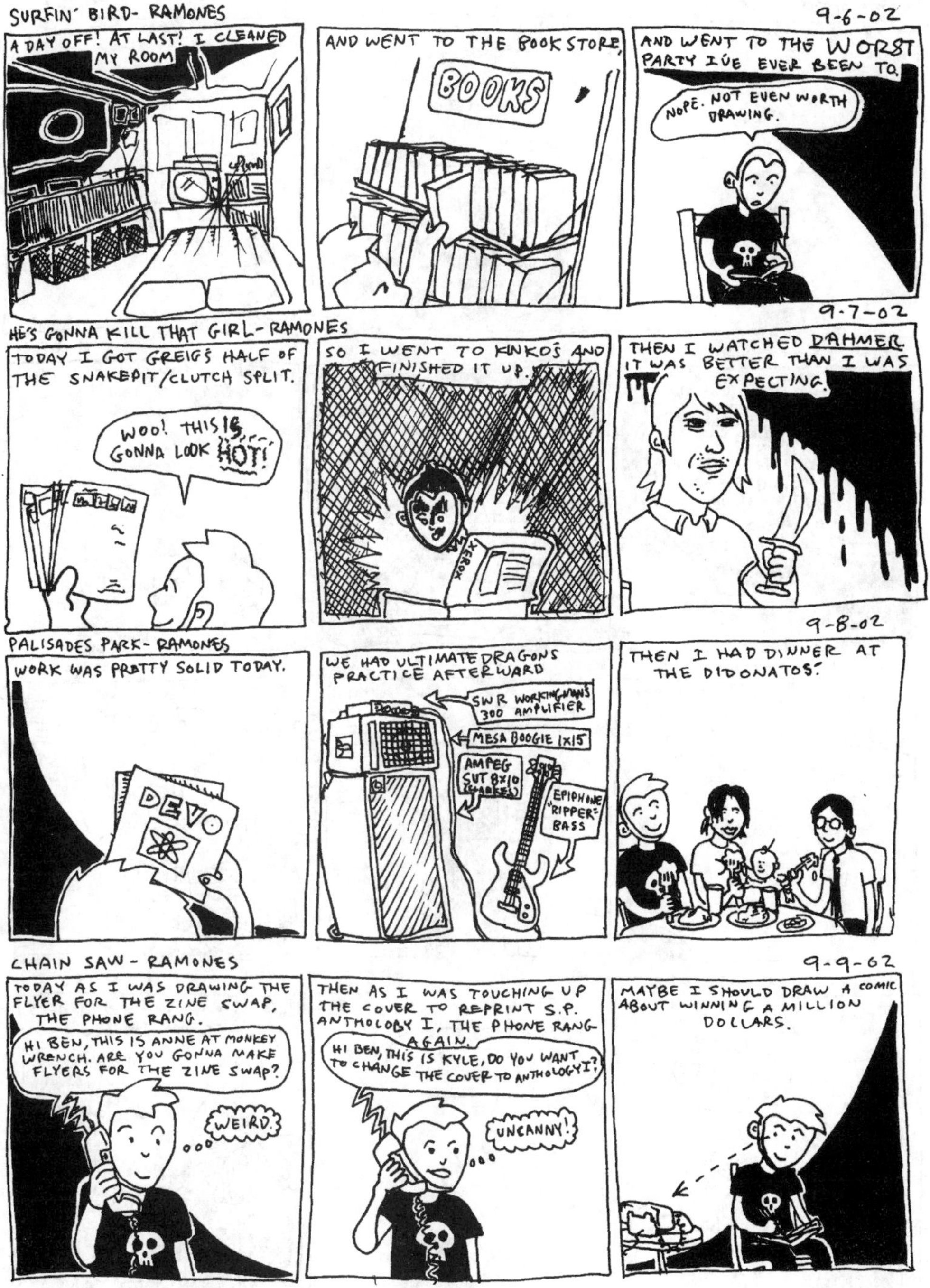
SURFIN' BIRD- RAMONES
9-6-02
A DAY OFF! AT LAST! I CLEANED MY ROOM
AND WENT TO THE BOOK STORE,
BOOKS
AND WENT TO THE WORST PARTY I'VE EVER BEEN TO.
NOPE. NOT EVEN WORTH DRAWING.
9-7-02
HE'S GONNA KILL THAT GIRL- RAMONES
TODAY I GOT GREIG'S HALF OF THE SNAKEPIT/CLUTCH SPLIT.
WOO! THIS IS GONNA LOOK HOT!
SO I WENT TO KINKO'S AND FINISHED IT UP.
XEROX
THEN I WATCHED DAHMER IT WAS BETTER THAN I WAS EXPECTING.
9-8-02
PALISADES PARK- RAMONES
WORK WAS PRETTY SOLID TODAY.
DEVO
WE HAD ULTIMATE DRAGONS PRACTICE AFTERWARD
SWR WORKINGMAN'S 300 AMPLIFIER
MESA BOOGIE 1x15
AMPEG SVT 8x10
EPIPHONE "RIPPER" BASS
THEN I HAD DINNER AT THE DIDONATOS'.
CHAIN SAW- RAMONES
9-9-02
TODAY AS I WAS DRAWING THE FLYER FOR THE ZINE SWAP, THE PHONE RANG.
HI BEN, THIS IS ANNE AT MONKEY WRENCH. ARE YOU GONNA MAKE FLYERS FOR THE ZINE SWAP?
WEIRD.
THEN AS I WAS TOUCHING UP THE COVER TO REPRINT S.P. ANTHOLOGY I, THE PHONE RANG AGAIN.
HI BEN, THIS IS KYLE, DO YOU WANT TO CHANGE THE COVER TO ANTHOLOGY I?
UNCANNY!
MAYBE I SHOULD DRAW A COMIC ABOUT WINNING A MILLION DOLLARS.

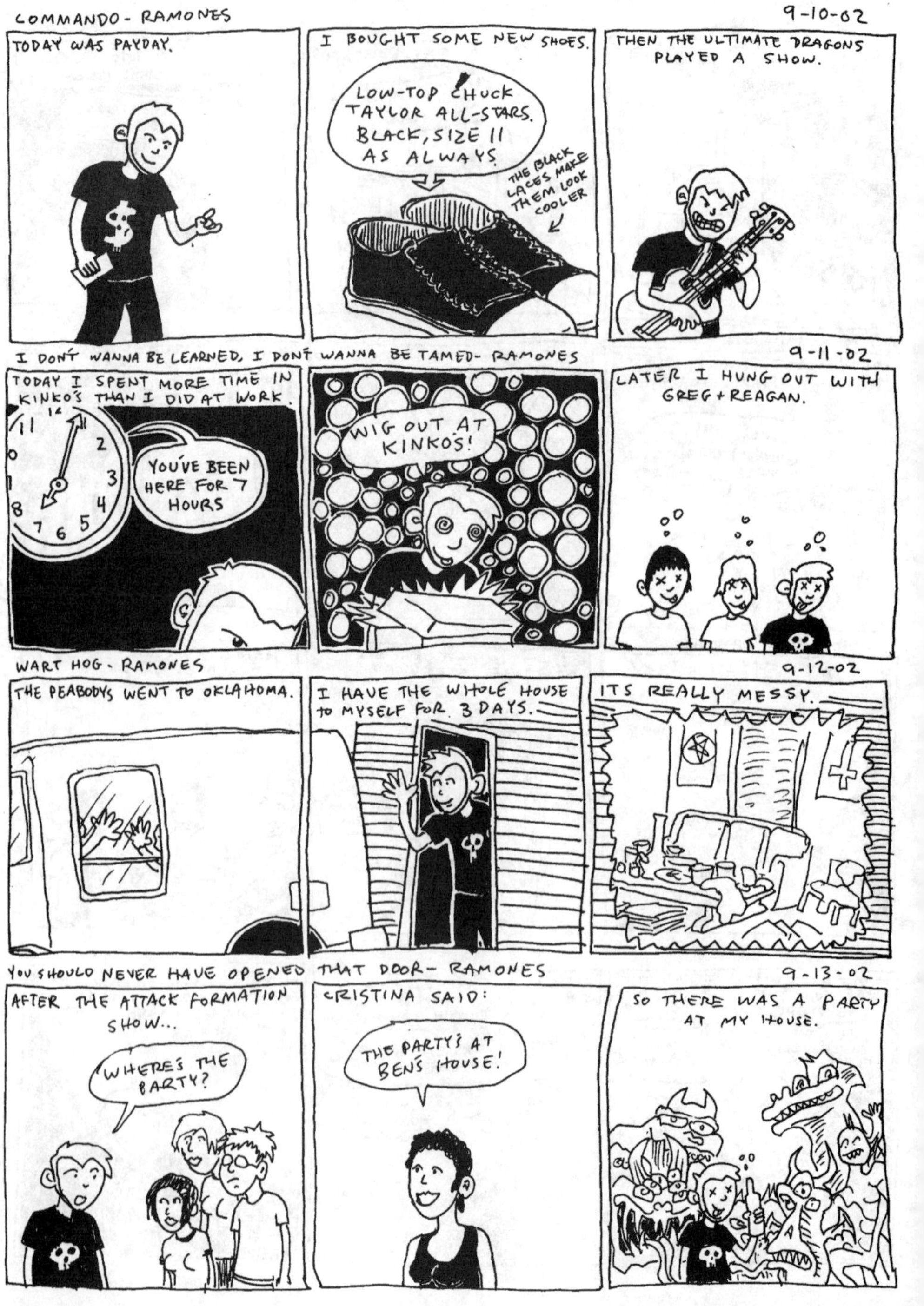
COMMANDO - RAMONES
9-10-02
TODAY WAS PAYDAY.
I BOUGHT SOME NEW SHOES.
LOW-TOP CHUCK TAYLOR ALL-STARS. BLACK, SIZE 11 AS ALWAYS.
THE BLACK LACES MAKE THEM LOOK COOLER
THEN THE ULTIMATE DRAGONS PLAYED A SHOW.
I DON'T WANNA BE LEARNED, I DON'T WANNA BE TAMED - RAMONES
9-11-02
TODAY I SPENT MORE TIME IN KINKO'S THAN I DID AT WORK.
YOU'VE BEEN HERE FOR 7 HOURS
WIG OUT AT KINKO'S!
LATER I HUNG OUT WITH GREG + REAGAN.
WART HOG - RAMONES
9-12-02
THE PEABODYS WENT TO OKLAHOMA.
I HAVE THE WHOLE HOUSE TO MYSELF FOR 3 DAYS.
ITS REALLY MESSY.
YOU SHOULD NEVER HAVE OPENED THAT DOOR - RAMONES
9-13-02
AFTER THE ATTACK FORMATION SHOW...
WHERE'S THE PARTY?
CRISTINA SAID:
THE PARTY'S AT BEN'S HOUSE!
SO THERE WAS A PARTY AT MY HOUSE.

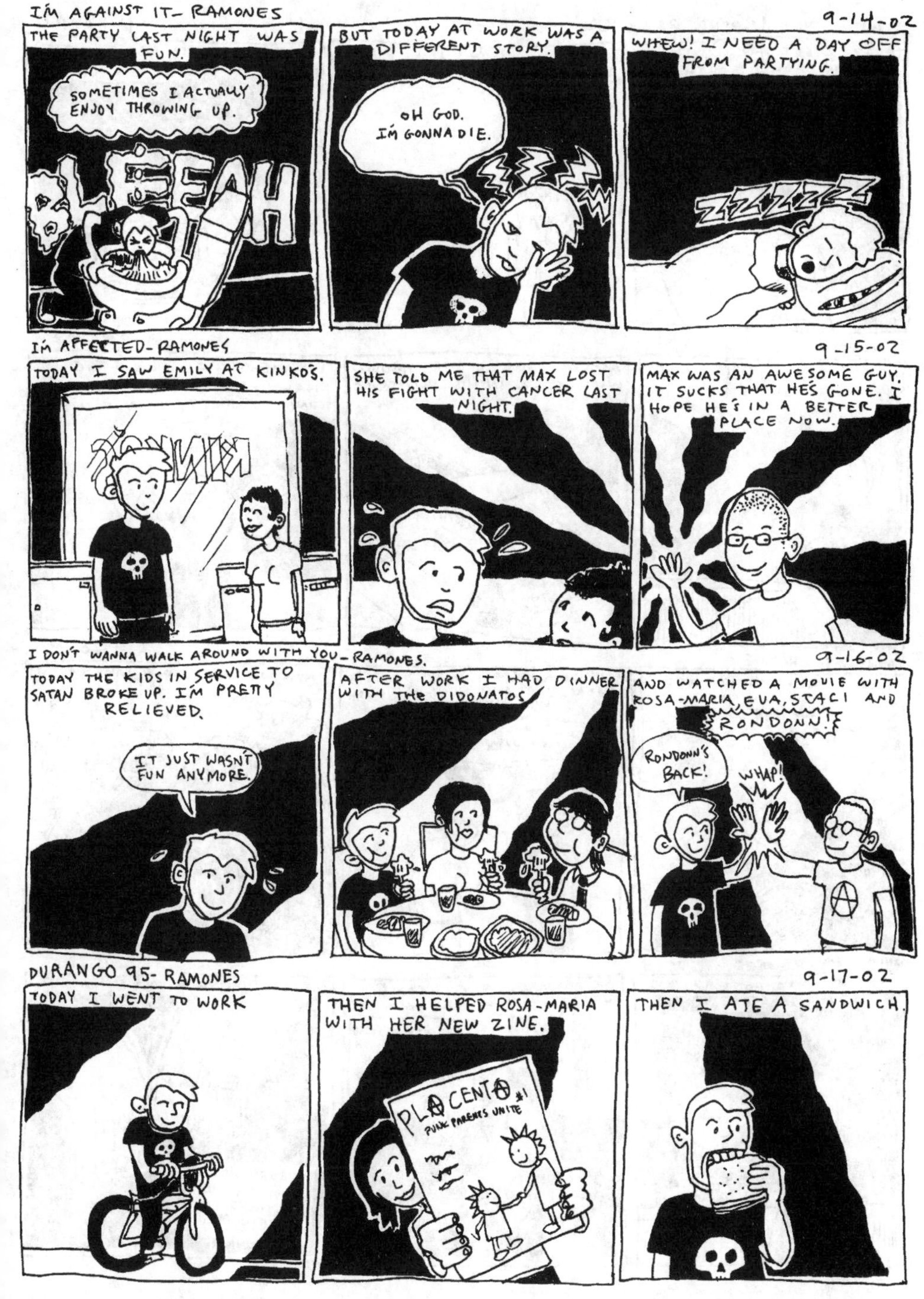
I'M AGAINST IT- RAMONES
9-14-02
THE PARTY LAST NIGHT WAS FUN.
SOMETIMES I ACTUALLY ENJOY THROWING UP.
BLEEAH
BUT TODAY AT WORK WAS A DIFFERENT STORY.
OH GOD. I'M GONNA DIE.
WHEW! I NEED A DAY OFF FROM PARTYING.
ZZZZZZ
I'M AFFECTED- RAMONES
9-15-02
TODAY I SAW EMILY AT KINKO'S.
SHE TOLD ME THAT MAX LOST HIS FIGHT WITH CANCER LAST NIGHT.
MAX WAS AN AWESOME GUY. IT SUCKS THAT HE'S GONE. I HOPE HE'S IN A BETTER PLACE NOW.
I DON'T WANNA WALK AROUND WITH YOU- RAMONES.
9-16-02
TODAY THE KIDS IN SERVICE TO SATAN BROKE UP. I'M PRETTY RELIEVED.
IT JUST WASN'T FUN ANYMORE.
AFTER WORK I HAD DINNER WITH THE DIDONATOS
AND WATCHED A MOVIE WITH ROSA-MARIA, EVA, STACI AND
RONDONN!
RONDONN'S BACK!
WHAP!
DURANGO 95- RAMONES
9-17-02
TODAY I WENT TO WORK
THEN I HELPED ROSA-MARIA WITH HER NEW ZINE.
PLACENTA #1
PUNK PARENTS UNITE
THEN I ATE A SANDWICH.

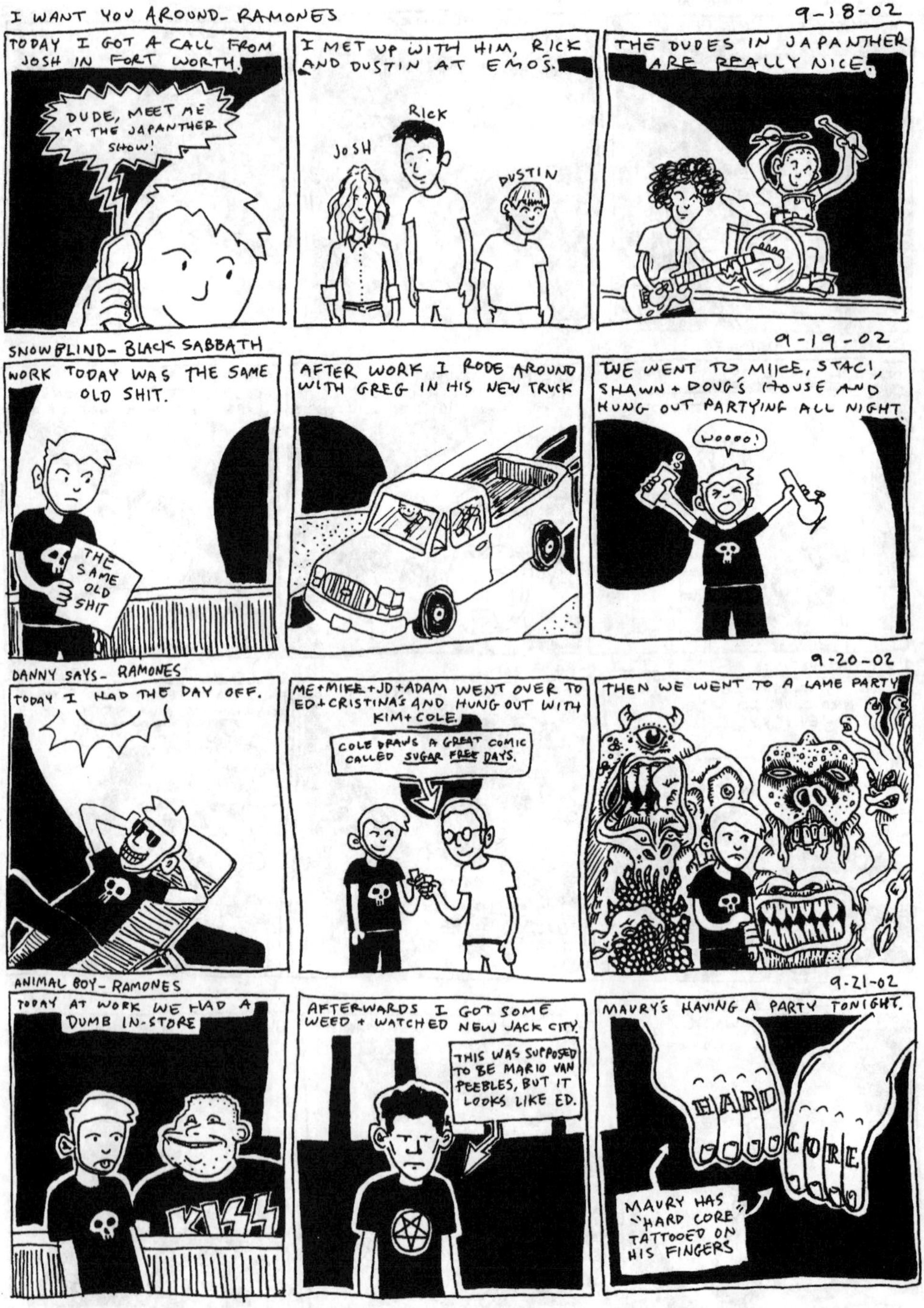
I WANT YOU AROUND- RAMONES
9-18-02
TODAY I GOT A CALL FROM JOSH IN FORT WORTH.
DUDE, MEET ME AT THE JAPANTHER SHOW!
I MET UP WITH HIM, RICK AND DUSTIN AT EMO'S.
RICK
JOSH
DUSTIN
THE DUDES IN JAPANTHER ARE REALLY NICE.
SNOWBLIND- BLACK SABBATH
9-19-02
WORK TODAY WAS THE SAME OLD SHIT.
THE SAME OLD SHIT
AFTER WORK I RODE AROUND WITH GREG IN HIS NEW TRUCK
WE WENT TO MIKE, STACI, SHAWN + DOUG'S HOUSE AND HUNG OUT PARTYING ALL NIGHT.
WOOOO!
DANNY SAYS- RAMONES
9-20-02
TODAY I HAD THE DAY OFF.
ME+MIKE+JD+ADAM WENT OVER TO ED+CRISTINA'S AND HUNG OUT WITH KIM+COLE.
COLE DRAWS A GREAT COMIC CALLED SUGAR FREE DAYS.
THEN WE WENT TO A LAME PARTY
ANIMAL BOY- RAMONES
9-21-02
TODAY AT WORK WE HAD A DUMB IN-STORE
KISS
AFTERWARDS I GOT SOME WEED + WATCHED NEW JACK CITY.
THIS WAS SUPPOSED TO BE MARIO VAN PEEBLES, BUT IT LOOKS LIKE ED.
MAURY'S HAVING A PARTY TONIGHT.
HARD
CORE
MAURY HAS "HARD CORE" TATTOOED ON HIS FINGERS

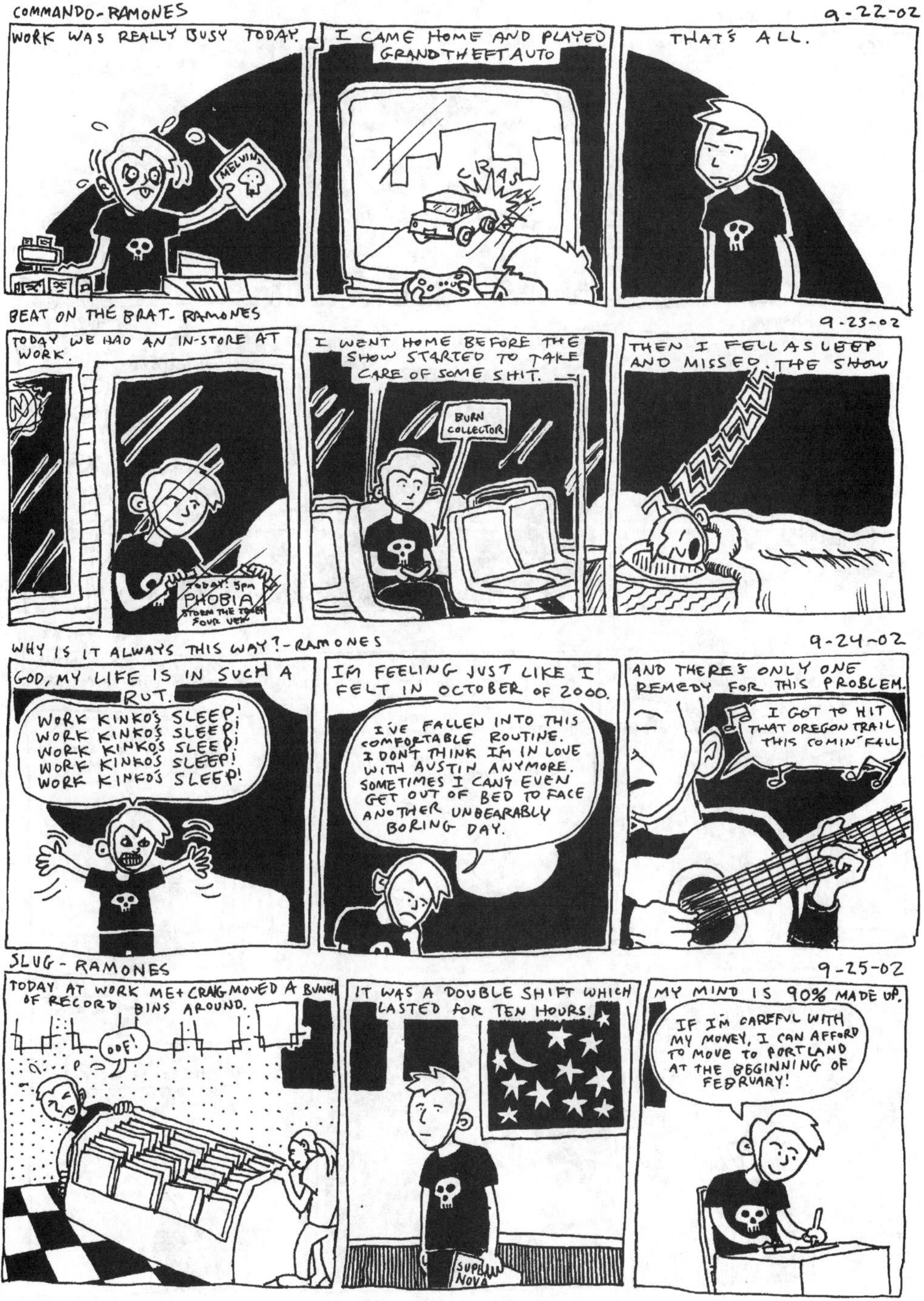
COMMANDO - RAMONES
9-22-02
WORK WAS REALLY BUSY TODAY.
MELVINS
I CAME HOME AND PLAYED GRANDTHEFTAUTO
CRAS
THAT'S ALL.
BEAT ON THE BRAT - RAMONES
9-23-02
TODAY WE HAD AN IN-STORE AT WORK.
TODAY: 5pm
PHOBIA
STORM THE TOWER
I WENT HOME BEFORE THE SHOW STARTED TO TAKE CARE OF SOME SHIT.
BURN COLLECTOR
THEN I FELL ASLEEP AND MISSED THE SHOW
WHY IS IT ALWAYS THIS WAY? - RAMONES
9-24-02
GOD, MY LIFE IS IN SUCH A RUT.
WORK KINKO'S SLEEP! WORK KINKO'S SLEEP! WORK KINKO'S SLEEP! WORK KINKO'S SLEEP! WORK KINKO'S SLEEP!
I'M FEELING JUST LIKE I FELT IN OCTOBER OF 2000.
I'VE FALLEN INTO THIS COMFORTABLE ROUTINE. I DON'T THINK I'M IN LOVE WITH AUSTIN ANYMORE. SOMETIMES I CAN'T EVEN GET OUT OF BED TO FACE ANOTHER UNBEARABLY BORING DAY.
AND THERE'S ONLY ONE REMEDY FOR THIS PROBLEM.
I GOT TO HIT THAT OREGON TRAIL THIS COMIN' FALL
SLUG - RAMONES
9-25-02
TODAY AT WORK ME + CRAIG MOVED A BUNCH OF RECORD BINS AROUND.
OOF!
IT WAS A DOUBLE SHIFT WHICH LASTED FOR TEN HOURS.
MY MIND IS 90% MADE UP.
IF I'M CAREFUL WITH MY MONEY, I CAN AFFORD TO MOVE TO PORTLAND AT THE BEGINNING OF FEBRUARY!

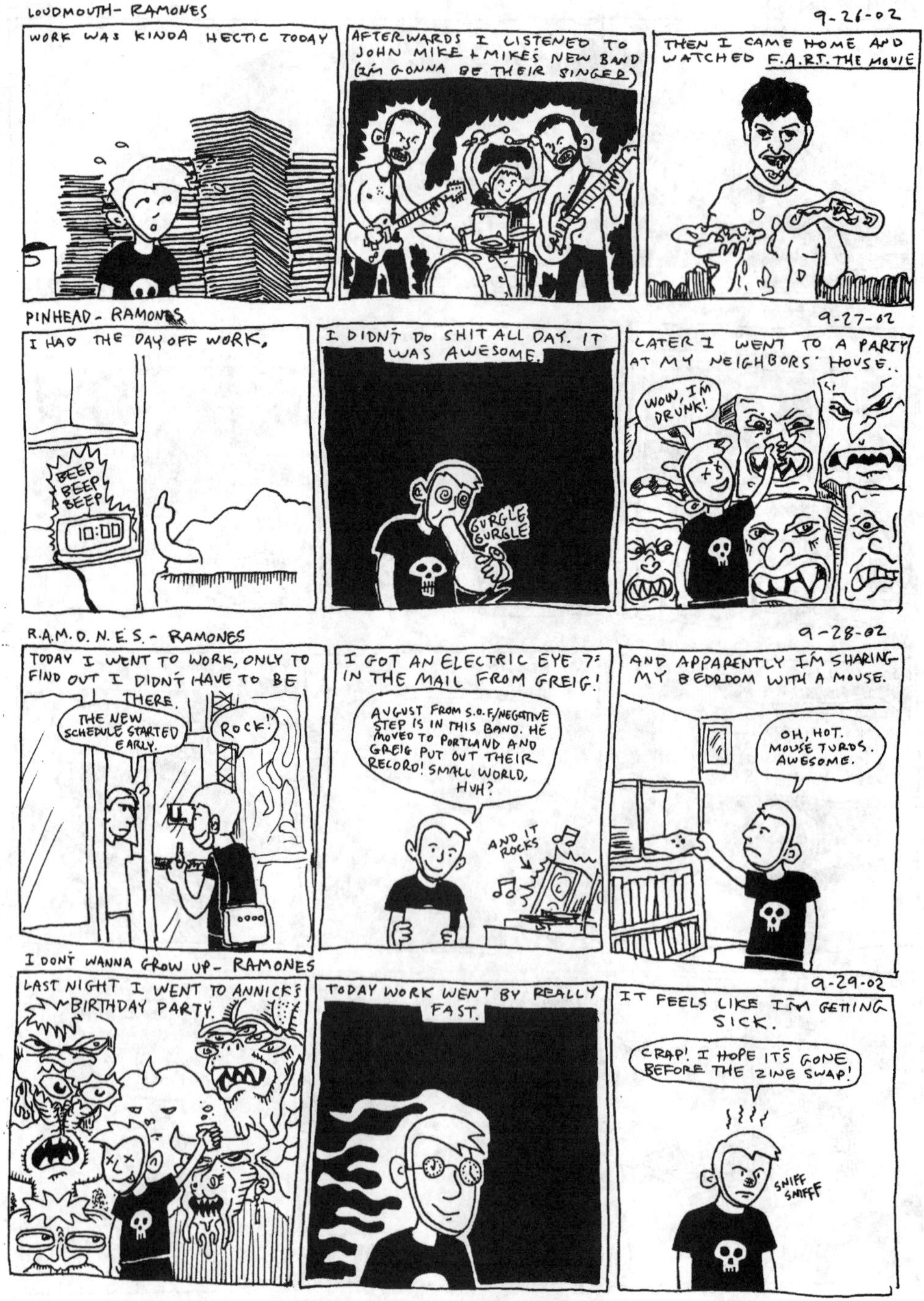
LOUDMOUTH - RAMONES
9-26-02
WORK WAS KINDA HECTIC TODAY
AFTERWARDS I LISTENED TO JOHN MIKE + MIKE'S NEW BAND (I'M GONNA BE THEIR SINGER)
THEN I CAME HOME AND WATCHED F.A.R.T. THE MOVIE
PINHEAD - RAMONES
9-27-02
I HAD THE DAY OFF WORK.
BEEP BEEP BEEP
10:00
I DIDN'T DO SHIT ALL DAY. IT WAS AWESOME.
GURGLE GURGLE
LATER I WENT TO A PARTY AT MY NEIGHBORS' HOUSE..
WOW, I'M DRUNK!
R.A.M.O.N.E.S. - RAMONES
9-28-02
TODAY I WENT TO WORK, ONLY TO FIND OUT I DIDN'T HAVE TO BE THERE.
THE NEW SCHEDULE STARTED EARLY.
ROCK!
I GOT AN ELECTRIC EYE 7" IN THE MAIL FROM GREIG!
AUGUST FROM S.O.F./NEGATIVE STEP IS IN THIS BAND. HE MOVED TO PORTLAND AND GREIG PUT OUT THEIR RECORD! SMALL WORLD, HUH?
AND IT ROCKS
AND APPARENTLY I'M SHARING MY BEDROOM WITH A MOUSE.
OH, HOT. MOUSE TURDS. AWESOME.
I DON'T WANNA GROW UP - RAMONES
9-29-02
LAST NIGHT I WENT TO ANNICK'S BIRTHDAY PARTY.
TODAY WORK WENT BY REALLY FAST.
IT FEELS LIKE I'M GETTING SICK.
CRAP! I HOPE IT'S GONE BEFORE THE ZINE SWAP!
SNIFF SNIFF

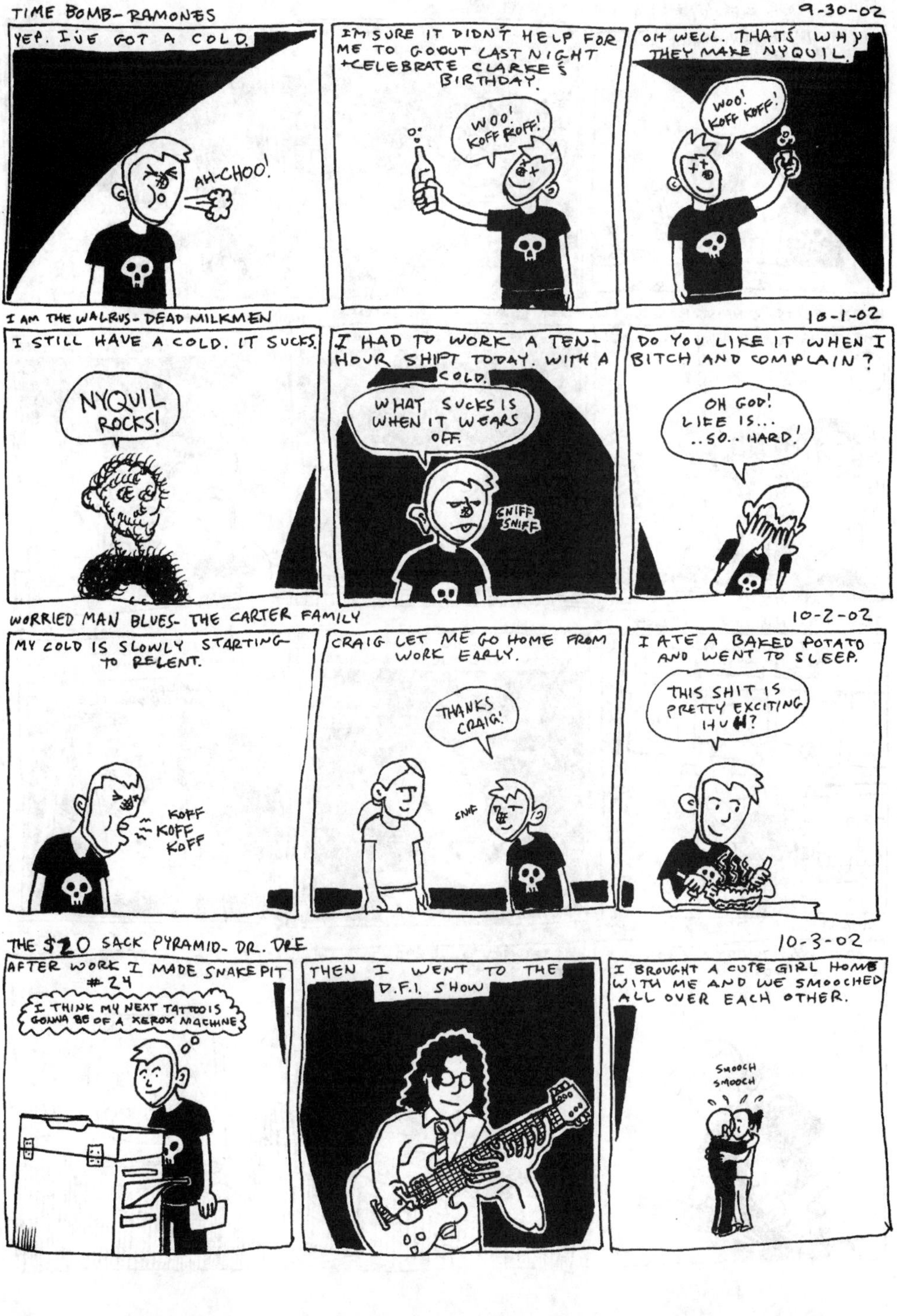
TIME BOMB - RAMONES
9-30-02
YEP. I'VE GOT A COLD.
AH-CHOO!
I'M SURE IT DIDN'T HELP FOR ME TO GO OUT LAST NIGHT + CELEBRATE CLARKE'S BIRTHDAY.
WOO! KOFF KOFF!
OH WELL. THAT'S WHY THEY MAKE NYQUIL.
WOO! KOFF KOFF!
I AM THE WALRUS - DEAD MILKMEN
10-1-02
I STILL HAVE A COLD. IT SUCKS.
NYQUIL ROCKS!
I HAD TO WORK A TEN-HOUR SHIFT TODAY. WITH A COLD.
WHAT SUCKS IS WHEN IT WEARS OFF.
SNIFF SNIFF
DO YOU LIKE IT WHEN I BITCH AND COMPLAIN?
OH GOD! LIFE IS... ..SO.. HARD!
WORRIED MAN BLUES - THE CARTER FAMILY
10-2-02
MY COLD IS SLOWLY STARTING TO RELENT.
KOFF KOFF KOFF
CRAIG LET ME GO HOME FROM WORK EARLY.
THANKS CRAIG!
SNIF
I ATE A BAKED POTATO AND WENT TO SLEEP.
THIS SHIT IS PRETTY EXCITING, HUH?
THE $20 SACK PYRAMID - DR. DRE
10-3-02
AFTER WORK I MADE SNAKEPIT #24
I THINK MY NEXT TATTOO IS GONNA BE OF A XEROX MACHINE
THEN I WENT TO THE D.F.I. SHOW
I BROUGHT A CUTE GIRL HOME WITH ME AND WE SMOOCHED ALL OVER EACH OTHER.
SMOOCH SMOOCH

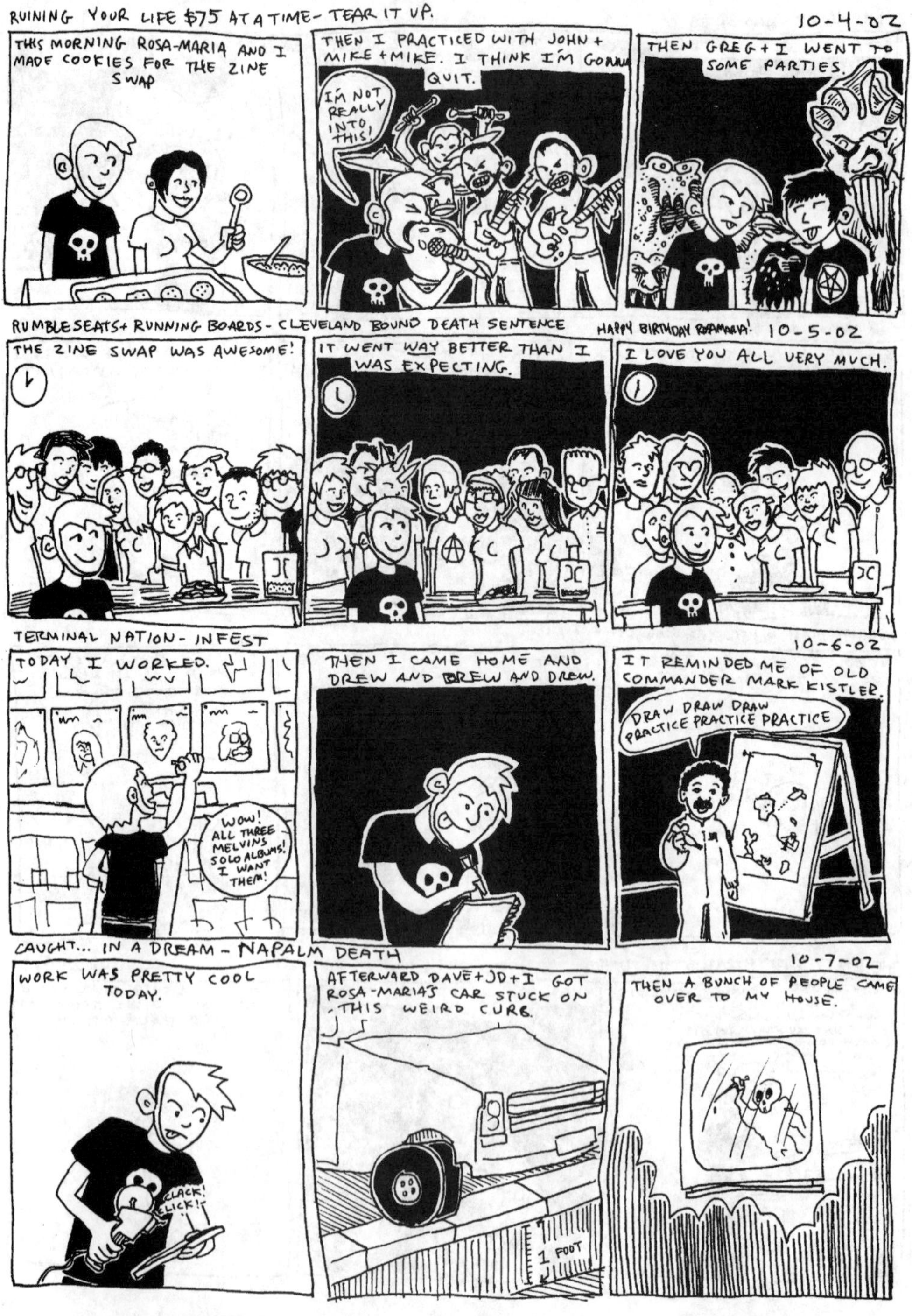

RUINING YOUR LIFE $75 AT A TIME - TEAR IT UP.
10-4-02
THIS MORNING ROSA-MARIA AND I MADE COOKIES FOR THE ZINE SWAP
THEN I PRACTICED WITH JOHN + MIKE + MIKE. I THINK I'M GONNA QUIT.
I'M NOT REALLY INTO THIS!
THEN GREG + I WENT TO SOME PARTIES.
RUMBLESEATS + RUNNING BOARDS - CLEVELAND BOUND DEATH SENTENCE
HAPPY BIRTHDAY ROSAMARIA!
10-5-02
THE ZINE SWAP WAS AWESOME!
IT WENT WAY BETTER THAN I WAS EXPECTING.
I LOVE YOU ALL VERY MUCH.
TERMINAL NATION - INFEST
10-6-02
TODAY I WORKED.
WOW! ALL THREE MELVINS SOLO ALBUMS! I WANT THEM!
THEN I CAME HOME AND DREW AND DREW AND DREW.
IT REMINDED ME OF OLD COMMANDER MARK KISTLER.
DRAW DRAW DRAW PRACTICE PRACTICE PRACTICE
CAUGHT... IN A DREAM - NAPALM DEATH
10-7-02
WORK WAS PRETTY COOL TODAY.
CLACK! CLICK!
AFTERWARD DAVE + JD + I GOT ROSA-MARIA'S CAR STUCK ON THIS WEIRD CURB.
1 FOOT
THEN A BUNCH OF PEOPLE CAME OVER TO MY HOUSE.

GARBAGEMAN - THE CRAMPS

TODAY WAS VERY RAINY.

THIS IS WHAT PORTLAND IS GONNA BE LIKE!

10-8-02

I WENT TO THE GROCERY STORE WITH JD + ADAM, BUT I DIDN'T BUY ANYTHING.

THE LINE IS TOO LONG.

THEN I GOT ALL STONED.

BODIES - SEX PISTOLS

TODAY THE NEW MAXIMUMROCKN ROLL CAME OUT...

MAXIMUMROCKNROLL

SNOBS

R.I.P. DEMON SYSTEM 13!

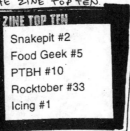

THEY GAVE SNAKEPIT A GREAT REVIEW AND LISTED IT IN THE ZINE TOP TEN.

ZINE TOP TEN

Snakepit #2
Food Geek #5
PTBH #10
Rocktober #33
Icing #1

10-9-02

AND THE SNOBS WERE ON THE COVER!!

THEY EVEN GAVE A SHOUT-OUT TO SOUND EXCHANGE!

PUNX ARE GOF   MRR

DICK ON A DOG - ROCKET FROM THE CRYPT

I SAW THIS CRAZY GUY AT THE GROCERY STORE

IT'S A MUNCHY-LUNCHY!

OH HUH.

10-10-02

THEN I WENT TO WORK. STACI WAS THERE (SHE JUST GOT BACK FROM A TRIP)

THEN I CAME HOME AND HUNG OUT WITH JD, CLARKE + GREG.

JEALOUS AGAIN - BLACK FLAG

THIS MORNING I WENT DOWN SOUTH TO THE THRIFT STORE.

NEW PANTS

THEN I CAME HOME AND PLAYED THE DRUMS.

10-11-02

AFTER THAT GREG AND I WENT TO A CRAPPY PARTY.

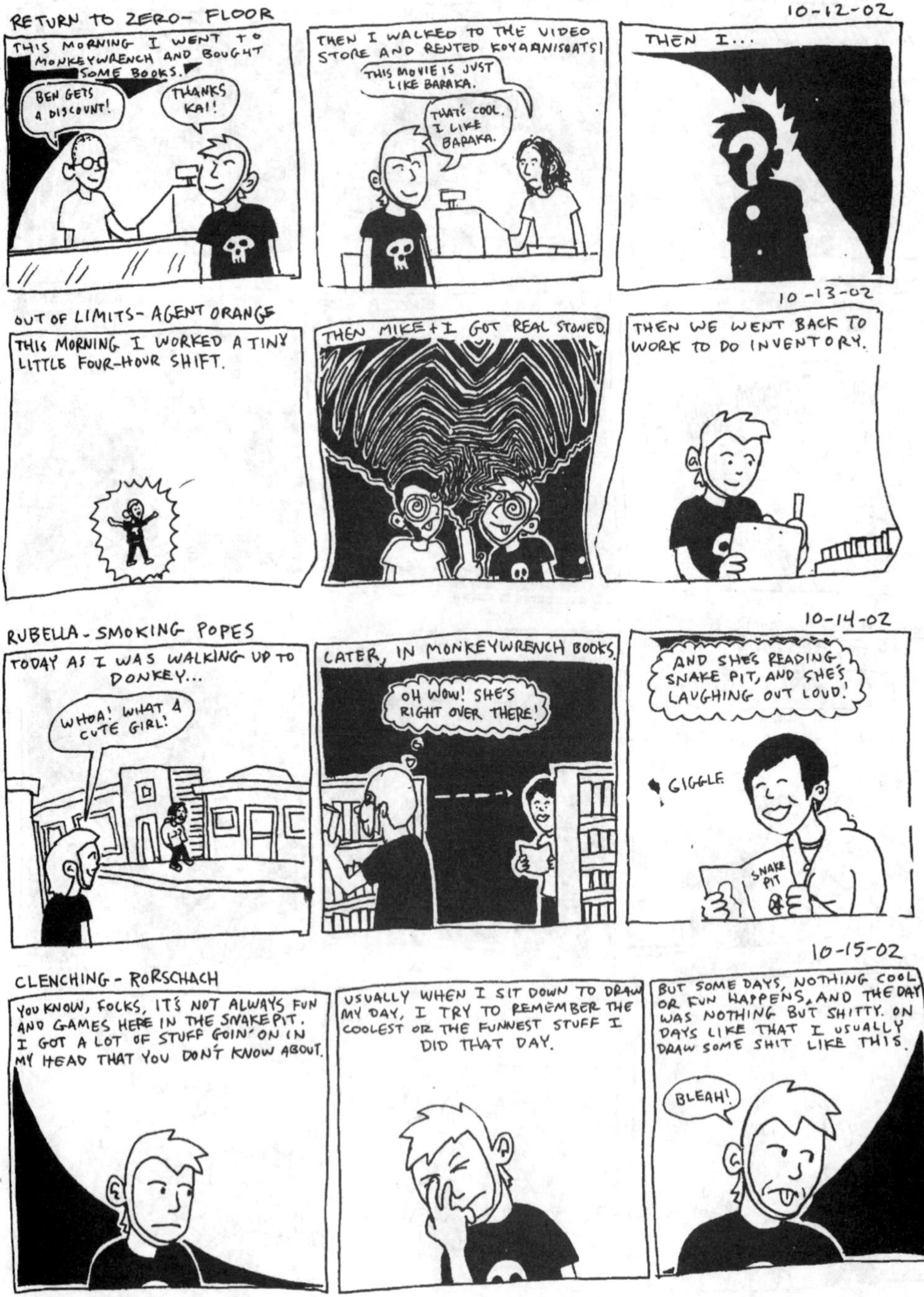

RETURN TO ZERO - FLOOR
10-12-02
THIS MORNING I WENT TO MONKEYWRENCH AND BOUGHT SOME BOOKS.
BEN GETS A DISCOUNT!
THANKS KAI!
THEN I WALKED TO THE VIDEO STORE AND RENTED KOYAANISQATSI
THIS MOVIE IS JUST LIKE BARAKA.
THAT'S COOL. I LIKE BARAKA.
THEN I...
OUT OF LIMITS - AGENT ORANGE
10-13-02
THIS MORNING I WORKED A TINY LITTLE FOUR-HOUR SHIFT.
THEN MIKE + I GOT REAL STONED.
THEN WE WENT BACK TO WORK TO DO INVENTORY.
RUBELLA - SMOKING POPES
10-14-02
TODAY AS I WAS WALKING UP TO DONKEY...
WHOA! WHAT A CUTE GIRL!
LATER, IN MONKEYWRENCH BOOKS.
OH WOW! SHE'S RIGHT OVER THERE!
AND SHE'S READING SNAKE PIT, AND SHE'S LAUGHING OUT LOUD!
GIGGLE
SNAKE PIT
CLENCHING - RORSCHACH
10-15-02
YOU KNOW, FOLKS, IT'S NOT ALWAYS FUN AND GAMES HERE IN THE SNAKEPIT. I GOT A LOT OF STUFF GOIN' ON IN MY HEAD THAT YOU DON'T KNOW ABOUT.
USUALLY WHEN I SIT DOWN TO DRAW MY DAY, I TRY TO REMEMBER THE COOLEST OR THE FUNNEST STUFF I DID THAT DAY.
BUT SOME DAYS, NOTHING COOL OR FUN HAPPENS, AND THE DAY WAS NOTHING BUT SHITTY. ON DAYS LIKE THAT I USUALLY DRAW SOME SHIT LIKE THIS.
BLEAH!

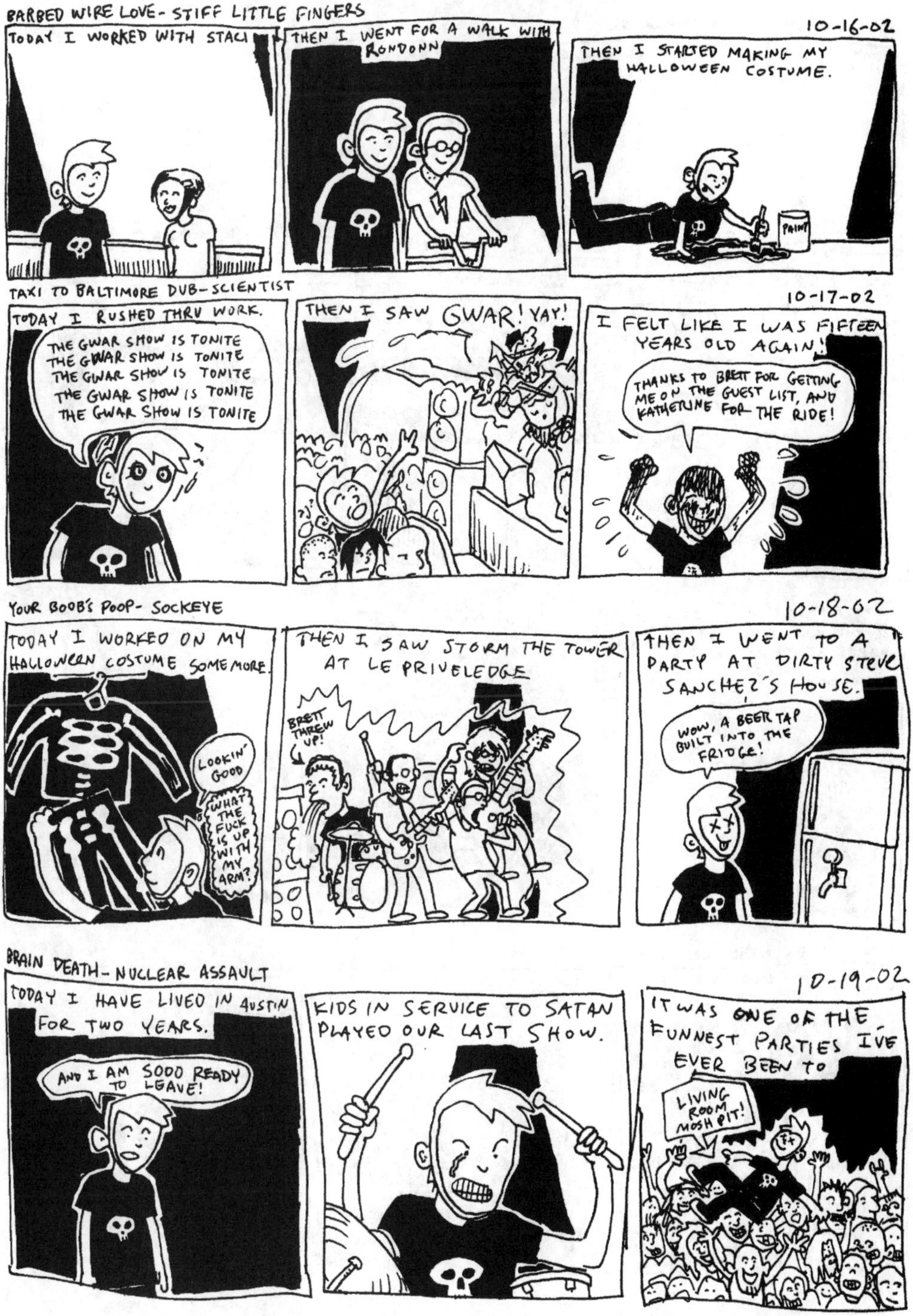
BARBED WIRE LOVE - STIFF LITTLE FINGERS
10-16-02
TODAY I WORKED WITH STACI
THEN I WENT FOR A WALK WITH RONDONN
THEN I STARTED MAKING MY HALLOWEEN COSTUME.
PAINT
TAXI TO BALTIMORE DUB-SCIENTIST
10-17-02
TODAY I RUSHED THRU WORK.
THE GWAR SHOW IS TONITE THE GWAR SHOW IS TONITE THE GWAR SHOW IS TONITE THE GWAR SHOW IS TONITE THE GWAR SHOW IS TONITE
THEN I SAW GWAR! YAY!
I FELT LIKE I WAS FIFTEEN YEARS OLD AGAIN!
THANKS TO BRETT FOR GETTING ME ON THE GUEST LIST, AND KATHERINE FOR THE RIDE!
YOUR BOOB'S POOP - SOCKEYE
10-18-02
TODAY I WORKED ON MY HALLOWEEN COSTUME SOME MORE.
LOOKIN' GOOD
WHAT THE FUCK IS UP WITH MY ARM?
THEN I SAW STORM THE TOWER AT LE PRIVELEDGE
BRETT THREW UP!
THEN I WENT TO A PARTY AT DIRTY STEVE SANCHEZ'S HOUSE.
WOW, A BEER TAP BUILT INTO THE FRIDGE!
BRAIN DEATH - NUCLEAR ASSAULT
10-19-02
TODAY I HAVE LIVED IN AUSTIN FOR TWO YEARS.
AND I AM SOOO READY TO LEAVE!
KIDS IN SERVICE TO SATAN PLAYED OUR LAST SHOW.
IT WAS ONE OF THE FUNNEST PARTIES I'VE EVER BEEN TO
LIVING ROOM MOSH PIT!

PRUNE BELLY - MAN IS THE BASTARD   10-20-02

 TODAY I WAS SITTING ON A BENCH, WAITING FOR A BUS.

 I WAS KINDA BUMMED OUT.

GOD THIS SUCKS. MY BAND JUST BROKE UP, AND IT DOESN'T SEEM LIKE I'LL EVER FIND THE RIGHT GIRL.

 THEN A BIRD SHIT ON ME.

GROSS.

DUMBOO DUB - THE SKATALITES

 THIS MORNING I WOKE UP FROM A DREAM WHERE I THOUGHT MY ALARM CLOCK WAS A CRYING BABY

THAT IS NOT THE CRY OF A HUNGRY BABY

I WENT TO EMO'S AND SAW DFI, STORM THE TOWER, SMALL TEAM OF EXPERTS, THE RISE + THOSE PEABODYS

HAPPY BIRTHDAY STACI!   10-21-02

 SO... MANY... BANDS...

 IT WAS FUN,

SO... MANY... BEERS...

IRON GIRL - FLOOR   10-22-02

 FOR THE PAST 2 DAYS, MY CHECK NUMBER AT TACO CABANA HAS BEEN 138!

WHAT AN AMAZING COINCIDENCE!

#138

 LAST NIGHT THE RISE'S VAN GOT BROKEN INTO AND ALL THEIR EQUIPMENT GOT STOLEN.

SUCKS! TRAGEDY SEEMS TO BE SYSTEMATICALLY BEFALLING SOUND EXCHANGE EMPLOYEES! HOPE I'M NOT NEXT.

 AFTER WORK I HAD ULTIMATE DRAGONS PRACTICE.

TOMORROW NIGHT'S GONNA BE FUN!

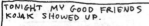

C'MON ~ NIKKI + THE CORVETTES   10-23-02

 TONIGHT MY GOOD FRIENDS KOJAK SHOWED UP.

KOJAK!

JASON   JOHN   BARRY

 THEY PLAYED A SHOW WITH THE ULTIMATE DRAGONS AT BEERLAND.

K

 IT WAS A LOT OF FUN!

I DON'T PLAY THE BASS SO GOOD WHEN I'M DRUNK

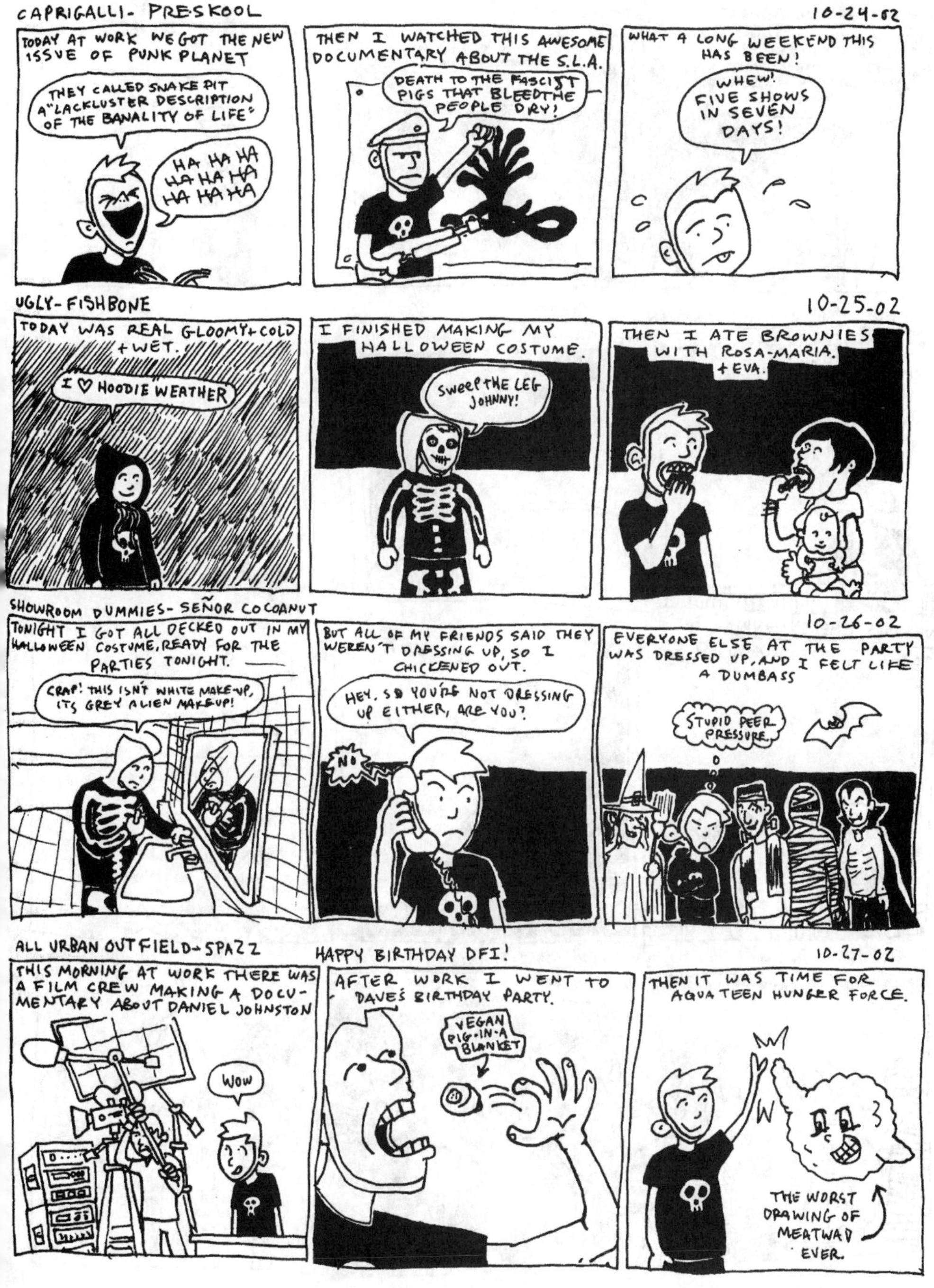

CAPRIGALLI- PRESKOOL
10-24-02
TODAY AT WORK WE GOT THE NEW ISSUE OF PUNK PLANET
THEY CALLED SNAKE PIT A "LACKLUSTER DESCRIPTION OF THE BANALITY OF LIFE"
HA HA HA HA HA HA HA HA HA
THEN I WATCHED THIS AWESOME DOCUMENTARY ABOUT THE S.L.A.
DEATH TO THE FASCIST PIGS THAT BLEED THE PEOPLE DRY!
WHAT A LONG WEEKEND THIS HAS BEEN!
WHEW! FIVE SHOWS IN SEVEN DAYS!
UGLY- FISHBONE
10-25-02
TODAY WAS REAL GLOOMY + COLD + WET.
I ♡ HOODIE WEATHER
I FINISHED MAKING MY HALLOWEEN COSTUME.
SWEEP THE LEG JOHNNY!
THEN I ATE BROWNIES WITH ROSA-MARIA. + EVA.
SHOWROOM DUMMIES- SEÑOR COCOANUT
10-26-02
TONIGHT I GOT ALL DECKED OUT IN MY HALLOWEEN COSTUME, READY FOR THE PARTIES TONIGHT.
CRAP! THIS ISN'T WHITE MAKE-UP, ITS GREY ALIEN MAKEUP!
BUT ALL OF MY FRIENDS SAID THEY WEREN'T DRESSING UP, SO I CHICKENED OUT.
HEY, SO YOU'RE NOT DRESSING UP EITHER, ARE YOU?
NO
EVERYONE ELSE AT THE PARTY WAS DRESSED UP, AND I FELT LIKE A DUMBASS
STUPID PEER PRESSURE.
ALL URBAN OUTFIELD- SPAZZ
HAPPY BIRTHDAY DFI!
10-27-02
THIS MORNING AT WORK THERE WAS A FILM CREW MAKING A DOCUMENTARY ABOUT DANIEL JOHNSTON
WOW
AFTER WORK I WENT TO DAVE'S BIRTHDAY PARTY.
VEGAN PIG-IN-A BLANKET
THEN IT WAS TIME FOR AQUA TEEN HUNGER FORCE.
THE WORST DRAWING OF MEATWAD EVER.

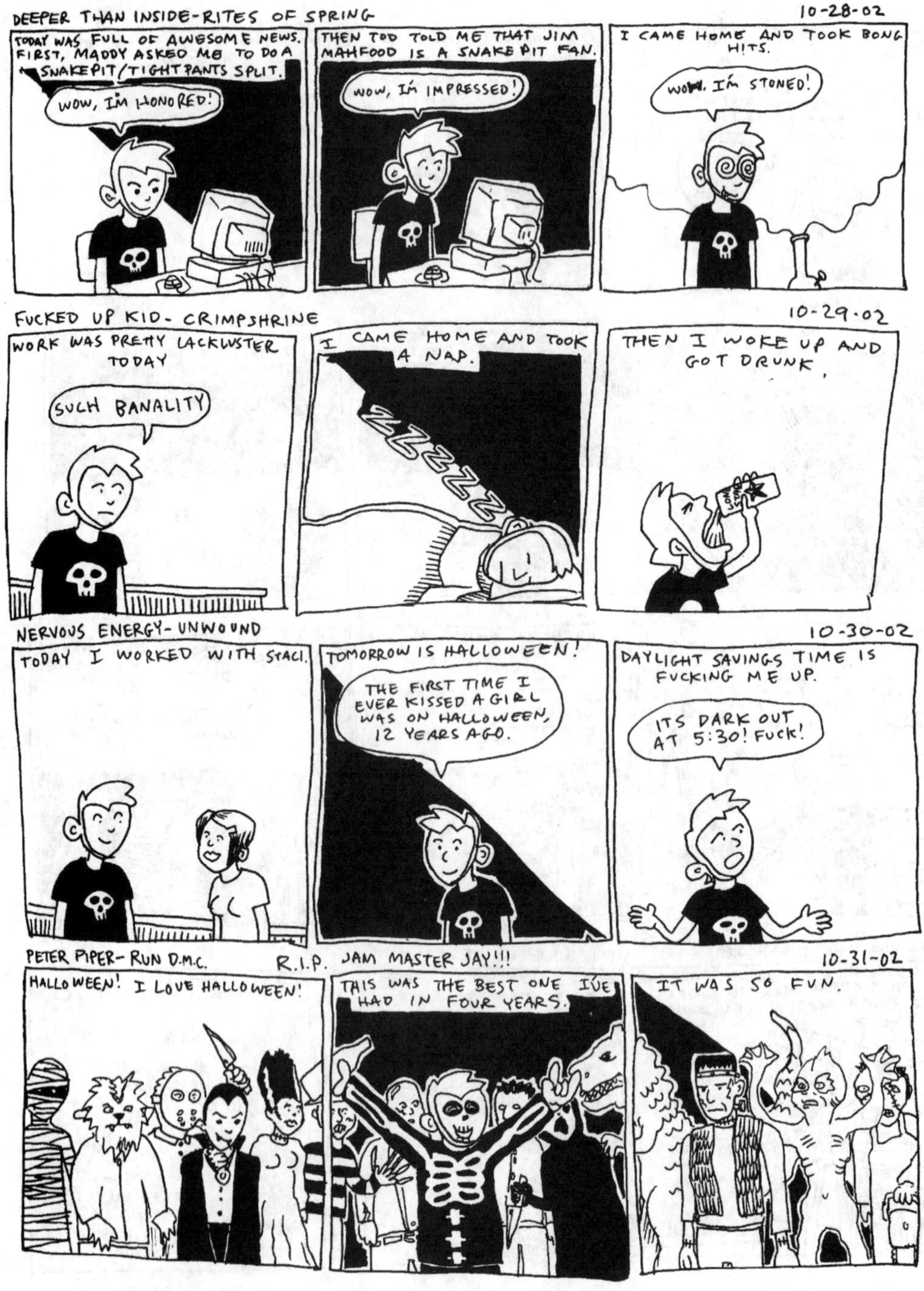
DEEPER THAN INSIDE-RITES OF SPRING
10-28-02
TODAY WAS FULL OF AWESOME NEWS. FIRST, MADDY ASKED ME TO DO A SNAKEPIT/TIGHT PANTS SPLIT.
WOW, I'M HONORED!
THEN TOD TOLD ME THAT JIM MAHFOOD IS A SNAKE PIT FAN.
WOW, I'M IMPRESSED!
I CAME HOME AND TOOK BONG HITS.
WOW. I'M STONED!
FUCKED UP KID- CRIMPSHRINE
10-29-02
WORK WAS PRETTY LACKLUSTER TODAY
SUCH BANALITY
I CAME HOME AND TOOK A NAP.
ZZZZZZ
THEN I WOKE UP AND GOT DRUNK,
NERVOUS ENERGY- UNWOUND
10-30-02
TODAY I WORKED WITH STACI.
TOMORROW IS HALLOWEEN!
THE FIRST TIME I EVER KISSED A GIRL WAS ON HALLOWEEN, 12 YEARS AGO.
DAYLIGHT SAVINGS TIME IS FUCKING ME UP.
ITS DARK OUT AT 5:30! FUCK!
PETER PIPER- RUN D.M.C.
R.I.P. JAM MASTER JAY!!!
10-31-02
HALLOWEEN! I LOVE HALLOWEEN!
THIS WAS THE BEST ONE I'VE HAD IN FOUR YEARS.
IT WAS SO FUN.

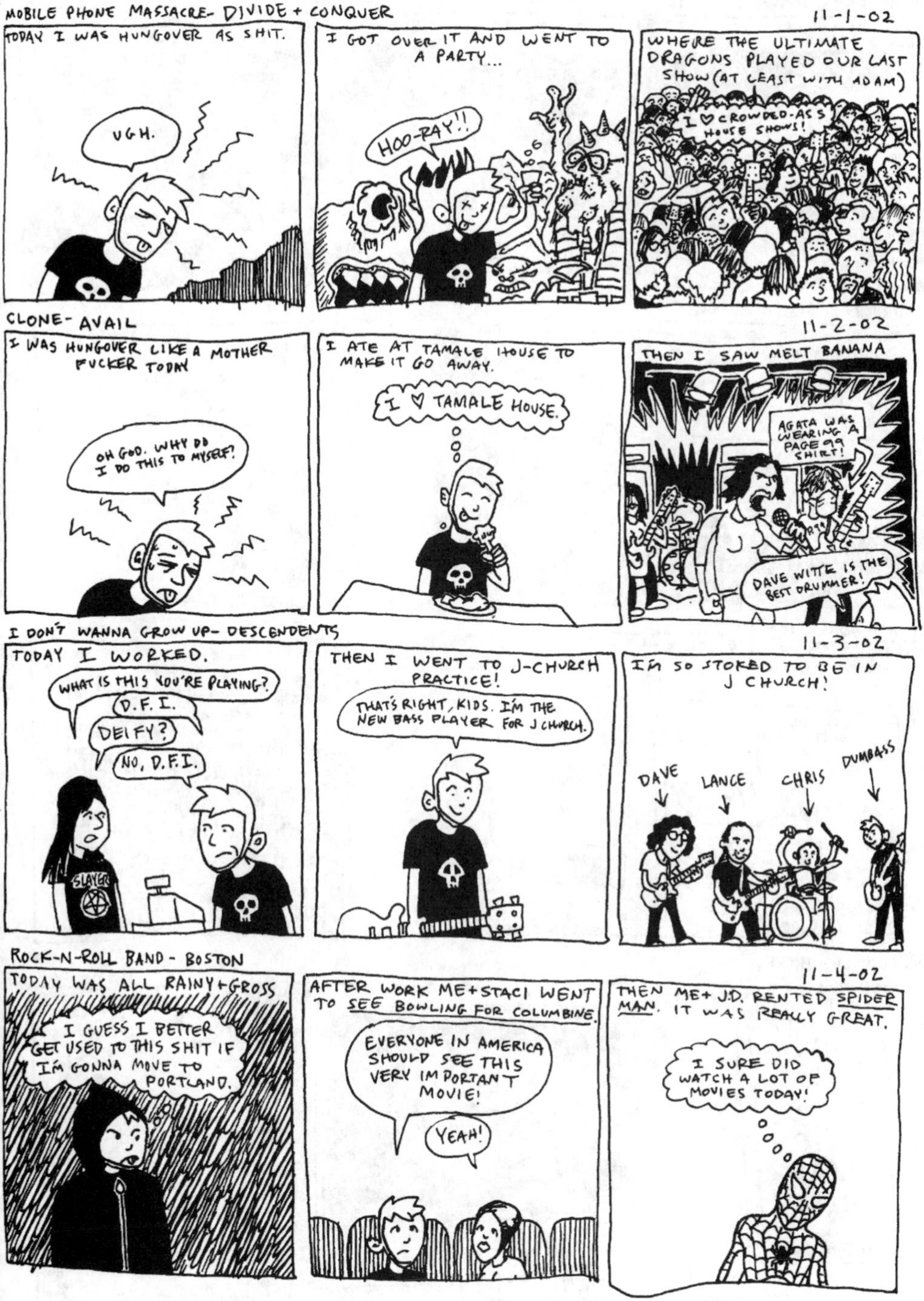
MOBILE PHONE MASSACRE- DIVIDE + CONQUER
11-1-02
TODAY I WAS HUNGOVER AS SHIT.
UGH.
I GOT OVER IT AND WENT TO A PARTY...
HOO-RAY!!
WHERE THE ULTIMATE DRAGONS PLAYED OUR LAST SHOW (AT LEAST WITH ADAM)
I ♡ CROWDED-ASS HOUSE SHOWS!
CLONE- AVAIL
11-2-02
I WAS HUNGOVER LIKE A MOTHER FUCKER TODAY
OH GOD. WHY DO I DO THIS TO MYSELF?
I ATE AT TAMALE HOUSE TO MAKE IT GO AWAY.
I ♡ TAMALE HOUSE.
THEN I SAW MELT BANANA
AGATA WAS WEARING A PAGE 99 SHIRT!
DAVE WITTE IS THE BEST DRUMMER!
I DON'T WANNA GROW UP- DESCENDENTS
11-3-02
TODAY I WORKED.
WHAT IS THIS YOU'RE PLAYING?
D.F.I.
DEIFY?
NO, D.F.I.
SLAYER
THEN I WENT TO J-CHURCH PRACTICE!
THAT'S RIGHT, KIDS. I'M THE NEW BASS PLAYER FOR J CHURCH.
I'M SO STOKED TO BE IN J CHURCH!
DAVE
LANCE
CHRIS
DUMBASS
ROCK-N-ROLL BAND- BOSTON
11-4-02
TODAY WAS ALL RAINY + GROSS
I GUESS I BETTER GET USED TO THIS SHIT IF I'M GONNA MOVE TO PORTLAND.
AFTER WORK ME + STACI WENT TO SEE BOWLING FOR COLUMBINE.
EVERYONE IN AMERICA SHOULD SEE THIS VERY IMPORTANT MOVIE!
YEAH!
THEN ME + J.D. RENTED SPIDER MAN. IT WAS REALLY GREAT.
I SURE DID WATCH A LOT OF MOVIES TODAY!

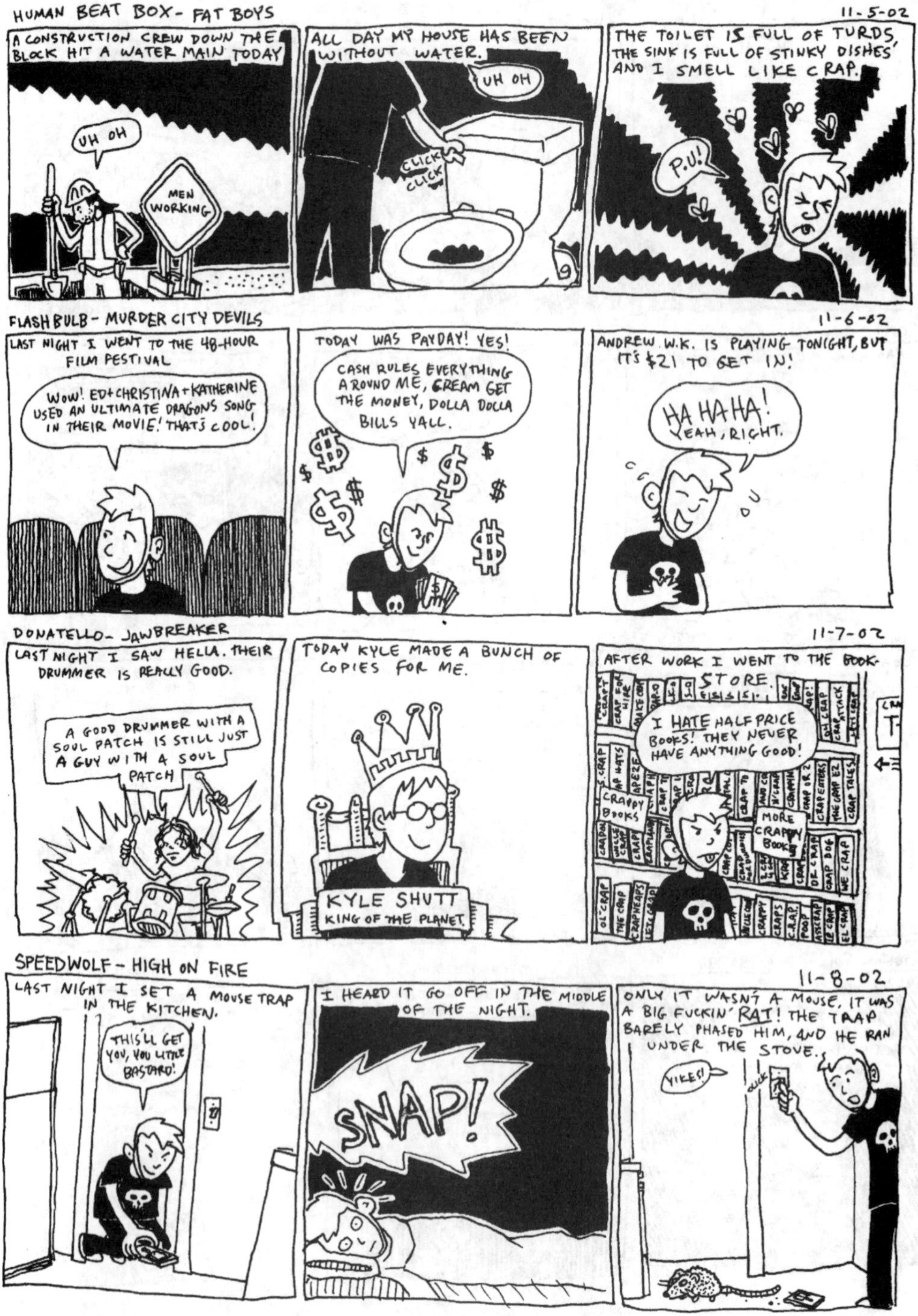

HUMAN BEAT BOX - FAT BOYS
11-5-02
A CONSTRUCTION CREW DOWN THE BLOCK HIT A WATER MAIN TODAY
UH OH
MEN WORKING
ALL DAY MY HOUSE HAS BEEN WITHOUT WATER.
UH OH
CLICK CLICK
THE TOILET IS FULL OF TURDS, THE SINK IS FULL OF STINKY DISHES AND I SMELL LIKE CRAP.
P.U!
FLASHBULB - MURDER CITY DEVILS
11-6-02
LAST NIGHT I WENT TO THE 48-HOUR FILM FESTIVAL
WOW! ED+CHRISTINA+KATHERINE USED AN ULTIMATE DRAGONS SONG IN THEIR MOVIE! THAT'S COOL!
TODAY WAS PAYDAY! YES!
CASH RULES EVERYTHING AROUND ME, CREAM GET THE MONEY, DOLLA DOLLA BILLS YALL.
ANDREW W.K. IS PLAYING TONIGHT, BUT IT'S $21 TO GET IN!
HA HAHA! YEAH, RIGHT.
DONATELLO - JAWBREAKER
11-7-02
LAST NIGHT I SAW HELLA. THEIR DRUMMER IS REALLY GOOD.
A GOOD DRUMMER WITH A SOUL PATCH IS STILL JUST A GUY WITH A SOUL PATCH
TODAY KYLE MADE A BUNCH OF COPIES FOR ME.
KYLE SHUTT
KING OF THE PLANET
AFTER WORK I WENT TO THE BOOK STORE.
I HATE HALF PRICE BOOKS! THEY NEVER HAVE ANYTHING GOOD!
CRAPPY BOOKS
MORE CRAPPY BOOKS
SPEEDWOLF - HIGH ON FIRE
11-8-02
LAST NIGHT I SET A MOUSE TRAP IN THE KITCHEN.
THIS'LL GET YOU, YOU LITTLE BASTARD!
I HEARD IT GO OFF IN THE MIDDLE OF THE NIGHT.
SNAP!
ONLY IT WASN'T A MOUSE, IT WAS A BIG FUCKIN' RAT! THE TRAP BARELY PHASED HIM, AND HE RAN UNDER THE STOVE.
YIKES!
CLICK

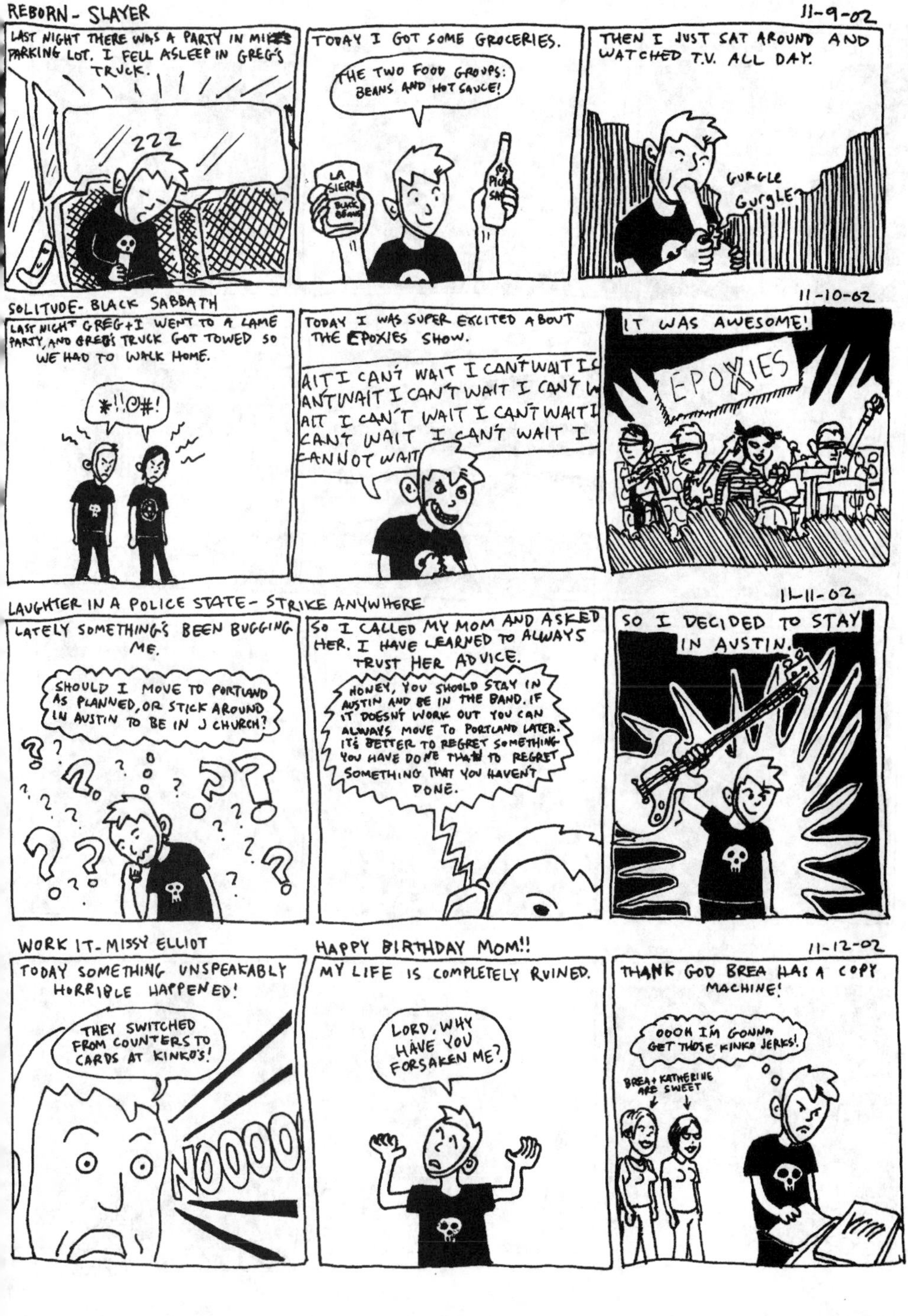
REBORN - SLAYER
11-9-02
LAST NIGHT THERE WAS A PARTY IN MIKE'S PARKING LOT. I FELL ASLEEP IN GREG'S TRUCK.
ZZZ
TODAY I GOT SOME GROCERIES.
THE TWO FOOD GROUPS: BEANS AND HOT SAUCE!
LA SIERRA BLACK BEANS
THEN I JUST SAT AROUND AND WATCHED T.V. ALL DAY.
GURGLE GURGLE
SOLITUDE - BLACK SABBATH
11-10-02
LAST NIGHT GREG+I WENT TO A LAME PARTY, AND GREG'S TRUCK GOT TOWED SO WE HAD TO WALK HOME.
*!!@#!
TODAY I WAS SUPER EXCITED ABOUT THE EPOXIES SHOW.
AIT I CAN'T WAIT I CAN'T WAIT I C ANT WAIT I CAN'T WAIT I CAN'T W AIT I CAN'T WAIT I CAN'T WAIT I CAN'T WAIT I CAN'T WAIT I CANNOT WAIT
IT WAS AWESOME!
EPOXIES
LAUGHTER IN A POLICE STATE - STRIKE ANYWHERE
11-11-02
LATELY SOMETHING'S BEEN BUGGING ME.
SHOULD I MOVE TO PORTLAND AS PLANNED, OR STICK AROUND IN AUSTIN TO BE IN J CHURCH?
SO I CALLED MY MOM AND ASKED HER. I HAVE LEARNED TO ALWAYS TRUST HER ADVICE.
HONEY, YOU SHOULD STAY IN AUSTIN AND BE IN THE BAND. IF IT DOESN'T WORK OUT YOU CAN ALWAYS MOVE TO PORTLAND LATER. IT'S BETTER TO REGRET SOMETHING YOU HAVE DONE THAN TO REGRET SOMETHING THAT YOU HAVEN'T DONE.
SO I DECIDED TO STAY IN AUSTIN.
WORK IT - MISSY ELLIOT
HAPPY BIRTHDAY MOM!!
11-12-02
TODAY SOMETHING UNSPEAKABLY HORRIBLE HAPPENED!
THEY SWITCHED FROM COUNTERS TO CARDS AT KINKO'S!
NOOOO
MY LIFE IS COMPLETELY RUINED.
LORD, WHY HAVE YOU FORSAKEN ME?
THANK GOD BREA HAS A COPY MACHINE!
OOOH I'M GONNA GET THOSE KINKO JERKS!
BREA + KATHERINE ARE SWEET

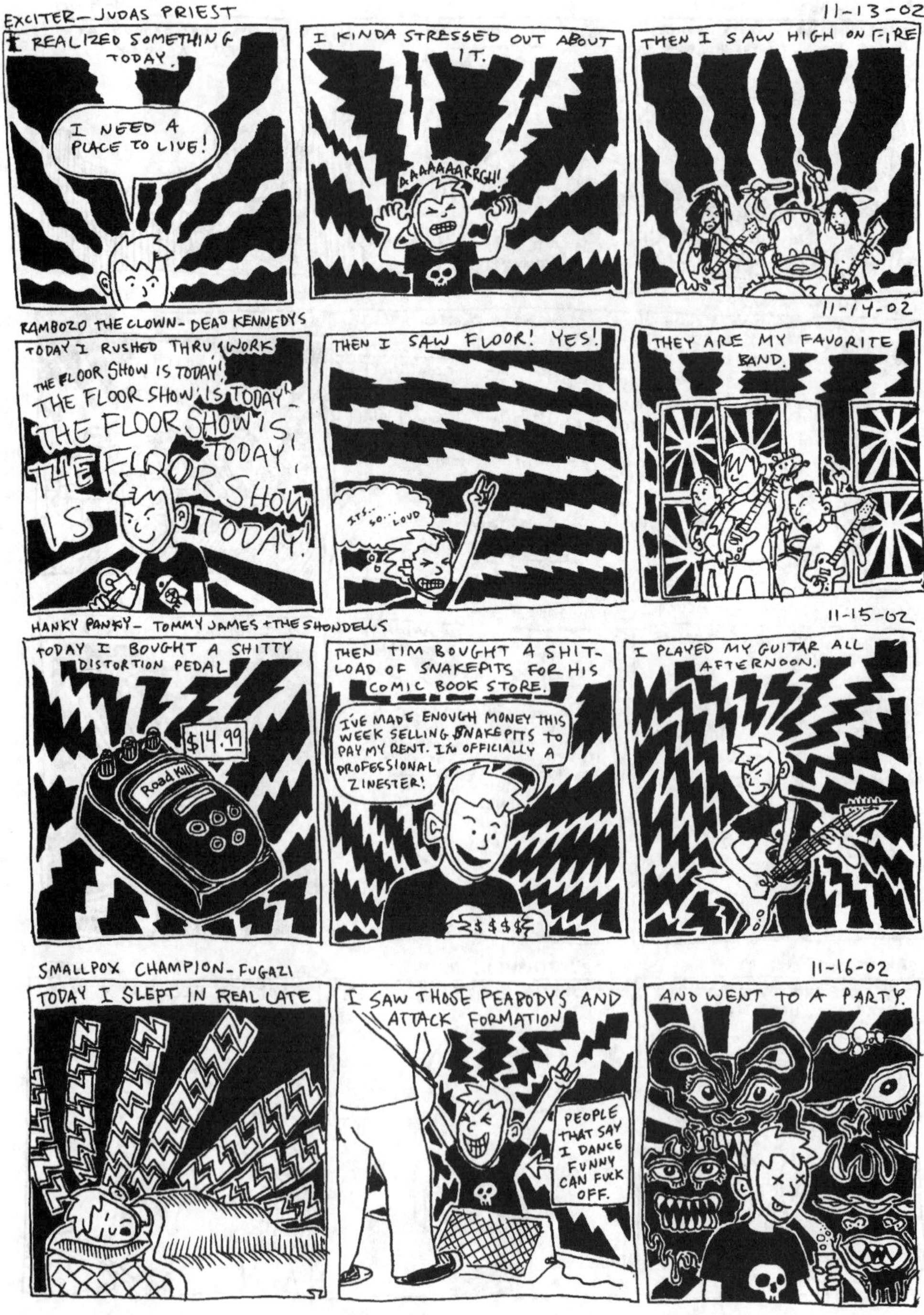
EXCITER—JUDAS PRIEST
11-13-02
I REALIZED SOMETHING TODAY.
I NEED A PLACE TO LIVE!
I KINDA STRESSED OUT ABOUT IT.
AAAAAAARRGH!
THEN I SAW HIGH ON FIRE
RAMBOZO THE CLOWN—DEAD KENNEDYS
11-14-02
TODAY I RUSHED THRU WORK
THE FLOOR SHOW IS TODAY!
THE FLOOR SHOW IS TODAY!
THE FLOOR SHOW IS TODAY!
THE FLOOR SHOW IS TODAY!
THEN I SAW FLOOR! YES!
ITS... SO... LOUD
THEY ARE MY FAVORITE BAND.
HANKY PANKY—TOMMY JAMES + THE SHONDELLS
11-15-02
TODAY I BOUGHT A SHITTY DISTORTION PEDAL
$14.99
Road Kill
THEN TIM BOUGHT A SHIT-LOAD OF SNAKEPITS FOR HIS COMIC BOOK STORE.
I'VE MADE ENOUGH MONEY THIS WEEK SELLING SNAKEPITS TO PAY MY RENT. I'M OFFICIALLY A PROFESSIONAL ZINESTER!
$$$$
I PLAYED MY GUITAR ALL AFTERNOON.
SMALLPOX CHAMPION—FUGAZI
11-16-02
TODAY I SLEPT IN REAL LATE
I SAW THOSE PEABODYS AND ATTACK FORMATION
PEOPLE THAT SAY I DANCE FUNNY CAN FUCK OFF.
AND WENT TO A PARTY.

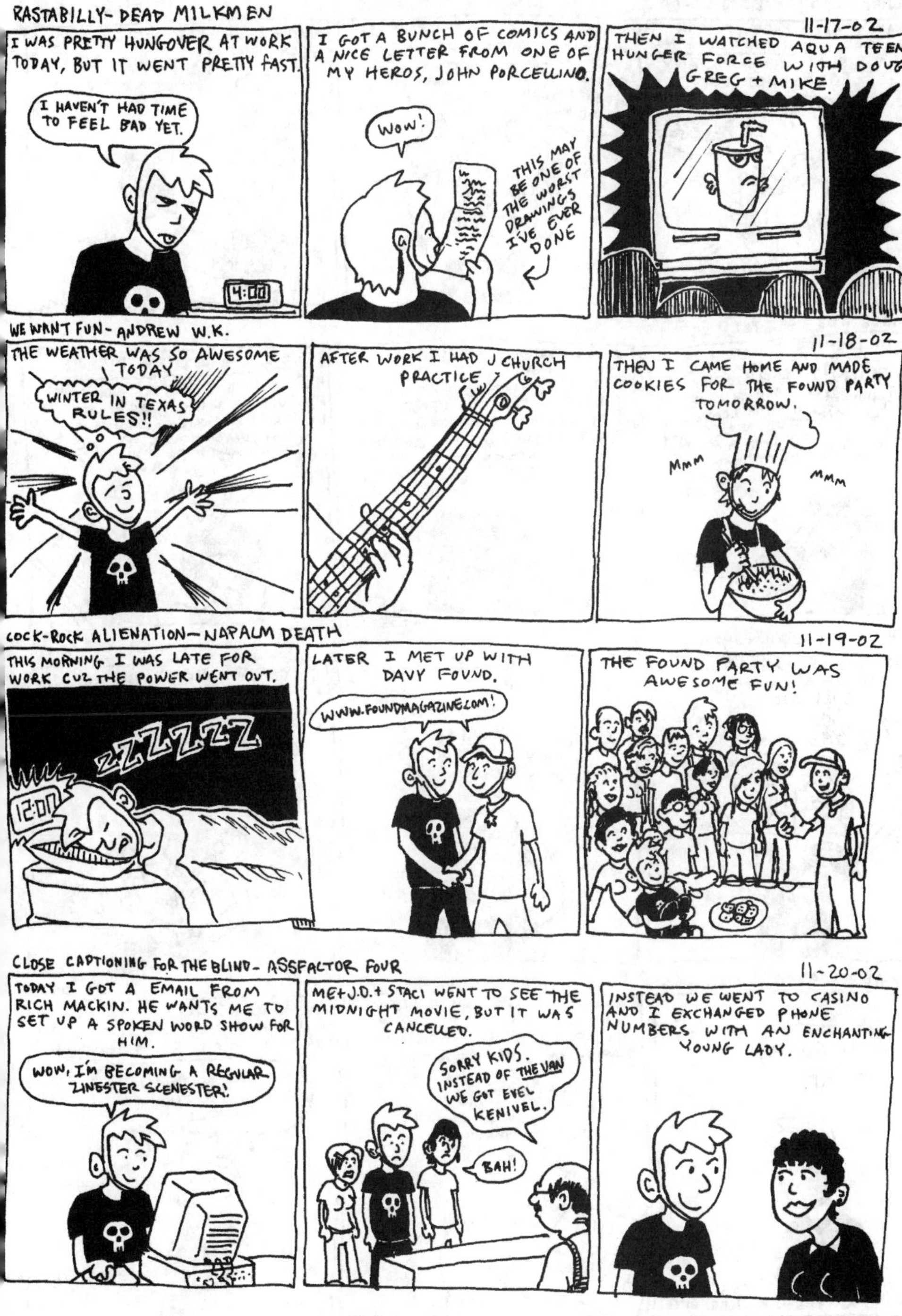

RASTABILLY- DEAD MILKMEN
11-17-02
I WAS PRETTY HUNGOVER AT WORK TODAY, BUT IT WENT PRETTY FAST.
I HAVEN'T HAD TIME TO FEEL BAD YET.
4:00
I GOT A BUNCH OF COMICS AND A NICE LETTER FROM ONE OF MY HEROS, JOHN PORCELLINO.
WOW!
THIS MAY BE ONE OF THE WORST DRAWINGS I'VE EVER DONE
THEN I WATCHED AQUA TEEN HUNGER FORCE WITH DOUG GREG + MIKE.
WE WANT FUN- ANDREW W.K.
11-18-02
THE WEATHER WAS SO AWESOME TODAY
WINTER IN TEXAS RULES!!
AFTER WORK I HAD J CHURCH PRACTICE
THEN I CAME HOME AND MADE COOKIES FOR THE FOUND PARTY TOMORROW.
MMM
MMM
COCK-ROCK ALIENATION- NAPALM DEATH
11-19-02
THIS MORNING I WAS LATE FOR WORK CUZ THE POWER WENT OUT.
ZZZZZZ
12:00
LATER I MET UP WITH DAVY FOUND.
WWW.FOUNDMAGAZINE.COM!
THE FOUND PARTY WAS AWESOME FUN!
CLOSE CAPTIONING FOR THE BLIND- ASSFACTOR FOUR
11-20-02
TODAY I GOT A EMAIL FROM RICH MACKIN. HE WANTS ME TO SET UP A SPOKEN WORD SHOW FOR HIM.
WOW, I'M BECOMING A REGULAR ZINESTER SCENESTER!
ME + J.D. + STACI WENT TO SEE THE MIDNIGHT MOVIE, BUT IT WAS CANCELLED.
SORRY KIDS. INSTEAD OF THE VAN WE GOT EVEL KENIVEL.
BAH!
INSTEAD WE WENT TO CASINO AND I EXCHANGED PHONE NUMBERS WITH AN ENCHANTING YOUNG LADY.

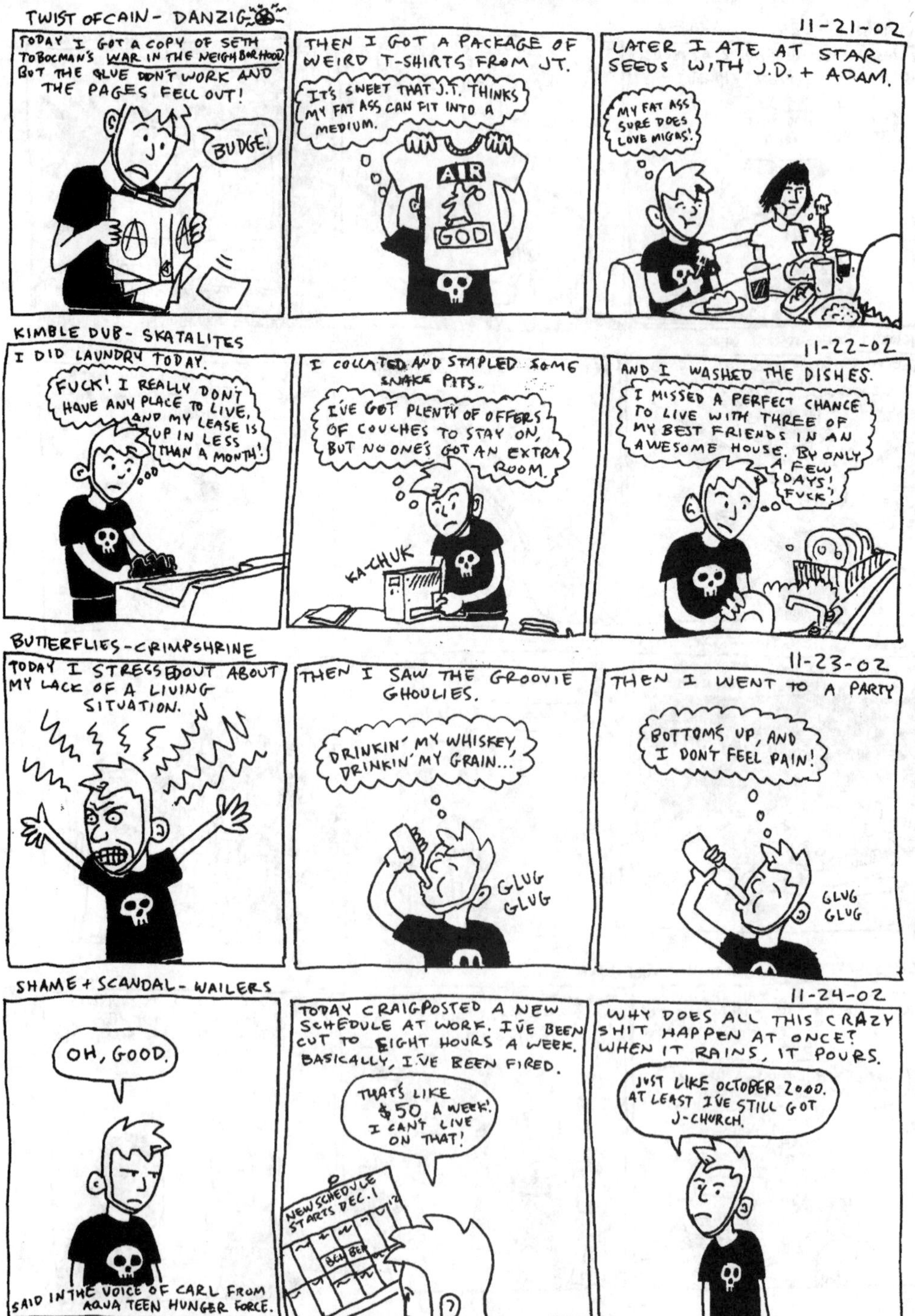
TWIST OF CAIN - DANZIG
11-21-02
TODAY I GOT A COPY OF SETH TOBOCMAN'S WAR IN THE NEIGHBORHOOD. BUT THE GLUE DON'T WORK AND THE PAGES FELL OUT!
BUDGE!
THEN I GOT A PACKAGE OF WEIRD T-SHIRTS FROM J.T.
IT'S SWEET THAT J.T. THINKS MY FAT ASS CAN FIT INTO A MEDIUM.
AIR GOD
LATER I ATE AT STAR SEEDS WITH J.D. + ADAM.
MY FAT ASS SURE DOES LOVE MIGAS!
KIMBLE DUB - SKATALITES
11-22-02
I DID LAUNDRY TODAY.
FUCK! I REALLY DON'T HAVE ANY PLACE TO LIVE, AND MY LEASE IS UP IN LESS THAN A MONTH!
I COLLATED AND STAPLED SOME SNAKE PITS.
I'VE GOT PLENTY OF OFFERS OF COUCHES TO STAY ON, BUT NO ONE'S GOT AN EXTRA ROOM.
KA-CHUK
AND I WASHED THE DISHES.
I MISSED A PERFECT CHANCE TO LIVE WITH THREE OF MY BEST FRIENDS IN AN AWESOME HOUSE. BY ONLY A FEW DAYS! FUCK!
BUTTERFLIES - CRIMPSHRINE
11-23-02
TODAY I STRESSED OUT ABOUT MY LACK OF A LIVING SITUATION.
THEN I SAW THE GROOVIE GHOULIES.
DRINKIN' MY WHISKEY, DRINKIN' MY GRAIN...
GLUG GLUG
THEN I WENT TO A PARTY
BOTTOMS UP, AND I DON'T FEEL PAIN!
GLUG GLUG
SHAME + SCANDAL - WAILERS
11-24-02
OH, GOOD.
SAID IN THE VOICE OF CARL FROM AQUA TEEN HUNGER FORCE.
TODAY CRAIG POSTED A NEW SCHEDULE AT WORK. I'VE BEEN CUT TO EIGHT HOURS A WEEK. BASICALLY, I'VE BEEN FIRED.
THAT'S LIKE $50 A WEEK! I CAN'T LIVE ON THAT!
NEW SCHEDULE STARTS DEC. 1
WHY DOES ALL THIS CRAZY SHIT HAPPEN AT ONCE? WHEN IT RAINS, IT POURS.
JUST LIKE OCTOBER 2000. AT LEAST I'VE STILL GOT J-CHURCH.

YOU'RE FIRED- STRIKE ANYWHERE

11-25-02

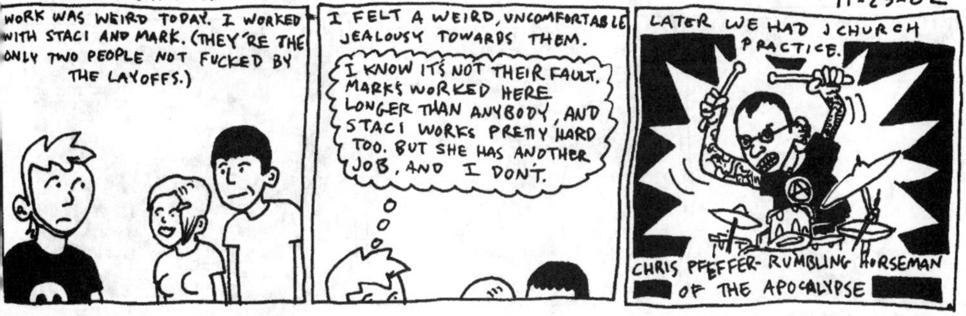
WORK WAS WEIRD TODAY. I WORKED WITH STACI AND MARK. (THEY'RE THE ONLY TWO PEOPLE NOT FUCKED BY THE LAYOFFS.)
I FELT A WEIRD, UNCOMFORTABLE JEALOUSY TOWARDS THEM.
I KNOW IT'S NOT THEIR FAULT. MARK'S WORKED HERE LONGER THAN ANYBODY, AND STACI WORKS PRETTY HARD TOO. BUT SHE HAS ANOTHER JOB, AND I DON'T.
LATER WE HAD J CHURCH PRACTICE.
CHRIS PFEFFER- RUMBLING HORSEMAN OF THE APOCALYPSE

CHICKEN STRUT- THE METERS

11-26-02

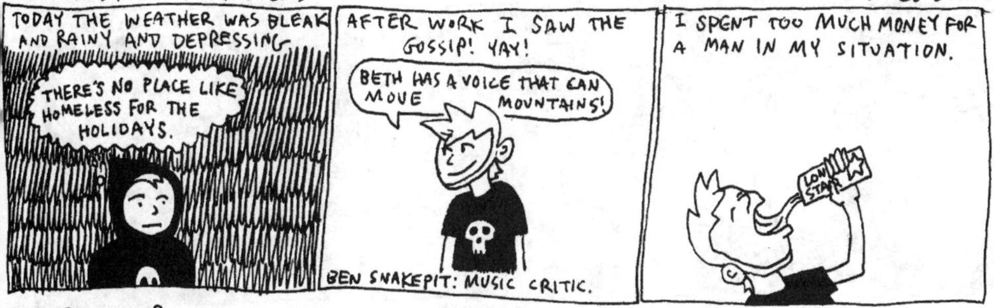
TODAY THE WEATHER WAS BLEAK AND RAINY AND DEPRESSING.
THERE'S NO PLACE LIKE HOMELESS FOR THE HOLIDAYS.
AFTER WORK I SAW THE GOSSIP! YAY!
BETH HAS A VOICE THAT CAN MOVE MOUNTAINS!
BEN SNAKEPIT: MUSIC CRITIC.
I SPENT TOO MUCH MONEY FOR A MAN IN MY SITUATION.
LONE STAR

JAMIE- WEEZER

11-27-02

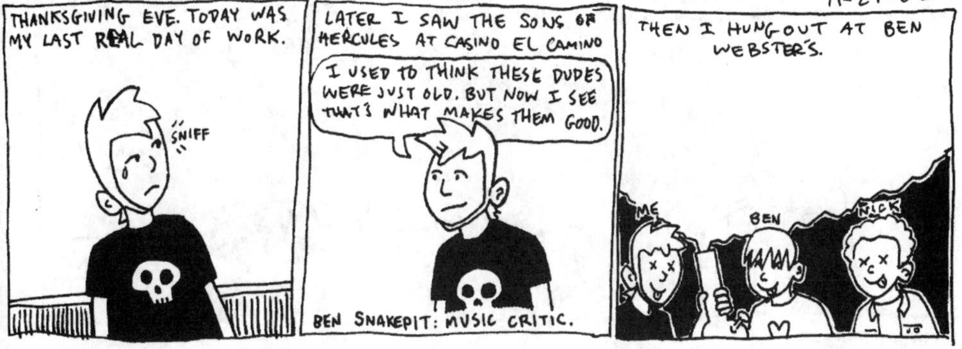
THANKSGIVING EVE. TODAY WAS MY LAST REAL DAY OF WORK.
SNIFF
LATER I SAW THE SONS OF HERCULES AT CASINO EL CAMINO
I USED TO THINK THESE DUDES WERE JUST OLD. BUT NOW I SEE THAT'S WHAT MAKES THEM GOOD.
BEN SNAKEPIT: MUSIC CRITIC.
THEN I HUNG OUT AT BEN WEBSTER'S.
ME
BEN
NICK

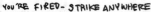

11-28-02

I AM THANKFUL THAT I AM HEALTHY AND THAT MY BODY WORKS CORRECTLY. I AM THANKFUL THAT I HAVE SO MANY AWESOME FRIENDS. I AM THANKFUL THAT I DIDN'T LOSE MY JOB COMPLETELY. I AM THANKFUL THAT I CAN ALWAYS GET INTO EMO'S FOR FREE. I'M THANKFUL TO BE IN J CHURCH. I AM THANKFUL THAT MY MOM LOVES ME. I AM THANKFUL TO LIVE IN AUSTIN. I AM THANKFUL THAT SO MANY PEOPLE LIKE SNAKEPIT. I AM THANKFUL TO HAVE LIVED AS FULL OF A LIFE AS I HAVE FOR A PERSON MY AGE. I AM THANKFUL THAT I DON'T HAVE A CELL PHONE. I AM THANKFUL TO GET THE MAIL EVERY DAY. I AM THANKFUL THAT I DON'T LIVE IN VIRGINIA ANYMORE. I AM THANKFUL THAT NO ONE IS TRYING TO KILL ME. I AM THANKFUL THAT THE DOWNTOWN KINKO'S STILL USES BLUE COUNTERS. I AM THANKFUL TO HAVE A GOOD RECORD COLLECTION. I AM THANKFUL THAT I GOT TO KISS SOME GIRLS THIS YEAR. I AM THANKFUL FOR AQUA TEEN HUNGER FORCE. I AM THANKFUL THAT I DON'T NEED A CAR. I AM THANKFUL THAT YOU ARE READING THIS.

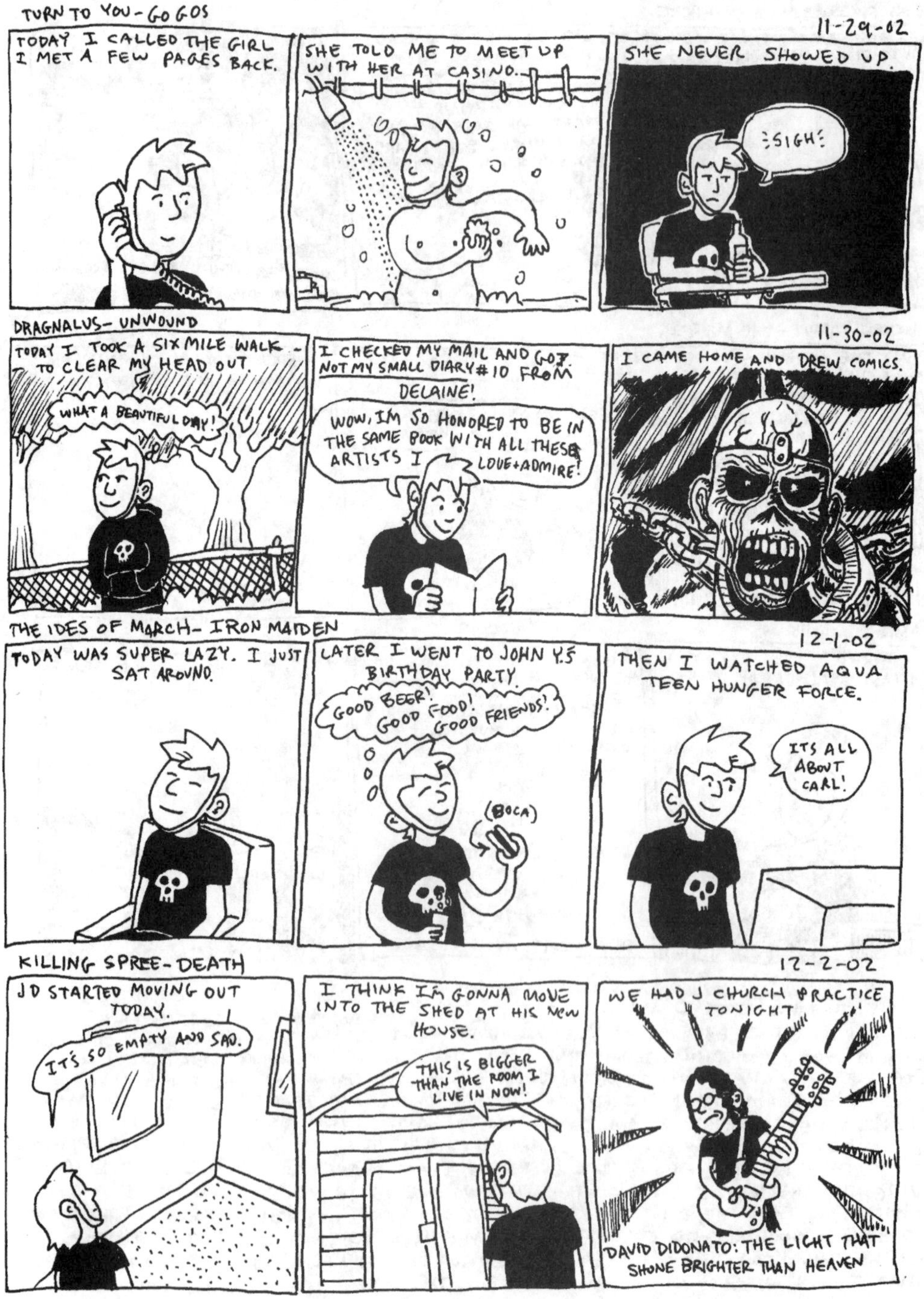
TURN TO YOU - GO GOS
11-29-02
TODAY I CALLED THE GIRL I MET A FEW PAGES BACK.
SHE TOLD ME TO MEET UP WITH HER AT CASINO.
SHE NEVER SHOWED UP.
SIGH
DRAGNALUS - UNWOUND
11-30-02
TODAY I TOOK A SIX MILE WALK - TO CLEAR MY HEAD OUT.
WHAT A BEAUTIFUL DAY!
I CHECKED MY MAIL AND GOT NOT MY SMALL DIARY #10 FROM DELAINE!
WOW, I'M SO HONORED TO BE IN THE SAME BOOK WITH ALL THESE ARTISTS I LOVE+ADMIRE!
I CAME HOME AND DREW COMICS.
THE IDES OF MARCH - IRON MAIDEN
12-1-02
TODAY WAS SUPER LAZY. I JUST SAT AROUND.
LATER I WENT TO JOHN Y.'S BIRTHDAY PARTY.
GOOD BEER! GOOD FOOD! GOOD FRIENDS!
(BOCA)
THEN I WATCHED AQUA TEEN HUNGER FORCE.
ITS ALL ABOUT CARL!
KILLING SPREE - DEATH
12-2-02
JD STARTED MOVING OUT TODAY.
IT'S SO EMPTY AND SAD.
I THINK I'M GONNA MOVE INTO THE SHED AT HIS NEW HOUSE.
THIS IS BIGGER THAN THE ROOM I LIVE IN NOW!
WE HAD J CHURCH PRACTICE TONIGHT
DAVID DIDONATO: THE LIGHT THAT SHONE BRIGHTER THAN HEAVEN

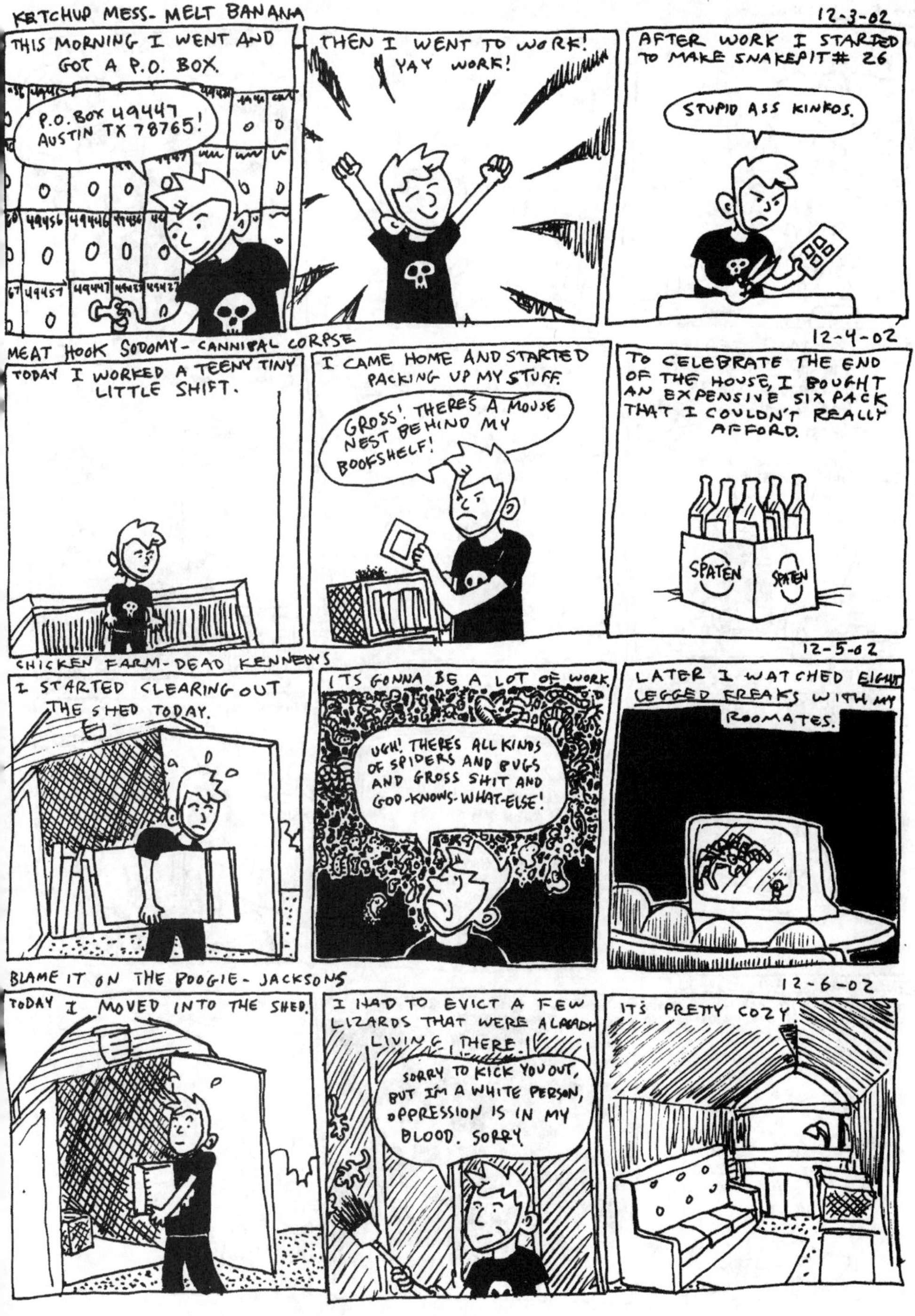

KETCHUP MESS- MELT BANANA
12-3-02
THIS MORNING I WENT AND GOT A P.O. BOX.
P.O. BOX 49447 AUSTIN TX 78765!
THEN I WENT TO WORK! YAY WORK!
AFTER WORK I STARTED TO MAKE SNAKEPIT # 26
STUPID ASS KINKOS.
MEAT HOOK SODOMY- CANNIBAL CORPSE
12-4-02
TODAY I WORKED A TEENY TINY LITTLE SHIFT.
I CAME HOME AND STARTED PACKING UP MY STUFF.
GROSS! THERE'S A MOUSE NEST BEHIND MY BOOKSHELF!
TO CELEBRATE THE END OF THE HOUSE, I BOUGHT AN EXPENSIVE SIX PACK THAT I COULDN'T REALLY AFFORD.
SPATEN
SPATEN
CHICKEN FARM-DEAD KENNEDYS
12-5-02
I STARTED CLEARING OUT THE SHED TODAY.
ITS GONNA BE A LOT OF WORK.
UGH! THERE'S ALL KINDS OF SPIDERS AND BUGS AND GROSS SHIT AND GOD-KNOWS-WHAT-ELSE!
LATER I WATCHED EIGHT LEGGED FREAKS WITH MY ROOMATES.
BLAME IT ON THE BOOGIE- JACKSONS
12-6-02
TODAY I MOVED INTO THE SHED.
I HAD TO EVICT A FEW LIZARDS THAT WERE ALREADY LIVING THERE.
SORRY TO KICK YOU OUT, BUT I'M A WHITE PERSON, OPPRESSION IS IN MY BLOOD. SORRY
IT'S PRETTY COZY.

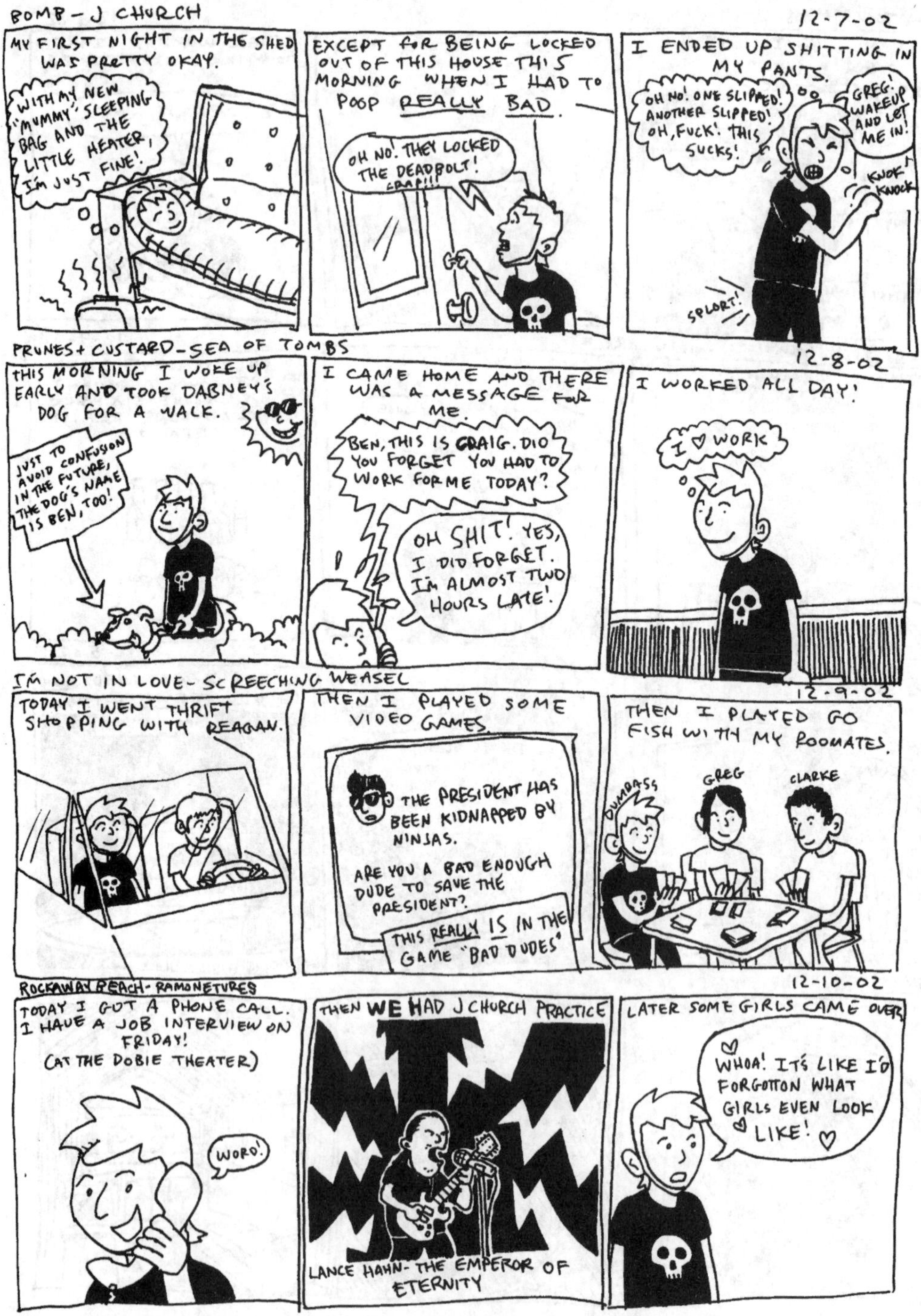
BOMB - J CHURCH
12-7-02
MY FIRST NIGHT IN THE SHED WAS PRETTY OKAY.
WITH MY NEW "MUMMY" SLEEPING BAG AND THE LITTLE HEATER, I'M JUST FINE!
EXCEPT FOR BEING LOCKED OUT OF THIS HOUSE THIS MORNING WHEN I HAD TO POOP REALLY BAD.
OH NO! THEY LOCKED THE DEADBOLT!
CRAP!!!
I ENDED UP SHITTING IN MY PANTS.
OH NO! ONE SLIPPED! ANOTHER SLIPPED! OH, FUCK! THIS SUCKS!
GREG! WAKEUP AND LET ME IN!
KNOK KNOCK
SPLORT!
PRUNES + CUSTARD - SEA OF TOMBS
12-8-02
THIS MORNING I WOKE UP EARLY AND TOOK DABNEY'S DOG FOR A WALK.
JUST TO AVOID CONFUSION IN THE FUTURE, THE DOG'S NAME IS BEN, TOO!
I CAME HOME AND THERE WAS A MESSAGE FOR ME.
BEN, THIS IS CRAIG. DID YOU FORGET YOU HAD TO WORK FOR ME TODAY?
OH SHIT! YES, I DID FORGET. I'M ALMOST TWO HOURS LATE!
I WORKED ALL DAY!
I ♡ WORK
I'M NOT IN LOVE - SCREECHING WEASEL
12-9-02
TODAY I WENT THRIFT SHOPPING WITH REAGAN.
THEN I PLAYED SOME VIDEO GAMES.
THE PRESIDENT HAS BEEN KIDNAPPED BY NINJAS.
ARE YOU A BAD ENOUGH DUDE TO SAVE THE PRESIDENT?
THIS REALLY IS IN THE GAME "BAD DUDES"
THEN I PLAYED GO FISH WITH MY ROOMATES.
DUMBASS
GREG
CLARKE
ROCKAWAY BEACH - RAMONETURES
12-10-02
TODAY I GOT A PHONE CALL. I HAVE A JOB INTERVIEW ON FRIDAY! (AT THE DOBIE THEATER)
WORD!
THEN WE HAD J CHURCH PRACTICE
LANCE HAHN - THE EMPEROR OF ETERNITY
LATER SOME GIRLS CAME OVER.
WHOA! IT'S LIKE I'D FORGOTTON WHAT GIRLS EVEN LOOK LIKE!

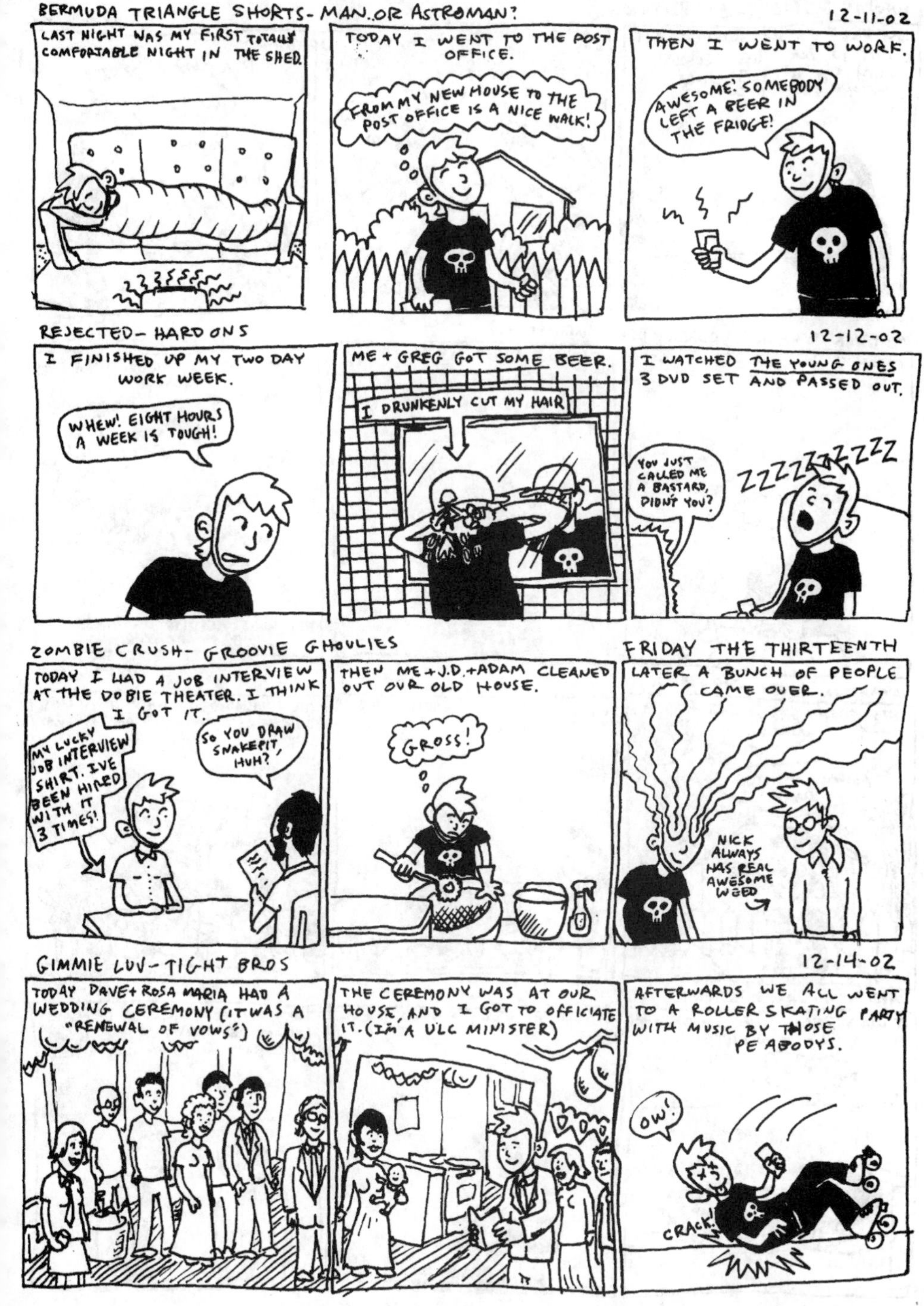

BERMUDA TRIANGLE SHORTS- MAN..OR ASTROMAN?
12-11-02
LAST NIGHT WAS MY FIRST TOTALLY COMFORTABLE NIGHT IN THE SHED.
TODAY I WENT TO THE POST OFFICE.
FROM MY NEW HOUSE TO THE POST OFFICE IS A NICE WALK!
THEN I WENT TO WORK.
AWESOME! SOMEBODY LEFT A BEER IN THE FRIDGE!
REJECTED- HARD ONS
12-12-02
I FINISHED UP MY TWO DAY WORK WEEK.
WHEW! EIGHT HOURS A WEEK IS TOUGH!
ME + GREG GOT SOME BEER.
I DRUNKENLY CUT MY HAIR
I WATCHED THE YOUNG ONES 3 DVD SET AND PASSED OUT.
YOU JUST CALLED ME A BASTARD, DIDN'T YOU?
ZZZZZZZZZZ
ZOMBIE CRUSH- GROOVIE GHOULIES
FRIDAY THE THIRTEENTH
TODAY I HAD A JOB INTERVIEW AT THE DOBIE THEATER. I THINK I GOT IT.
MY LUCKY JOB INTERVIEW SHIRT. I'VE BEEN HIRED WITH IT 3 TIMES!
SO YOU DRAW SNAKEPIT, HUH?
THEN ME + J.D. + ADAM CLEANED OUT OUR OLD HOUSE.
GROSS!
LATER A BUNCH OF PEOPLE CAME OVER.
NICK ALWAYS HAS REAL AWESOME WEED
GIMMIE LUV- TIGHT BROS
12-14-02
TODAY DAVE + ROSA MARIA HAD A WEDDING CEREMONY (IT WAS A "RENEWAL OF VOWS")
THE CEREMONY WAS AT OUR HOUSE, AND I GOT TO OFFICIATE IT. (I'M A ULC MINISTER)
AFTERWARDS WE ALL WENT TO A ROLLER SKATING PARTY WITH MUSIC BY THOSE PEABODYS.
OW!
CRACK!

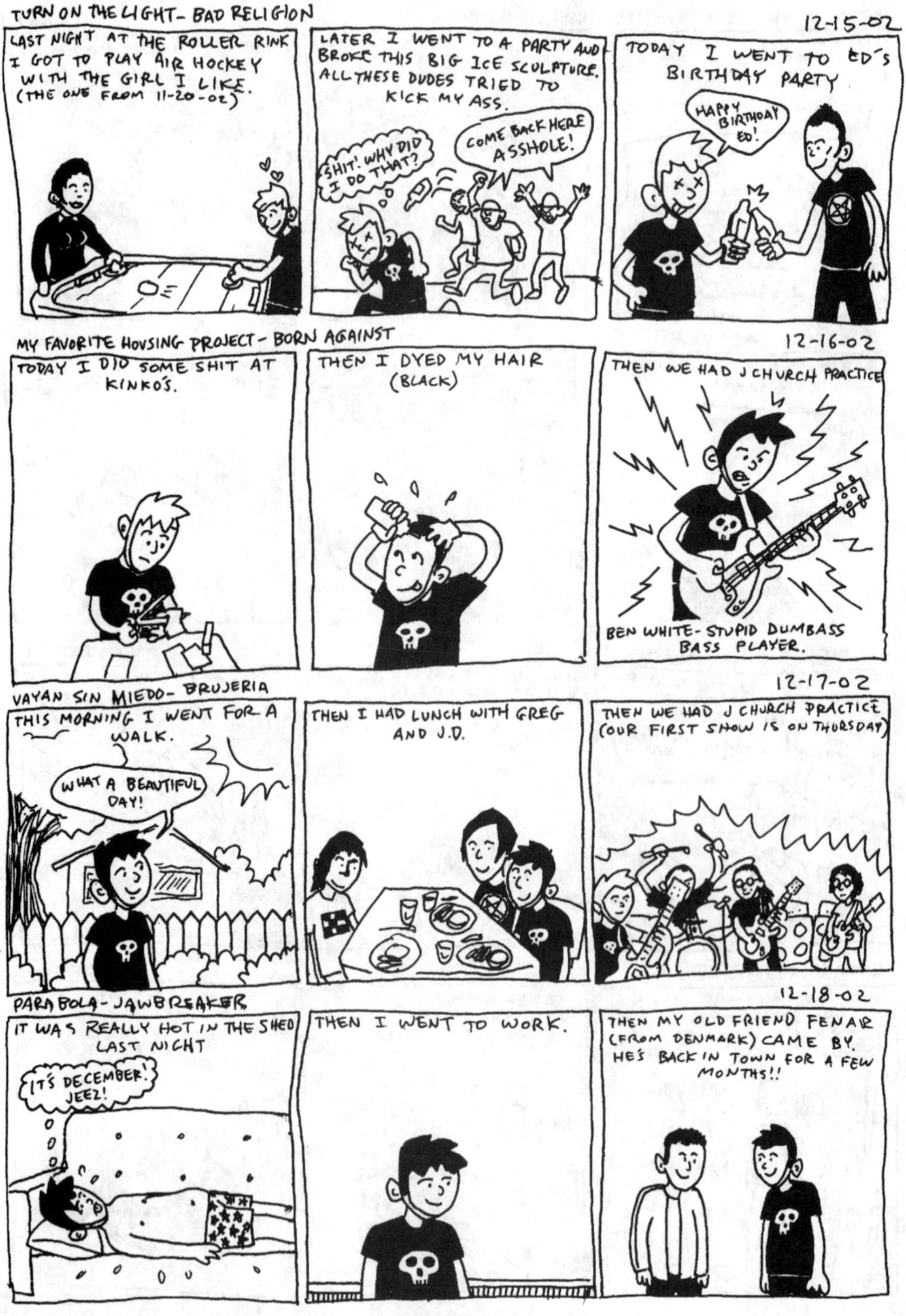
TURN ON THE LIGHT - BAD RELIGION
12-15-02
LAST NIGHT AT THE ROLLER RINK I GOT TO PLAY AIR HOCKEY WITH THE GIRL I LIKE. (THE ONE FROM 11-20-02)
LATER I WENT TO A PARTY AND BROKE THIS BIG ICE SCULPTURE. ALL THESE DUDES TRIED TO KICK MY ASS.
SHIT! WHY DID I DO THAT?
COME BACK HERE ASSHOLE!
TODAY I WENT TO ED'S BIRTHDAY PARTY
HAPPY BIRTHDAY ED!
MY FAVORITE HOUSING PROJECT - BORN AGAINST
12-16-02
TODAY I DID SOME SHIT AT KINKO'S.
THEN I DYED MY HAIR (BLACK)
THEN WE HAD J CHURCH PRACTICE
BEN WHITE - STUPID DUMBASS BASS PLAYER.
VAYAN SIN MIEDO - BRUJERIA
12-17-02
THIS MORNING I WENT FOR A WALK.
WHAT A BEAUTIFUL DAY!
THEN I HAD LUNCH WITH GREG AND J.D.
THEN WE HAD J CHURCH PRACTICE (OUR FIRST SHOW IS ON THURSDAY)
PARABOLA - JAWBREAKER
12-18-02
IT WAS REALLY HOT IN THE SHED LAST NIGHT
IT'S DECEMBER! JEEZ!
THEN I WENT TO WORK.
THEN MY OLD FRIEND FENAR (FROM DENMARK) CAME BY. HE'S BACK IN TOWN FOR A FEW MONTHS!!

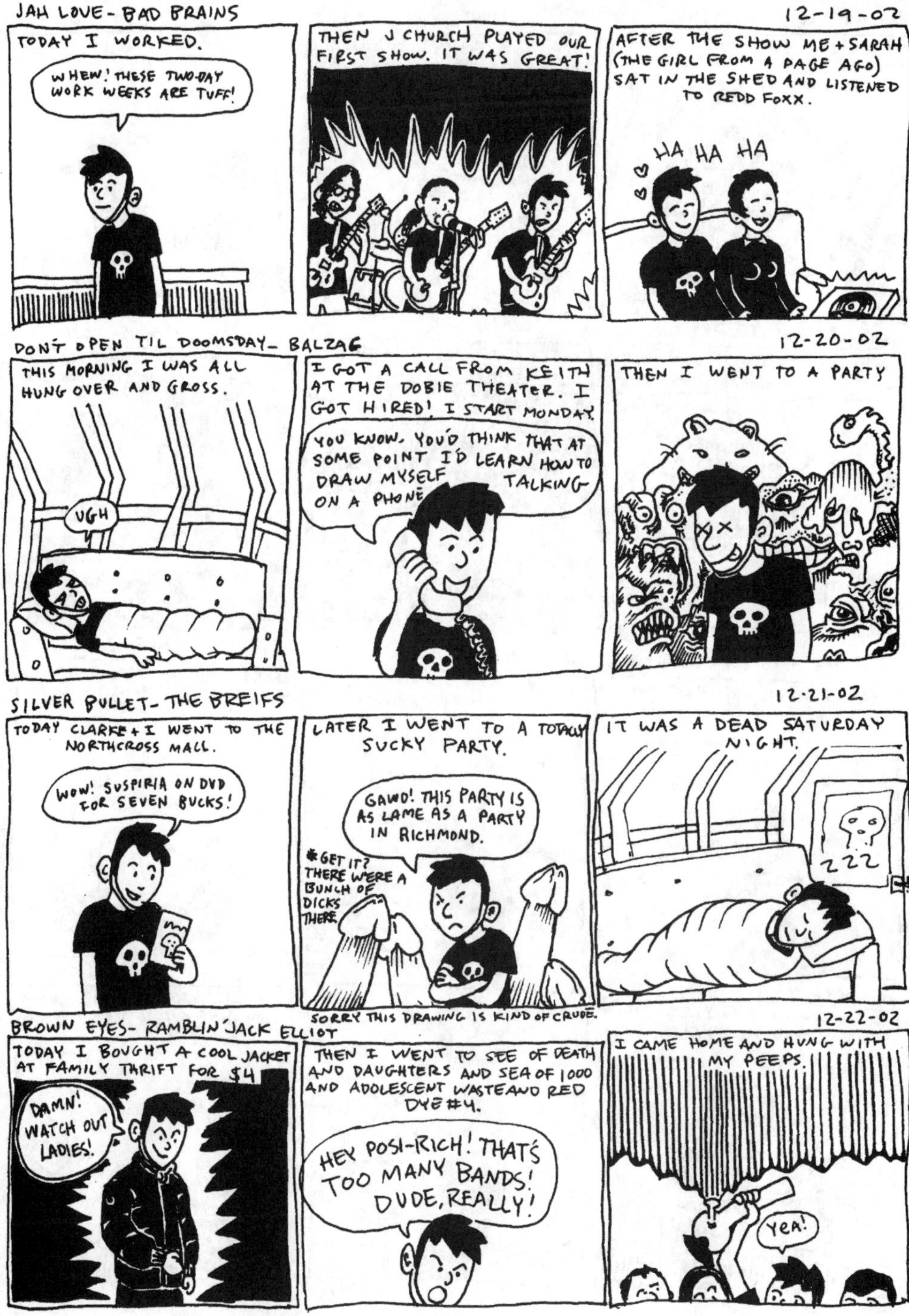
JAH LOVE - BAD BRAINS
12-19-02
TODAY I WORKED.
WHEW! THESE TWO-DAY WORK WEEKS ARE TUFF!
THEN J CHURCH PLAYED OUR FIRST SHOW. IT WAS GREAT!
AFTER THE SHOW ME + SARAH (THE GIRL FROM A PAGE AGO) SAT IN THE SHED AND LISTENED TO REDD FOXX.
HA HA HA
DON'T OPEN TIL DOOMSDAY - BALZAC
12-20-02
THIS MORNING I WAS ALL HUNG OVER AND GROSS.
UGH
I GOT A CALL FROM KEITH AT THE DOBIE THEATER. I GOT HIRED! I START MONDAY.
YOU KNOW. YOU'D THINK THAT AT SOME POINT I'D LEARN HOW TO DRAW MYSELF TALKING ON A PHONE
THEN I WENT TO A PARTY
SILVER BULLET - THE BREIFS
12-21-02
TODAY CLARKE + I WENT TO THE NORTHCROSS MALL.
WOW! SUSPIRIA ON DVD FOR SEVEN BUCKS!
LATER I WENT TO A TOTALLY SUCKY PARTY.
GAWD! THIS PARTY IS AS LAME AS A PARTY IN RICHMOND.
*GET IT? THERE WERE A BUNCH OF DICKS THERE.
SORRY THIS DRAWING IS KIND OF CRUDE.
IT WAS A DEAD SATURDAY NIGHT.
ZZZ
BROWN EYES - RAMBLIN' JACK ELLIOT
12-22-02
TODAY I BOUGHT A COOL JACKET AT FAMILY THRIFT FOR $4
DAMN! WATCH OUT LADIES!
THEN I WENT TO SEE OF DEATH AND DAUGHTERS AND SEA OF 1000 AND ADOLESCENT WASTE AND RED DYE #4.
HEY POSI-RICH! THAT'S TOO MANY BANDS! DUDE, REALLY!
I CAME HOME AND HUNG WITH MY PEEPS.
YEA!

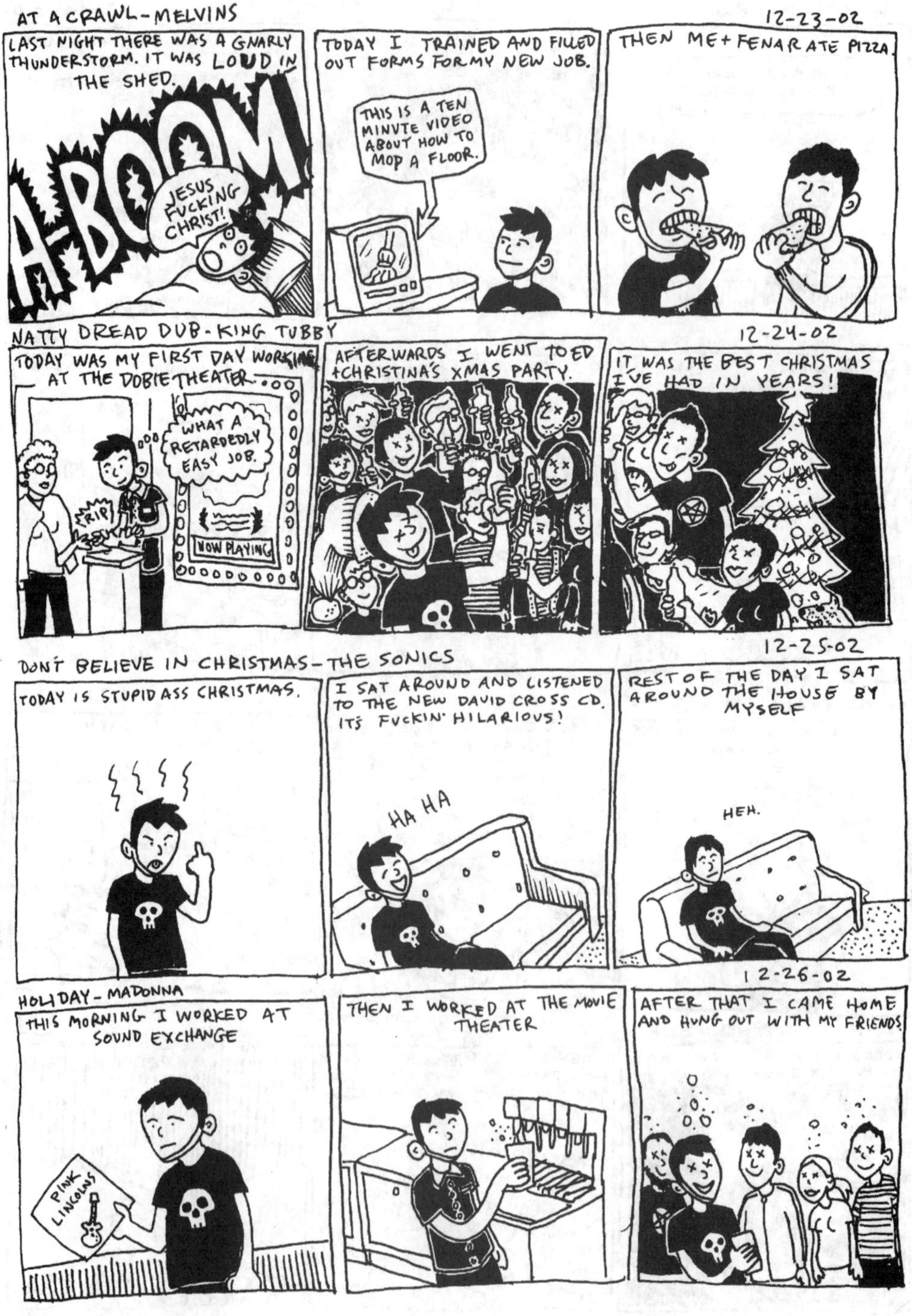
AT A CRAWL - MELVINS
12-23-02
LAST NIGHT THERE WAS A GNARLY THUNDERSTORM. IT WAS LOUD IN THE SHED.
A-BOOM!
JESUS FUCKING CHRIST!
TODAY I TRAINED AND FILLED OUT FORMS FOR MY NEW JOB.
THIS IS A TEN MINUTE VIDEO ABOUT HOW TO MOP A FLOOR.
THEN ME + FENAR ATE PIZZA.
NATTY DREAD DUB - KING TUBBY
12-24-02
TODAY WAS MY FIRST DAY WORKING AT THE DOBIE THEATER.
RIP!
WHAT A RETARDEDLY EASY JOB.
NOW PLAYING
AFTERWARDS I WENT TO ED + CHRISTINA'S XMAS PARTY.
IT WAS THE BEST CHRISTMAS I'VE HAD IN YEARS!
DON'T BELIEVE IN CHRISTMAS - THE SONICS
12-25-02
TODAY IS STUPID ASS CHRISTMAS.
I SAT AROUND AND LISTENED TO THE NEW DAVID CROSS CD. IT'S FUCKIN' HILARIOUS!
HA HA
REST OF THE DAY I SAT AROUND THE HOUSE BY MYSELF
HEH.
HOLIDAY - MADONNA
12-26-02
THIS MORNING I WORKED AT SOUND EXCHANGE
PINK LINCOLNS
THEN I WORKED AT THE MOVIE THEATER
AFTER THAT I CAME HOME AND HUNG OUT WITH MY FRIENDS.

URSULA FINALLY HAS TITS- THE QUEERS   12-27-02

TODAY I DID LAUNDRY AND GOT SOME GROCERIES

WOW! LIVING IN HYDE PARK IS SO CONVENIENT!

FRESH PLUS   LAUNDRETTE

THEN I WENT TO WORK AT THE MOVIE THEATER.

NOW PLAYING
the flower that drank the MOON
WINNER

THEN THERE WAS A SMALL PARTY AT MY HOUSE.

KEEP ON THE SUNNY SIDE- CARTER FAMILY.   12-28-02

J.D. GOT VICE CITY FOR CHRISTMAS. I PLAYED IT ALL DAY!

AWESOME!

THEN I WORKED AT THE THEATER.

FLOWER DRANK MOON

BLIP!

THEN I HUNG OUT WITH SARAH.

LOVEJOY'S

INTO THE MIST 2 - LIGHTNING & BOLT   12-29-02

TODAY I WORKED A DOUBLE SHIFT AT SOUND EXCHANGE.

KISS

I MISS THE GOOD OL' DAYS.

SIGH

LATER ME + CLARKE + ALEX GOT VERY DRUNK MAKING MARGARITAS.

FIGURED OUT -FLOOR   12-30-02

TODAY I WORKED WITH STACI AT SOUND EXCHANGE. IT WAS COOL (WE HAVEN'T BEEN TALKING TO EACH OTHER MUCH LATELY)

I'M GLAD WE'RE FRIENDS AGAIN.

I CAME HOME AND PLAYED VIDEO GAMES.

VICE CITY!

TOMORROW IS GONNA BE FUN!

JAGERMEISTER
MD 20/20
BLUE NUN
SOCO
LONE STAR

END OF A YEAR- EMBRACE

12-31-02

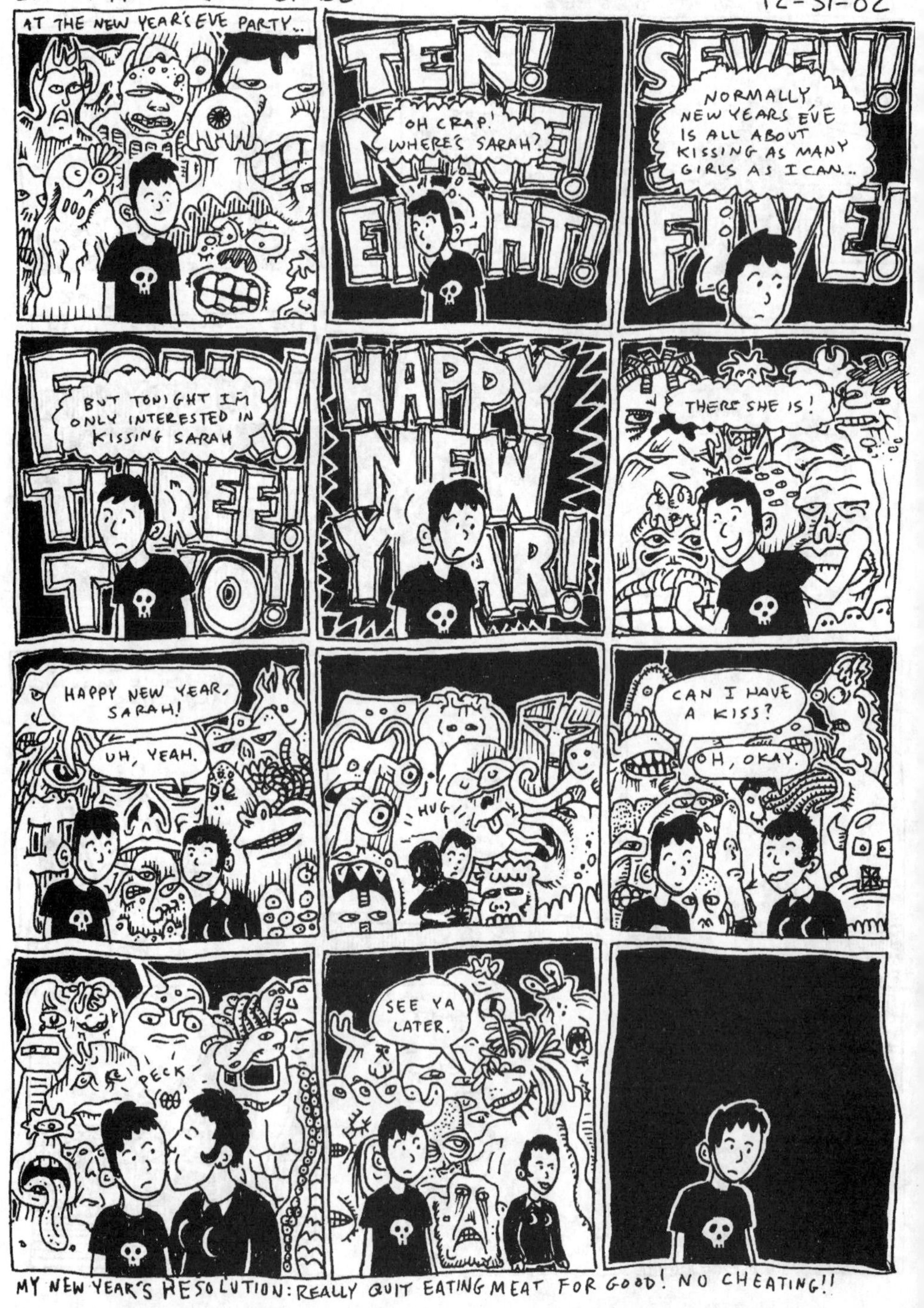
AT THE NEW YEAR'S EVE PARTY..
TEN! NINE! EIGHT!
OH CRAP! WHERE'S SARAH?
SEVEN! FIVE!
NORMALLY NEW YEARS EVE IS ALL ABOUT KISSING AS MANY GIRLS AS I CAN..
FOUR! THREE! TWO!
BUT TONIGHT I'M ONLY INTERESTED IN KISSING SARAH
HAPPY NEW YEAR!
THERE SHE IS!
HAPPY NEW YEAR, SARAH!
UH, YEAH.
HUG
CAN I HAVE A KISS?
OH, OKAY.
PECK
SEE YA LATER.

MY NEW YEAR'S RESOLUTION: REALLY QUIT EATING MEAT FOR GOOD! NO CHEATING!!

2003

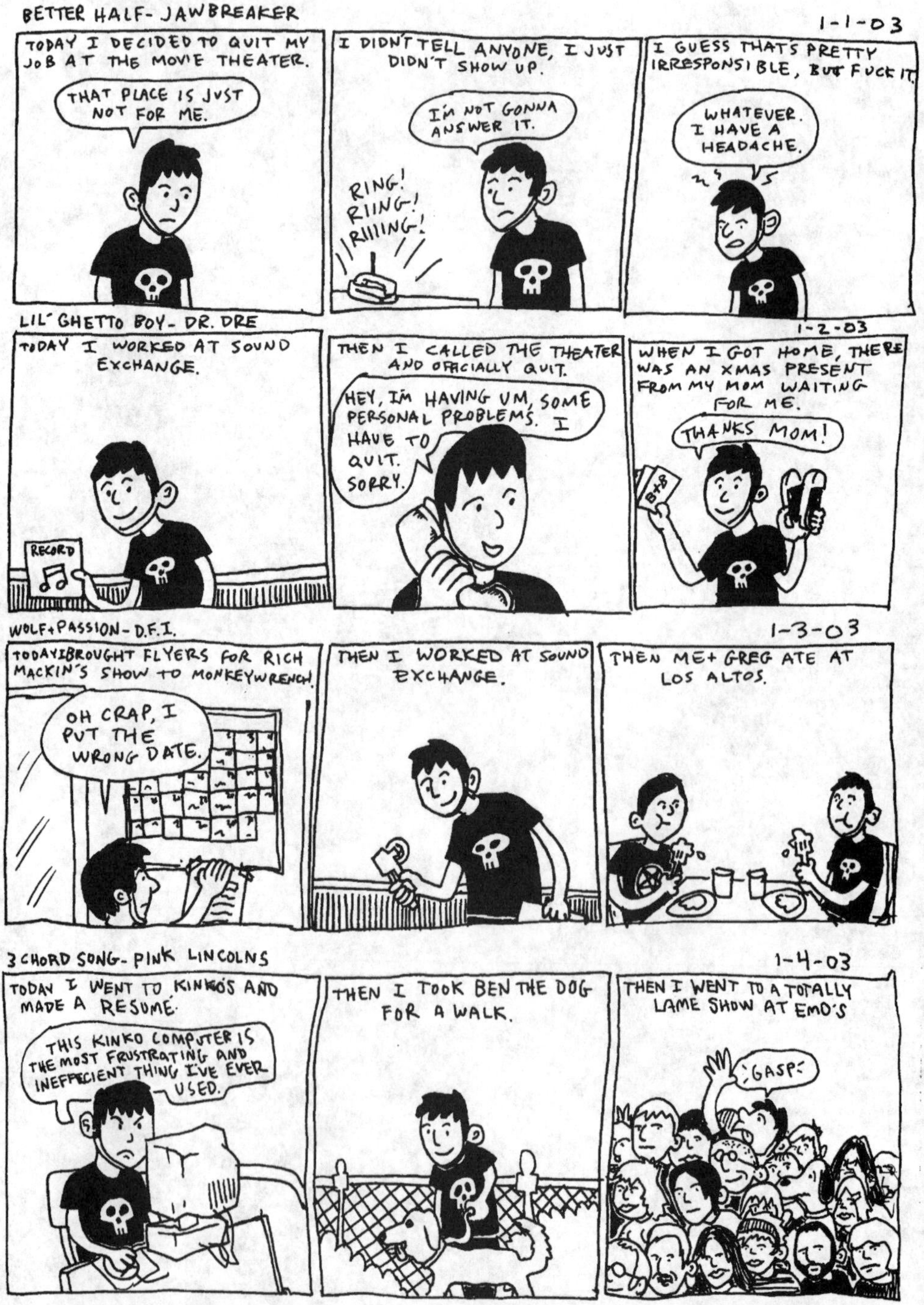
BETTER HALF- JAWBREAKER
1-1-03
TODAY I DECIDED TO QUIT MY JOB AT THE MOVIE THEATER.
THAT PLACE IS JUST NOT FOR ME.
I DIDN'T TELL ANYONE, I JUST DIDN'T SHOW UP.
I'M NOT GONNA ANSWER IT.
RING! RIING! RIIIING!
I GUESS THAT'S PRETTY IRRESPONSIBLE, BUT FUCK IT.
WHATEVER. I HAVE A HEADACHE.
LIL' GHETTO BOY- DR. DRE
1-2-03
TODAY I WORKED AT SOUND EXCHANGE.
RECORD
THEN I CALLED THE THEATER AND OFFICIALLY QUIT.
HEY, I'M HAVING UM, SOME PERSONAL PROBLEMS. I HAVE TO QUIT. SORRY.
WHEN I GOT HOME, THERE WAS AN XMAS PRESENT FROM MY MOM WAITING FOR ME.
THANKS MOM!
B+B
WOLF+PASSION- D.F.I.
1-3-03
TODAY I BROUGHT FLYERS FOR RICH MACKIN'S SHOW TO MONKEYWRENCH.
OH CRAP, I PUT THE WRONG DATE.
THEN I WORKED AT SOUND EXCHANGE.
THEN ME + GREG ATE AT LOS ALTOS.
3 CHORD SONG- PINK LINCOLNS
1-4-03
TODAY I WENT TO KINKO'S AND MADE A RESUME.
THIS KINKO COMPUTER IS THE MOST FRUSTRATING AND INEFFECIENT THING I'VE EVER USED.
THEN I TOOK BEN THE DOG FOR A WALK.
THEN I WENT TO A TOTALLY LAME SHOW AT EMO'S
GASP

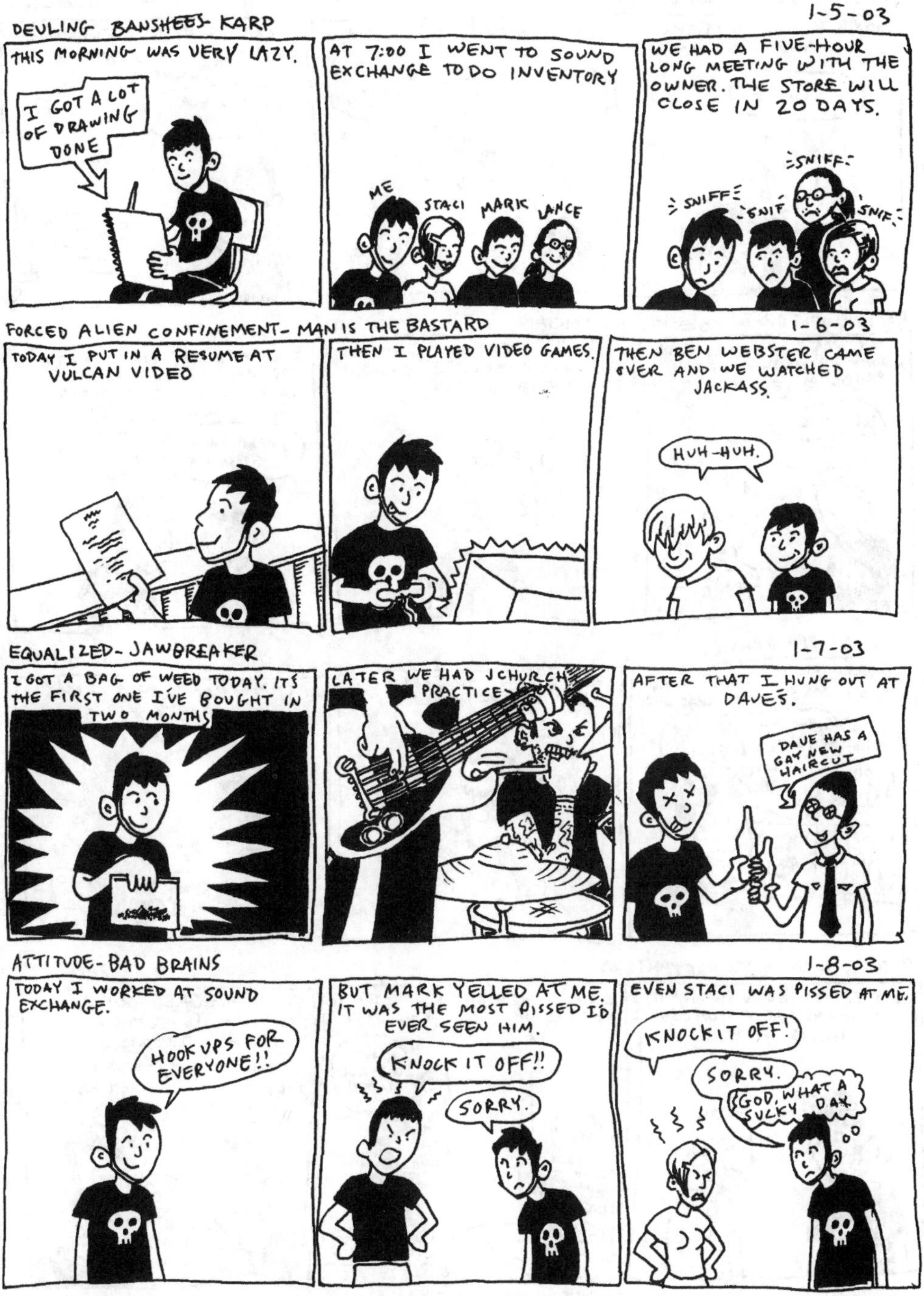
DEULING BANSHEES- KARP
1-5-03
THIS MORNING WAS VERY LAZY.
I GOT A LOT OF DRAWING DONE
AT 7:00 I WENT TO SOUND EXCHANGE TO DO INVENTORY
ME
STACI
MARK
LANCE
WE HAD A FIVE-HOUR LONG MEETING WITH THE OWNER. THE STORE WILL CLOSE IN 20 DAYS.
SNIFF
SNIFF
SNIF
SNIF
FORCED ALIEN CONFINEMENT- MAN IS THE BASTARD
1-6-03
TODAY I PUT IN A RESUME AT VULCAN VIDEO
THEN I PLAYED VIDEO GAMES.
THEN BEN WEBSTER CAME OVER AND WE WATCHED JACKASS.
HUH-HUH.
EQUALIZED- JAWBREAKER
1-7-03
I GOT A BAG OF WEED TODAY. IT'S THE FIRST ONE I'VE BOUGHT IN TWO MONTHS
LATER WE HAD J CHURCH PRACTICE
AFTER THAT I HUNG OUT AT DAVE'S.
DAVE HAS A GAY NEW HAIRCUT
ATTITUDE- BAD BRAINS
1-8-03
TODAY I WORKED AT SOUND EXCHANGE.
HOOK UPS FOR EVERYONE!!
BUT MARK YELLED AT ME. IT WAS THE MOST PISSED I'D EVER SEEN HIM.
KNOCK IT OFF!!
SORRY.
EVEN STACI WAS PISSED AT ME.
KNOCK IT OFF!
SORRY.
GOD, WHAT A SUCKY DAY

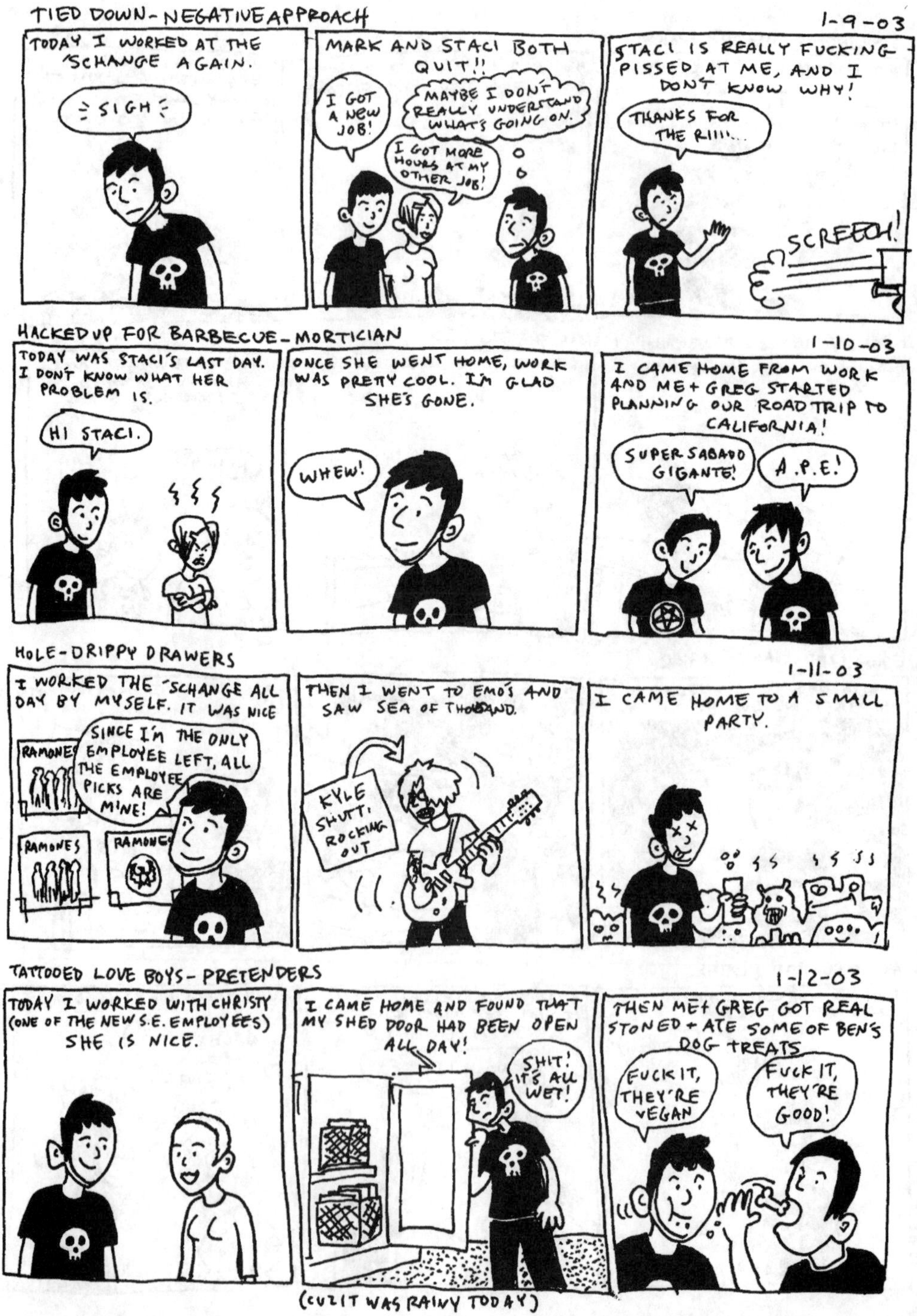
TIED DOWN - NEGATIVE APPROACH
1-9-03
TODAY I WORKED AT THE 'SCHANGE AGAIN.
SIGH
MARK AND STACI BOTH QUIT!!
I GOT A NEW JOB!
MAYBE I DON'T REALLY UNDERSTAND WHAT'S GOING ON.
I GOT MORE HOURS AT MY OTHER JOB!
STACI IS REALLY FUCKING PISSED AT ME, AND I DON'T KNOW WHY!
THANKS FOR THE RIIII...
SCREECH!
HACKED UP FOR BARBECUE - MORTICIAN
1-10-03
TODAY WAS STACI'S LAST DAY. I DON'T KNOW WHAT HER PROBLEM IS.
HI STACI.
ONCE SHE WENT HOME, WORK WAS PRETTY COOL. I'M GLAD SHE'S GONE.
WHEW!
I CAME HOME FROM WORK AND ME + GREG STARTED PLANNING OUR ROAD TRIP TO CALIFORNIA!
SUPER SABADO GIGANTE!
A.P.E.!
HOLE - DRIPPY DRAWERS
1-11-03
I WORKED THE 'SCHANGE ALL DAY BY MYSELF. IT WAS NICE
SINCE I'M THE ONLY EMPLOYEE LEFT, ALL THE EMPLOYEE PICKS ARE MINE!
RAMONES
RAMONES
RAMONES
THEN I WENT TO EMO'S AND SAW SEA OF THOUSAND.
KYLE SHUTT: ROCKING OUT
I CAME HOME TO A SMALL PARTY.
TATTOOED LOVE BOYS - PRETENDERS
1-12-03
TODAY I WORKED WITH CHRISTY (ONE OF THE NEW S.E. EMPLOYEES) SHE IS NICE.
I CAME HOME AND FOUND THAT MY SHED DOOR HAD BEEN OPEN ALL DAY!
SHIT! IT'S ALL WET!
(CUZ IT WAS RAINY TODAY)
THEN ME + GREG GOT REAL STONED + ATE SOME OF BEN'S DOG TREATS
FUCK IT, THEY'RE VEGAN
FUCK IT, THEY'RE GOOD!

CHEETAH - RFTC 1-13-03

I STARTED WORKING AT SOUND EXCHANGE TODAY, BUT THE OWNER TOLD ME TO GO HOME.

BUT THESE GIRLS BARELY KNOW HOW TO RUN THE STORE!

OH WELL.

SO I WENT TO KINKO'S INSTEAD.

THEN WE HAD J CHURCH PRACTICE

MYKEL+CARLI - WEEZER 1-14-03

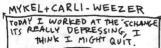

TODAY I WORKED AT THE 'SCHANGE. ITS REALLY DEPRESSING, I THINK I MIGHT QUIT.

=) SIGH. (=

LATER ED CAME OVER AND WE LISTENED TO BURNING WITCH

ITS... SO... ...SLOOOOW...

SARAH IS HAVING A BIRTHDAY PARTY TONIGHT, BUT I DON'T FEEL LIKE GOING.

I HAVE SUCH BAD FUCKING LUCK WITH GIRLS NAMED SARAH.

GLUG GLUG

VAMPIRE OF DUSSELDORF - MACABRE 1-15-03

TODAY I QUIT SOUND EXCHANGE.

IT'S JUST TOO SAD.

ALMOST AS IF ON CUE, WHEN I GOT HOME THERE WAS A MESSAGE FROM I ♡ VIDEO.

WORD!

COME IN FOR AN INTERVIEW TOMORROW

LATER GREG AND I TOOK SOME DRUGS THAT MADE ME CRAP IN MY PANTS.

I DIDN'T KNOW XANAX COULD DO THAT.

SPLORTCH

TURBO LOVER - JUDAS PRIEST 1-16-03

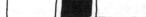

I WAS IN TWO DIFFERENT NEWSPAPERS TODAY!

UM. WOW. THIS ONE IS A LAME, ILL-INFORMED ARTICLE ABOUT "AUSTIN PEACE PUNKS"

AND THIS IS JUST A TINY MENTION IN AN ARTICLE ABOUT TIM DOYLE. WHAT A BITTERSWEET VICTORY.

STATESMAN

CHRONICLE

THEN I WENT TO A JOB INTERVIEW AT I ♡ VIDEO. ✱

I HOPE THIS IS GOING WELL, I CAN'T REALLY TELL.

THEN I WENT TO BED REALLY EARLY.

ITS SUPPOSED TO HIT FREEZING TONIGHT, BUT I DON'T CARE!

✱ I DIDN'T WEAR MY LUCKY JOB INTERVIEW SHIRT BECAUSE IT DOESN'T GO WITH MY BROWN PANTS. MY GREEN PANTS HAVE SHIT IN THEM.

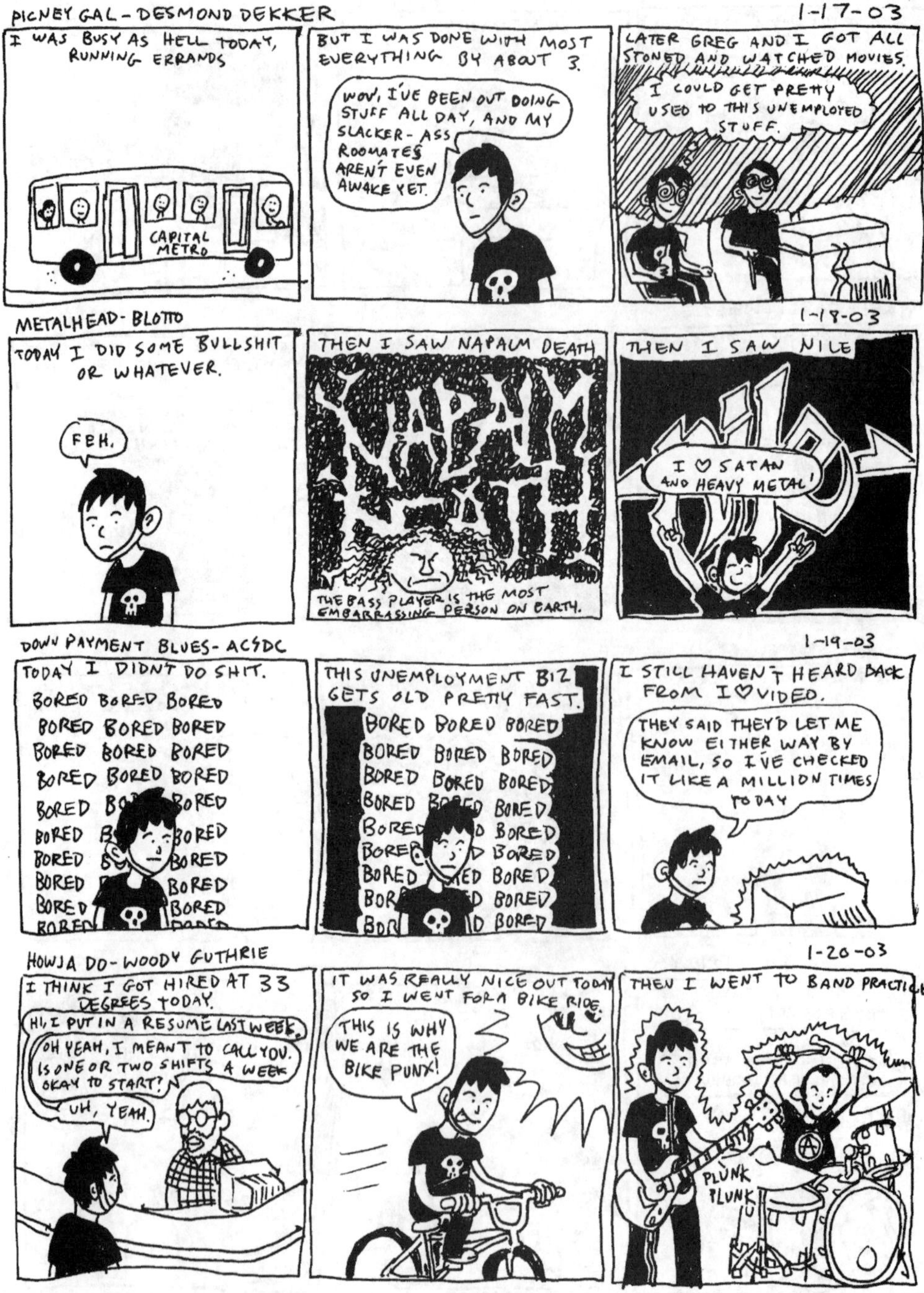
PICNEY GAL - DESMOND DEKKER
1-17-03
I WAS BUSY AS HELL TODAY, RUNNING ERRANDS
CAPITAL METRO
BUT I WAS DONE WITH MOST EVERYTHING BY ABOUT 3.
WOW, I'VE BEEN OUT DOING STUFF ALL DAY, AND MY SLACKER-ASS ROOMATES AREN'T EVEN AWAKE YET.
LATER GREG AND I GOT ALL STONED AND WATCHED MOVIES.
I COULD GET PRETTY USED TO THIS UNEMPLOYED STUFF.
METALHEAD - BLOTTO
1-18-03
TODAY I DID SOME BULLSHIT OR WHATEVER.
FEH.
THEN I SAW NAPALM DEATH
THE BASS PLAYER IS THE MOST EMBARRASSING PERSON ON EARTH.
THEN I SAW NILE
I ♡ SATAN AND HEAVY METAL!
DOWN PAYMENT BLUES - AC/DC
1-19-03
TODAY I DIDN'T DO SHIT.
BORED BORED
THIS UNEMPLOYMENT BIZ GETS OLD PRETTY FAST.
BORED BORED BORED BORED BORED BORED BORED BORED BORED BORED BORED BORED BORED BORED BORED BORED BORED BORED BORED BORED
I STILL HAVEN'T HEARD BACK FROM I♡VIDEO.
THEY SAID THEY'D LET ME KNOW EITHER WAY BY EMAIL, SO I'VE CHECKED IT LIKE A MILLION TIMES TODAY
HOWJA DO - WOODY GUTHRIE
1-20-03
I THINK I GOT HIRED AT 33 DEGREES TODAY.
HI, I PUT IN A RESUMÉ LAST WEEK.
OH YEAH, I MEANT TO CALL YOU. IS ONE OR TWO SHIFTS A WEEK OKAY TO START?
UH, YEAH.
IT WAS REALLY NICE OUT TODAY SO I WENT FOR A BIKE RIDE.
THIS IS WHY WE ARE THE BIKE PUNX!
THEN I WENT TO BAND PRACTICE.
PLUNK PLUNK

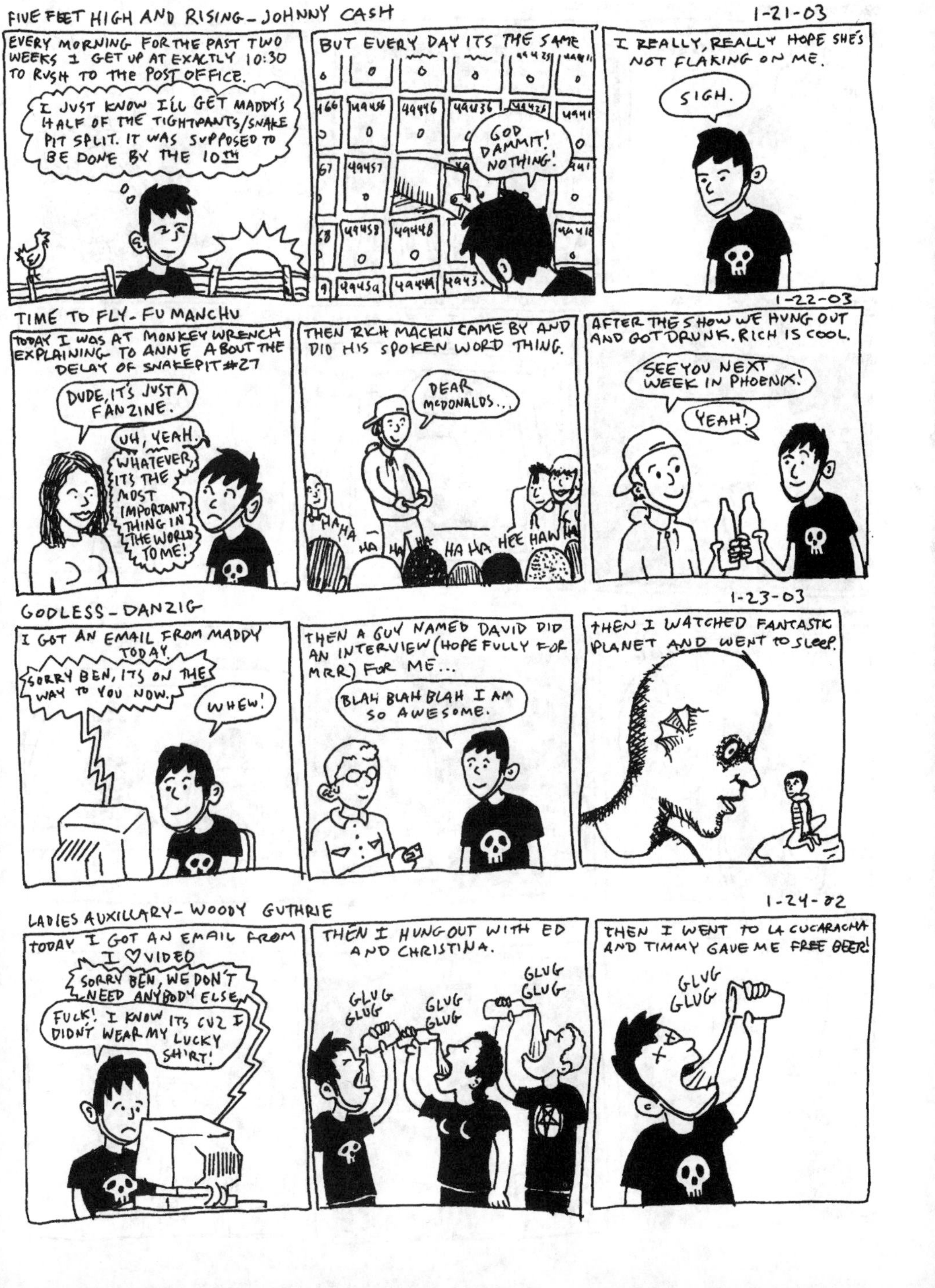
FIVE FEET HIGH AND RISING - JOHNNY CASH
1-21-03
EVERY MORNING FOR THE PAST TWO WEEKS I GET UP AT EXACTLY 10:30 TO RUSH TO THE POST OFFICE.
I JUST KNOW I'LL GET MADDY'S HALF OF THE TIGHTPANTS/SNAKE PIT SPLIT. IT WAS SUPPOSED TO BE DONE BY THE 10TH
BUT EVERY DAY ITS THE SAME
GOD DAMMIT! NOTHING!
I REALLY, REALLY HOPE SHE'S NOT FLAKING ON ME.
SIGH.
TIME TO FLY - FU MANCHU
1-22-03
TODAY I WAS AT MONKEY WRENCH EXPLAINING TO ANNE ABOUT THE DELAY OF SNAKEPIT #27
DUDE, IT'S JUST A FANZINE.
UH, YEAH.
WHATEVER, ITS THE MOST IMPORTANT THING IN THE WORLD TO ME!
THEN RICH MACKIN CAME BY AND DID HIS SPOKEN WORD THING.
DEAR McDONALDS...
HA HA
HA HA HA
HA HA HEE HAW
AFTER THE SHOW WE HUNG OUT AND GOT DRUNK. RICH IS COOL.
SEE YOU NEXT WEEK IN PHOENIX!
YEAH!
GODLESS - DANZIG
1-23-03
I GOT AN EMAIL FROM MADDY TODAY.
SORRY BEN, ITS ON THE WAY TO YOU NOW.
WHEW!
THEN A GUY NAMED DAVID DID AN INTERVIEW (HOPEFULLY FOR MRR) FOR ME...
BLAH BLAH BLAH I AM SO AWESOME.
THEN I WATCHED FANTASTIC PLANET AND WENT TO SLEEP.
LADIES AUXILLARY - WOODY GUTHRIE
1-24-02
TODAY I GOT AN EMAIL FROM I ♡ VIDEO
SORRY BEN, WE DON'T NEED ANYBODY ELSE.
FUCK! I KNOW ITS CUZ I DIDN'T WEAR MY LUCKY SHIRT!
THEN I HUNG OUT WITH ED AND CHRISTINA.
GLUG GLUG
GLUG GLUG
GLUG GLUG
THEN I WENT TO LA CUCARACHA AND TIMMY GAVE ME FREE BEER!
GLUG GLUG

DR. DOOM IS IN THE ROOM- KOOL KEITH   1-25-03

YAY! I FINALLY GOT MADDY'S HALF OF THE TIGHTPANTS SPLIT!
FUCK YEAH! THIS IS GONNA LOOK AWESOME!

LATER I SAW STORM THE TOWER AND SBITCH
I LOVE SHOWS AT THE SACRED CUP. THEY GIVE ME SUCH A WARM COMFORTING FEELING OF COMMUNITY. AUSTIN HAS AN AWESOME PUNK SCENE.

THEN I WENT TO A BIG PARTY.
DRUNK AGAIN!

RAT SALAD- BLACK SABBATH   HAPPY BIRTHDAY LEI LEEN!   1-26-03

TODAY I BORROWED RUN RONNIE RUN FROM DAVE SO I COULD DUB IT.

I WATCHED IT 3 TIMES IN A ROW.
AAAAAH!

THEN I WENT TO LEI LEEN'S BIRTHDAY PARTY

ASS KICKIN' FAT KID- PUSCIFER   1-27-03

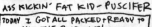
TODAY I GOT ALL PACKED + READY TO HIT THE ROAD WITH GREG.

LET'S HIT THE FUCKIN' ROAD!

WE HIT THE ROAD AT 11:00 PM
VROOOM!
LEAVING AUSTIN

AND MADE IT TO EL PASO BY SUN-UP!

RUDE BOY TRAIN- DESMOND DEKKER   LIZ + MARK ARE AWESOME!!   1-28-03

NO SLEEP TIL PHOENIX!!!
POOR MAN'S ACID (NO SLEEP)

WE STAYED WITH MY FRIEND LIZ. SHE IS COOL.
LIZ   DEFIANCE!

ALSO STAYING THERE WERE SHAWN GRANTON, RICH MACKIN AND LIZ'S BOYFRIEND MARK.
SHAWN   RICH   MARK

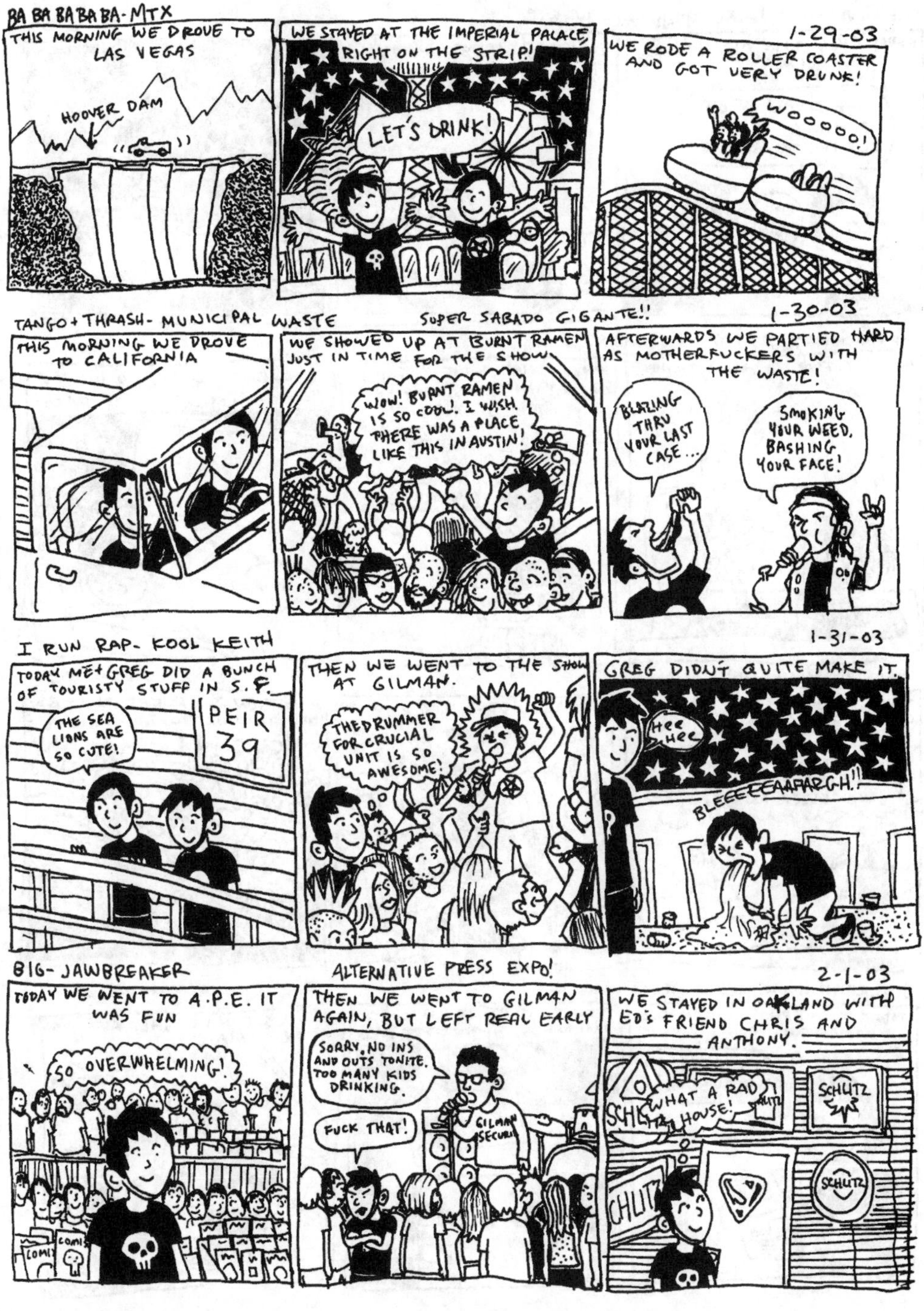
BA BA BA BA BA - MTX
1-29-03
THIS MORNING WE DROVE TO LAS VEGAS
HOOVER DAM
WE STAYED AT THE IMPERIAL PALACE, RIGHT ON THE STRIP!
LET'S DRINK!
WE RODE A ROLLER COASTER AND GOT VERY DRUNK!
WOOOOO!
TANGO + THRASH - MUNICIPAL WASTE
SUPER SABADO GIGANTE!!
1-30-03
THIS MORNING WE DROVE TO CALIFORNIA
WE SHOWED UP AT BURNT RAMEN JUST IN TIME FOR THE SHOW
WOW! BURNT RAMEN IS SO COOL! I WISH THERE WAS A PLACE LIKE THIS IN AUSTIN!
AFTERWARDS WE PARTIED HARD AS MOTHERFUCKERS WITH THE WASTE!
BLAZING THRU YOUR LAST CASE...
SMOKING YOUR WEED, BASHING YOUR FACE!
I RUN RAP - KOOL KEITH
1-31-03
TODAY ME + GREG DID A BUNCH OF TOURISTY STUFF IN S.F.
THE SEA LIONS ARE SO CUTE!
PEIR 39
THEN WE WENT TO THE SHOW AT GILMAN.
THE DRUMMER FOR CRUCIAL UNIT IS SO AWESOME!
GREG DIDN'T QUITE MAKE IT.
HEE HEE
BLEEEEEAARGH!!
BIG - JAWBREAKER
ALTERNATIVE PRESS EXPO!
2-1-03
TODAY WE WENT TO A.P.E. IT WAS FUN
SO OVERWHELMING!
COMIX
COMIX
THEN WE WENT TO GILMAN AGAIN, BUT LEFT REAL EARLY
SORRY, NO INS AND OUTS TONITE. TOO MANY KIDS DRINKING.
FUCK THAT!
GILMAN SECURI
WE STAYED IN OAKLAND WITH ED'S FRIEND CHRIS AND ANTHONY.
WHAT A RAD HOUSE!
SCHLITZ
SCHLITZ

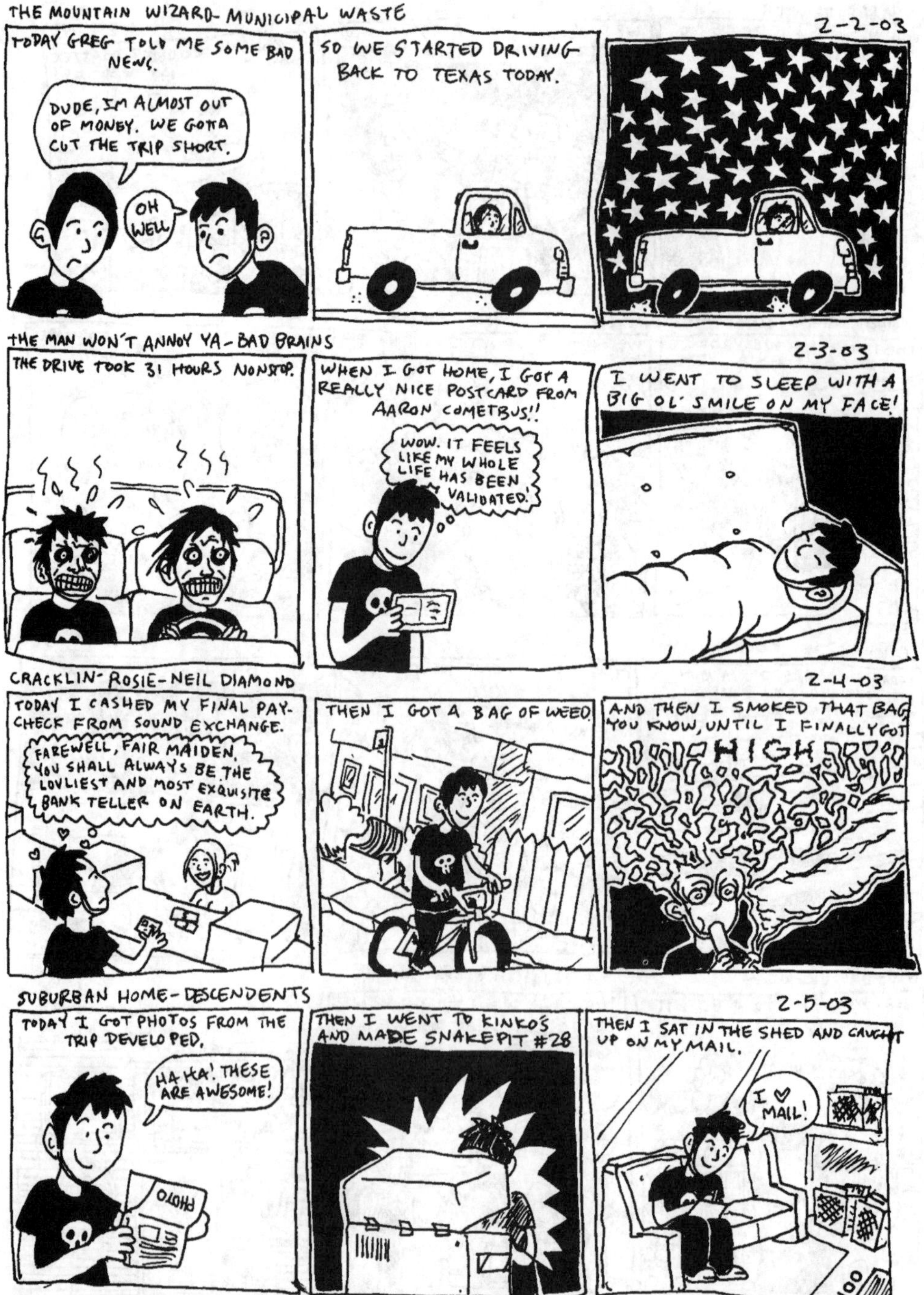
THE MOUNTAIN WIZARD - MUNICIPAL WASTE
2-2-03
TODAY GREG TOLD ME SOME BAD NEWS.
DUDE, I'M ALMOST OUT OF MONEY. WE GOTTA CUT THE TRIP SHORT.
OH WELL
SO WE STARTED DRIVING BACK TO TEXAS TODAY.
THE MAN WON'T ANNOY YA - BAD BRAINS
2-3-03
THE DRIVE TOOK 31 HOURS NONSTOP.
WHEN I GOT HOME, I GOT A REALLY NICE POSTCARD FROM AARON COMETBUS!!
WOW. IT FEELS LIKE MY WHOLE LIFE HAS BEEN VALIDATED!
I WENT TO SLEEP WITH A BIG OL' SMILE ON MY FACE!
CRACKLIN' ROSIE - NEIL DIAMOND
2-4-03
TODAY I CASHED MY FINAL PAYCHECK FROM SOUND EXCHANGE.
FAREWELL, FAIR MAIDEN. YOU SHALL ALWAYS BE THE LOVLIEST AND MOST EXQUISITE BANK TELLER ON EARTH.
THEN I GOT A BAG OF WEED.
AND THEN I SMOKED THAT BAG YOU KNOW, UNTIL I FINALLY GOT
HIGH
SUBURBAN HOME - DESCENDENTS
2-5-03
TODAY I GOT PHOTOS FROM THE TRIP DEVELOPED.
HA HA! THESE ARE AWESOME!
PHOTO
THEN I WENT TO KINKO'S AND MADE SNAKEPIT #28
THEN I SAT IN THE SHED AND CAUGHT UP ON MY MAIL.
I ♥ MAIL!
400

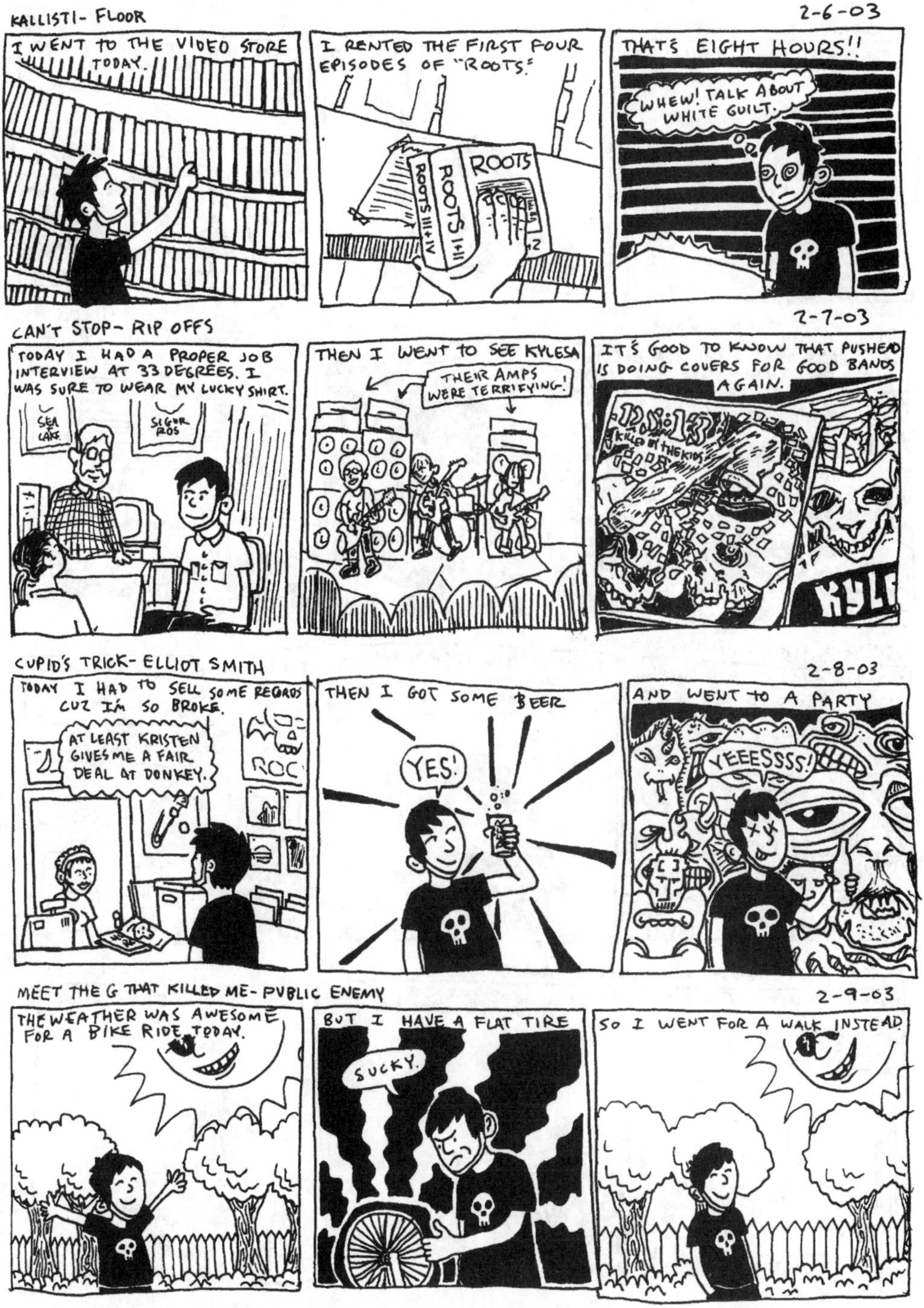
KALLISTI- FLOOR
2-6-03
I WENT TO THE VIDEO STORE TODAY.
I RENTED THE FIRST FOUR EPISODES OF "ROOTS."
ROOTS
ROOTS I+II
ROOTS III+IV
THAT'S EIGHT HOURS!!
WHEW! TALK ABOUT WHITE GUILT.
CAN'T STOP- RIP OFFS
2-7-03
TODAY I HAD A PROPER JOB INTERVIEW AT 33 DEGREES. I WAS SURE TO WEAR MY LUCKY SHIRT.
SIGUR ROS
THEN I WENT TO SEE KYLESA
THEIR AMPS WERE TERRIFYING!
IT'S GOOD TO KNOW THAT PUSHEAD IS DOING COVERS FOR GOOD BANDS AGAIN.
CUPID'S TRICK- ELLIOT SMITH
2-8-03
TODAY I HAD TO SELL SOME RECORDS CUZ I'M SO BROKE.
AT LEAST KRISTEN GIVES ME A FAIR DEAL AT DONKEY.
THEN I GOT SOME BEER
YES!
AND WENT TO A PARTY
YEEESSSS!
MEET THE G THAT KILLED ME- PUBLIC ENEMY
2-9-03
THE WEATHER WAS AWESOME FOR A BIKE RIDE TODAY.
BUT I HAVE A FLAT TIRE
SUCKY.
SO I WENT FOR A WALK INSTEAD

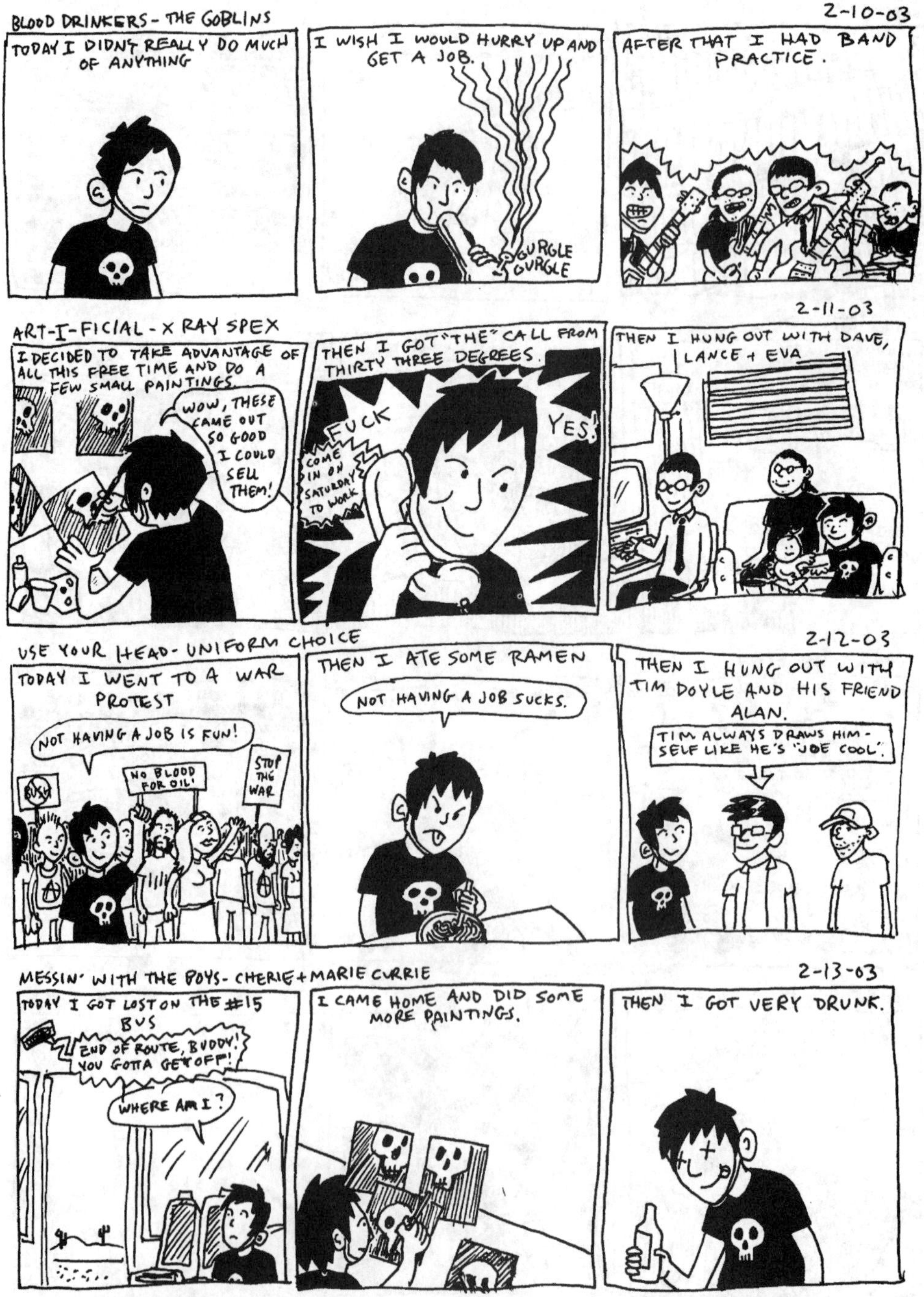
BLOOD DRINKERS - THE GOBLINS
2-10-03
TODAY I DIDN'T REALLY DO MUCH OF ANYTHING
I WISH I WOULD HURRY UP AND GET A JOB.
GURGLE GURGLE
AFTER THAT I HAD BAND PRACTICE.
ART-I-FICIAL - X RAY SPEX
2-11-03
I DECIDED TO TAKE ADVANTAGE OF ALL THIS FREE TIME AND DO A FEW SMALL PAINTINGS.
WOW, THESE CAME OUT SO GOOD I COULD SELL THEM!
THEN I GOT "THE" CALL FROM THIRTY THREE DEGREES.
FUCK
COME IN ON SATURDAY TO WORK
YES!
THEN I HUNG OUT WITH DAVE, LANCE + EVA
USE YOUR HEAD - UNIFORM CHOICE
2-12-03
TODAY I WENT TO A WAR PROTEST
NOT HAVING A JOB IS FUN!
BUSH
NO BLOOD FOR OIL!
STOP THE WAR
THEN I ATE SOME RAMEN
NOT HAVING A JOB SUCKS.
THEN I HUNG OUT WITH TIM DOYLE AND HIS FRIEND ALAN.
TIM ALWAYS DRAWS HIMSELF LIKE HE'S "JOE COOL".
MESSIN' WITH THE BOYS - CHERIE + MARIE CURRIE
2-13-03
TODAY I GOT LOST ON THE #15 BUS
END OF ROUTE, BUDDY! YOU GOTTA GET OFF!
WHERE AM I?
I CAME HOME AND DID SOME MORE PAINTINGS.
THEN I GOT VERY DRUNK.

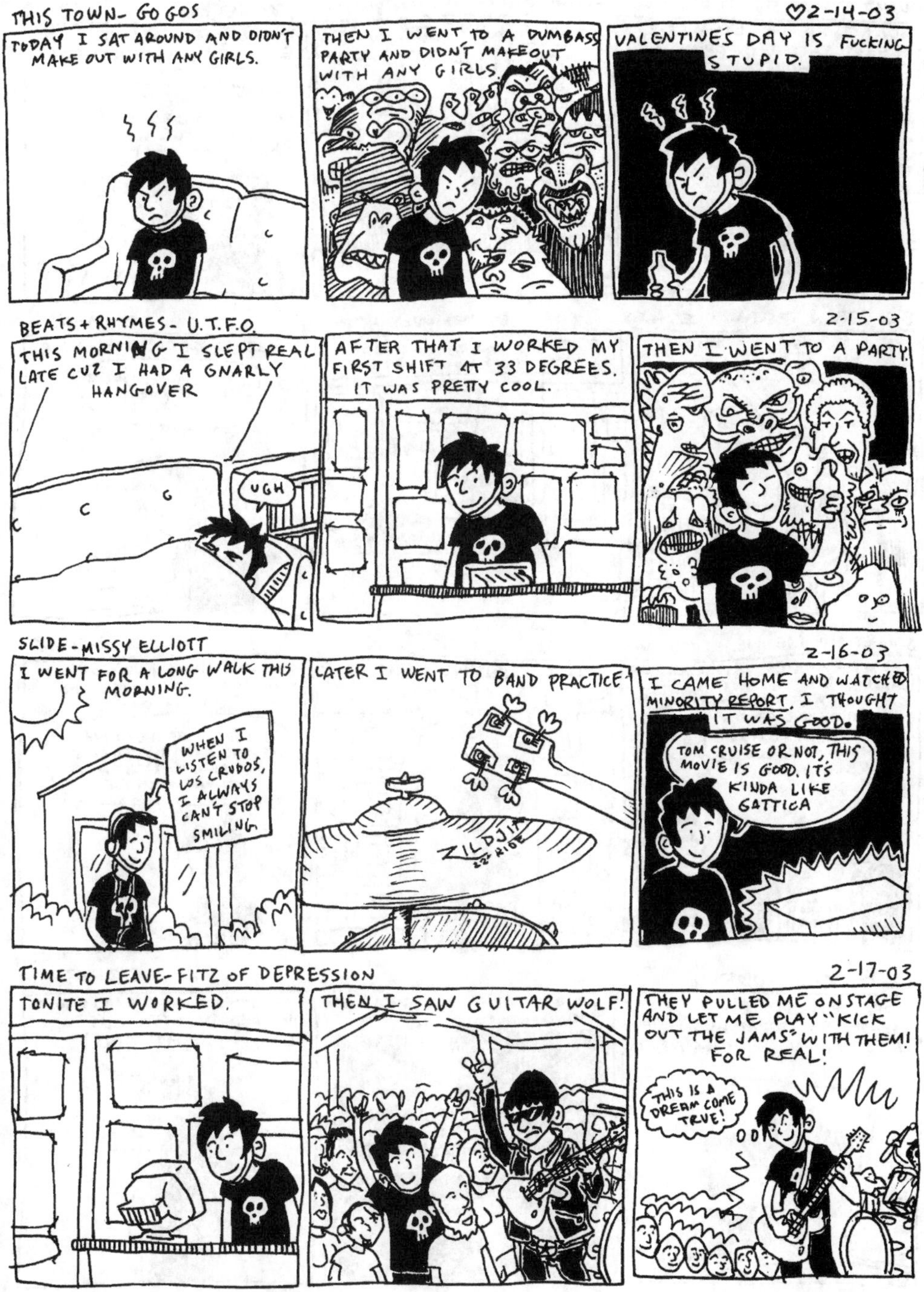
THIS TOWN- GO GOS
♡2-14-03
TODAY I SAT AROUND AND DIDN'T MAKE OUT WITH ANY GIRLS.
THEN I WENT TO A DUMBASS PARTY AND DIDN'T MAKEOUT WITH ANY GIRLS.
VALENTINE'S DAY IS FUCKING STUPID.
BEATS + RHYMES - U.T.F.O.
2-15-03
THIS MORNING I SLEPT REAL LATE CUZ I HAD A GNARLY HANGOVER
UGH
AFTER THAT I WORKED MY FIRST SHIFT AT 33 DEGREES. IT WAS PRETTY COOL.
THEN I WENT TO A PARTY.
SLIDE-MISSY ELLIOTT
2-16-03
I WENT FOR A LONG WALK THIS MORNING.
WHEN I LISTEN TO LOS CRUDOS, I ALWAYS CAN'T STOP SMILING.
LATER I WENT TO BAND PRACTICE
ZILDJIAN 22" RIDE
I CAME HOME AND WATCHED MINORITY REPORT. I THOUGHT IT WAS GOOD.
TOM CRUISE OR NOT, THIS MOVIE IS GOOD. IT'S KINDA LIKE GATTICA
TIME TO LEAVE- FITZ OF DEPRESSION
2-17-03
TONITE I WORKED.
THEN I SAW GUITAR WOLF!
THEY PULLED ME ONSTAGE AND LET ME PLAY "KICK OUT THE JAMS" WITH THEM! FOR REAL!
THIS IS A DREAM COME TRUE!

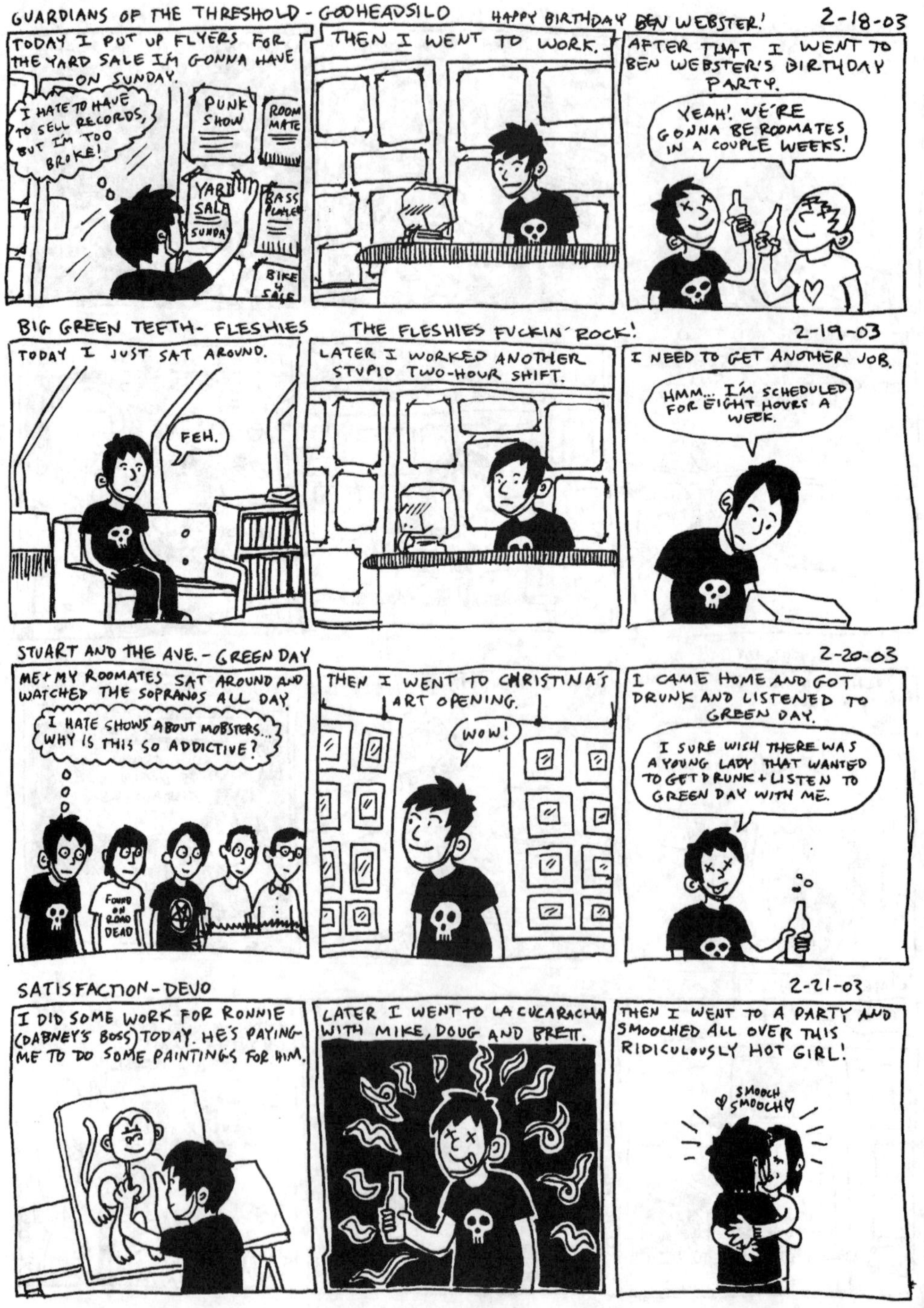
GUARDIANS OF THE THRESHOLD - GODHEADSILO
HAPPY BIRTHDAY BEN WEBSTER!
2-18-03
TODAY I PUT UP FLYERS FOR THE YARD SALE I'M GONNA HAVE ON SUNDAY.
I HATE TO HAVE TO SELL RECORDS, BUT I'M TOO BROKE!
PUNK SHOW
ROOM MATE
YARD SALE SUNDAY
BASS PLAYER
BIKE 4 SALE
THEN I WENT TO WORK.
AFTER THAT I WENT TO BEN WEBSTER'S BIRTHDAY PARTY.
YEAH! WE'RE GONNA BE ROOMATES IN A COUPLE WEEKS!
BIG GREEN TEETH - FLESHIES
THE FLESHIES FUCKIN' ROCK!
2-19-03
TODAY I JUST SAT AROUND.
FEH.
LATER I WORKED ANOTHER STUPID TWO-HOUR SHIFT.
I NEED TO GET ANOTHER JOB.
HMM... I'M SCHEDULED FOR EIGHT HOURS A WEEK.
STUART AND THE AVE. - GREEN DAY
2-20-03
ME + MY ROOMATES SAT AROUND AND WATCHED THE SOPRANOS ALL DAY.
I HATE SHOWS ABOUT MOBSTERS... WHY IS THIS SO ADDICTIVE?
FOUND ON ROAD DEAD
THEN I WENT TO CHRISTINA'S ART OPENING.
WOW!
I CAME HOME AND GOT DRUNK AND LISTENED TO GREEN DAY.
I SURE WISH THERE WAS A YOUNG LADY THAT WANTED TO GET DRUNK + LISTEN TO GREEN DAY WITH ME.
SATISFACTION - DEVO
2-21-03
I DID SOME WORK FOR RONNIE (DABNEY'S BOSS) TODAY. HE'S PAYING ME TO DO SOME PAINTINGS FOR HIM.
LATER I WENT TO LA CUCARACHA WITH MIKE, DOUG AND BRETT.
THEN I WENT TO A PARTY AND SMOOCHED ALL OVER THIS RIDICULOUSLY HOT GIRL!
SMOOCH SMOOCH

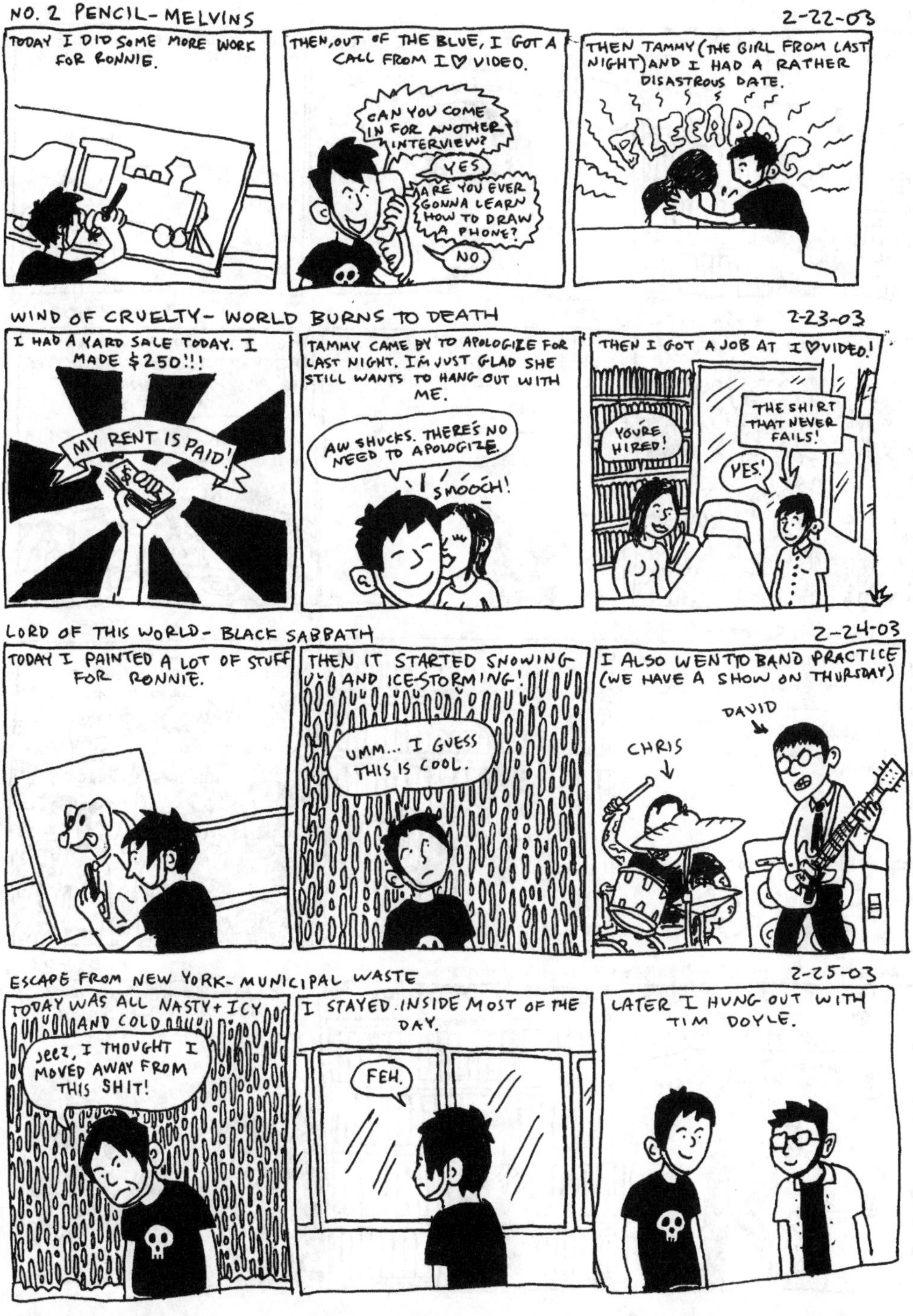
NO. 2 PENCIL- MELVINS
2-22-03
TODAY I DID SOME MORE WORK FOR RONNIE.
THEN, OUT OF THE BLUE, I GOT A CALL FROM I ♥ VIDEO.
CAN YOU COME IN FOR ANOTHER INTERVIEW?
YES.
ARE YOU EVER GONNA LEARN HOW TO DRAW A PHONE?
NO.
THEN TAMMY (THE GIRL FROM LAST NIGHT) AND I HAD A RATHER DISASTROUS DATE.
BLEEARGG
WIND OF CRUELTY- WORLD BURNS TO DEATH
2-23-03
I HAD A YARD SALE TODAY. I MADE $250!!!
MY RENT IS PAID!
TAMMY CAME BY TO APOLOGIZE FOR LAST NIGHT. I'M JUST GLAD SHE STILL WANTS TO HANG OUT WITH ME.
AW SHUCKS. THERE'S NO NEED TO APOLOGIZE.
SMOOCH!
THEN I GOT A JOB AT I ♥ VIDEO!
YOU'RE HIRED!
THE SHIRT THAT NEVER FAILS!
YES!
LORD OF THIS WORLD- BLACK SABBATH
2-24-03
TODAY I PAINTED A LOT OF STUFF FOR RONNIE.
THEN IT STARTED SNOWING AND ICE-STORMING!
UMM... I GUESS THIS IS COOL.
I ALSO WENT TO BAND PRACTICE (WE HAVE A SHOW ON THURSDAY)
DAVID
CHRIS
ESCAPE FROM NEW YORK- MUNICIPAL WASTE
2-25-03
TODAY WAS ALL NASTY + ICY AND COLD
JEEZ, I THOUGHT I MOVED AWAY FROM THIS SHIT!
I STAYED INSIDE MOST OF THE DAY.
FEH.
LATER I HUNG OUT WITH TIM DOYLE.

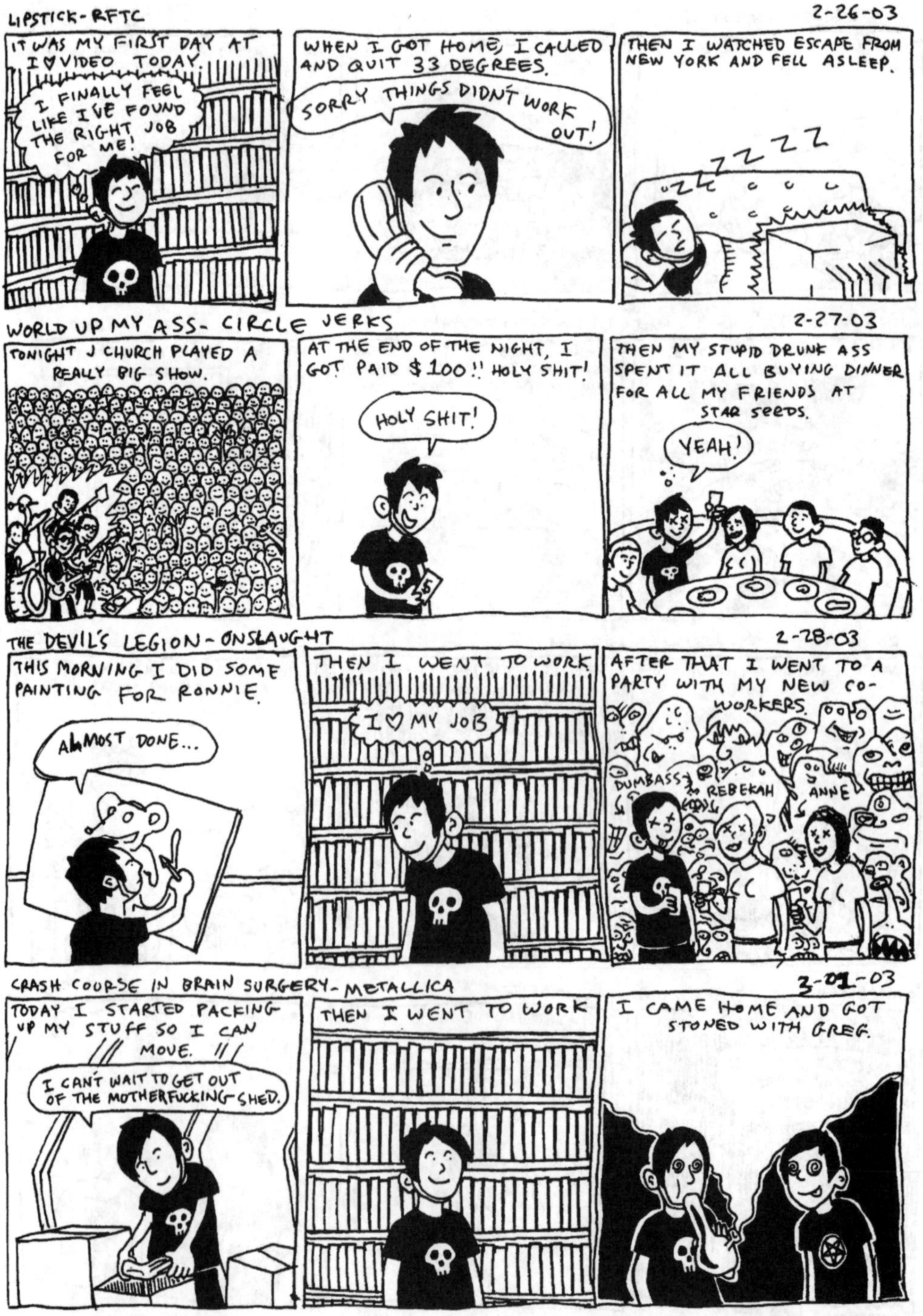
LIPSTICK - RFTC
2-26-03
IT WAS MY FIRST DAY AT I ♥ VIDEO TODAY.
I FINALLY FEEL LIKE I'VE FOUND THE RIGHT JOB FOR ME!
WHEN I GOT HOME, I CALLED AND QUIT 33 DEGREES.
SORRY THINGS DIDN'T WORK OUT!
THEN I WATCHED ESCAPE FROM NEW YORK AND FELL ASLEEP.
ZZZZZZ
WORLD UP MY ASS - CIRCLE JERKS
2-27-03
TONIGHT J CHURCH PLAYED A REALLY BIG SHOW.
AT THE END OF THE NIGHT, I GOT PAID $100!! HOLY SHIT!
HOLY SHIT!
THEN MY STUPID DRUNK ASS SPENT IT ALL BUYING DINNER FOR ALL MY FRIENDS AT STAR SEEDS.
YEAH!
THE DEVIL'S LEGION - ONSLAUGHT
2-28-03
THIS MORNING I DID SOME PAINTING FOR RONNIE.
ALMOST DONE...
THEN I WENT TO WORK
I ♥ MY JOB
AFTER THAT I WENT TO A PARTY WITH MY NEW CO-WORKERS.
DUMBASS
REBEKAH
ANNE
CRASH COURSE IN BRAIN SURGERY - METALLICA
3-01-03
TODAY I STARTED PACKING UP MY STUFF SO I CAN MOVE.
I CAN'T WAIT TO GET OUT OF THE MOTHERFUCKING SHED.
THEN I WENT TO WORK
I CAME HOME AND GOT STONED WITH GREG.

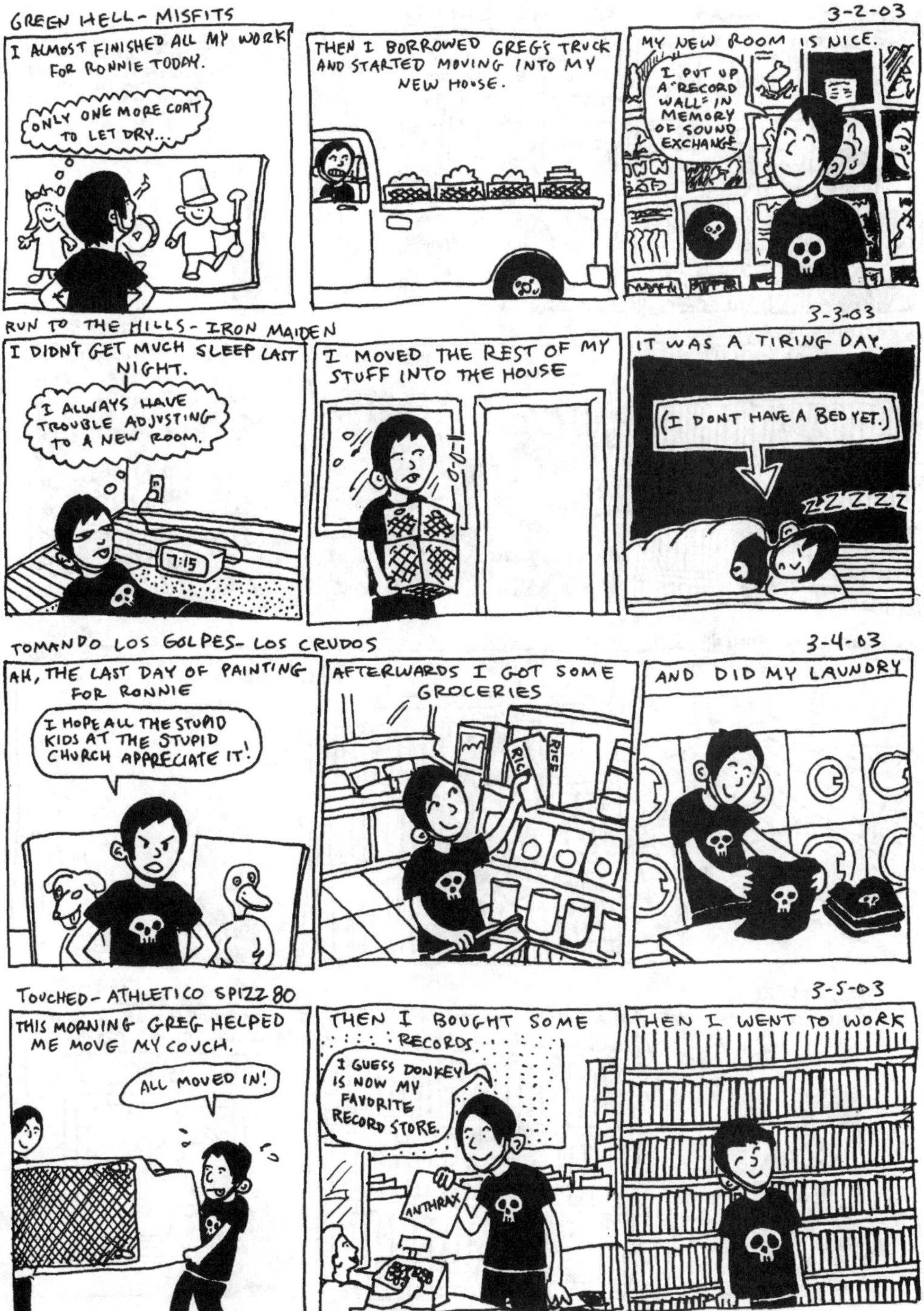
GREEN HELL - MISFITS
3-2-03
I ALMOST FINISHED ALL MY WORK FOR RONNIE TODAY.
ONLY ONE MORE COAT TO LET DRY...
THEN I BORROWED GREG'S TRUCK AND STARTED MOVING INTO MY NEW HOUSE.
MY NEW ROOM IS NICE.
I PUT UP A "RECORD WALL" IN MEMORY OF SOUND EXCHANGE.
RUN TO THE HILLS - IRON MAIDEN
3-3-03
I DIDN'T GET MUCH SLEEP LAST NIGHT.
I ALWAYS HAVE TROUBLE ADJUSTING TO A NEW ROOM.
7:15
I MOVED THE REST OF MY STUFF INTO THE HOUSE
IT WAS A TIRING DAY.
(I DONT HAVE A BED YET.)
ZZZZZ
TOMANDO LOS GOLPES - LOS CRUDOS
3-4-03
AH, THE LAST DAY OF PAINTING FOR RONNIE
I HOPE ALL THE STUPID KIDS AT THE STUPID CHURCH APPRECIATE IT!
AFTERWARDS I GOT SOME GROCERIES
RICE
AND DID MY LAUNDRY
TOUCHED - ATHLETICO SPIZZ 80
3-5-03
THIS MORNING GREG HELPED ME MOVE MY COUCH.
ALL MOVED IN!
THEN I BOUGHT SOME RECORDS.
I GUESS DONKEY IS NOW MY FAVORITE RECORD STORE.
ANTHRAX
THEN I WENT TO WORK

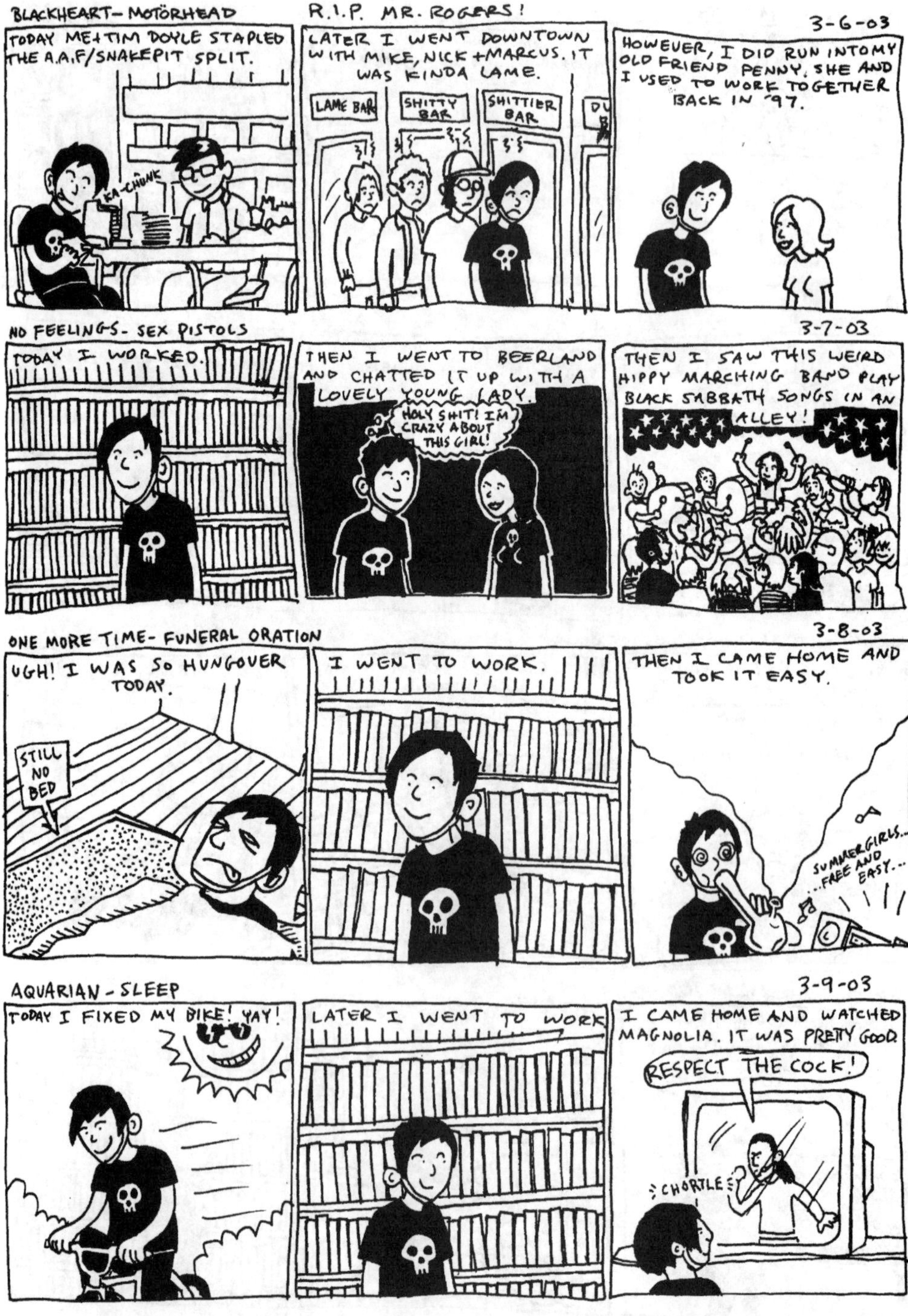
BLACKHEART – MOTÖRHEAD
R.I.P. MR. ROGERS!
3-6-03
TODAY ME + TIM DOYLE STAPLED THE A.A.F/SNAKEPIT SPLIT.
KA-CHUNK
LATER I WENT DOWNTOWN WITH MIKE, NICK + MARCUS. IT WAS KINDA LAME.
LAME BAR
SHITTY BAR
SHITTIER BAR
HOWEVER, I DID RUN INTO MY OLD FRIEND PENNY. SHE AND I USED TO WORK TOGETHER BACK IN '97.
NO FEELINGS – SEX PISTOLS
3-7-03
TODAY I WORKED.
THEN I WENT TO BEERLAND AND CHATTED IT UP WITH A LOVELY YOUNG LADY.
HOLY SHIT! I'M CRAZY ABOUT THIS GIRL!
THEN I SAW THIS WEIRD HIPPY MARCHING BAND PLAY BLACK SABBATH SONGS IN AN ALLEY!
ONE MORE TIME – FUNERAL ORATION
3-8-03
UGH! I WAS SO HUNGOVER TODAY.
STILL NO BED
I WENT TO WORK.
THEN I CAME HOME AND TOOK IT EASY.
SUMMER GIRLS... ...FREE AND EASY...
AQUARIAN – SLEEP
3-9-03
TODAY I FIXED MY BIKE! YAY!
LATER I WENT TO WORK
I CAME HOME AND WATCHED MAGNOLIA. IT WAS PRETTY GOOD
RESPECT THE COCK!
CHORTLE

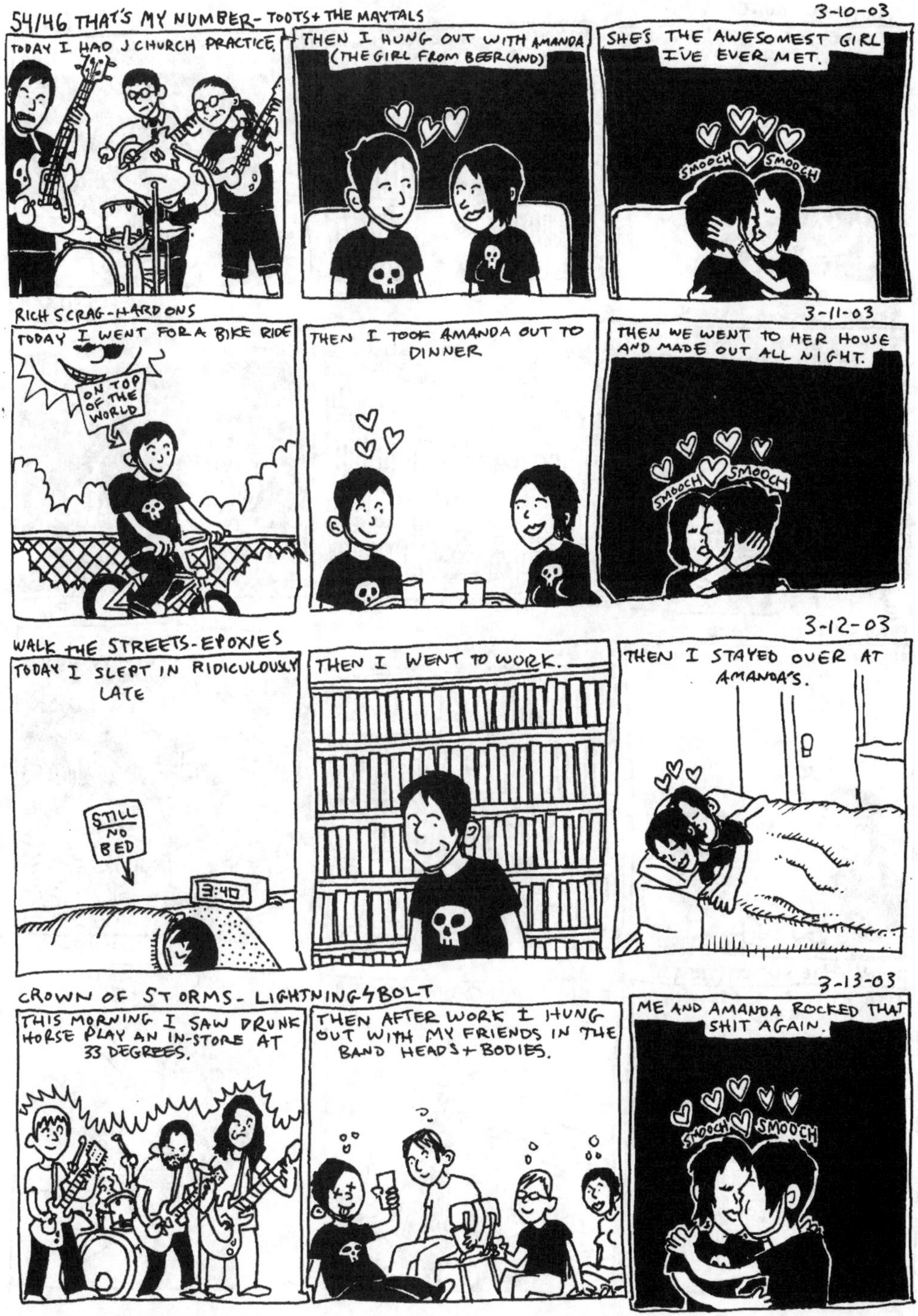
54/46 THAT'S MY NUMBER - TOOTS + THE MAYTALS
3-10-03
TODAY I HAD J CHURCH PRACTICE.
THEN I HUNG OUT WITH AMANDA (THE GIRL FROM BEERLAND)
SHE'S THE AWESOMEST GIRL I'VE EVER MET.
SMOOCH SMOOCH
RICH SCRAG - HARD ONS
3-11-03
TODAY I WENT FOR A BIKE RIDE
ON TOP OF THE WORLD
THEN I TOOK AMANDA OUT TO DINNER
THEN WE WENT TO HER HOUSE AND MADE OUT ALL NIGHT.
SMOOCH SMOOCH
WALK THE STREETS - EPOXIES
3-12-03
TODAY I SLEPT IN RIDICULOUSLY LATE
STILL NO BED
3:40
THEN I WENT TO WORK.
THEN I STAYED OVER AT AMANDA'S.
CROWN OF STORMS - LIGHTNING BOLT
3-13-03
THIS MORNING I SAW DRUNK HORSE PLAY AN IN-STORE AT 33 DEGREES.
THEN AFTER WORK I HUNG OUT WITH MY FRIENDS IN THE BAND HEADS + BODIES.
ME AND AMANDA ROCKED THAT SHIT AGAIN.
SMOOCH SMOOCH

MUSTAPHA - QUEEN

3-14-03

MY BIKE GOT ANOTHER FUCKING FLAT TIRE TODAY!

IF I WASNT THE HAPPIEST DUDE ON EARTH I'D PROBABLY BE PISSED ABOUT THIS.

AT WORK I WATCHED DAWN OF THE DEAD. ITS ONE OF MY FAVORITE MOVIES.

FUCK YEAH! HIS WHOLE HEAD BLEW UP!

ME AND AMANDA WATCHED A MOVIE OR SOMETHING.

3-15-03

DRUNKEN WISDOM - OVER KILL

I HAD TO WALK TO WORK. IT TOOK AN HOUR

WHO CARES. ITS A BEAUTIFUL DAY!

WORK WAS PRETTY CHILL

HEY EVERYONE, SORRY ALL THESE DRAWINGS OF ME AT WORK ARE KINDA LAME AND BORING. I HAVEN'T REALLY FIGURED OUT WHAT TO DO WITH IT. YET.

I CAME HOME AND HUNG OUT WITH AMANDA.

3-16-03

PUSSY WHIPPED - S.O.D.

THIS MORNING AMANDA AND I ATE AT ARANDAS.

THEN I WENT TO WORK

AFTER THAT I WENT TO A FUN PARTY.

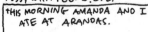

3-17-03

SPRINGTIME - LEATHERFACE

YAY! A DAY OFF! I CLEANED MY ROOM.

I FINALLY GOT A BED, TOO!

THEN I MADE DINNER FOR AMANDA.

AND WENT TO BAND PRACTICE.

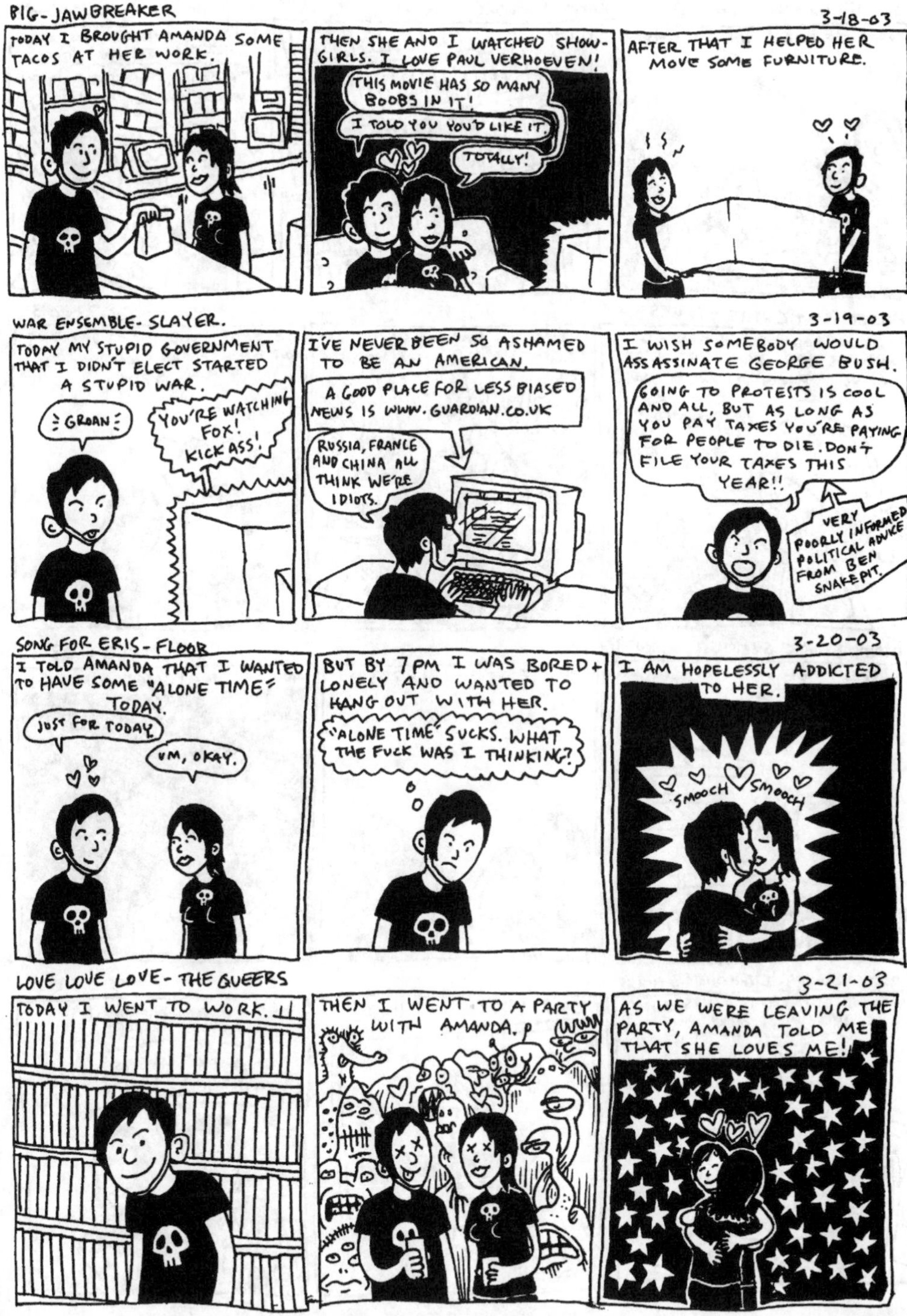
BIG-JAWBREAKER
3-18-03
TODAY I BROUGHT AMANDA SOME TACOS AT HER WORK.
THEN SHE AND I WATCHED SHOW-GIRLS. I LOVE PAUL VERHOEVEN!
THIS MOVIE HAS SO MANY BOOBS IN IT!
I TOLD YOU YOU'D LIKE IT.
TOTALLY!
AFTER THAT I HELPED HER MOVE SOME FURNITURE.
WAR ENSEMBLE-SLAYER.
3-19-03
TODAY MY STUPID GOVERNMENT THAT I DIDN'T ELECT STARTED A STUPID WAR.
GROAN
YOU'RE WATCHING FOX! KICK ASS!
I'VE NEVER BEEN SO ASHAMED TO BE AN AMERICAN.
A GOOD PLACE FOR LESS BIASED NEWS IS WWW.GUARDIAN.CO.UK
RUSSIA, FRANCE AND CHINA ALL THINK WE'RE IDIOTS.
I WISH SOMEBODY WOULD ASSASSINATE GEORGE BUSH.
GOING TO PROTESTS IS COOL AND ALL, BUT AS LONG AS YOU PAY TAXES YOU'RE PAYING FOR PEOPLE TO DIE. DON'T FILE YOUR TAXES THIS YEAR!!
VERY POORLY INFORMED POLITICAL ADVICE FROM BEN SNAKEPIT.
SONG FOR ERIS-FLOOR
3-20-03
I TOLD AMANDA THAT I WANTED TO HAVE SOME "ALONE TIME" TODAY.
JUST FOR TODAY.
UM, OKAY.
BUT BY 7PM I WAS BORED + LONELY AND WANTED TO HANG OUT WITH HER.
"ALONE TIME" SUCKS. WHAT THE FUCK WAS I THINKING?
I AM HOPELESSLY ADDICTED TO HER.
SMOOCH SMOOCH
LOVE LOVE LOVE-THE QUEERS
3-21-03
TODAY I WENT TO WORK.
THEN I WENT TO A PARTY WITH AMANDA.
AS WE WERE LEAVING THE PARTY, AMANDA TOLD ME THAT SHE LOVES ME!

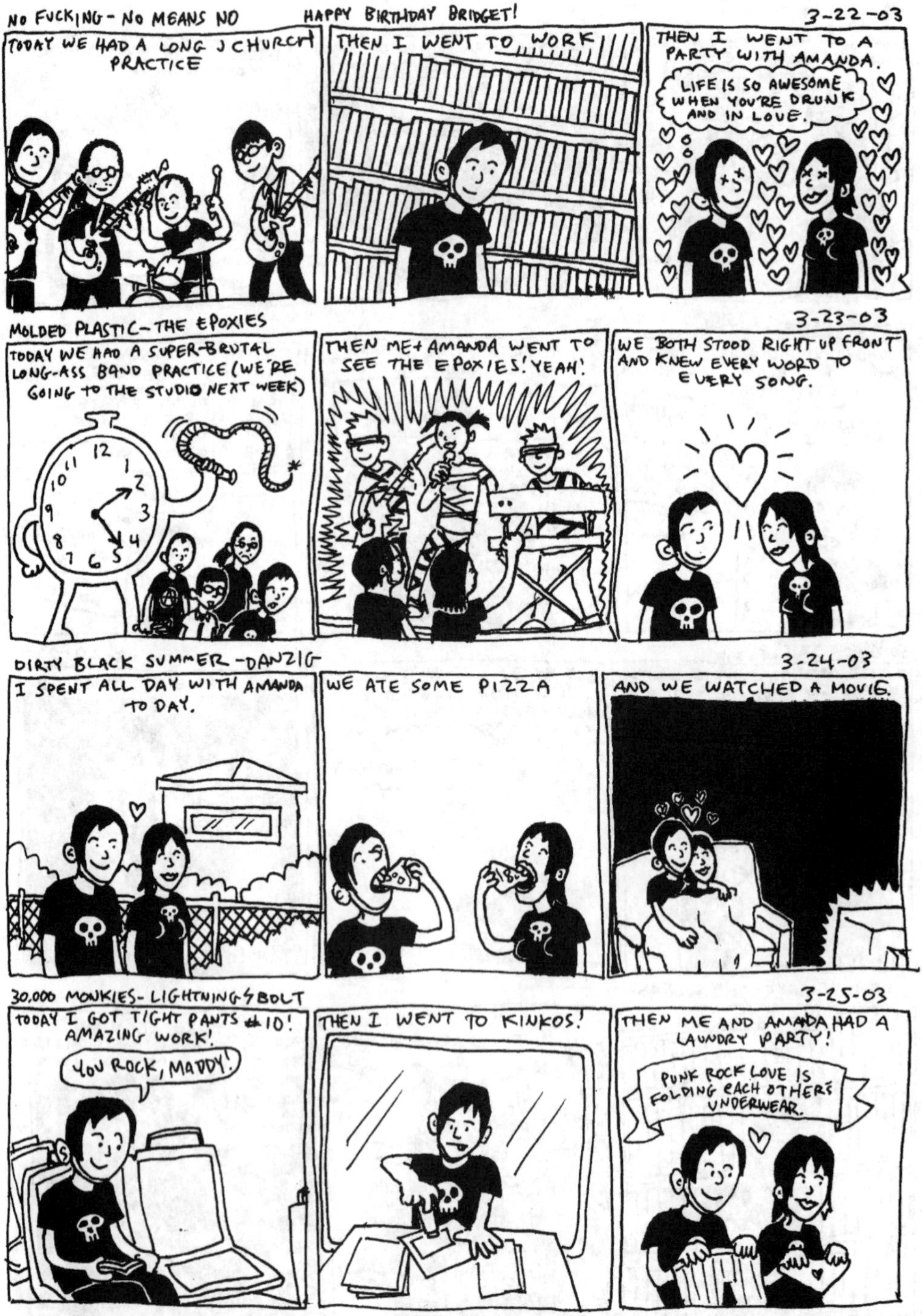
NO FUCKING - NO MEANS NO
HAPPY BIRTHDAY BRIDGET!
3-22-03
TODAY WE HAD A LONG J CHURCH PRACTICE
THEN I WENT TO WORK
THEN I WENT TO A PARTY WITH AMANDA.
LIFE IS SO AWESOME WHEN YOU'RE DRUNK AND IN LOVE.
MOLDED PLASTIC - THE EPOXIES
3-23-03
TODAY WE HAD A SUPER-BRUTAL LONG-ASS BAND PRACTICE (WE'RE GOING TO THE STUDIO NEXT WEEK)
THEN ME + AMANDA WENT TO SEE THE EPOXIES! YEAH!
WE BOTH STOOD RIGHT UP FRONT AND KNEW EVERY WORD TO EVERY SONG.
DIRTY BLACK SUMMER - DANZIG
3-24-03
I SPENT ALL DAY WITH AMANDA TODAY.
WE ATE SOME PIZZA
AND WE WATCHED A MOVIE.
30,000 MONKIES - LIGHTNING BOLT
3-25-03
TODAY I GOT TIGHT PANTS #10! AMAZING WORK!
YOU ROCK, MADDY!
THEN I WENT TO KINKOS!
THEN ME AND AMANDA HAD A LAUNDRY PARTY!
PUNK ROCK LOVE IS FOLDING EACH OTHER'S UNDERWEAR.

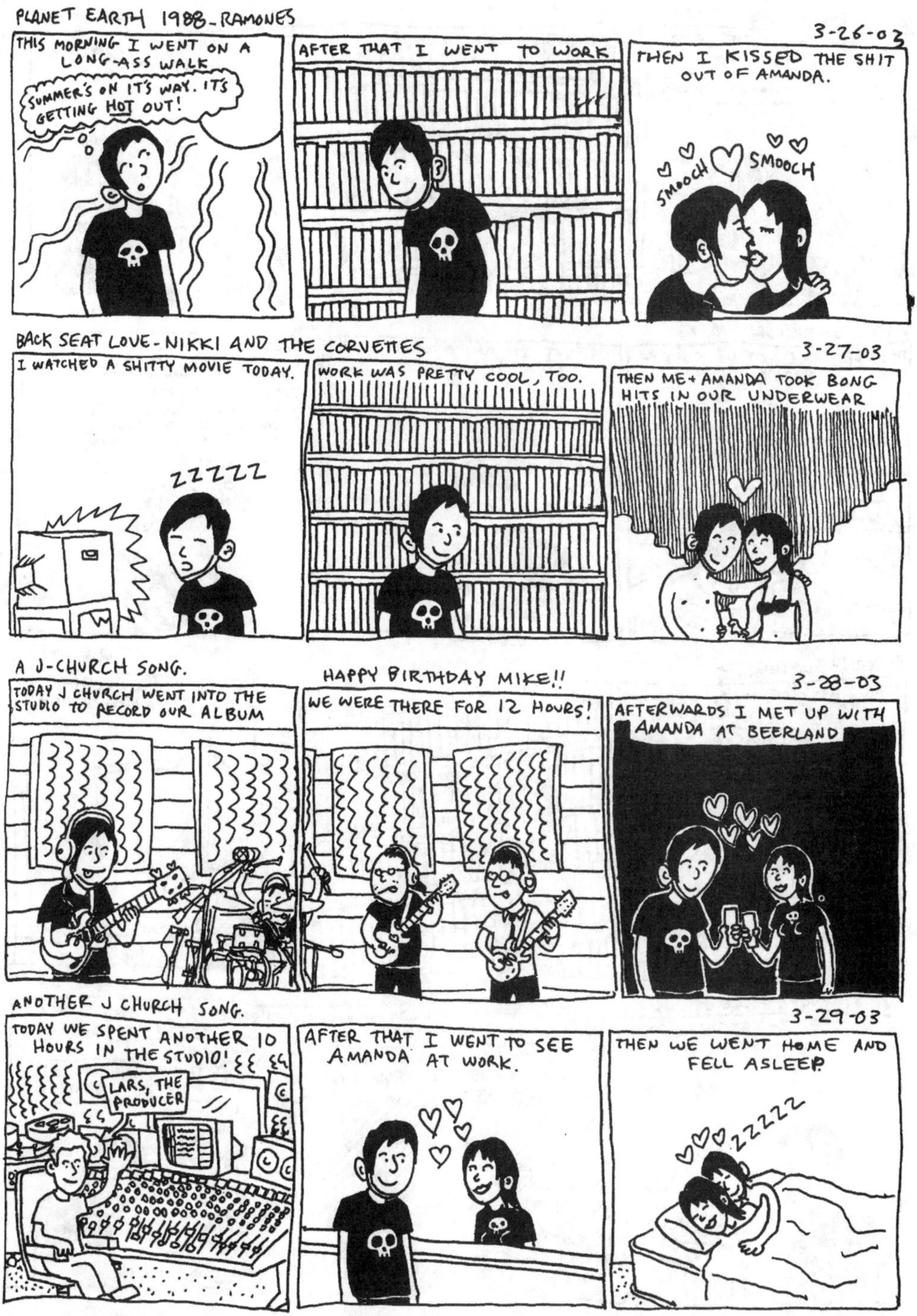
PLANET EARTH 1988 - RAMONES
3-26-03
THIS MORNING I WENT ON A LONG-ASS WALK
SUMMER'S ON IT'S WAY. IT'S GETTING HOT OUT!
AFTER THAT I WENT TO WORK
THEN I KISSED THE SHIT OUT OF AMANDA.
SMOOCH
SMOOCH
BACK SEAT LOVE - NIKKI AND THE CORVETTES
3-27-03
I WATCHED A SHITTY MOVIE TODAY.
ZZZZZ
WORK WAS PRETTY COOL, TOO.
THEN ME + AMANDA TOOK BONG HITS IN OUR UNDERWEAR
A J-CHURCH SONG.
HAPPY BIRTHDAY MIKE!!
3-28-03
TODAY J CHURCH WENT INTO THE STUDIO TO RECORD OUR ALBUM
WE WERE THERE FOR 12 HOURS!
AFTERWARDS I MET UP WITH AMANDA AT BEERLAND
ANOTHER J CHURCH SONG.
3-29-03
TODAY WE SPENT ANOTHER 10 HOURS IN THE STUDIO!
LARS, THE PRODUCER
AFTER THAT I WENT TO SEE AMANDA AT WORK.
THEN WE WENT HOME AND FELL ASLEEP.
ZZZZZ

MY MICHELLE - GUNS N ROSES   3-30-03

THIS MORNING I WENT RECORD SHOPPING WITH AMANDA

GOD, I MISS SOUND EXCHANGE

ME TOO

THEN I WENT TO WORK

THEN I MET AMANDA AT BARFLY'S.

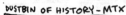

DUSTBIN OF HISTORY - MTX   3-31-03

THIS MORNING I GOT UP SUPER EARLY.

I WENT TO KINKO'S AND MADE SNAKEPIT #30

THEN AMANDA + I WATCHED EASY RIDER.

I'M GLAD WE ALWAYS WATCH MOVIES THAT I'VE SEEN BEFORE BECAUSE WE NEVER ACTUALLY GET ANY MOVIE-WATCHING DONE!

7:22   ZZZ   WIDE AWAKE

REBORN - SLAYER   4-1-03

TODAY I HUNG OUT WITH GREG AND J.D. FOR A LITTLE WHILE.

DUDE, NOW THAT YOU HAVE A GIRLFRIEND, YOU NEVER HANG OUT ANYMORE.

I KNOW. SORRY.

FIRST OR RACE DAY

THEN I WENT TO WORK.

AFTER THAT I WATCHED TV WITH AMANDA, MIKE + PENNY.

WONDERFUL - CIRCLE JERKS   4-2-03

A DAY OFF! I WATCHED SOME MOVIES.

LATER I HAD A VERY EMBARRASSING JAM SESH WITH KYLE.

SORRY KYLE, BUT YOUR SONGS ARE TOO HARD. I CAN'T KEEP UP!

OH.

THEN AMANDA AND I MADE BAKED POTATOES.

THESE KINDA SUCK

I THINK WE'RE MORE BAKED THAN THEY ARE

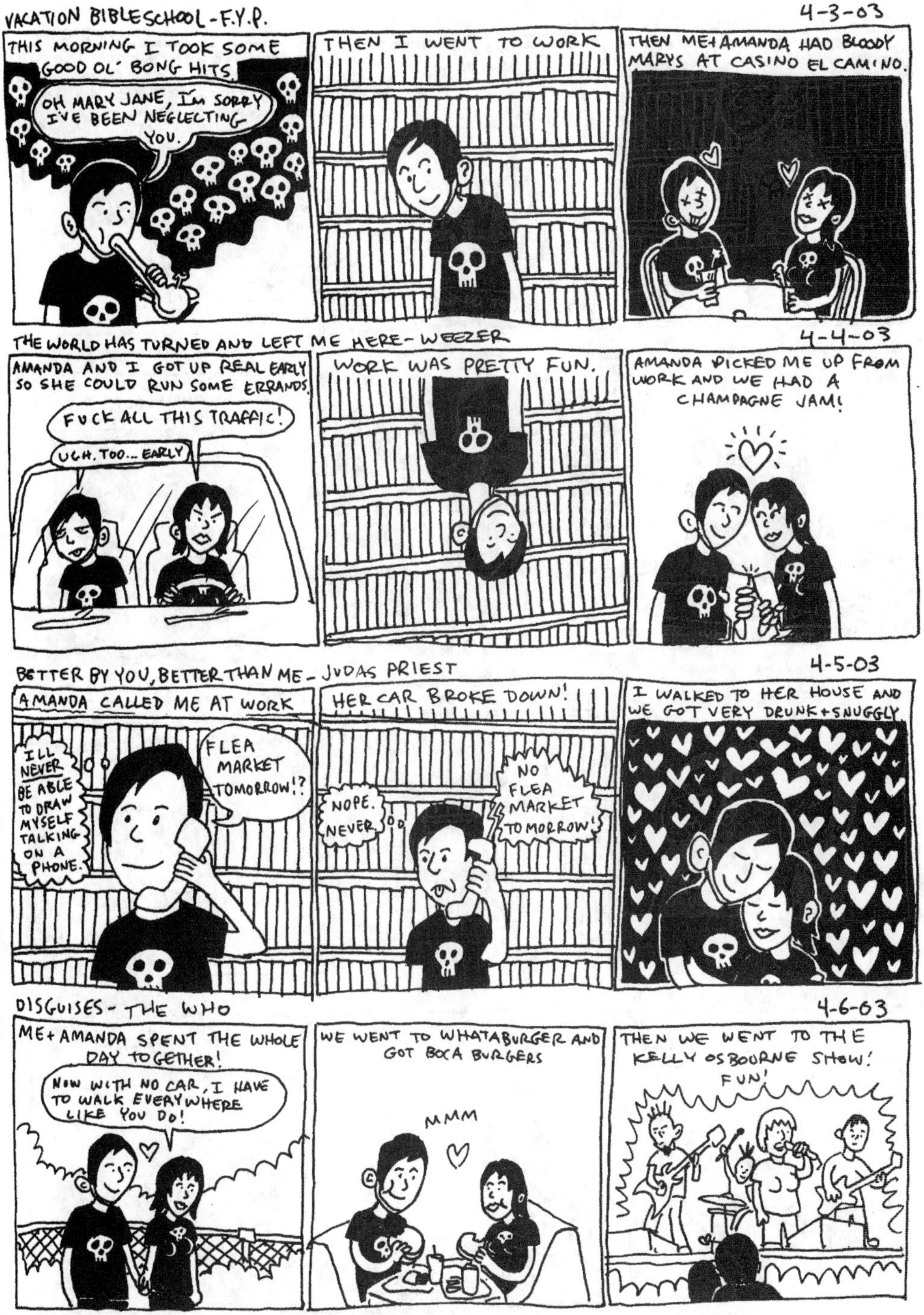
VACATION BIBLESCHOOL - F.Y.P.
4-3-03
THIS MORNING I TOOK SOME GOOD OL' BONG HITS.
OH MARY JANE, I'M SORRY I'VE BEEN NEGLECTING YOU.
THEN I WENT TO WORK
THEN ME+AMANDA HAD BLOODY MARYS AT CASINO EL CAMINO.
THE WORLD HAS TURNED AND LEFT ME HERE - WEEZER
4-4-03
AMANDA AND I GOT UP REAL EARLY SO SHE COULD RUN SOME ERRANDS.
FUCK ALL THIS TRAFFIC!
UGH. TOO... EARLY
WORK WAS PRETTY FUN.
AMANDA PICKED ME UP FROM WORK AND WE HAD A CHAMPAGNE JAM!
BETTER BY YOU, BETTER THAN ME - JUDAS PRIEST
4-5-03
AMANDA CALLED ME AT WORK
I'LL NEVER BE ABLE TO DRAW MYSELF TALKING ON A PHONE.
FLEA MARKET TOMORROW!?
HER CAR BROKE DOWN!
NOPE. NEVER.
NO FLEA MARKET TOMORROW!
I WALKED TO HER HOUSE AND WE GOT VERY DRUNK + SNUGGLY
DISGUISES - THE WHO
4-6-03
ME+AMANDA SPENT THE WHOLE DAY TOGETHER!
NOW WITH NO CAR, I HAVE TO WALK EVERYWHERE LIKE YOU DO!
WE WENT TO WHATABURGER AND GOT BOCA BURGERS
MMM
THEN WE WENT TO THE KELLY OSBOURNE SHOW! FUN!

ANTI-PLEASURE DISSERTATION— BIKINI KILL

4-7-03

THIS MORNING I CLEANED MY ROOM.

THEN AMANDA AND I WENT ON A LONG WALK.

LATER WE ATE QUESO AND FELL ASLEEP.

HAVING A GIRLFRIEND IS SO AWESOME.

WE ATE SAND— KARP

4-8-03

TODAY I WENT TO THE GROCERY STORE.

I CAME HOME AND WATCHED T.V.

THEN I WENT TO AMANDA'S AND MADE DINNER FOR HER.

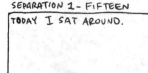

SEPARATION 1— FIFTEEN

4-9-03

TODAY I SAT AROUND.

FEH.

THEN I WENT TO WORK.

THEN I WATCHED AMAZON WOMEN ON THE MOON WITH AMANDA

COVERED WITH SORES— CANNIBAL CORPSE

4-10-03

I GOT A LOT OF DRAWING DONE TODAY.

AMANDA CAME OVER AFTER WORK AND I MADE DINNER FOR HER.

THE SECRET INGREDIENT IS LOVE

THEN WE WENT TO HER HOUSE AND GOT DRUNK.

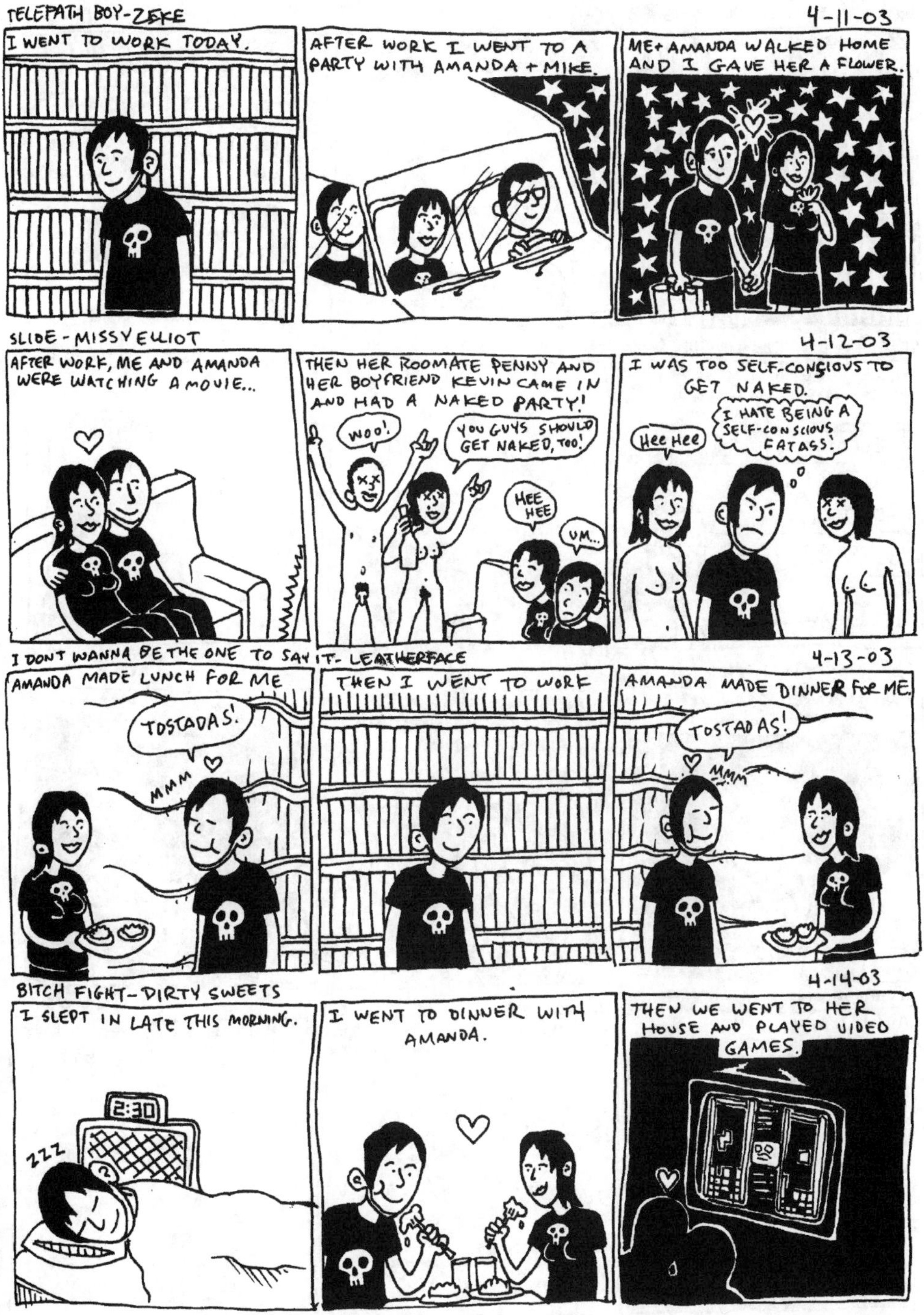
TELEPATH BOY-ZEKE
4-11-03
I WENT TO WORK TODAY.
AFTER WORK I WENT TO A PARTY WITH AMANDA + MIKE.
ME+ AMANDA WALKED HOME AND I GAVE HER A FLOWER.
SLIDE - MISSY ELLIOT
4-12-03
AFTER WORK, ME AND AMANDA WERE WATCHING A MOVIE...
THEN HER ROOMATE PENNY AND HER BOYFRIEND KEVIN CAME IN AND HAD A NAKED PARTY!
WOO!
YOU GUYS SHOULD GET NAKED, TOO!
HEE HEE
UM...
I WAS TOO SELF-CONSCIOUS TO GET NAKED.
HEE HEE
I HATE BEING A SELF-CONSCIOUS FATASS!
I DONT WANNA BE THE ONE TO SAY IT - LEATHERFACE
4-13-03
AMANDA MADE LUNCH FOR ME
TOSTADAS!
MMM
THEN I WENT TO WORK
AMANDA MADE DINNER FOR ME.
TOSTADAS!
MMM
BITCH FIGHT - DIRTY SWEETS
4-14-03
I SLEPT IN LATE THIS MORNING.
2:30
ZZZ
I WENT TO DINNER WITH AMANDA.
THEN WE WENT TO HER HOUSE AND PLAYED VIDEO GAMES.

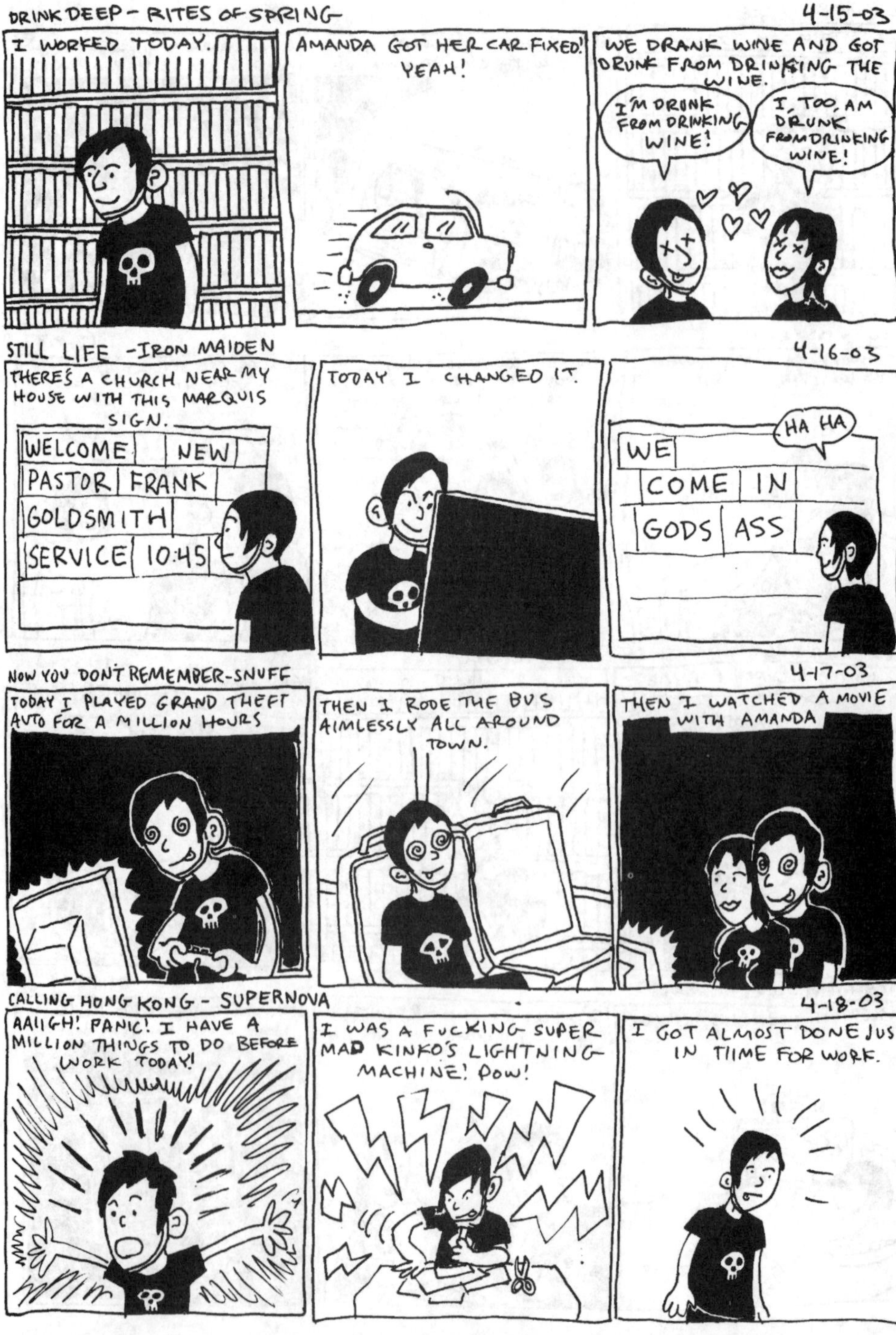

DRINK DEEP - RITES OF SPRING
4-15-03
I WORKED TODAY.
AMANDA GOT HER CAR FIXED! YEAH!
WE DRANK WINE AND GOT DRUNK FROM DRINKING THE WINE.
I'M DRUNK FROM DRINKING WINE!
I, TOO, AM DRUNK FROM DRINKING WINE!
STILL LIFE - IRON MAIDEN
4-16-03
THERE'S A CHURCH NEAR MY HOUSE WITH THIS MARQUIS SIGN.
WELCOME NEW PASTOR FRANK GOLDSMITH SERVICE 10:45
TODAY I CHANGED IT.
WE COME IN GODS ASS
HA HA
NOW YOU DON'T REMEMBER - SNUFF
4-17-03
TODAY I PLAYED GRAND THEFT AUTO FOR A MILLION HOURS
THEN I RODE THE BUS AIMLESSLY ALL AROUND TOWN.
THEN I WATCHED A MOVIE WITH AMANDA
CALLING HONG KONG - SUPERNOVA
4-18-03
AAIIGH! PANIC! I HAVE A MILLION THINGS TO DO BEFORE WORK TODAY!
I WAS A FUCKING SUPER MAD KINKO'S LIGHTNING MACHINE! POW!
I GOT ALMOST DONE JUST IN TIIME FOR WORK.

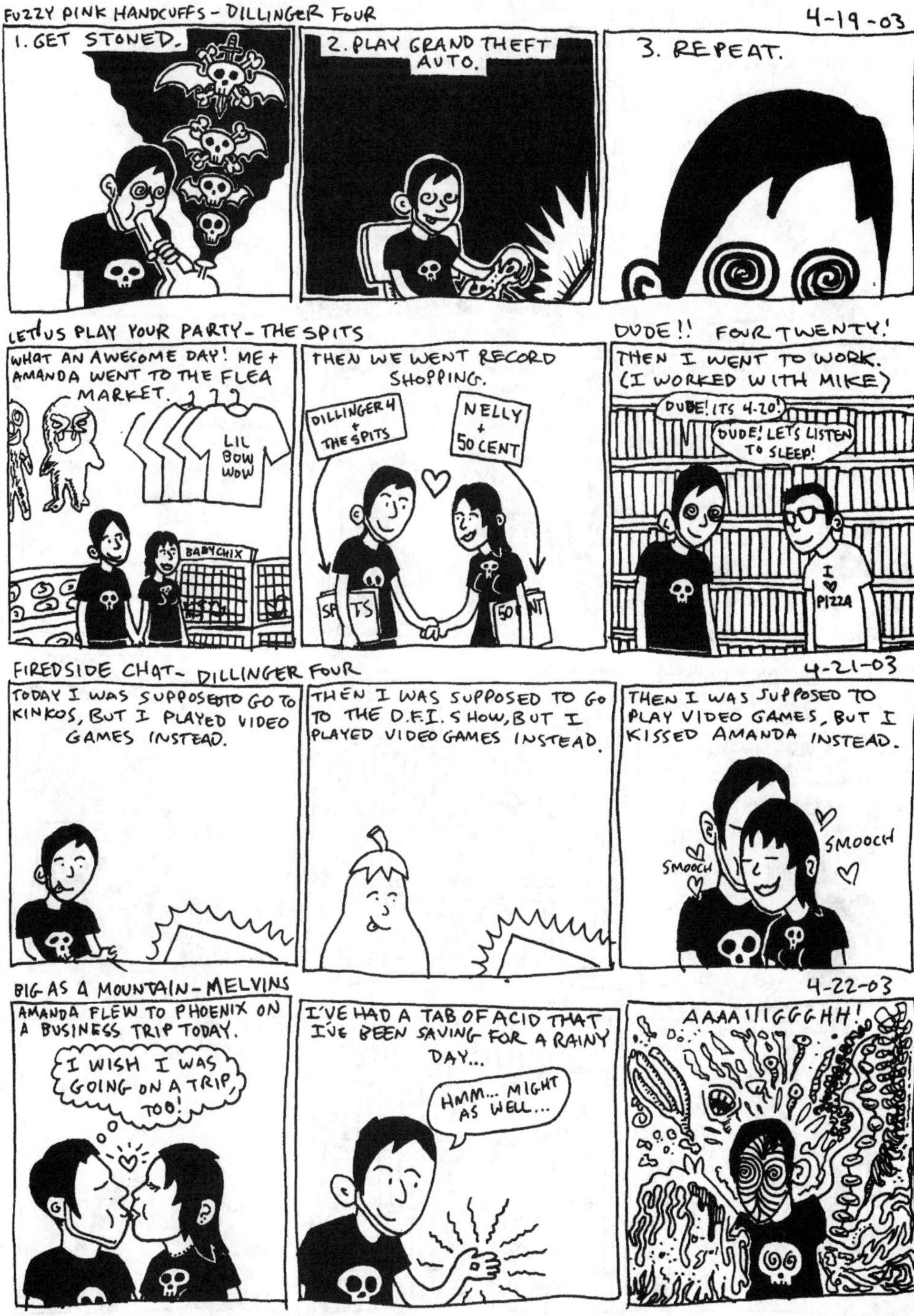
FUZZY PINK HANDCUFFS - DILLINGER FOUR
4-19-03
1. GET STONED.
2. PLAY GRAND THEFT AUTO.
3. REPEAT.
LET US PLAY YOUR PARTY - THE SPITS
DUDE!! FOUR TWENTY!
WHAT AN AWESOME DAY! ME + AMANDA WENT TO THE FLEA MARKET.
LIL BOW WOW
BABY CHIX
THEN WE WENT RECORD SHOPPING.
DILLINGER 4 + THE SPITS
NELLY + 50 CENT
SPITS
50 CENT
THEN I WENT TO WORK. (I WORKED WITH MIKE)
DUDE! ITS 4-20!
DUDE! LETS LISTEN TO SLEEP!
I ♥ PIZZA
FIREDSIDE CHAT - DILLINGER FOUR
4-21-03
TODAY I WAS SUPPOSED TO GO TO KINKOS, BUT I PLAYED VIDEO GAMES INSTEAD.
THEN I WAS SUPPOSED TO GO TO THE D.F.I. SHOW, BUT I PLAYED VIDEO GAMES INSTEAD.
THEN I WAS SUPPOSED TO PLAY VIDEO GAMES, BUT I KISSED AMANDA INSTEAD.
SMOOCH
SMOOCH
BIG AS A MOUNTAIN - MELVINS
4-22-03
AMANDA FLEW TO PHOENIX ON A BUSINESS TRIP TODAY.
I WISH I WAS GOING ON A TRIP, TOO!
I'VE HAD A TAB OF ACID THAT I'VE BEEN SAVING FOR A RAINY DAY...
HMM... MIGHT AS WELL...
AAAAIIIGGGHH!

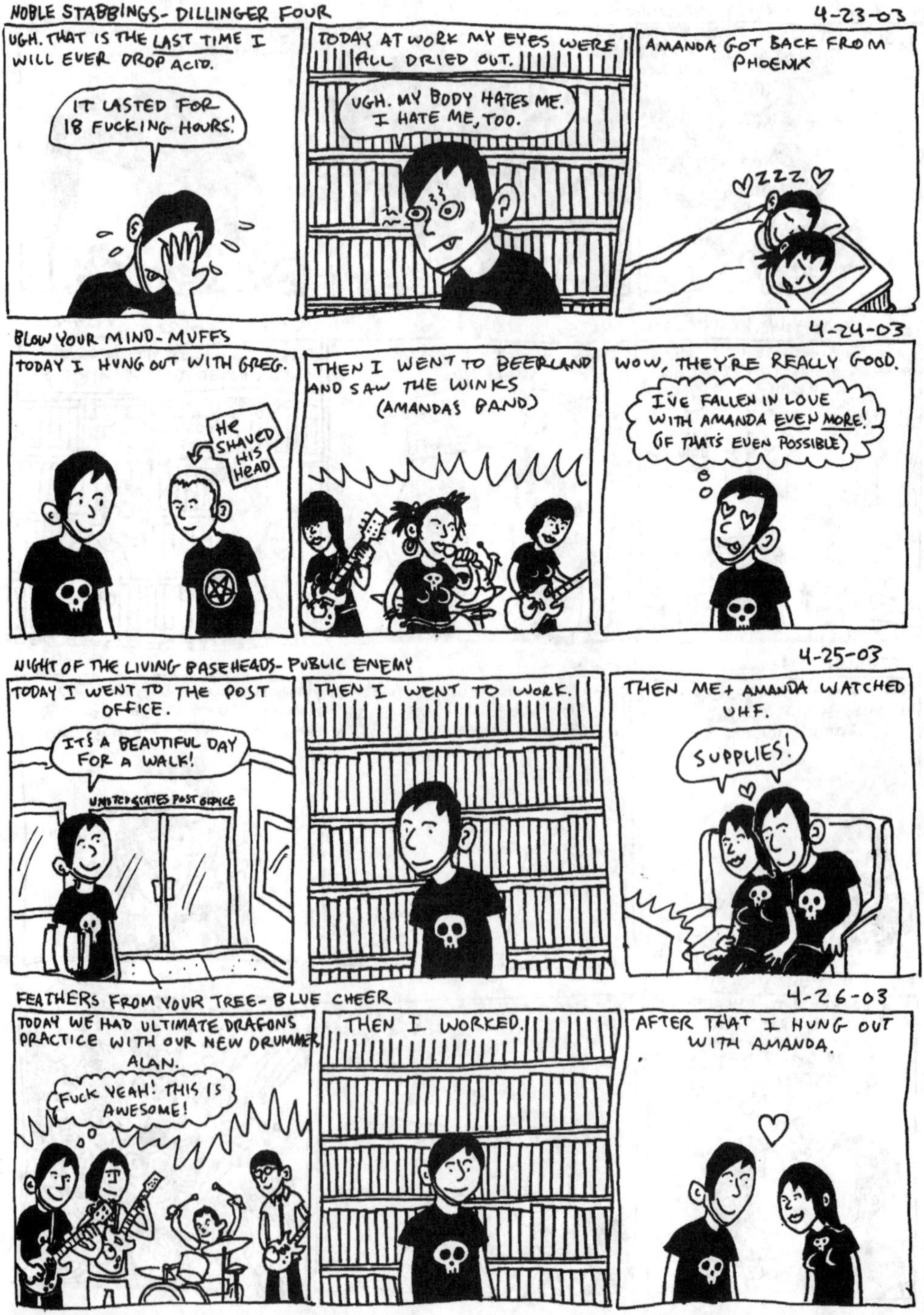
NOBLE STABBINGS - DILLINGER FOUR
4-23-03
UGH. THAT IS THE LAST TIME I WILL EVER DROP ACID.
IT LASTED FOR 18 FUCKING HOURS!
TODAY AT WORK MY EYES WERE ALL DRIED OUT.
UGH. MY BODY HATES ME. I HATE ME, TOO.
AMANDA GOT BACK FROM PHOENIX
ZZZ
BLOW YOUR MIND - MUFFS
4-24-03
TODAY I HUNG OUT WITH GREG.
HE SHAVED HIS HEAD
THEN I WENT TO BEERLAND AND SAW THE WINKS (AMANDA'S BAND)
WOW, THEY'RE REALLY GOOD.
I'VE FALLEN IN LOVE WITH AMANDA EVEN MORE! (IF THAT'S EVEN POSSIBLE)
NIGHT OF THE LIVING BASEHEADS - PUBLIC ENEMY
4-25-03
TODAY I WENT TO THE POST OFFICE.
IT'S A BEAUTIFUL DAY FOR A WALK!
UNITED STATES POST OFFICE
THEN I WENT TO WORK.
THEN ME + AMANDA WATCHED UHF.
SUPPLIES!
FEATHERS FROM YOUR TREE - BLUE CHEER
4-26-03
TODAY WE HAD ULTIMATE DRAGONS PRACTICE WITH OUR NEW DRUMMER, ALAN.
FUCK YEAH! THIS IS AWESOME!
THEN I WORKED.
AFTER THAT I HUNG OUT WITH AMANDA.

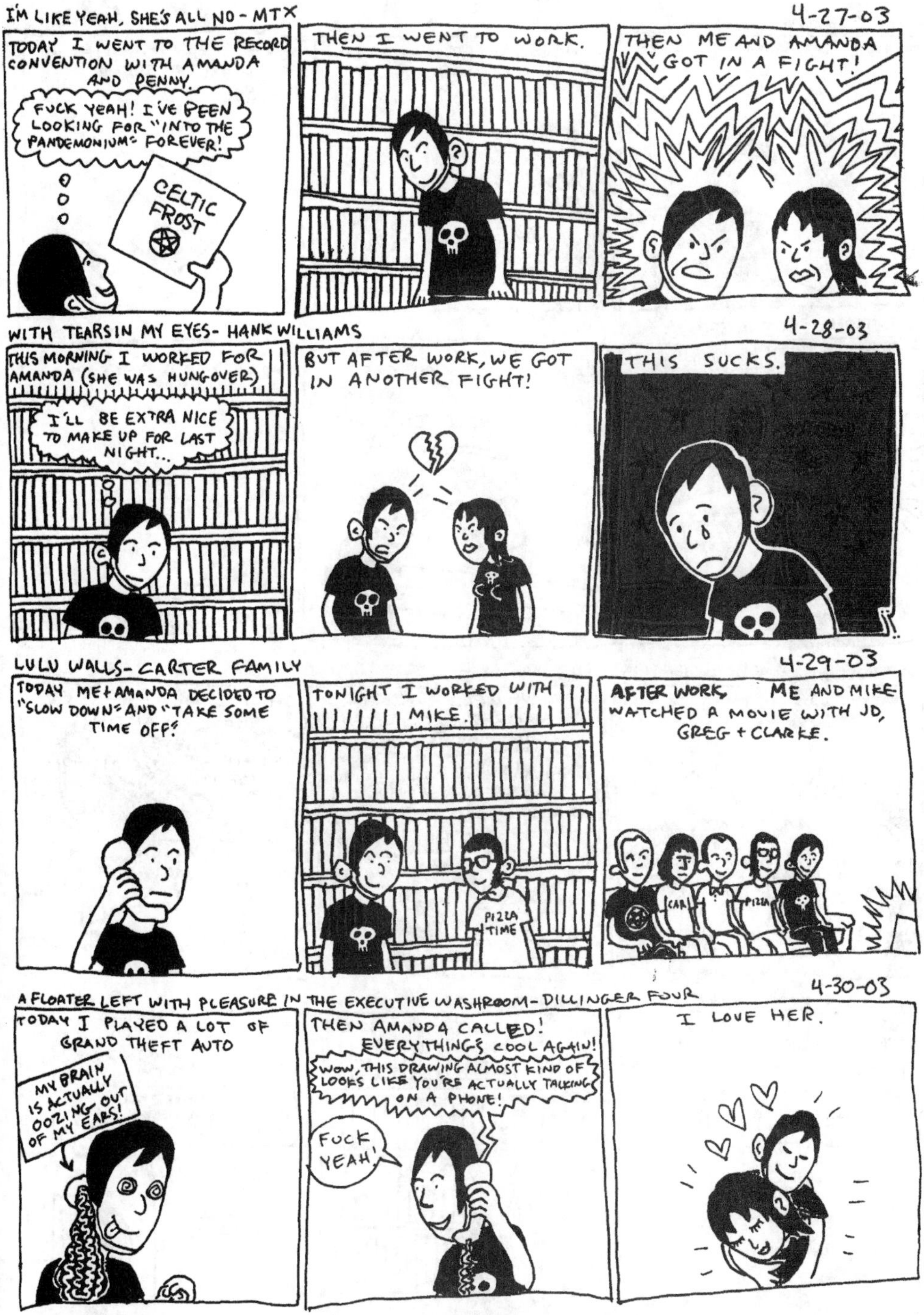
I'M LIKE YEAH, SHE'S ALL NO - MTX
4-27-03
TODAY I WENT TO THE RECORD CONVENTION WITH AMANDA AND PENNY.
FUCK YEAH! I'VE BEEN LOOKING FOR "INTO THE PANDEMONIUM" FOREVER!
CELTIC FROST
THEN I WENT TO WORK.
THEN ME AND AMANDA GOT IN A FIGHT!
WITH TEARS IN MY EYES - HANK WILLIAMS
4-28-03
THIS MORNING I WORKED FOR AMANDA (SHE WAS HUNGOVER)
I'LL BE EXTRA NICE TO MAKE UP FOR LAST NIGHT...
BUT AFTER WORK, WE GOT IN ANOTHER FIGHT!
THIS SUCKS.
LULU WALLS - CARTER FAMILY
4-29-03
TODAY ME + AMANDA DECIDED TO "SLOW DOWN" AND "TAKE SOME TIME OFF"
TONIGHT I WORKED WITH MIKE.
PIZZA TIME
AFTER WORK, ME AND MIKE WATCHED A MOVIE WITH JD, GREG + CLARKE.
A FLOATER LEFT WITH PLEASURE IN THE EXECUTIVE WASHROOM - DILLINGER FOUR
4-30-03
TODAY I PLAYED A LOT OF GRAND THEFT AUTO
MY BRAIN IS ACTUALLY OOZING OUT OF MY EARS!
THEN AMANDA CALLED! EVERYTHING'S COOL AGAIN!
WOW, THIS DRAWING ALMOST KIND OF LOOKS LIKE YOU'RE ACTUALLY TALKING ON A PHONE!
FUCK YEAH!
I LOVE HER.

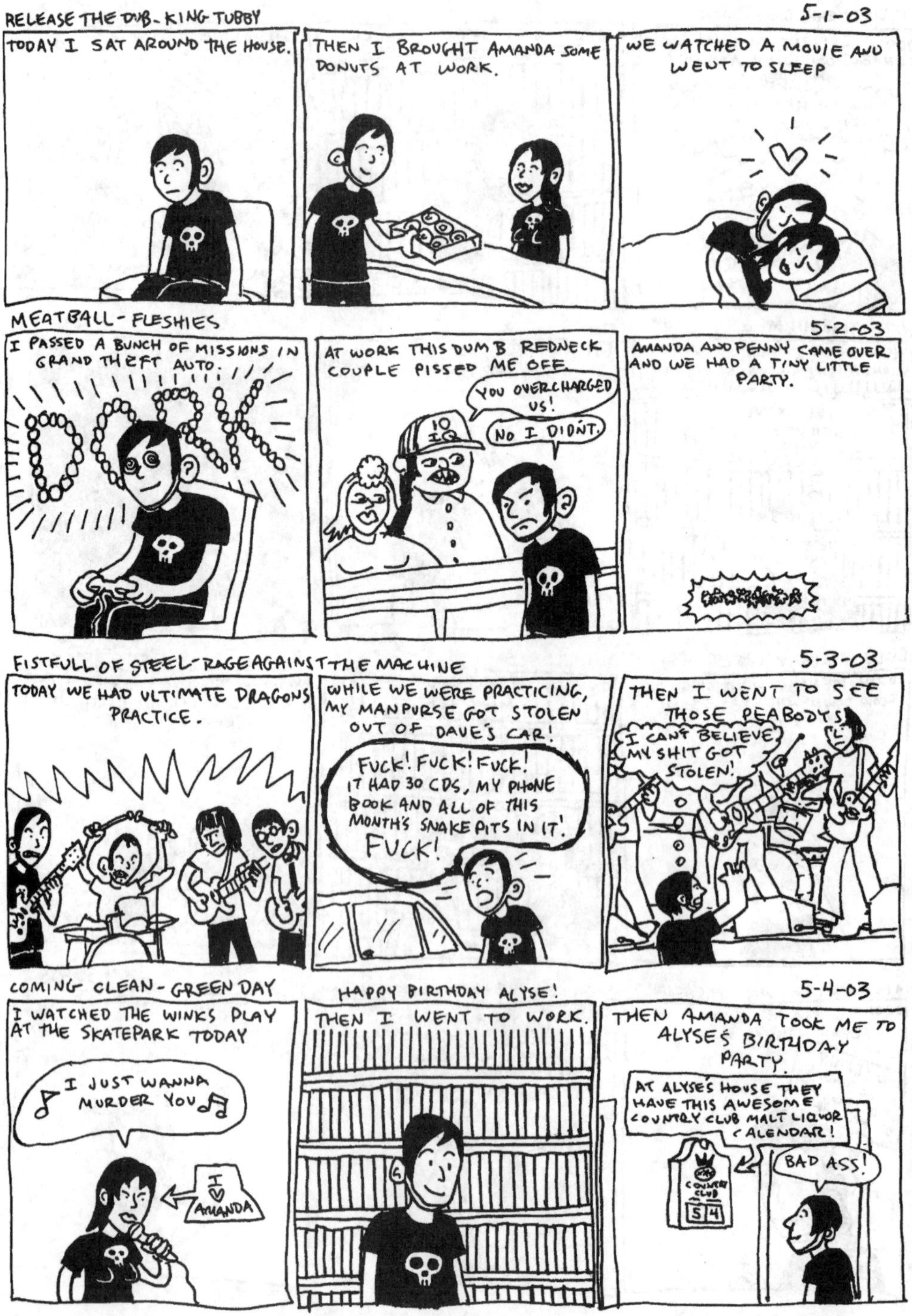
RELEASE THE DUB - KING TUBBY
5-1-03
TODAY I SAT AROUND THE HOUSE.
THEN I BROUGHT AMANDA SOME DONUTS AT WORK.
WE WATCHED A MOVIE AND WENT TO SLEEP
MEATBALL - FLESHIES
5-2-03
I PASSED A BUNCH OF MISSIONS IN GRAND THEFT AUTO.
DORK
AT WORK THIS DUMB REDNECK COUPLE PISSED ME OFF.
YOU OVERCHARGED US!
NO I DIDNT.
IQ 10
AMANDA AND PENNY CAME OVER AND WE HAD A TINY LITTLE PARTY.
FISTFULL OF STEEL - RAGE AGAINST THE MACHINE
5-3-03
TODAY WE HAD ULTIMATE DRAGONS PRACTICE.
WHILE WE WERE PRACTICING, MY MANPURSE GOT STOLEN OUT OF DAVE'S CAR!
FUCK! FUCK! FUCK! IT HAD 30 CDS, MY PHONE BOOK AND ALL OF THIS MONTH'S SNAKE PITS IN IT! FUCK!
THEN I WENT TO SEE THOSE PEABODYS!
I CANT BELIEVE MY SHIT GOT STOLEN!
COMING CLEAN - GREEN DAY
HAPPY BIRTHDAY ALYSE!
5-4-03
I WATCHED THE WINKS PLAY AT THE SKATEPARK TODAY
I JUST WANNA MURDER YOU
I ♡ AMANDA
THEN I WENT TO WORK.
THEN AMANDA TOOK ME TO ALYSE'S BIRTHDAY PARTY.
AT ALYSE'S HOUSE THEY HAVE THIS AWESOME COUNTRY CLUB MALT LIQUOR CALENDAR!
COUNTRY CLUB
5 4
BAD ASS!

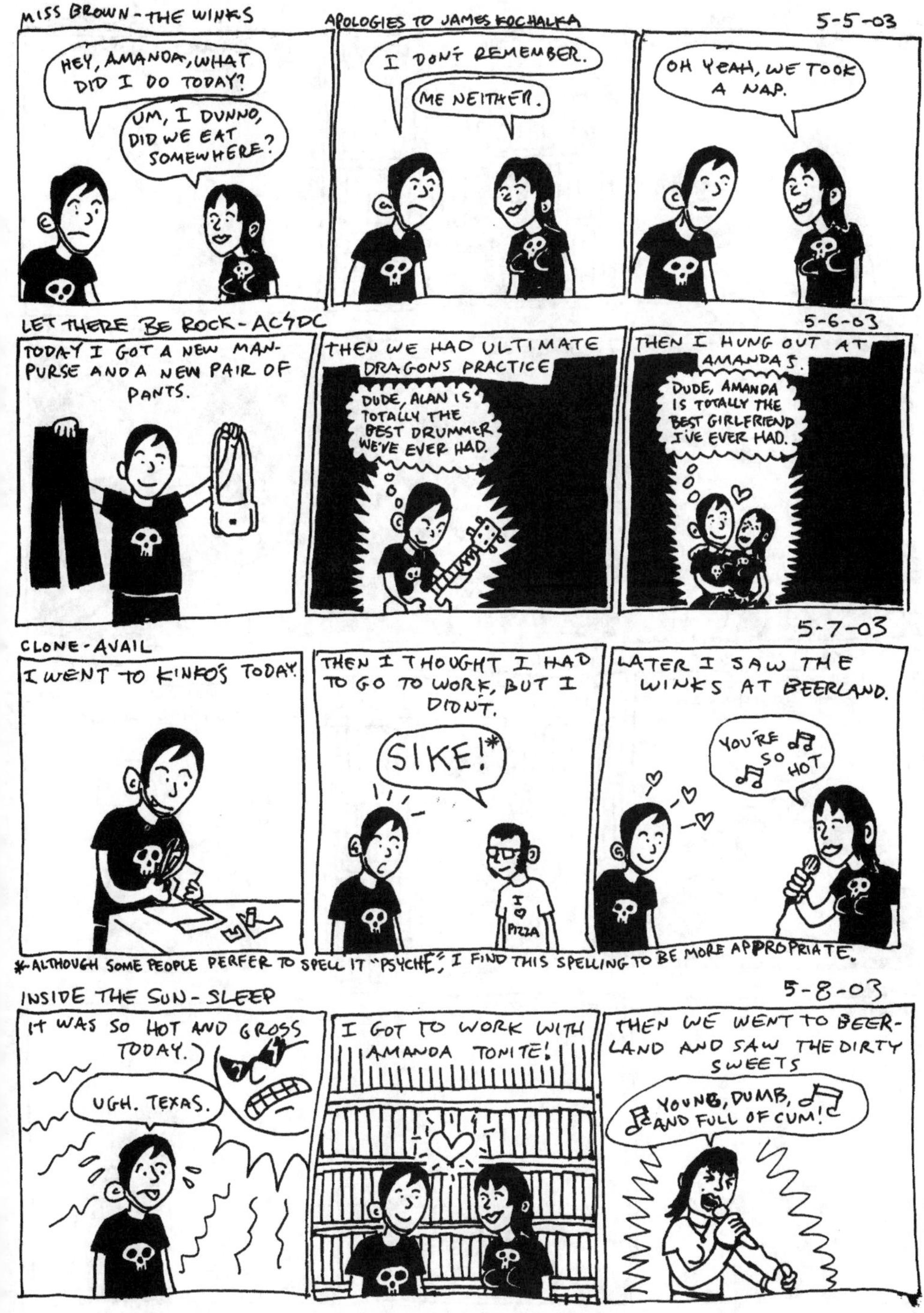
MISS BROWN - THE WINKS
APOLOGIES TO JAMES KOCHALKA
5-5-03
HEY, AMANDA, WHAT DID I DO TODAY?
UM, I DUNNO, DID WE EAT SOMEWHERE?
I DON'T REMEMBER.
ME NEITHER.
OH YEAH, WE TOOK A NAP.
LET THERE BE ROCK - AC/DC
5-6-03
TODAY I GOT A NEW MAN-PURSE AND A NEW PAIR OF PANTS.
THEN WE HAD ULTIMATE DRAGONS PRACTICE
DUDE, ALAN IS TOTALLY THE BEST DRUMMER WE'VE EVER HAD.
THEN I HUNG OUT AT AMANDA'S.
DUDE, AMANDA IS TOTALLY THE BEST GIRLFRIEND I'VE EVER HAD.
5-7-03
CLONE - AVAIL
I WENT TO KINKO'S TODAY.
THEN I THOUGHT I HAD TO GO TO WORK, BUT I DIDN'T.
SIKE!*
I ♥ PIZZA
LATER I SAW THE WINKS AT BEERLAND.
YOU'RE SO HOT
*ALTHOUGH SOME PEOPLE PERFER TO SPELL IT "PSYCHE", I FIND THIS SPELLING TO BE MORE APPROPRIATE.
INSIDE THE SUN - SLEEP
5-8-03
IT WAS SO HOT AND GROSS TODAY.
UGH. TEXAS.
I GOT TO WORK WITH AMANDA TONITE!
THEN WE WENT TO BEER-LAND AND SAW THE DIRTY SWEETS
YOUNG, DUMB, AND FULL OF CUM!

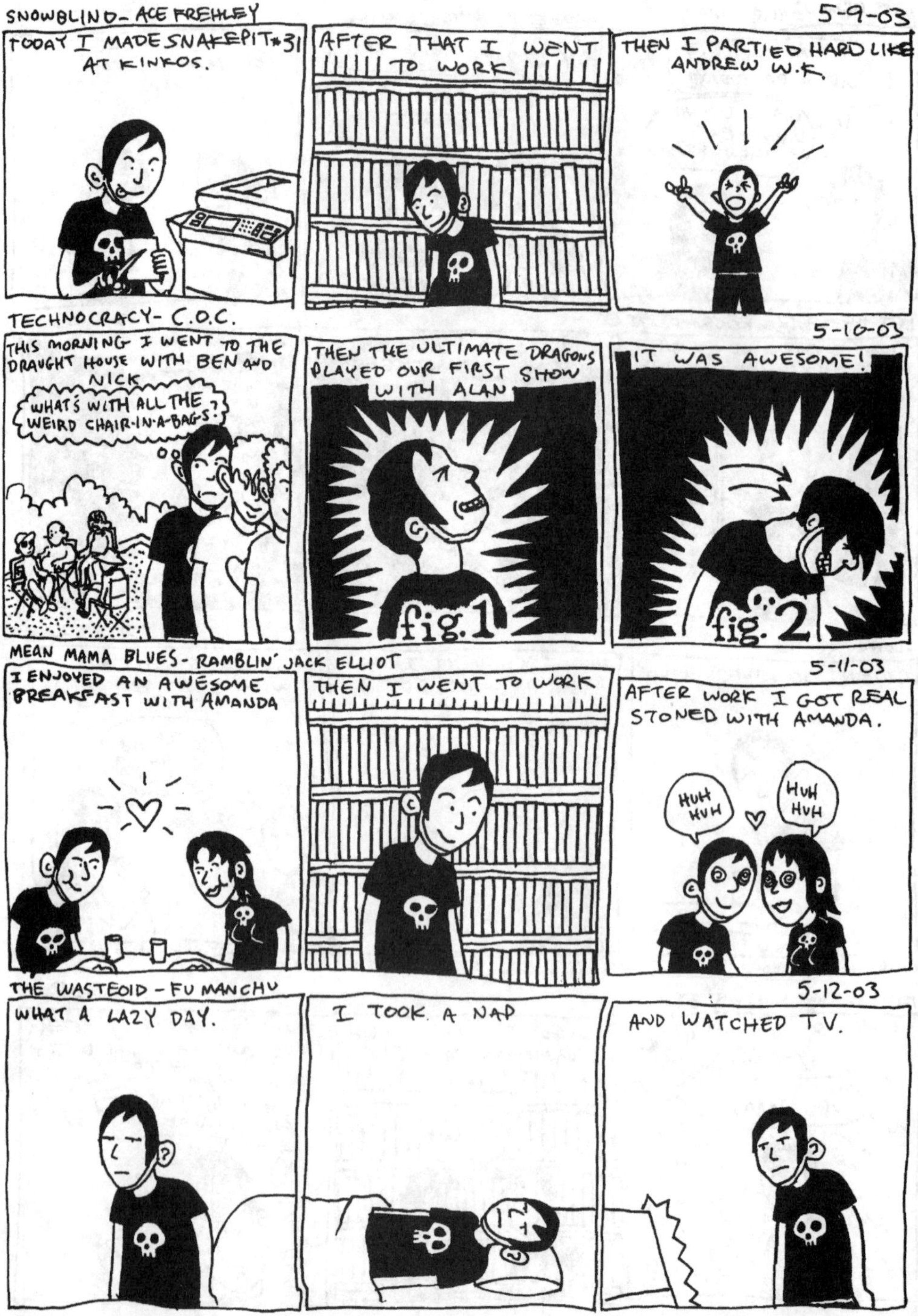
SNOWBLIND- ACE FREHLEY
5-9-03
TODAY I MADE SNAKEPIT #31 AT KINKOS.
AFTER THAT I WENT TO WORK
THEN I PARTIED HARD LIKE ANDREW W.K.
TECHNOCRACY- C.O.C.
5-10-03
THIS MORNING I WENT TO THE DRAUGHT HOUSE WITH BEN AND NICK
WHAT'S WITH ALL THE WEIRD CHAIR-IN-A-BAGS?
THEN THE ULTIMATE DRAGONS PLAYED OUR FIRST SHOW WITH ALAN
fig. 1
IT WAS AWESOME!
fig. 2
MEAN MAMA BLUES- RAMBLIN' JACK ELLIOT
5-11-03
I ENJOYED AN AWESOME BREAKFAST WITH AMANDA
THEN I WENT TO WORK
AFTER WORK I GOT REAL STONED WITH AMANDA.
HUH HUH
HUH HUH
THE WASTEOID - FU MANCHU
5-12-03
WHAT A LAZY DAY.
I TOOK A NAP
AND WATCHED T.V.

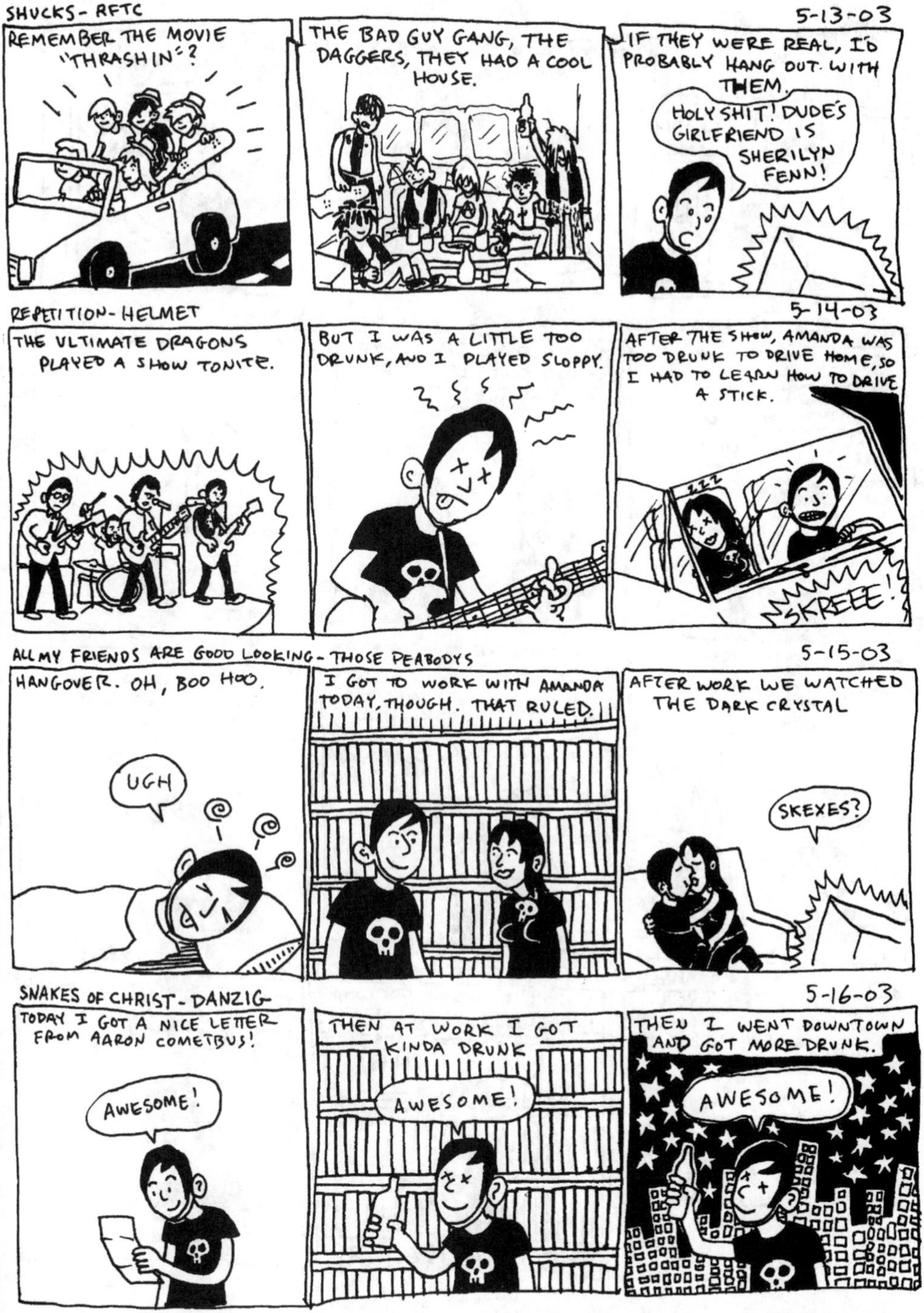
SHUCKS - RFTC
5-13-03
REMEMBER THE MOVIE "THRASHIN'"?
THE BAD GUY GANG, THE DAGGERS, THEY HAD A COOL HOUSE.
IF THEY WERE REAL, I'D PROBABLY HANG OUT WITH THEM.
HOLY SHIT! DUDE'S GIRLFRIEND IS SHERILYN FENN!
REPETITION - HELMET
5-14-03
THE ULTIMATE DRAGONS PLAYED A SHOW TONITE.
BUT I WAS A LITTLE TOO DRUNK, AND I PLAYED SLOPPY.
AFTER THE SHOW, AMANDA WAS TOO DRUNK TO DRIVE HOME, SO I HAD TO LEARN HOW TO DRIVE A STICK.
ZZZ
SKREEE!
ALL MY FRIENDS ARE GOOD LOOKING - THOSE PEABODYS
5-15-03
HANGOVER. OH, BOO HOO.
UGH
I GOT TO WORK WITH AMANDA TODAY, THOUGH. THAT RULED.
AFTER WORK WE WATCHED THE DARK CRYSTAL
SKEXES?
SNAKES OF CHRIST - DANZIG
5-16-03
TODAY I GOT A NICE LETTER FROM AARON COMETBUS!
AWESOME!
THEN AT WORK I GOT KINDA DRUNK
AWESOME!
THEN I WENT DOWNTOWN AND GOT MORE DRUNK.
AWESOME!

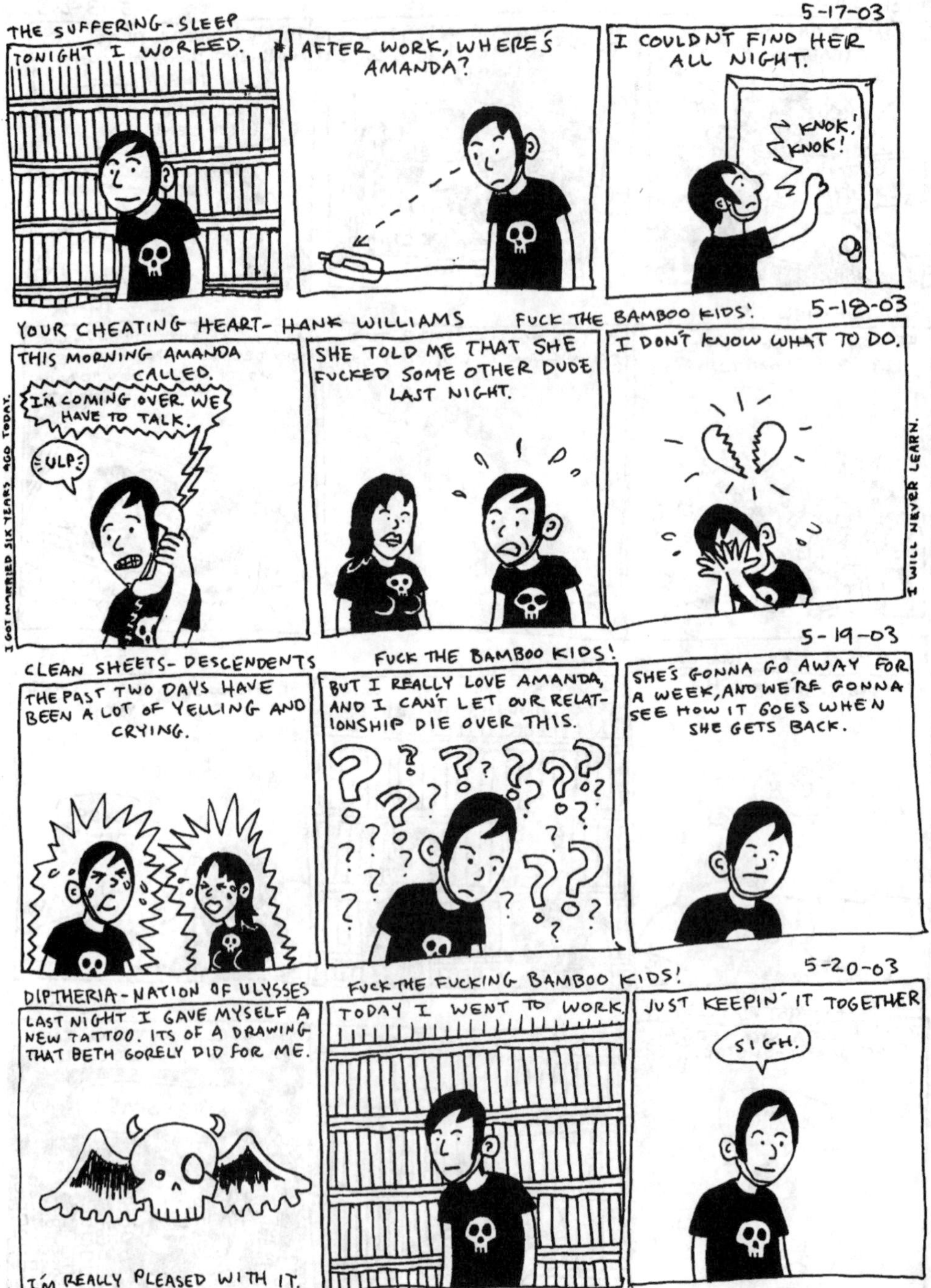
5-17-03
THE SUFFERING-SLEEP
TONIGHT I WORKED.
AFTER WORK, WHERE'S AMANDA?
I COULDNT FIND HER ALL NIGHT.
KNOK! KNOK!
5-18-03
YOUR CHEATING HEART- HANK WILLIAMS
FUCK THE BAMBOO KIDS!
THIS MORNING AMANDA CALLED.
I'M COMING OVER. WE HAVE TO TALK.
ULP.
I GOT MARRIED SIX YEARS AGO TODAY.
SHE TOLD ME THAT SHE FUCKED SOME OTHER DUDE LAST NIGHT.
I DON'T KNOW WHAT TO DO.
I WILL NEVER LEARN.
5-19-03
CLEAN SHEETS- DESCENDENTS
FUCK THE BAMBOO KIDS!
THE PAST TWO DAYS HAVE BEEN A LOT OF YELLING AND CRYING.
BUT I REALLY LOVE AMANDA, AND I CAN'T LET OUR RELATIONSHIP DIE OVER THIS.
SHE'S GONNA GO AWAY FOR A WEEK, AND WE'RE GONNA SEE HOW IT GOES WHEN SHE GETS BACK.
5-20-03
DIPTHERIA- NATION OF ULYSSES
FUCK THE FUCKING BAMBOO KIDS!
LAST NIGHT I GAVE MYSELF A NEW TATTOO. ITS OF A DRAWING THAT BETH GORELY DID FOR ME.
I'M REALLY PLEASED WITH IT.
TODAY I WENT TO WORK.
JUST KEEPIN' IT TOGETHER
SIGH.

WHERE DID YOU SLEEP LAST NIGHT? - LEADBELLY   KILL THE BAMBOO KIDS!   5-21-03

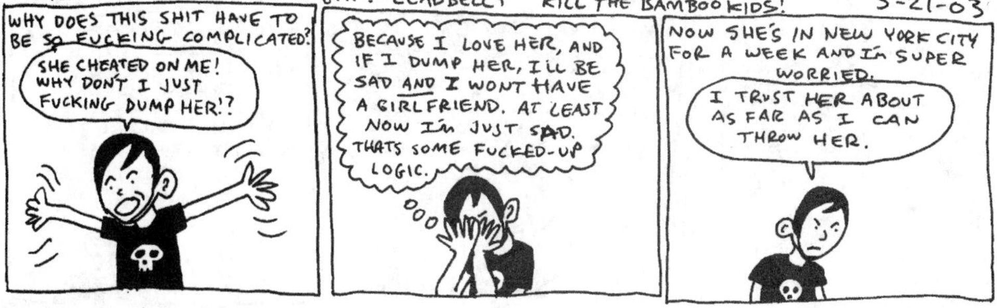
WHY DOES THIS SHIT HAVE TO BE SO FUCKING COMPLICATED?
SHE CHEATED ON ME! WHY DON'T I JUST FUCKING DUMP HER!?
BECAUSE I LOVE HER, AND IF I DUMP HER, I'LL BE SAD AND I WONT HAVE A GIRLFRIEND. AT LEAST NOW I'M JUST SAD. THATS SOME FUCKED-UP LOGIC.
NOW SHE'S IN NEW YORK CITY FOR A WEEK AND I'M SUPER WORRIED.
I TRUST HER ABOUT AS FAR AS I CAN THROW HER.

DONT NEED YOU - BIKINI KILL   HAPPY 1ST BIRTHDAY EVA DIDONATO!   5-22-03

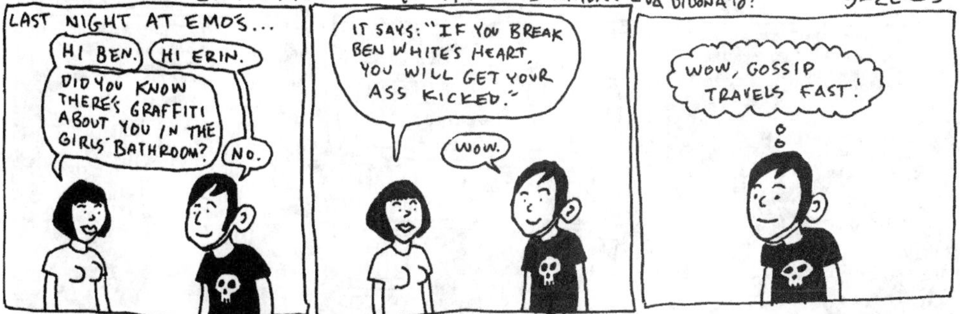
LAST NIGHT AT EMO'S...
HI BEN.
HI ERIN.
DID YOU KNOW THERE'S GRAFFITI ABOUT YOU IN THE GIRLS' BATHROOM?
NO.
IT SAYS: "IF YOU BREAK BEN WHITE'S HEART, YOU WILL GET YOUR ASS KICKED."
WOW.
WOW, GOSSIP TRAVELS FAST!

NIGHT FULL OF KICKS - FLOOR   5-23-03

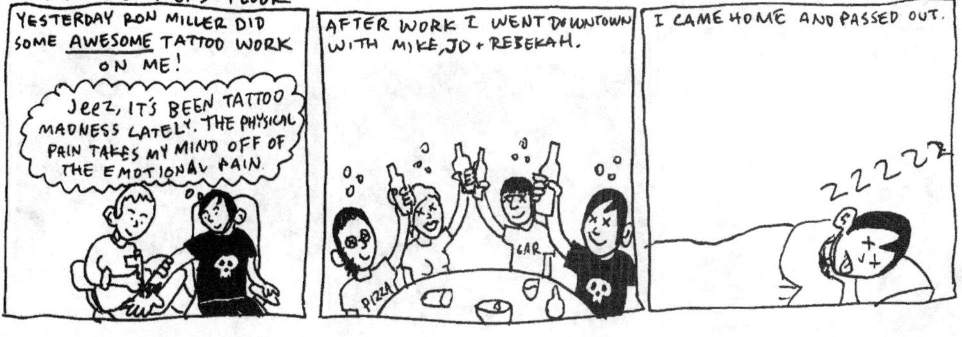
YESTERDAY RON MILLER DID SOME AWESOME TATTOO WORK ON ME!
JEEZ, IT'S BEEN TATTOO MADNESS LATELY. THE PHYSICAL PAIN TAKES MY MIND OFF OF THE EMOTIONAL PAIN.
AFTER WORK I WENT DOWNTOWN WITH MIKE, JD + REBEKAH.
PIZZA
CAR
I CAME HOME AND PASSED OUT.
ZZZZZ

PARTY TIL YOU PUKE - ANDREW W.K.   5-24-03

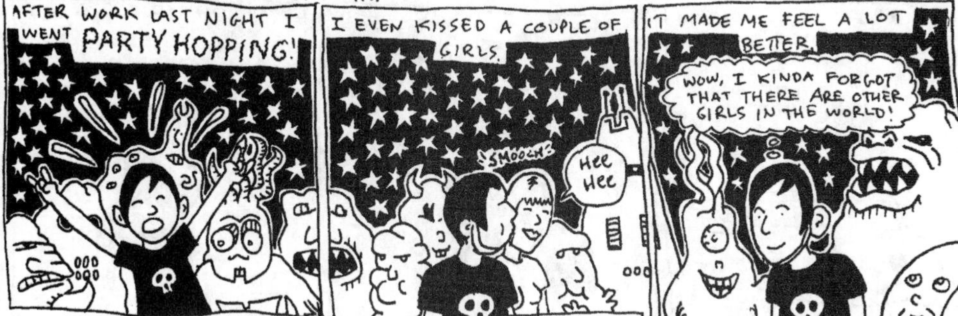
AFTER WORK LAST NIGHT I WENT PARTY HOPPING!
I EVEN KISSED A COUPLE OF GIRLS.
SMOOCH
HEE HEE
IT MADE ME FEEL A LOT BETTER.
WOW, I KINDA FORGOT THAT THERE ARE OTHER GIRLS IN THE WORLD!

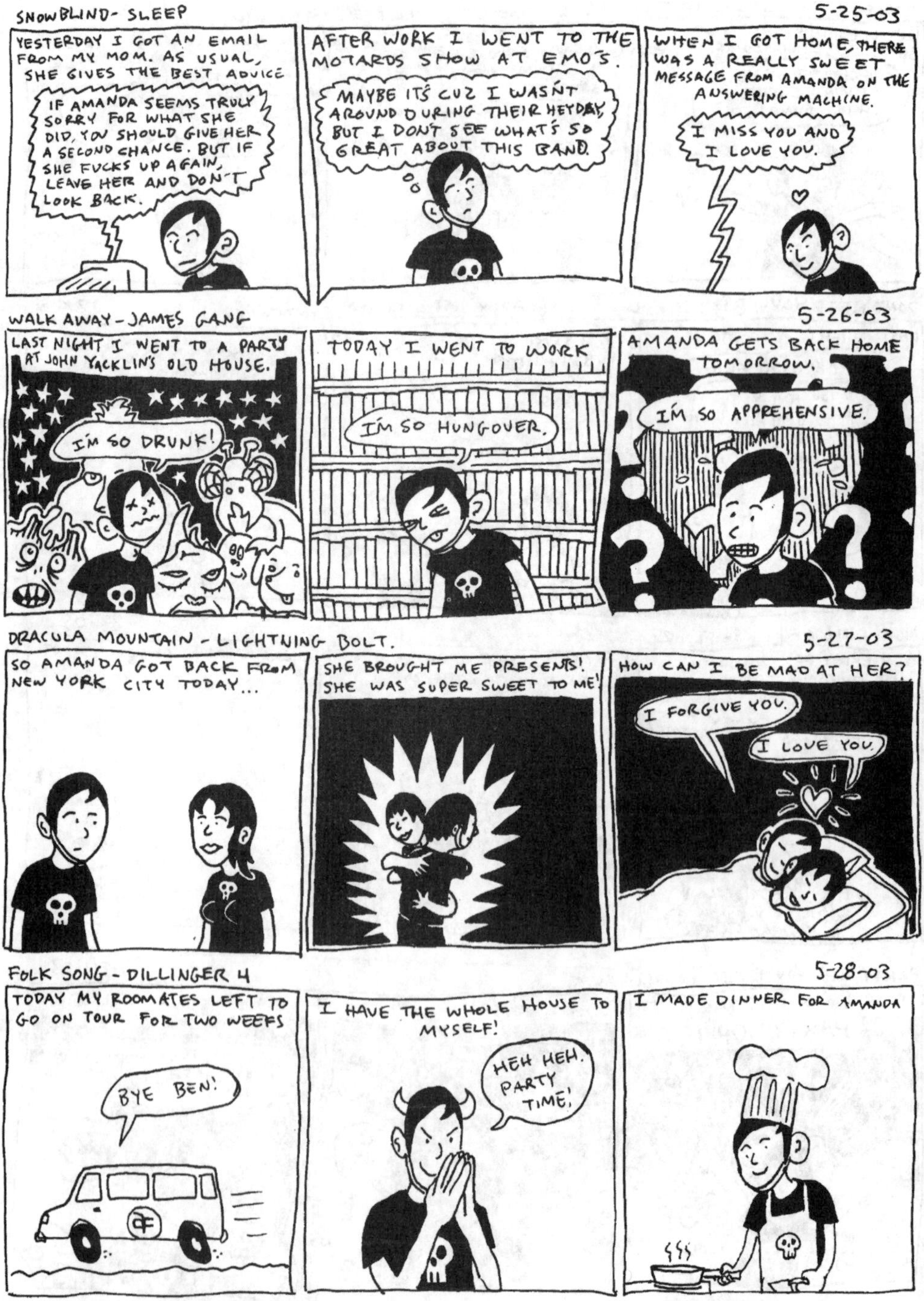
SNOWBLIND - SLEEP
5-25-03
YESTERDAY I GOT AN EMAIL FROM MY MOM. AS USUAL, SHE GIVES THE BEST ADVICE
IF AMANDA SEEMS TRULY SORRY FOR WHAT SHE DID, YOU SHOULD GIVE HER A SECOND CHANCE. BUT IF SHE FUCKS UP AGAIN, LEAVE HER AND DON'T LOOK BACK.
AFTER WORK I WENT TO THE MOTARDS SHOW AT EMO'S.
MAYBE IT'S CUZ I WASN'T AROUND DURING THEIR HEYDAY, BUT I DON'T SEE WHAT'S SO GREAT ABOUT THIS BAND.
WHEN I GOT HOME, THERE WAS A REALLY SWEET MESSAGE FROM AMANDA ON THE ANSWERING MACHINE.
I MISS YOU AND I LOVE YOU.
WALK AWAY - JAMES GANG
5-26-03
LAST NIGHT I WENT TO A PARTY AT JOHN YACKLIN'S OLD HOUSE.
I'M SO DRUNK!
TODAY I WENT TO WORK
I'M SO HUNGOVER.
AMANDA GETS BACK HOME TOMORROW.
I'M SO APPREHENSIVE.
DRACULA MOUNTAIN - LIGHTNING BOLT.
5-27-03
SO AMANDA GOT BACK FROM NEW YORK CITY TODAY...
SHE BROUGHT ME PRESENTS! SHE WAS SUPER SWEET TO ME!
HOW CAN I BE MAD AT HER?
I FORGIVE YOU.
I LOVE YOU.
FOLK SONG - DILLINGER 4
5-28-03
TODAY MY ROOMATES LEFT TO GO ON TOUR FOR TWO WEEKS
BYE BEN!
I HAVE THE WHOLE HOUSE TO MYSELF!
HEH HEH. PARTY TIME!
I MADE DINNER FOR AMANDA

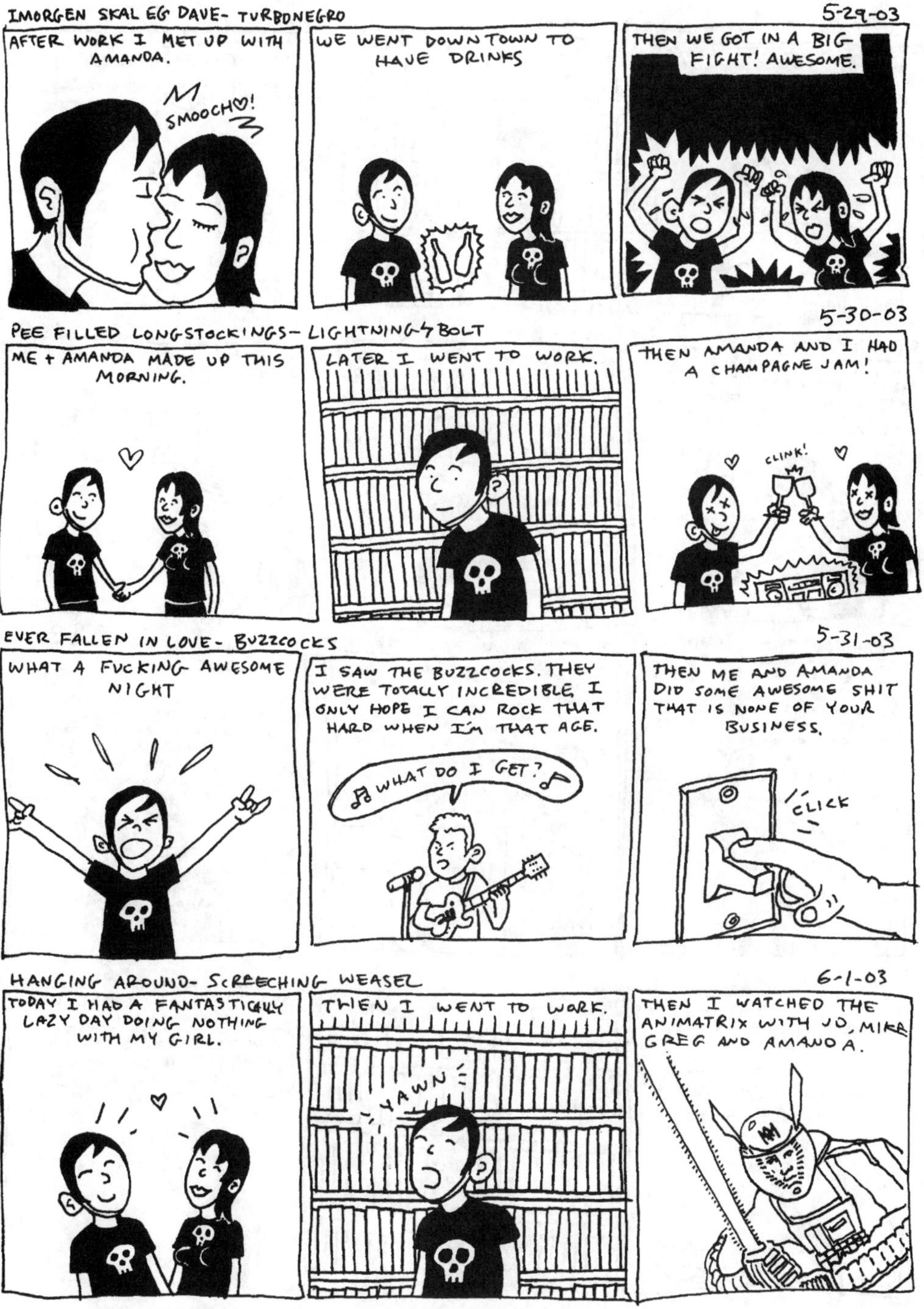
IMORGEN SKAL EG DAVE- TURBONEGRO
5-29-03
AFTER WORK I MET UP WITH AMANDA.
SMOOCH♡!
WE WENT DOWNTOWN TO HAVE DRINKS
THEN WE GOT IN A BIG FIGHT! AWESOME.
PEE FILLED LONGSTOCKINGS- LIGHTNING BOLT
5-30-03
ME + AMANDA MADE UP THIS MORNING.
LATER I WENT TO WORK.
THEN AMANDA AND I HAD A CHAMPAGNE JAM!
CLINK!
EVER FALLEN IN LOVE- BUZZCOCKS
5-31-03
WHAT A FUCKING AWESOME NIGHT
I SAW THE BUZZCOCKS. THEY WERE TOTALLY INCREDIBLE. I ONLY HOPE I CAN ROCK THAT HARD WHEN I'M THAT AGE.
♫ WHAT DO I GET? ♪
THEN ME AND AMANDA DID SOME AWESOME SHIT THAT IS NONE OF YOUR BUSINESS.
CLICK
HANGING AROUND- SCREECHING WEASEL
6-1-03
TODAY I HAD A FANTASTICALLY LAZY DAY DOING NOTHING WITH MY GIRL.
THEN I WENT TO WORK.
YAWN
THEN I WATCHED THE ANIMATRIX WITH JO, MIKE GREG AND AMANDA.

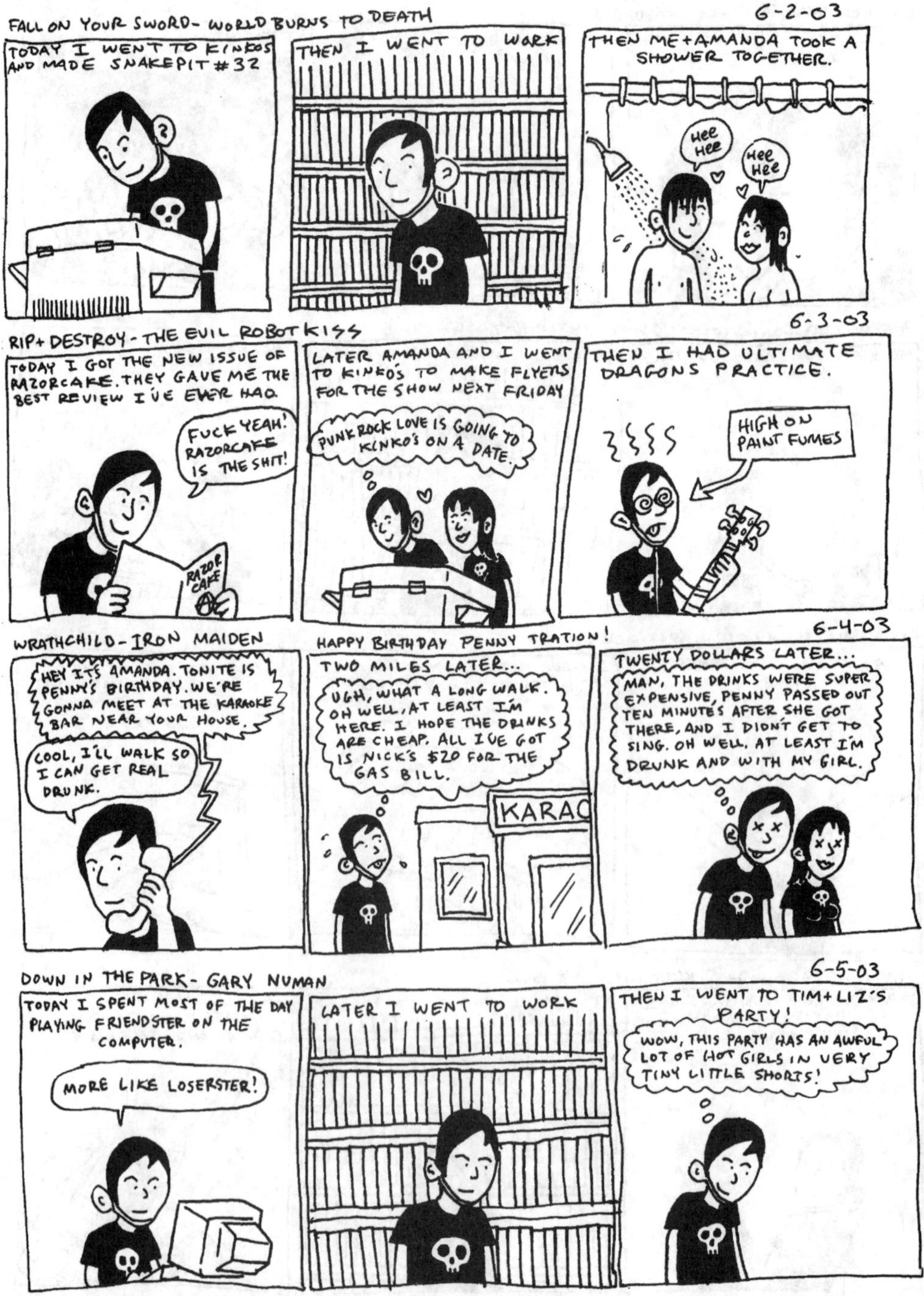
FALL ON YOUR SWORD- WORLD BURNS TO DEATH
6-2-03
TODAY I WENT TO KINKOS AND MADE SNAKEPIT #32
THEN I WENT TO WORK
THEN ME+AMANDA TOOK A SHOWER TOGETHER.
HEE HEE
HEE HEE
RIP+ DESTROY- THE EVIL ROBOT KISS
6-3-03
TODAY I GOT THE NEW ISSUE OF RAZORCAKE. THEY GAVE ME THE BEST REVIEW I'VE EVER HAD.
FUCK YEAH! RAZORCAKE IS THE SHIT!
RAZOR CAKE
LATER AMANDA AND I WENT TO KINKO'S TO MAKE FLYERS FOR THE SHOW NEXT FRIDAY
PUNK ROCK LOVE IS GOING TO KINKO'S ON A DATE.
THEN I HAD ULTIMATE DRAGONS PRACTICE.
HIGH ON PAINT FUMES
WRATHCHILD- IRON MAIDEN
HAPPY BIRTHDAY PENNY TRATION!
6-4-03
HEY IT'S AMANDA. TONITE IS PENNY'S BIRTHDAY. WE'RE GONNA MEET AT THE KARAOKE BAR NEAR YOUR HOUSE.
COOL, I'LL WALK SO I CAN GET REAL DRUNK.
TWO MILES LATER...
UGH, WHAT A LONG WALK. OH WELL, AT LEAST I'M HERE. I HOPE THE DRINKS ARE CHEAP. ALL I'VE GOT IS NICK'S $20 FOR THE GAS BILL.
KARAO
TWENTY DOLLARS LATER...
MAN, THE DRINKS WERE SUPER EXPENSIVE, PENNY PASSED OUT TEN MINUTES AFTER SHE GOT THERE, AND I DIDN'T GET TO SING. OH WELL, AT LEAST I'M DRUNK AND WITH MY GIRL.
DOWN IN THE PARK- GARY NUMAN
6-5-03
TODAY I SPENT MOST OF THE DAY PLAYING FRIENDSTER ON THE COMPUTER.
MORE LIKE LOSERSTER!
LATER I WENT TO WORK
THEN I WENT TO TIM+LIZ'S PARTY!
WOW, THIS PARTY HAS AN AWFUL LOT OF HOT GIRLS IN VERY TINY LITTLE SHORTS!

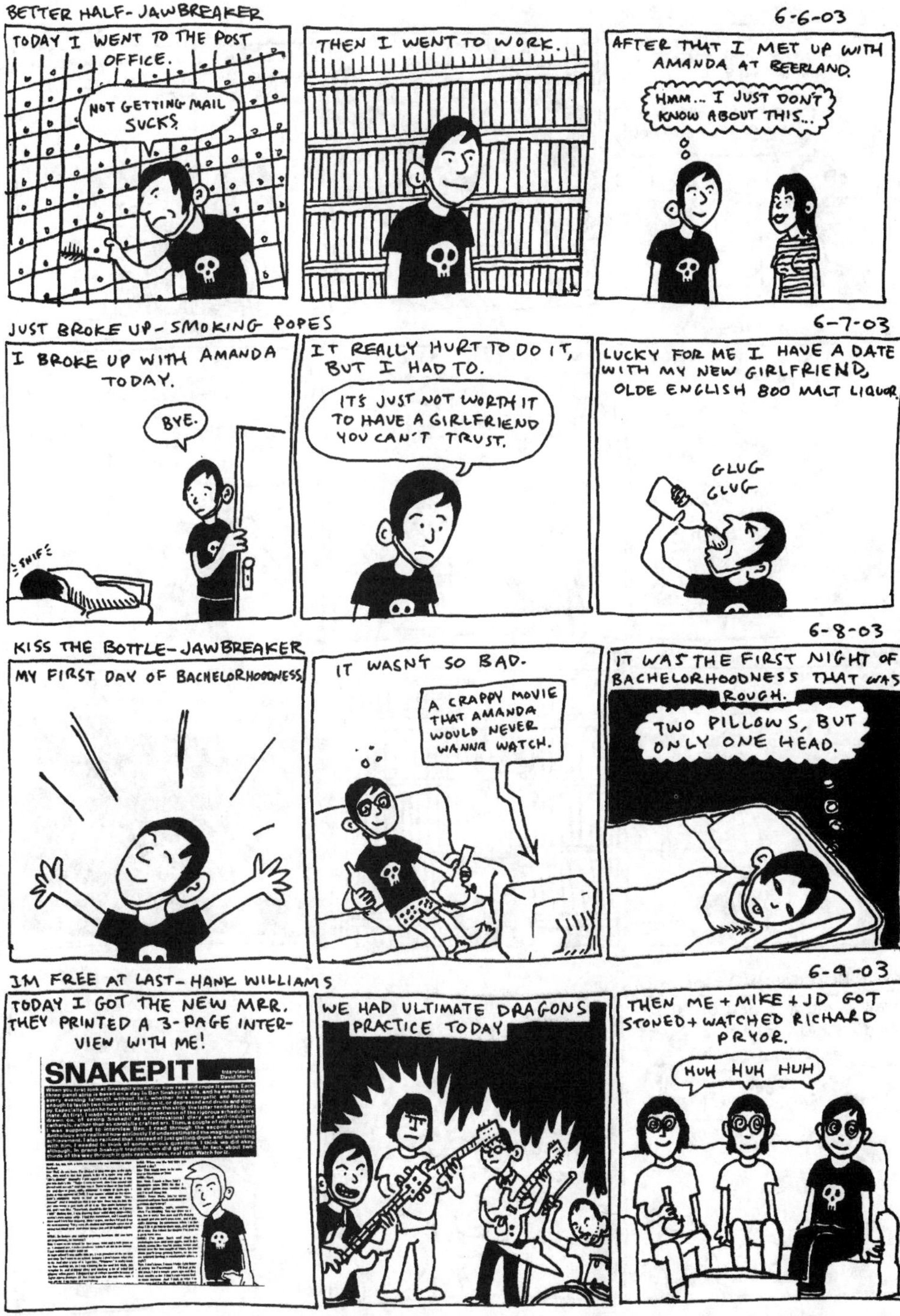
BETTER HALF- JAWBREAKER
6-6-03
TODAY I WENT TO THE POST OFFICE.
NOT GETTING MAIL SUCKS.
THEN I WENT TO WORK.
AFTER THAT I MET UP WITH AMANDA AT BEERLAND.
HMM... I JUST DON'T KNOW ABOUT THIS...
JUST BROKE UP- SMOKING POPES
6-7-03
I BROKE UP WITH AMANDA TODAY.
BYE.
SNIF
IT REALLY HURT TO DO IT, BUT I HAD TO.
IT'S JUST NOT WORTH IT TO HAVE A GIRLFRIEND YOU CAN'T TRUST.
LUCKY FOR ME I HAVE A DATE WITH MY NEW GIRLFRIEND, OLDE ENGLISH 800 MALT LIQUOR.
GLUG GLUG
6-8-03
KISS THE BOTTLE- JAWBREAKER
MY FIRST DAY OF BACHELORHOODNESS.
IT WASN'T SO BAD.
A CRAPPY MOVIE THAT AMANDA WOULD NEVER WANNA WATCH.
IT WAS THE FIRST NIGHT OF BACHELORHOODNESS THAT WAS ROUGH.
TWO PILLOWS, BUT ONLY ONE HEAD.
I'M FREE AT LAST- HANK WILLIAMS
6-9-03
TODAY I GOT THE NEW MRR. THEY PRINTED A 3-PAGE INTERVIEW WITH ME!
SNAKEPIT
WE HAD ULTIMATE DRAGONS PRACTICE TODAY
THEN ME + MIKE + JD GOT STONED + WATCHED RICHARD PRYOR.
HUH HUH HUH

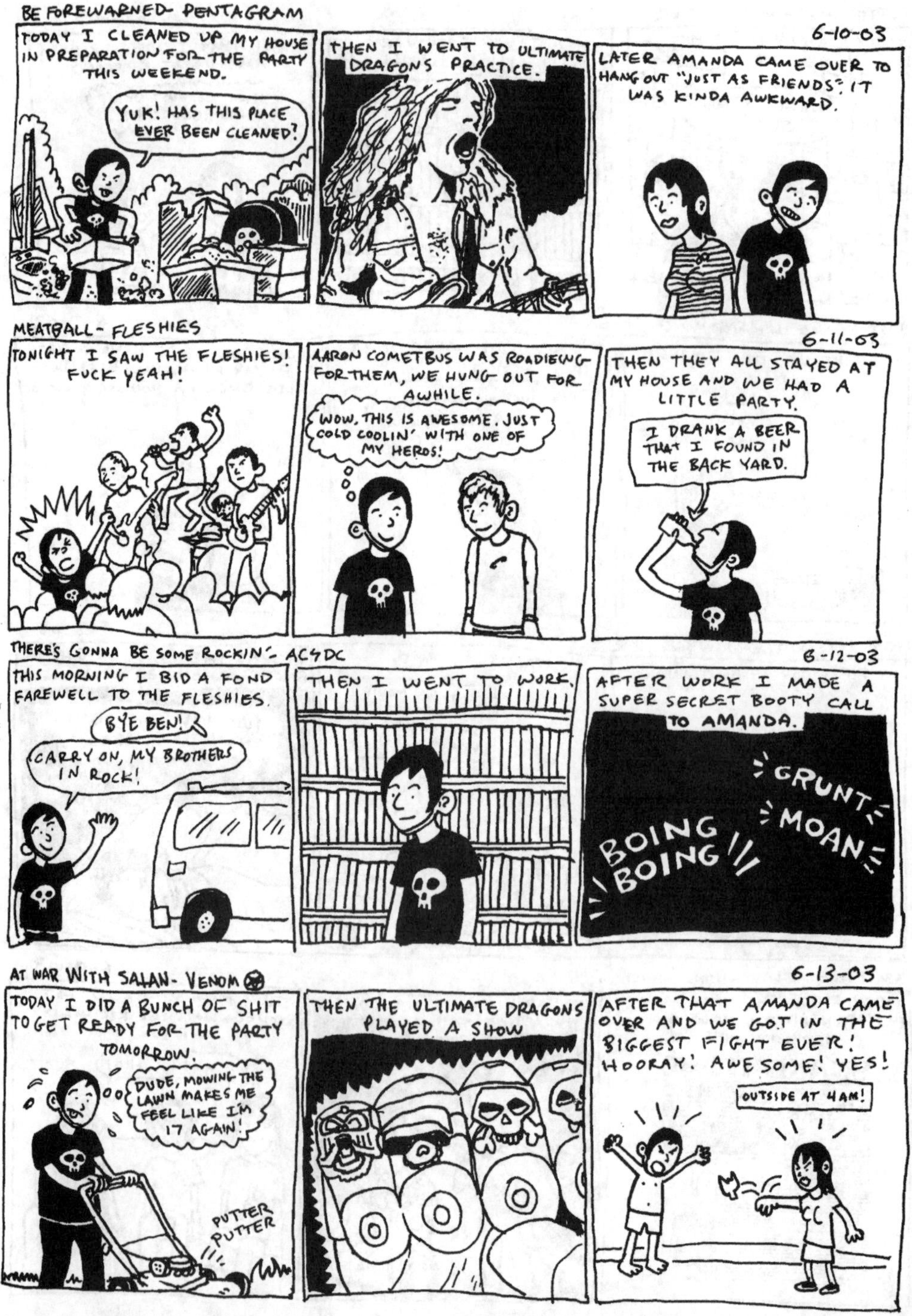
BE FOREWARNED- PENTAGRAM
6-10-03
TODAY I CLEANED UP MY HOUSE IN PREPARATION FOR THE PARTY THIS WEEKEND.
YUK! HAS THIS PLACE EVER BEEN CLEANED?
THEN I WENT TO ULTIMATE DRAGONS PRACTICE.
LATER AMANDA CAME OVER TO HANG OUT "JUST AS FRIENDS." IT WAS KINDA AWKWARD.
MEATBALL- FLESHIES
6-11-03
TONIGHT I SAW THE FLESHIES! FUCK YEAH!
AARON COMETBUS WAS ROADIEING FOR THEM, WE HUNG OUT FOR AWHILE.
WOW, THIS IS AWESOME. JUST COLD COOLIN' WITH ONE OF MY HEROS!
THEN THEY ALL STAYED AT MY HOUSE AND WE HAD A LITTLE PARTY.
I DRANK A BEER THAT I FOUND IN THE BACK YARD.
THERE'S GONNA BE SOME ROCKIN'- AC/DC
6-12-03
THIS MORNING I BID A FOND FAREWELL TO THE FLESHIES.
BYE BEN!
CARRY ON, MY BROTHERS IN ROCK!
THEN I WENT TO WORK.
AFTER WORK I MADE A SUPER SECRET BOOTY CALL TO AMANDA.
GRUNT
MOAN
BOING BOING
AT WAR WITH SATAN- VENOM
6-13-03
TODAY I DID A BUNCH OF SHIT TO GET READY FOR THE PARTY TOMORROW.
DUDE, MOWING THE LAWN MAKES ME FEEL LIKE I'M 17 AGAIN!
PUTTER PUTTER
THEN THE ULTIMATE DRAGONS PLAYED A SHOW
AFTER THAT AMANDA CAME OVER AND WE GOT IN THE BIGGEST FIGHT EVER! HOORAY! AWESOME! YES!
OUTSIDE AT 4AM!

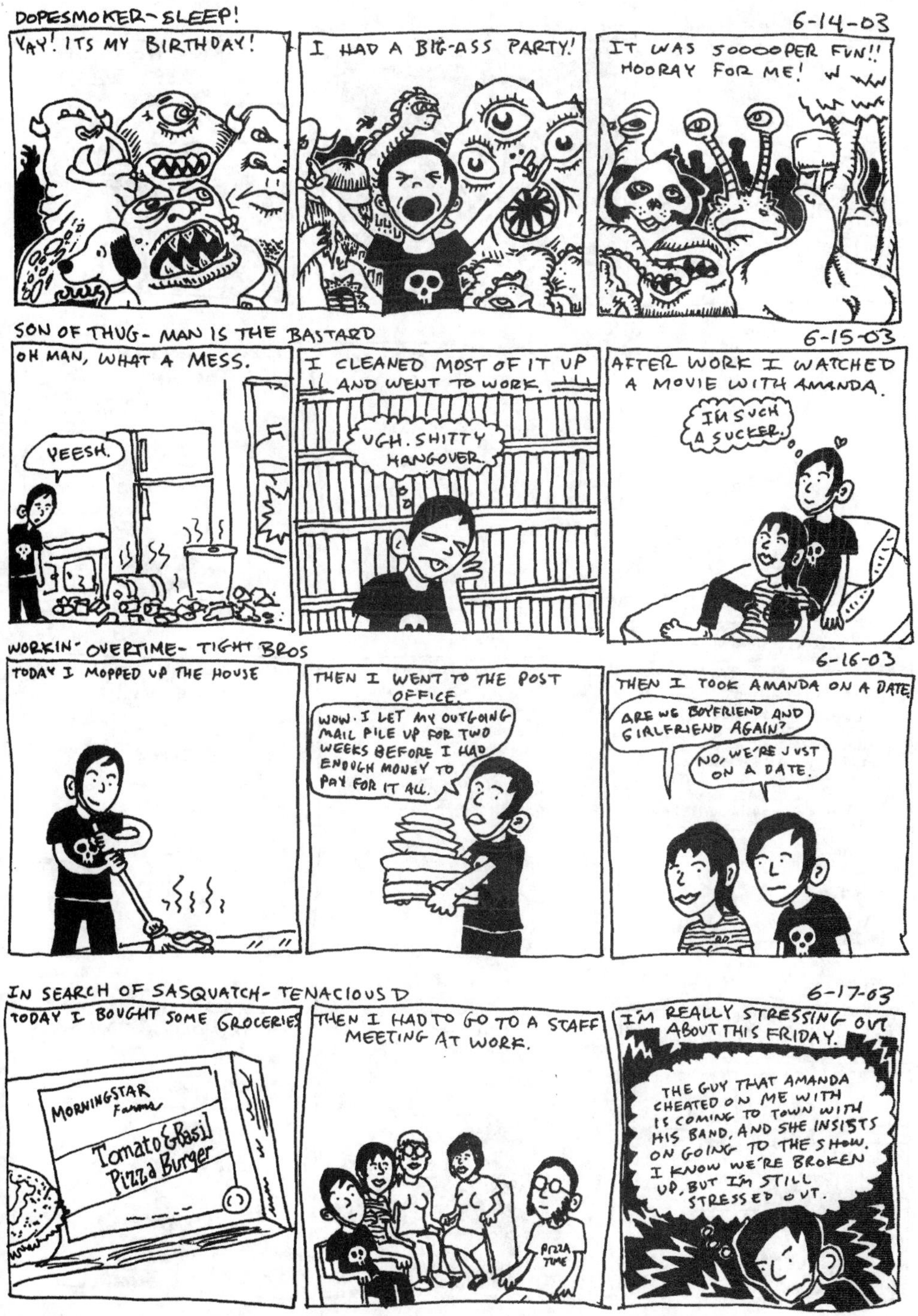
DOPESMOKER- SLEEP!
6-14-03
YAY! ITS MY BIRTHDAY!
I HAD A BIG-ASS PARTY!
IT WAS SOOOOPER FUN!! HOORAY FOR ME!
SON OF THUG- MAN IS THE BASTARD
6-15-03
OH MAN, WHAT A MESS.
YEESH.
I CLEANED MOST OF IT UP AND WENT TO WORK.
UGH. SHITTY HANGOVER.
AFTER WORK I WATCHED A MOVIE WITH AMANDA.
I'M SUCH A SUCKER.
WORKIN' OVERTIME- TIGHT BROS
6-16-03
TODAY I MOPPED UP THE HOUSE
THEN I WENT TO THE POST OFFICE.
WOW. I LET MY OUTGOING MAIL PILE UP FOR TWO WEEKS BEFORE I HAD ENOUGH MONEY TO PAY FOR IT ALL.
THEN I TOOK AMANDA ON A DATE.
ARE WE BOYFRIEND AND GIRLFRIEND AGAIN?
NO, WE'RE JUST ON A DATE.
IN SEARCH OF SASQUATCH- TENACIOUS D
6-17-03
TODAY I BOUGHT SOME GROCERIES
MORNINGSTAR Farms
Tomato & Basil Pizza Burger
THEN I HAD TO GO TO A STAFF MEETING AT WORK.
PIZZA TIME
I'M REALLY STRESSING OUT ABOUT THIS FRIDAY.
THE GUY THAT AMANDA CHEATED ON ME WITH IS COMING TO TOWN WITH HIS BAND, AND SHE INSISTS ON GOING TO THE SHOW. I KNOW WE'RE BROKEN UP, BUT I'M STILL STRESSED OUT.

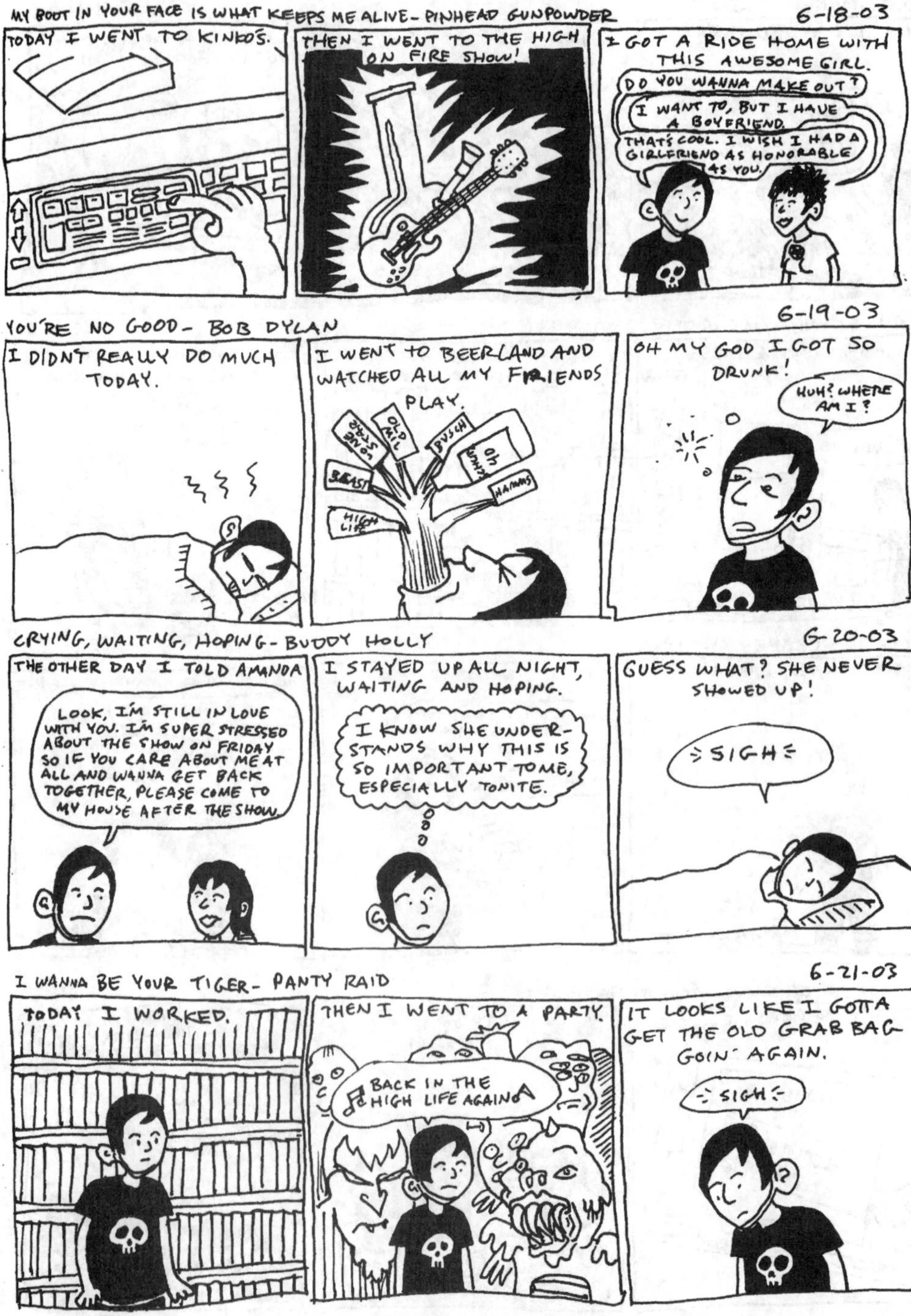
MY BOOT IN YOUR FACE IS WHAT KEEPS ME ALIVE- PINHEAD GUNPOWDER
6-18-03
TODAY I WENT TO KINKO'S.
THEN I WENT TO THE HIGH ON FIRE SHOW!
I GOT A RIDE HOME WITH THIS AWESOME GIRL.
DO YOU WANNA MAKE OUT?
I WANT TO, BUT I HAVE A BOYFRIEND.
THAT'S COOL. I WISH I HAD A GIRLFRIEND AS HONORABLE AS YOU.
YOU'RE NO GOOD- BOB DYLAN
6-19-03
I DIDN'T REALLY DO MUCH TODAY.
I WENT TO BEERLAND AND WATCHED ALL MY FRIENDS PLAY.
LONE STAR
OLD MIL
BUSCH
BEAST
HAMMS
HIGH LIFE
OH MY GOD I GOT SO DRUNK!
HUH? WHERE AM I?
CRYING, WAITING, HOPING- BUDDY HOLLY
6-20-03
THE OTHER DAY I TOLD AMANDA
LOOK, I'M STILL IN LOVE WITH YOU. I'M SUPER STRESSED ABOUT THE SHOW ON FRIDAY SO IF YOU CARE ABOUT ME AT ALL AND WANNA GET BACK TOGETHER, PLEASE COME TO MY HOUSE AFTER THE SHOW.
I STAYED UP ALL NIGHT, WAITING AND HOPING.
I KNOW SHE UNDERSTANDS WHY THIS IS SO IMPORTANT TO ME, ESPECIALLY TONITE.
GUESS WHAT? SHE NEVER SHOWED UP!
SIGH
I WANNA BE YOUR TIGER- PANTY RAID
6-21-03
TODAY I WORKED.
THEN I WENT TO A PARTY.
BACK IN THE HIGH LIFE AGAIN
IT LOOKS LIKE I GOTTA GET THE OLD GRAB BAG GOIN' AGAIN.
SIGH

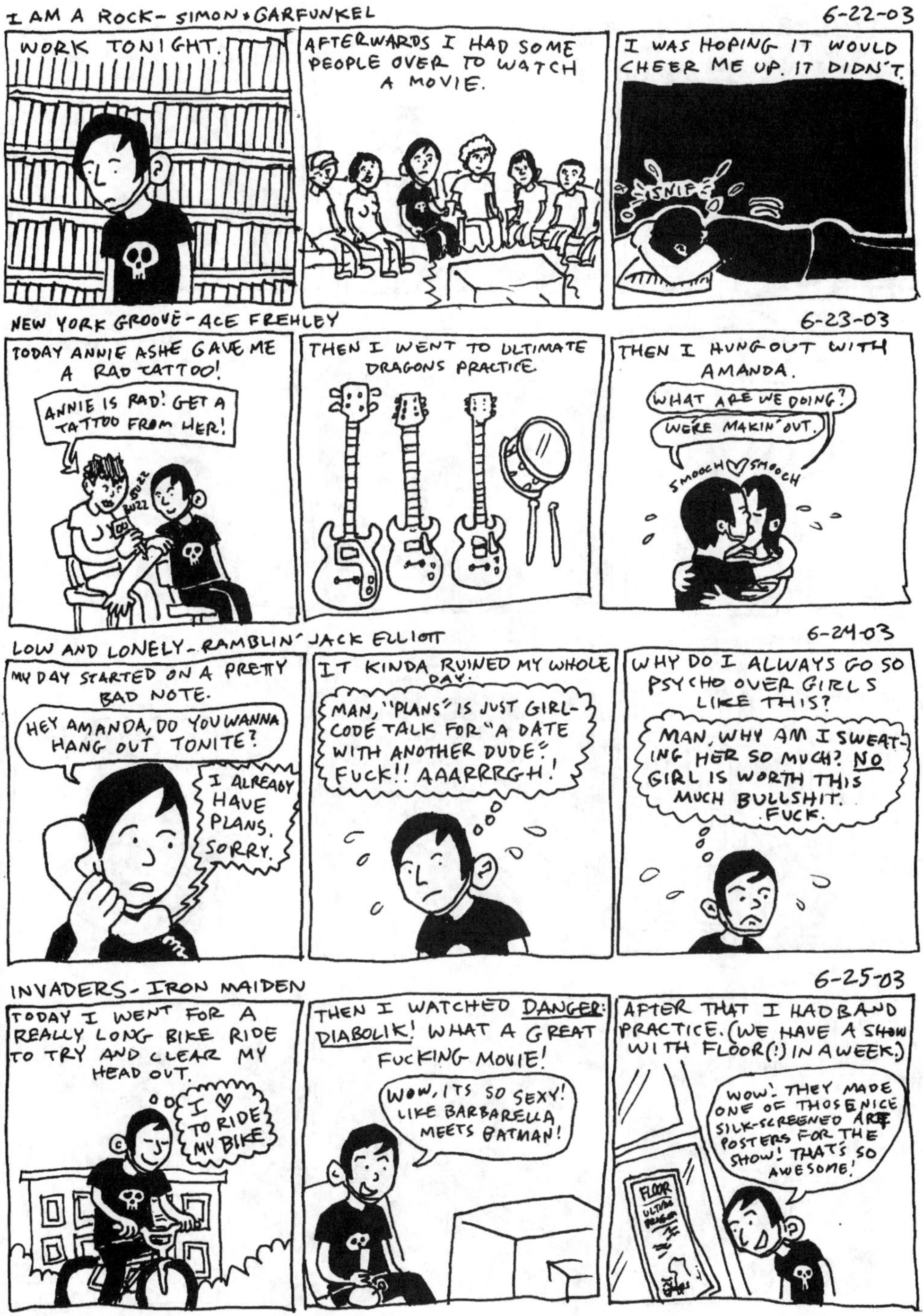
I AM A ROCK - SIMON + GARFUNKEL
6-22-03
WORK TONIGHT.
AFTERWARDS I HAD SOME PEOPLE OVER TO WATCH A MOVIE.
I WAS HOPING IT WOULD CHEER ME UP. IT DIDN'T.
SNIF
NEW YORK GROOVE - ACE FREHLEY
6-23-03
TODAY ANNIE ASHE GAVE ME A RAD TATTOO!
ANNIE IS RAD! GET A TATTOO FROM HER!
BUZZ BUZZ
THEN I WENT TO ULTIMATE DRAGONS PRACTICE.
THEN I HUNG OUT WITH AMANDA.
WHAT ARE WE DOING?
WE'RE MAKIN' OUT.
SMOOCH SMOOCH
LOW AND LONELY - RAMBLIN' JACK ELLIOTT
6-24-03
MY DAY STARTED ON A PRETTY BAD NOTE.
HEY AMANDA, DO YOU WANNA HANG OUT TONITE?
I ALREADY HAVE PLANS. SORRY.
IT KINDA RUINED MY WHOLE DAY.
MAN, "PLANS" IS JUST GIRL-CODE TALK FOR "A DATE WITH ANOTHER DUDE". FUCK!! AAARRRGH!
WHY DO I ALWAYS GO SO PSYCHO OVER GIRLS LIKE THIS?
MAN, WHY AM I SWEATING HER SO MUCH? NO GIRL IS WORTH THIS MUCH BULLSHIT. FUCK.
INVADERS - IRON MAIDEN
6-25-03
TODAY I WENT FOR A REALLY LONG BIKE RIDE TO TRY AND CLEAR MY HEAD OUT.
I ♥ TO RIDE MY BIKE
THEN I WATCHED DANGER: DIABOLIK! WHAT A GREAT FUCKING MOVIE!
WOW, ITS SO SEXY! LIKE BARBARELLA MEETS BATMAN!
AFTER THAT I HAD BAND PRACTICE. (WE HAVE A SHOW WITH FLOOR(!) IN A WEEK.)
WOW! THEY MADE ONE OF THOSE NICE SILK-SCREENED ART POSTERS FOR THE SHOW! THAT'S SO AWESOME!
FLOOR
ULTIMATE DRAGONS

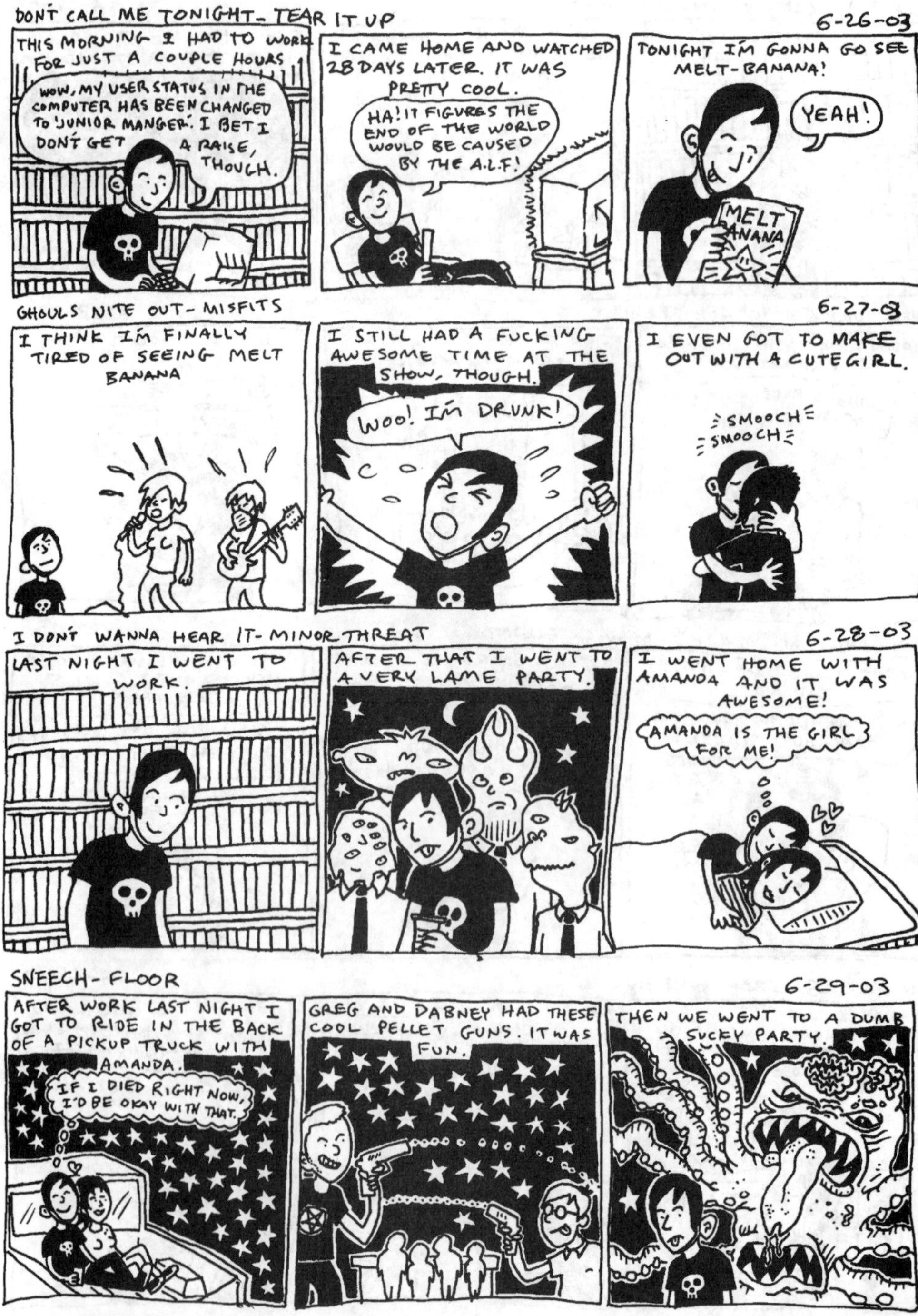
DON'T CALL ME TONIGHT - TEAR IT UP
6-26-03
THIS MORNING I HAD TO WORK FOR JUST A COUPLE HOURS
WOW, MY USER STATUS IN THE COMPUTER HAS BEEN CHANGED TO 'JUNIOR MANGER'. I BET I DON'T GET A RAISE, THOUGH.
I CAME HOME AND WATCHED 28 DAYS LATER. IT WAS PRETTY COOL.
HA! IT FIGURES THE END OF THE WORLD WOULD BE CAUSED BY THE A.L.F!
TONIGHT I'M GONNA GO SEE MELT-BANANA!
YEAH!
MELT BANANA
GHOULS NITE OUT - MISFITS
6-27-03
I THINK I'M FINALLY TIRED OF SEEING MELT BANANA
I STILL HAD A FUCKING AWESOME TIME AT THE SHOW, THOUGH.
WOO! I'M DRUNK!
I EVEN GOT TO MAKE OUT WITH A CUTE GIRL.
SMOOCH
SMOOCH
I DON'T WANNA HEAR IT - MINOR THREAT
6-28-03
LAST NIGHT I WENT TO WORK.
AFTER THAT I WENT TO A VERY LAME PARTY.
I WENT HOME WITH AMANDA AND IT WAS AWESOME!
AMANDA IS THE GIRL FOR ME!
SNEECH - FLOOR
6-29-03
AFTER WORK LAST NIGHT I GOT TO RIDE IN THE BACK OF A PICKUP TRUCK WITH AMANDA.
IF I DIED RIGHT NOW, I'D BE OKAY WITH THAT.
GREG AND DABNEY HAD THESE COOL PELLET GUNS. IT WAS FUN.
THEN WE WENT TO A DUMB SUCKY PARTY.

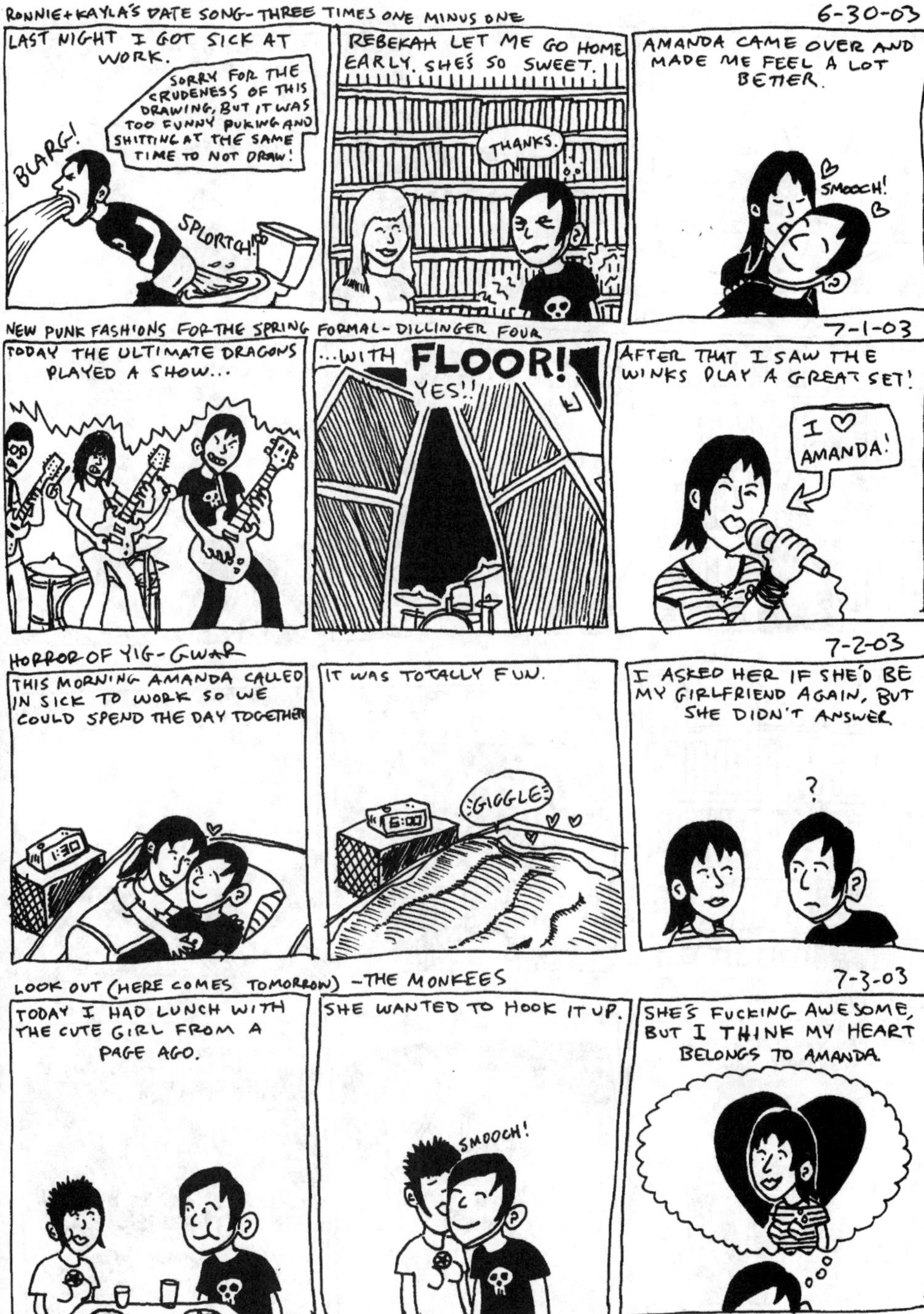
RONNIE+KAYLA'S DATE SONG - THREE TIMES ONE MINUS ONE
6-30-03
LAST NIGHT I GOT SICK AT WORK.
SORRY FOR THE CRUDENESS OF THIS DRAWING, BUT IT WAS TOO FUNNY PUKING AND SHITTING AT THE SAME TIME TO NOT DRAW!
BLARG!
SPLORTCH!
REBEKAH LET ME GO HOME EARLY. SHE'S SO SWEET.
THANKS.
AMANDA CAME OVER AND MADE ME FEEL A LOT BETTER.
SMOOCH!
NEW PUNK FASHIONS FOR THE SPRING FORMAL - DILLINGER FOUR
7-1-03
TODAY THE ULTIMATE DRAGONS PLAYED A SHOW...
...WITH FLOOR!
YES!!
AFTER THAT I SAW THE WINKS PLAY A GREAT SET!
I ♡ AMANDA!
HORROR OF YIG-GWAR
7-2-03
THIS MORNING AMANDA CALLED IN SICK TO WORK SO WE COULD SPEND THE DAY TOGETHER
1:30
IT WAS TOTALLY FUN.
6:00
GIGGLE
I ASKED HER IF SHE'D BE MY GIRLFRIEND AGAIN, BUT SHE DIDN'T ANSWER.
?
LOOK OUT (HERE COMES TOMORROW) - THE MONKEES
7-3-03
TODAY I HAD LUNCH WITH THE CUTE GIRL FROM A PAGE AGO.
SHE WANTED TO HOOK IT UP.
SMOOCH!
SHE'S FUCKING AWESOME, BUT I THINK MY HEART BELONGS TO AMANDA.

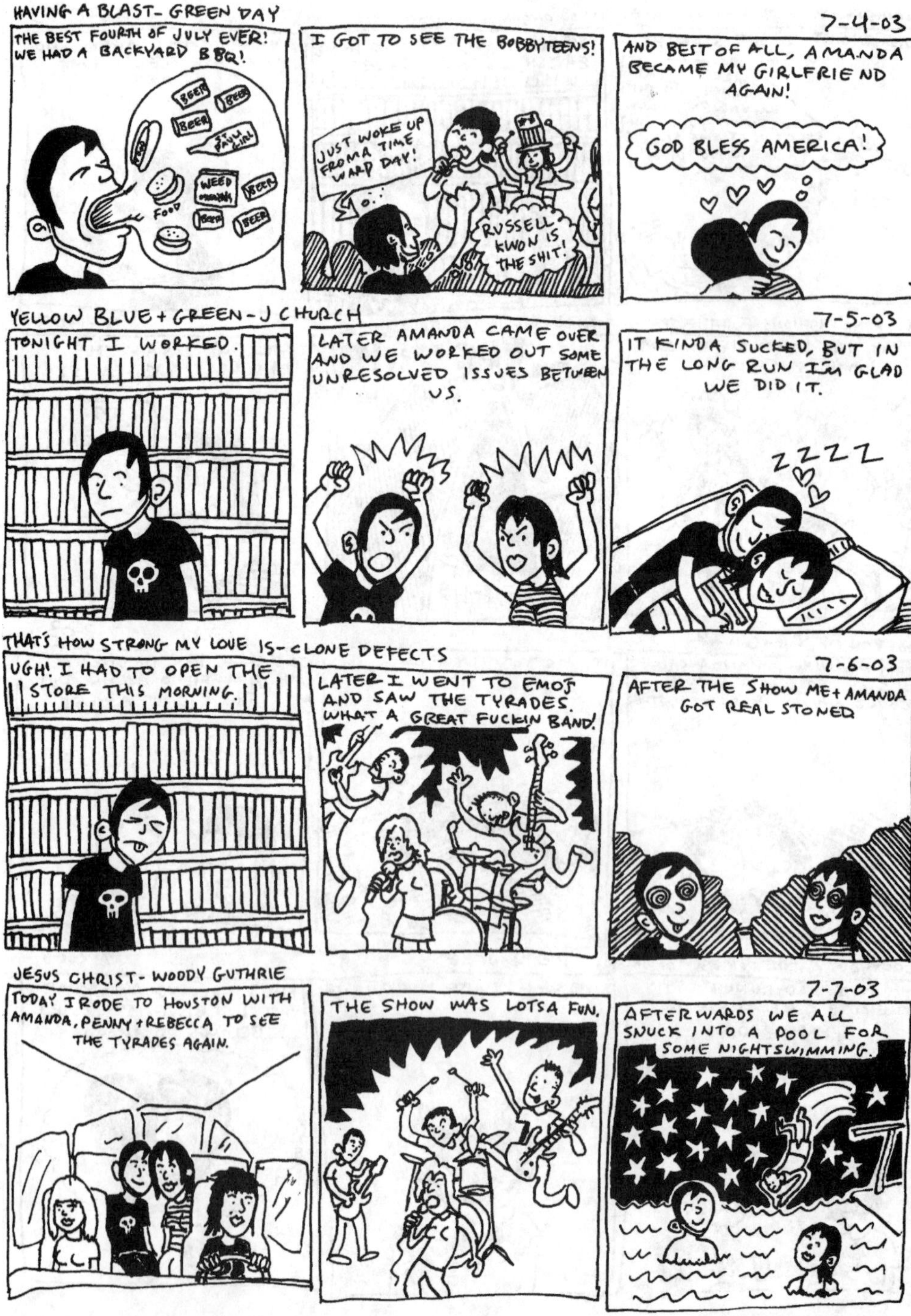

HAVING A BLAST- GREEN DAY
7-4-03
THE BEST FOURTH OF JULY EVER! WE HAD A BACKYARD BBQ!
BEER
BEER
BEER
BEER
BEER
ST PAULI GIRL
WEED
FOOD
I GOT TO SEE THE BOBBYTEENS!
JUST WOKE UP FROM A TIME WARP DAY!
RUSSELL KWON IS THE SHIT!
AND BEST OF ALL, AMANDA BECAME MY GIRLFRIEND AGAIN!
GOD BLESS AMERICA!
YELLOW BLUE + GREEN - J CHURCH
7-5-03
TONIGHT I WORKED.
LATER AMANDA CAME OVER AND WE WORKED OUT SOME UNRESOLVED ISSUES BETWEEN US.
IT KINDA SUCKED, BUT IN THE LONG RUN I'M GLAD WE DID IT.
ZZZZ
THAT'S HOW STRONG MY LOVE IS - CLONE DEFECTS
7-6-03
UGH! I HAD TO OPEN THE STORE THIS MORNING.
LATER I WENT TO EMO'S AND SAW THE TYRADES. WHAT A GREAT FUCKIN BAND!
AFTER THE SHOW ME + AMANDA GOT REAL STONED
JESUS CHRIST - WOODY GUTHRIE
7-7-03
TODAY I RODE TO HOUSTON WITH AMANDA, PENNY + REBECCA TO SEE THE TYRADES AGAIN.
THE SHOW WAS LOTSA FUN.
AFTERWARDS WE ALL SNUCK INTO A POOL FOR SOME NIGHTSWIMMING.

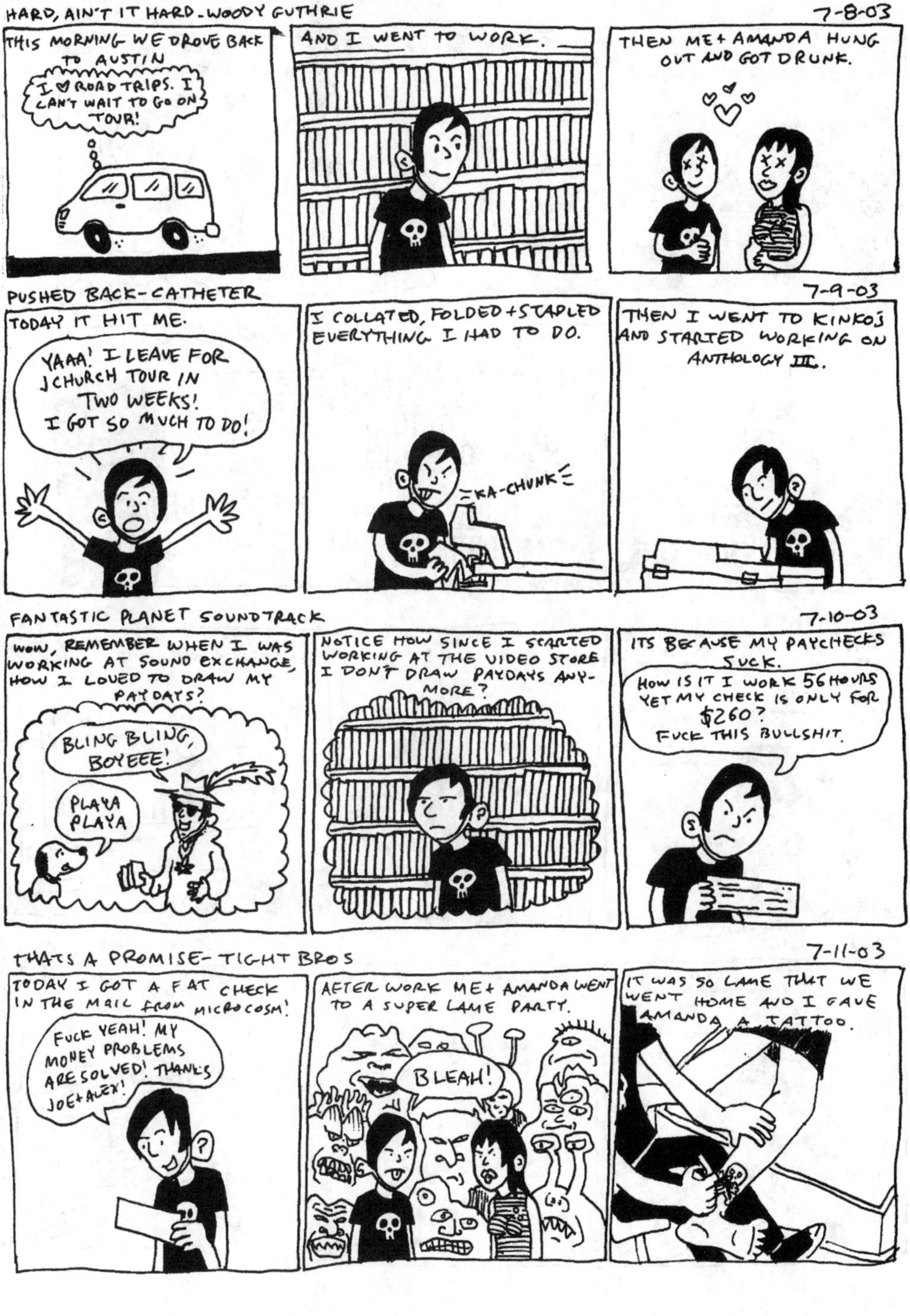
HARD, AIN'T IT HARD - WOODY GUTHRIE
7-8-03
THIS MORNING WE DROVE BACK TO AUSTIN
I ♥ ROAD TRIPS. I CAN'T WAIT TO GO ON TOUR!
AND I WENT TO WORK.
THEN ME + AMANDA HUNG OUT AND GOT DRUNK.
PUSHED BACK - CATHETER
7-9-03
TODAY IT HIT ME.
YAAA! I LEAVE FOR J CHURCH TOUR IN TWO WEEKS! I GOT SO MUCH TO DO!
I COLLATED, FOLDED + STAPLED EVERYTHING I HAD TO DO.
KA-CHUNK
THEN I WENT TO KINKO'S AND STARTED WORKING ON ANTHOLOGY III.
FANTASTIC PLANET SOUNDTRACK
7-10-03
WOW, REMEMBER WHEN I WAS WORKING AT SOUND EXCHANGE, HOW I LOVED TO DRAW MY PAYDAYS?
BLING BLING, BOYEEE!
PLAYA PLAYA
NOTICE HOW SINCE I STARTED WORKING AT THE VIDEO STORE I DON'T DRAW PAYDAYS ANYMORE?
ITS BECAUSE MY PAYCHECKS SUCK.
HOW IS IT I WORK 56 HOURS YET MY CHECK IS ONLY FOR $260? FUCK THIS BULLSHIT.
THATS A PROMISE - TIGHT BROS
7-11-03
TODAY I GOT A FAT CHECK IN THE MAIL FROM MICROCOSM!
FUCK YEAH! MY MONEY PROBLEMS ARE SOLVED! THANKS JOE + ALEX!
AFTER WORK ME + AMANDA WENT TO A SUPER LAME PARTY.
BLEAH!
IT WAS SO LAME THAT WE WENT HOME AND I GAVE AMANDA A TATTOO.

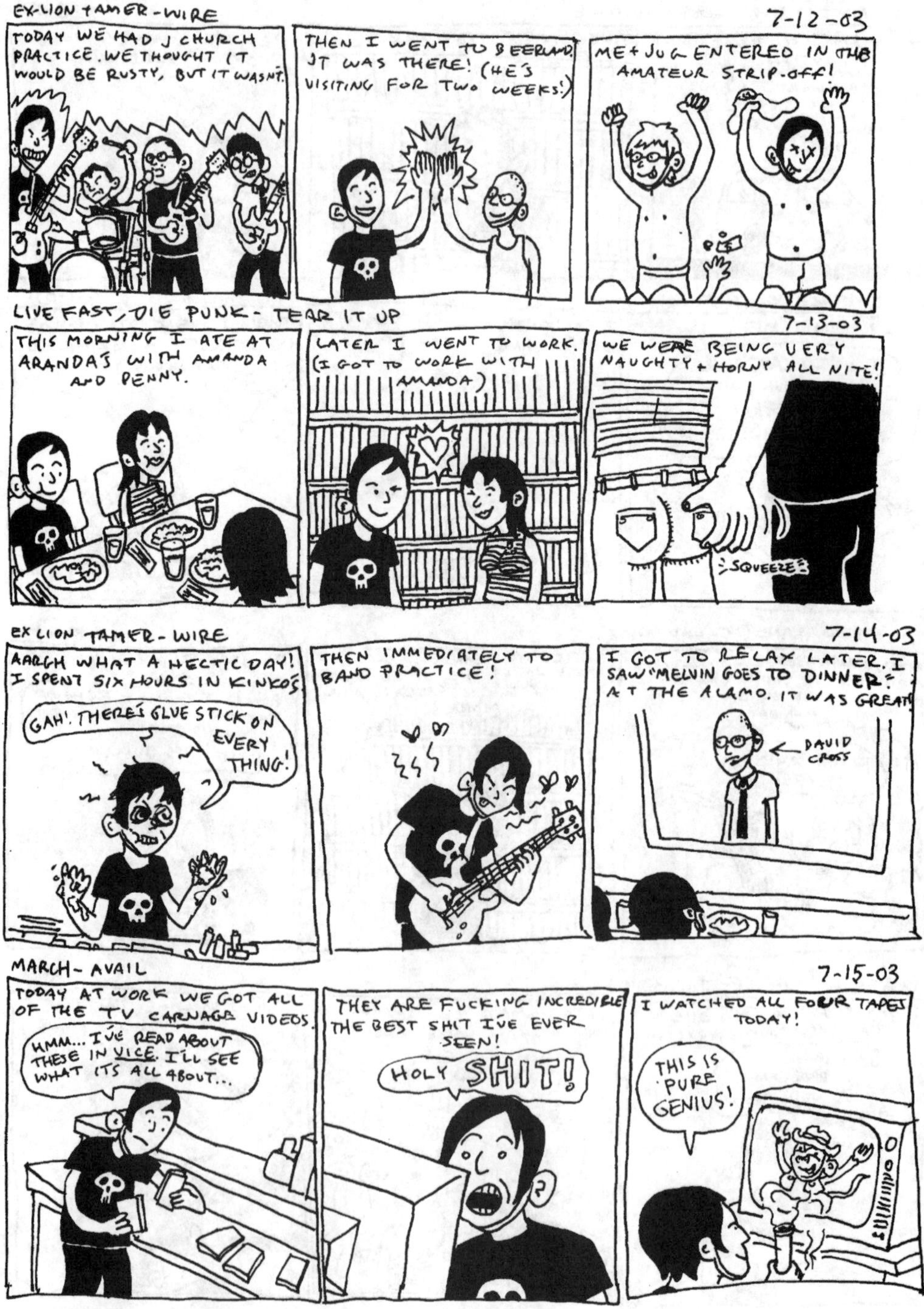
EX-LION TAMER - WIRE
7-12-03
TODAY WE HAD J CHURCH PRACTICE. WE THOUGHT IT WOULD BE RUSTY, BUT IT WASN'T.
THEN I WENT TO BEERLAND. JT WAS THERE! (HE'S VISITING FOR TWO WEEKS!)
ME + JUG ENTERED IN THE AMATEUR STRIP-OFF!
LIVE FAST, DIE PUNK - TEAR IT UP
7-13-03
THIS MORNING I ATE AT ARANDA'S WITH AMANDA AND PENNY.
LATER I WENT TO WORK. (I GOT TO WORK WITH AMANDA)
WE WERE BEING VERY NAUGHTY + HORNY ALL NITE!
SQUEEZE
EX LION TAMER - WIRE
7-14-03
AARGH WHAT A HECTIC DAY! I SPENT SIX HOURS IN KINKO'S.
GAH! THERE'S GLUE STICK ON EVERY THING!
THEN IMMEDIATELY TO BAND PRACTICE!
I GOT TO RELAX LATER. I SAW "MELVIN GOES TO DINNER" AT THE ALAMO. IT WAS GREAT!
DAVID CROSS
MARCH - AVAIL
7-15-03
TODAY AT WORK WE GOT ALL OF THE TV CARNAGE VIDEOS.
HMM... I'VE READ ABOUT THESE IN VICE. I'LL SEE WHAT ITS ALL ABOUT...
THEY ARE FUCKING INCREDIBLE THE BEST SHIT I'VE EVER SEEN!
HOLY SHIT!
I WATCHED ALL FOUR TAPES TODAY!
THIS IS PURE GENIUS!

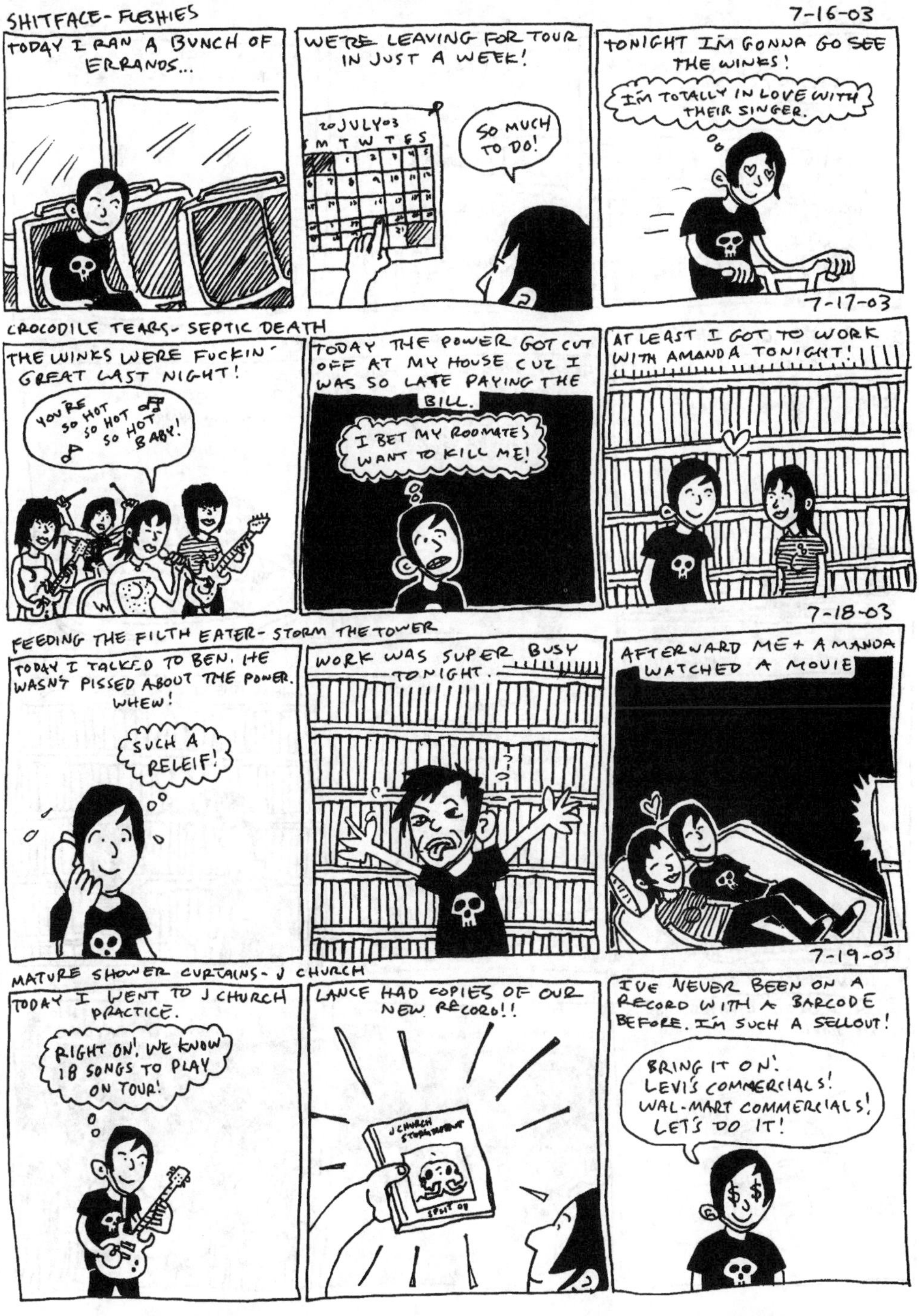

SHITFACE- FLESHIES
7-16-03
TODAY I RAN A BUNCH OF ERRANDS...
WE'RE LEAVING FOR TOUR IN JUST A WEEK!
JULY 03
SO MUCH TO DO!
TONIGHT I'M GONNA GO SEE THE WINKS!
I'M TOTALLY IN LOVE WITH THEIR SINGER.
7-17-03
CROCODILE TEARS- SEPTIC DEATH
THE WINKS WERE FUCKIN' GREAT LAST NIGHT!
YOU'RE SO HOT SO HOT SO HOT BABY!
TODAY THE POWER GOT CUT OFF AT MY HOUSE CUZ I WAS SO LATE PAYING THE BILL.
I BET MY ROOMATES WANT TO KILL ME!
AT LEAST I GOT TO WORK WITH AMANDA TONIGHT!
7-18-03
FEEDING THE FILTH EATER- STORM THE TOWER
TODAY I TALKED TO BEN. HE WASN'T PISSED ABOUT THE POWER. WHEW!
SUCH A RELEIF!
WORK WAS SUPER BUSY TONIGHT.
AFTERWARD ME + AMANDA WATCHED A MOVIE
7-19-03
MATURE SHOWER CURTAINS- J CHURCH
TODAY I WENT TO J CHURCH PRACTICE.
RIGHT ON! WE KNOW 18 SONGS TO PLAY ON TOUR!
LANCE HAD COPIES OF OUR NEW RECORD!!
J CHURCH
I'VE NEVER BEEN ON A RECORD WITH A BARCODE BEFORE. I'M SUCH A SELLOUT!
BRING IT ON! LEVI'S COMMERCIALS! WAL-MART COMMERCIALS! LET'S DO IT!

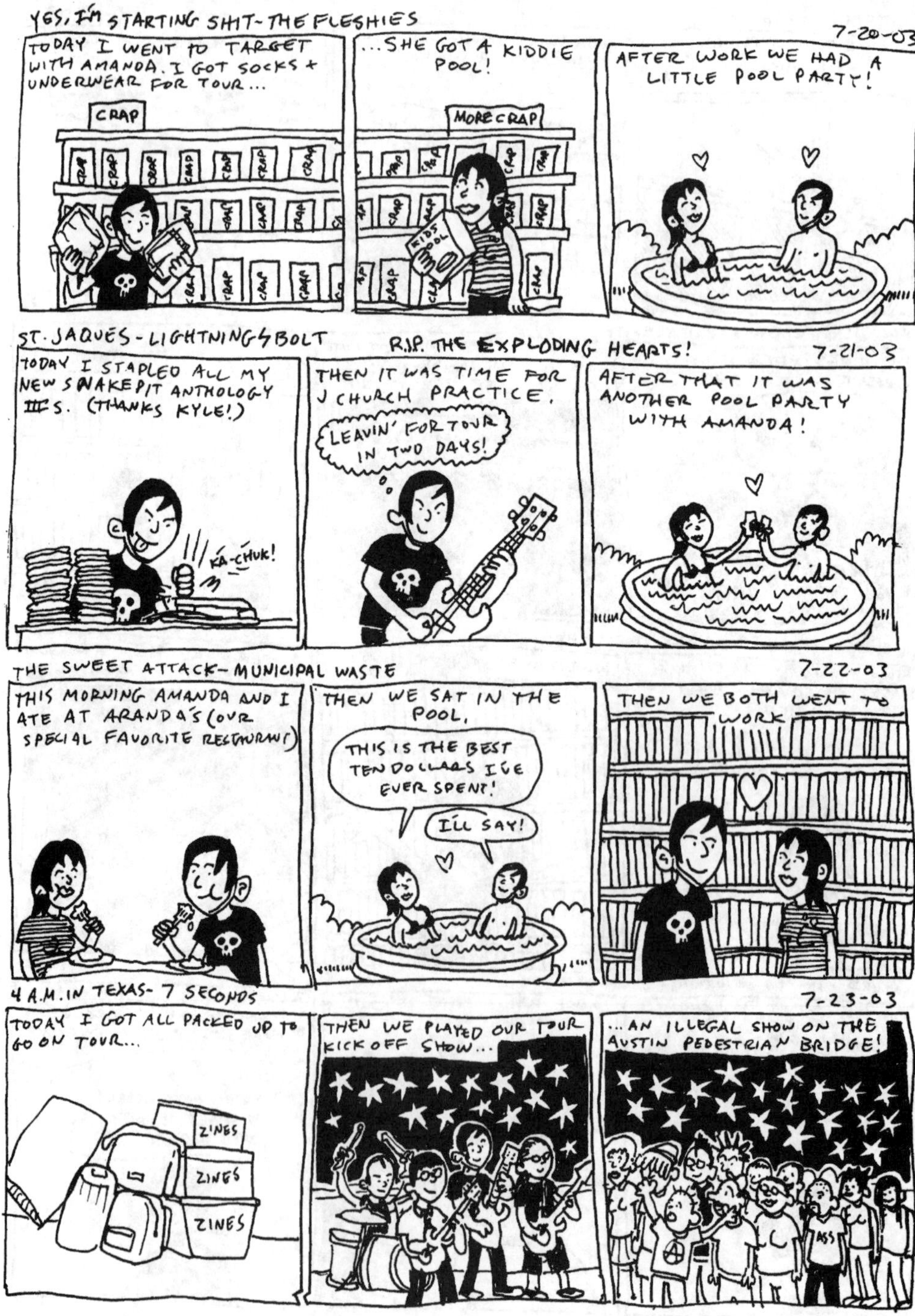
YES, I'M STARTING SHIT - THE FLESHIES
7-20-03
TODAY I WENT TO TARGET WITH AMANDA. I GOT SOCKS + UNDERWEAR FOR TOUR...
CRAP
...SHE GOT A KIDDIE POOL!
MORE CRAP
KIDS POOL
AFTER WORK WE HAD A LITTLE POOL PARTY!
ST. JAQUES - LIGHTNING BOLT
R.I.P. THE EXPLODING HEARTS!
7-21-03
TODAY I STAPLED ALL MY NEW SNAKEPIT ANTHOLOGY III'S. (THANKS KYLE!)
KA-CHUK!
THEN IT WAS TIME FOR J CHURCH PRACTICE.
LEAVIN' FOR TOUR IN TWO DAYS!
AFTER THAT IT WAS ANOTHER POOL PARTY WITH AMANDA!
THE SWEET ATTACK - MUNICIPAL WASTE
7-22-03
THIS MORNING AMANDA AND I ATE AT ARANDA'S (OUR SPECIAL FAVORITE RESTAURANT)
THEN WE SAT IN THE POOL.
THIS IS THE BEST TEN DOLLARS I'VE EVER SPENT!
I'LL SAY!
THEN WE BOTH WENT TO WORK
4 A.M. IN TEXAS - 7 SECONDS
7-23-03
TODAY I GOT ALL PACKED UP TO GO ON TOUR...
ZINES
ZINES
ZINES
THEN WE PLAYED OUR TOUR KICKOFF SHOW...
...AN ILLEGAL SHOW ON THE AUSTIN PEDESTRIAN BRIDGE!
ASS

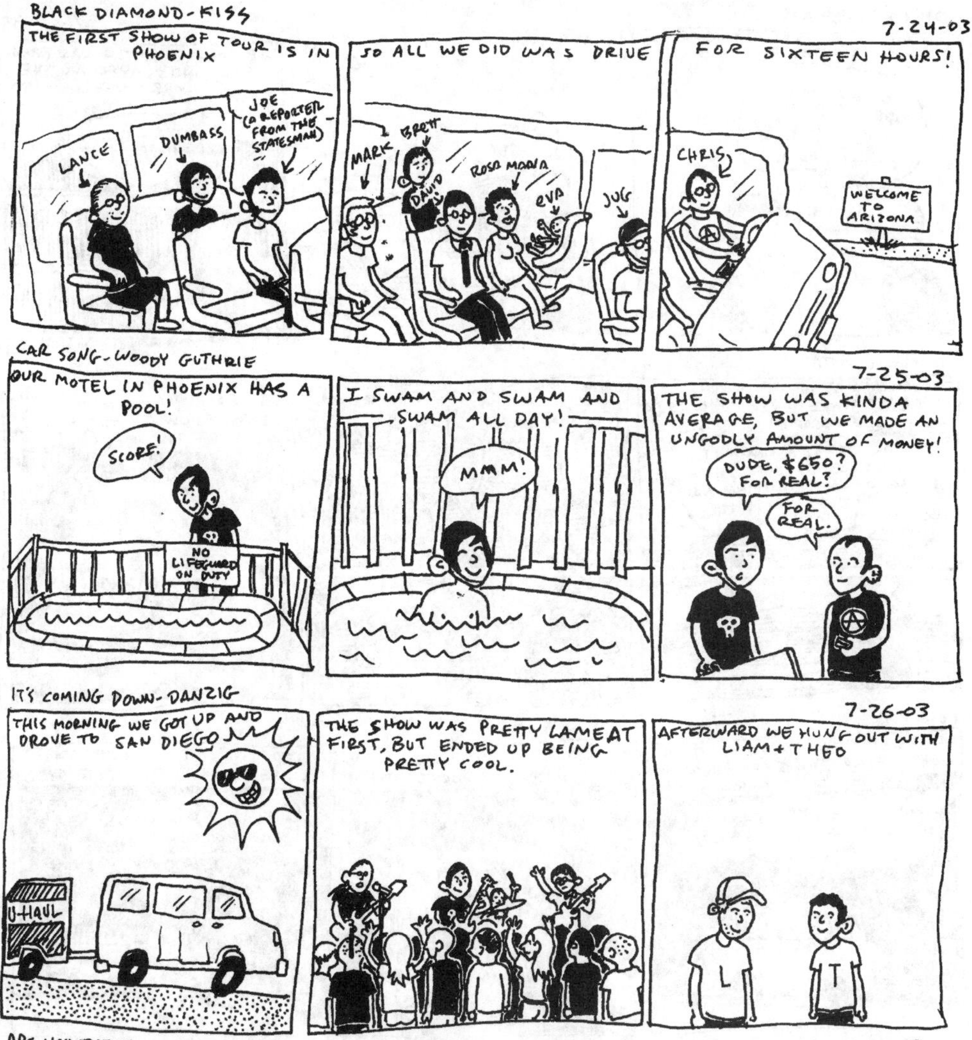
BLACK DIAMOND - KISS
7-24-03
THE FIRST SHOW OF TOUR IS IN PHOENIX
LANCE
DUMBASS
JOE (A REPORTER FROM THE STATESMAN)
SO ALL WE DID WAS DRIVE
MARK
BRETT
DAVID
ROSA MARIA
EVA
JUG
FOR SIXTEEN HOURS!
CHRIS
WELCOME TO ARIZONA
CAR SONG - WOODY GUTHRIE
7-25-03
OUR MOTEL IN PHOENIX HAS A POOL!
SCORE!
NO LIFEGUARD ON DUTY
I SWAM AND SWAM AND SWAM ALL DAY!
MMM!
THE SHOW WAS KINDA AVERAGE, BUT WE MADE AN UNGODLY AMOUNT OF MONEY!
DUDE, $650? FOR REAL?
FOR REAL.
IT'S COMING DOWN - DANZIG
7-26-03
THIS MORNING WE GOT UP AND DROVE TO SAN DIEGO
U-HAUL
THE SHOW WAS PRETTY LAME AT FIRST, BUT ENDED UP BEING PRETTY COOL.
AFTERWARD WE HUNG OUT WITH LIAM + THEO
L
T
ARE YOU THE MOTHERFUCKER WITH THE BANANA? - DILLINGER FOUR
7-27-03
THIS MORNING I GOT TO SWIM IN THE PACIFIC OCEAN!
THIS IS WHY I DIDN'T MOVE TO PORTLAND!
THEN WE PLAYED A REALLY WEAK SHOW IN L.A.
FUCK! MY BASS HAS A SHORT IN THE WIRING! IT KEEPS CUTTING OUT!
I STAYED WITH TODD AND MEGAN FROM RAZORCAKE. THEY ARE SUPER NICE PEOPLE!
LET'S DRINK!

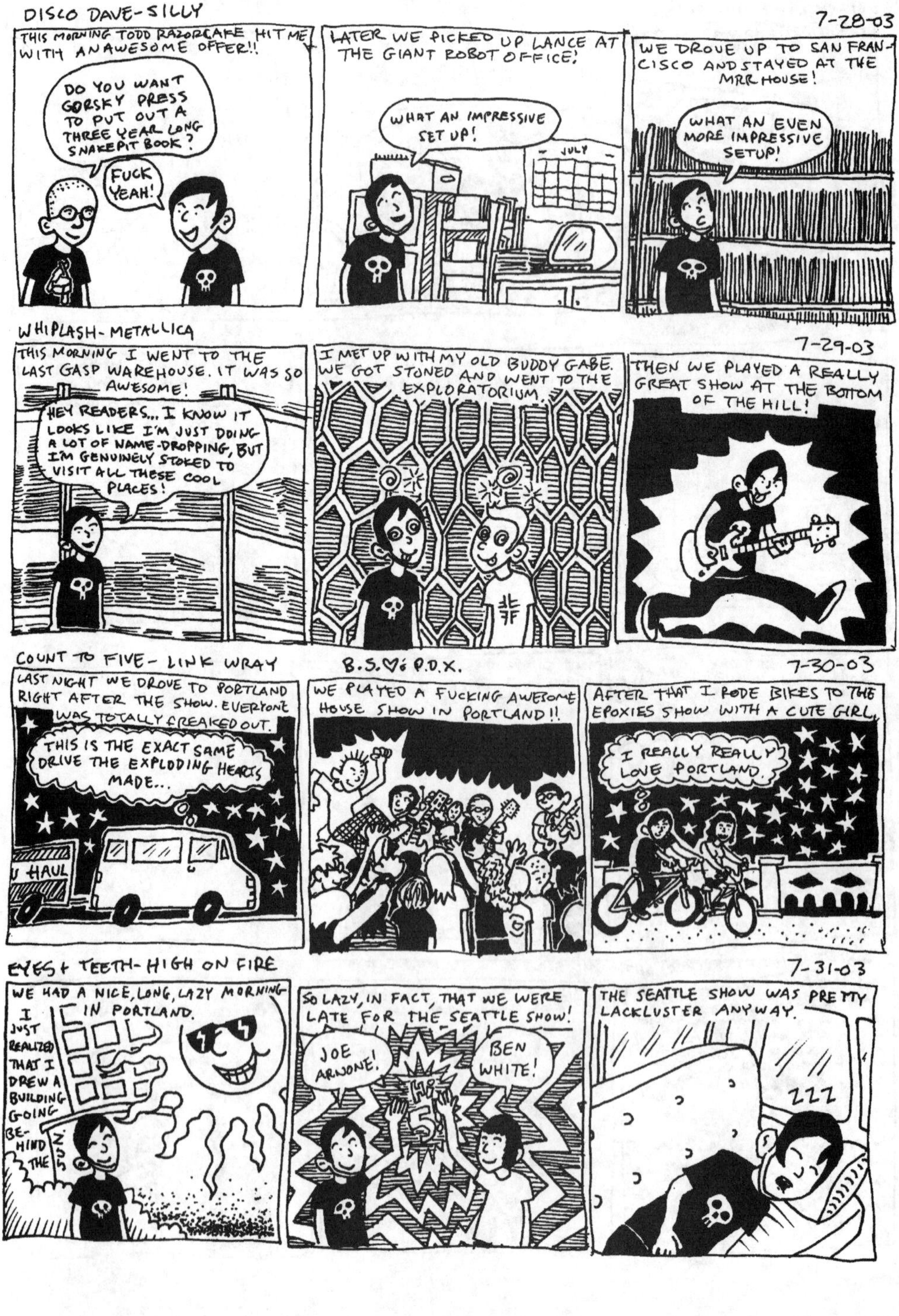
DISCO DAVE-SILLY
7-28-03
THIS MORNING TODD RAZORCAKE HIT ME WITH AN AWESOME OFFER!!
DO YOU WANT GORSKY PRESS TO PUT OUT A THREE YEAR LONG SNAKEPIT BOOK?
FUCK YEAH!
LATER WE PICKED UP LANCE AT THE GIANT ROBOT OFFICE!
WHAT AN IMPRESSIVE SET UP!
JULY
WE DROVE UP TO SAN FRANCISCO AND STAYED AT THE MRR HOUSE!
WHAT AN EVEN MORE IMPRESSIVE SETUP!
WHIPLASH-METALLICA
7-29-03
THIS MORNING I WENT TO THE LAST GASP WAREHOUSE. IT WAS SO AWESOME!
HEY READERS... I KNOW IT LOOKS LIKE I'M JUST DOING A LOT OF NAME-DROPPING, BUT I'M GENUINELY STOKED TO VISIT ALL THESE COOL PLACES!
I MET UP WITH MY OLD BUDDY GABE. WE GOT STONED AND WENT TO THE EXPLORATORIUM.
THEN WE PLAYED A REALLY GREAT SHOW AT THE BOTTOM OF THE HILL!
COUNT TO FIVE-LINK WRAY
B.S.♡:P.D.X.
7-30-03
LAST NIGHT WE DROVE TO PORTLAND RIGHT AFTER THE SHOW. EVERYONE WAS TOTALLY FREAKED OUT.
THIS IS THE EXACT SAME DRIVE THE EXPLODING HEARTS MADE...
U HAUL
WE PLAYED A FUCKING AWESOME HOUSE SHOW IN PORTLAND!!
AFTER THAT I RODE BIKES TO THE EPOXIES SHOW WITH A CUTE GIRL.
I REALLY REALLY LOVE PORTLAND.
EYES + TEETH-HIGH ON FIRE
7-31-03
WE HAD A NICE, LONG, LAZY MORNING IN PORTLAND.
I JUST REALIZED THAT I DREW A BUILDING GOING BEHIND THE SUN
SO LAZY, IN FACT, THAT WE WERE LATE FOR THE SEATTLE SHOW!
JOE ARNONE!
BEN WHITE!
HI 5!
THE SEATTLE SHOW WAS PRETTY LACKLUSTER ANYWAY.
ZZZ

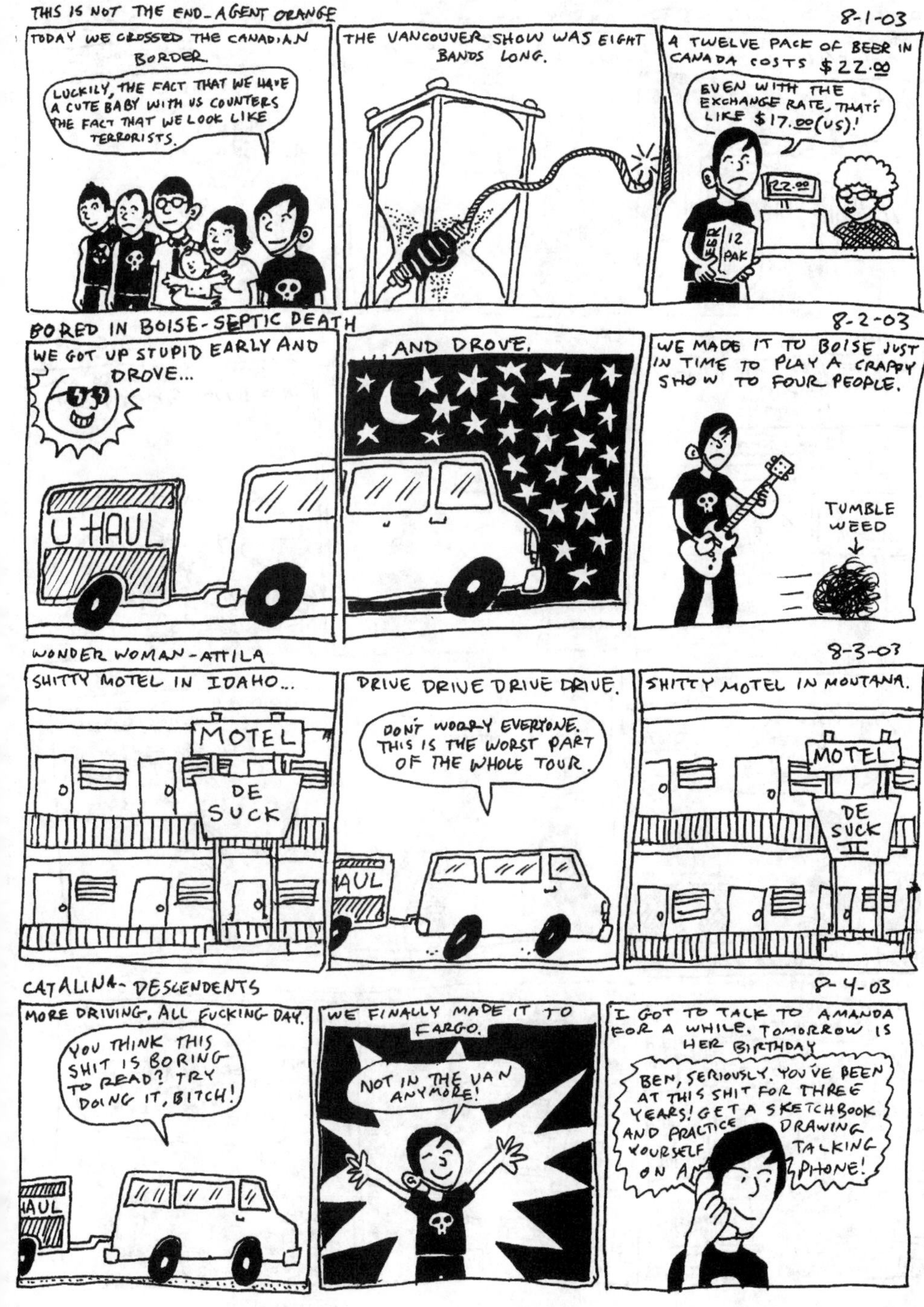
THIS IS NOT THE END_AGENT ORANGE
8-1-03
TODAY WE CROSSED THE CANADIAN BORDER
LUCKILY, THE FACT THAT WE HAVE A CUTE BABY WITH US COUNTERS THE FACT THAT WE LOOK LIKE TERRORISTS.
THE VANCOUVER SHOW WAS EIGHT BANDS LONG.
A TWELVE PACK OF BEER IN CANADA COSTS $22.00
EVEN WITH THE EXCHANGE RATE, THAT'S LIKE $17.00 (US)!
22.00
12 PAK
BORED IN BOISE-SEPTIC DEATH
8-2-03
WE GOT UP STUPID EARLY AND DROVE...
U HAUL
AND DROVE.
WE MADE IT TO BOISE JUST IN TIME TO PLAY A CRAPPY SHOW TO FOUR PEOPLE.
TUMBLE WEED
WONDER WOMAN-ATTILA
8-3-03
SHITTY MOTEL IN IDAHO...
MOTEL
DE SUCK
DRIVE DRIVE DRIVE DRIVE.
DON'T WORRY EVERYONE. THIS IS THE WORST PART OF THE WHOLE TOUR.
HAUL
SHITTY MOTEL IN MONTANA.
MOTEL
DE SUCK II
CATALINA-DESCENDENTS
8-4-03
MORE DRIVING. ALL FUCKING DAY.
YOU THINK THIS SHIT IS BORING TO READ? TRY DOING IT, BITCH!
HAUL
WE FINALLY MADE IT TO FARGO.
NOT IN THE VAN ANYMORE!
I GOT TO TALK TO AMANDA FOR A WHILE. TOMORROW IS HER BIRTHDAY
BEN, SERIOUSLY. YOU'VE BEEN AT THIS SHIT FOR THREE YEARS! GET A SKETCHBOOK AND PRACTICE DRAWING YOURSELF TALKING ON A PHONE!

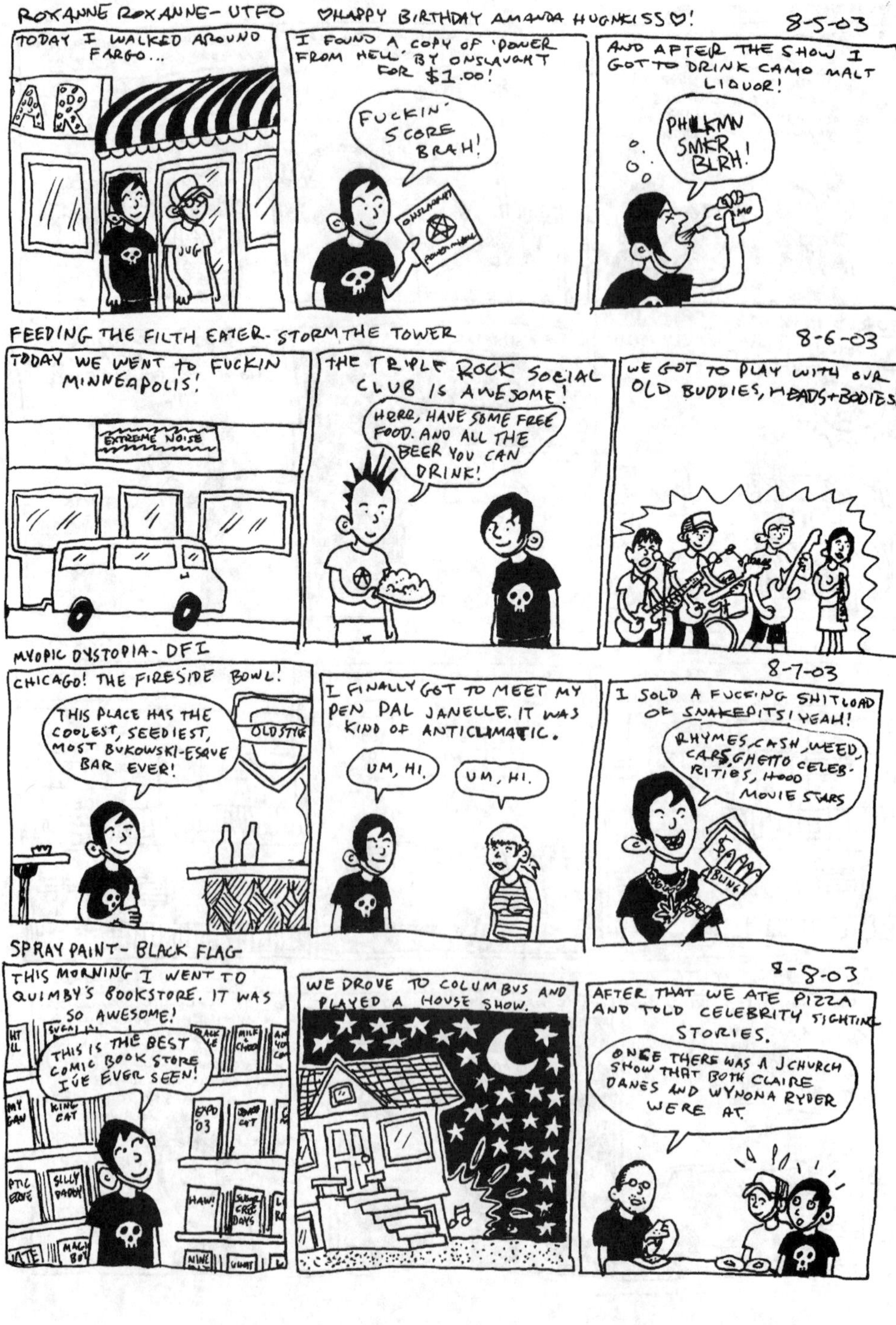
ROXANNE ROXANNE - UTFO
♡HAPPY BIRTHDAY AMANDA HUGNKISS♡!
8-5-03
TODAY I WALKED AROUND FARGO...
JUG
I FOUND A COPY OF 'POWER FROM HELL' BY ONSLAUGHT FOR $1.00!
FUCKIN' SCORE BRAH!
ONSLAUGHT
POWER FROM HELL
AND AFTER THE SHOW I GOT TO DRINK CAMO MALT LIQUOR!
PHKMN SMKR BLRH!
CAMO
FEEDING THE FILTH EATER - STORM THE TOWER
8-6-03
TODAY WE WENT TO FUCKIN MINNEAPOLIS!
EXTREME NOISE
THE TRIPLE ROCK SOCIAL CLUB IS AWESOME!
HERE, HAVE SOME FREE FOOD. AND ALL THE BEER YOU CAN DRINK!
WE GOT TO PLAY WITH OUR OLD BUDDIES, HEADS+BODIES!
MYOPIC DYSTOPIA - DFI
8-7-03
CHICAGO! THE FIRESIDE BOWL!
THIS PLACE HAS THE COOLEST, SEEDIEST, MOST BUKOWSKI-ESQUE BAR EVER!
OLD STYLE
I FINALLY GOT TO MEET MY PEN PAL JANELLE. IT WAS KIND OF ANTICLIMATIC.
UM, HI.
UM, HI.
I SOLD A FUCKING SHITLOAD OF SNAKEPITS! YEAH!
RHYMES, CASH, WEED, CARS, GHETTO CELEBRITIES, HOOD MOVIE STARS
$
BLING
SPRAY PAINT - BLACK FLAG
8-8-03
THIS MORNING I WENT TO QUIMBY'S BOOKSTORE. IT WAS SO AWESOME!
THIS IS THE BEST COMIC BOOK STORE I'VE EVER SEEN!
KING CAT
EXPO '03
SILLY DADDY
HAW!
WE DROVE TO COLUMBUS AND PLAYED A HOUSE SHOW.
AFTER THAT WE ATE PIZZA AND TOLD CELEBRITY SIGHTING STORIES.
ONCE THERE WAS A JCHURCH SHOW THAT BOTH CLAIRE DANES AND WYNONA RYDER WERE AT.

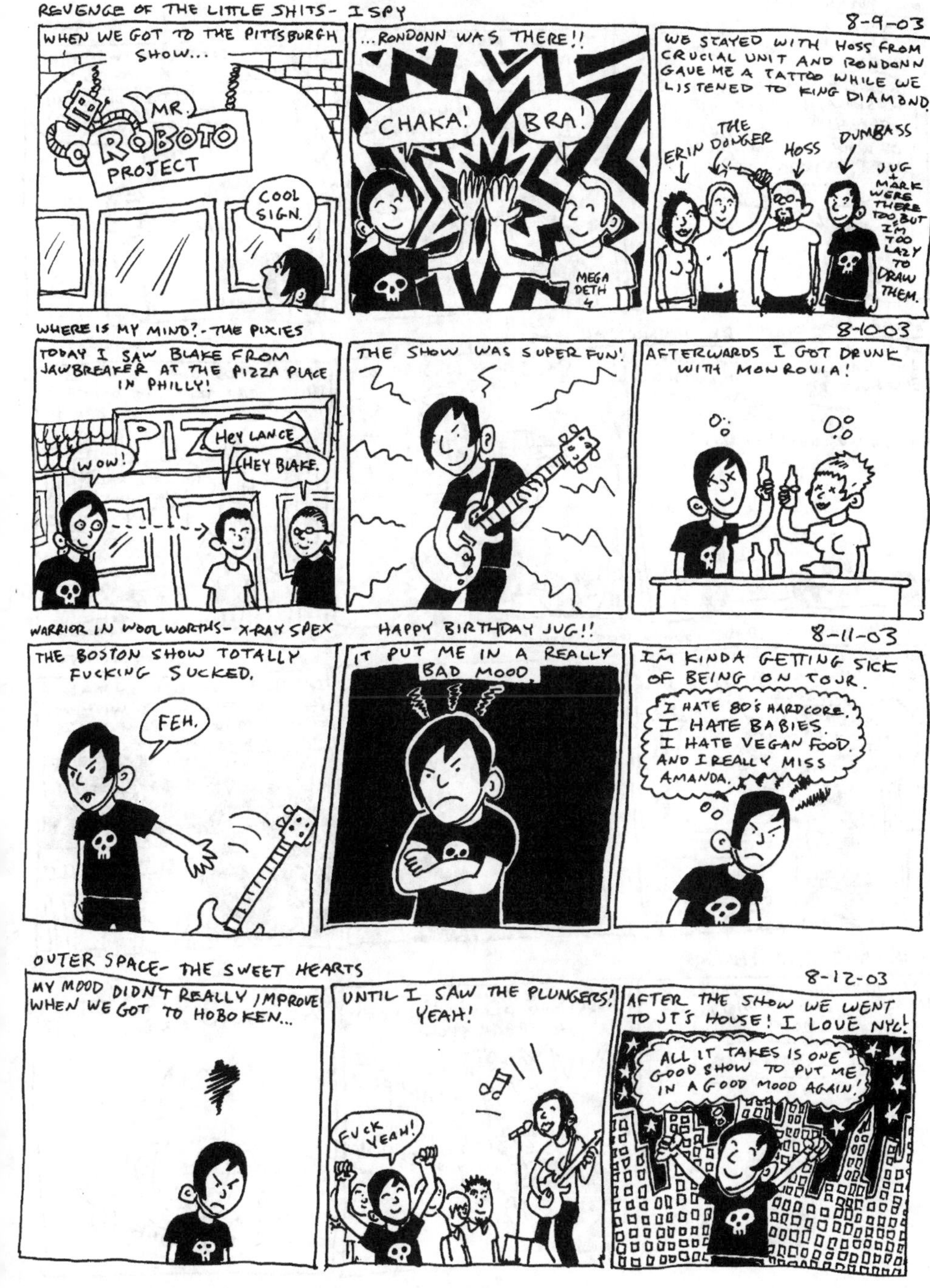
REVENGE OF THE LITTLE SHITS - I SPY
8-9-03
WHEN WE GOT TO THE PITTSBURGH SHOW...
MR. ROBOTO PROJECT
COOL SIGN.
...RONDONN WAS THERE!!
CHAKA!
BRA!
MEGA DETH
WE STAYED WITH HOSS FROM CRUCIAL UNIT AND RONDONN GAVE ME A TATTOO WHILE WE LISTENED TO KING DIAMOND.
ERIN
THE DONGER
HOSS
DUMBASS
JUG + MARK WERE THERE TOO, BUT I'M TOO LAZY TO DRAW THEM.
WHERE IS MY MIND? - THE PIXIES
8-10-03
TODAY I SAW BLAKE FROM JAWBREAKER AT THE PIZZA PLACE IN PHILLY!
PIZ
WOW!
HEY LANCE
HEY BLAKE.
THE SHOW WAS SUPER FUN!
AFTERWARDS I GOT DRUNK WITH MONROVIA!
WARRIOR IN WOOLWORTHS - X-RAY SPEX
HAPPY BIRTHDAY JUG!!
8-11-03
THE BOSTON SHOW TOTALLY FUCKING SUCKED.
FEH.
IT PUT ME IN A REALLY BAD MOOD.
I'M KINDA GETTING SICK OF BEING ON TOUR.
I HATE 80'S HARDCORE.
I HATE BABIES.
I HATE VEGAN FOOD.
AND I REALLY MISS AMANDA.
OUTER SPACE - THE SWEET HEARTS
8-12-03
MY MOOD DIDN'T REALLY IMPROVE WHEN WE GOT TO HOBOKEN...
UNTIL I SAW THE PLUNGERS! YEAH!
FUCK YEAH!
AFTER THE SHOW WE WENT TO JT'S HOUSE! I LOVE NYC!
ALL IT TAKES IS ONE GOOD SHOW TO PUT ME IN A GOOD MOOD AGAIN!

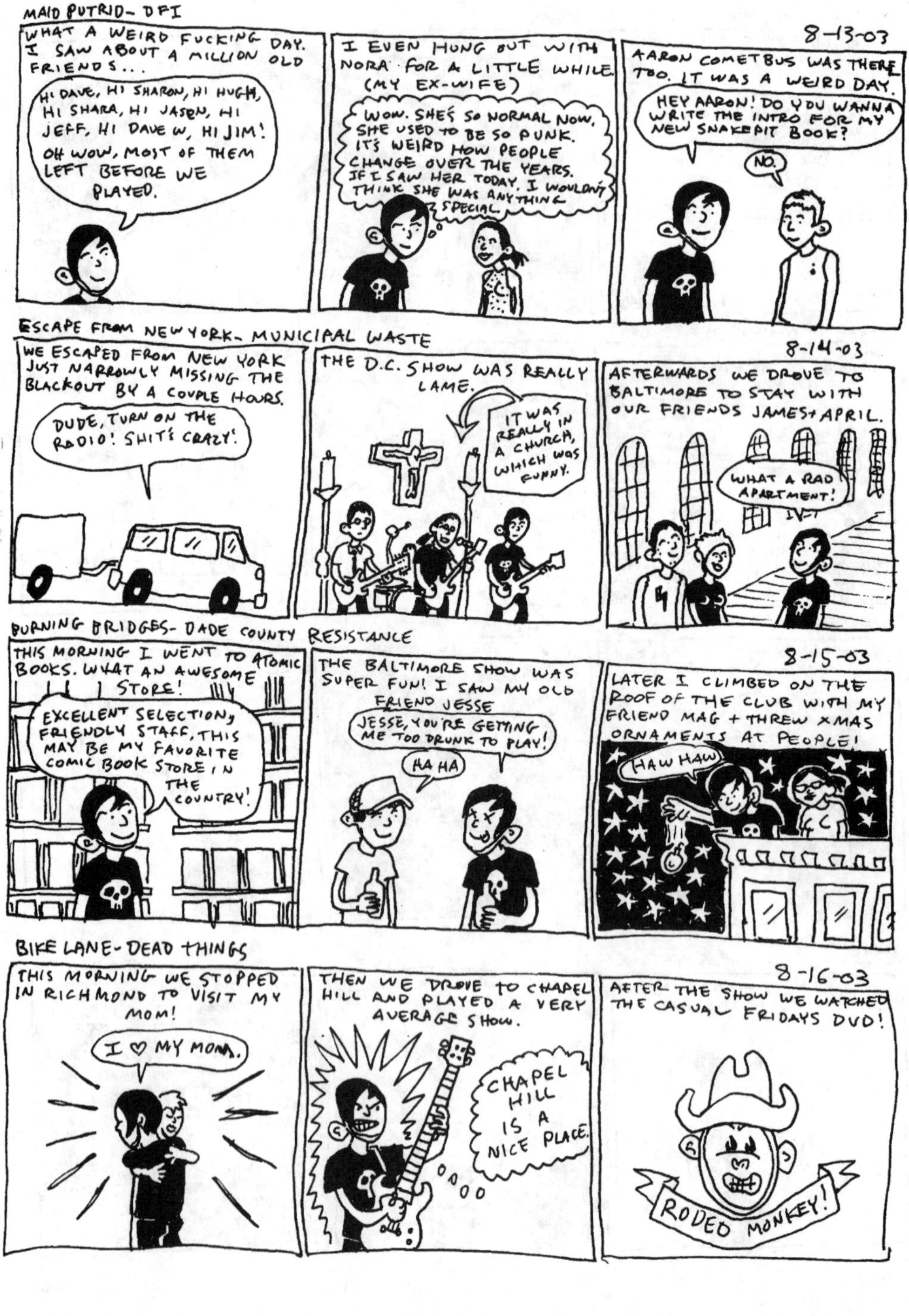
MAID PUTRID - DFI
8-13-03
WHAT A WEIRD FUCKING DAY. I SAW ABOUT A MILLION OLD FRIENDS...
HI DAVE, HI SHARON, HI HUGH, HI SHARA, HI JASON, HI JEFF, HI DAVE W, HI JIM! OH WOW, MOST OF THEM LEFT BEFORE WE PLAYED.
I EVEN HUNG OUT WITH NORA FOR A LITTLE WHILE. (MY EX-WIFE)
WOW. SHE'S SO NORMAL NOW, SHE USED TO BE SO PUNK. IT'S WEIRD HOW PEOPLE CHANGE OVER THE YEARS. IF I SAW HER TODAY, I WOULDN'T THINK SHE WAS ANYTHING SPECIAL.
AARON COMETBUS WAS THERE TOO. IT WAS A WEIRD DAY.
HEY AARON! DO YOU WANNA WRITE THE INTRO FOR MY NEW SNAKEPIT BOOK?
NO.
ESCAPE FROM NEW YORK - MUNICIPAL WASTE
8-14-03
WE ESCAPED FROM NEW YORK JUST NARROWLY MISSING THE BLACKOUT BY A COUPLE HOURS.
DUDE, TURN ON THE RADIO! SHIT'S CRAZY!
THE D.C. SHOW WAS REALLY LAME.
IT WAS REALLY IN A CHURCH, WHICH WAS FUNNY.
AFTERWARDS WE DROVE TO BALTIMORE TO STAY WITH OUR FRIENDS JAMES + APRIL.
WHAT A RAD APARTMENT!
BURNING BRIDGES - DADE COUNTY RESISTANCE
8-15-03
THIS MORNING I WENT TO ATOMIC BOOKS. WHAT AN AWESOME STORE!
EXCELLENT SELECTION, FRIENDLY STAFF, THIS MAY BE MY FAVORITE COMIC BOOK STORE IN THE COUNTRY!
THE BALTIMORE SHOW WAS SUPER FUN! I SAW MY OLD FRIEND JESSE
JESSE, YOU'RE GETTING ME TOO DRUNK TO PLAY!
HA HA
LATER I CLIMBED ON THE ROOF OF THE CLUB WITH MY FRIEND MAG + THREW XMAS ORNAMENTS AT PEOPLE!
HAW HAW
BIKE LANE - DEAD THINGS
8-16-03
THIS MORNING WE STOPPED IN RICHMOND TO VISIT MY MOM!
I ♥ MY MOM.
THEN WE DROVE TO CHAPEL HILL AND PLAYED A VERY AVERAGE SHOW.
CHAPEL HILL IS A NICE PLACE.
AFTER THE SHOW WE WATCHED THE CASUAL FRIDAYS DVD!
RODEO MONKEY!

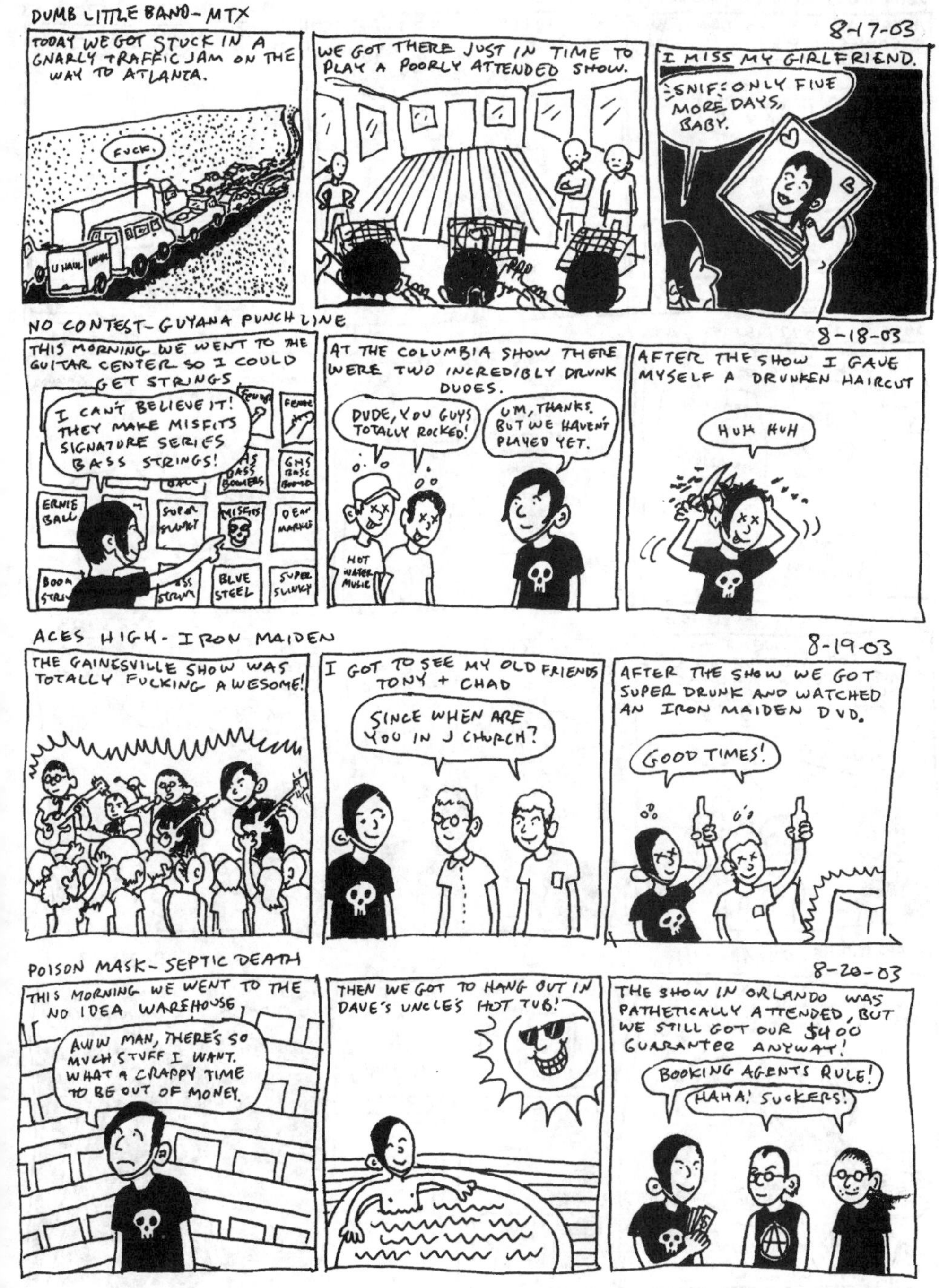

DUMB LITTLE BAND - MTX
8-17-03
TODAY WE GOT STUCK IN A GNARLY TRAFFIC JAM ON THE WAY TO ATLANTA.
FUCK.
U HAUL
WE GOT THERE JUST IN TIME TO PLAY A POORLY ATTENDED SHOW.
I MISS MY GIRLFRIEND.
SNIF. ONLY FIVE MORE DAYS, BABY.
NO CONTEST - GUYANA PUNCH LINE
8-18-03
THIS MORNING WE WENT TO THE GUITAR CENTER SO I COULD GET STRINGS
I CAN'T BELIEVE IT! THEY MAKE MISFITS SIGNATURE SERIES BASS STRINGS!
ERNIE BALL
SUPER SLINKY
MISFITS
BASS BOOMERS
BLUE STEEL
SUPER SLINKY
AT THE COLUMBIA SHOW THERE WERE TWO INCREDIBLY DRUNK DUDES.
DUDE, YOU GUYS TOTALLY ROCKED!
UM, THANKS. BUT WE HAVEN'T PLAYED YET.
HOT WATER MUSIC
AFTER THE SHOW I GAVE MYSELF A DRUNKEN HAIRCUT
HUH HUH
ACES HIGH - IRON MAIDEN
8-19-03
THE GAINESVILLE SHOW WAS TOTALLY FUCKING AWESOME!
I GOT TO SEE MY OLD FRIENDS TONY + CHAD
SINCE WHEN ARE YOU IN J CHURCH?
AFTER THE SHOW WE GOT SUPER DRUNK AND WATCHED AN IRON MAIDEN DVD.
GOOD TIMES!
POISON MASK - SEPTIC DEATH
8-20-03
THIS MORNING WE WENT TO THE NO IDEA WAREHOUSE
AWW MAN, THERE'S SO MUCH STUFF I WANT. WHAT A CRAPPY TIME TO BE OUT OF MONEY.
THEN WE GOT TO HANG OUT IN DAVE'S UNCLE'S HOT TUB!
THE SHOW IN ORLANDO WAS PATHETICALLY ATTENDED, BUT WE STILL GOT OUR $400 GUARANTEE ANYWAY!
BOOKING AGENTS RULE!
HAHA! SUCKERS!

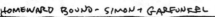

HOMEWARD BOUND - SIMON + GARFUNKEL
8-21-03
AFTER ORLANDO WE DROVE BACK TO GAINESVILLE TO STAY WITH DAVE'S UNCLE.
SOMEBODY IN ORLANDO RAN INTO THE VAN!
U HAUL
THEN WE DROVE TO PENSACOLA AND PLAYED A DUMB SHOW.
WELL, THOSE TWO FRAT BOYS IN THE FRONT LIKE IT.
WE LEFT IMMEDIATELY AFTER FOR TEXAS!!
UHAUL
BACK IN BABY'S ARMS - PATSY CLINE
8-22-03
THIS MORNING WE GOT TO HOUSTON AND WENT TO SLEEP.
WHO WANTS TO SEE A ROPE TRICK?
MARK'S DAD, THE AMAZING GENE-O
INTL BROTHERHOOD OF MAGICIANS
AFTER THE SHOW I HITCHED A RIDE HOME WITH STACEY.
EVERYONE ELSE HAS TO STAY ALL DAY TOMORROW TO GET THE VAN FIXED. I KNOW IT'S SHITTY TO DITCH OUT, BUT I DON'T CARE!
BYE, GUYS!
I GOT BACK TO AUSTIN AND CRAWLED INTO BED WITH AMANDA. IT WAS AWESOME.
GORILLAS IN THE MIST - ICE CUBE
8-23-03
THIS MORNING I WENT TO MY HOUSE FOR A LITTLE WHILE (I HAVE TO STAY AT AMANDA'S UNTIL THE FIRST CUZ I RENTED OUT MY ROOM)
BEN + NICK!
BEN!
THEN WE PLAYED THE LAST SHOW OF THE TOUR. FOR SOME REASON WE PLAYED FOR AN HOUR AND A HALF.
LET'S PLAY THE 15 MINUTE SONG AS AN ENCORE!
DO WE HAVE TO?
AFTER THAT ME + AMANDA WATCHED "URGH: A MUSIC WAR"
I'M SO GLAD TO BE HOME!
HELLO THERE - CHEAP TRICK
8-24-03
WHAT AN AMAZING DAY. IT STARTED WITH ME + AMANDA HAVING A COOKOUT AND A POOL PARTY.
LATER I TOOK HER OUT TO DINNER
thai kitchen
THEN WE GOT DRUNK AND WENT TO A PLAYGROUND IN THE MIDDLE OF THE NIGHT.

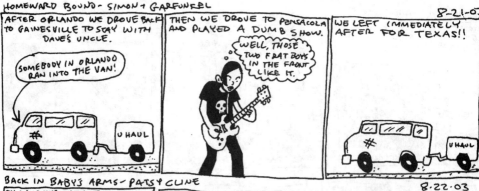

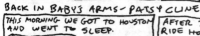

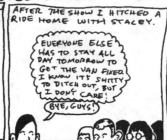

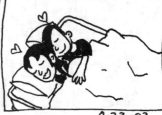

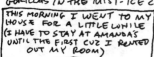

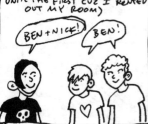

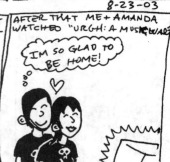

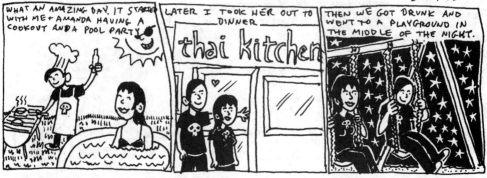

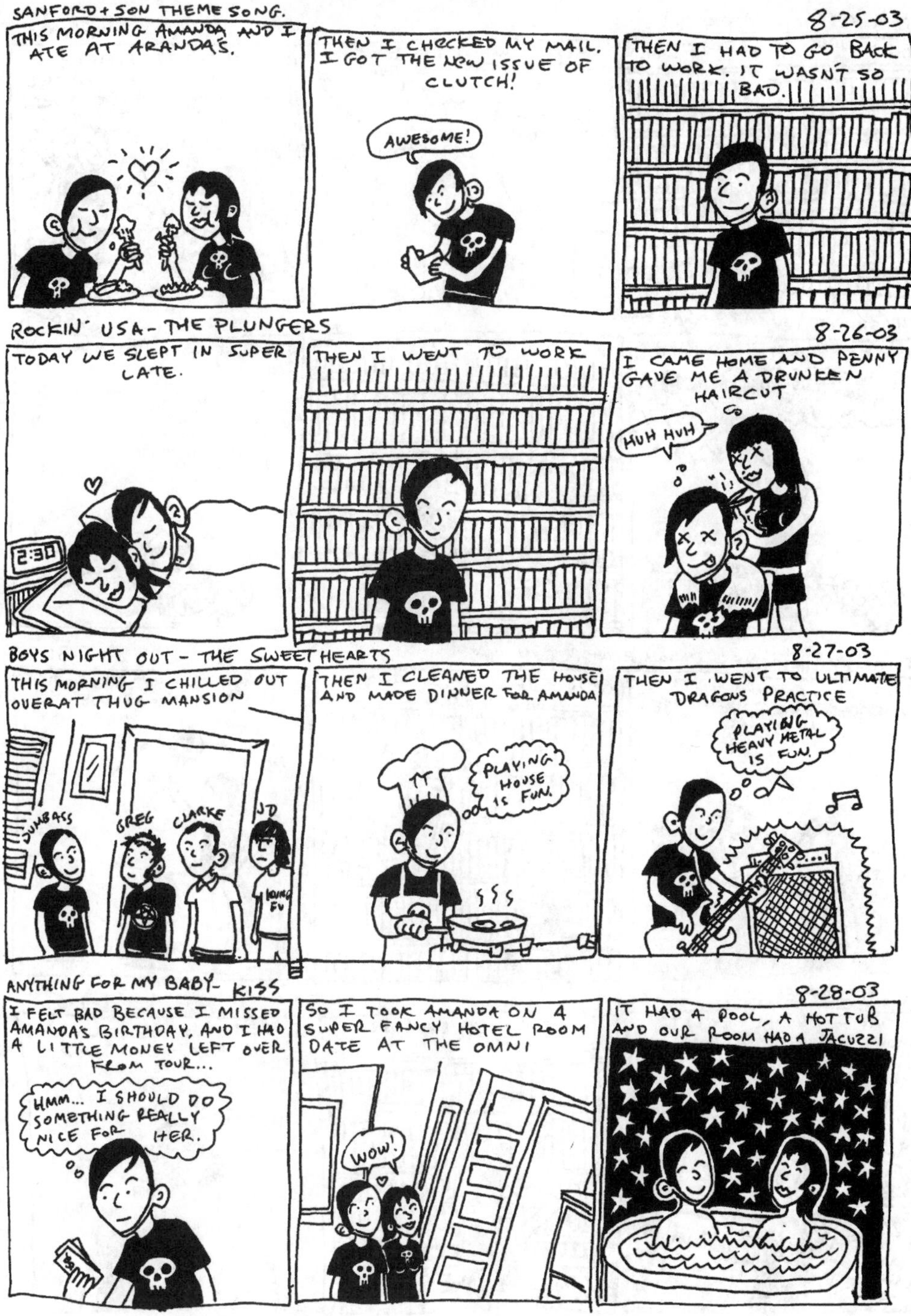
SANFORD + SON THEME SONG.
8-25-03
THIS MORNING AMANDA AND I ATE AT ARANDA'S.
THEN I CHECKED MY MAIL. I GOT THE NEW ISSUE OF CLUTCH!
AWESOME!
THEN I HAD TO GO BACK TO WORK. IT WASN'T SO BAD.
ROCKIN' USA - THE PLUNGERS
8-26-03
TODAY WE SLEPT IN SUPER LATE.
2:30
THEN I WENT TO WORK
I CAME HOME AND PENNY GAVE ME A DRUNKEN HAIRCUT
HUH HUH
BOYS NIGHT OUT - THE SWEETHEARTS
8-27-03
THIS MORNING I CHILLED OUT OVER AT THUG MANSION
JUMBASS
GREG
CLARKE
JD
THEN I CLEANED THE HOUSE AND MADE DINNER FOR AMANDA
PLAYING HOUSE IS FUN.
THEN I WENT TO ULTIMATE DRAGONS PRACTICE
PLAYING HEAVY METAL IS FUN.
ANYTHING FOR MY BABY - KISS
8-28-03
I FELT BAD BECAUSE I MISSED AMANDA'S BIRTHDAY, AND I HAD A LITTLE MONEY LEFT OVER FROM TOUR...
HMM... I SHOULD DO SOMETHING REALLY NICE FOR HER.
SO I TOOK AMANDA ON A SUPER FANCY HOTEL ROOM DATE AT THE OMNI
WOW!
IT HAD A POOL, A HOT TUB AND OUR ROOM HAD A JACUZZI

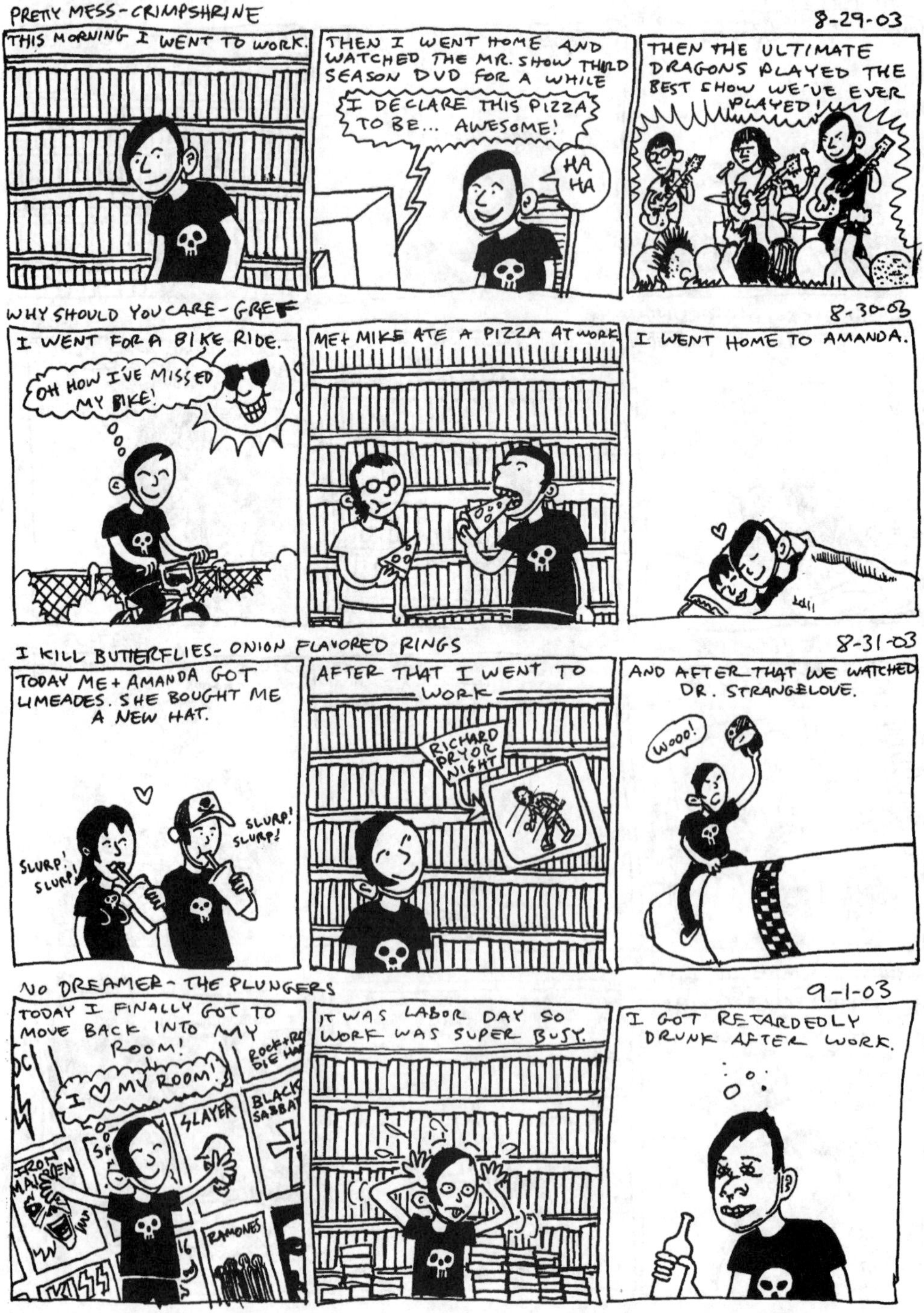
PRETTY MESS - CRIMPSHRINE
8-29-03
THIS MORNING I WENT TO WORK.
THEN I WENT HOME AND WATCHED THE MR. SHOW THIRD SEASON DVD FOR A WHILE
I DECLARE THIS PIZZA TO BE... AWESOME!
HA HA
THEN THE ULTIMATE DRAGONS PLAYED THE BEST SHOW WE'VE EVER PLAYED!
WHY SHOULD YOU CARE - GREF
8-30-03
I WENT FOR A BIKE RIDE.
OH HOW I'VE MISSED MY BIKE!
ME + MIKE ATE A PIZZA AT WORK
I WENT HOME TO AMANDA.
I KILL BUTTERFLIES - ONION FLAVORED RINGS
8-31-03
TODAY ME + AMANDA GOT LIMEADES. SHE BOUGHT ME A NEW HAT.
SLURP! SLURP!
SLURP! SLURP!
AFTER THAT I WENT TO WORK
RICHARD PRYOR NIGHT
AND AFTER THAT WE WATCHED DR. STRANGELOVE.
WOOO!
NO DREAMER - THE PLUNGERS
9-1-03
TODAY I FINALLY GOT TO MOVE BACK INTO MY ROOM!
I ♥ MY ROOM!
SLAYER
BLACK SABBATH
IRON MAIDEN
RAMONES
KISS
IT WAS LABOR DAY SO WORK WAS SUPER BUSY.
I GOT RETARDEDLY DRUNK AFTER WORK.

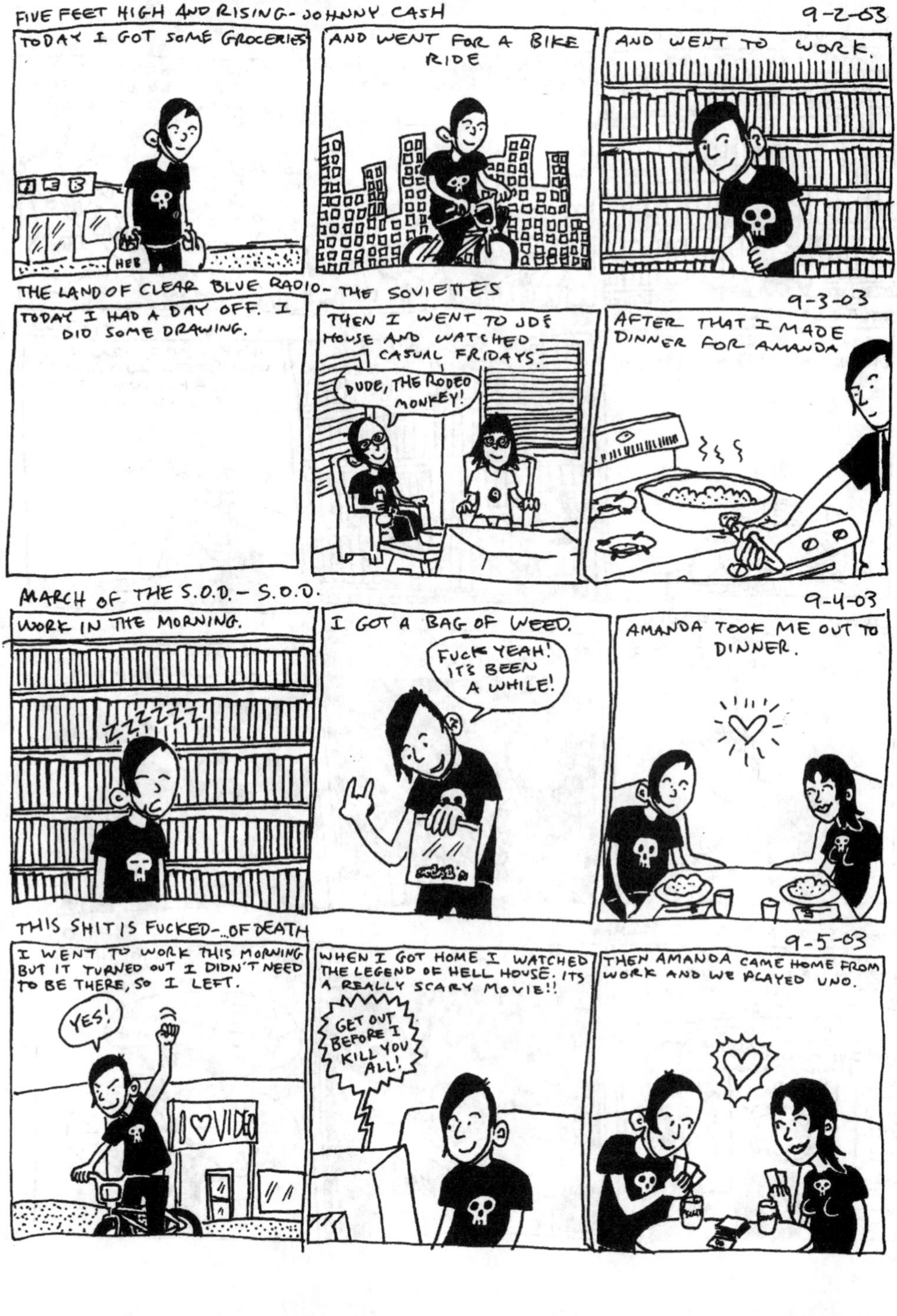
FIVE FEET HIGH AND RISING - JOHNNY CASH
9-2-03
TODAY I GOT SOME GROCERIES
HEB
HEB
AND WENT FOR A BIKE RIDE
AND WENT TO WORK.
THE LAND OF CLEAR BLUE RADIO - THE SOVIETTES
9-3-03
TODAY I HAD A DAY OFF. I DID SOME DRAWING.
THEN I WENT TO JDS HOUSE AND WATCHED CASUAL FRIDAYS.
DUDE, THE RODEO MONKEY!
AFTER THAT I MADE DINNER FOR AMANDA
MARCH OF THE S.O.D. - S.O.D.
9-4-03
WORK IN THE MORNING.
ZZZZZZ
I GOT A BAG OF WEED.
FUCK YEAH! IT'S BEEN A WHILE!
AMANDA TOOK ME OUT TO DINNER.
THIS SHIT IS FUCKED - ...OF DEATH
9-5-03
I WENT TO WORK THIS MORNING BUT IT TURNED OUT I DIDN'T NEED TO BE THERE, SO I LEFT.
YES!
I ♥ VIDEO
WHEN I GOT HOME I WATCHED THE LEGEND OF HELL HOUSE. ITS A REALLY SCARY MOVIE!!
GET OUT BEFORE I KILL YOU ALL!
THEN AMANDA CAME HOME FROM WORK AND WE PLAYED UNO.

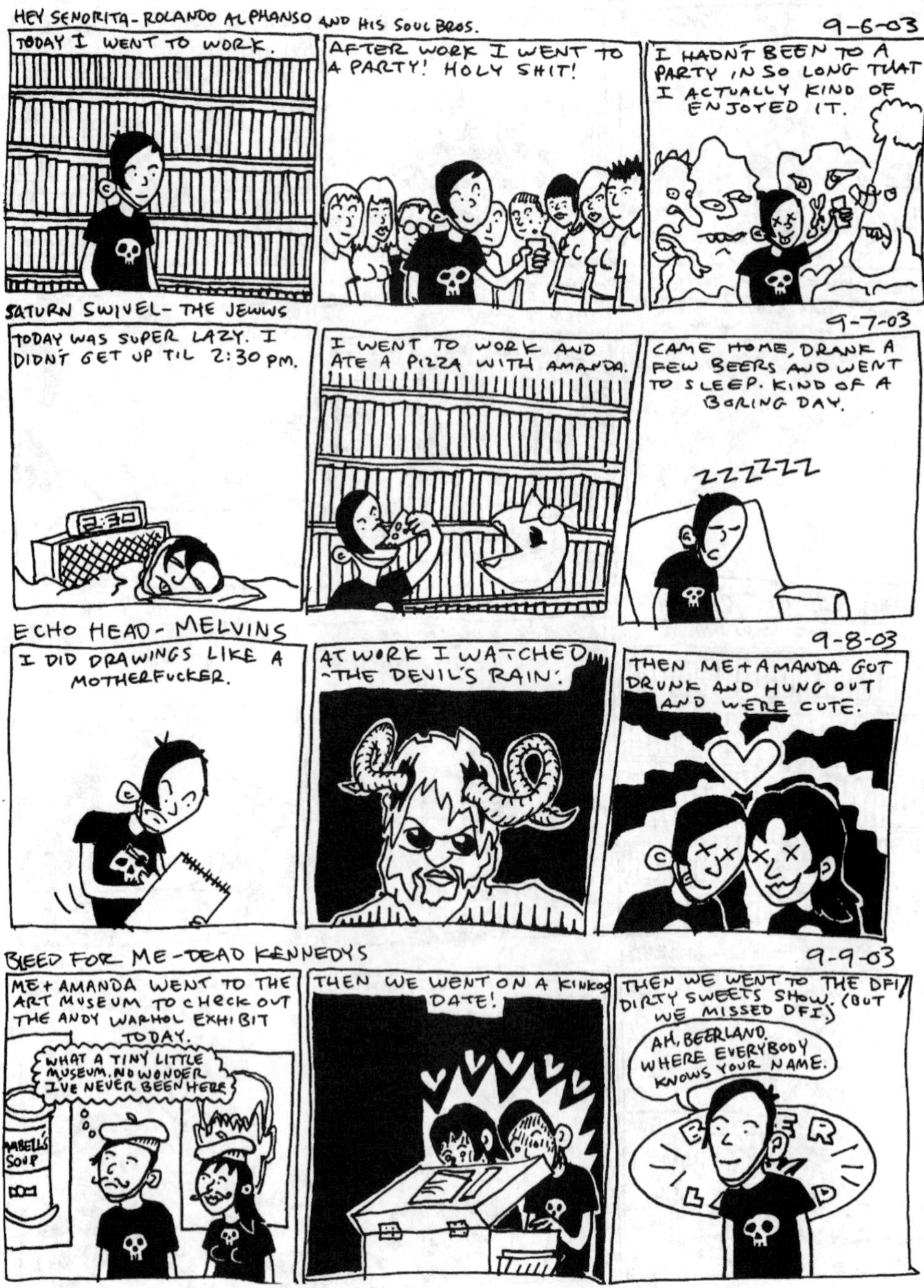

HEY SENORITA - ROLANDO ALPHANSO AND HIS SOUL BROS.
9-6-03
TODAY I WENT TO WORK.
AFTER WORK I WENT TO A PARTY! HOLY SHIT!
I HADN'T BEEN TO A PARTY IN SO LONG THAT I ACTUALLY KIND OF ENJOYED IT.
SATURN SWIVEL - THE JEWWS
9-7-03
TODAY WAS SUPER LAZY. I DIDN'T GET UP TIL 2:30 PM.
2:30
I WENT TO WORK AND ATE A PIZZA WITH AMANDA.
CAME HOME, DRANK A FEW BEERS AND WENT TO SLEEP. KIND OF A BORING DAY.
ZZZZZZ
ECHO HEAD - MELVINS
9-8-03
I DID DRAWINGS LIKE A MOTHERFUCKER.
AT WORK I WATCHED "THE DEVIL'S RAIN".
THEN ME + AMANDA GOT DRUNK AND HUNG OUT AND WERE CUTE.
BLEED FOR ME - DEAD KENNEDYS
9-9-03
ME + AMANDA WENT TO THE ART MUSEUM TO CHECK OUT THE ANDY WARHOL EXHIBIT TODAY.
WHAT A TINY LITTLE MUSEUM. NO WONDER I'VE NEVER BEEN HERE
SOUP
THEN WE WENT ON A KINKOS DATE!
THEN WE WENT TO THE DFI / DIRTY SWEETS SHOW. (BUT WE MISSED DFI.)
AH, BEERLAND. WHERE EVERYBODY KNOWS YOUR NAME.

BAD MOON - HELMET

YESTERDAY PENNY'S DOG ATE SOME DIRTY TAMPONS OUT OF THE TRASH AND THEN PUKED THEM ONTO THE COUCH. IT WAS AMAZING.

HORK!

THIS MORNING I TALKED ON THE PHONE TO SEAN + TODD AT GORSKY ABOUT MY BOOK.

FUCK YEAH!

9-10-03

THEN I WENT TO WORK

SYNTHESIZED - EPOXIES

THIS MORNING I MADE SNAKEPIT #33.

WOW. IT'S BEEN AWHILE. I'D FORGOTTEN HOW MUCH I LOVE DOING THIS SHIT!

KA-CHUNK

WORK WAS PRETTY SLOW.

I HAVE NO IDEA WHAT THIS IS SUPPOSED TO BE.

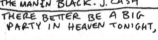

9-11-03

AFTER WORK I WATCHED A MOVIE WITH AMANDA

WAS IT SUPPOSED TO BE A SNAIL?

UH, YEAH, UM, SHUT UP!

HEE HEE

THE MAN IN BLACK - J. CASH

THERE BETTER BE A BIG PARTY IN HEAVEN TONIGHT,

NEWS PAPER

OH NO!

WE MISS YOU.

BECAUSE JOHNNY CASH DIED TODAY.

=SNIF=

RING OF FIRE

SPLOOSH!

9-12-03

GOD BLESS YOU, JOHNNY. THANKS FOR EVERYTHING.

RABID DOGS - C.O.C.

TODAY WAS JUST FUCKING AWFUL. I MISSED MUNICIPAL WASTE BECAUSE I HAD TO WORK.

THERE'S NO ONE TO COVER MY SHIFT AND IF I DON'T SHOW UP I'LL GET FIRED.

FUCK FUCK FUCK!!!

I MADE IT TO THE EPOXIES SHOW IN TIME, BUT IT WAS NO FUN EITHER

HMM. THIS IS LIKE THE 7TH TIME I'VE SEEN THE EPOXIES. I STILL LIKE THEM, BUT THEY'RE GETTING TOO POPULAR FOR ME TO ENJOY THEIR SHOWS ANYMORE.

9-13-03

ME + AMANDA GOT IN A BIG FIGHT!

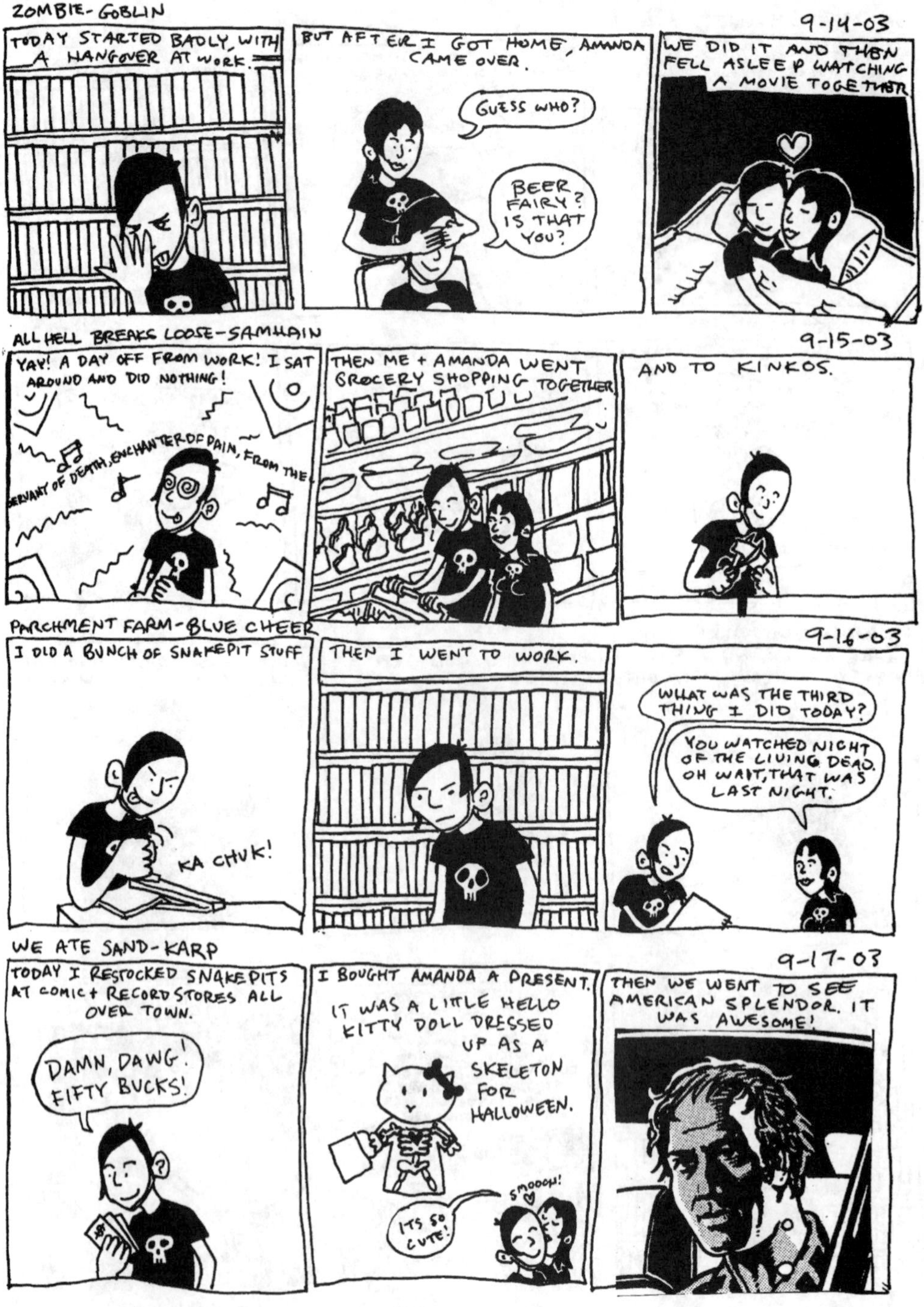
ZOMBIE- GOBLIN
9-14-03
TODAY STARTED BADLY, WITH A HANGOVER AT WORK.
BUT AFTER I GOT HOME, AMANDA CAME OVER.
GUESS WHO?
BEER FAIRY? IS THAT YOU?
WE DID IT AND THEN FELL ASLEEP WATCHING A MOVIE TOGETHER
ALL HELL BREAKS LOOSE-SAMHAIN
9-15-03
YAY! A DAY OFF FROM WORK! I SAT AROUND AND DID NOTHING!
SERVANT OF DEATH, ENCHANTER OF PAIN, FROM THE
THEN ME + AMANDA WENT GROCERY SHOPPING TOGETHER
AND TO KINKOS.
PARCHMENT FARM-BLUE CHEER
9-16-03
I DID A BUNCH OF SNAKEPIT STUFF
KA CHUK!
THEN I WENT TO WORK.
WHAT WAS THE THIRD THING I DID TODAY?
YOU WATCHED NIGHT OF THE LIVING DEAD. OH WAIT, THAT WAS LAST NIGHT.
WE ATE SAND-KARP
9-17-03
TODAY I RESTOCKED SNAKEPITS AT COMIC + RECORD STORES ALL OVER TOWN.
DAMN, DAWG! FIFTY BUCKS!
I BOUGHT AMANDA A PRESENT.
IT WAS A LITTLE HELLO KITTY DOLL DRESSED UP AS A SKELETON FOR HALLOWEEN.
ITS SO CUTE!
SMOOCH!
THEN WE WENT TO SEE AMERICAN SPLENDOR. IT WAS AWESOME!

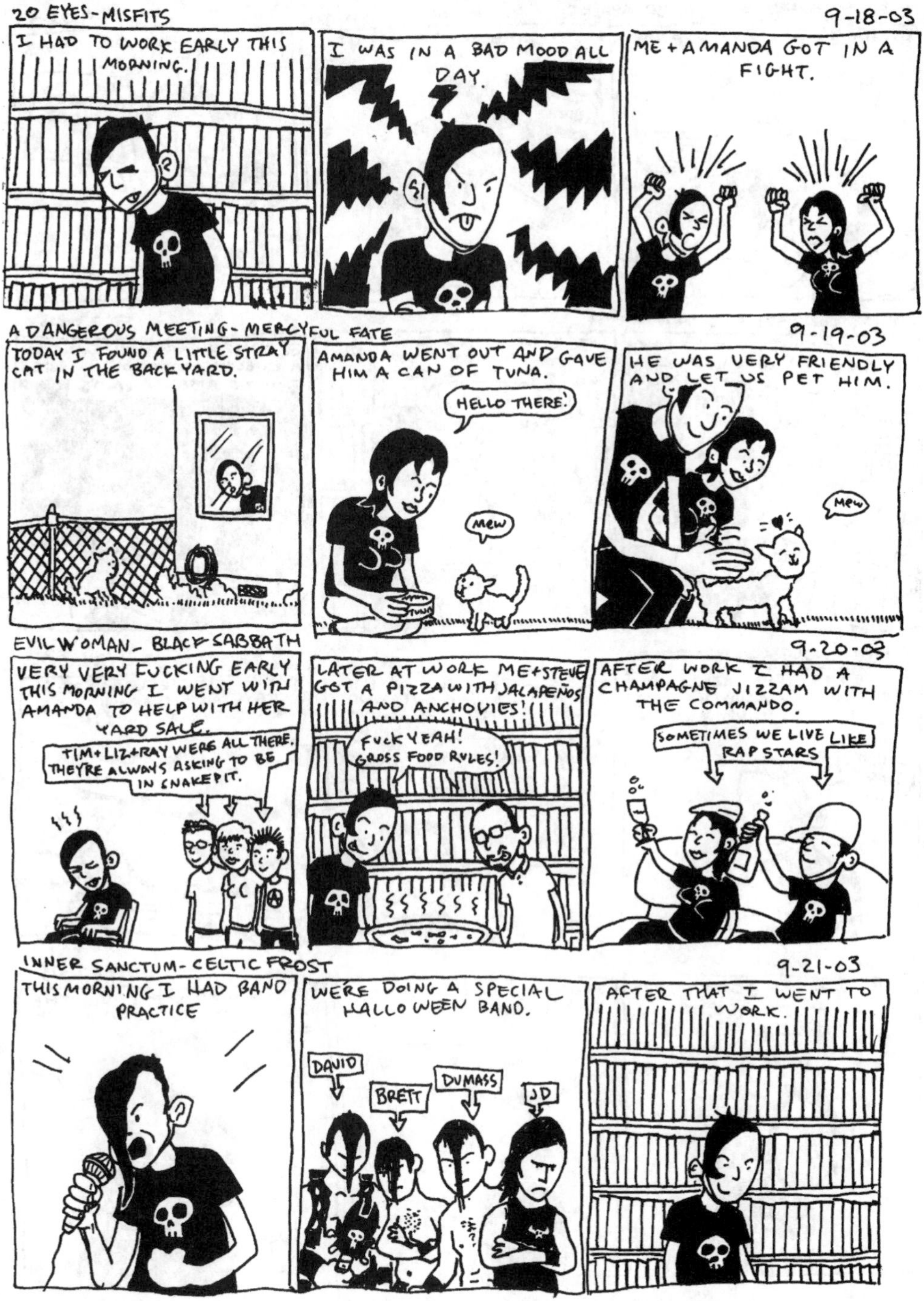

20 EYES-MISFITS
9-18-03
I HAD TO WORK EARLY THIS MORNING.
I WAS IN A BAD MOOD ALL DAY.
ME + AMANDA GOT IN A FIGHT.
A DANGEROUS MEETING-MERCYFUL FATE
9-19-03
TODAY I FOUND A LITTLE STRAY CAT IN THE BACKYARD.
AMANDA WENT OUT AND GAVE HIM A CAN OF TUNA.
HELLO THERE!
MEW
HE WAS VERY FRIENDLY AND LET US PET HIM.
MEW
EVIL WOMAN-BLACK SABBATH
9-20-03
VERY VERY FUCKING EARLY THIS MORNING I WENT WITH AMANDA TO HELP WITH HER YARD SALE.
TIM+LIZ+RAY WERE ALL THERE. THEY'RE ALWAYS ASKING TO BE IN SNAKEPIT.
LATER AT WORK ME+STEVE GOT A PIZZA WITH JALAPEÑOS AND ANCHOVIES!
FUCK YEAH! GROSS FOOD RULES!
AFTER WORK I HAD A CHAMPAGNE JIZZAM WITH THE COMMANDO.
SOMETIMES WE LIVE LIKE RAP STARS
INNER SANCTUM-CELTIC FROST
9-21-03
THIS MORNING I HAD BAND PRACTICE
WE'RE DOING A SPECIAL HALLOWEEN BAND.
DAVID
BRETT
DUMASS
JD
AFTER THAT I WENT TO WORK.

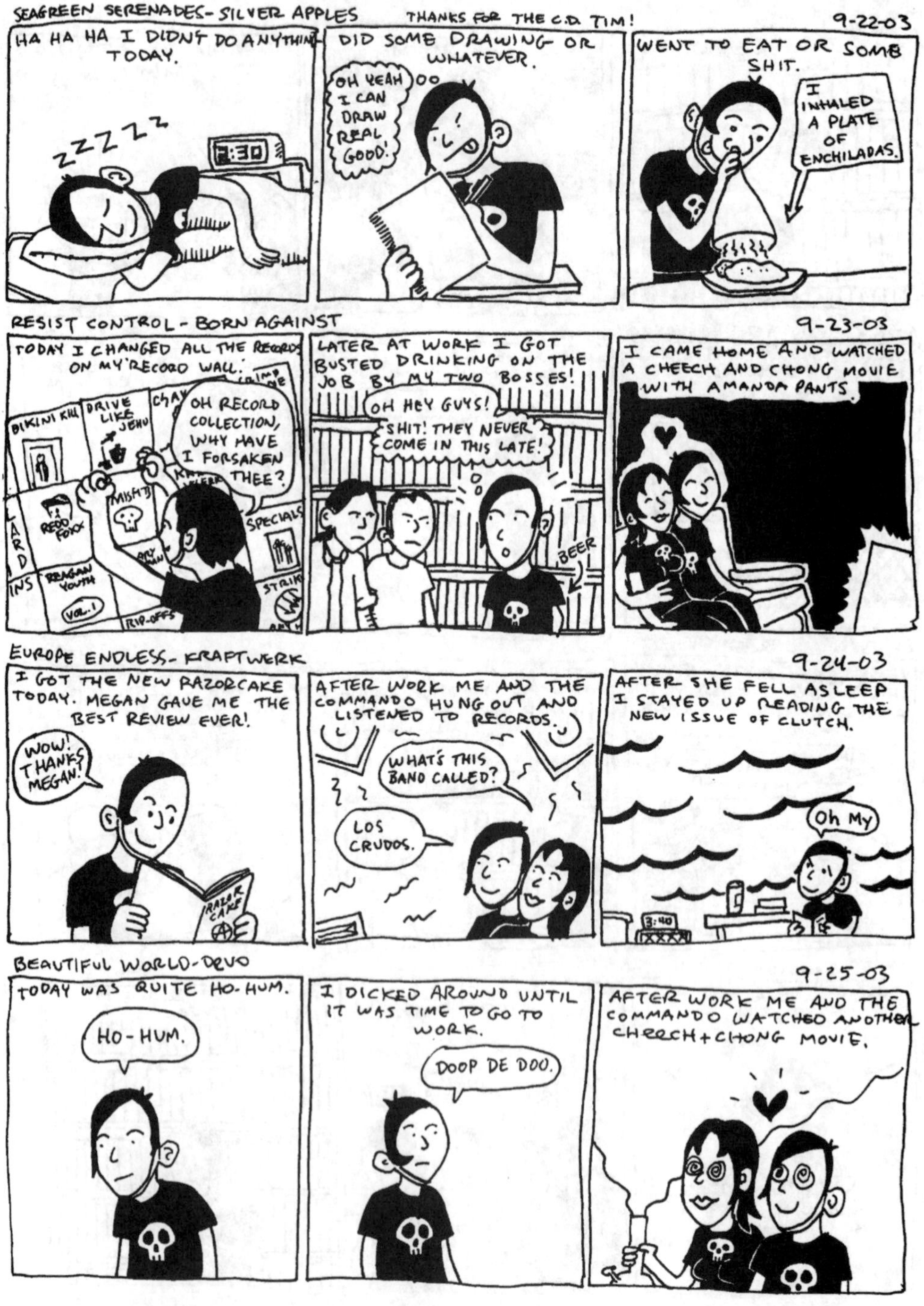
SEAGREEN SERENADES- SILVER APPLES
THANKS FOR THE C.D. TIM!
9-22-03
HA HA HA I DIDN'T DO ANYTHING TODAY.
ZZZZZ
2:30
DID SOME DRAWING OR WHATEVER.
OH YEAH I CAN DRAW REAL GOOD!
WENT TO EAT OR SOME SHIT.
I INHALED A PLATE OF ENCHILADAS.
RESIST CONTROL - BORN AGAINST
9-23-03
TODAY I CHANGED ALL THE RECORDS ON MY RECORD WALL.
BIKINI KILL
DRIVE LIKE JEHU
MISFITS
REDD FOXX
REAGAN YOUTH
VOL. 1
RIP-OFFS
SPECIALS
OH RECORD COLLECTION, WHY HAVE I FORSAKEN THEE?
LATER AT WORK I GOT BUSTED DRINKING ON THE JOB BY MY TWO BOSSES!
OH HEY GUYS!
SHIT! THEY NEVER COME IN THIS LATE!
BEER
I CAME HOME AND WATCHED A CHEECH AND CHONG MOVIE WITH AMANDA PANTS.
EUROPE ENDLESS- KRAFTWERK
9-24-03
I GOT THE NEW RAZORCAKE TODAY. MEGAN GAVE ME THE BEST REVIEW EVER!
WOW! THANKS MEGAN!
RAZOR CAKE
AFTER WORK ME AND THE COMMANDO HUNG OUT AND LISTENED TO RECORDS.
WHAT'S THIS BAND CALLED?
LOS CRUDOS.
AFTER SHE FELL ASLEEP I STAYED UP READING THE NEW ISSUE OF CLUTCH.
Oh My
3:40
BEAUTIFUL WORLD- DEVO
9-25-03
TODAY WAS QUITE HO-HUM.
HO-HUM.
I DICKED AROUND UNTIL IT WAS TIME TO GO TO WORK.
DOOP DE DOO.
AFTER WORK ME AND THE COMMANDO WATCHED ANOTHER CHEECH + CHONG MOVIE.

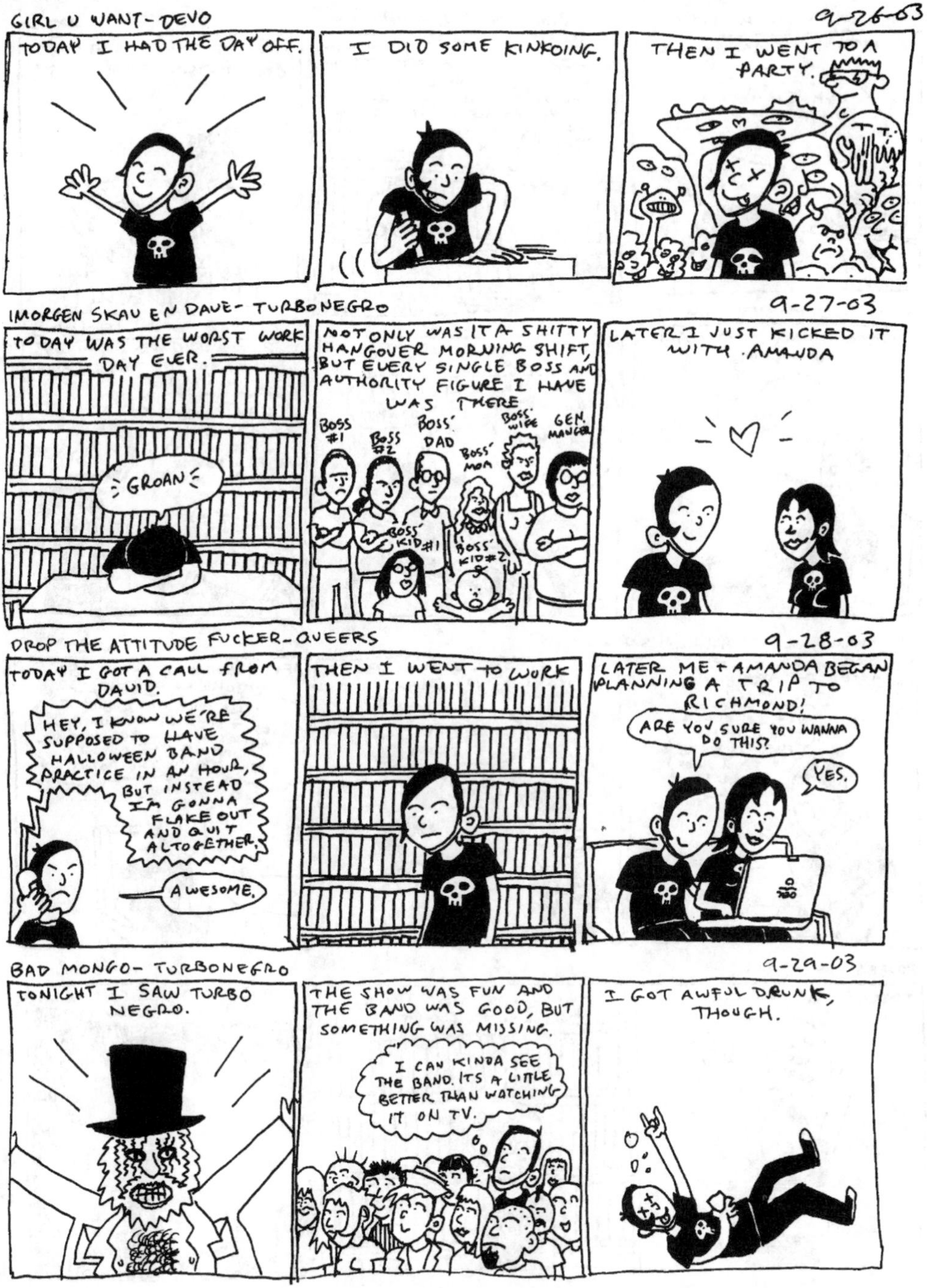

GIRL U WANT- DEVO
9-26-03
TODAY I HAD THE DAY OFF.
I DID SOME KINKOING.
THEN I WENT TO A PARTY.
IMORGEN SKAU EN DAVE- TURBONEGRO
9-27-03
TODAY WAS THE WORST WORK DAY EVER.
GROAN
NOT ONLY WAS IT A SHITTY HANGOVER MORNING SHIFT, BUT EVERY SINGLE BOSS AND AUTHORITY FIGURE I HAVE WAS THERE
BOSS #1
BOSS #2
BOSS' DAD
BOSS' MOM
BOSS' WIFE
GEN. MANGER
BOSS' KID #1
BOSS' KID #2
LATER I JUST KICKED IT WITH AMANDA
DROP THE ATTITUDE FUCKER- QUEERS
9-28-03
TODAY I GOT A CALL FROM DAVID.
HEY, I KNOW WE'RE SUPPOSED TO HAVE HALLOWEEN BAND PRACTICE IN AN HOUR, BUT INSTEAD I'M GONNA FLAKE OUT AND QUIT ALTOGETHER.
AWESOME.
THEN I WENT TO WORK
LATER ME + AMANDA BEGAN PLANNING A TRIP TO RICHMOND!
ARE YOU SURE YOU WANNA DO THIS?
YES.
BAD MONGO- TURBONEGRO
9-29-03
TONIGHT I SAW TURBO NEGRO.
THE SHOW WAS FUN AND THE BAND WAS GOOD, BUT SOMETHING WAS MISSING.
I CAN KINDA SEE THE BAND. ITS A LITTLE BETTER THAN WATCHING IT ON TV.
I GOT AWFUL DRUNK, THOUGH.

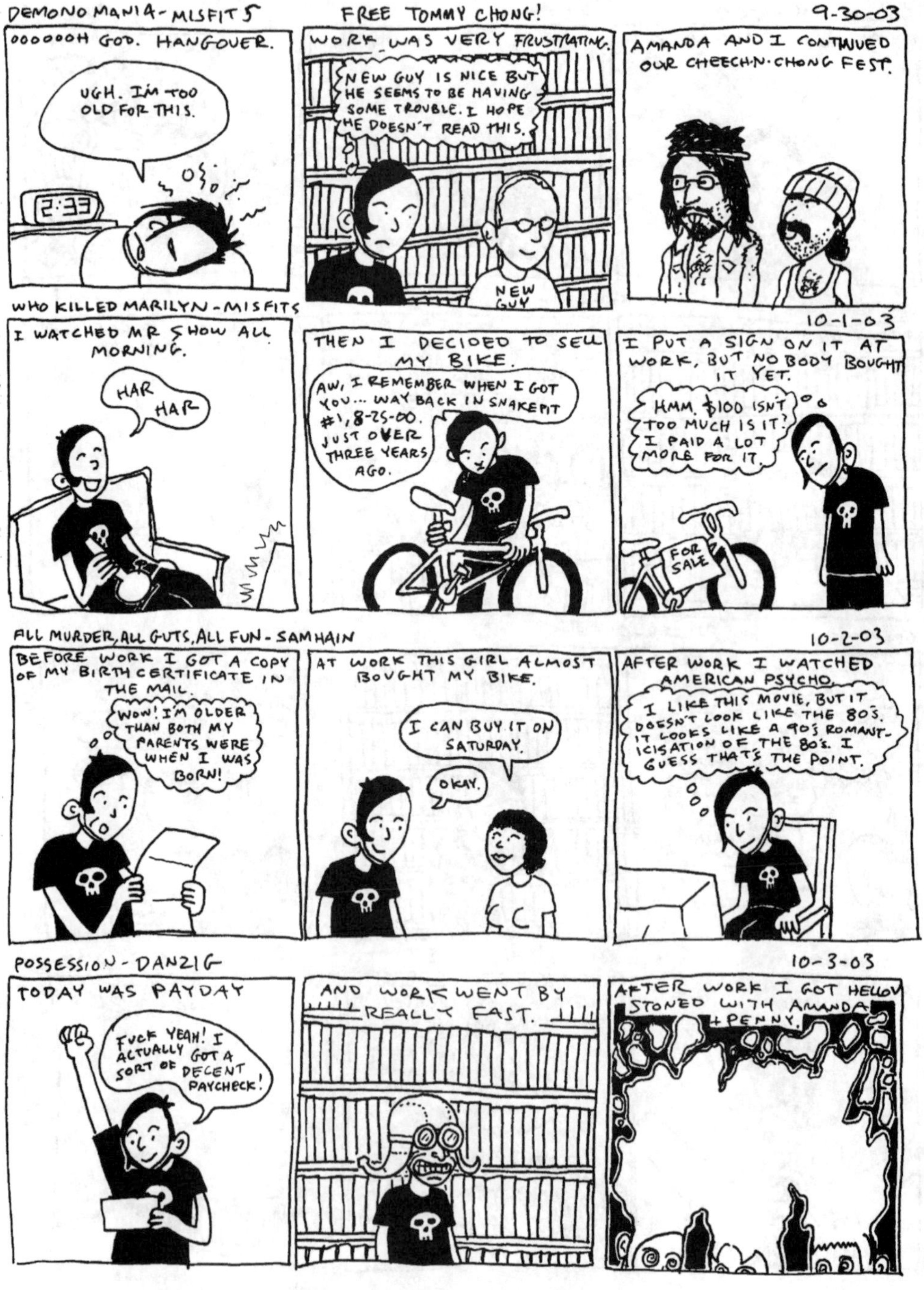
DEMONOMANIA - MISFITS
FREE TOMMY CHONG!
9-30-03
OOOOOOH GOD. HANGOVER.
UGH. I'M TOO OLD FOR THIS.
2:33
WORK WAS VERY FRUSTRATING.
NEW GUY IS NICE BUT HE SEEMS TO BE HAVING SOME TROUBLE. I HOPE HE DOESN'T READ THIS.
NEW GUY
AMANDA AND I CONTINUED OUR CHEECH-N-CHONG FEST.
WHO KILLED MARILYN - MISFITS
10-1-03
I WATCHED MR SHOW ALL MORNING.
HAR HAR
THEN I DECIDED TO SELL MY BIKE.
AW, I REMEMBER WHEN I GOT YOU... WAY BACK IN SNAKEPIT #1, 8-25-00. JUST OVER THREE YEARS AGO.
I PUT A SIGN ON IT AT WORK, BUT NOBODY BOUGHT IT YET.
HMM. $100 ISN'T TOO MUCH IS IT? I PAID A LOT MORE FOR IT.
FOR SALE
ALL MURDER, ALL GUTS, ALL FUN - SAMHAIN
10-2-03
BEFORE WORK I GOT A COPY OF MY BIRTH CERTIFICATE IN THE MAIL.
WOW! I'M OLDER THAN BOTH MY PARENTS WERE WHEN I WAS BORN!
AT WORK THIS GIRL ALMOST BOUGHT MY BIKE.
I CAN BUY IT ON SATURDAY.
OKAY.
AFTER WORK I WATCHED AMERICAN PSYCHO.
I LIKE THIS MOVIE, BUT IT DOESN'T LOOK LIKE THE 80'S. IT LOOKS LIKE A 90'S ROMANTICISATION OF THE 80'S. I GUESS THAT'S THE POINT.
POSSESSION - DANZIG
10-3-03
TODAY WAS PAYDAY
FUCK YEAH! I ACTUALLY GOT A SORT OF DECENT PAYCHECK!
AND WORK WENT BY REALLY FAST.
AFTER WORK I GOT HELLOV STONED WITH AMANDA + PENNY.

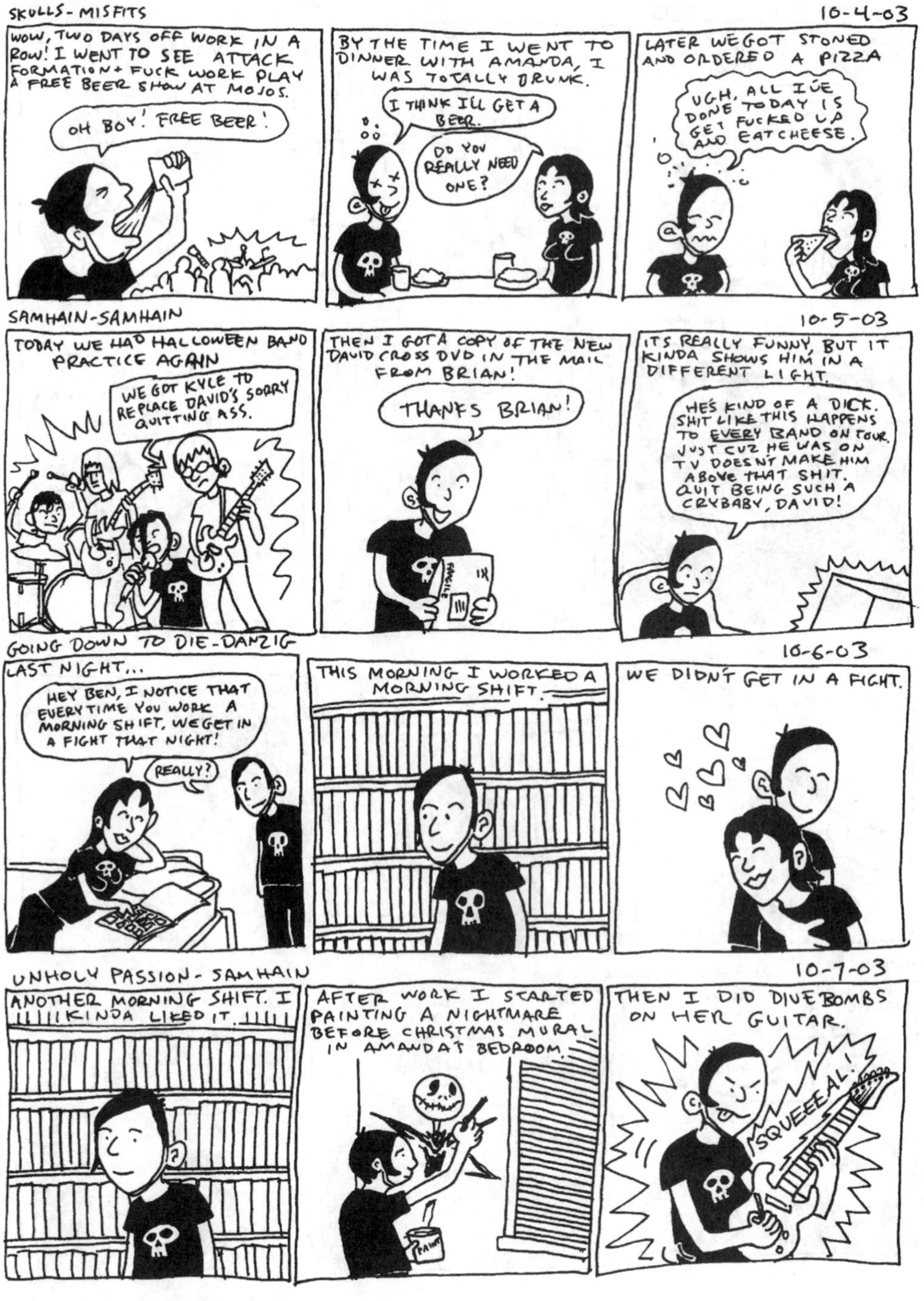
SKULLS - MISFITS
10-4-03
WOW, TWO DAYS OFF WORK IN A ROW! I WENT TO SEE ATTACK FORMATION + FUCK WORK PLAY A FREE BEER SHOW AT MOJOS.
OH BOY! FREE BEER!
BY THE TIME I WENT TO DINNER WITH AMANDA, I WAS TOTALLY DRUNK.
I THINK I'LL GET A BEER.
DO YOU REALLY NEED ONE?
LATER WE GOT STONED AND ORDERED A PIZZA
UGH, ALL I'VE DONE TODAY IS GET FUCKED UP AND EAT CHEESE.
SAMHAIN - SAMHAIN
10-5-03
TODAY WE HAD HALLOWEEN BAND PRACTICE AGAIN
WE GOT KYLE TO REPLACE DAVID'S SORRY QUITTING ASS.
THEN I GOT A COPY OF THE NEW DAVID CROSS DVD IN THE MAIL FROM BRIAN!
THANKS BRIAN!
FRAGILE
IX
ITS REALLY FUNNY, BUT IT KINDA SHOWS HIM IN A DIFFERENT LIGHT.
HE'S KIND OF A DICK. SHIT LIKE THIS HAPPENS TO EVERY BAND ON TOUR. JUST CUZ HE WAS ON TV DOESN'T MAKE HIM ABOVE THAT SHIT. QUIT BEING SUCH A CRYBABY, DAVID!
GOING DOWN TO DIE - DANZIG
10-6-03
LAST NIGHT...
HEY BEN, I NOTICE THAT EVERY TIME YOU WORK A MORNING SHIFT, WE GET IN A FIGHT THAT NIGHT!
REALLY?
THIS MORNING I WORKED A MORNING SHIFT.
WE DIDN'T GET IN A FIGHT.
UNHOLY PASSION - SAMHAIN
10-7-03
ANOTHER MORNING SHIFT. I KINDA LIKED IT.
AFTER WORK I STARTED PAINTING A NIGHTMARE BEFORE CHRISTMAS MURAL IN AMANDA'S BEDROOM.
PAINT
THEN I DID DIVE BOMBS ON HER GUITAR.
SQUEEEAL!

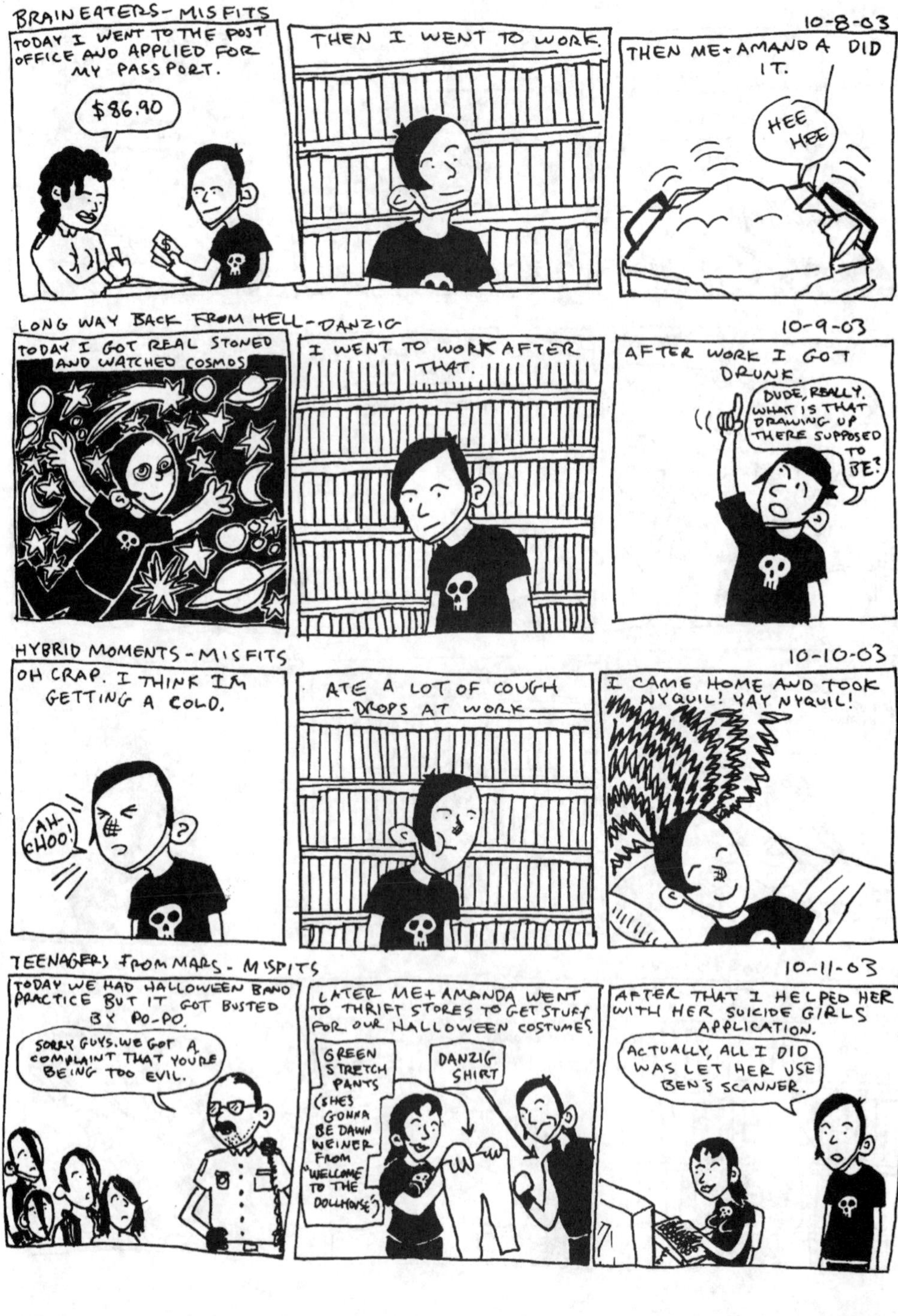

BRAINEATERS - MISFITS
10-8-03
TODAY I WENT TO THE POST OFFICE AND APPLIED FOR MY PASSPORT.
$86.90
THEN I WENT TO WORK.
THEN ME + AMANDA DID IT.
HEE HEE
LONG WAY BACK FROM HELL - DANZIG
10-9-03
TODAY I GOT REAL STONED AND WATCHED COSMOS
I WENT TO WORK AFTER THAT.
AFTER WORK I GOT DRUNK.
DUDE, REALLY. WHAT IS THAT DRAWING UP THERE SUPPOSED TO BE?
HYBRID MOMENTS - MISFITS
10-10-03
OH CRAP. I THINK I'M GETTING A COLD.
AH-CHOO!
ATE A LOT OF COUGH DROPS AT WORK
I CAME HOME AND TOOK NYQUIL! YAY NYQUIL!
TEENAGERS FROM MARS - MISFITS
10-11-03
TODAY WE HAD HALLOWEEN BAND PRACTICE BUT IT GOT BUSTED BY PO-PO.
SORRY GUYS, WE GOT A COMPLAINT THAT YOU'RE BEING TOO EVIL.
LATER ME + AMANDA WENT TO THRIFT STORES TO GET STUFF FOR OUR HALLOWEEN COSTUMES.
GREEN STRETCH PANTS
(SHE'S GONNA BE DAWN WEINER FROM "WELCOME TO THE DOLLHOUSE")
DANZIG SHIRT
AFTER THAT I HELPED HER WITH HER SUICIDE GIRLS APPLICATION.
ACTUALLY, ALL I DID WAS LET HER USE BEN'S SCANNER.

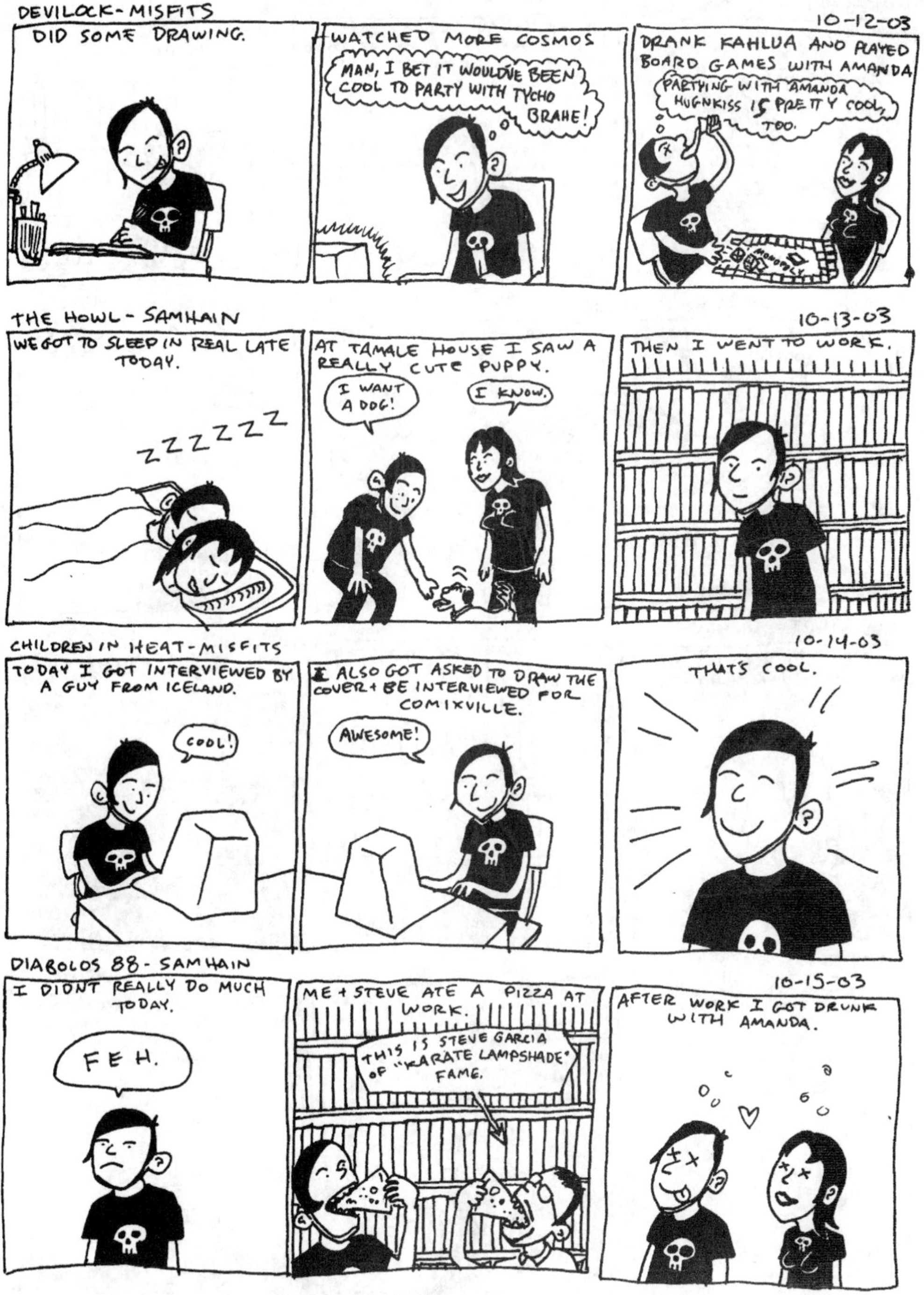
DEVILOCK - MISFITS
10-12-03
DID SOME DRAWING.
WATCHED MORE COSMOS
MAN, I BET IT WOULD'VE BEEN COOL TO PARTY WITH TYCHO BRAHE!
DRANK KAHLUA AND PLAYED BOARD GAMES WITH AMANDA
PARTYING WITH AMANDA HUGNKISS IS PRETTY COOL, TOO.
MONOPOLY
THE HOWL - SAMHAIN
10-13-03
WE GOT TO SLEEP IN REAL LATE TODAY.
ZZZZZZ
AT TAMALE HOUSE I SAW A REALLY CUTE PUPPY.
I WANT A DOG!
I KNOW.
THEN I WENT TO WORK.
CHILDREN IN HEAT - MISFITS
10-14-03
TODAY I GOT INTERVIEWED BY A GUY FROM ICELAND.
COOL!
I ALSO GOT ASKED TO DRAW THE COVER + BE INTERVIEWED FOR COMIXVILLE.
AWESOME!
THAT'S COOL.
DIABOLOS 88 - SAMHAIN
10-15-03
I DIDNT REALLY DO MUCH TODAY.
FEH.
ME + STEVE ATE A PIZZA AT WORK.
THIS IS STEVE GARCIA OF "KARATE LAMPSHADE" FAME.
AFTER WORK I GOT DRUNK WITH AMANDA.

SNAKES OF CHRIST - DANZIG.

10-16-03

MAN, I'M BROKE.

FUCK. 82¢.

I THINK AFTER I GET BACK FROM JAPAN, I'M GONNA LOOK FOR A NEW JOB.

YEAH.

CLIK CLIK

THE VIDEO STORE ISN'T AS COOL AS IT USED TO BE ANYWAY.

LONG WAY BACK FROM HELL - DANZIG

10-17-03

WOW, PAYDAY! AND A FRIDAY OFF!

MONEY IS AWESOME!

WE HAD HALLOWEEN BAND PRACTICE

THEN I SAW THE WINKS AND 5-WAY ACTION PLAY A SHOW.

BEEN A LONG TIME SINCE I'VE ROCKED AND ROLLED.

THE SHIFT - SAMHAIN

10-18-03

THIS MORNING I WENT TO EAT WITH BEN, NICK + REAGAN.

THEN I WENT TO WORK.

THEN I REALIZED SOMETHING.

MAN, SNAKEPIT'S REALLY BEEN BORING LATELY. IS MY LIFE STARTING TO GET BORING? AM I GETTING TOO OLD?

DIRTY BLACK SUMMER - DANZIG

10-19-03

TODAY ME + AMANDA WENT THRIFT STORE HOPPIN'.

THEN WE WENT TO WATERLOO AND THEY DIDN'T HAVE A GOD DAMNED THING I WANTED.

FUCK! I WISH JUG WOULD HURRY UP AND OPEN HIS RECORD STORE!

AFTER WORK I WATCHED TV CARNAGE WITH AMANDA, PENNY AND JOSH.

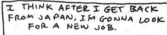

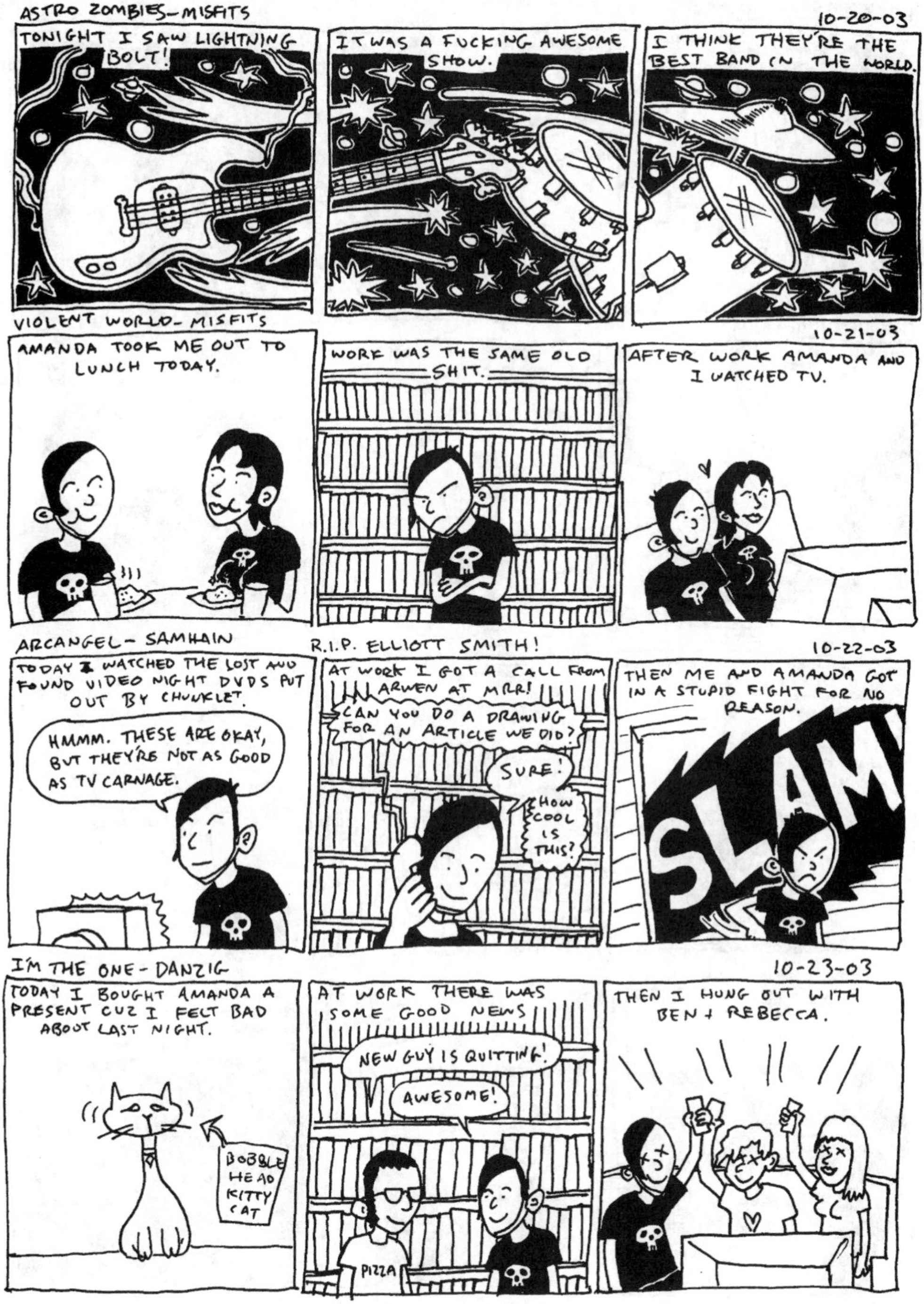
ASTRO ZOMBIES – MISFITS
10-20-03
TONIGHT I SAW LIGHTNING BOLT!
IT WAS A FUCKING AWESOME SHOW.
I THINK THEY'RE THE BEST BAND IN THE WORLD.
VIOLENT WORLD – MISFITS
10-21-03
AMANDA TOOK ME OUT TO LUNCH TODAY.
WORK WAS THE SAME OLD SHIT.
AFTER WORK AMANDA AND I WATCHED TV.
ARCANGEL – SAMHAIN
R.I.P. ELLIOTT SMITH!
10-22-03
TODAY I WATCHED THE LOST AND FOUND VIDEO NIGHT DVDS PUT OUT BY CHUNKLET.
HMMM. THESE ARE OKAY, BUT THEY'RE NOT AS GOOD AS TV CARNAGE.
AT WORK I GOT A CALL FROM ARWEN AT MRR!
CAN YOU DO A DRAWING FOR AN ARTICLE WE DID?
SURE!
HOW COOL IS THIS?
THEN ME AND AMANDA GOT IN A STUPID FIGHT FOR NO REASON.
SLAM
I'M THE ONE – DANZIG
10-23-03
TODAY I BOUGHT AMANDA A PRESENT CUZ I FELT BAD ABOUT LAST NIGHT.
BOBBLE HEAD KITTY CAT
AT WORK THERE WAS SOME GOOD NEWS
NEW GUY IS QUITTING!
AWESOME!
PIZZA
THEN I HUNG OUT WITH BEN + REBECCA.

HATE BREEDERS - MISFITS   10-24-03

HALLOWEEN IS JUST A WEEK AWAY!

I LOVE HALLOWEEN. IT'S MY FAVORITE HOLIDAY.

THAT'S ALL.

THE BIRTHING - SAMHAIN   10-25-03

THIS MORNING I HUNG OUT WITH ED.

THEN I MADE SOME FAKE BLOOD FOR HALLOWEEN.

LATER I HUNG OUT WITH AMANDA AND HER CAT.

WOLF'S BLOOD - MISFITS

TODAY WE HAD HALLOWEEN BAND PRACTICE AGAIN.

I MIGHT HAVE TO PLAY BASS FOR THE DANZIG SONGS CUZ BEN FUCKED HIS HAND UP IN A SKATEBOARD CRASH.

HAPPY BIRTHDAY TO D.F.I.   10-26-03

AT WORK MY FRIEND AARON BOUGHT ME A TALL BOY OF SCHLITZ BLUE BULL.

THANKS AARON!

NO SWEAT!

AFTER WORK I WATCHED INDIANA JONES AND THE TEMPLE OF DOOM.

GOD, I CAN'T BELIEVE HOW RACIST THIS IS. INDIAN PEOPLE DON'T EAT SNAKES AND BUGS AND EYBALLS AND BRAINS!

NOVEMBER'S FIRE - SAMHAIN   10-27-03

TODAY ME + BRETT PAINTED A BACKDROP FOR THE HALLOWEEN SHOW.

THEN I WENT TO THE GROCERY STORE WITH AMANDA.

PICKLED ASPARAGUS!

FAKE BACON!

LATER WE WATCHED THE BLAIR WITCH PROJECT. I'D FORGOTTEN HOW SCARY IT WAS.

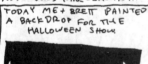

HORROR HOTEL - MISFITS

10-28-03

BEFORE WORK I PLAYED VIDEO GAMES.

AT WORK I DRANK A 40 OF OLDE ENGLISH

AFTER WORK ME+AMANDA CARVED A JACK-O-LANTERN

KILLER WOLF - DANZIG

10-29-03

I SPENT MOST OF MY MORNING GETTING READY FOR HALLOWEEN.

AM I DEMON?

THEN I WENT TO WORK.

YEAH! I DON'T HAVE TO WORK AGAIN UNTIL NOVEMBER!

THEN A BAND CALLED THE ORPHANS STAYED AT MY HOUSE.

WE ARE 138 - MISFITS

10-30-03

TODAY I CARVED ANOTHER JACK-O-LANTERN AND MADE SOME MORE FAKE BLOOD.

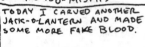

THEN I WATCHED THE HULK. IT SUCKED.

ZZZZ

THEN I WENT TO THE ORPHANS SHOW. THEY ROCKED!

HALLOWEEN - DEAD KENNEDYS

FUCK SKINHEADS!

10-31-03

TODAY DURING HALLOWEEN BAND PRACTICE BEN'S GUITAR AMP THAT WE WERE BORROWING BLEW UP!

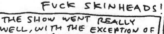

THE SHOW WENT REALLY WELL, WITH THE EXCEPTION OF SOME DUMBASS SKINHEADS.

INFINITE SLEEP HAS ENDED AND I LIVE AGAIN!

I DUMPED A GALLON OF FAKE BLOOD ON MY HEAD.

AFTER THE SHOW I CUT MY DEVILOCK OFF.

LATER, DUDE.

SNIP

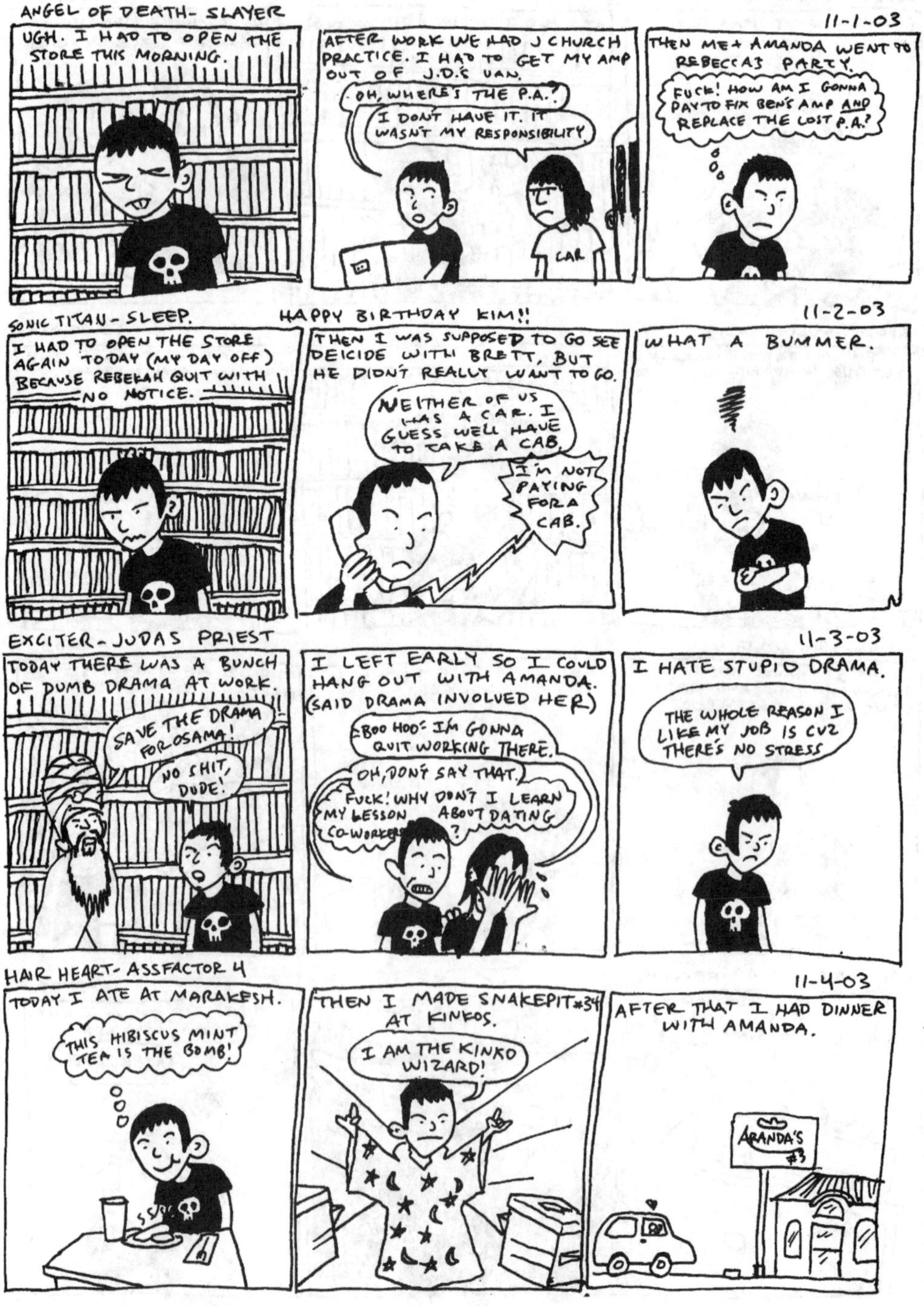
ANGEL OF DEATH - SLAYER
11-1-03
UGH. I HAD TO OPEN THE STORE THIS MORNING.
AFTER WORK WE HAD J CHURCH PRACTICE. I HAD TO GET MY AMP OUT OF J.D.'S VAN.
OH, WHERE'S THE P.A.?
I DON'T HAVE IT. IT WASN'T MY RESPONSIBILITY.
CAR
THEN ME + AMANDA WENT TO REBECCA'S PARTY.
FUCK! HOW AM I GONNA PAY TO FIX BEN'S AMP AND REPLACE THE LOST P.A.?
SONIC TITAN - SLEEP.
HAPPY BIRTHDAY KIM!!
11-2-03
I HAD TO OPEN THE STORE AGAIN TODAY (MY DAY OFF) BECAUSE REBEKAH QUIT WITH NO NOTICE.
THEN I WAS SUPPOSED TO GO SEE DEICIDE WITH BRETT, BUT HE DIDN'T REALLY WANT TO GO.
NEITHER OF US HAS A CAR. I GUESS WE'LL HAVE TO TAKE A CAB.
I'M NOT PAYING FOR A CAB.
WHAT A BUMMER.
EXCITER - JUDAS PRIEST
11-3-03
TODAY THERE WAS A BUNCH OF DUMB DRAMA AT WORK.
SAVE THE DRAMA FOR OSAMA!
NO SHIT, DUDE!
I LEFT EARLY SO I COULD HANG OUT WITH AMANDA. (SAID DRAMA INVOLVED HER)
BOO HOO I'M GONNA QUIT WORKING THERE.
OH, DON'T SAY THAT.
FUCK! WHY DON'T I LEARN MY LESSON ABOUT DATING CO-WORKERS?
I HATE STUPID DRAMA.
THE WHOLE REASON I LIKE MY JOB IS CUZ THERE'S NO STRESS
HAIR HEART - ASSFACTOR 4
11-4-03
TODAY I ATE AT MARAKESH.
THIS HIBISCUS MINT TEA IS THE BOMB!
THEN I MADE SNAKEPIT #34 AT KINKOS.
I AM THE KINKO WIZARD!
AFTER THAT I HAD DINNER WITH AMANDA.
ARANDA'S #3

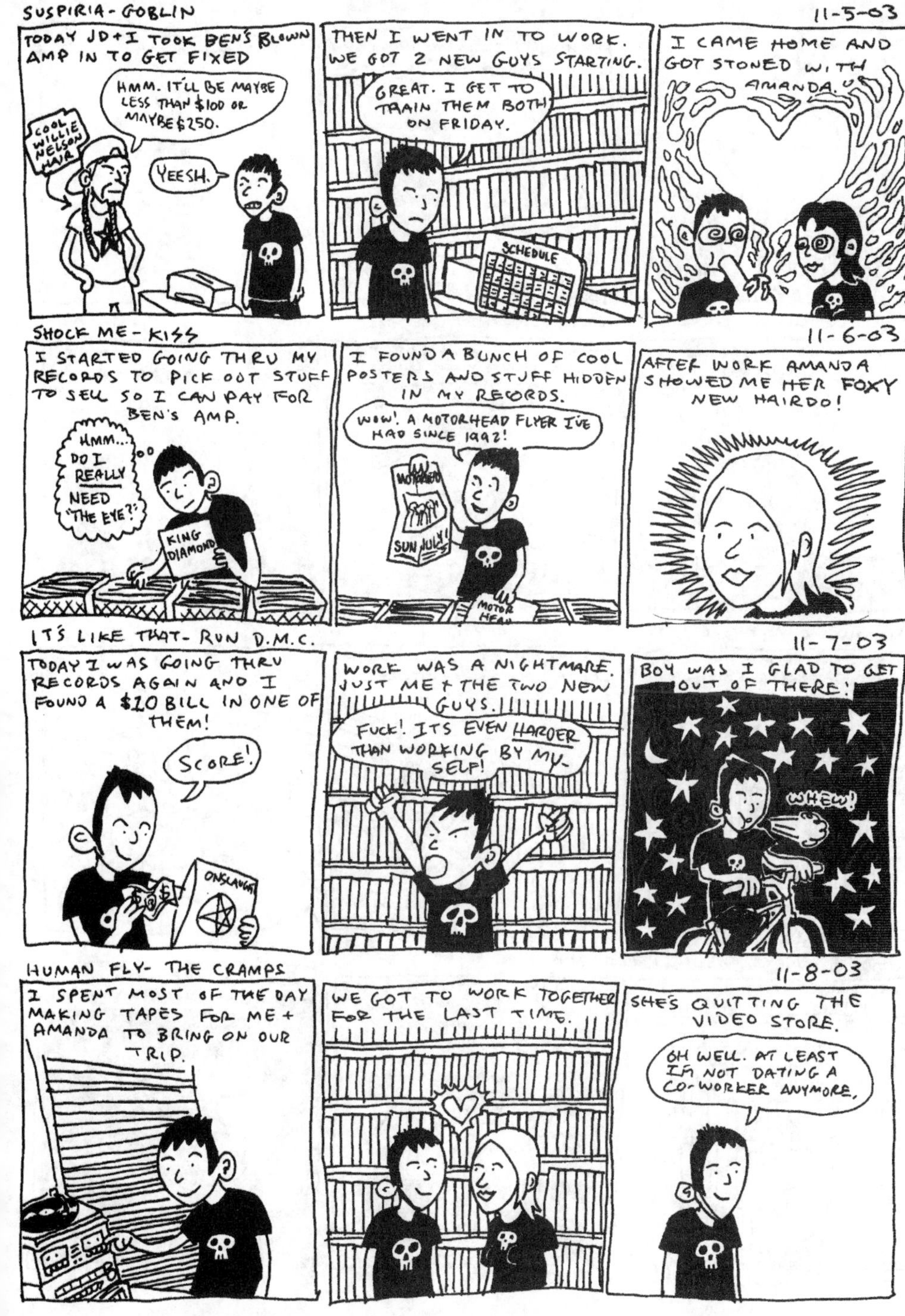

SUSPIRIA - GOBLIN
11-5-03
TODAY JD + I TOOK BEN'S BLOWN AMP IN TO GET FIXED
HMM. IT'LL BE MAYBE LESS THAN $100 OR MAYBE $250.
COOL WILLIE NELSON HAIR
YEESH.
THEN I WENT IN TO WORK. WE GOT 2 NEW GUYS STARTING.
GREAT. I GET TO TRAIN THEM BOTH ON FRIDAY.
SCHEDULE
I CAME HOME AND GOT STONED WITH AMANDA.
SHOCK ME - KISS
11-6-03
I STARTED GOING THRU MY RECORDS TO PICK OUT STUFF TO SELL SO I CAN PAY FOR BEN'S AMP.
HMM... DO I REALLY NEED "THE EYE?"
KING DIAMOND
I FOUND A BUNCH OF COOL POSTERS AND STUFF HIDDEN IN MY RECORDS.
WOW! A MOTORHEAD FLYER I'VE HAD SINCE 1992!
SUN JULY!
AFTER WORK AMANDA SHOWED ME HER FOXY NEW HAIRDO!
IT'S LIKE THAT - RUN D.M.C.
11-7-03
TODAY I WAS GOING THRU RECORDS AGAIN AND I FOUND A $20 BILL IN ONE OF THEM!
SCORE!
ONSLAUGHT
WORK WAS A NIGHTMARE. JUST ME + THE TWO NEW GUYS.
FUCK! ITS EVEN HARDER THAN WORKING BY MY-SELF!
BOY WAS I GLAD TO GET OUT OF THERE!
WHEW!
HUMAN FLY - THE CRAMPS
11-8-03
I SPENT MOST OF THE DAY MAKING TAPES FOR ME + AMANDA TO BRING ON OUR TRIP.
WE GOT TO WORK TOGETHER FOR THE LAST TIME.
SHE'S QUITTING THE VIDEO STORE.
OH WELL. AT LEAST I'M NOT DATING A CO-WORKER ANYMORE.

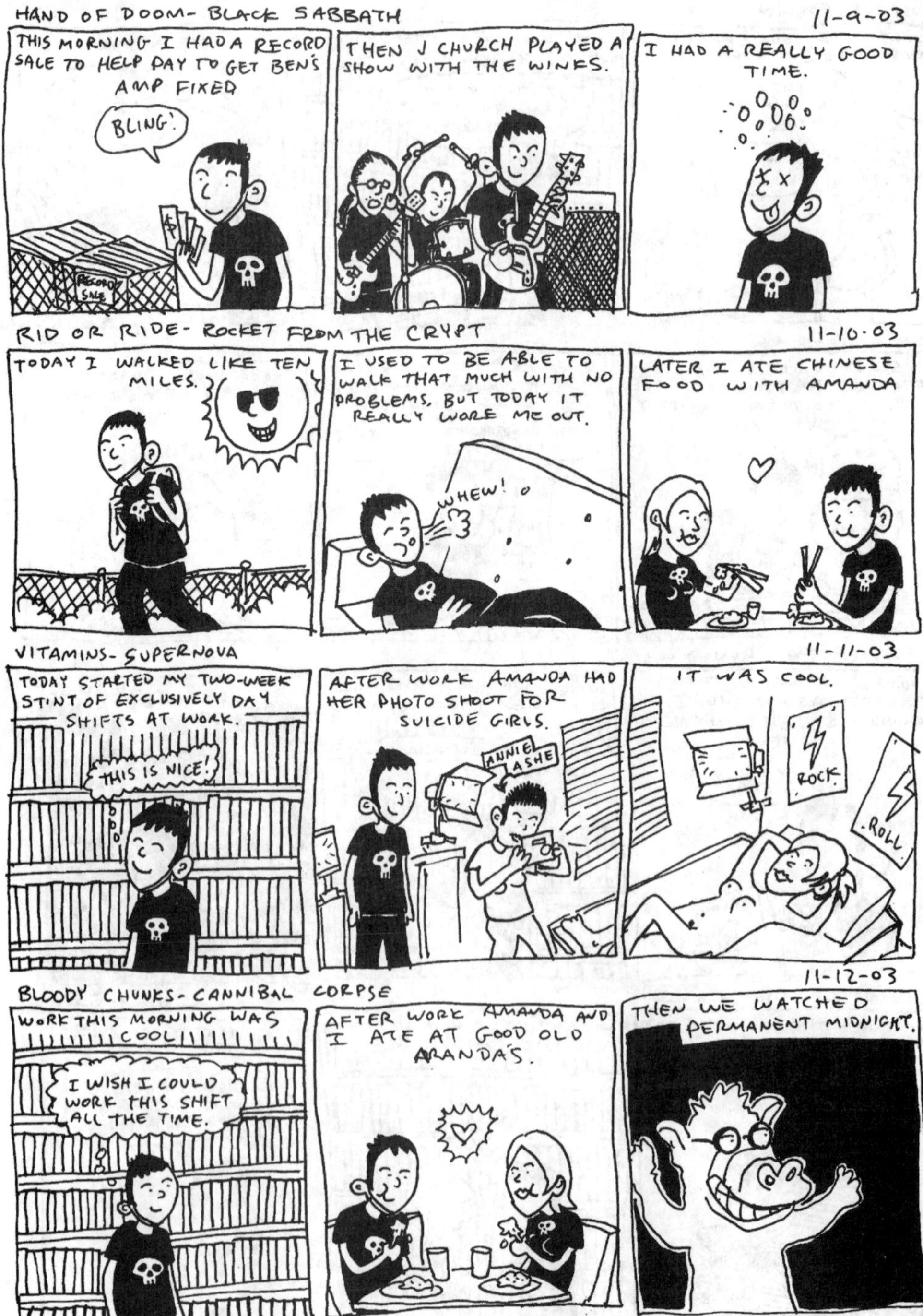
HAND OF DOOM- BLACK SABBATH
11-9-03
THIS MORNING I HAD A RECORD SALE TO HELP PAY TO GET BEN'S AMP FIXED
BLING!
RECORD SALE
THEN J CHURCH PLAYED A SHOW WITH THE WINKS.
I HAD A REALLY GOOD TIME.
RID OR RIDE- ROCKET FROM THE CRYPT
11-10-03
TODAY I WALKED LIKE TEN MILES.
I USED TO BE ABLE TO WALK THAT MUCH WITH NO PROBLEMS, BUT TODAY IT REALLY WORE ME OUT.
WHEW!
LATER I ATE CHINESE FOOD WITH AMANDA
VITAMINS- SUPERNOVA
11-11-03
TODAY STARTED MY TWO-WEEK STINT OF EXCLUSIVELY DAY SHIFTS AT WORK.
THIS IS NICE!
AFTER WORK AMANDA HAD HER PHOTO SHOOT FOR SUICIDE GIRLS.
ANNIE ASHE
IT WAS COOL.
ROCK
ROLL
11-12-03
BLOODY CHUNKS- CANNIBAL CORPSE
WORK THIS MORNING WAS COOL
I WISH I COULD WORK THIS SHIFT ALL THE TIME.
AFTER WORK AMANDA AND I ATE AT GOOD OLD ARANDA'S.
THEN WE WATCHED PERMANENT MIDNIGHT.

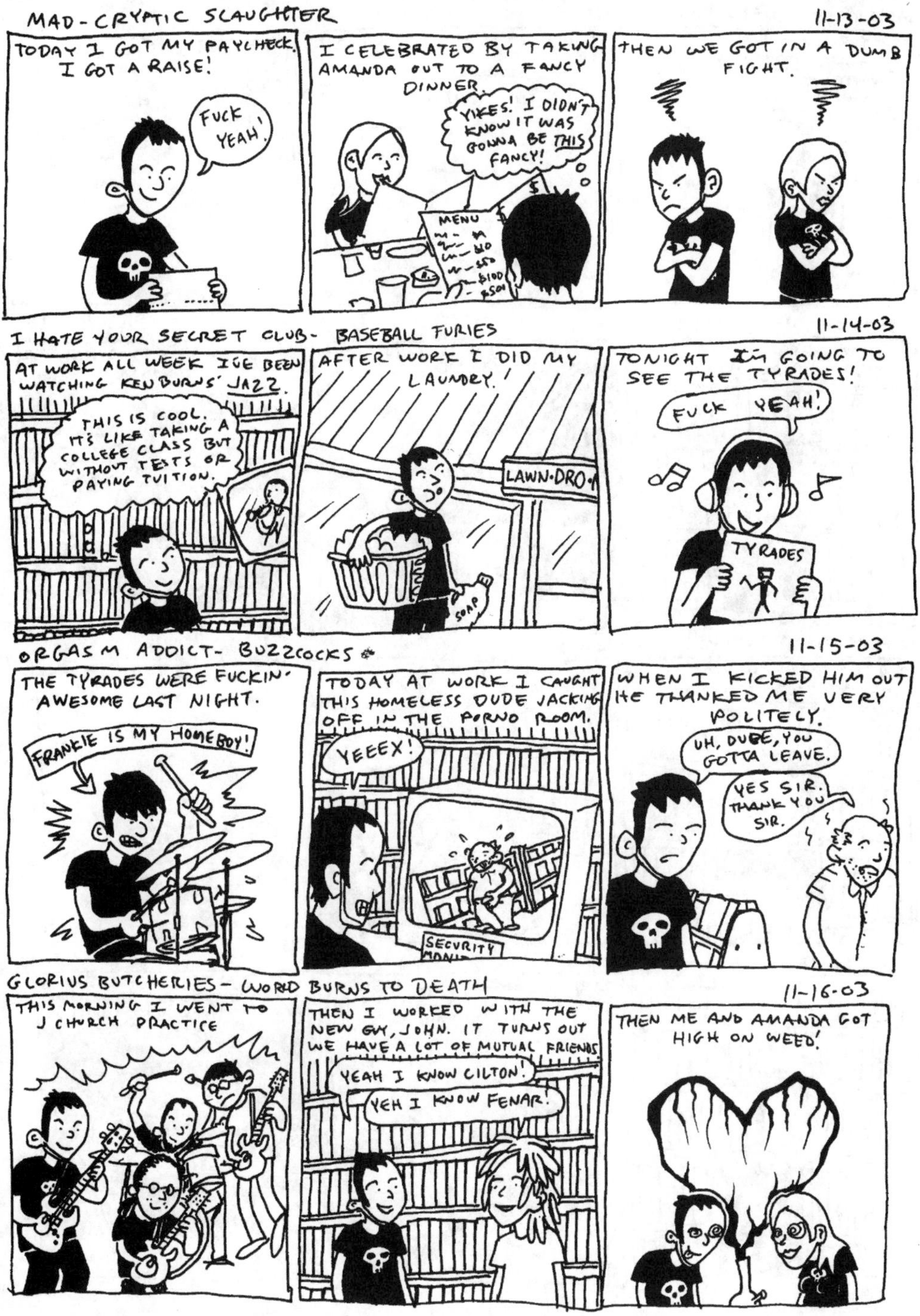
MAD-CRYPTIC SLAUGHTER
11-13-03
TODAY I GOT MY PAYCHECK. I GOT A RAISE!
FUCK YEAH!
I CELEBRATED BY TAKING AMANDA OUT TO A FANCY DINNER.
YIKES! I DIDN'T KNOW IT WAS GONNA BE THIS FANCY!
$
MENU
$10
$50
$100
$500
THEN WE GOT IN A DUMB FIGHT.
I HATE YOUR SECRET CLUB- BASEBALL FURIES
11-14-03
AT WORK ALL WEEK I'VE BEEN WATCHING KEN BURNS' JAZZ.
THIS IS COOL. IT'S LIKE TAKING A COLLEGE CLASS BUT WITHOUT TESTS OR PAYING TUITION.
AFTER WORK I DID MY LAUNDRY.
LAWN•DRO•
SOAP
TONIGHT I'M GOING TO SEE THE TYRADES!
FUCK YEAH!
TYRADES
ORGASM ADDICT- BUZZCOCKS
11-15-03
THE TYRADES WERE FUCKIN' AWESOME LAST NIGHT.
FRANKIE IS MY HOMEBOY!
TODAY AT WORK I CAUGHT THIS HOMELESS DUDE JACKING OFF IN THE PORNO ROOM.
YEEEX!
SECURITY MONI
WHEN I KICKED HIM OUT HE THANKED ME VERY POLITELY.
UH, DUDE, YOU GOTTA LEAVE.
YES SIR. THANK YOU SIR.
GLORIUS BUTCHERIES- WORD BURNS TO DEATH
11-16-03
THIS MORNING I WENT TO J CHURCH PRACTICE
THEN I WORKED WITH THE NEW GUY, JOHN. IT TURNS OUT WE HAVE A LOT OF MUTUAL FRIENDS.
YEAH I KNOW CILTON!
YEH I KNOW FENAR!
THEN ME AND AMANDA GOT HIGH ON WEED!

MISS EASY RIDER - ORPHANS
11-17-03
TODAY I RAN A BUNCH OF ERRANDS.
SOMETIMES I REALLY WISH I HAD A CAR.
THEN AMANDA CALLED ME UP CRYING.
OH NO! WHAT'S WRONG?
SHE WAS SUPPOSED TO QUIT THE VIDEOSTORE TODAY, BUT SHE GOT FIRED INSTEAD.
THAT SUCKS!
BUT IT'S FUNNY!
PEACE OF MIND - BOSTON
11-18-03
WORK THIS MORNING WAS PRETTY LACKLUSTER.
AFTER WORK I GOT VERY STONED.
AND I MADE DINNER FOR THE COMMANDO.
WIPE IT TIL IT BLEEDS - TURBONEGRO
11-19-03
I WASTE SO MUCH OF MY LIFE AT STUPID DUMBASS WORK.
I HAVE A WHOLE LOT OF DRAWING TO GET DONE, TOO.
NOV.
URK..
DEADLINE 12/03
FUCK IT.
12 PAK
COOL PLACE TO PARK - GWAR
11-20-03
WORK. WHATEVER.
I DID SOME DRAWING WHILE AMANDA DID SOME KNITTING.
IN THE MIDDLE OF THE NIGHT AMANDA'S ROOMATE DRUNKENLY CRAWLED INTO BED WITH US.
MOVE, BEN!
WHY?
SO I CAN GO OUTSIDE.
UH, THERE'S NO DOOR IN THIS ROOM.

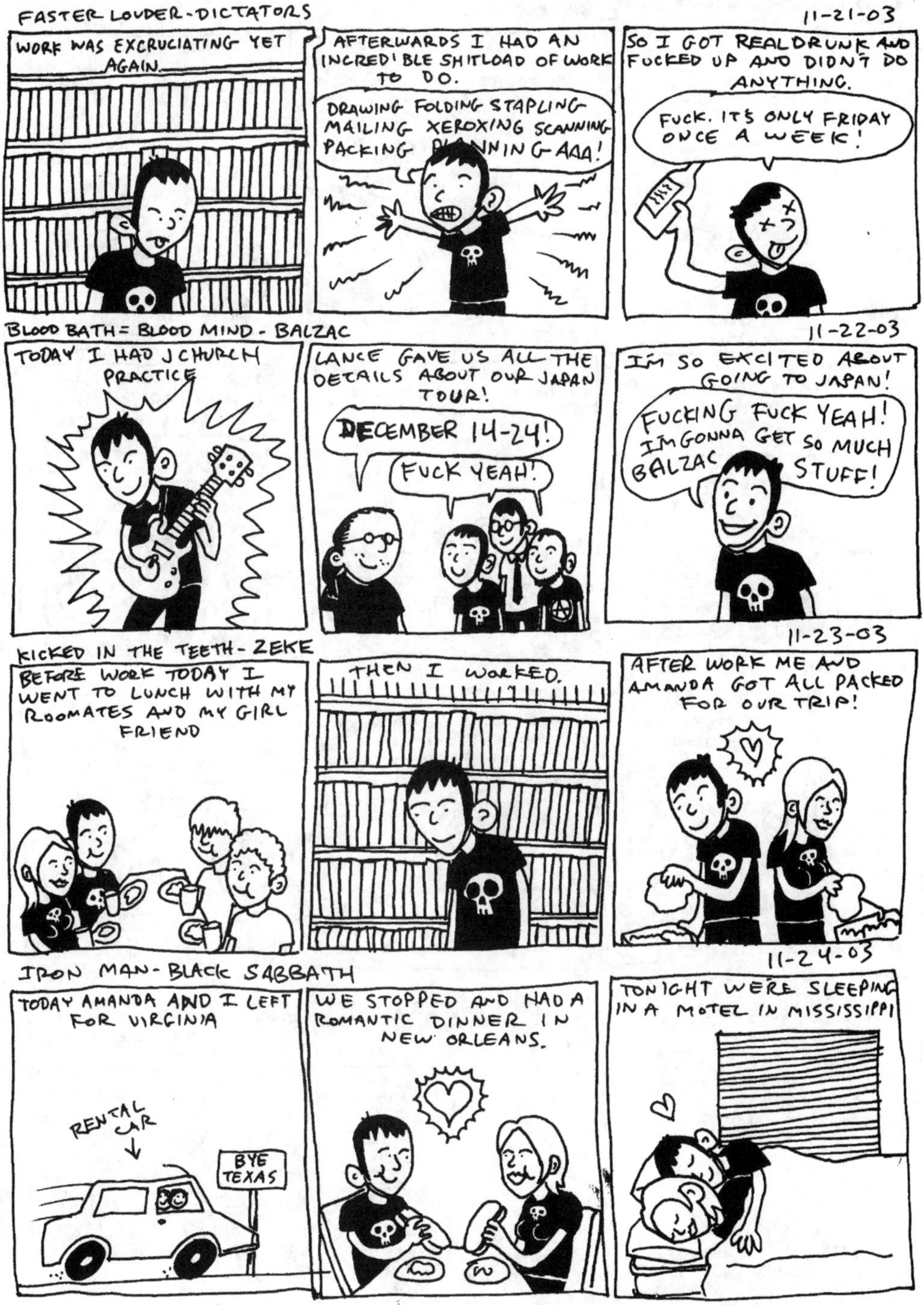
FASTER LOUDER - DICTATORS
11-21-03
WORK WAS EXCRUCIATING YET AGAIN.
AFTERWARDS I HAD AN INCREDIBLE SHITLOAD OF WORK TO DO.
DRAWING FOLDING STAPLING MAILING XEROXING SCANNING PACKING PLANNING AAA!
SO I GOT REAL DRUNK AND FUCKED UP AND DIDN'T DO ANYTHING.
FUCK. IT'S ONLY FRIDAY ONCE A WEEK!
BLOOD BATH = BLOOD MIND - BALZAC
11-22-03
TODAY I HAD J CHURCH PRACTICE
LANCE GAVE US ALL THE DETAILS ABOUT OUR JAPAN TOUR!
DECEMBER 14-24!
FUCK YEAH!
I'M SO EXCITED ABOUT GOING TO JAPAN!
FUCKING FUCK YEAH! I'M GONNA GET SO MUCH BALZAC STUFF!
11-23-03
KICKED IN THE TEETH - ZEKE
BEFORE WORK TODAY I WENT TO LUNCH WITH MY ROOMATES AND MY GIRL FRIEND
THEN I WORKED.
AFTER WORK ME AND AMANDA GOT ALL PACKED FOR OUR TRIP!
11-24-03
IRON MAN - BLACK SABBATH
TODAY AMANDA AND I LEFT FOR VIRGINIA
RENTAL CAR
BYE TEXAS
WE STOPPED AND HAD A ROMANTIC DINNER IN NEW ORLEANS.
TONIGHT WE'RE SLEEPING IN A MOTEL IN MISSISSIPPI

DAY THE EARTH CAUGHT FIRE- BALZAC

11-25-03

WE DROVE ALL DAY LONG TODAY.

WELCOME TO GEORGIA

WE GOT STUCK IN TRAFFIC IN ATLANTA AND AMANDA HAD TO PEE IN A BOTTLE. IT WAS FUNNY.

AAH! IT'S GETTING ALL OVER THE SEAT!

WE FINALLY GOT TO RICHMOND AT 5:00 AM.

BORNEO JIMMY- DICTATORS

11-26-03

THIS MORNING I SHOWED AMANDA AROUND RICHMOND

I USED TO LIVE IN THAT HOUSE, AND THAT ONE, AND THAT ONE THERE....

JEEZ, YOU'VE LIVED ALL OVER THIS TOWN.

THEN WE WENT OUT TO EAT WITH MY MOM. IT WAS FUN.

AFTER THAT WE HUNG OUT WITH TONY, JOHN, AND JESSIE KELLEY.

TONY HAS LONG HAIR NOW. LIKE A GIRL.

NINA- THE MUFFS

11-27-03

TODAY IS THANKSGIVING. WE ATE DINNER WITH MY MOM, TONY, AND SOME NORMAL PEOPLE.

COOL PUNK ROCKERS

MY MOM

LAME NORMAL PEOPLE

I THOUGHT THE NORMAL PEOPLE WERE GONNA MAKE IT SUCK, BUT TONY SAVED THE DAY.

BLAHAH! I'M TOTALLY WASTED.

YEEK!

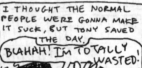

AFTERWARDS WE HUNG OUT WITH JAY

HEY DUDE, I'M MOVING TO AUSTIN. CAN I STAY ON YOUR COUCH FOR A WHILE?

SURE.

ARNIE- WARLOCK PINCHERS

11-28-03

THIS MORNING ME+ AMANDA+ TONY WENT TO THE FLEA MARKET.

AWW, IT'S SO SAD. IT LOOKS LIKE THIS PLACE IS DYING.

AFTER WE ATE A VEGGIE MONSTER PIZZA, WE WENT HOME AND WATCHED A MOVIE.

YOUR MOM'S FIREPLACE ROCKS!

YEAH

THEN WE MET UP WITH TONY AT THE VILLAGE.

OH HOW I MISS THINGS LIKE PABST IN A PITCHER

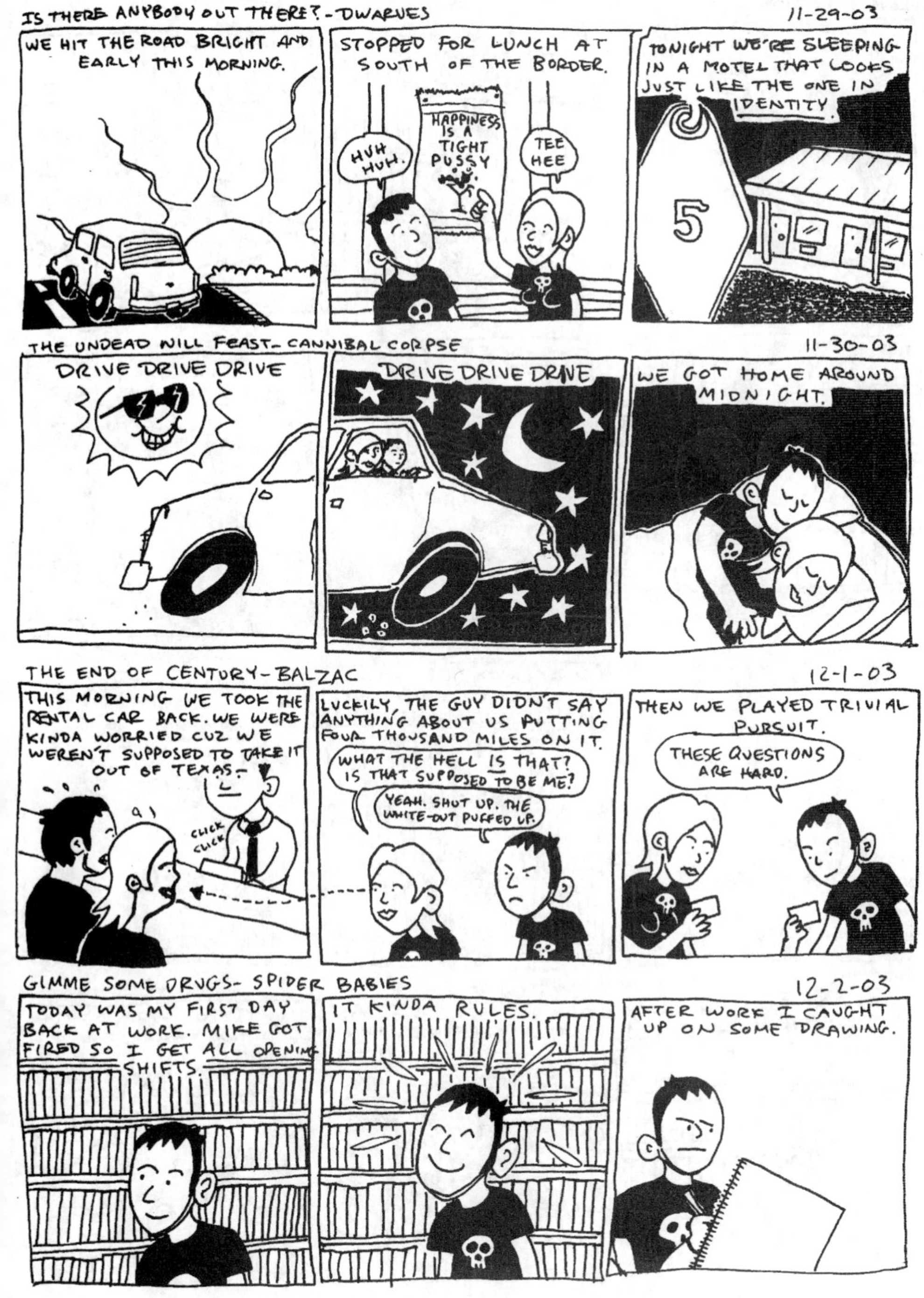
IS THERE ANYBODY OUT THERE? - DWARVES
11-29-03
WE HIT THE ROAD BRIGHT AND EARLY THIS MORNING.
STOPPED FOR LUNCH AT SOUTH OF THE BORDER.
HUH HUH.
HAPPINESS IS A TIGHT PUSSY
TEE HEE
TONIGHT WE'RE SLEEPING IN A MOTEL THAT LOOKS JUST LIKE THE ONE IN IDENTITY.
5
THE UNDEAD WILL FEAST - CANNIBAL CORPSE
11-30-03
DRIVE DRIVE DRIVE
DRIVE DRIVE DRIVE
WE GOT HOME AROUND MIDNIGHT.
THE END OF CENTURY - BALZAC
12-1-03
THIS MORNING WE TOOK THE RENTAL CAR BACK. WE WERE KINDA WORRIED CUZ WE WEREN'T SUPPOSED TO TAKE IT OUT OF TEXAS -
CLICK CLICK
LUCKILY, THE GUY DIDN'T SAY ANYTHING ABOUT US PUTTING FOUR THOUSAND MILES ON IT.
WHAT THE HELL IS THAT? IS THAT SUPPOSED TO BE ME?
YEAH. SHUT UP. THE WHITE-OUT PUFFED UP.
THEN WE PLAYED TRIVIAL PURSUIT.
THESE QUESTIONS ARE HARD.
GIMME SOME DRUGS - SPIDER BABIES
12-2-03
TODAY WAS MY FIRST DAY BACK AT WORK. MIKE GOT FIRED SO I GET ALL OPENING SHIFTS.
IT KINDA RULES.
AFTER WORK I CAUGHT UP ON SOME DRAWING.

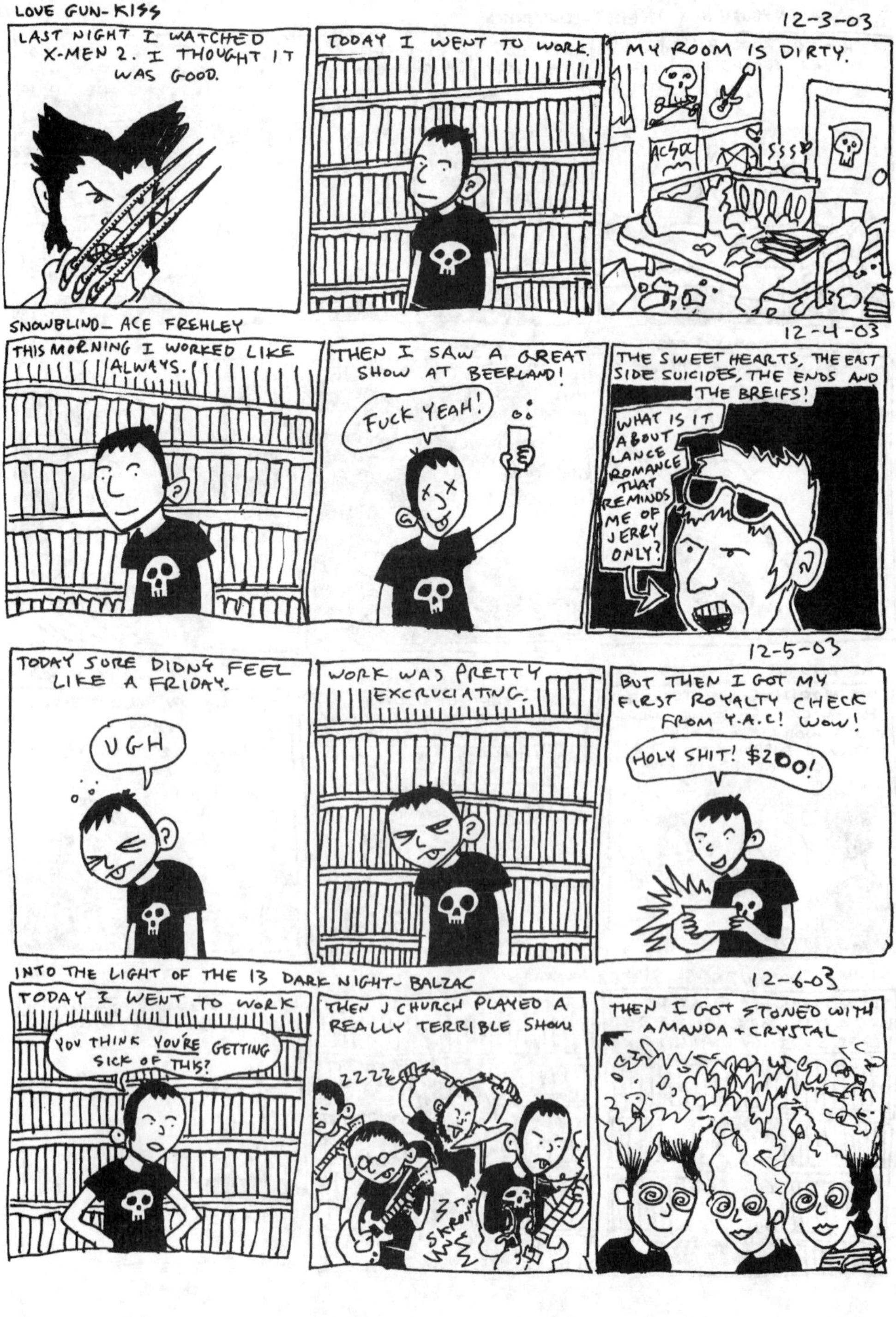

LOVE GUN- KISS
12-3-03
LAST NIGHT I WATCHED X-MEN 2. I THOUGHT IT WAS GOOD.
TODAY I WENT TO WORK.
MY ROOM IS DIRTY.
AC/DC
SNOWBLIND- ACE FREHLEY
12-4-03
THIS MORNING I WORKED LIKE ALWAYS.
THEN I SAW A GREAT SHOW AT BEERLAND!
FUCK YEAH!
THE SWEET HEARTS, THE EAST SIDE SUICIDES, THE ENDS AND THE BREIFS!
WHAT IS IT ABOUT LANCE ROMANCE THAT REMINDS ME OF JERRY ONLY?
12-5-03
TODAY SURE DIDN'T FEEL LIKE A FRIDAY.
UGH
WORK WAS PRETTY EXCRUCIATING.
BUT THEN I GOT MY FIRST ROYALTY CHECK FROM Y.A.C! WOW!
HOLY SHIT! $200!
INTO THE LIGHT OF THE 13 DARK NIGHT- BALZAC
12-6-03
TODAY I WENT TO WORK
YOU THINK YOU'RE GETTING SICK OF THIS?
THEN J CHURCH PLAYED A REALLY TERRIBLE SHOW
ZZZZ
SKRONK
THEN I GOT STONED WITH AMANDA + CRYSTAL

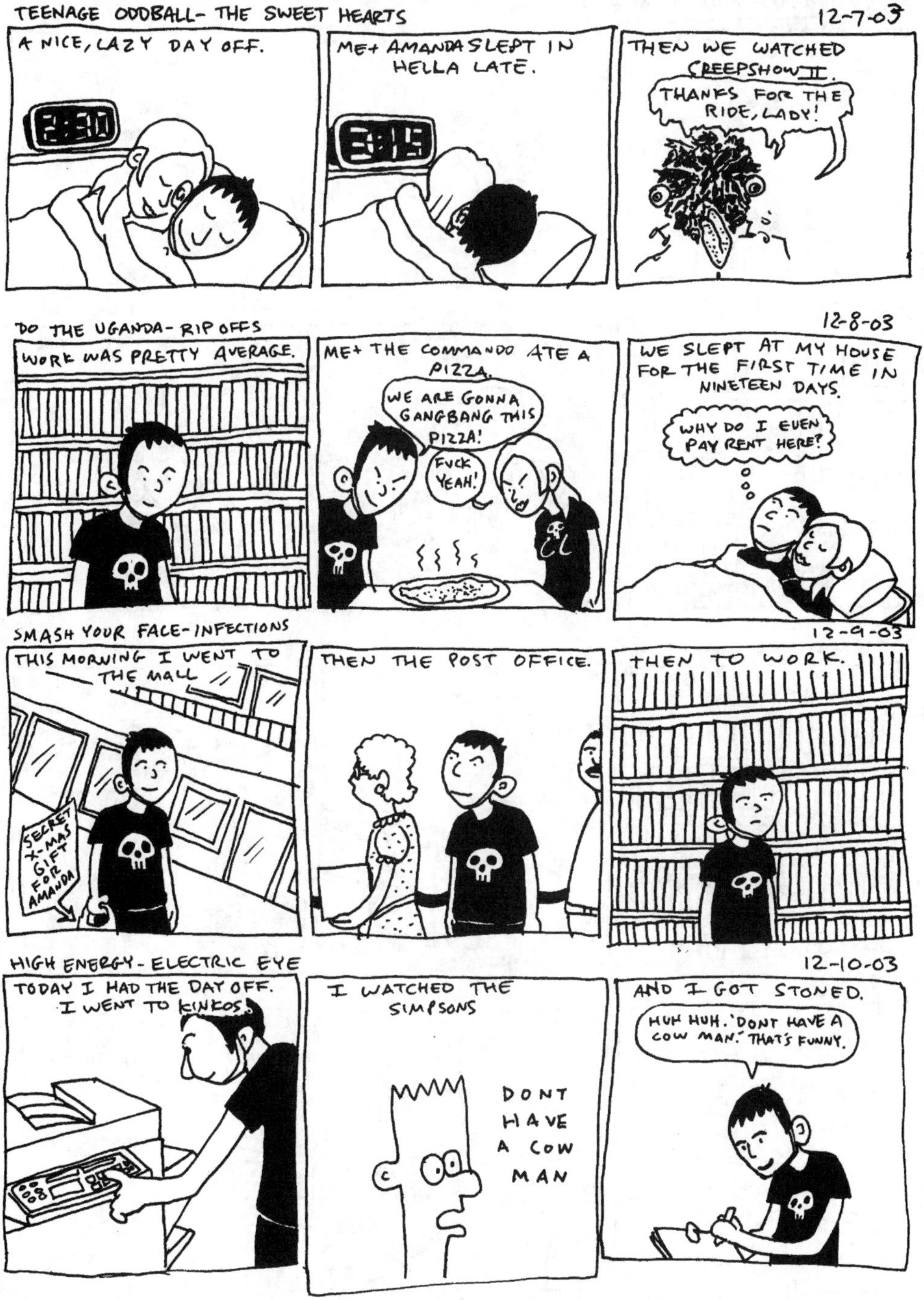
TEENAGE ODDBALL- THE SWEET HEARTS
12-7-03
A NICE, LAZY DAY OFF.
ME+ AMANDA SLEPT IN HELLA LATE.
THEN WE WATCHED CREEPSHOW II.
THANKS FOR THE RIDE, LADY!
DO THE UGANDA- RIP OFFS
12-8-03
WORK WAS PRETTY AVERAGE.
ME+ THE COMMANDO ATE A PIZZA.
WE ARE GONNA GANGBANG THIS PIZZA!
FUCK YEAH!
WE SLEPT AT MY HOUSE FOR THE FIRST TIME IN NINETEEN DAYS.
WHY DO I EVEN PAY RENT HERE?
SMASH YOUR FACE- INFECTIONS
12-9-03
THIS MORNING I WENT TO THE MALL
SECRET X-MAS GIFT FOR AMANDA
THEN THE POST OFFICE.
THEN TO WORK.
HIGH ENERGY- ELECTRIC EYE
12-10-03
TODAY I HAD THE DAY OFF. I WENT TO KINKOS.
I WATCHED THE SIMPSONS
DONT HAVE A COW MAN
AND I GOT STONED.
HUH HUH. 'DONT HAVE A COW MAN.' THAT'S FUNNY.

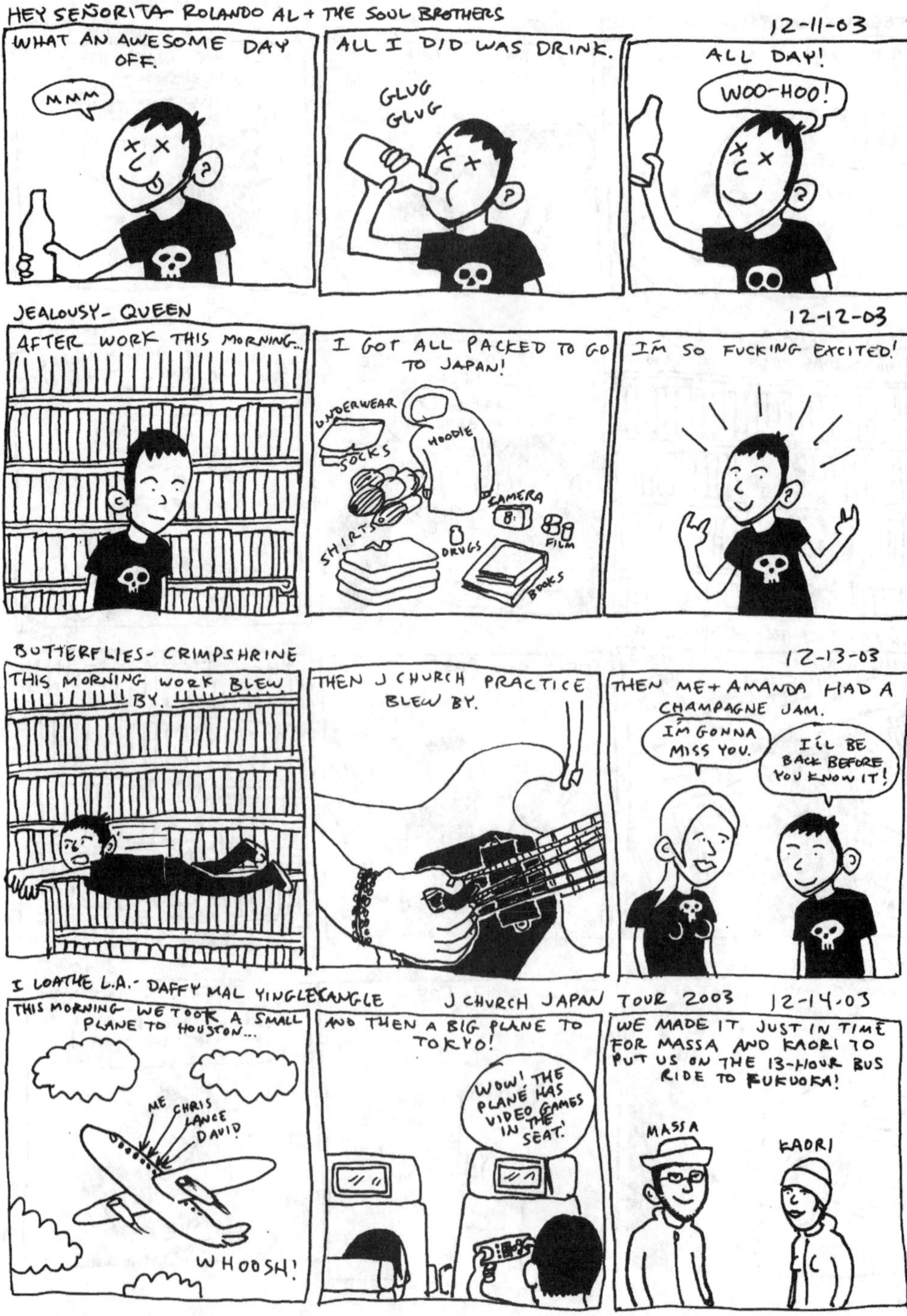
HEY SEÑORITA- ROLANDO AL + THE SOUL BROTHERS
12-11-03
WHAT AN AWESOME DAY OFF.
MMM
ALL I DID WAS DRINK.
GLUG GLUG
ALL DAY!
WOO-HOO!
JEALOUSY- QUEEN
12-12-03
AFTER WORK THIS MORNING...
I GOT ALL PACKED TO GO TO JAPAN!
UNDERWEAR
HOODIE
SOCKS
CAMERA
SHIRTS
DRUGS
FILM
BOOKS
I'M SO FUCKING EXCITED!
BUTTERFLIES- CRIMPSHRINE
12-13-03
THIS MORNING WORK BLEW BY.
THEN J CHURCH PRACTICE BLEW BY.
THEN ME + AMANDA HAD A CHAMPAGNE JAM.
I'M GONNA MISS YOU.
I'LL BE BACK BEFORE YOU KNOW IT!
I LOATHE L.A.- DAFFY MAL YINGLEKANGLE
J CHURCH JAPAN TOUR 2003
12-14-03
THIS MORNING WE TOOK A SMALL PLANE TO HOUSTON...
ME
CHRIS
LANCE
DAVID
WHOOSH!
AND THEN A BIG PLANE TO TOKYO!
WOW! THE PLANE HAS VIDEO GAMES IN THE SEAT!
WE MADE IT JUST IN TIME FOR MASSA AND KAORI TO PUT US ON THE 13-HOUR BUS RIDE TO FUKUOKA!
MASSA
KAORI

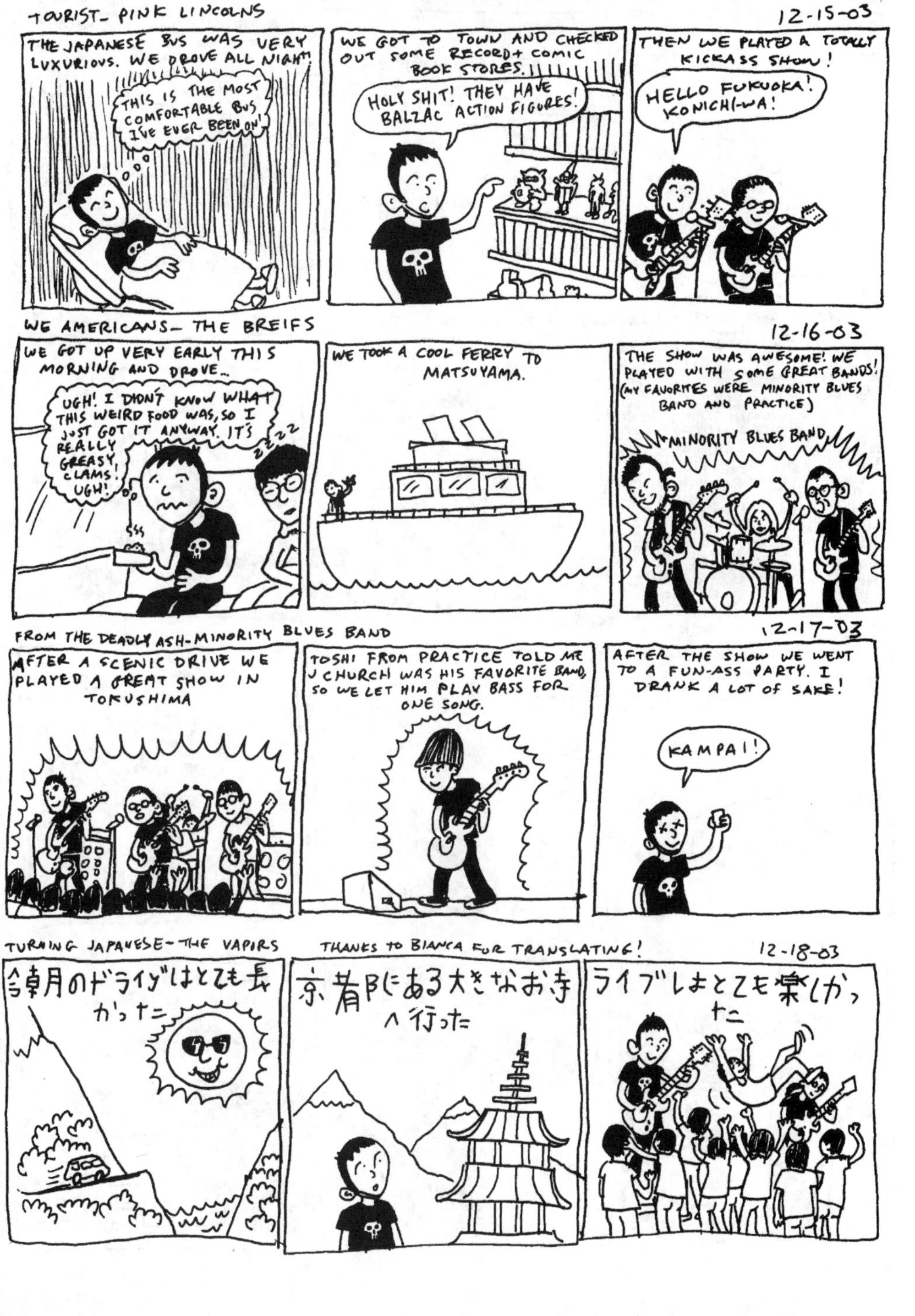
TOURIST_ PINK LINCOLNS
12-15-03
THE JAPANESE BUS WAS VERY LUXURIOUS. WE DROVE ALL NIGHT.
THIS IS THE MOST COMFORTABLE BUS I'VE EVER BEEN ON!
WE GOT TO TOWN AND CHECKED OUT SOME RECORD + COMIC BOOK STORES.
HOLY SHIT! THEY HAVE BALZAC ACTION FIGURES!
THEN WE PLAYED A TOTALLY KICKASS SHOW!
HELLO FUKUOKA! KONICHI-WA!
WE AMERICANS_ THE BREIFS
12-16-03
WE GOT UP VERY EARLY THIS MORNING AND DROVE...
UGH! I DIDN'T KNOW WHAT THIS WEIRD FOOD WAS, SO I JUST GOT IT ANYWAY. IT'S REALLY GREASY CLAMS! UGH!
ZZZZ
WE TOOK A COOL FERRY TO MATSUYAMA.
THE SHOW WAS AWESOME! WE PLAYED WITH SOME GREAT BANDS! (MY FAVORITES WERE MINORITY BLUES BAND AND PRACTICE)
MINORITY BLUES BAND
FROM THE DEADLY ASH-MINORITY BLUES BAND
12-17-03
AFTER A SCENIC DRIVE WE PLAYED A GREAT SHOW IN TOKUSHIMA
TOSHI FROM PRACTICE TOLD ME J CHURCH WAS HIS FAVORITE BAND, SO WE LET HIM PLAY BASS FOR ONE SONG.
AFTER THE SHOW WE WENT TO A FUN-ASS PARTY. I DRANK A LOT OF SAKE!
KAMPAI!
TURNING JAPANESE- THE VAPIRS
THANKS TO BIANCA FOR TRANSLATING!
12-18-03
今朝のドライブはとても長かった
京都にある大きなお寺へ行った
ライブはとても楽しかった

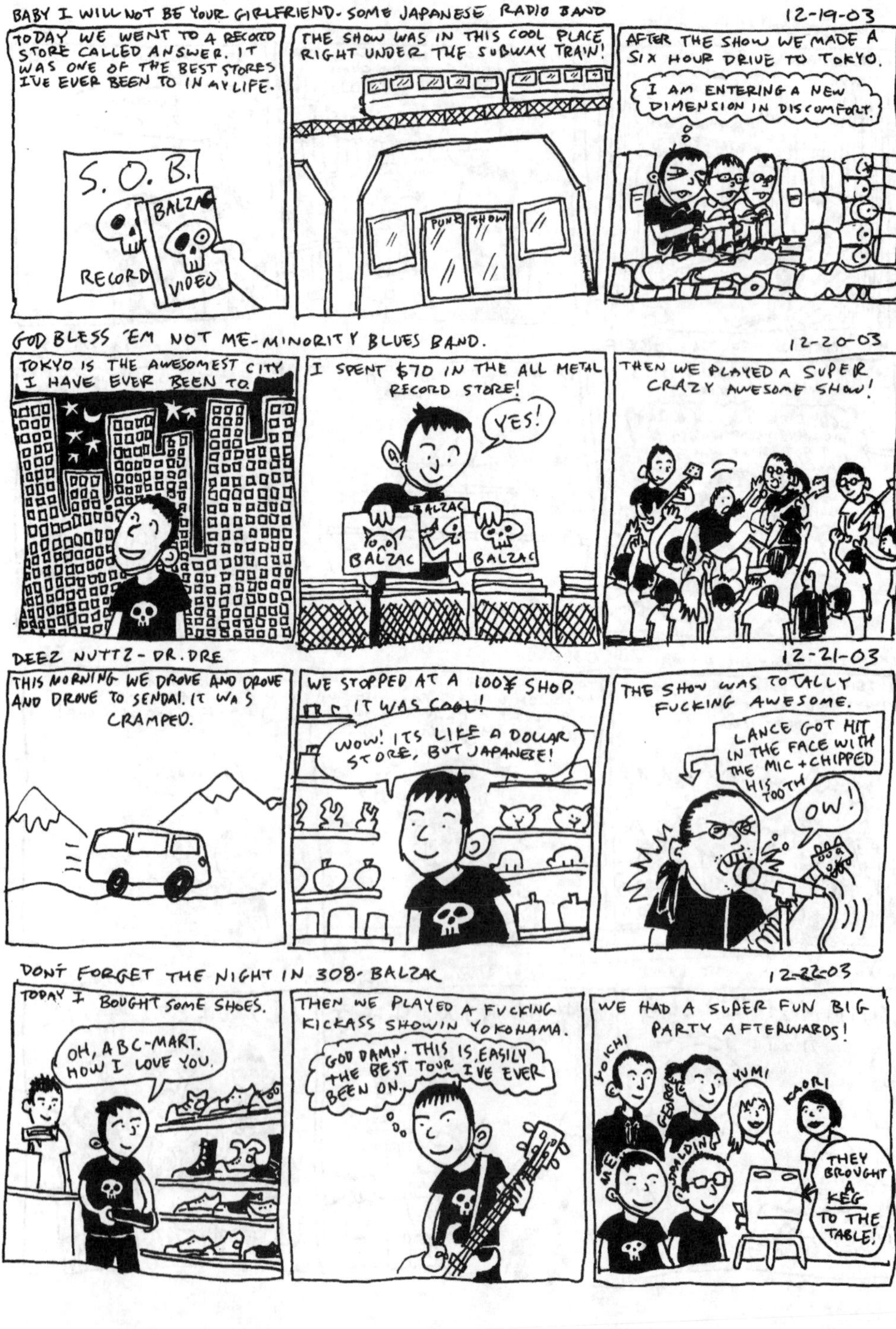
BABY I WILL NOT BE YOUR GIRLFRIEND - SOME JAPANESE RADIO BAND
12-19-03
TODAY WE WENT TO A RECORD STORE CALLED ANSWER. IT WAS ONE OF THE BEST STORES I'VE EVER BEEN TO IN MY LIFE.
S.O.B.
RECORD
BALZAC
VIDEO
THE SHOW WAS IN THIS COOL PLACE RIGHT UNDER THE SUBWAY TRAIN!
PUNK SHOW
AFTER THE SHOW WE MADE A SIX HOUR DRIVE TO TOKYO.
I AM ENTERING A NEW DIMENSION IN DISCOMFORT.
GOD BLESS 'EM NOT ME - MINORITY BLUES BAND.
12-20-03
TOKYO IS THE AWESOMEST CITY I HAVE EVER BEEN TO.
I SPENT $70 IN THE ALL METAL RECORD STORE!
YES!
BALZAC
BALZAC
BALZAC
THEN WE PLAYED A SUPER CRAZY AWESOME SHOW!
DEEZ NUTTZ - DR. DRE
12-21-03
THIS MORNING WE DROVE AND DROVE AND DROVE TO SENDAI. IT WAS CRAMPED.
WE STOPPED AT A 100¥ SHOP. IT WAS COOL!
WOW! ITS LIKE A DOLLAR STORE, BUT JAPANESE!
THE SHOW WAS TOTALLY FUCKING AWESOME.
LANCE GOT HIT IN THE FACE WITH THE MIC + CHIPPED HIS TOOTH
OW!
DON'T FORGET THE NIGHT IN 308 - BALZAC
12-22-03
TODAY I BOUGHT SOME SHOES.
OH, ABC-MART. HOW I LOVE YOU.
THEN WE PLAYED A FUCKING KICKASS SHOW IN YOKOHAMA.
GOD DAMN. THIS IS EASILY THE BEST TOUR I'VE EVER BEEN ON.
WE HAD A SUPER FUN BIG PARTY AFTERWARDS!
YOICHI
GEORGE
YUMI
KAORI
ME
SPALDING
THEY BROUGHT A KEG TO THE TABLE!

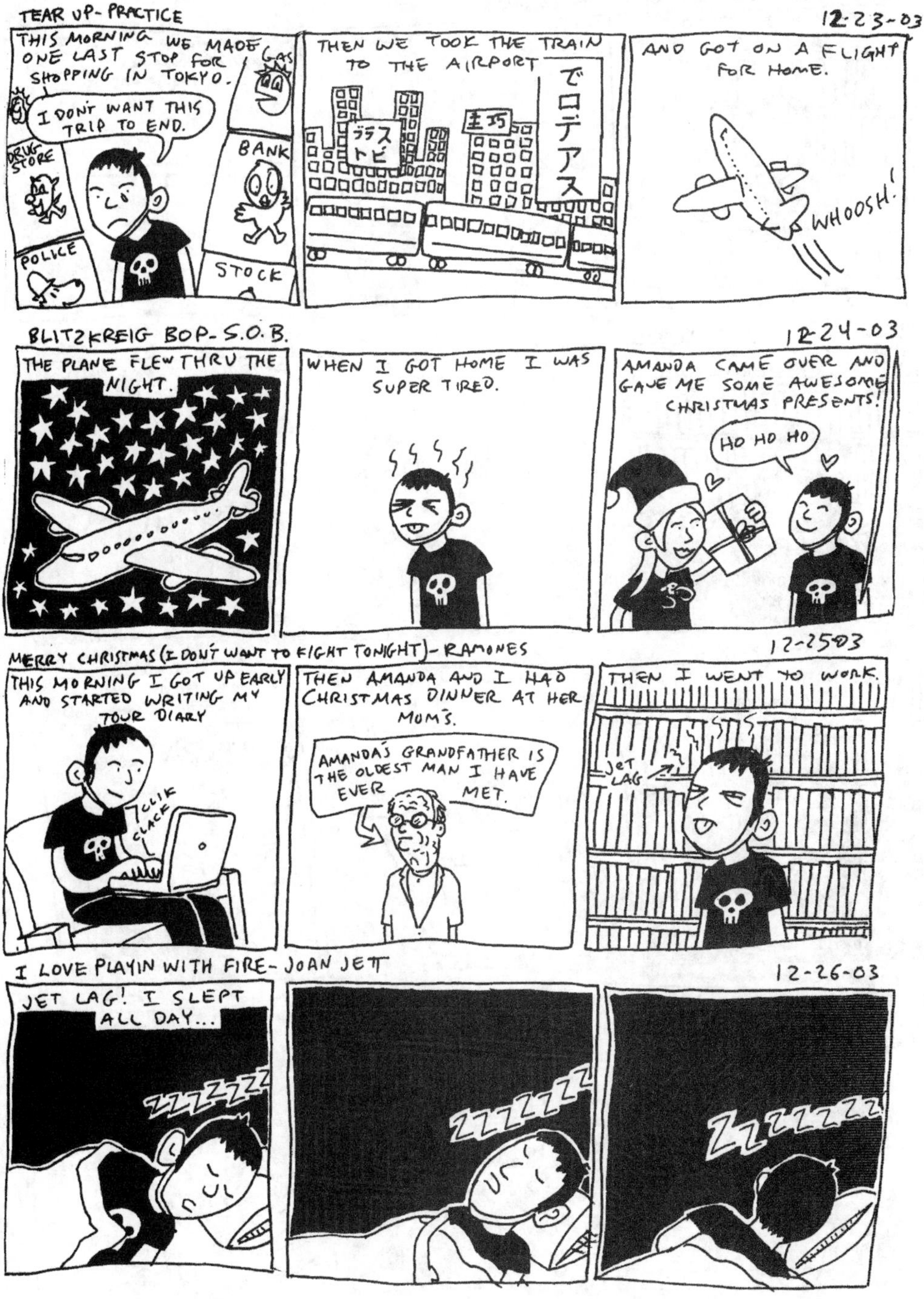
TEAR UP - PRACTICE
12-23-03
THIS MORNING WE MADE ONE LAST STOP FOR SHOPPING IN TOKYO.
I DON'T WANT THIS TRIP TO END.
GAS
DRUG STORE
BANK
POLICE
STOCK
THEN WE TOOK THE TRAIN TO THE AIRPORT
AND GOT ON A FLIGHT FOR HOME.
WHOOSH!
BLITZKREIG BOP - S.O.B.
12-24-03
THE PLANE FLEW THRU THE NIGHT.
WHEN I GOT HOME I WAS SUPER TIRED.
AMANDA CAME OVER AND GAVE ME SOME AWESOME CHRISTMAS PRESENTS!
HO HO HO
MERRY CHRISTMAS (I DON'T WANT TO FIGHT TONIGHT) - RAMONES
12-25-03
THIS MORNING I GOT UP EARLY AND STARTED WRITING MY TOUR DIARY
CLIK CLACK
THEN AMANDA AND I HAD CHRISTMAS DINNER AT HER MUM'S.
AMANDA'S GRANDFATHER IS THE OLDEST MAN I HAVE EVER MET.
THEN I WENT TO WORK.
JET LAG
I LOVE PLAYIN WITH FIRE - JOAN JETT
12-26-03
JET LAG! I SLEPT ALL DAY...
ZZZZZZZ
ZZZZZZZ
ZZZZZZZ

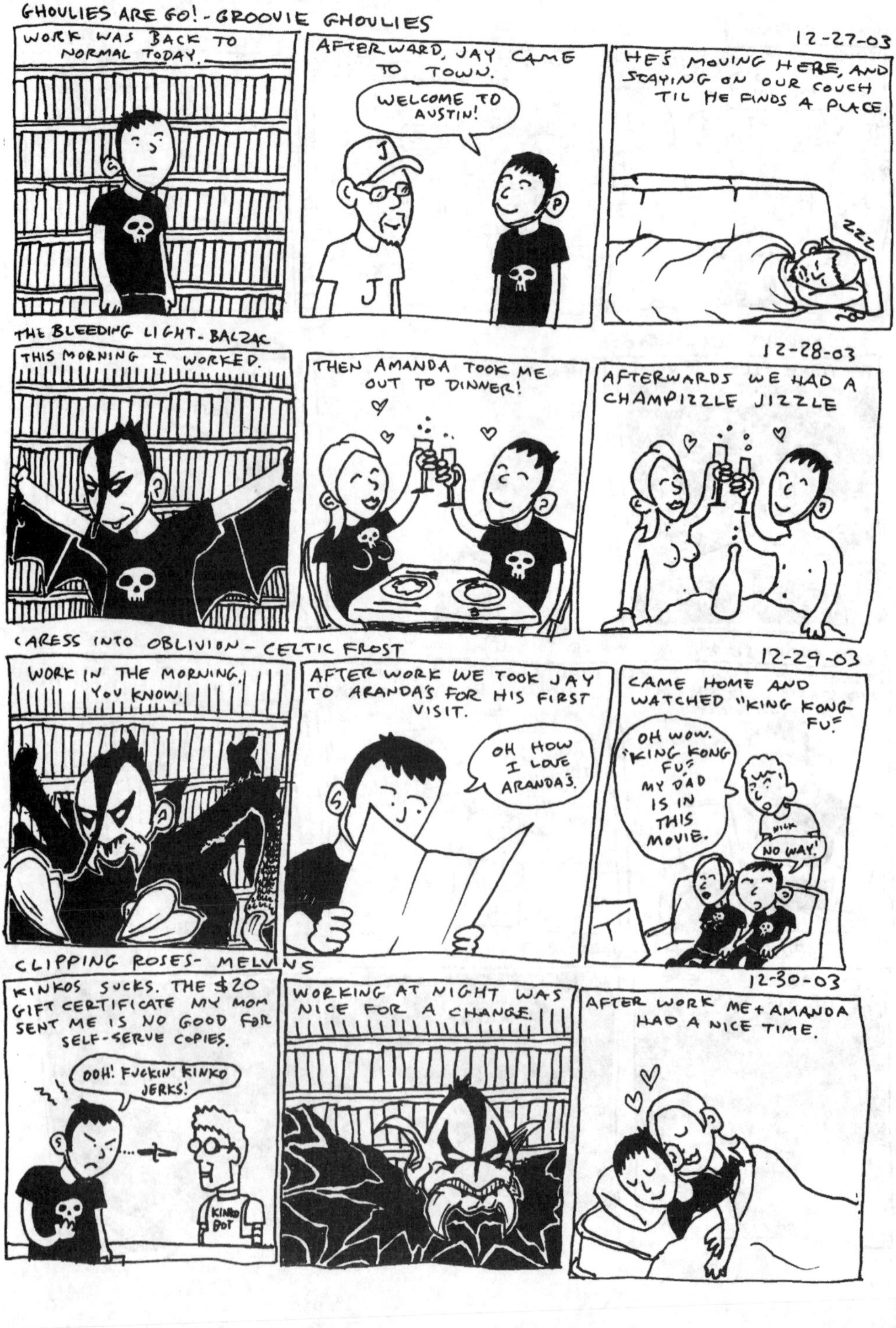
GHOULIES ARE GO! - GROOVIE GHOULIES
12-27-03
WORK WAS BACK TO NORMAL TODAY.
AFTERWARD, JAY CAME TO TOWN.
WELCOME TO AUSTIN!
J
J
P
HE'S MOVING HERE, AND STAYING ON OUR COUCH TIL HE FINDS A PLACE.
ZZZ
THE BLEEDING LIGHT - BALZAC
12-28-03
THIS MORNING I WORKED.
THEN AMANDA TOOK ME OUT TO DINNER!
AFTERWARDS WE HAD A CHAMPIZZLE JIZZLE
CARESS INTO OBLIVION - CELTIC FROST
12-29-03
WORK IN THE MORNING. YOU KNOW.
AFTER WORK WE TOOK JAY TO ARANDA'S FOR HIS FIRST VISIT.
OH HOW I LOVE ARANDA'S.
CAME HOME AND WATCHED "KING KONG FU"
OH WOW. "KING KONG FU" MY DAD IS IN THIS MOVIE.
NO WAY!
CLIPPING ROSES - MELVINS
12-30-03
KINKOS SUCKS. THE $20 GIFT CERTIFICATE MY MOM SENT ME IS NO GOOD FOR SELF-SERVE COPIES.
OOH! FUCKIN' KINKO JERKS!
KINKO BOT
WORKING AT NIGHT WAS NICE FOR A CHANGE.
AFTER WORK ME + AMANDA HAD A NICE TIME.

DO YOU REMEMBER ROCK-N-ROLL RADIO? - RAMONES. 12-31-03

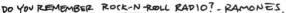

7:00pm BUY A SIX PACK.
PABST
PABST
PABST
PABST
BY 8:30 PM, THREE BEERS ARE LEFT. GO TO AMANDAS.
BY 9:30 PM, SIX PACK IS GONE. RIDE TO BEER LAND WITH AMANDA.
ARE YOU SURE YOU'RE NOT DRINKING TOO FAST?
10:30 PM. THE FIRST BAND STARTS AND I'VE HAD 2 MORE BEERS.
GAWD! THIS BAND SUCKS!
AT MIDNIGHT, BILLY HALFHEARTEDLY TAKES THE STAGE...
HEY EVERYBODY, ITS MIDNIGHT.
OH, I MEAN... FIVE, FOUR, THREE, TWO, ONE. ITS MIDNIGHT.
RANDALL AND DONYA GIVE OUT FREE CHAMPAGNE.
HAPPY NEW YEAR!
I DRINK THREE LITTLE CUPS OF IT.
TIM BUYS ME TWO MORE BEERS.
THANKS TIM!
NO SWEAT!
THE VELVET UNDERGROUND COVER BAND PLAYS. AMANDA GO-GO DANCES AND I DRINK TWO MORE BEERS.
WE DRIVE TO AMANDA'S HOUSE

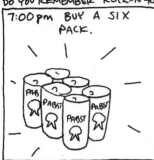

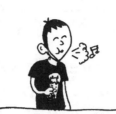

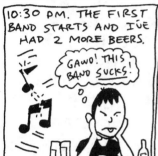

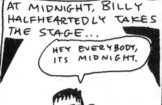

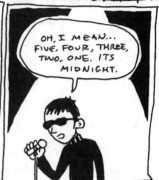

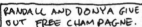

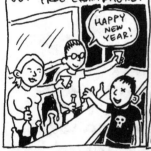

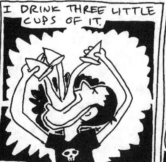

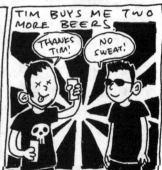

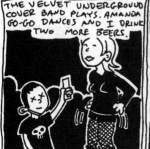

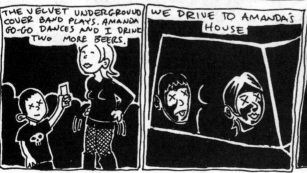

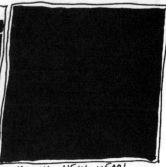

HAPPY NEW YEAR!

AFTERWARD
(WRITTEN TEN YEARS LATER)

IT'S FUNNY HOW OVER THE LAST DECADE, I'VE KINDA ROMANTICIZED THE TIMES IN THIS BOOK AS BEING WHEN I LIVED THE MOST WILD AND FREE, BUT LOOKING BACK ON THEM NOW, FROM THE PERSPECTIVE OF BEING A BORING SQUARE WITH A GOOD JOB, A DECENT PLACE TO LIVE AND A WIFE WHOM I TRUST IMPLICITLY, I REALIZE THIS WAS A HORRIBLE TIME IN MY LIFE. I WAS DEPRESSED AND LONELY, HEAVILY SELF-MEDICATING AND DESPERATELY SEEKING THE COMPANIONSHIP OF WHOEVER WAS AROUND. THESE WERE NOT WILD, FREE TIMES. THESE WERE SAD, AWFUL TIMES.

SEVERAL PEOPLE HAVE WRITTEN TO ME OVER THE LAST TEN YEARS AND SAID THAT THIS BOOK HELPED THEM THROUGH SIMILAR DARK PERIODS IN THEIR LIVES. I'M GLAD THAT I WAS ABLE TO CHANNEL MY MISERY INTO "ART," (I USE THE TERM LOOSELY BECAUSE, WELL, JUST LOOK AT SOME OF THESE SLOPPY BULLSHIT DRAWINGS) AND WHILE I HAVE NO REGRETS, I WOULD NEVER WANT TO LIVE THESE DAYS OVER AGAIN.

— BEN SNAKEPIT
MARCH 2013

THANKS LIST

SUPER SPECIAL THANKS TO MY MOM, SEAN + TODD AND
THE WHOLE RAZORCAKE/GORSKY FAMILY, TOD PARKHILL
AND YOUNG AMERICAN COMICS, KYLE SHUTT FOR ALL
HIS AWESOME HELP OVER THE YEARS, AND OF COURSE TO
AMANDA. REGULAR THANKS IN ROUGHLY CHRONOLOGICAL
ORDER GO TO SHAWN SHANKLIN, JESSE GREGORY, MARK
PROTAS, THE GAY HAÜS, ANNICK, AMANDA ROADS, TONY BITCH,
CRAIG KOON, MARK TWISTWORTHY, STACEY PRIDHAM, KATHRYN
STRICKLAND, ADAM HATLEY, J.D. CRONISE, J.T. YOST, CLARKE WILSON,
AARON FRANKLIN, SHARAN, CARMEN, DIRTY STEVE SANCHEZ AND
HIS PINK SWORDS, NORA ROBINSON, STEFANIE NGUYEN, CHRIS
PFEFFER, JILL, MICHELLE, CORY KILDUFF, THE ENIGMA, BETH
GORELY, MAX (R.I.P.) KELLY PETRASH, MARTY KEY, DAVID DIDONATO,
GENEVIEVE, MUNICIPAL WASTE, CHARLIE + ANDY GREENLEES,
SMALL KATHRYN, ROSA-MARIA DIDONATO, SAM, MIKE RODRIGUEZ, HOLLY,
MOSES, JEFF LEWIS, PAUL PETERSAN, NICK MOULOS, JOHNNY WALKER,
BRETT BAYS, HARLEY, JOHN PORCELLINO, HEIDI DICKSON, JOSH ROOFTOP,
VICTORIA, KATE, LAURA, JAMES KOCHALKA, THE WEDNESDAYS, ALEX +
THE FEAST OF SNAKES, WELLS, ED DAVIS, CHRISTINA SIMON,
PAGE99 (R.I.P.), JOE ARNONE, SUZANNE BISHOP, OLLIE, BEN WEBSTER,
PAUL RIFFE, JENNY SMITH, TIM DOYLE, LANCE HAHN, ANGELA
PILAND (R.I.P.), BEN BATEMAN, GABE BALDWIN, DAVE WAFFORD, DOUG
HART, KOJAK, PCP ROADBLOCK, MR. BEN, DANNY WOOD, FONTAINE
STEPHANIE MANN, REAGAN VAN MATRE, MATTY MATT, MIKE MEHIGAN,
MARTIN DEAL (R.I.P.), JOE FRANKE, MIKE + SUSAN, BEN CISSNER,
JESSY SCHWARTZ, FACE DOWN IN SHIT, JOSH BROWN, STACI MYERS,
KAREN SILVERMAN, WILLIE + NATALIA, THE SNOBS (R.I.P.), GREG TIFFIN,
ATTACK FORMATION, FRISTY DAVIS, NICOLE, EMPLOYEE EMPLOYEE
(R.I.P.) ALISON GOODMAN, LEN, JOHN YACKLIN, MARTINA, PAUL
CURRAN, SARA DOUBEARS, JENNIFER STAFFORD, JAY METZLER,
DANIELLE, SARAH LIPSCOMB, DABNEY, ... OF DEATH, THE SWEET
HEARTS, SOUND EXCHANGE (R.I.P.), AUSTIN BOOKS, MONKEYWRENCH
BOOKS, THIRTY THREE DEGREES, FUNNY PAPERS, DONKEY, ACE,
BATTLE UNICRON, JEREMY, ERIN MILLER, RONDONN DELORIAN,
STORM THE TOWER, RICK VEE, DUSTIN PILKINGTON, BETH
SCHINDLER, AUBREY, JUG, LACY WEATHERS BEE, ALEX LANE,
TIMMY HEFNER, STRIKE ANYWHERE, JOSH CATES, FENAR,
DELAINE, EMOS, BEERLAND, MADDY BARAN, FLIP, EMILY,
EVA DIDONATO, BRIEN WHITE, TONY GUARDRAIL, POPS RECORD
ROUND-UP TASHA, ALMITRA, CHRISSY, FREEMAN, CASEY,
GARUDA, ROSALEE, MEASON WILEY, CHRISTOFFER, JOHN LOWE,
LEI-LEEN CHOO, DAN MACHOLD, PAT MASTERSON, JOHN MISSISSIPPI,

MIKE + LORI, BREA GRANT, CATHERINE, KATHRYN,
CHRIS BULTMAN, SWEET TOOTH, BEAU, CLUTCH MC
BASTARD, WHITNEY, CATHETER, ANDREA, JOE,
BRIDGET, ANNE, JAPANTHER, KIM CANTON, COLE
JOHNSON, MAURY, MIKE ALFERD, LANDON, LYZ + KAI,
DAVEY FOUND, RICH MACKIN, SARA DILLON, THE
SHED, NICK, DOBIE THEATER, DAVID MORRIS, LIZ
DEFIANCE, MARK, SHAWN GRANTON, BURNT RAMEN,
HOSS + CRUCIAL UNIT, ANTHONY + CHRIS IN OAKLAND,
AARON COMETBUS, KELLY THE BANE TELLER, GUITAR
WOLF, TAMMY, ANNE SCHROLL, REBEKAH O'PRESKA,
TIM SHOCKEY, RONNIE, HEADS + BODIES, PENNY
TRATION, JENNY TALIA + JOHN MOTARD, ALYSE,
BILLY BEERLAND, LARS, KEVIN, ALAN ROWE,
THE DIRTY SWEETS, ERIN, ANNIE ASHE, AIKI,
TIM STORM + LIZ BUHAY, RAY, ARWEN CURRY,
MIKE THORN AND THE MRR CREW, THE FLESHIES,
CELINA, FLOOR, THE BOBBYTEENS, THE TYRADES,
REBECCA + OMARI + THE JEWWS (R.I.P.) LIAM, THEO,
MEGAN PANTS, JANELLE BLARG, SHOSH C, QUIMBYS
BOOKSTORE, MON ROVIA, THE PLUNGERS, DAVE CHOI,
SHARON MOONEY, HUGH WALLACE, SHARA, JEFF
WINTERBERG, JIM + NOREEN CROSLEY, JAMES +
APRIL, JESSE LYELL, MAG, TONY WEINBENDER
CHAD SMITH, TALENA, STEVE GARCIA, JOSH, JASON,
PAT, AARON, THE ORPHANS, JOHN, JESSIE KELLEY,
MELTY, ATOMIC BOOKS (BALTIMORE) MASSA + THE
URCHIN, KAORI AND THE HAPPENING, YOICHI SNUFFY
SMILE, SPALDING, GEORGIE, YUMI, BIANCA,
EVERYONE FROM THE THANKS LISTS IN ANTHOLOGY
NUMBER ONE - THREE, AND ALL THE PEOPLE
I FORGOT. SORRY I ALWAYS FORGET STUFF.

THIS BOOK IS DEDICATED
TO THE PUNX.

SUBSCRIBE TO EVERYTHING WE PUBLISH!

Do you love what Microcosm publishes?

Do you want us to publish more great stuff?

Would you like to receive each new title as it's published?

Subscribe as a BFF to our new titles and we'll mail them all to you as they are released!

$10-30/mo, pay what you can afford. Include your t-shirt size and month/date of birthday for a possible surprise! Subscription begins the month after it is purchased.

microcosmpublishing.com/bff

...AND HELP US GROW YOUR SMALL WORLD!